The administrative structure

The development and functions of the Department of Education and local school systems, the financing of education, and the educational activities of provincial and federal governments are studied in this volume. The emphasis is on current issues and problems. Dr Fleming delves into the activities of the department since 1965, giving a thorough analysis of the consolidation of local administrative units in 1969. He describes in detail the financing of education, the budgetary practices of the department, and the system of federal and provincial grants. The last section gives a description of every type of educational activity of the provincial and federal governments.

W.G. FLEMING studied at Queen's University and the University of Toronto (MEd, Ed D). He has taught elementary (1941–3) and high school (1948–54) and was principal of an intermediate school in the province of Quebec (1943–5). He joined the faculty of the University of Toronto in 1954 and since that time has been a researcher and instructor in the graduate school. He was assistant director of the Department of Educational Research from 1962 to 1966 and was the first coordinator of research and assistant director of the Ontario Institute for Studies in Education. At present he is professor of education at the University of Toronto and at OISE. He has travelled widely, studying and making recommendations on educational planning, and other matters.

ONTARIO'S EDUCATIVE SOCIETY / II

The administrative structure

W.G. FLEMING

UNIVERSITY OF TORONTO PRESS

Reprinted in paperback 2017

Volume II

ISBN 978-0-8020-3268-3 (cloth)
ISBN 978-1-4875-9861-7 (paper)

Volumes I–V
ISBN 0-8020-3258-3
Microfiche ISBN 0-8020-0079-7
LC 77-166928

Preface

The series entitled ONTARIO'S EDUCATIVE SOCIETY, of which this volume is the second, deals with many formal and informal aspects of education as they have developed in Ontario in recent years. The province of Ontario is particularly suitable for a study of this kind. Its population of approximately 7.5 million, the largest of any Canadian province, demonstrates a rich and varied mosaic of cultures and traditions. Its extended territory includes a wide range of topographical and climatic features shaping the lives of its people in many different ways. During the post-war period it has surged with unprecedented life and vitality, striding ahead in population, in resource development, in technology, and in culture. As both a highly developed and a rapidly developing society, it offers examples of many of the problems and difficulties involved in meeting the challenges of the modern world.

Recent educational progress in Ontario has been impressive in both quantity and quality. Such a judgment has been made by numerous observers from other provinces and from abroad. This does not mean, of course, that the province has become the universal model; in some respects it is in the process of catching up with developments already completed elsewhere. It is perhaps not unreasonable to suggest, however, that many of its achievements are at least worthy of attention, if not of emulation, in other parts of the world.

Education is defined in a broad sense to include training activities of many kinds, even those with very limited goals. Such treatment does not imply that there is no value in distinguishing between education and training as concepts. The danger in dwelling excessively on such distinctions is that it becomes difficult to discern the larger pattern in which both types of activity have a part. They are often in practice so inextricably intertwined that any effort at separate treatment becomes highly artificial.

The reader will be conscious of two somewhat different approaches, one for the great majority of events and developments, where I have been largely or exclusively a bystander, and the other for situations where I have had some significant personal involvement. Examples of the latter are the operation of the departmental grade 13 examination system and the origin and early expansion of the Ontario Institute for Studies in Education. No matter what the topic, I have attempted to present an objective factual account. However, where direct experience has seemed to justify it, I have been much freer about offering opinions and assessments than where my material has been obtained at second hand. I trust that I have been successful in keeping fact separated from opinion. A second feature distinguishing the two types of material is that I have presented a relatively large amount of information about the developments in which I have had a substantial role. As a result, my attempt to present a fairly complete overview of education in Ontario has perhaps been somewhat distorted. I can only hope that there is value in the more thorough treatment which I have felt particularly qualified to provide.

For the whole series I have used the title ONTARIO'S EDUCATIVE SOCIETY. In doing so, I have deliberately obscured a valid distinction between the ideal and the actual. Imperfect human society will not soon be truly educative in the sense that education in all its manifestations is universally accepted as the central activity to which all others are subordinated. Yet if modern civilization, and even humanity itself, is to survive, I firmly believe that there will have to be a strong and consistent move in that direction. Future generations, if any, will have to ask themselves first of any activity: "Is it educative?" Only when they have answered affirmatively will they then be justified in asking: "Is it productive of material goods?" "Is it entertaining?"

If Ontario does not yet, strictly speaking, have an educative society, a study of the record of recent years suggests that remarkable strides have been made toward that objective. The extension of formal opportunities for learning has been impressive enough in itself. When one also considers the multiplicity of informal influences that are actually or potentially educative, the over-all effect is awesome. It is possible to feel in moments of optimism that the ultimate ideal is not completely unattainable.

Volume I, *The expansion of the educational system*, provides an introduction to the whole series, in which some of the major contemporary issues and problems in education are discussed briefly, followed by seven chapters containing most of the quantitative information in compact form. For many readers it may serve chiefly for reference purposes. Volume II, *The administrative structure*, deals with the development and functions of the Department of Education and of local school systems, the financing of education, and the educational activities of the provincial and federal governments. Volume III, *Schools, pupils, and teachers*, covers the evolution of the school structure and curriculum, and attempts to show how the process of education has operated up to the end of secondary school. Volume IV, *Post-secondary and adult education*, deals with the development and activities of universities, colleges of applied arts and technology, and other institutions of post-secondary education, as well as with public and private training activities in business and industry. Volume V, *Supporting institutions and services*, relates to a variety of institutions and activities such as teacher preparation, research and development, educational television services, and externally administered examinations. Volume VI, *Significant developments in local school systems*, indicates some of the educational contributions arising chiefly from local initiative. Volume VII, *Educational contributions of associations*, attempts to demonstrate the extent to which educative activities in Ontario are initiated and conducted through voluntary effort as a supplement to formal and official services. A companion volume to the series, *Education: Ontario's preoccupation*, contains a review of the main highlights of educational development in Ontario, with less emphasis on fact and more on interpretation.

The main focus of the series is on the recent period. An attempt was made to record developments of major importance up to early 1970, just before the first five volumes were delivered to the publisher. Volumes VI and VII, which were written during the latter part of the same year, contain a certain amount of more recent material. Very few additions or changes were made during the editorial stage. The result is that a number of the speculations about future developments have already lost some of the value they might have had earlier.

The treatment of the topic is essentially descriptive. As a means of conveying a reasonable understanding of recent developments, it was thought desirable to trace the origins of many current institutions and practices back into the nineteenth century. For the relevant material in the earlier period, I have relied almost exclusively on secondary sources. Treatment of the last four decades, particularly the period since the Second World War, involved increasing use of primary data.

Acknowledgments

I am deeply indebted to the Honourable William G. Davis, Minister of Education and of University Affairs at the time of writing, for providing me the full co-operation of his departments in the production of the series of volumes constituting ONTARIO'S EDUCATIVE SOCIETY. In this task I was given access to all pertinent material in the two departments under his direction. His officials at the time of writing, headed by Dr J.R. McCarthy, Deputy Minister of Education, and Dr E.E. Stewart, Deputy Minister of University Affairs, were also extraordinarily co-operative and helpful. I am particularly grateful to these officials for enabling me to pursue the work in a way that most appeals to a member of the university community: that is, I was completely free to choose, present, and interpret the facts according to my own best judgment. I did not feel the slightest pressure to adapt or modify the material in any way so as to present an "official" version of educational developments in Ontario. As a consequence, I am completely responsible for any opinions or interpretations of the facts that the work contains. The generous assistance for the project provided by the Ontario government, without which publication would have been impossible, does not involve any responsibility for the contents.

I would like to express my particular gratitude to those who assisted me so devotedly in the project: Miss L. McGuire, my loyal secretary, who served from the time the work began in the spring of 1968, Mrs E. West, who also served with extraordinary devotion and competence during most of the same period, and Mrs S. Constable, Miss D. McDowell, and Mrs G.J. Moore, each of whom participated during an extended period. Mr C.H. Westcott, who served as Executive Assistant to the Minister of Education and University Affairs, gave me continuous encouragement and helped to deal with practical problems relating to production and publication. Particularly helpful advice and information were given by Dr C.A. Brown, Professor E.B. Rideout, and Dr. J.A. Keddy. Arrangements by Dr. G.E. Flower to relieve me of the majority of my other professional obligations during most of a three-year period are also greatly appreciated. In addition, I would like to acknowledge my general indebtedness to the hundreds of people who supplied information so willingly in a variety of forms. That I am unable to name them all individually does not mean that I am any the less grateful for their contributions.

W.G. FLEMING
May 1971

Contents

ONTARIO'S EDUCATIVE SOCIETY / II

The administrative structure

ONE

The evolution of the structure of the Department of Education

ORIGIN AND EARLY DEVELOPMENT

Although government initiative was evident in the establishment of the district grammar schools in 1808, the earliest common schools developed as an expression of local interest in education. It was inevitable that the wide variation in the quality of services provided by community effort would lead to the creation of a regulatory governmental agency designed initially to correct the most glaring deficiencies. There is a natural tendency for such an agency to become increasingly powerful as it discovers the need for one improvement after another, and as it follows what usually appears to be the most convenient and effective approach – that of direct intervention. As this process unfolded during the nineteenth century, it appeared to be a constructive one, and most recent observers feel that it was necessary. It also seems apparent that centralization went too far, and that its deadening effects had to become very pronounced before an effective counterattack could be launched.

According to Phillips, the steps by which central authority was instituted were as follows: 1 / the establishment of a regular grant system; 2 / the setting up of boards in a position intermediate between the local area and the government to examine and license teachers; 3 / the establishment of a provincial board with wider powers; 4 / the employment of a provincial superintendent and supporting staff; and 5 / the subjection of the central administration to the elected legislature. Upper Canada departed from this order by reversing the third and fourth steps.[1]

The first grants to common schools were made in 1816. There was an attempt to establish a central authority in 1823 with the appointment of a General Board of Education under the presidency of John Strachan. Its purpose was to promote uniformity of standards among the schools. It was the duty of the president to visit the districts in order to obtain first-hand knowledge of school conditions. The board lasted only until 1833, when its functions were transferred to the Council of King's College. Although these functions ceased to be exercised, a significant precedent had been established.

For a brief period after 1841, the situation was one of extreme decentralization. Elected township officials were given the right, held earlier by the General Board of Education, to choose texts, to decide on courses of study, and to determine the qualifications of teachers. Arrangements were made in 1841 to have a Superintendent of Education for the whole of the united province of Canada, with an assistant superintendent in charge of each of the former provinces. The Provincial Secretary acted as superintendent until 1846, when Egerton Ryerson, who had been appointed as assistant superintendent for Canada West in 1844, was elevated to that position. At first, the superintendent was responsible only for making suggestions designed to further uniform practices in the schools. Ryerson, who held the office until 1876, conducted a patient but determined effort during his long tenure of office to establish strong central control.

Significant steps were taken toward the development of a centralized school system by the passing of the Acts of 1846 and 1850. The first gave major powers to a General Board of Education and to the Superintendent of Schools. The second provided for a newly constituted Council of Public Instruction to replace the General Board of Education. At the same time, county boards of public instruction were established, each consisting of grammar school trustees and the county superintendent. This measure did not represent a move toward decentralization, since the board members were almost entirely appointed by the governor. They were authorized to certify teachers and to select textbooks from lists approved by the Council of Public Instruction. The first of these functions declined in importance as professional training developed, and the second as the Council of Public Instruction reduced the list of textbooks from which selections could be made.[2]

These developments meant that, when the Grammar School Act of 1853 provided for the appointment of trustees by the local municipal authorities, there was no real diminution of central powers. After 1871, county inspectors were substituted for county superintendents. Like their predecessors, they were appointed by the county councils, but they had to obtain qualifications specified by the central authority.

Ryerson built up a nucleus of a Department of Education from the executive of the Council of Public Instruction. At the same time, there was increasing criticism of the council, which at first consisted of prominent men from Toronto and vicinity, and at a later stage largely of university teachers. It seemed to have nothing of any great importance to do until 1874, when it was given the power to prescribe courses of study and to appoint secondary school inspectors. At that time elected members were added, and the total membership was increased from nine to eighteen. Ryerson was opposed to this arrangement and soon succeeded in getting it changed. When he retired in 1876, the council and the office of the chief superintendent were abolished, the functions of the former being assumed by the Department of Education, and those of the latter by a Minister of Education.

A reorganization of the Department of Education was carried out in 1906. The office of Superintendent of Education was revived, but with advisory rather than administrative powers. The incumbent was supposed to provide the minister with expert professional counsel in order to assist with the development of educational policy. The deputy minister exercised the direct responsibility of ensuring that accepted policies were carried out. The same reorganization involved the establishment of an Advisory Council on Education, which was intended to provide the minister with a means of keeping in close touch with opinion in different educational constituencies. It had representatives from the universities, the high, public, and separate schools, the inspectors, and the trustees. It did not assume a role of any great importance, partly because it could consider only those questions that were referred to it by the minister. Rather than accede to the teachers' attempt to have its powers extended, the government abolished it in 1915. Its lack of success was partly attributed to the attitude of John Seath, who held the superintendency from 1906 until his death in 1919.[3] He so dominated education during his term of office that there was little opportunity for the council to gain prestige and influence. The superintendency lapsed in 1919, but was revived in 1923 when F.W. Merchant was appointed under the title Chief Director of Education. For the next twenty years, the positions of the chief director and the deputy minister remained unstable in relation to one another.

An important move away from central control was made in the 1930s, when the departmental middle school and lower school examinations were abandoned, and the schools were given the responsibility for evaluating students at these levels. For a time it appeared that this development would encompass the upper school level as well, but the recommendation system was discontinued after a brief trial. There was no sign of a conscious resolution at this stage to relax the department's control. The changes merely signified a desire to reduce costs during a period of financial stringency. The abolition of the high school entrance examinations in 1949 and of the departmental grade 13 examinations in 1967, on the other hand, reflected a feeling that they had become anomalous.

Despite the appraisals of many observers at the time, as well as of those viewing the situation from a longer perspective, the *Report of the Minister, 1947* identified the system as a decentralized one. The local authorities were said to exercise "much control" in terms of engaging teachers, erecting and maintaining schools, and raising money for educational purposes. It was acknowledged, however, that the provincial authorities also exercised considerable control through regulations dealing with school accommodation, courses of study, and textbooks, through the training and certification of teachers, and through legislative grants.[4]

During his term as chief director from 1944 to 1956, J.G. Althouse gave evidence of a sincere desire to relax departmental control. Inspection, for example, was performed with increasing frequency by officials selected and paid by the larger boards. Provincial inspectors were said to be delivering fewer adverse reports on local authorities. There was more freedom for local selection of textbooks within certain limits. Teachers' colleges gained the privilege of setting and marking their own examinations. The Porter Plan for decentralizing the process of curriculum construction was instituted about the time the report of the Royal Commission appeared. Dana Porter, who held the portfolio of education from 1948 to 1951, was interested in breaking down some of the rigidities of the system as he found it. On the other hand, his successor, W.J. Dunlop, who had a highly paternalistic outlook, did almost nothing to reduce the department's authority. By discouraging the efforts of his inspectors to induce smaller school boards to amalgamate, he helped to perpetuate the weakness of the latter, and thus their dependence on the department.

CHANGES IN ORGANIZATION AND FUNCTIONS, 1943–65

Structure

In 1943 the newly-elected Conservative government attempted to restore the intended organizational plan of 1906, with a chief director responsible for educational policy and a deputy minister responsible for administration. In 1944 George Drew, who retained the education portfolio, issued a memorandum designed to distinguish between the roles of the two officials.

The Chief Director is the educational adviser of the Minister, the officer whose duty it is to learn the Minister's plans and aims in education and see that they are realized. Under the Minister it is his responsibility to develop such a system of education as will tend to produce citizens who will conform to the ideal citizen envisaged by the Minister as the proper product of education. School administration, courses of study, text-books and the training and control of teachers and inspectors are his special concern. He is also concerned with institutions such as the Universities, the Ontario College of Art and the Conservatories of Music when their courses or policy affect the education of the young. He should help to mould public opinion and should guide and direct officials and inspectors in the development of the Minister's educational policy.

The Deputy Minister is the administrative officer who should keep the Department running smoothly and efficiently, so that the Chief Director may be free to work out the policy of the Minister. Under the Minister, the Deputy Minister's duties and powers are:

(1) to oversee and direct staff as provided for under section 9 (3) of the Public Service Act:

(a) to pass (i) recommendations for the appointment of officials and inspectors submitted by the Chief Director and approved by the Minister, and (ii) approved recommendations for the appointment of other personnel to the Civil Service Commissioner for consideration and certificates and to the Council for appointment;

(b) to approve recommendations of the heads of the branches concerned for the appointment of casual and temporary employees to be paid at a rate of less than $1,200 a year (this would include appointments of maids, etc., to the staffs of the Ontario School for the Deaf and the Ontario School for the Blind, summer temporary clerical staffs required for Summer School and examination work) and sessional appointments recommended by the Dean of the Ontario College of Education, and to sign for the Minister letters of appointment to the staff of the Canadian Vocational Training;

(c) to arrange leave, holidays, etc. of staff in accordance with the Regulations;

(d) to assign office accommodation and provide necessary equipment;

(e) to maintain proper staff records;

(2) to direct in all matters where policy and practice are clearly established the work of the following branches: Archives, Legislative Library, Examination Branch, Accountant's Branch, Statistics, Correspondence and Filing;

(3) to oversee finances:

(a) in preparing the Estimates in consultation with the Chief Director and the Adviser on School Finance;

(b) in approving expenditures covered by regulations or orders-in-council and provided for in the Estimates;

(c) in approving special expenditures on the satisfactory recommendation of the Chief Director, the Superintendent of Elementary Education, or the Superintendent of Secondary Education, not specifically covered by the regulations, such as assisted school grants, but not in amounts exceeding $500.00.

(4) to approve contracts for the transportation of pupils when in line with the regulations;

(5) to route Departmental mail and conduct official correspondence on all matters concerning administration in which an official statement of Departmental policy is involved;

(6) to supervise the preparation of Recommendations to Council, Regulations, and School Law amendments;

(7) to provide for the necessary printing of text-books, forms, pamphlets, circulars, etc.;

(8) to sign for the Minister when specially directed, as, for example, letters of appointment to the Canadian Vocational Training as mentioned in (1) (b) above, cheques and letters connected with the Woodruff Trust Fund or other scholarships or bursaries, and to approve the appointments of boards and committees provided for by regulations or established practice of the Department;

(9) to consult the Chief Director in any matter where policy and practice do not seem to be definitely established, and to refer special circumstances, appointments and recommendations to the Minister.[5]

According to the organization plan for the department in 1944, shown

CHART 1-1
Organization chart for the Ontario Department of Education, 1944

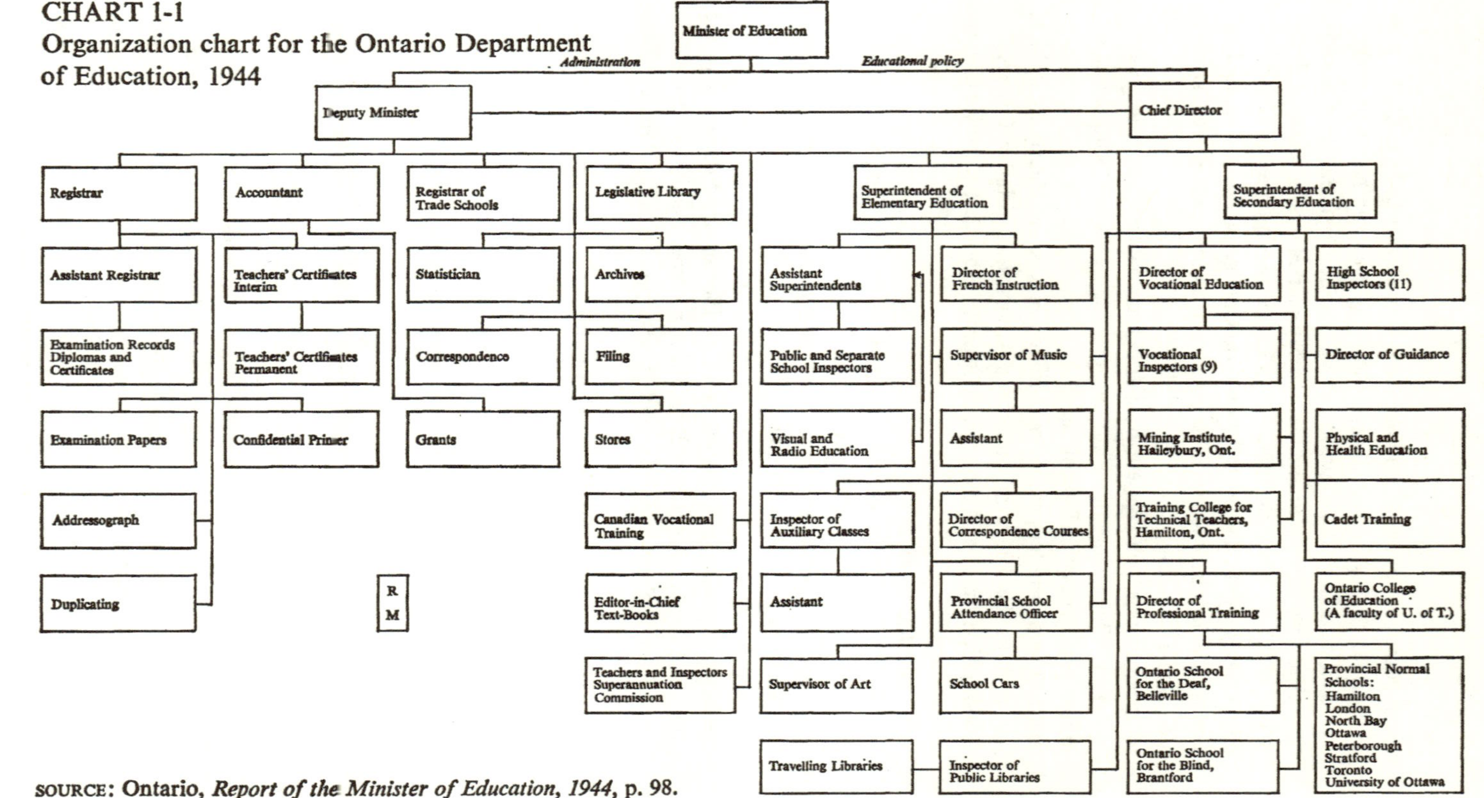

SOURCE: Ontario, *Report of the Minister of Education, 1944*, p. 98.

in Chart 1-1, the positions of chief director and deputy minister were on the same level. Two years later, as shown in Chart 1-2, the position of the chief director had been raised above that of the deputy minister. The two-fold division of functions was bound to be an unstable one unless the minister not only possessed a strong personality but also maintained active control over the affairs of the department. There was no doubt that Drew met the first qualification, but he was too busy with other matters to exercise much direct supervision over the department. It was perhaps inevitable that the new chief director, J.G. Althouse, who was a forceful and competent leader, would assume the dominant role. In contrast to his unbroken period of service, the position of deputy minister was vacated by G.F. Rogers in 1945, and held for a single year by J.P. Cowles, for five years (1946–51) by F.S. Rutherford, and for the subsequent five-year period by C.F. Cannon.

According to the organization chart of 1946, the chief officials having direct responsibility to the chief director and the deputy minister were the Superintendents of Elementary Education, Secondary Education, and Professional Training. Also reporting to one or the other, or both, were the Provincial Archivist, the Inspector of Public Libraries, the Directors of Art, Guidance, Physical and Health Education, and Music, the Editor of Text Books, the Registrar, the Chief Accountant, the Statistician, and the Librarian of the Legislative Library. These observations should be tempered with the general comment that organization charts are not a very good reflection of the way things actually operate, and by the specific comments of more than one person with long experience in the department that the charts were particularly far off the track as far as that organization was concerned.

Direct services

Although the preponderance of departmental activity during that period was regulatory, several direct educational services were provided. The most important of these was the professional preparation of teachers. Others included correspondence courses, begun in 1926, which in 1947 included instruction in subjects in grades 1 to 10; railway school cars to bring schooling to scattered groups in shifting settlements; citizenship training offered in various centres; provincial technical institutes, including the Provincial Institute of Mining at Haileybury, established in 1944, and the Provincial Institute of Textiles, established in 1946, to which were added the Lakehead Technical Institute and the Ryerson Institute of Technology in 1948; schools for the handicapped, namely, the Ontario School for the Blind and the Ontario School for the Deaf; a library of films; radio broadcasts given in co-operation with the Canadian Broadcasting Corporation; and travelling libraries. Also, departmental interest in such areas as guidance has always taken the form of service.

During the immediate post-war period, the Physical and Health Education Branch developed and maintained two types of summer course for specially selected high school students. An athletic leadership training course was offered at Longford Mills to give the participants practical training in the development of basic athletic skills, the knowledge of game rules, the art of officiating, and the organization of a physical education program. The two-weeks' course was also intended to be a useful experience in living, working, and playing together. The second type of program was one to train camp counsellors for non-profit camping organizations. Courses for girls were offered at Belwood Lake Camp near Fergus and those for boys at Bark Lake Camp at Irondale. The numbers of students attending these courses increased regularly from year to year.

During a visit to the Longford Mills and Bark Lake camps on July 27, 1969, the minister observed the activities of the participants with satisfaction. He was reported to have said that the Department of Education was not doing enough in the field of athletic development. He expressed the view that existing accommodation should be doubled so that at least four students from each of Ontario's 540 secondary schools could attend. Robert Secord, Director of the Youth and Recreation Branch, indicated that there were plans for two $6 million extensions to the Longford Mills camp, the first involving the construction of a conference and training centre with an indoor pool and track, and the second an outdoor track, three gymnasiums, and a swimming pool. These projects were not, apparently, high on the government's priority list, and it was impossible to say how soon they would be undertaken.[6]

The establishment of the Community Programs Branch in April 1948 was one of the most important developments of the immediate post-war period. It combined services in recreation and adult education previously provided by the Physical and Health Education Branch of the department and by the Ontario Adult Education Board. It was intended to be primarily a service organization, assisting on request with community activities conducted under community auspices. It co-operated with other government departments and with various associations, with particular emphasis on municipal recreation programs. It maintained a centrally-based technical staff as well as a field staff situated throughout the province. A large part of the efforts of the branch were devoted to the training of local leaders through the promotion of leadership training institutes and the provision of appropriate courses. In 1948–9 such courses were given in art, audio-visual problems, citizenship teaching, parent education and family relations, general leadership, handicrafts, physical recreation, rural composite programs, social recreation, and theatre. Rural community night schools were offered by joint efforts of the Department of Agriculture and the Community Programs Branch. There were fifteen such schools in 1949, offering classes in woodworking, public speaking, sewing, motor mechanics, folk dancing and singing, farm engineering, drama, weaving, farm science, farm machinery, music, wood refinishing,

CHART 1-2
Organization chart for the Ontario Department of Education, 1946

SOURCE: Ontario, *Report of the Minister of Education, 1946.*

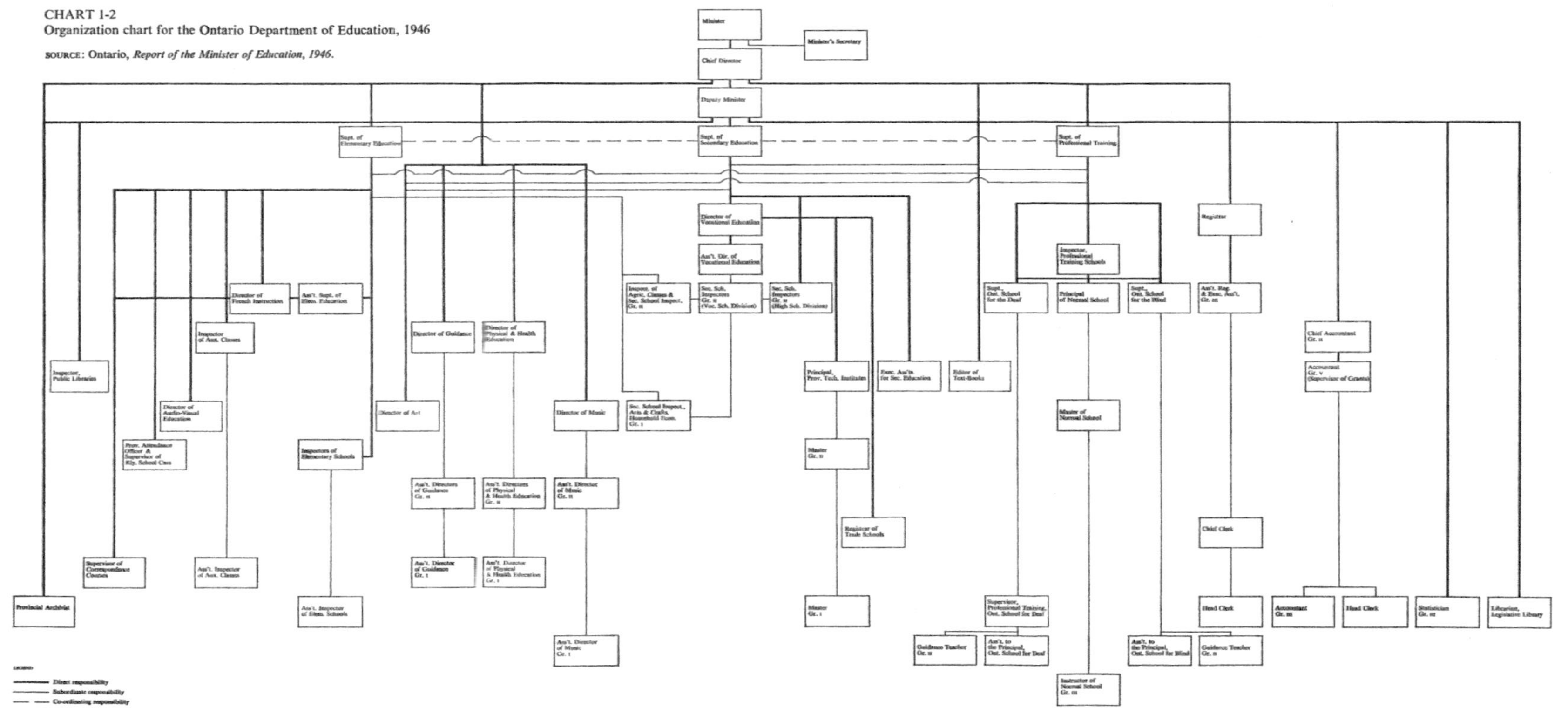

CHART 1-3
Organization chart for the Ontario Department of Education, 1964

SOURCE: Ontario, Department of Education

Minister of Education

Executive Assistant to the Minister

Chief Director of Education

Ministerial agencies

Deputy Minister

Deputy Minister

Personnel Director
School Planning and Buildings Research
Technical Advisor

Superintendent Business Administration
Assistant Superintendent Business Administration
Finance & Administration
Chief Grants Office

Superintendent Elementary Education
Assistant Superintendents Elementary Education
Elementary School Inspectors
Director Elementary School Library Services
Director of French for English-Speaking Students
Director French Instruction

Superintendent Special Education
Assistant Superintendent
Director Auxiliary Education
Director Correspondence Courses
Director Guidance Services
Director Statistical Services
School for the Blind, Brantford
Schools for the Deaf, Belleville, Milton

Superintendent Teacher Education
Assistant Superintendents
Teachers' Colleges: Hamilton, Lakehead, Lakeshore, London, North Bay, Ottawa, Peterborough, Stratford, Sudbury, Toronto, Windsor, University of Ottawa

Superintendent Professional Development
Assistant Superintendents
Summer Courses for Teachers

Superintendent Curriculum & Text-Books
Assistant Superintendents
Director Information Branch

Superintendent Secondary Education
Assistant Superintendent
Secondary School Inspectors
Director Music Education
Director Physical & Health Education
Ontario Athletic Leadership Camps
Director Art Education
Director Audio-Visual Education

Superintendent Technological & Trades Training
Assistant Superintendent
Co-Ordinator Technical Institutes
Provincial Technological Institutes: Haileybury, Hamilton, Ottawa, Kirkland Lake, Windsor
Co-ordinator of Institutes of Trades and Programme 5
Trade Schools Toronto 3
Vocational Centres: London, Ottawa
Director Curriculum & Standards

Director Provincial Library Service
Travelling Libraries

Registrar & Superintendent of Examinations
Assistant Superintendent of Examinations
Assistant Registrar
Departmental Examinations
Certificates & Diplomas
Correspondence & Filing

Director Community Programmes

Director Youth Branch

Teachers' Superannuation Commission
Ontario College of Education
Defence Training Board
Ontario College of Art
Ontario Council for the Arts
Ryerson Polytechnical Institute
Lakehead College of Arts, Science & Technology

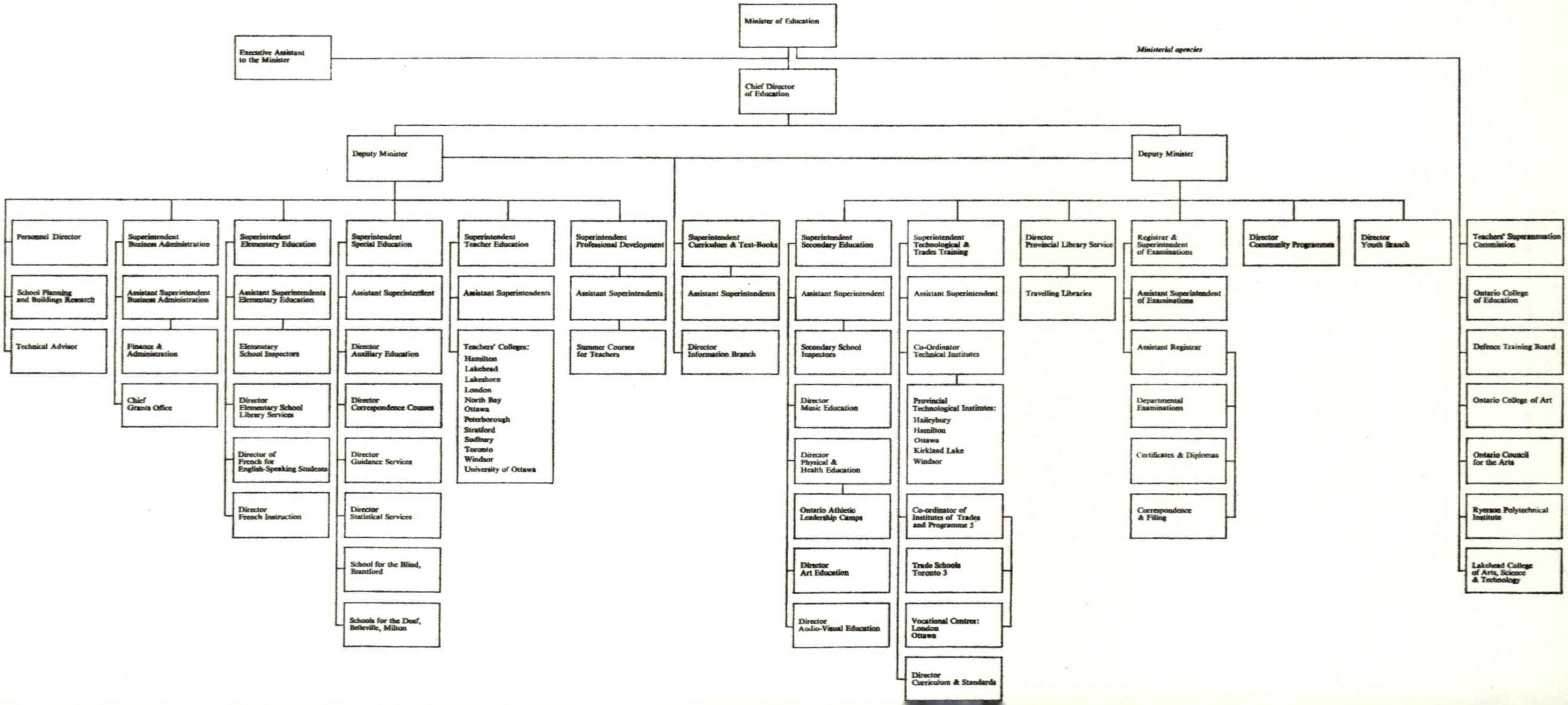

leathercraft, radio, electricity, shop work, art, plastics, and art metalwork. Citizenship training was placed under the management of the branch, and constituted one of its major activities.

Recommendations of the Royal Commission for Structural Changes
The Royal Commission made some recommendations in 1950 about the organization of the department, specifically, that there should be a grouping of branches into seven divisions, each headed by a superintendent or by an official of the same rank. The recommended divisions were Elementary Education, Secondary Education, Further Education, Professional Education, Curriculum, Business Administration, and the Registrar's Division. Each of the senior officials in charge of one of these respective branches would report to an associate deputy minister, a position that would have to be created. It was also recommended that these officials constitute a Committee of Superintendents, which would meet regularly for the following purposes:

(i) to devise ways and means of implementing policies determined by the Minister;
(ii) to collate and integrate recommendations for submission to the Associate Deputy Minister;
(iii) to resolve problems arising in one division which have involutions or implications for other divisions.[7]

Changes of 1956 and 1957
There were no major structural changes in the department until 1956. When C.F. Cannon was promoted to the position of chief director, he was succeeded by two deputy ministers: C.W. Booth, who was responsible for secondary school affairs, and F.S. Rivers, responsible for elementary school affairs. This development had unfortunate symbolic implications, since it seemed to sharpen the distinction between the two levels and to indicate a full retreat from the attempts made while Dana Porter was minister to bridge the gap with an intermediate division. The responsibility for final co-ordination was pushed up one level to the chief director. There was probably no greater actual split in departmental operations than there had been before, since the personalities of the new appointees were conducive to co-operation. Other significant developments during the same year were the creation of the offices of Superintendent of Curriculum and Superintendent of Special Services, to which S.A. Watson and H.R. Beattie were appointed. The former development represented a rather grudging recognition of the importance of curriculum, since it was many years before the Curriculum Branch had more than a small handful of staff. Beattie had previously held the rank of assistant superintendent, with responsibility for auxiliary, guidance, and statistical services. The new title represented an upgrading of this particular group of interests. Reporting to him in 1956 were the Director of Guidance, the Director of

Auxiliary Education Services, the Provincial Attendance Officer, the Statistician, and the Superintendents of the Ontario School for the Blind and the Ontario School for the Deaf. In the area of departmental administration, 1956 also saw the promotion of the Chief Accountant to the position of Superintendent of Business Administration, with an assistant superintendent and the Chief of the Grants Office reporting to him.

In 1957 a Professional Development Branch was created apart from the Teacher Education Branch. It was designed to give assistance, particularly to inexperienced teachers, at both the elementary and secondary levels. Whether or not it was a good idea to put initial and in-service teacher preparation in separate branches was a matter of some question. There was an argument for giving the latter special emphasis at a time when it seemed to be in particular need of building up. The work of the branch has been particularly significant in the area of departmental summer courses.

Changes immediately preceding the reorganization of 1965

The appointment of W.G. Davis as Minister of Education on October 25, 1962, was followed, after a brief period while he got his bearings, by the creation of new departmental organs for the more effective performance of existing functions and for the handling of new ones. The extension of the structure helped to point up some of its deficiencies and to speed the coming reorganization.

The Technological and Trades Training Branch was established in 1963 to give leadership in the development of provincial institutes of technology and provincial institutes of trades and to supervise the programs under the Federal-Provincial Technical and Vocational Training Agreement. It was responsible for the training of the unemployed, training in co-operation with industry, advanced technical evening classes, and training involving federal departments and agencies. It co-operated with the Department of Labour in providing the formal course work component of apprenticeship training. The functions of the new branch were previously exercised by the Secondary Education Branch of the department. The development of the new structure and the establishment of so many new departmental relationships owed a great deal to the work of the first superintendent, L.M. Johnston, whose innovative talents also played an outstanding part in the evolution of Technological and Trades Training Branch into the Applied Arts and Technology Branch.

The Youth Branch was organized in 1963, with W.F. Koerber, temporarily seconded from the Scarborough Board, as acting director. It was seen as an agency for co-ordinating and encouraging public and private agencies devoted to providing educational services for young people. According to the *Report of the Minister, 1963*, it was to deal with special problems that had arisen as a result of "automation, increased leisure time, the progress of urbanization, premature withdrawals from school, and changes in the social and family patterns."[8] Its focus of attention was young people who were not in full-time attendance at an educational institution. Early plans were made for a research program to help to clarify some possible courses of action.

A recommendation for the establishment of a Personnel Branch emerged from the study of the structure and organization of the department, to be dealt with in more detail later. Appropriate action was taken in August, 1963, with the appointment of T. Campbell as Director of Personnel. This development led to studies and definitions of job requirements and to a more satisfactory matching of personnel and responsibilities. A further result was that government salaries became more competitive, enabling the department to acquire the staff for the developments ahead.

In September 1963 the department called a conference on school construction and design, at which educational and administrative officials, school trustees, teachers, architects, and administrators exchanged experiences in dealing with building problems and devoted their attention to a search for guidelines for the future. Interest in this area led in June 1964 to the establishment of a Division of School Planning and Building Research, which came into full operation by the following November. Its main purpose was to study all aspects of the construction of school buildings and their equipment. A Minister's Committee on School Planning was set up in December 1964 "to keep the Department informed on all factors which affect school design under rapidly changing conditions."[9] Two other major developments of the same year were the creation of the Policy and Development Council and the Information Branch, both reserved for later treatment.

DEVELOPMENTS LEADING TO THE REORGANIZATION OF 1965

Despite the efforts of a great many highly competent officials, the department had a poor image during the 1950s. It seemed to be characterized by defensiveness, negativism, and resistance to change. Responses to initiatives from outside were typically, although by no means always, unenthusiastic. There was an inordinate concern with secrecy, even about quite trivial matters. This policy was, of course, self-defeating; the more such columnists as Bascom St John of the *Globe and Mail* ran into what appeared to be quite unnecessary barriers, the more critical they became.

Much of the immediate responsibility rested on the shoulders of W.J. Dunlop, who made no real effort to defend his officials. They thus drew together and erected barriers to defend themselves. In the absence of sufficient policy directions from him, they tended to think in terms of a self-generated department policy. There was a sense of alienation, reinforced by certain qualities in Dunlop that made him difficult to approach with anything but reinforcement for his own well solidified ideas. The writer recalls assisting a highly placed official in preparing a memorandum for his eyes, and being warned in the process that two words he preferred not to see were "American" and "social." If the many unfavourable views of Dunlop's performance are valid, Premier Frost must certainly assume most of the ultimate responsibility. He could hardly have been favourably impressed when he participated in meetings to work out school grant policy which Dunlop failed to attend. Yet it must be recorded that some of those who worked with Dunlop, and a large number who knew him, had a very high regard for him. One of the former asserts that he worshipped him – surely not an insignificant tribute to any man.

When J.P. Robarts became minister in 1959, he was immediately aware of the air of the defensiveness about the department, and he attempted to dispel it. Described as a "fresh breeze," he was particularly eager to open lines of communication with non-official educational interests and to encourage the flow of new ideas. In debates in the Legislature, he dealt with the faults of the educational system with the kind of candour that had not been heard from a government spokesman for a long time, and yet managed to ensure that his officials felt supported and encouraged. He found that, in many respects, the department was not an effective instrument for the implementation of new policies. There is no record that he ever said, as Khrushchev is reported to have done: "I sit here and give orders, and nothing happens." But he must have felt that there were innumerable ways by which a proposed departure from traditional practice could be held up, sidetracked, or smothered.

During the two years in which he was able to devote full time to the department, Robarts did not make any radical changes in its structure or organization. Such action was hardly to be expected during the following year, when he retained the education portfolio along with the prime ministership. His contributions to change, which were of crucial importance, consisted in establishing an atmosphere that was conducive to it, in selecting a successor in the person of William G. Davis with the determination to carry it through, and in giving him the kind of support that was necessary for success. It takes nothing away from the extraordinary achievements of the Davis ministry to point out that they occurred in a decade during which education had been placed at the top of the government's priority list, and that they had the active and firm backing of a sympathetic Prime Minister.

The contributions of the two successive ministers were praised in 1964 by their political opponent, Donald MacDonald, in these words: "I think that he [Davis] and his predecessor before him, the hon. Prime Minister, have rescued The Department of Education from a process of ossification, which was little short of terrifying in its later stages."[10]

Certain difficulties began to come to a head in the late 1950s and developed apace in the early 1960s. Salaries in the department, which adhered to civil service scales, rose more slowly than those paid by local school systems. The department was thus at a competitive disadvantage in recruiting replacements and the additional staff needed for its expanding supervisory and service programs. Remedies were sought in the creation of new job categories commanding relatively high salaries, to which large numbers of people were appointed. Two years after an assistant superintendency was created to accommodate a single individual, there were about thirty people in comparable positions. These developments caused considerable concern in the Treasury Board and the Civil Service Commission. It seemed questionable that so many high-priced educators were needed to carry out many of the administrative functions of the department.

An early survey of the situation was made in April 1962 by T. Campbell, then employed by the Civil Service Commission. The immediate occasion for his study was a request by the department for salary increases for secondary school inspectors to permit recruitment from among secondary school principals who were at that time earning from $13,000 to $14,000 a year, as compared with $10,000 to $12,000 for inspectors. Since increases for one category would affect salaries in related categories, it was thought necessary to obtain additional information about the kinds of activities and responsibilities involved at each level.

It was obvious that the problem was more fundamental than that of meeting salary competition from local boards. The department was relying on an outdated structure and mode of operations to meet the proliferating demands being made upon it. Many of these demands were attributable to the rapid growth in the school population and the expanded building program. The professional staff, in their efforts to keep the machinery operating effectively, were working long hours and often assuming inordinate burdens. There was an obvious need to eliminate unnecessary tasks, to avoid duplication, and to ensure that the responsibility for decision-making was located where it could be exercised most effectively.

One of the chief problems was that there was too little specific delegation of authority to the six superintendents and twenty-four assistant superintendents then on the departmental staff. Before a definite recommendation was made by the person best qualified to do so, there was a great deal of committee work and consultation, and then the matter had to go up two or three levels for official approval. This process often involved the writing of detailed explanations to superiors justifying the recommendation. Often a great deal of time was consumed in getting a series of initials on a particular document.

Another aspect of the same problem was the lack of clear-cut responsibility for specific functions such as curriculum, examinations, and inspection. Decisions thus had to be a group responsibility rather than an individual one. It was thus difficult to hold anyone specifically accountable for results. It was also very difficult for an individual with innovative ideas to get an opportunity to put them into practice. Campbell observed that the department was not making efficient use of the many highly talented people it had at its disposal.

A consequence of the rapid expansion in the school system and of its increasing complexity was that many assistant superintendents were spending the greater part of their time on clerical-administrative work such as school grants and business operations of school boards. In terms of the conservation and optimum utilization of professional talent, this development was very undesirable. It was also becoming less and less defensible from the financial point of view. Salaries of chartered accountants were at a maximum of $7,200, as compared with $12,500 for assistant superintendents. Campbell suggested a school affairs branch staffed with clerical-administrative personnel in order to give professional staff more time to control standards of education, to plan, and to recommend policy and legislation. This arrangement might be extended to secondary school field inspectors and to elementary school inspectors.

The collection of information on various aspects of the operation of the school system demonstrated some of the most serious defects in the department's organization. It was often considered easier for a particular branch to go directly to the school system for some item of information that it needed rather than to get it from another branch that already had it. A study done under the present writer's supervision in 1964 showed that, in extreme cases, the same item might be collected as often as seventeen times. It was hardly surprsing that there was a considerable degree of irritation and frustration in schools and in local systems.

Campbell anticipated some later developments in a revised organization chart for the department based on four principles. 1 / Unnecessary levels of supervision would be eliminated. 2 / Clear-cut responsibility would be delegated to seven or eight strong branch heads, who would have the authority to make administrative decisions in their own spheres of operations. 3 / The dichotomy between elementary and secondary education would be eliminated. 4 / There would be an emphasis on organization along functional lines, with all adult education managed by one branch, all teacher training under another, and a similar arrangement for other areas of concern.

Davis interested himself in departmental reform soon after his appointment. On May 21, 1963, he wrote to the Provincial Treasurer, J.N. Allan, as follows:

In my report to his Honour the Lieutenant-Governor covering the activities of the Department of Education for 1962, I referred to the tremendous expansion of the school system and to the new educational demands being made upon this Department. I am particularly concerned that it should be staffed and administratively organized to meet this challenge most effectively.

There have been conversations between officials of this Department and the Civil Service Commission regarding the possibility of having a member of the Commission's staff conduct a survey in this field for our Department. I should now like to submit a formal request that you make the services of an appropriate officer in your Department available to us to engage in such a study of our staffing in relation to organization and administration.[11]

The terms of reference for the study were as follows.

A. *Purpose of the Study*
To examine, report, and recommend staffing procedures wtih a view to achieving optimum efficiency in the operation of the Department of Education. "Staffing procedures" are interpreted to include determination of personnel needs, recruitment, selection, placement, orientation, promotion, career development, and the maintenance of favourable working conditions.

B. *Scope of the Study*

1. To examine first generally, and then in detail, the present organization of the Department.
2. To examine the existing techniques of administration including the allocation of work load, delegation of authority and responsibility, decision making, accountability, signing authority, communication, and workflow.
3. To examine in detail staffing objectives, techniques and procedures with particular reference to the ratio of administrators to educators.
4. To study the possibility of extending the decentralization of administration to district offices.
5. To review job content and classification structure for all positions in the Department.
6. To make such recommendations as may seem advisable with a view to improving efficiency in the operation of the Department.

C. *Report and Recommendations*
Periodic reports to be made from time to time, discussed with the Chief Director of Education, and submitted to the Minister of Education.

Allan immediately responded by naming J.S. Stephen, Executive Director of the Department of Civil Service, to conduct the study. Stephen was obviously well qualified for the task, not only because of his training but also by reason of his familiarity with the problem as seen from the civil service point of view. During the period of the study he was on leave from his regular position.

At the same time there was widespread recognition of the weaknesses, already identified by Campbell, attributable to the sharp division between elementary and secondary school affairs. Such a division produced a wasteful duplication of services and structures. It was confusing to the school systems and to the public because of differing policies and procedures at the two levels. It confined administrators to a limited field of operations, thus preventing them from developing a broad view of the educational process.

The absence of provision for co-ordination between elementary and secondary education at any administrative level below that of the chief director was balanced by an equally undesirable lack of distinction in functions at the inspectors' level. Inspectors had obligations with respect to the two main departmental functions: 1 / to offer guidance in the provision of instruction and in the maintenance of standards, and 2 / to provide assistance to school systems with respect to such *externa* as finances, legal requirements, and physical facilities. To handle both sets of obligations effectively placed an extraordinary burden on inspectors. There was considerable risk that the arrangement would fail to ensure that policy formulated in the department would be carried out effectively at the local level. Sound organizational principles suggested that the two functions should be separated at the inspectoral level and co-ordinated at the top.

Stephen felt that the situation called for the establishment of a major division of the department to deal with school administration. It would be responsible for administrative control over legislative grants, school building programs, transportation agreements, school jurisdictional problems, and other matters of concern to the secretary of the board at the local level. It could be staffed by people with business training and experience who need not necessarily come from the teaching profession. Through them there would be a possibility of exercising some control over the costs that were assuming increasing importance in the provincial budget. Under the proposed arrangement, inspectors could concentrate on classroom supervision, professional development of teachers, and liaison with principals. Among internal departmental functions, it seeemed appropriate to have the school administration division look after the central file registry and the mailing office.

Changing views of the importance of various departmental functions called for an enlargement and upgrading of the Curriculum Branch. Because of the way in which the department had developed, responsibility for various aspects of curriculum had become scattered to a certain extent through various branches, with a resulting lack of co-ordination. Stephen thought that the Curriculum Branch should be staffed with subject specialists who would draw on the experience of those involved in teacher training, inspection, and examinations. They, in turn, without actually engaging in inspection, would provide subject inspectors with assistance and guidance.

Stephen suggested the possibility of grouping all direct teaching programs in one division. Such a development would facilitate an arrangement by which difficulties over civil service salaries might be avoided. Teachers could be employed on contract just as they were by local school boards.

H.R. Beattie, who served for many years as Superintendent of Special Services and Provincial School Attendance Officer, and retired on December 21, 1965, after acting as Director of the Special Schools and Services

Branch during the first year after the reorganization went into effect, recalls some of the conditions in the department that gave rise to criticism.[12] He cites his own varied interests, ranging through guidance, special education, and data processing, as an example of the tendency for responsibilities to become associated with individuals, to the distress of those who felt that the organization should be rational, neat, and explainable to the outsider. Beattie did not feel unduly constrained in his efforts to achieve things he regarded as desirable and important. He was generally acknowledged, however, to be unusually skilled in departmental diplomacy, and doors were probably opened to him that at best creaked on very rusty hinges in the face of the efforts of others. There is little doubt that serious losses in efficiency resulted from the mingling of disparate functions, especially when a position which had been built up around the individual characteristics of one man had to be filled by another.

The same defects in the decision-making process which Campbell had noted earlier were very obvious to Stephen. Lack of clearly defined objectives and of specific delegation of authority meant that far too many matters were pushed upward beyond the levels where they could most appropriately be settled. Too many people were engaged in preparing letters for someone else's signature rather than for their own. Where the signature was that of a top official, follow-up communication was difficult or impossible. Thus the objective of effective communication was defeated. Furthermore, a ruling from the minister or the chief director was excessively difficult to reopen or challenge, even though circumstances might justify it. Ideally, policy and its applications should be so definitely and clearly outlined that most inquiries could be handled well down the line, and only exceptional questions would have to be referred to upper echelons. (See chart opposite p. 9.)

As an effective administrative procedure, Stephen favoured the use of written directions in the form of manuals on the procedures to be followed and the decisions to be made. These tended to be particularly useful where similar duties were performed by large numbers of officials such as principals of teachers' colleges, inspectors, or examination clerks. They could save a great deal of the time then being spent in supplying the same information over and over again on an individual basis.

Stephen's report, entitled "Staffing in Relation to Organization and Administration in the Department of Education"[13] was completed in December 1963 and made a major contribution to the planning for departmental reorganization. Particularly active in this process were the minister's Executive Assistant, C.H. Westcott, and the youthful Directors of Personnel and of Information, T. Campbell and C.H. Williams. Their position was not an easy one, since in the eyes of many officials their activities constituted a threat to a familiar and in many respects a comfortable regime. Although there was widespread agreement that changes were needed, there was a great variety of opinions as to what should be done, and an awareness that all interests could not be satisfied simultaneously. In an organization where long experience and tradition were highly regarded, there was bound to be suspicion of an in-group consisting of relative newcomers.

In an account that emphasizes events and results rather than the process by which they were achieved, it is particularly difficult to give adequate recognition to the contributions of a man in Westcott's position. He did not make policy announcements, deliver tradition-shattering addresses, or produce articles for educational journals, but worked behind the scenes to get things done. The record of his achievements is largely to be found in the work of others, particularly that of the minister he served. Some of the ideas that lay behind the major educational reforms of the period may be assumed to have originated with him, while the way in which others were actually implemented bore the stamp of his influence.

The reorganization inevitably meant that certain officials had to assume less prestigious positions and titles than they had previously enjoyed. An effort was made to compensate them by providing for salary increases.

The period was something of a tragedy for F.S. Rivers, who served as deputy minister from 1956 to 1961, and as chief director from 1961 to 1965. His outstanding abilities were perhaps most conspicuously in evidence in the production of the report of the Royal Commission, completed in 1950. During his last few years of service, however, it was evident that he had failed to catch Davis's vision of educational progress and reform. There was a suggestion of weariness in his reputed remark that he knew drastic changes had to come, but that he hoped they would be delayed until he had passed from the scene. The departmental reorganization, involving the abolition of his position, seemed a kind of rebuff to him. While continuing to serve in a consultative capacity during the period before Z.S. Phimister, the newly appointed deputy minister, could assume his responsibilities on a full-time basis, Rivers suddenly died.

THE REORGANIZED STRUCTURE

Announcement of the reorganization

Davis held a press conference on January 7, 1965, to announce and explain the new departmental structure. He defined two major objectives of the changes. The first was to streamline the organization for more efficient and effective operation in an era of rapid change and great expansion. Educators were to be free to devote their time exclusively to educational problems, while administrative specialists were to handle business matters. The second objective was to recognize more clearly the increasing emphasis on technical and vocational training throughout the entire departmental program. Davis mentioned the probability that nearly 50 per cent of secondary school students would enrol in the

Business and Commerce Branch or the Science, Technology and Trades Branch under the Reorganized Programs of Study. He also referred to the program of constructing institutes of technology and Ontario vocational centres in various parts of the province.

The main features of the new organization were described in terms of three key words: integration, decentralization, and re-allocation. Integration would apply to elementary and secondary education as a means of strengthening the concept of the two as part of a continuing process. The main justification for the original administrative separation had disappeared now that education at both levels was regarded as basic. A second aspect of integration would be the bringing together of school supervision, curriculum, and examinations in a new Programs Branch. It was hoped that the efforts centred on the student in the classroom would be part of a harmonious pattern. Integration also involved the merging of many small specialist branches into larger units based on a logical grouping of functions. The supervision of subjects such as music, art, and guidance, which had become established in schools as part of the regular program, was to be integrated with the supervision of regular subjects in the curriculum.

Decentralization was a somewhat more distant objective, to be achieved by an orderly progression from the existing organization. Davis mentioned the setting up of what he called "districts" in various parts of the province, in which superintendents, responsible for both elementary and secondary education, would operate with staffs of inspectors in various specialties. It would thus be possible to make prompt decisions in accordance with local conditions and needs.

Re-allocation of functions involved changing the title of the chief director to deputy minister in harmony with accepted practice elsewhere. Reporting directly to him would be three assistant deputy ministers responsible respectively for instruction, administration, and provincial schools and further education. As a second aspect of re-allocation, school inspectors and other educators were to be relieved of many functions that did not require the attention of professional educators. Such functions would henceforth be exercised by officials in the School Business Administration Branch.

Davis referred to the diagram shown on Chart 1-4, and made brief comments on the responsibilities of various officials and on the functions of different parts of the organization. An inspection of the diagram shows that the ten units at the level next to that of assistant deputy minister were called branches, and that those at the level beyond that were called divisions. The officials in charge of branches were designated directors, and, except for the Registrar, those in charge of divisions were superintendents. For most of the units, the reorganization involved a continuation of substantially the same basic function. These units included the Registrar's Division, formerly the Registrar's Branch; the Curriculum Division, form-

CHART 1-4
Organization chart for the Ontario Department of Education, 1965

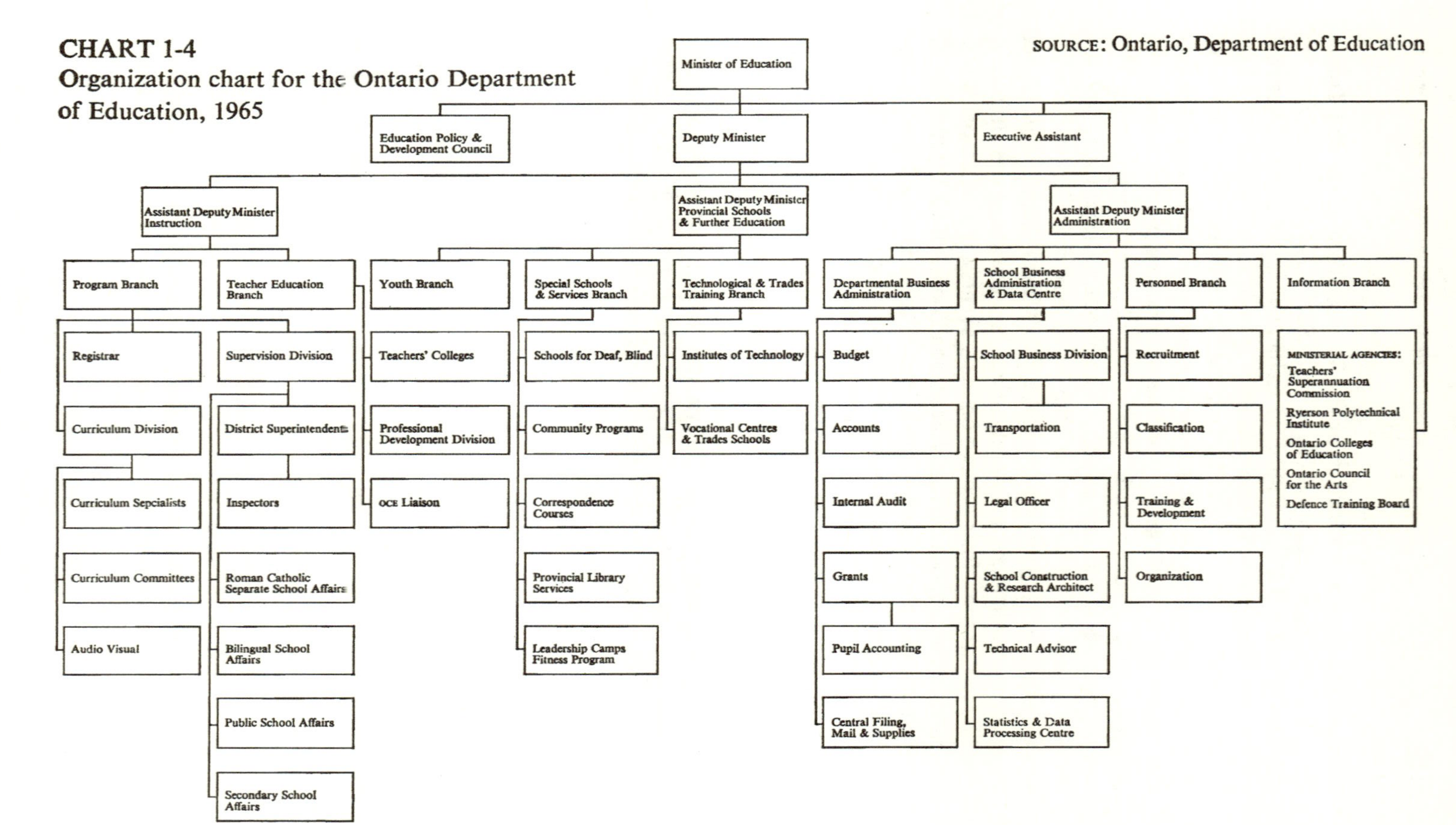

SOURCE: Ontario, Department of Education

erly the Curriculum and Text-books Branch; the Teacher Education Branch; the Professional Development Division, formerly the Professional Development Branch; the Technological and Trades Training Branch; the Youth Branch; the Provincial Library Service Branch; the Personnel Branch; and the Information Branch. The Supervision Division absorbed the major part of the functions of the former Elementary Education and Secondary Education Branches. The Special Schools and Services Branch was the successor to the Special Services Branch. The former Business Administration Branch was divided into Departmental Business Administration and School Business Administration Branches. The version of the diagram in the *Report of the Minister, 1965* appears to have been in error in showing the chairman of what was at that time designated the Education Policy and Development Council, and later simply the Policy and Development Council, responsible to the deputy minister. This body was clearly set up to give advice directly to the minister. Confusion appears to have arisen because the minister did not see it in the light of other agencies where the imposition of line authority was a major factor, but rather as a means of generating ideas and suggestions that he hoped would flow directly to the deputy minister as well as to himself. The organization diagram for 1966 was changed to show the chairman responsible directly to the minister.

At a further press conference on January 13, Davis indicated the names of the appointees to the new positions. On that occasion, he paid tribute to Rivers, and announced that Z.S. Phimister, Director of Education for the city of Toronto during the previous six years, would be the new deputy minister. The respective Assistant Deputy Ministers for Instruction, for Provincial Schools and Further Education, and for Administration were H.E. Elborn, W.R. Stewart, and J.S. Stephen. The first two had been deputy ministers for elementary and secondary education respectively in the previous organization. Stephen, whose ideas had been so influential in the planning process of the previous two years, was appropriately given an opportunity to help make the scheme work despite the fact that he had recommended that the assistant deputy minister be chosen from among outstanding business administrators employed by the larger school boards. The minister referred to those who would hold new or continued appointments: L.M. Johnston, Director of the Program Branch; M.B. Parnall, Superintendent of the Curriculum Division; A.H. McKague, Superintendent of the Supervision Division; J.B. St John, Director of the Education Policy and Development Council, to be joined by C.A. Mustard; C.H. Westcott, Executive Assistant; G.L. Duffin, Director of the Teacher Education Branch; H.R. Beattie, Director of the Special Schools and Services Branch; N.A. Sisco, Director of the Technological and Trades Training Branch; P.H. Cunningham, Director of Departmental Business Administration; T. Campbell, Director of the Personnel Branch; and C.H. Williams, Director of the Information Branch. The position of Director of School Business Administration and the Data Centre had not yet been filled.

Further evolution of the organization

The departmental organization continued the process of adaptation, partly as certain features of the reorganized structure proved in practice to need adjustment, but more perhaps to accommodate changing needs. Later in 1965 the first steps were taken toward decentralization with the establishment of the first five Regional Offices (or Area Offices, as they were called until 1967). These five were in Port Arthur, Sudbury, North Bay, London, and Waterloo. The network was completed in 1966 when additional offices were established in St Catharines, Metropolitan Toronto (two offices), Kingston, and Eastview. A structural development in the Special Schools and Services Branch in 1965 was the creation of a Schools for Retarded Children Division. A new Educational Television Section began a brief period of incubation in the Curriculum Division during the same year.

One of the major changes in 1966 was the creation of the Applied Arts and Technology Branch, which absorbed the Technological and Trades Training Branch. The name of the new unit and its extended area of concern reflected the rapidly developing plans for the provincial system of colleges of applied arts and technology. During the same year, the Educational Television Section was established as a branch headed by a director who was responsible to the Assistant Deputy Minister for Instruction. Changes were also made in administrative organization. The Financial Administration Office was carved off from the Departmental Business Administration Branch, and given a staff in budgeting and internal auditing as well as a legal adviser and a special adviser in data processing. At the same time, the Grants Division was transferred from the Departmental Business Administration Branch to the School Business Administration Branch.

The deputy ministers

Z.S. Phimister's brief term of office came to an end with his sudden death on November 20, 1966. His appointment less than two years before had come as a result of a thorough appraisal of possible candidates for the top administrative post of deputy minister. Davis had been particularly anxious to secure the best possible leadership in his newly-organized department, and Phimister had appeared to tower over all others, not only physically but also in terms of the force and originality of his ideas and the wealth of his administrative experience. The last stage of his distinguished career is not generally regarded as a success. His new post differed greatly from the highly structured situation in the Toronto school system, and he did not know the location of the levers of power. According to some inside views, he lacked the firmness to deal with opposition. The opinion was also expressed, however, that he was overcoming some of his initial difficulties and that, had he been in office for a longer period, the story might have been different.

Phimister's successor was J.R. McCarthy, who had been Deputy Minister of University Affairs from the time that department was established, and previously Superintendent of Curriculum and Text-books. Having come up through the ranks, McCarthy possessed the kind of familiarity with official procedure that Phimister lacked. His strongly held and eloquently expounded progressive views had survived through the 1950s when the tide was running in the other direction. He had advocated freedom for teachers in the choice of curricula and textbooks, denounced the tyranny of external examinations, and in general opposed the imposition of unnecessary restrictions and regulations of all kinds. He favoured decentralization of departmental powers and the maximum encouragement of local initiative and responsibility. In short, his philosophical orientation seemed very much in harmony with Davis's own.

Changes after McCarthy's appointment

A change in terminology was introduced in 1967. What were previously called divisions were renamed sections, and the term "division" was applied to the areas under the three assistant deputy ministers. There was thus an Instruction Division, a Provincial Schools and Further Education Division, and an Administration Division.

In January 1967 the Cultural Exchange Office was created with C.E. Rathé as Co-ordinator, reporting directly to the deputy minister. In 1968 News and Information Service (formerly the Information Branch) was given a similar status in the organization, as was also the newly created Special Services Section.

In a statement of major importance in the Legislature on June 4, 1968, the minister outlined the changing role of the department. After reviewing the steps already taken toward decentralization, he said:

> The function of departmental officials is to develop and continuously review a comprehensive philosophy of public education. This educational planning – which must cover an extremely broad spectrum, taking into account the social and economic needs of all citizens – is then expressed as policy in two principal ways: through the medium of the educational laws, which form the framework for publicly supported education, and through the distribution of funds, which are not unlimited and therefore must be invested with some wisdom. Being centrally located, the department is also specially qualified to be a resource centre for new information and a clearing house for worthwhile ideas emanating from within and outside the province.
>
> These are ... the three basic or principal responsibilities of the department,

and all other involvements, it seems to me, can only have the effect of diluting the considerable effort required to do those jobs well. With the decentralization of many of the traditional departmental functions to local authorities which are situated more closely to the public they serve, departmental officials will be better able to concentrate on those responsibilities which they are best equipped to perform.

The main condition needed to bring about this ideal situation is that local educational authorities should be large enough to be able to provide a full range of programmes plus the highly specialized staff of psychologists, reading consultants, speech therapists, and others that are required if all children are to be given the opportunity to achieve their maximum potential.

Realization of such an aim will call for co-operation, highmindedness and quite frankly, some sacrifice. This centralization at the local level is in no way inconsistent with the philosophy of decentralization at the provincial level. We should strive for an optimum local organization which is close enough to the local scene to be fully conversant with its problems, yet large enough and well enough staffed to receive delegation of responsibility from the department. This delegation of duties will provide the local staff and specialists with the flexibility and freedom from artificial constraints which will enable them to operate at maximum effectiveness.

The point I wish to stress here is that a distinction must be drawn between "operating" functions and "policy-making" functions. I am suggesting that, in a highly developed and mature educational system such as we have in this province, "operating" functions are most effectively and appropriately the responsibility of local agencies such as boards of education and boards of governors. The central Department of Education, on the other hand, must be responsible for overall planning ...

I would suggest that we can best focus the role of a central Department of Education by investigating some of its broad strategic objectives and resulting responsibilities. These might be stated as follows, and not necessarily in order of priority.

1. The department is responsible for ensuring that all citizens have suitable educational opportunities. This involves the setting of objectives, the provision of leadership and the establishment and involvement of appropriate authorities to implement the necessary programmes.

Leadership cannot take the form of dictation from a superior authority to other levels. To be effective, it must be based on mutual respect and recognition of the special contributions which can be made by all parties to the total educational enterprise. For example, classroom teachers and local authorities are particularly qualified to take part in the development and implementation of new approaches to meet specific circumstances with which they are familiar. The department, on the other hand, because of its central location, is uniquely equipped to disseminate locally developed techniques to other parts of the province.

2. The department should delegate the operation of institutions to other

bodies, for example, local education authorities, which, through legislation, are given sufficiently wide powers to ensure that all educational needs of society are met.

From this premise, it follows that the department must encourage the establishment of authorities suitable for the task; such authorities as large local education jurisdictions, colleges and institutions, to which responsibility can be delegated. Such agencies should be given encouragement to innovate, with as much freedom from regulation as is consistent with the central authority's responsibility.

3. The department must provide financial resources to local education authorities and establish priorities so that resources which are scarce may be allocated in the most judicious manner. Here, the primary needs are analysis and long-term planning.

4. The department has a responsibility for research, whether it engages in it directly or encourages local education authorities and other agencies to search for fresh approaches and better educational methods.

5. The department must provide assistance to local education agencies in the form of consultative services, proposals and new ideas for curriculum development, and must assist in providing suitably qualified personnel.

These suggestions concerning the appropriate role of a Department of Education are based on a number of assumptions. The first is that the true strength of a democracy lies in the opportunities which it provides for individual growth and development, and that this can best be achieved through the scale of diversity and flexibility which is only possible in a decentralized system.

Another assumption is that, in educational matters, locally elected representatives working with professional teachers can be counted on not only to maintain existing standards but to achieve new heights of excellence, which will ultimately be of benefit to all.

The response from the press to the minister's statement was favourable. On June 10, 1968, the *Sarnia Observer* printed an editorial under the heading "Change in Policy" which began as follows:

Ontario Education Minister William Davis, appears to be a practical man. With the new county and district school boards not far in the offing, he is going to decentralize his department and leave only the brass in Toronto to determine policies.

That is probably the most thought-provoking word to come out of Queen's Park for a long time. Imagine cutting down on the horde of people swarming around the education department and putting them out in selected spots throughout the province, where they could be more accessible!

An aspect of the department's functions on which the minister enlarged in November 1969 was the necessity of directing provincial support to those projects which had high priority from the provincial point of view.[14] He had established a departmental task force to propose ways and means of ensuring that grants made to local authorities would achieve this purpose. There was a somewhat cryptically worded warning that the department would not abdicate its essential responsibilities: "If local authorities, because of their limited jurisdiction, should find it difficult to implement fiscal policies which are in line with provincial priorities, they would be required to revise their fiscal requirements according to norms which would be formulated by the Department."[15]

TWO

The role and functions of the department after 1965

THE MINISTER

The reorganization of 1965 did not involve any substantial change in the position or powers of the minister himself, but rather in the apparatus through which he discharged his responsibilities. His legal powers and duties had accumulated since the establishment of the office in 1876. That event, which was of great significance, occurred on Ryerson's urging at the time of his retirement. It had previously been thought that an arrangement which left the superintendent as the highest responsible official was a desirable way of keeping partisan political influences out of education. But Ryerson had found it frustrating and difficult to get his bills passed when he had to depend on the sponsorship of others. For this and other reasons, education was placed in the hands of a responsible minister.

McCutcheon expressed approval of the change made in 1876 for the reasons noted.[1] He also suggested that the minister's position in the cabinet and in the Legislature enhanced his power and prestige and that he was much better placed than any appointed official to whom such duties might be delegated. He thought that public opinion was an adequate check on one endowed with so much power. When Frank MacKinnon dealt with the proposition in general terms, without specific reference to Ontario, twenty years later, he took quite a different view. He declared that a minister of education all too often finds it difficult to resist going beyond his responsibility of policy making and general direction, and gets into all kinds of activities for which he is unfitted. Having asked rhetorically who there is to check a minister of education, MacKinnon answered that the schools and the teachers, who were most directly concerned with education, had no power or independence, and the minister could consult, direct, or ignore them at will.[2]

The powers of the minister in Ontario are indeed very great. *The Department of Education Act* defines a large part of them, although many are also specified in other legislation. The main areas covered by ministerial powers are as follows: 1 / the establishment and administration of schools and other educational institutions at all levels; 2 / the prescription of courses of study and textbooks in all provincial educational institutions; 3 / the definition of school attendance requirements; 4 / the definition of qualifications and duties of teachers and their conditions of service, and the making of arrangements for the professional preparation of teachers; 5 / the setting, conducting, and marking of examinations and the reporting of the results; 6 / the handling of complaints and disputes arising from the school acts; 7 / the provision of educational services for children with physical and mental handicaps; 8 / the establishment of educational facilities for children living on Crown lands or other tax-exempt property; 9 / the distribution of school grants and defraying of other expenses entailed in operating the provincial educational system; 10 / the provision of adult educational and recreational services; 11 / the conduct of negotiations with federal government agencies with respect to technical and vocational training; and 12 / the regulation of private schools. There is a considerable list of additional functions that do not fall under these headings.

DAVIS AS A PUBLIC FIGURE

Davis's appointment as minister in 1962 was an event of such importance that it can hardly be exaggerated. There has been nothing comparable since the days of Egerton Ryerson to the surge of innovations he has sent sweeping through the educational system. It is difficult to avoid comparisons with the Ryerson era, even though they have been made so often that they have come to seem trite. Both Ryerson and Davis set about creating new structures to meet the compelling needs of their respective eras. Both have seemed to be constantly hovering on the edge of forward positions into which a cautious public was not yet quite prepared to be led. The fact of his being, unlike Ryerson, an elected official has meant that Davis has had to develop and push through his programs in a much shorter period of time. The necessity for speed has put a premium on the political finesse which he possesses to a marked degree.

Davis strikes observers as an unusual combination of ambition and idealism. There is no point in denying the ambition, since no one becomes a minister of the Crown without some measure of it. Society goes only so far in recognizing and availing itself of outstanding executive and administrative talents; unless their possessor gives some very positive evidence of willingness to use them, they remain untapped. The idealism is also unmistakable, and, in the opinion of Davis's close associates, predominant. Davis is profoundly convinced of the importance of education – and education of a particular kind. There is some reason to wonder why he has not come out with a ringing endorsement of the report of the Hall-Dennis Committee, since so many of his actions before its appearance reflected a similar orientation. He encourages every move to give pupils and teachers more freedom, more responsibility, more chance for constructive initiative. He backs every development that promises to make school experiences more humane, more stimulating, and more in tune with the positive features of modern life.

He appears to see life as a compelling challenge, with real rewards for sincere and honest effort, and to believe that children and young people can be brought up to view things in the same light. Although he displays far more sympathy with student activists than many officials particularly appreciate, he tells the extremists among them with firm conviction that society, despite its defects, is not rotten and corrupt.

Davis seems to have come to his position with no blueprint for a reformed educational structure. Some associates even claim that he has developed his program with little idea of what he is going to do next. But he has from the beginning been extremely receptive to new ideas, especially if they are expressed with confidence and enthusiasm. He has seemed almost passive as he has waited for a show of initiative, but has constantly stood ready to open doors for those with the determination and perception to push against them. More than one person, ready with his contribution, has tarried in the background waiting for a signal that has not come. Davis seems to feel that impulses that lack the force to break in upon him are too weak to merit encouragement. The situation is difficult for those who have been too long steeped in bureaucratic protocol.

Davis's general orientation has been sharp enough to enable him to identify the proposals that fit into an acceptable pattern of development. This does not mean that he has shown an unerring ability to select the enterprises that will succeed and to reject those that will fail. While his major programs have been largely successful or at least, like the reorganization of the local system in 1969, highly desirable in principle, some of the less conspicuous projects to which he has given his blessing have not worked out particularly well.

Perhaps his most extraordinary talent is his ability to secure support for a controversial proposal in order to get it implemented or, if opposition cannot be overcome, to override it with a minimum of rancour. This talent is displayed most conspicuously in the Legislature and in contacts with the public. In the legislative debates, Davis is unfailingly courteous and unruffled. On the rare occasions when he has been subjected to bitter attacks, as when his integrity was impugned in the debate over the University of Western Ontario Bill in 1957, he has handled himself with such dignity that members of the opposition have rallied strongly to his defence. He has maintained good relations with most opposition critics by giving informative and straightforward answers to their questions and by expressing appreciation for their positive contributions. At the same time, he makes sure to present the best case for the government that the facts justify. A number of highly placed members of the opposition, with the reservation that one of their own members might do even better, have expressed the opinion that he is the best Minister of Education the province has ever had.

Placing a strong emphasis on the value of good public relations, he has been extremely receptive to delegations from educational associations and from local school systems. He has persuaded innumerable dissatisfied individuals and groups that, if he could not accede to their wishes, he was at least sympathetic to their cause, and valued the opportunity to hear their views. His investment in communication has done more than anything else to change the image of remoteness and lack of responsiveness of the department in the 1950s.

Since he obtained offices in the Parliament Buildings in 1965, Davis has largely withdrawn in a physical sense from the Department of Education. At the same time, his contacts with departmental officials have considerably narrowed. As the organization has increasingly come under the control of people of his own choosing, this mode of operating may well be justifiable on practical grounds. But there is certainly a feeling of neglect on the part of middle-level officials, which could be dispelled by an occasional semi-formal or informal group meeting with the minister. Those who never see him except on television have difficulty persuading themselves that they are really part of his team.

Davis's extraordinary achievements are not the result of what are normally considered to be orderly or organized work habits. Although the really essential things manage to get done on time, he sometimes seems bent, like the hero of the comic strip of old, on snatching the fair maiden from destruction at the very last possible moment. For one who does not know all the circumstances, it is difficult to tell whether he is an incurable procrastinator or whether he has a finely attuned sense of the most strategic moment to act.

His addresses achieve a positive effect on the basis of their content rather than because of inspirational or emotional appeal. His delivery is often noticeably flat, and loses force through his propensity for inserting qualifying words and phrases as if he were determined to avoid the inaccuracy of the bold assertion. More than anyone else, he can claim credit for spreading the Ontario usage of the word "jurisdiction" as an equivalent for "place." Despite this contribution, he is conspicuous among political leaders in the appeal he makes to an intelligent and thoughtful audience.

As an appraisal of Davis in his public role, the foregoing comments are profusely supplemented by the account in the present series of volumes of the many impressive achievements in Ontario education since 1962. In a sense, they are all Davis achievements, and few will begrudge calling the period the Davis era.

THE DEPUTY MINISTER

The establishment of the position of deputy minister as the senior one in the department was in accord with a recommendation of the Royal Commission in 1950. The commission advised that this official be freed as far as possible from routine duties so that he could devote himself to educational statesmanship. It was therefore recommended that he be assisted by an associate deputy minister, who would be responsible for the co-ordination of the work of the chief officials of the department.

In recent years, the trend has been toward greater centralization of control by the deputy minister of that part of the departmental apparatus remaining in Toronto, along with the delegation of powers to the Regional Offices. This trend may be attributable to two main factors: 1 / the particular leadership style of the incumbent, J.R. McCarthy, and 2 / the waning interest of the minister in the specifics of departmental administration. In the earlier days of his ministry, Davis held regular meetings of an informal minister's council in which he sought ideas and encouraged the expression of points of view from people below the top organizational level. When he became Minister of University Affairs as well as Minister of Education in 1964, he acquired an office in the Parliament Buildings, and thereafter spent little time in the Department of Education quarters. It was perhaps only natural that he would give the machinery a chance to run once he had reconstructed it in a fashion more to his liking.

THE ASSISTANT DEPUTY MINISTERS

The functions of the assistant deputy ministers are to be understood mainly in terms of the activities of the part of the department responsible to each of them. These activities are dealt with in the pages that follow. The assistant deputy ministers interpret policy at the appropriate level, make decisions on certain matters, and pass others on to the deputy minister to deal with. They sometimes represent the minister on ceremonial occasions. Since the reorganization in 1965, the assistant deputy ministership for instruction has been held successively by H.E. Elborn, G.L. Duffin, and J.F. Kinlin; that for provincial schools and further education by W.R. Stewart and L.M. Johnston; and that for administration by J.S. Stephen.

THE PROGRAM BRANCH

The Program Branch was intended to provide a framework for the co-ordination of the entire educational program, including that at the elementary and secondary school levels. Its functions were really those of the three constituent divisions. After the death of its director, M.B. Parnall, in 1968, the co-ordinating function at that level was left in abeyance, and the superintendents of the three divisions, by now called sections, reported directly to the assistant deputy minister.

The Curriculum Division (Section)

The Curriculum Division absorbed part of the functions of branches that formerly had responsibility for individual subjects and subject areas such as art, guidance, music, and physical and health education. The former directors of those branches became assistant superintendents in the Curriculum Division, and the inspectors concerned with these subjects were assigned to the Supervision Division. The former Audio-Visual Education Branch became a section of the Curriculum Division.

According to the *Report of the Minister, 1965* the objectives of the Curriculum Division were as follows:

(1) to articulate courses of study for Grades 1 to 13;
(2) to provide new courses and programs designed to meet a wide variety of student needs;
(3) to promote the best of new teaching methods, materials and techniques, including educational television and other audio-visual media and technological devices;
(4) to carry out a continuing revision of curriculum publications in order that the school program may benefit from the findings of educational research, from the latest developments in scholarship, and from contacts with business and industry;
(5) to redirect emphasis in the curriculum so as to prepare students for life in a technologically advanced society;
(6) to ensure, within the limits of the school program, that the sense of identity and integrity of the individual and the values of society are preserved and enhanced.[3]

Whether the grandiose generalities at the end of this statement were realized or not, there was a great expansion of departmental activity in the curriculum area, and curriculum became the important concern that earlier critics had suggested it should be.

Since the 1950s there have been profound changes in the department's concept of its responsibilities in the curriculum area and in its procedures for achieving its objectives. These changes have owed a great deal to a succession of enlightened leaders, including J.R. McCarthy, M.B. Parnall, J.F. Kinlin, and J.K. Crossley. As each in turn has headed the branch, division, or section, according to the current terminology, he has strengthened a growing staff group sharing the same outlook. While it is appropriate to touch on some aspects of the work of these people in a discussion of the development of the departmental organization, the influence of the changes is much wider, and affects many other topics dealt with in the present series of volumes.

In an article in the *Ontario Mathematics Gazette* in 1966, J.F. Kinlin indicated some of the most significant changes in the departmental approach beginning in 1956.[4] Although he was dealing specifically with mathematics, many of the developments he referred to had a much broader application. In some ways, in fact, new approaches in that subject foreshadowed progress in curriculum reform in general. Kinlin identified the adoption of the policy in late 1956 of appointing staff inspectors for academic subjects as the first significant departmental change of the period. Some hint of future efforts to integrate elementary and secondary education was provided by his own experience in that he was the first elementary school inspector to be appointed as an inspector of an academic subject at the secondary school level. Integration of the two levels became a stated objective as early as 1960. Two years later, a single specialist became responsible for mathematics in the full range of grades from kindergarten to grade 13.

The early 1960s saw the beginning of active co-operation between the department and outside associations in the curriculum field. Kinlin referred to negotiations between the chief director, F.S. Rivers, and A.J. Coleman of the Ontario Mathematics Commission to enable departmental officials to become full-fledged members of the latter organization. Some idea of the extent of the department's self-imposed isolation in the previous period can be gained by his comments.

Only those close to the situation at that time can appreciate the difficulties associated with the development of this cooperation between the Department and the Commission. Such a development caused surprise outside the Department and consternation within. No such thing had ever been attempted before and acceptance (or tolerance) of the situation by certain senior officials required considerable tact and diplomacy. Timing of approaches, forms of presentations, even strategy in keeping certain persons apart at crucial times – all required careful planning.[5]

The Social Sciences Study Committee of the Joint Committee of the Toronto Board of Education and the University of Toronto expressed considerable dissatisfaction with the way the department handled curriculum construction and revision around 1961. The committee claimed that the existing method too often consisted of "slow deliberation by Departmental officials interspersed with sudden and hurried consultations of an *ad hoc* group of active teachers."[6] The rather tart observation was made that a new curriculum could not be drafted in three or four Saturdays by any group of teachers. Consultation seemed too little and too late to overcome the deficiencies attributable to the remoteness of departmental officials from teaching and to their lack of up-to-date knowledge in the various disciplines. The committee also charged that changes initiated by the department were inclined to involve only changes in the sequence of courses or in the prescription of their factual content. The department was given credit for extending to local boards and teachers freedom of interpretation and room to experiment, but was urged to devise more effective procedures for continuous consultation and to encourage more initiative from below.

The new outlook of the 1960s was articulated by J.R. McCarthy at the

Ontario Conference on Education at Windsor in November 1961. This outlook involved a recognition 1 / that the fundamental purposes of education must be examined as a background for the development of curriculum; 2 / that the whole educational program, from kindergarten through grade 13 and into further education, must be considered as a unit; and 3 / that the widest possible range of resources must be utilized, including consultation and the results of research. McCarthy put it this way:

> The most pressing and vital problems in education today are those having to do with the experiences of our students in the classrooms of this province. That this fact is fully recognized is indicated by the announcement in the speech from the Throne in the Ontario legislature this week when it was stated that revisions of the courses in kindergarten and grades 1 to 6 will be undertaken in 1962. It should be fully understood that this task cannot be accomplished without a thorough examination of the purposes of the elementary school in the 1960's and its place in the overall educational programme from kindergarten to grade 13, and indeed into further education whether it be in trade schools, technical institutes, universities, teachers' colleges or other institutions.
>
> Since it is the desire to produce courses that will serve the best interests of all our boys and girls, time will be needed to study new developments, to examine new research, to consider recent experimentation and to consult those who are likely to be affected by any changes that may be adopted. In other words, adequate opportunity will be given to all those who have suggestions to offer, to make their views known and every consideration will be given to them. Committees to do this work will be set up at the provincial level and local committees and organizations will be encouraged to consider problems which they have encountered and about which they may wish to submit their views. This revision is seen as a cooperative venture in education across this province that can make a major contribution to a better understanding, not only by educators, but by all our citizens of our educational goals and the means by which they can be achieved.[7]

An acceptance of the need for field trials was another aspect of the process noted by Kinlin in the article referred to earlier. He gave credit to the Ontario Mathematics Commission, in co-operation with the department, for setting the pattern in this area. Pre-trials of mathematics materials began as early as 1959–60, and increased quickly in subsequent years. This development was associated with the abandonment of the policy of keeping the deliberations of curriculum committees confidential until the courses of study was actually distributed to the teachers. Kinlin traced the beginning of the new practice to an occasion in 1961 when he and A.W. Bishop, later Registrar of the department, interviewed a thousand teachers, reporting to them the proposals of an active committee, and eliciting their reactions for referral back to the latter. The approach was beneficial, not only because it elicited helpful information, but also because it gave many teachers an opportunity to prepare to handle the topics long before the new outlines were released.

Kinlin commented that departmental courses of study were traditionally developed to last, and that in some cases they had lasted for a generation. The idea had more recently become accepted that they would normally be of short duration. Thus the process of examination, trial, and revision had become a continuous one. Obviously this development emphasized the importance of familiarizing teachers as quickly as possible with the latest changes. Tradition was broken in the summer of 1963 when a certificate course was offered for teachers of grades 7 and 8 before there was an officially approved course of study. In the same year and in the year following, there was unprecedented co-operation among the Teacher Education, Professional Development, and Curriculum and Textbooks Branches to assist teachers in courses organized by inspectors and federation groups. In 1964 the same branches pooled their efforts to offer the first short course for elementary school inspectors to assist them in improving classroom instruction.

There was a further development of the organizational structure of the Curriculum Section in August 1967, in that subjects were grouped in four main areas: 1 / humanities, including English, Français,[8] modern languages (French, German, Italian, Russian, and Spanish), the classical languages (Latin and Greek), and specialist work in primary reading; 2 / mathematics and science (physics, chemistry, and biology); 3 / social sciences (history, geography, social studies, government, and economics); and 4 / the general group (art, music, physical education, commercial, technical, and industrial arts, and home economics). Where applicable, treatment of the subjects extended from kindergarten to the end of grade 13. A group chairman was appointed to co-ordinate the work of each area. The initial appointments to the chairmanships of the groups in the order listed were C.H. Williams, A.T. Carnahan, G. Kaye, and J.K. Crossley. The new arrangement was intended to meet the need for integration of certain aspects of several subjects and to lay the foundation for a more flexible grouping of options in school programs.

The change in departmental supervisory practices in 1967 was of major importance to the Curriculum Section. As of September 1, 113 former subject inspectors became program consultants attached to Regional Offices, but looking for inspiration to the Curriculum Section. They had formerly had a dual role, encompassing inspection and consulting, but now they were confined to the latter. They visited schools only on the invitation of local authorities, and made no reports on the quality of the teaching they observed during their classroom visits. For the most part, their work tended to involve group assistance rather than individual counselling. Although the latter type of activity came within their terms of reference, there were far too few of them to fill the need adequately. Requests for individual assistance had to go through the local officials, a procedure that some reports from the field in 1968–9 indicated was excessively cumbersome. There were predictions that provision would have to be made for direct appeals from teachers.

In 1969–70 there were approximately 150 program consultants working from the Regional Offices. The department was following a policy of increasing the number of generalist consultants, who were expected to look at the over-all impact of groups of subjects ranging over several grades, and to assume special responsibility in matters of school organization.

The 1967–8 school year was regarded as one of transition from the old to the new function. The Curriculum Section offered sensitivity training courses and other forms of assistance organized by subject chairman in the department. It was intended that the program consultants would be either giving or taking courses during the summer in a continuous process of teaching and learning. The Curriculum Section found some administrative difficulties at the beginning in providing the necessary instructional program. When the Regional Offices were first established in 1965 there was no budgetary allocation specifically for them, and people on the department payroll were simply assigned to work there. Funds for their direct maintenance were provided later, but it was not until 1969–70 that the Curriculum Section was given an allocation specifically for upgrading courses.

The reaction of former subject inspectors to their new role varied considerably. Most of them found that there were more demands on them than they could meet. For those whose services were not in great demand, the department undertook to find other positions. The extent to which the new divisional boards would attempt to meet their own need for consultative as well as for supervisory services was not easily predicted. The prospects were that the boards in the less populous and less wealthy areas would be eager to accept all the assistance the department cared to provide.

The establishment of the Ontario Curriculum Institute, in which there was substantial representation from the department, had important implications for the Curriculum and Text-books Branch. An account of the organization and activities of this institute is given in volume v, chapter 11, in connection with the treatment of research and development. The exact division of functions between the two agencies was never entirely clear in many minds, but the major distinction was that the institute was supposed to explore fundamental curriculum principles from an independent point of view, and the departmental branch would utilize its findings, and those from other sources, to develop actual courses of study for classroom use. At a time when the department was following a policy of accepting an increasing variety of alternatives in the schools, and the line between an experimental and a regular program was becoming less distinct, the two roles were not entirely easy to separate. When the institute began to consider having an experiment involving up to one hundred schools, there was some feeling that the department's role was being usurped.

The institute was undoubtedly in a position to take a critically appraising look at the efforts of the department and the schools. Davis mentioned this possibility in answer to some probing questions from Donald MacDonald about possible overlap.

I am just taking one area as an example – in reading or the instruction of reading in the elementary schools. There is a certain school of thought in the province which would indicate that the view taken by the department is not correct. In order to be completely objective, and realizing the great importance of this particular area at the elementary level, we have asked the curriculum institute to do an objective and independent study and to assess what the department is doing in relation to what other groups are suggesting and what classroom teachers are suggesting.[9]

During the middle 1960s the departmental curriculum committees were both numerous and active. They typically involved a wide range of people, including university professors, classroom teachers, supervisors and inspectors, and teachers' college staff members, as well as department officials. There was an increasing interest in what was happening in other places, and more opportunities were provided for visits abroad. There was also regular consultation with the appropriate committee of the Ontario Teachers' Federation. By 1967 Davis was able to report that the Curriculum Division maintained liaison with more than seventy institutions whose activities and projects were considered to have a direct bearing on the programs of Ontario schools. Among those he mentioned were the Albion Hills Conservation School, the Canadian Association of Physicists, the Canadian Broadcasting Corporation, and the Canadian Institute of International Affairs.[10]

The *Report of the Minister, 1964* indicated that some nineteen curriculum committees involving over 225 participants were active during the year. They had completed course outlines in home economics, mathematics for grades 8 and 12, chemistry, Spanish for grades 10 through 13, and in several of the four-year options such as biology, geology, world politics, and man in society. Committee work was going on in music for grades 7 through 12, health for grades 7 through 12, marketing, data processing, mathematics for grades 9, 10, and 13, and courses for nursing assistants and dietary supervisors.[11] By 1967 the number of active committees had reached fifty, with something like six hundred members. At the grade 13 level alone there were eight language committees as well as some in other subjects.[12]

Curriculum construction moved away from the production of specific, detailed courses of study to that of guidelines within which local authorities, in co-operation with departmental program consultants, could prepare specific courses of study based on local needs. The aim was to provide a maximum of inspiration from those with specialized knowledge who had devoted intensive thought to a particular area of study, while at the same time leaving plenty of room for initiative and originality of treatment on the part of the teacher and the class.

The Supervision Division (Section)

The evolution of the supervisory function

A brief review of some of the salient developments in the provisions for school supervision in Ontario seems in order at this point. For the first initiative in this direction, we must go back to 1823, when the General Board of Education was established, as mentioned earlier. The President of the Board, John Strachan, became, by virtue of this office, the first Superintendent of Education for Upper Canada. He included among his functions that of visiting the district public schools and the common schools. This precedent was of lasting importance even though the board disappeared in 1833.

The first permanent arrangement for the systematic inspection of schools was that made by Ryerson in 1846, when provision was made for the appointment of district superintendents. County and local superintendents replaced these officials in 1850. Much of the inspection that went on under this arrangement was apparently not very serious. Political factors rather than any demonstrated capacity for the job often accounted for an appointment, and the appointees were frequently considered to be inferior in academic standing to teachers whom they visited. We are told in *Centennial Story* of the first inspection of Toronto schools that was sufficiently serious to make the teachers nervous. It was conducted in 1865 and was made not by the local superintendent, to whom the responsibility normally belonged, but by the Management Committee of the board. Fortunately it is said to have been conducted in a thorough, kindly, and intelligent manner.[18] The offices of superintendent and secretary of the Toronto Board were combined from 1844 to 1857, a clergyman superintendent served until 1874, and a professional inspector took over in that year.

The establishment of a system of county school inspectors in 1871 was significant because of the requirement that appointees must have specified qualifications. Appointments continued, however, to be influenced by factors other than that of professional competence. Many appointees were older teachers who served for a brief period before retirement. An attempt was made to improve the situation in 1908 by the creation of the office of Chief Inspector of Public and Separate Schools. Adequate steps were not taken, however, to create a really professional body of inspectors until arrangements were made in 1930 to have all inspectors, except those employed by city boards, appointed by Order-in-Council on the recommendation of the minister. By 1930 an inspector had to be a university graduate, to hold a Permanent First Class Certificate, to have had adequate teaching experience, and to pass a comprehensive examination.

The right of city boards to appoint their own supervisory officers dates from 1847. At the time the Royal Commission on Education surveyed the situation, twelve of the larger cities were taking advantage of this provision. The twenty-five officials so appointed went under a variety of titles such as "director of education," "superintendent of schools," and "inspector of public schools." Some had responsibility for both public elementary and secondary schools and others for public schools only.[14]

The Royal Commission identified supervision of educational programs in publicly supported schools as the main function of the department. It recognized four types of supervisory services: inspection, the improvement of instruction, organizational activities and public relations, and business administration. Two methods of supervision were identified: that by field workers who conducted on-the-spot evaluations and engaged in consultation, and that by officials in the central offices of the department, who co-ordinated the work of the field workers and assisted in the formulation and implementation of new policies.[15]

When provision was first made for the inspection of vocational secondary school programs in composite schools, there was no co-ordination with general course inspection. Inspectors from the High School and Vocational School Branches might accidentally encounter one another in the same school without having known beforehand of each other's plans. In a typical reflection of traditional academic snobbery, vocational inspectors were regarded as inferior in status, and at one time were paid according to a lower scale. L.S. Beattie, who served as Superintendent of Secondary Education from 1952 until his retirement in 1956, took particular pride in his efforts to bridge the gap between the two groups. The co-ordination of inspection was already developing at the time of his appointment. Inspectors from the two branches would select a group of composite schools and direct their attention particularly to matters of organization, accommodation, promotion standards, optional subjects, guidance, and the relationship between the school and the community. In 1952 the designations "high school inspector" and "vocational school inspector" were dropped in favour of the uniform title "secondary school inspector."

A new approach to secondary school inspection was inaugurated on an experimental basis in 1950 in schools with at least five teachers. There was less classroom inspection, and more time was spent with principals, heads of departments, and staff members in discussing administration, organization, optional subjects, and local educational problems. There was also more opportunity for inspectors to acquaint themselves with the work of local curriculum committees which were being organized enthusiastically in many parts of the province.

An important step was taken in 1951, when the province was divided into fifteen high school inspectoral areas, with the intention of assigning a member of the high school inspectional staff to each. The first such appointments were those of A.H. McKague, whose headquarters were at the Lakehead, and W.T. Laing, who operated from Wallaceburg. Each local "generalist" inspector was responsible for the schools in his area, and might invite others to assist him. Inspectors of special subjects were on call, but did not attempt to make annual visits. The scheme was based on the hope that greater familiarity with a limited area would enable the inspector to give improved service. It was also felt that it was too awkward and inconvenient for inspectors to visit all parts of the province from headquarters in Toronto, although specialist inspectors were still not relieved of this obligation. As the plan developed, arrangements were made for a thorough joint general inspection every four years of schools with twenty or more teachers, while the local inspector would pay at least one visit in each of the intervening years.

As a result of the passing of the act to create a new municipal structure in Metropolitan Toronto in 1953, a new impetus was given to the local assumption of supervisory responsibilities. Boards of Education were created in North York and Scarborough, with their own supervisory officials. In 1954 there were twenty-one cities with this type of arrangement, and fifty-eight officials were employed. Arrangements were made during that year to enable any city or town to appoint an inspector for specifically high school purposes.

The *Report of the Minister, 1952* describes the growing obligations of school inspectors which studies of the departmental organization in the early 1960s, already referred to, identified as excessively burdensome. Elementary school inspectors checked the annual financial reports of school boards and completed the grant forms which served as a basis for distributing legislative grants to no fewer than 3,887 elementary school boards. They prepared additional reports of a special statistical nature or on local problems. They were responsible for the proper observance of school acts and regulations. They assisted school boards in preparing budgets, estimating grants, selecting school sites, arranging for transportation contracts, improving school grounds, building new schools, interpreting acts and regulations, selecting teachers, and arbitrating disputes among boards, parents, and teachers. They assisted municipal councils by drafting by-laws for the establishment and alteration of school sections, by issuing warrants for the payment of school taxes and township grants, by acting as arbitrators in connection with school boundary or equalization disputes, and by acting as secretaries to consultative committees.

In performing their duties with respect to teachers, they supervised methods of instruction, assisted in the selection of teachers for curriculum committees, served on committees to select candidates for entrance to normal schools, taught summer school, conducted in-service teacher training programs, checked qualifications for permanent certificates, and often assisted teachers to secure the positions for which they were best suited. They also supervised the promotion of pupils, ensured as far as possible that classrooms were properly heated, lighted, and ventilated, and generally concerned themselves with the standards attained in various aspects of the school program. Many inspectors also participated actively in community organizations, serving on committees of library boards and boards of health, recreation, and conservation, as well as taking part in the activities of Home and School Associations, trustees' organizations, children's aid societies, and others.[16]

Concern was expressed in the department at intervals over the growing demands on inspectors' time, and efforts were made to curtail those duties regarded as of peripheral importance. G.A. Pearson, in his final year as Superintendent of Elementary Education in 1963, sent out a memorandum in which he noted with some disfavour the number of conferences that appeared to require inspectors' attendance. The memorandum suggested that each inspector should be in the schools at least 60 per cent of the time during which they were open. While the benefits of attendance at conferences were acknowledged, the department proposed to place a limit on the time that could be spent in this way. Inspectors were accordingly required to secure prior approval from the department to absent themselves from their inspectorate except for attendance at the sessions of the Ontario Educational Association or the regional conferences of inspectors and teachers' college staffs arranged by the department. They were warned that they should not assume that authority would be granted each request for absence from an inspectorate, or that, where approval was given for attendance at a conference of trustees or teachers, the department would necessarily pay the expenses involved.[17]

At an earlier stage, inspectors' reports on secondary school teachers were made in descriptive, qualitative terms, and kept on file in the department. In the mid-1950s the use of a quantitative scale was adopted with numbers ranging from 1 for the poorest teachers to 7 for the best. A rating of 1 was considered unacceptable and 2 definitely questionable. Secondary school inspectors received a memorandum in 1960 instructing them on how to deal with a teacher who received either of these ratings. They were to give such a teacher a detailed oral report in the presence of the principal. A printed copy of this report was also to be given to the teacher and one to the Superintendent of Secondary Education. A staff or subject inspector was to give a copy to the district secondary school inspector or to the local superintendent of secondary schools. The latter was responsible for taking further action, including steps to obtain a report from another inspector. Except for beginning teachers, the minister was prepared after March 10, 1959, to cancel the certificates of teachers with a rating of 1, and after May 1, 1960, to relieve school boards of the necessity of giving preference to the applications of teachers with a rating of 2 over those from suitable unqualified applicants.[18] The visit of the inspector was thus a serious matter for a teacher who was not doing too well.

Elementary school inspectors were made responsible, beginning in 1965, for applying the same seven-point rating scale to teachers in their inspectorates. The specifications for the rating categories were defined as follows:

Rating 7 – Outstanding
An outstanding teacher and educational leader, whose influence extends beyond his own school. A person who is a credit to the profession, who displays fine personal qualities and scholarship.
Rating 6 – Excellent
An excellent classroom teacher who organizes his work well, teaches with ease, skill and precision and exerts an excellent influence on his pupils. This is the teacher who does superior work in school, who is willing to accept responsibility and is highly prized by his principal.
Rating 5 – Very good
A very good teacher who may range from good to excellent in the various phases of his work with the overall level well above average.
Rating 4 – Good
A steady, dependable teacher. His teaching skills are satisfactory although he may have some weaknesses. He gets good results. He is a good staff member and exerts a good influence in the school.
Rating 3 – Fair
A fair but usually dull teacher, lacking imagination and inspiration. He plods along and gets reasonable results. If he is an older teacher he will probably continue his routine performance until retirement. On the other hand if he is a beginner he has made a reasonably *fair* start and can be expected to improve.
Rating 2 – Poor
A weak teacher below the acceptable level. This teacher should not be recommended for a permanent certificate.
Rating 1 – Very poor or Failure
This rating should be assigned only after determined efforts to help the teacher have not produced acceptable results. The teacher will have been made well aware of the weaknesses in his teaching and will have received concrete suggestions with respect to improvements.[19]

Each teacher was to be rated by January 31, and the result entered on his Teacher's Record Card, along with the date. During his first two years of experience, he was to be designated a beginner, and his status as such was to be specially indicated. The ratings were to be available solely to other inspectors, and not to school boards or to federation officials. However, each teacher who was rated 1 or 2 was, at the request of the Ontario

Teachers' Federation, to be notified in writing that his performance was considered poor or very poor. A rating of 3 was required for a recommendation for a permanent certificate. Each inspector was notified that, during 1965, he would be expected to complete a summary for his inspectorate indicating the number of teachers in each category to provide the basis for a study of the situation. As things turned out, this scheme proved to be remarkably short-lived.

A growing recognition of the complexities of the inspector's work led to the establishment in 1955 of the Internship Plan in Supervision under the sponsorship of the Ontario College of Education. Each teacher who participated spent two weeks with an experienced inspector engaging in a first hand study of various aspects of the supervision of classrooms and the administration of elementary schools. A considerable number of the participants received subsequent appointments as elementary school inspectors. An in-service program was also initiated for newly-appointed inspectors by the department. The participants met department officials and had an opportunity to learn something about departmental administration. In the 1960s the program involved lectures on new developments in curriculum.

There were sporadic objections to the extent and nature of supervisory appraisals during the early 1960s. J.M. Paton took this line in the study paper he prepared for the second Canadian Conference on Education, held in 1962.[20] Although he was dealing with the situation in Canada in general, his comments had as much application to Ontario as to most other provinces. He noted the common observation that teachers should have more freedom and be subjected to less supervision as they became better qualified and more competent. But in practice there did not seem to be any diminution in departmental inspection of the experienced. Paton thought that much of this inspection ought to be disappearing if teachers were to have full professional status. He cited the experience of a teacher in Nova Scotia who had taught for about twenty years, and had been asked to recommend textbooks and to outline a course for use in the province, her recommendations being accepted in both cases. Yet she was not permitted to select textbooks or a course of study for use in her own classroom. Every year, the written reports of laboratory work done by her students were inspected, and there was never an adverse criticism or a suggestion for improvement. Despite this fact, annual inspections continued. Paton may not have seen much sign of concern about such practices, but a reaction against them was incubating even then.

Research in the area of supervision was also producing results that may seem to have exerted little immediate effect in Ontario but were to contribute to a gradual erosion of confidence in the inspector's ability to appraise a teacher with any degree of accuracy during the often brief period he spent in a single classroom. One of the best known of such studies was conducted in Alberta in 1961, involving sixty-three superintendents who attended the Canadian Education Association's short course for superintendents at Banff, as well as sixty-five principals who attended Alberta's short course for principals. The results were reported by W.W. Worth.[21] The experiment involved the presentation by kinescope of a fifteen-minute lesson by a grade 1 teacher. Each of the participating administrators then made an independent appraisal of the teacher and completed a probationary report form. The result of their rating on a seven-point scale was a remarkable lack of agreement. While no one thought the teacher was unsuited for teaching, 3 per cent rated her as doubtful, 6 per cent as weak, 17 per cent as barely satisfactory, 40 per cent as generally satisfactory, 26 per cent as proficient, and 3 per cent as exceptional. The unstructured responses of the raters with respect to what they observed were equally varied. Contrary to expectations, the amount of experience the individual administrators had did not affect the variation in their responses.

Many individual inspectors, especially those with no great confidence in research, tend to reject findings of this kind, or at least to decline to apply them to themselves. But the point, especially if supported by further research, gradually wins a degree of acceptance. While there is continued belief in Ontario in the necessity of removing certain misfits from the classroom, the later years of the 1960s saw a remarkably rapid shift away from the mentality that supports wholesale inspection for the purpose of rating and categorization.

The major changes in arrangements for school supervision in the late 1960s were closely tied in with the development of the administrative regions. In 1967, when subject inspectors became program consultants, as previously mentioned, the district inspectors were designated "area superintendents of schools" and were made directly responsible to the regional superintendents of education. As before, they dealt with public, Roman Catholic separate, or secondary schools. The emphasis shifted away from inspection in favour of positive measures to improve the quality of the educational program. Area superintendents were expected to keep in touch with new developments in many subject areas and to concentrate on in-service activities. Responsibility for necessary supervision was shifted to principals, department heads, and officials appointed by local boards. It was hoped that the boards would not rush in to impose the kind of inspection that the department was in the process of abandoning. Davis expressed this hope in the Legislature:

> The traditional concept of inspection is disappearing and these individuals will act as resource people to assist the teachers, not to inspect them in that sense of the word. We really feel that this will become the philosophy of the divisional boards as they become established. And certainly, we will, as a department, make every effort to see that this becomes the approach.[22]

A year after the new arrangement went into operation, G.P. Wilkinson, Executive Officer of the Ontario Secondary School Teachers' Federation, expressed satisfaction with the way things were working.

In the matter of *Inspection and Supervision* the Federation gave repeated assurances to Department officials that the professional staffs of the secondary schools of the province needed no more supervision than they could provide for themselves out of the ranks of their own members. Again it needed faith and courage on the part of the Minister and his senior officials to accept these assurances as being supported by an effective majority within the profession. As with the change in Grade 13, the first year has made a good beginning. Consultants have provided valuable advice and assistance to teachers, department heads and principals. No longer are the needs of the vast majority of competent teachers to develop confident working relationships with knowledgeable visitors, such as the consultants, left unmet because of the fear of the little black book and the rating system.[23]

As of December 31, 1968, provincial inspection ceased entirely, except for private schools. Local superintendents were left with the responsibility of reporting teacher appraisals to the department only for the purpose of recommending permanent certificates. This they were required to do even though they were municipal employees. Program consultants were the only departmental officials entering the schools, and they were forbidden to make any appraisal of the teacher's work even to the principal.

In the twilight era of departmental supervision, school department heads were expected to work with, help, and advise teachers, but not to give the principal any formal appraisal of their work. They were supposed to be on the teacher's side if the concept of opposing interests had to be acknowledged. If they thought there was a serious weakness that they were unable to remedy, they might ask the principal to look into the situation and make his own appraisal. They might also go so far as to say that they would not want a particular teacher in their department the following year. As far as the principal was concerned, he was not expected to increase his classroom visits unless there was trouble.

One of the problems commented on by those who were apprehensive about the new arrangement was that there remained no way for a prospective employer to get an objective rating of a teacher. Local superintendents might be assumed not to want to give the kind of rating that would result in the loss of a good teacher. On the other hand, it was thought likely that they would over-praise one whom they would not seriously object to losing. Sceptics also suggested that school boards would object to having so little objective knowledge about the quality of the system they were operating, and might resort to employing independent appraisers on contract.

There is no question that the new arrangement constituted a tremendous expression of confidence in the ability and willingness of teachers to use the kind of freedom they had never previously enjoyed in the Ontario school system. The change also involved a confidence that local authorities would resist pressure to snatch away what had been surrendered by the central authority by imposing new restrictions of their own. The results of the new approach can become apparent only over a period of years, but those who believe in the creative power of liberty will be confident of the outcome.

In 1970 there were thirteen assistant superintendents in the Supervision Section, of whom most concerned themselves with public and secondary school affairs, while one dealt with matters concerning Indian and Eskimo children, and two devoted their attention to the affairs of the Roman Catholic separate schools.

In the summer of 1969, A.H. McKague, who had played a leading part in integrating the former Elementary and Secondary School Branches during and after the reorganization of 1965, retired from the position of Superintendent of Supervision. He was succeeded by G.H. Waldrum, who had been an assistant superintendent since 1965. While occupying that position, he had directed the departmental courses for elementary school principals, and had chaired the departmental committee on larger units of administration.

The Special Education Service

In the consolidation of scattered units in the department in 1965, the former Auxiliary Education Services Division became the Special Education Service of the Supervision Division, Program Branch. The first steps toward decentralization of this service were taken with the appointment of inspectors in special education to the East Central, West Central, and Eastern Ontario Regional Offices.

The section was concerned with the educational development of all exceptional children of school age, including those with superior learning capacity, those with limited educational ability, the educationally retarded, the socially immature, the emotionally disturbed, and those with orthopaedic, neurological, physical, or speech disabilities. According to the *Report of the Minister, 1966*, special education inspectors assisted local school authorities by performing the following functions:

(1) visiting special classes, teachers, and schools, where units are established to aid the teachers concerned;
(2) working with local staff and school boards, conducting surveys and assessing children, thereby rendering assistance in the establishment of new services;
(3) assisting in the diagnosis of the exceptional child's problems and developing appropriate educational programs;

(4) participating in teacher in-service training programs based on education topics relevant to special classes and to atypical pupils in regular grades.[24]

In August 1968 the Schools for Retarded Children Section was dissolved and the staff were integrated into the Supervision Section. F.J. Reynolds, formerly administrator, Schools for Retarded Children Section, was appointed Assistant Superintendent of Supervision, with responsibility for the co-ordination and development of all aspects of special education. The seven specialists in this area were concerned respectively with the emotionally disturbed, the neurologically impaired, the perceptually handicapped, the educationally retarded, the physically handicapped, the trainable retarded, and children in the Ontario Hospital Schools.

The Northern Corps of Teachers

The Northern Corps of Teachers, established in 1966, provided competent teachers for isolated schools in northern Ontario where the boards had been unable to secure or retain qualified people. Many of them had non-treaty Indian pupils for whom the Department of Indian Affairs was not responsible. According to the scheme, teachers who were willing to serve in these areas were given special preparation, and their salaries were augmented by contributions from the department. Teachers were initially placed at Auden, Mine Centre, Savant Lake, Shining Tree, Ramsey, Oba, Mosher, Gogama, Franz, Bear Island, and Menapia. The service was subsequently extended so that in 1968–9, twenty communities were being served by twenty-five teachers. The number of teachers rose to twenty-nine in 1969–70, but the number of schools involved dropped to seventeen. For the first time two communities with four-room schools were included.

The orientation course in the summer of 1969 was held at the University of Western Ontario. It was attended by sixty-nine other teachers who were undertaking employment with the Department of Indian Affairs in reserve communities.

The Moosonee Education Centre

The Moosonee Education Centre developed as a joint project involving both the provincial and the federal governments. Provincial responsibilities were shared by the Department of Education and the Department of Social and Family Services, and federal responsibilities were assumed by the Department of Indian Affairs and Northern Development. The project arose out of an awareness of the depressed conditions of the area, in particular among the Cree Indian residents. There had been an influx of population in the 1940s with the establishment by the federal government of a hospital on Moose Factory Island and in the early 1960s with the building of a Canadian Forces Radar Station. But many of the people of the area failed to secure adequate employment, and problems of poor housing and sanitation were acute. Many of the difficulties seemed traceable to inadequate facilities for education, and the failure to break the traditional apathy of the Indians toward the value of the educational process itself.

Plans for the new development were made in 1964 and 1965 when two survey teams did preliminary studies. A board of governors for the centre was set up in April 1966, with three representatives from the Department of Education, one from the Department of Social and Family Services, one from the Ontario Northland Railway, and four from Moosonee and Moose Factory. At the time of the official opening of the new building by Davis on June 15, 1969, five of the members were from the Moosonee-Moose Factory area, of whom three were Cree Indians. The minister declared that, as time went on, the outside representatives would be replaced by people from the area.

The Education Centre, a 3.5 million dollar project, was actually in operation from November 1968. In 1969–70 the director and eighteen teachers were working with nearly four hundred adults on courses in heavy equipment and preventive maintenance, building construction, and home-hospital services. Upgrading courses were also being offered in English, mathematics, science, and citizenship. Full-time students spent half of each day in upgrading and half in skill courses. There were evening courses for adults in English, mathematics, sewing, handicrafts, office skills, small motors, woodwork, building construction, and welding.

There was also a nursery school where Cree-speaking children were introduced to English. Elementary school pupils from the local public and separate schools attended regular gymnasium, library, home economics, and woodworking classes, and learned to handle small motors. As a community service, the library and gymnasium were kept open six nights a week, and on weekends and holidays the gymnasium was available to children, young people, and adults for a variety of recreational and cultural activities.

The Young Voyageurs Program

The Young Voyageurs travel and exchange program, begun by the Centennial Commission in 1964, involved the participation of over fifteen thousand secondary school students during its first five years. Its purpose was to enable them to visit provinces other than their own during the summer in order to learn at first hand about Canada's geography, its political and educational institutions, and its cultural and industrial achievements. As the program operated in 1969, participating students were chosen on a regional basis, ordinarily no more than one to a school, on the nomination of their principal and teachers. Preference was given to those in grade 11, who had to be between fifteen and seventeen years of age. The Department of Education organized the groups and acted as host for visiting students from other provinces. The federal government paid the cost of transportation and reimbursed the province for certain other expenditures. It also determined the places to be visited.

Regional decentralization
The boundaries of the administrative regions are shown on Chart 2-1. Except for West Central Region no. 7 and East Central Region no. 8, they followed the boundaries of counties and territorial districts. This factor proved to be important when the divisional school boards were established in 1969.

As has already been mentioned, the formation of the first five regions was announced in early 1965, and of the other five during the following year. The initial set-up was as follows.

Region / First Superintendent	*Territory Included*
1 Northwestern Ontario R. R. Steele	Territorial districts of Rainy River, Kenora, and Thunder Bay
2 Midnorthern Ontario G. R. Allan	Territorial districts of Algoma, Sudbury, and Manitoulin
3 Northeastern Ontario J. H. Kennedy	Territorial districts of Cochrane, Timiskaming, Nipissing, Parry Sound, and Muskoka
4 Western Ontario W. T. Laing	Counties of Essex, Kent, Lambton, Elgin, Middlesex, Huron, and Bruce
5 Midwestern Ontario R. F. Bornhold	Counties of Grey, Wellington, Waterloo, Brant, Norfolk, Oxford, and Perth
6 Niagara H. B. Henderson	Counties of Haldimand, Lincoln, Welland, and Wentworth
7 West Central Ontario G. P. Hillmer	Counties of Dufferin, Halton, Peel, Simcoe, and the city of Toronto and the municipalities of Metropolitan Toronto situated wholly west of Yonge Street
8 East Central Ontario J. F. Kinlin	Counties of Durham, Ontario, Victoria, and York, the township of York, and the municipalities of Metropolitan Toronto situated wholly east of Yonge Street
9 Eastern Ontario R. W. Froates	Counties of Frontenac, Haliburton, Hastings, Leeds, Lennox and Addington, Northumberland, Peterborough, and Prince Edward
10 Ottawa Valley J. O. Proulx	Counties of Carleton, Dundas, Stormont, Glengarry, Grenville, Lanark, Prescott, Russell, and Renfrew

There were difficulties as a result of the fact that Metropolitan Toronto was split. The Metropolitan Toronto school authorities found it awkward to deal with the two offices. Some consideration was given to having the Metropolitan Toronto School Board deal with one and the Metropolitan Toronto Separate School Board with the other. No change had been announced at the time of writing.

In each of the regions the superintendent was to co-ordinate the work of all provincial school inspectors (later area superintendents of schools), and to maintain close association with the directors, superintendents, and inspectors of municipal inspectorates. All inspectors, school officials,

CHART 2-1
Administrative regions of the Department of Education

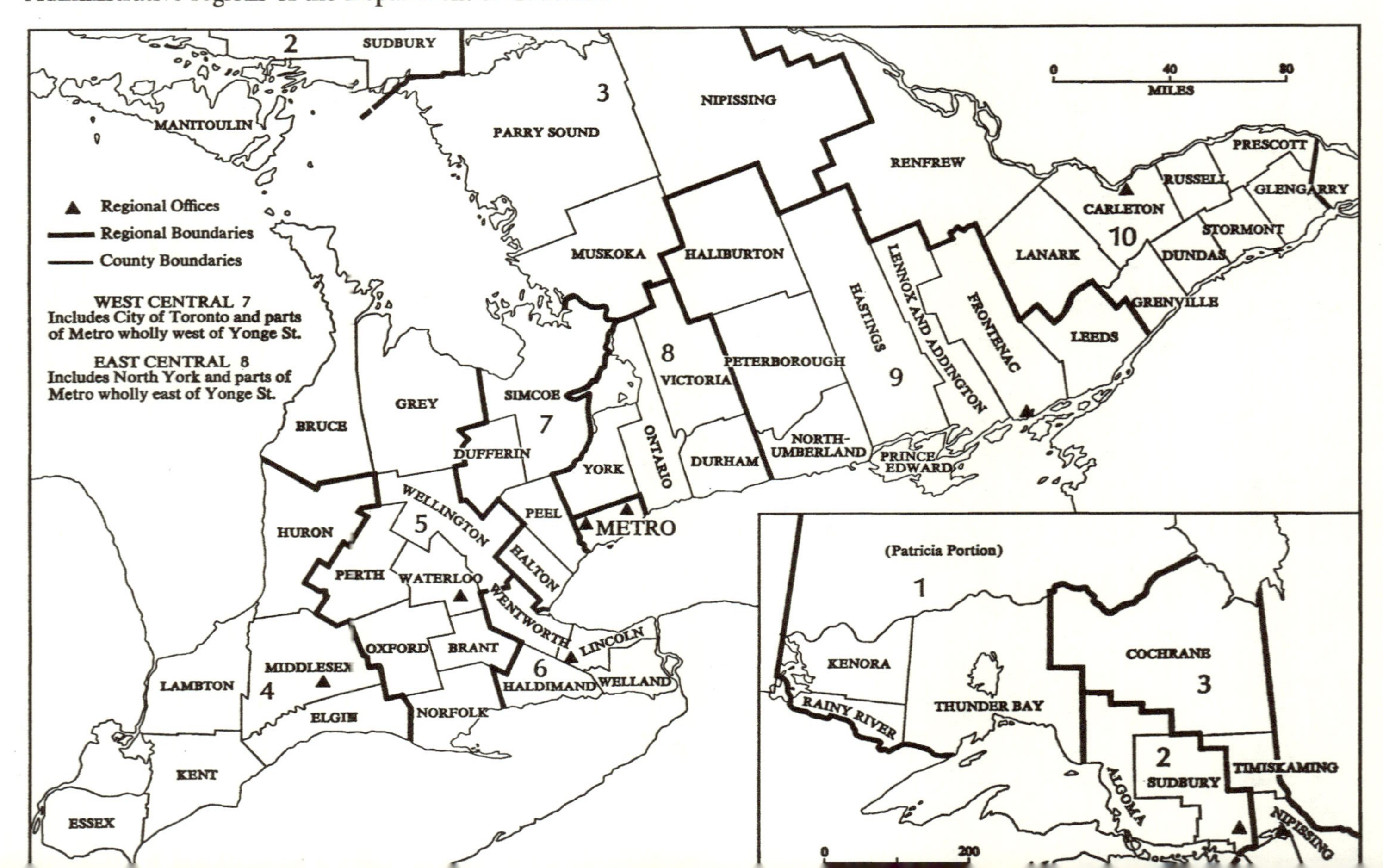

and secretaries of school boards were asked to communicate with the department through the regional superintendents, except in replying to correspondence received directly from the main office at Toronto. There were expected to be considerable advantages in terms of speed and adequacy of communication. Departmental files indicate, however, that some people in the field were not easily persuaded against seeking responses, even to routine inquiries, from top officials.

At the time the first regional offices were set up, J.F. Kinlin was a member of the Policy and Development Council. He was seconded from that position to make a study of administrative units and supervisory practices in the ten regions, with particular reference to the East Central Region, which he also administered for a brief period. The functions of the regional offices and their relationship to the central authorities remained somewhat in question until J.R. McCarthy assumed the deputy ministership in January 1967. The pattern that emerged involved staffing initially for three purposes: supervision, assistance with program development, and advice on business matters. As already indicated, the traditional approach to supervision was rather rapidly phased out, and the area superintendents were encouraged to seek positions with the district school boards. Most of this process was completed in 1969. Program consultation during the same period was a flourishing activity, and promised to remain so. There were consultants in the school subjects, in educational television, and in various aspects of special education. Business administrators were attached to the offices to assume many of the responsibilities formerly discharged by inspectors, such as offering assistance to local boards on financial and legal matters. This function seemed likely to diminish in importance as the large district boards employed highly trained officials of their own. The regional offices were also centres for the collection of certain types of data, such as those required as a basis for awarding grants, and are likely to assume an increased role in this area. Another type of function consisted in the issuing of departmental approvals for transportation grants, site purchases, and building proposals.

D. Spry, appointed as Director of the School Business Administration Branch in 1966, showed considerable interest in ensuring that the business administrators and assistants appointed to the Regional Offices had the kind of competence and knowledge that would enable them to be of maximum assistance to local school board officials. Candidates were sought with a professional accounting affiliation, a degree in commerce, or substantial experience in school administration. Those who lacked the latter qualification spent six weeks at central headquarters familiarizing themselves with departmental functions and problems. They also worked for three months with local school boards as assistants to business administrators before assignment to the Regional Offices.

The Regional Centres had a very important, if transitory, role in 1968 when a tremendous amount of planning had to be done in a relatively short time to prepare for the school board reorganization which took effect on January 1, 1969. The regional superintendents, or "regional directors," as they were renamed, typically took the lead in organizing the interim school organization committees (the ISOCs), and in guiding their activities. They also offered instructions and advice to the small boards on the procedures to be followed in winding up their affairs. In the new structure, the regional directors met with the directors of the boards of education and the superintendents of the combined separate school boards at appropriate times to discuss matters involving responsibility of board officials to the minister. The regional directors acted as chairmen of these councils.

In an address to the Legislature on May 17, 1967, the minister referred to plans to open a Resources Centre at the Regional Office at Sudbury. He promised that, in addition to the usual library reference materials, there would be films, recordings, tapes, projectors, and other teaching aids provided for circulation. Workshops would be available for teachers to devise many of their own technical aids. Experienced staff would be on hand to help pupils with reading disabilities.[25] These plans were quickly put into effect. Less than two years later the centre had accumulated about 3,500 books, 2,300 films, and a large number of other materials. The centre's library consultants were said to have visited every school in the region, and to have designed twenty libraries for district schools. Consultants from the remedial reading unit were working with classroom teachers, recommending appropriate programs and materials. A remedial reading van, carrying the latest equipment and materials, visited smaller centres throughout the region, remaining a month at a time, and dealing with children from grades 3 to 7 who had been identified by their teachers as having special difficulty. The centre's psychological service unit, during the same period, had dealt with 1,200 children from the region. A child referred there by his school principal had the help of social workers, psychologists, child development consultants, and psychometrists.[26]

In his announcement of May 1967 the minister referred to plans by the Department of Health to establish diagnostic and treatment centres for pupils with emotional disturbances or with physical handicaps that might lead to emotional problems. Davis said that the Department of Education was appointing an educational officer in each centre to work with the medical specialists in order to ensure that diagnosis and treatment were followed by appropriate educational procedures. The work of these eight officers was to be co-ordinated by a provincial education director.[27]

With the virtual abandonment of provincial school supervision, and with the ability of the new district school boards to manage most of their business affairs, the Regional Offices are obviously becoming primarily service centres. In theory, this role should also decline as the boards employ their own specialist consultants in various aspects of the school program and provide their own special services for exceptional children. But this course of action has appealed thus far only to the larger of the boards. Services provided by the department show every evidence of being enthusiastically received. In 1968–9 the Western Regional Office, with headquarters at London, reported a 50 per cent increase over the previous year in requests for consultants to visit the secondary schools of the region, and a 500 per cent increase in requests to visit elementary schools. There was some suggestion that departmental consultants were better received than the master teachers who went around offering assistance in their own areas.

The centres may well have an important role to play in countering the effects of in-breeding in some of the local areas. Some boards are said to employ and promote almost entirely from within their own systems. Such a practice could lead to stagnation if there were not special means of ensuring the penetration of new ideas. There is a real opportunity for the centres to promote enlightenment and progress.

The Registrar's Division (Section)

The Registrar's Section, as it is now called, was once best known for its management of departmental examination programs. These activities, described in volume v, chapter 15, disappeared during the latter part of the 1960s. There has also been a long list of other responsibilities which tend to increase greatly in volume, and in some respects in variety, as the years pass. Many of them involve issuing certificates, a process which may not be entirely automatic, but may require a check to ensure that the specified requirements have been met. The following list, which was adapted from one compiled in the Registrar's Section in June 1968, indicates the functions of the section at that time.

1 It received recommendations from teachers' colleges and colleges of education, and issued interim certificates.

2 It received recommendations and issued permanent teaching certificates. A check had to be made to ensure that a candidate for a specialist's certificate had taught at least a year in grade 11, 12, or 13. Local officials sometimes signed the recommendation without making certain that this condition had been met.

3 It received recommendations from principals of departmental summer courses and board-sponsored winter courses, and from deans of colleges of education, and issued special certificates.

4 It maintained accurate cumulative records of certificates held by individual teachers. These records were being put on tape in co-operation with the Education Data Centre in 1969.

5 It received applications from elementary school teachers to raise their certificates to a higher standard. Their additional qualifications had to be checked to ensure that the issuing of the new certificates was justified.

6 It received applications for admission to teachers' colleges from people educated outside Ontario, and evaluated their standing.
7 It received applications for admission to departmental summer courses, checked qualifications, and issued statements of admission.
8 It received applications for Letters of Standing from teachers trained to teach and qualified outside Ontario, evaluated their documents, and issued Letters of Standing.
9 It received applications from secondary school boards for Letters of Permission for unqualified teachers, checked their qualifications, and issued Letters of Permission.
10 It received copies of Letters of Permission issued by regional superintendents to engage unqualified teachers for elementary schools, checked the contents, and placed them in the teacher records.
11 It issued letters announcing the suspension and cancellation of teaching certificates. Twice a year, it issued a list of invalid certificates to educational officials in Ontario and to the deputy ministers of education in other provinces.
12 It received applications for elementary school superintendents' examinations; checked the qualifications of the applicants; issued acceptance letters; arranged for examiners for the written and oral examinations, for the printing of the papers, and for the holding of the examinations; received the results; and issued the certificates.
13 It arranged for extramural candidates to write the teachers' college examinations.
14 It examined qualifications and issued standings and certificates under the Internship Plan for elementary school teachers.
15 It issued Recreation Director and Arena Manager Certificates, and others of a similar nature, on recommendation.
16 It conducted interviews, examined documents, and issued for the minister statements of comparable Ontario elementary and secondary school standing for individuals from anywhere in the world for the purpose of obtaining work or for admission to courses in areas such as embalming, chiropractic, or nursing assistance. It arranged with the Office of the Provincial Secretary for the translation of documents written in foreign languages.
17 It arranged for the printing of forms for diplomas, certificates of standing, and certificates of training, which the schools filled in and issued.
18 It arranged for the submission of grade 13 teachers' marks and recommendations for diplomas.
19 It issued to all Ontario universities lists of marks in book form and on magnetic tape for all grade 13 candidates in the province.
20 It supplied the Department of University Affairs with a list of Ontario Scholarship winners, after checking to ensure that each recommendation was based on an 80 per cent average, as indicated in the formula.

21 It determined the winners of Carter scholarships and authorized the Provincial Treasurer to issue cheques to the winners. There were three of these scholarships awarded in each of several counties. They were formerly awarded on the basis of the grade 13 departmental examinations.
22 It received grade 12 marks and recommendations for diplomas from the schools.
23 It issued to provincial secondary schools blank forms for diplomas, certificates of standing, and certificates of training, with directions for their completion.
24 It issued Secondary School Graduation Diplomas and Secondary School Honour Graduation Diplomas to candidates from inspected private schools.
25 It issued statements of equivalent secondary school standing to individuals trained under the manpower program. As the colleges of applied arts and technology took over these courses, they also assumed the responsibility for issuing certificates.
26 It maintained records of student achievement at high school entrance and at lower, middle, and upper school, beginning in the 1800s, and continuing for various levels to the present day. It issued duplicate statements and transcripts of marks, as well as proof of age, from these records.
27 It assembled information and prepared a *Directory of Schools* for the elementary, secondary, and Department of Education schools.
28 It maintained archives of examination papers, courses of study, *Schools and Teachers*, Ministers' reports, textbook regulations, certificate regulations, and other such material from the 1800s on.
29 It registered private schools according to *The Department of Education Act.*
30 It received applications and fees for the inspection of private schools, received reports of such inspection, and forwarded these to the schools.
31 It received and screened applications from teachers for scholarships for study outside Ontario. On the advice of a committee, and with the approval of the deputy minister, it awarded the scholarships and received reports from the recipients.
32 It publicized the program of teacher exchange, received and screened applications, and forwarded these to the Canadian Education Association. It received suggestions from overseas regarding the possibility of specific exchanges, contacted applicants and carried through negotiations until an agreement was reached, and assisted in problems raised by hospitalization, withdrawal from the agreement, and death.
33 It received requests from the universities for decisions regarding new courses satisfying Circular 649, which indicated the requirements for Type A certification.
34 It maintained liaison with the colleges of education regarding recommendations for certification.

35 It arranged for committees to interview candidates for Letters of Standing and for admission to teachers' colleges for decisions on the acceptability of their use of English.
36 It maintained a library of university calendars from Canada and the United States.
37 It supervised examinations set by other provinces and countries for candidates temporarily or permanently residing in Ontario.

THE TEACHER EDUCATION BRANCH

Before the reorganization of 1965, the Teacher Education Branch was responsible only for the supervision of the teachers' colleges. Under the new arrangements, it was also given the task of maintaining liaison with the colleges of education. The Professional Development Branch became a subordinate division. The activities of these administrative units are dealt with largely in connection with the account of the development of teacher education in volume V. The trend has been away from close supervision of the activities of the teachers' colleges, as exemplified by their increased responsibility for developing their own curriculum. As they move into the universities, it will become unnecessary to ensure the enforcement of many existing regulations, and the main function of the branch will be to ensure that the minister's specifications for certification are met. Agreements between the minister and the universities with respect to the colleges of education have involved increasing control on the part of the universities, and a consequent decline in the obligations of the Teacher Education Branch.

A structural change of some interest was made in the branch in 1967 by the appointment of D.A. MacTavish as Assistant Director, Special Education. It was announced that the department planned to establish a new institution in co-operation with some Ontario university where teachers could be trained in various areas of special education. Since more immediate action was needed, the initial responsibility of the new assistant director was to visit institutions in the United States in order to identify acceptable programs in these areas as a preliminary to having them accredited by the department. The intention was that teachers holding a basic teaching certificate in Ontario could attend such institutions in order to qualify for an Ontario certificate in the special area of their training.

THE PROFESSIONAL DEVELOPMENT DIVISION (SECTION)

A Professional Development Branch was first organized in 1957, with the responsibility for promoting in-service education for teachers in elementary schools. It co-operated with school inspectors in setting up various types of in-service education programs, particularly for teachers with limited training and experience. It also assumed responsibility for the departmental summer course program, which is dealt with at some length in volume V, chapter 9. These courses involved co-operation with the Registrar's Branch, the Elementary Education Branch, and the Teacher Education Branch.

It became the policy in 1957 to hold the summer courses in a larger number of locations scattered about the province. This development was of symbolic significance in that it indicated a greater willingness on the part of the department to meet the convenience of teachers. It presented certain organizational problems, including the added difficulty of finding suitable instructors in smaller places. During the same period, an experiment with "helping teachers" was introduced. These teachers worked with inspectors to provide assistance to inexperienced teachers. Their work was seen as an extension of the summer courses offered for grade 12 graduates in the emergency program.

Enrolment in the departmental summer courses increased greatly when the four standards were introduced for the certification of elementary school teachers. The provision of some form of recognized credit constitutes a strong incentive for attendance. Despite constantly increasing enrolment, the future of the courses in their present form is doubtful. There is growing support for the proposition that the universities should assume full responsibility for offering such courses. This development may occur as the teachers' colleges are integrated into the universities. There would still be an important role for the department in professional development, however, in view of the increasingly accepted concept of teaching as a profession requiring continuous upgrading.

THE EDUCATIONAL TELEVISION BRANCH

The development of educational television is dealt with more fully in volume v, chapter 19, and reference is made there to the origin and expanding activities of the branch. Thus only the briefest treatment is needed here. The beginning of adequate organizational provision for the utilization of the powerful educational medium of television began in 1965, when the first specialists were appointed to the Curriculum Division. Their initial task was to conduct a wide-ranging study of educational television systems in different parts of the world. The removal of the operation from the Curriculum Division in 1966, and the establishment of an Educational Television Branch with a director reporting to the assistant deputy minister, instruction, signified the minister's intention of making a major thrust in this area.

As set up in 1966 under the direction of T.R. Ide, the branch was divided into two major areas, education and operations. The function of the educators was to study the needs, propose areas where television could make a contribution, and originate ideas for programs. They maintained contact with the technical specialists during the production of approved programs, and gave or denied final approval to the finished product. It was assumed that their recent experience in the classroom enabled them to ensure that programs were suitable for a particular viewing audience.

The producers were expected to understand thoroughly the special qualities of television as a means of communication. In the words of a brochure issued by the branch:

> It is important to know a variety of ways whereby television can involve the viewer; what kind of artistry will capture the imagination of the viewer and encourage the desire to search elsewhere for more information; what techniques will permit the viewer to see each important detail most clearly.[28]

The script writer became involved at an early stage in order to become immersed in the content. His task was to achieve the purposes formulated by the educators. A curriculum consultant, also a participant from the early stages, helped to ensure that these purposes were achieved, and prepared a teachers' guide.

Supplementing the regular staff of the branch were an Advisory Council and a Consultative Committee. The first of these represented the various sections of the Department of Education, and the second had representation from the Ontario Teachers' Federation, the Ontario School Trustees' Council, and school administrators. These agencies helped to establish priorities among educational interests as a basis for determining what programs would be produced.

Among the promotional activities of the branch was the organization of teams of educational and technical experts who toured the province in vans, giving demonstrations in the uses of educational television. Experts were attached to the Regional Offices of the department to act as consultants to the schools. Contact with the field also involved evaluation, designed to determine how many schools used the programs and what teachers and pupils thought of their content. The results of surveys were considered in the planning of new programs.

In the Third Session of the Twenty-eighth Legislature in 1970, the government introduced the long-expected *Act to Establish The Ontario Educational Communications Authority* which, at the time the present volume went to press, had received first reading.[29] The act proposed to place the activities of the Educational Television Branch under the control of a board consisting of members appointed by the Lieutenant-Governor-in-Council. The provisions and implications of this act are reserved for more complete discussion in volume v, chapter 19.

THE TECHNOLOGICAL AND TRADES TRAINING (APPLIED ARTS AND TECHNOLOGY) BRANCH

The Technological and Trades Training Branch survived under that name only into 1966, when it became the new Applied Arts and Technology Branch. Under both names it had responsibility for the supervision of all aspects of formal post-secondary and adult education, except for teacher education and university courses. It also administered the various programs under the Federal-Provincial Technical and Vocational Training Agreement. The change in the name of the branch recognized the creation of the network of colleges of applied arts and technology. Most aspects of the activities of the branch are dealt with in volume IV in connection with the institutions with which it has been concerned. In 1965, just before most of these were absorbed into the new colleges, they were as follows: the Provincial Institute of Mining at Haileybury, the Hamilton Institute of Technology, the Eastern Ontario Institute of Technology at Ottawa, the Northern Ontario Institute of Technology at Kirkland Lake, the Western Ontario Institute of Technology at Windsor, the Provincial Institutes of Trades, of Automotive and Allied Trades, and of Trades and Occupations, all at Toronto, and the Ontario Vocational Centres at London, Ottawa, and Sault Ste Marie. The branch sponsored Advanced Technical Evening Classes at a number of these institutions.

The branch became involved in a Business Management Program in 1963 under Program 4 of the Federal-Provincial Technical and Vocational Training Agreement. Under the supervision of J.A. Wright, these activities expanded rapidly among small industries across the province. The role of the department officials was largely one of assisting local sponsors, which might be groups of local businessmen, trade associations, service clubs, or others, in organizing and presenting the courses. Chambers of Commerce were particularly active in this regard. As a first step a sponsoring committee was set up to select a suitable course or courses, to choose a date, a time, and a location, to promote course attendance through publicity, to seek support from other groups, to suggest a suitable course leader, to set registration targets, and to collect registration fees. The provincial supervisor assumed the responsibility for designating the course leader or instructor and for ensuring that he was properly trained. An attempt was made to enrol a group ranging from fifteen to twenty-five for each course. Sponsors were encouraged to arrange for courses in series rather than presenting a single one in isolation.

Course materials were prepared by the Department of Education and by the federal Department of Manpower and Immigration. The supervisor of the Business Management Program supplied these to the local groups along with promotional material. The following courses were among those offered: Management Accounting, which attempted to show a businessman how he could use information in his own books to operate more profitably; Retail Management, which was designed for independent retailers to help them improve their marketing knowledge and decision-making skills; Marketing for Manufacturers, which dealt with approaches and techniques by which owner-managers could promote their products and sell more effectively in competitive markets; Marketing for Service Businesses, which was designed to solve marketing problems encountered by service businesses in such areas as service to be offered, pricing, and advertising; Exporting, which showed the independent manufacturer how to take advantage of foreign sales opportunities by finding markets and by gaining familiarity with them; Personnel, which dealt with methods by which owner-managers could get, keep, and make the best use of personnel; Purchasing for Manufacturers, which showed the owner how to take advantage of opportunities for cost saving and profit in the purchase of raw materials, components, and supplies; Bookkeeping, which taught the fundamentals of the subject and showed the businessman how to appraise his accounting system and make needed improvements; Finance and Taxation, which was designed to help businessmen improve their current financial position and take advantage of profitable investment opportunities; Business Law, which helped the owner-manager deal more effectively with the legal aspects of his business problems. Those who attended at least 80 per cent of the sessions received a Department of Education certificate.

The branch also offered supervisory courses under the title "Effective Supervision," the materials for which were prepared for the federal Department of Manpower and Immigration. There were four courses dealing respectively with the specific applications of supervisory techniques in production, construction, administration, and mining. The ten sessions in the Effective Supervision-Production course were devoted to the following topics: the role of the supervisor, principles of effective supervision, taking proper action, motivation of the worker, setting objectives and goals, planning, scheduling, measuring results and evaluating efficiency, improvements, and getting a day's work done. The topics in the other three variations of the same course were adapted to the specific problems of the respective areas of concern. Use was made of the case study approach, with cases taken from actual practice. The supervisory program also included follow-up courses in human relations, communications, labour relations, and work study.

With the firm establishment of the colleges of applied arts and technology, as many of the courses as possible were given in college buildings. In some cases the colleges acted as co-sponsors of the courses along with the community organizations. The offering of such courses was likely to have important implications for the extension departments of the colleges.

A third type of training begun under Program 4 was a series of upgrading courses for employees. These involved departmental co-operation to provide courses in basic academic subjects such as English, mathematics, and science, and courses in skill areas.

The Applied Arts and Technology Branch was responsible for meeting the province's obligations for training and retraining of the unemployed under what was known at successive stages as Program 5 and the Ontario Manpower Retraining Program. The changing roles of the federal and provincial governments, as well as the content and effects of this program, are explored in chapter 11 of the present volume and in volume IV, chapter 20. A development of major significance during 1968 and 1969 was the transfer of the administration of this program from local school boards to the colleges of applied arts and technology.

THE SPECIAL SCHOOLS AND SERVICES BRANCH

The Special Schools and Services Branch was the successor to the Special Educational Services Branch in the reorganization of 1965. As already mentioned, the policy of consolidating supervisory activities resulted in the transfer of the Auxiliary Education Services Division to the Program Branch. The Special Schools and Services Branch consisted of the Blind and Deaf Division, the Schools for Retarded Children Division, the Community Programs Division, and the Correspondence Courses Division. There was provision for assistance to the handicapped for whom no other form of help was available. Such services included contributions toward the cost of tutoring blind students, transportation for temporarily physically handicapped children, fees for blind and deaf children attending schools outside the province, and correspondence courses for patients in sanatoria.

The Schools for the Blind and Deaf Division (Section)

The Schools for the Blind and Deaf Division was responsible for the administration and supervision of the residential schools for the blind and deaf: the Ontario School for the Blind at Brantford and the two Ontario Schools for the Deaf at Belleville and Milton respectively. The division also supervised day classes for the deaf operated by local school boards and provided consultative services to school boards for the establishment and administration of such classes. Liaison was maintained with the Canadian Hearing Society and the Canadian National Institute for the Blind in order to ensure optimum training for deaf and blind children.

As described in the *Report of the Minister, 1965*, the program at the Ontario School for the Blind, involving the use of the Ontario courses of study for grades 1 to 12 as a base, consisted of a variety of academic, vocational, physical, cultural, and social activities aimed at preparing the student for independent, self-supporting adulthood. The academic courses led to university and the vocational courses to appropriate types of employment. Emphasis was placed on home economics for girls, on music for those with suitable talent and interest, and on physical education for all except those who were medically disqualified. There were opportunities for engaging in many types of team sports and in extracurricular activities such as Cubs, Scouts, Guides, Brownies, social clubs, a United Nations club, and a French club.[30] During the next few years the character of the school was modified by an increase in the number of blind children with multiple handicaps, which resulted in a lowering of the pupil-teacher ratio, and by an increase in the secondary school enrolment. Growing enrolment allowed for more staff specialization.[31]

The program in the Ontario Schools for the Deaf also stressed physical education, recreation, and social development through participation in extra-curricular activities. The instructional program concentrated on overcoming the effects of language deprivation resulting from early deafness. Basic academic courses were offered to the grade 10 level, along with a variety of vocational courses. The school at Milton was in the process of developing a curriculum paralleling that at Belleville. The latter school provided for the training of a home-visiting teacher, whose responsibility it was to help parents develop early language skills in their young deaf children and prepare them for the school program. The school at Milton also maintained the same kind of service.[32] It instituted night school classes for graduates of the school and for deaf adults living in the immediate area. In 1968 these consisted of commercial work, dressmaking and sewing, language, graphic arts, drafting, carpentry, welding, and machine shop work.

The Schools for Retarded Children Division

The Schools for Retarded Children Division was established in September 1965 to supervise day schools operated by the Retarded Children's Education Authorities. The department had gradually, over the years, assumed an increasing amount of responsibility for the financial support of such schools. At this stage, the authorities received a departmental grant covering 80 per cent of the operating cost, and the municipalities where the schools were located supplied the rest. The department paid half the cost of capital construction, and the Associations for Retarded Children were responsible for the remainder. The division also conducted the educational program for mentally retarded children in Ontario hospital schools, and organized and operated a summer course for teachers of trainable retarded children. As already mentioned, the division was dissolved in 1968.

The Community Programs Division (Section)

Mention has been made of the establishment in 1948 of what was called the Community Programs Branch. It had a major responsibility in its earlier years for providing assistance to immigrants. By 1958, there were 1,096 citizenship classes with an enrolment of over 26,000. In addition to evening classes, daytime classes were provided in English and citizenship for unemployed newcomers. Responsibility for these functions was assumed by the Provincial Secretary's department in 1961.

The purposes of the Community Programs Branch, in broad terms, were to assist with the provision of opportunities for people to use their leisure time constructively in recreational and educational activities. Communities received grants, advice, guidance, and leadership training, and help in conducting conferences, seminars, clinics, and surveys. The staff worked with municipal recreation committees, school boards, national, provincial, and local organizations, and other departments of government. In 1965 there were offices in Belleville, Dryden, Fort William, Hamilton,

Hanover, London, North Bay, Oakville, Ottawa, Sudbury, and Toronto, from which field staff kept contact with local agencies. There were also special advisers in art, crafts, drama, music, puppetry, programs for "senior citizens," recreation buildings and areas, rural programs, and women's physical fitness activities. The branch produced a number of publications and operated a loan service in films, slides, reference books, and material for use in dramatic and musical activities. These operations continued under successive organizational changes.

Grants were made to municipalities that set up municipal recreation authorities. By 1965 these grants amounted to $725,895, and were paid to 356 municipalities. For the most part, it was not the department's intention to pay a large proportion of the cost of projects it sponsored, but rather to stimulate local communities to look after their own needs, and to provide them with the necessary leadership training. During 1965, 364 leadership courses were offered, either directly or in co-operation with other agencies, to train volunteer and semi-professional leaders in art, crafts, drama, music, executive skills, sports, and group leadership. Between 1951 and 1965 a three-year in-service training course, initiated by the branch, was offered at the University of Western Ontario to train workers in municipal recreation. A two-year diploma course at the University of Guelph began to turn out graduates in the latter year. Later the colleges of applied arts and technology entered the field with considerable enthusiasm, and the Guelph program was transferred to them. The Universities of Ottawa and Waterloo began to offer a degree program in recreation in 1968.

According to regulations made in 1966 under *The Department of Education Act*, an Interim Municipal Recreation Director's Certificate, Type A, might be granted by the minister, on the recommendation of the Administrator of the Community Programs Division, to a candidate submitting 1 / evidence of having obtained a degree from an approved university and having successfully completed the certification course, or 2/ evidence of having obtained a degree in a course in recreation from an approved university, or 3 / evidence of having completed, before January 1, 1966, the in-service training course in recreation approved by the Administrator of the Community Programs Division. After at least three years of full-time experience as a municipal recreation director, the holder of an Interim Type A Certificate might apply for a Permanent Municipal Recreation Director's Certificate, Type A. The Interim Type B Certificate was granted on successful completion of the two-year diploma course, and might be made permanent after the same period of successful experience as a municipal recreation director.[33]

After successful completion of an in-service training course in arena management conducted by the Ontario Arenas Association and approved by the Administrator of the Community Programs Division, a candidate could, under the terms of regulations passed in 1967, apply for an Interim

Arena Manager's Certificate. After at least two years of successful full-time experience, the holder of this interim certificate might be granted a Permanent Arena Manager's Certificate.[34]

Under the Federal-Provincial Agreement on Fitness and Amateur Sport, the branch sponsored a large number of projects to train coaches, referees, and leaders in a wide variety of athletic activities. Bursaries were provided for students enrolled in physical and health education courses in universities. Grants were made to non-profit camps, and a consultative service was provided for them in addition to workshops for camp directors. The Ontario Athletic Leadership Camp and the Ontario Camp Leadership Centre, whose earlier establishment has already been mentioned, were administered through the branch.

Among services to rural communities conducted in co-operation with the Department of Agriculture has been the provision of assistance in the establishment of rural community night schools. The Community Programs Branch has helped local agencies to organize these, and has given financial assistance. Active assistance normally lasts for two years, and then the community assumes the entire responsibility.

The Youth Branch

From the beginning the purpose of the Youth Branch was seen as one of encouraging co-operation among public and private agencies in the interests of improving services to young people, particularly those with insufficient schooling. Much of the effort of the branch was devoted to research activities. It was not given a large budget, and had only a small staff. During its first year of operations, it undertook a survey to determine the full extent of existing services to youth, the agencies that were providing such services, the cost, and the sources of funds being provided.

The minister outlined some of the possibilities open to the branch in discussing the estimates in the Legislature in 1964.

If we know the nature and extent of a problem there is a better chance that we can do something about it than if the problem is loosely defined, full of information gaps, and a mixture of truths, half-truths, and one or two distortions. The delinquency picture and the school drop-out problem are areas which come under scrutiny at once in this regard. Rumours about increases in the obsolescence of certain jobs are not helping our young people to develop the necessary courage and drive. At the same time, there is much said about new kinds of jobs growing out of the discarding of the old kinds. There is an air of uncertainty. If this new kind of world is to be an automated one, there will have to be borne in mind the implications of the comment that society is quick to be proud of its developments in the area of automation but is hesitant to accept the social consequences of such automation.

The youth branch may be able to give a real service by sharpening the uncertain edges of the economic trends of the very immediate future. It may be able to help the curriculum and course builders; it may be able to foresee certain trends. I am hopeful that the counsel it may be able to provide indirectly to concerned youth may contribute elements of stability in a situation which at present is somewhat vague and uneasy.[35]

Two days later, Davis again returned to the topic of the Youth Branch. He said that the new unit had begun as a rather nebulous idea, and suggested that a good deal of information was needed before effective programs could be devised. Decisions were being made at that time about what areas should be tackled.[36]

The branch received some rough treatment at the hands of Robert Nixon the following year. He claimed that it already showed signs of being moribund. Among the suggestions he made for it was that it might provide jobs for post-secondary school students. The requirements of every department of government might be brought together in a co-ordinated list which would be available to the students. At that time students were looking for jobs mainly during the summer, but when the trimester system got well established, there might be numbers of them seeking short-term work throughout the year. Those studying engineering and science might be employed by Hydro, the Department of Highways, and the Department of Public Works, while those with more general interests might serve as hospital assistants and assistant welfare officers with the Children's Aid Society, the Canadian National Institute for the Blind, the Red Cross, and community welfare councils. Nixon extended this list with a considerable number of further suggestions.[37] The department did not, however, see fit to move in this direction.

The account of the activities of the branch in the *Report of the Minister, 1965*, stressed its advisory and research role.[38] Under the direction of H.E. Thomas, it was said to be assisting communities in identifying the factors which influenced the development of youth, such as population movements, employment, education, social adjustment, and recreation. The communities had the responsibility of using the information thus obtained to undertake the appropriate programs. The branch had completed the study already referred to, which was entitled "Continuing Education in Ontario: Opportunities by Sources," as well as two others designated respectively "Population, Labour and Educational Statistics for Ontario" and "Preparation of a Bibliography and Evaluation of Films on Sex Education." In order to expand these activities, the branch was seeking additional research officers in economics and sociology. The department was making funds available for research on unreached youth in Metropolitan Toronto at the request of the Social Planning Council of Metropolitan Toronto, acting in consultation with the Youth Branch. Members of the staff of the branch were participating in conferences and acting as consultants to a large number of organizations.

During the following year, the research officer in sociology was added, but not the one in economics. The branch developed an approach for identifying the social, educational, and unemployment problems of young people by community study teams, with representation from youth, education, industry, labour, municipal councils, Canada Manpower Centres, police, and those with responsibility for probation, recreation, religion, and welfare. This approach was employed successively in northwestern and northern Ontario in two-year studies consisting of six phases: 1 / field work, involving visits in the communities to discuss the project with leaders and to encourage their involvement; 2 / an initial four-day residential seminar to provide understanding of the region, to develop research methods of gathering data, and to outline future commitments; 3 / community surveys; 4 / a second four-day seminar to interpret the community data collected and ultimately to develop specific programs for youth; 5 / community implementation with advisory help from the Youth Branch; 6 / a third seminar to evaluate the study and its implementation.

In 1967 two studies were published entitled respectively *A Study of Walpole Island Indian Reserve* and *Now That You've Left School*, an information booklet for unemployed youth. A study of youth in South Peel County was also carried out, and the youth and resources study in northern and northwestern Ontario proceeded through successive phases.

The Youth and Recreation Branch

The Community Programs Section, as it was then called, was merged with the Youth Branch in June 1968 to form the Youth and Recreation Branch. It had been obvious that the two agencies had a great many common interests, although the Youth Branch was concerned with a more limited group, and involved the research orientation that the Community Programs Section lacked.

New responsibilities were assumed in addition to those inherited from the two parent organizations. In the Ontario Youth-in-Action program, thirty-five university, college, and senior high school students were employed in the late summer of 1968 to help young people in certain municipalities to participate in activities affecting their lives in their own communities. The Youth-in-Action teams initiated the activities, which were carried out under the supervision of members of the branch. In 1968 and 1969 measures were taken to provide public information about educational and employment opportunities for young people, and about welfare policies, recreational programs, and other services. The branch undertook to identify gaps in existing youth and recreation services, and to offer practical solutions for the problem of unmet needs.

One of the highlights of 1968–9 was the holding of two sports conferences under the sponsorship of the branch. The first, convened in November 1968, involved representatives of the governing bodies of seventy-two Ontario sports, who undertook to identify and study the problems of amateur sport in the province and to set priorities for action. A committee was set up to devise the structure and outline the functions of an Ontario Sports Council. A second conference was held in May 1969 to vote on the formation of the council.

T.L. Wells, then Minister without Portfolio, but with special responsibilities in the educational field, discussed the role of the new branch on February 25, 1969. He expressed the view that the amalgamation of the two parent units was very much in keeping with the spirit and thinking of the Legislature's Select Committee on Youth, which had advocated the establishment of a separate Department of Youth. His over-all appraisal was as follows:

> As a member of this select committee on youth I travelled to all these other provinces in Canada and saw the organizations that they have. And in my own mind I am convinced that our youth and recreation branch, as it now stands organized, and as it will develop, is the equal or better of any department of youth in any other government in this country.[39]

Wells went on to review some of the activities in which the branch was currently engaged. Among the most significant was the formation of a Provincial Youth Council along the lines suggested by the select committee. Initially, it was to be composed of one young person under twenty-five years of age from each of the nineteen areas of the province covered by field staff from the branch. Its purpose would be to advise the branch on programs and services required by young people. From time to time it would meet with the interdepartmental committee on youth to discuss common concerns. In addition to the council at the provincial level, long-range plans called for the ultimate establishment of local community and regional youth councils. The local community councils would select representatives for the regional councils, and these in turn would choose representatives to serve on the provincial council. Ideas for the role and functions of the local councils were being obtained from the Ontario Youth-in-Action program. Commenting on the placement of the extension staff of the branch in the Regional Offices of the Department of Education as of January 1, 1969, Wells noted that they would be able to use their expertise in advising boards of education on such matters as the optimum community use of schools, leadership training courses for teachers of adult avocational programs, and the development of continuing education programs.

An Ontario Recreation Research Committee had been established under the chairmanship of J.R. Kidd to provide for research services recommended by the Select Committee on Youth. Its initial task would be to consolidate existing research, after which it would identify areas in which research was required as a guide for research-conducting agencies.

An Ontario Recreation Society, then in the planning stages, was to include all professional recreationists, whether in public or private practice. It would provide training opportunities for its membership and encourage co-operation among agencies to ensure the maximum of opportunities for the creative use of leisure.

The Speech from the Throne introducing the Third Session of the Twenty-eighth Legislature on February 24, 1970, foreshadowed certain changes in governmental organization, with possible implications for the Youth and Recreation Branch:

> Through the years, the government of Ontario has developed a broad programme of essential services for the people of our province in fields such as health, education, housing, industry and agriculture. At the same time, it has created special programmes related directly to the role of the individual within the larger society. Many of these special programmes, such as the integration of newcomers into the mainstream of life in our province, respect for human rights, leisure, recreation, and cultural activities, enable the individual to enjoy a full and meaningful life and to make a positive contribution to our province and to Canada. ...
>
> To achieve these purposes, it is the intention of the government to consolidate and co-ordinate in a reorganized Department of Citizenship many such activities now directed to individual groups of residents. ... This ministry will encourage interests in community affairs and an increased awareness of the challenges which we face and the community goals which must be attained. By drawing together all of these programmes in a single department and by giving emphasis to total involvement, a comprehensive citizenship programme can be developed to further enrich the quality of life in our province.[40]

At the time of writing, there was no definite information as to whether or not these rather cryptic lines meant that the Youth and Recreation Branch would actually be transferred to the Department of Citizenship. More specific indications of the government's intentions were expected later in the session.

The Provincial Library Service

The report of Francis R. St John Library Consultants Inc. was released in 1965, shortly after the departmental reorganization.[41] At that time the staff of the Provincial Library Service consisted of a director, W.A. Roedde, a Chief Librarian-Supervisor of Adult Service, a Supervisor of Children's Service, a Supervisor of Extension Service, an additional librarian, and a clerical staff of eight. The Chief Librarian-Supervisor of Adult Service acted in an advisory capacity with other supervisors and specialized in book services which involved lending to Department of Education staff, teachers, and members of the staffs of provincial libraries. The fifth librarian on the provincial library staff acted as her assistant, assuming special responsibility for travelling libraries and for the

Teachers' Reference Service. The Supervisor of Extension Service organized institutes and workshops and offered advice to librarians and trustees. The Supervisor of Children's Service performed similar functions, but with emphasis on work with children. There was close co-operation with organizations interested in children's reading, such as Home and School Associations and the Children's Recreational Reading Council, and with branches of the Department of Education concerned with elementary education.

The responsibilities of the director and supervisors involved travelling around the province to visit, evaluate, and report on libraries and to attend meetings of municipal councils, library boards, and other bodies to deal with matters such as grants on capital expenditure, personnel, and the co-ordination of public library service with that of school boards and other agencies. The St John report indicated that these staff members were too few in number to fill the province's needs for consultative service, and recommended that the group be enlarged.[42] This recommendation was not acted upon, since by 1969 the professional staff had been increased by only one librarian.

Between ten and twenty library institutes were held each year, dealing with such topics as regional reference centres, technical services in the public library, and the role of the library trustee. Courses of from three to six weeks were offered, as well as shorter workshops, with lectures followed by a program of assignments. After a similar course the following year, a Class D Certificate of Library Service might be obtained.

The service published the *Ontario Library Review*, a quarterly periodical dating from 1916 which contained articles written by librarians, library trustees, and others, as well as certain statistics relating to circulation of library materials, costs, and other factors. The Teachers' Reference Library, a direct mailing service for rural teachers, distributed books, filmstrips, picture study prints, and records. Its resources included a modest collection of books for use in university extension courses. The Teachers' Reference Library was promoted through mailings to inspectors, displays at teachers' colleges, and articles in educational journals. Travelling library services had been initiated at the beginning of the century as a means of providing books to areas without library facilities. The need for these services was diminishing rapidly as larger schools with adequate libraries replaced the one- and two-room units, and as association libraries gave way to county and regional libraries. The report recommended that travelling library services be terminated.

The organizational structure of the Provincial Library Service had not undergone any substantial change by 1969. The nature of its activities was of course affected by the development of provincial library facilities, which are dealt with in volume V, chapter 20. Among extended services to Department of Education staff and others was the production of EDEX, a monthly periodical copying service of educational journals.

Correspondence courses

Correspondence courses were first offered in 1926 to meet the needs of children who lived in isolated areas where they had no access to schools, and of children whom illness or physical disability prevented from attending school. From the beginning, the service was provided free of charge. At first, only academic school subjects were offered, closely following the provincial course of study, and enrolment was restricted to children and young people between the ages of six and twenty-one, and to a restricted number of parents who wished to keep ahead of their children. Not only was the age limit eventually removed, but courses began also to be written especially for adults. According to the *Report of the Minister, 1951*, courses were reaching homes in all parts of the province; patients in hospitals and sanatoria; inmates of penitentiaries and reformatories; and children of businessmen, government officials, and missionaries abroad.[43]

The courses began with basic subjects in the eight elementary school grades. Subjects in grades 9 and 10 were added in 1935, and bilingual lessons for French-speaking pupils at the elementary school level were introduced in 1942. Eight years later, the process of extending the offerings through grade 13 was begun, and a revision of courses from grades 1 to 10 was undertaken. At the same time, the program was extended to cover additional subjects at all levels.

By 1956–7 the categories of individuals who were eligible for enrolment in the courses were as follows: 1 / children between six and fifteen years of age inclusive living in Ontario who were unable to attend school and who were recommended for the courses by the local elementary school inspector, or the secondary school principal if the courses were at the secondary school level; 2 / individuals sixteen years of age and over who were unable to attend school; 3 / persons normally resident in Ontario, but temporarily living outside Canada; 4 / members of the Canadian Armed Services and their dependents when stationed outside Canada where it was impossible to attend a school where the Ontario curriculum was taught; 5 / secondary school students in Ontario who found it impossible to complete grades 11, 12, or 13 within the school year because the required subjects were not taught in the school attended, provided they had the approval of the local secondary school principal, the secondary school inspector, and the provincial Superintendent of Secondary Education. It was clearly intended that the courses would not be allowed to become a substitute for attendance at school in cases where facilities could reasonably be expected to be used. The schools were also forbidden to use the courses as teaching aids except where the teacher was unqualified and the local inspector and the provincial Superintendent of Elementary or Secondary Education gave specific approval.

Courses for children were available at this time in all subjects up to the end of grade 8, and for adults in English, arithmetic, and social studies at the same level. A child was given a certificate of promotion as he completed the work of each grade satisfactorily. An adult who had achieved success in grade 8 English and arithmetic was eligible to enrol in any course in the grade 9 program. Courses in grades 11 and 12 that counted toward the Ontario Secondary School Graduation Diploma involved a supervised test. The correspondence course in grade 13 was a preparation for the departmental examination, which had to be written at one of the regular centres.

For children studying at the elementary school level, the department lent textbooks and provided all other necessary materials. Students at the secondary level and all adults had to secure and pay for their own books and materials. The courses could be begun at any time during the year, although students were advised to plan work undertaken in grade 13 in such a way as to be ready for the departmental examinations. Considerable efforts were made to accommodate students living outside Ontario by setting up special centres where they could write the departmentals.

In the 1950s Canadian Vocational Correspondence Courses began to be offered in a number of fields as a result of co-operation involving the federal government and the departments of education in the provinces. These courses could be taken by adults in any part of Canada on payment of a nominal fee. Prepared primarily for tradesmen, they did not yield credit towards an Ontario Secondary School Graduation Diploma.

While conditions under which the academic courses were given did not change substantially over the years, there were minor alterations in the scheme. In 1963 registration at the elementary level was limited to the period between September 1 and May 15. After September 1964 the practice of lending free textbooks was extended to students in grades 9 and 10, and after September 1965 to those in grades 11 and 12. As schools became increasingly accessible to children in remote areas, the distribution of students shifted steadily toward the adult age groups. The courses increasingly became a means whereby employed people could upgrade their academic education. In 1965 there were more applications from the twenty to twenty-four-year age group than from any other, and more were taking work in grade 13 than in any other grade.

In 1966 courses in the subjects of the five-year program of the Business and Commerce Branch were added to those of the five-year program of the Arts and Science Branch. With the further addition of thirty secondary school subjects in 1967, it became possible to complete the requirements for departmental Statements of Standing and diplomas in any branch of the secondary school four- or five-year programs. Commenting in the Legislature on the extended range of offerings, the minister foresaw an even more rapid increase in enrolment than that recorded in previous years.[44]

In 1968 grade 13 courses were made available for the first time during the summer months, and students who had been attending school in that grade during the previous year could enrol at any time after the results of the grade 13 examinations had been announced. While they could not expect to complete the work in a subject by the time the colleges and universities opened in the fall, they might do so by December. Thus they might qualify for the winter semester where the trimester system prevailed, if they needed only one or two subjects. Students attending school in any one of grades 9 to 12 could not enrol in correspondence courses in the summer immediately following, but might do so in September.

After the abolition of the grade 13 departmental examinations in 1967, there was no longer a final examination for correspondence students at that level. The mark was based on performance on twenty lesson assignments in all subjects except accountancy practice, where there were ten assignments, plus the results of two supervised tests.

During the fall of 1969 new unit courses were introduced consisting of ten lessons, replacing some of the twenty-lesson courses. Two of the new units carried credit equivalent to that of a regular course. It was hoped that the shorter units would better retain the interest of the students. Courses introduced for the first time included those on archaeology, ecology, pollution, and contemporary science fiction, as well as readings on flight. In the process of preparation was a unit on the mathematics of finance designed to give students a basic understanding of mortgage rates, interest rates on loans and charge accounts, and techniques of dealing with mortgages, bonds, and annuities.

At this time over 90 per cent of those taking the courses were adults who were unable to attend regular or night school classes. The most popular subjects were English and mathematics, which constituted the base for most other studies. Many parents were taking the new mathematics in order to be able to help their children with their homework.

ADMINISTRATIVE SERVICES

The Departmental Business Administration Branch

In the reorganized plan, the Departmental Business Administration Branch was given the responsibility for preparing the departmental budget estimates, in connection with which it conducted an increasing number of studies on current and planned program costs. It was responsible for establishing and maintaining internal controls, accounting procedures, and systems to ensure proper adherence to government regulations with respect to the receipt and disbursement of funds. It administered funds for vocational building projects and various vocational and technical training programs and services under the Federal-Provincial Technical and Vocational Training Agreement. This responsibility included payments to school boards, trainees, and others, and subsequently recovering the agreed share of the costs from the federal government. The Accounts and Payroll Unit processed, controlled, and recorded all financial transactions, including the collection of loans under the provincial Student-Aid Loan

Program. It also prepared the relevant section of the Public Accounts. The Administrative Services Division provided liaison between the department and certain outside agencies, as well as maintaining services for different parts of the department, such as printing, central filing of teachers' documents and departmental records, and the distribution and dispatch of mail.

Initially the Grants Division operated under the Departmental Business Administration Branch. It was responsible for ensuring the calculation and distribution of grants to school boards, public libraries, Retarded Children's Authorities, municipalities (for recreation programs), and non-profit camps. It also calculated the amount of provincial reimbursement to school boards for the education of non-resident pupils in the territorial districts. In June 1966 the Grants Division was transferred, as indicated earlier, to the School Business Administration Branch.

The *Report of the Minister of Education, 1968* recorded a number of significant developments in the branch during that year.[45] One of these was the adoption of a computerized accounting system for classifying, recording, and reporting departmental expenditures, designed to give faster and better service. Payroll functions were reorganized to improve work flow through better workload distribution, and revised accounting systems were introduced to improve internal control and increase productivity. The printing units formerly located in the Registrar's Section, the Correspondence Courses Section, the Community Programs Section, and Administrative Services were combined in a single unit to achieve a reduction in printing expenditures and increased efficiency in production and distribution services.

The School Business Administration Branch

The School Business Administration Branch had a varied assortment of functions within the reorganized departmental structure. These included research into school planning, designing facilities for schools, and developing procedures for allocating financial assistance for school building projects. It was also responsible for the administration of data processing facilities. Through business administrators appointed to Regional Offices, it took over many of the non-academic advisory functions hitherto carried out by school inspectors, relating to transportation agreements, boundaries, and the like.

The Education Data Centre

The Education Data Centre was established in 1965 under the supervision of J.A. Keddy. Much of the information which follows is from an address which Keddy delivered to the Golden Horseshoe Section of the Computer Society of Canada at Hamilton on May 21, 1968, under the title "Data Processing in Education in Ontario." When he joined the department in October 1964, he had a keypunch staff of sixteen to operate a small unit record installation which was used only for statistical purposes. At that time the Department of Educational Research of the Ontario College of Education was performing two main service functions for the department: the compilation of grade 13 examination results and the calculation of provincial grants to school boards.

Expansion of the department's operations was preceded by the activities of a Data Processing Committee charged by Howard Beattie, on which the present writer was privileged to serve. Whatever the results of the deliberations and recommendations of this committee, the minister threw considerable weight behind the development of more adequate facilities in the department. By October 1965 Keddy had an authorized establishment of forty and an actual staff of thirty-two, including assistant managers, systems analysts, programmers, and computer operators. The centre was equipped with a 16k IBM 1460 with a console, a console typewriter, two disc drives, two tape drives (later increased successively to four and six), and a 1402 for card input and output.

In order to establish an information system by which the major items of data needed by the department could be obtained, updated, and made available without duplication of effort, the centre organized a master identification, or Mident, file. This file involved a system of numbers for a hierarchy of units beginning with schools and working up through boards, superintendencies, and regional superintendencies. Also identified were the municipality and county or district in which each school was located, along with the population of the former. Provision was made for the grouping of counties and districts into economic regions. For some applications, pupils and teacher numbers could be related to the appropriate school number, and through it to the rest of the file. The teacher's superannuation number, which was used at first, was later replaced by the social insurance number.

In expanding its activities, the centre stressed the external activities of the department in relation to school boards by concentrating on the collection of provincial data from schools, boards, or larger units of school administration. It assisted the boards that were equipped for data processing by giving them an early indication of the data they should collect for transmission to the department. With their co-operation, it was possible to perform certain tabulations and analyses of data, not only for the province as a whole, but also for counties, municipalities, educational administrative regions, or even individual schools. The results were particularly useful to regional superintendents.

It was considered that the full potential range of useful data covered pupils, teachers, curriculum, facilities, and finances. The centre confined its initial efforts largely to pupils, teachers, and finances. Enrolment data were collected and categorized by sex as well as grade. A means was devised by which the analysis of the school population by age, grade, and sex, previously compiled every five years, could be handled by the computer for the first time. A further plan was implemented for the conduct of a major study of student retirement from secondary schools, the first data for which were collected in 1964–5. Information was obtained to indicate the grade, course, branch, and program the student last attended, the certificate he received, and his employment or further training immediately after he left school. Each school was given tables based on an analysis of its own student retirements corresponding to that for the province as a whole.

The centre entered two fields of teacher data. One of these had to do with certification, degrees held, experience, employment, and other items which constituted a common core that would be useful to the various branches of the department, to the Ontario Teachers' Federation, and to the Teachers' Superannuation Commission. The plan for the second field, that of superannuation, was implemented in three phases. These were 1 / the calculation of payments made to pensioners, begun on January 1, 1966; 2 / the recording of current contributions; and 3 / the placing on record of all contributions to date.

Entry into the financial area involved the assumption of the responsibility for calculating provincial grants to school boards, a function which had been assumed by the Ontario Institute for Studies in Education when it absorbed the Department of Educational Research. The centre's first step was to recommend the installation of an Addo-x to record in the Grants Office the necessary details of each school board's audited financial return and its attendance data. A recommendation was made, and later implemented, that the attendance base for grants be changed from actual attendance to average enrolment. During the first year of the centre's move toward full responsibility in the area, the input data were turned over to the OISE, where the calculations were made according to the methods used previously. At the same time a study was conducted with a view to devising a more flexible computer system so that estimates of cost might easily be prepared for any proposed changes. The result was a considerable improvement in the operation.

Another continuing function of major proportions conducted by the centre was the calculation of various payments made by the Business Administration Branch to students or employees in training under various vocational programs. There were also non-recurring projects such as the analysis of questionnaire data on grants to secondary schools for textbooks, and occasional questionnaire studies for the Curriculum Branch. Responsibility for such projects was assumed only if they did not interfere with normal obligations.

In April 1968 the Education Data Centre absorbed the Regional Data Processing Centre that had been operated during the previous two-year period under the aegis of the Ontario Institute for Studies in Education. The new unit was called the Education Data Processing Centre. The Regional Data Processing Centre had begun with the ambitious hope of developing a central facility to provide for the needs of the school boards of the Metropolitan Toronto area, the Department of Education, and possibly of one or more post-secondary educational institutions. Most of the school boards were understandably reluctant to rely on an untried agency outside their control, and chose to develop their own facilities. The regional centre proceeded to work on several projects, including the following: 1 / a student administration system covering registration, attendance reporting, report cards, and other administrative requirements; 2 / a teacher payroll system; and 3 / a computerized timetabling service. The new branch assumed responsibility for these, as well as for the calculation of school grants, the scoring of objective tests for the Ontario Admission to College and University (OACU) program, and the processing of post-secondary student loans and grants for the Department of University Affairs. The branch was placed under the direction of Z.R. Patterson.

In 1969 the following additional systems were under development: 1 / extension of the department's business administration system to include other functions; 2 / conversion of certification information as the first phase in establishing a teacher information file; 3 / feasibility studies in the area of a computer-based guidance system, audio-visual library systemization, and a school board administration system.

The departmental Statistical Unit

These changes were accompanied by the creation of a departmental Statistical Unit under the direction of J.A. Keddy, who was named Chief Statistician. It had responsibility for the annual minister's report and for the collection of other statistical information needed for departmental purposes, including planning. It acted as a source of ideas for the productive use of quantitative data for the improvement of the educational system.

Division of School Planning and Building Research

The Division of School Planning and Building Research, which was established in 1964 as a sequel to the Minister's Conference on School Design, had four primary objectives: 1 / to investigate the facilities needed to house new teaching media; 2 / to study quality control of school buildings, with particular attention to materials and construction methods as related to costs; 3 / to determine how early obsolescence of school buildings might be avoided; and 4 / to determine how greater use might be made of the schools for community purposes. Shortly after its formation, the division organized a series of regional workshops to study the problems of school design. The first five of these, held in Sudbury, the Lakehead, Windsor, Kingston, and Niagara Falls, involved a discussion of local building needs, problems of the professional building team, the meaning of construction quality, control of the environment, the effect of teaching aids, and the function of the building committee.[46]

The purposes of the division, or section, as it came to be called, were met in part through publication. The booklets, produced over a period of several years, were intended to provide guidelines for architects, planners, officials, and administrators, rather than detailed prescriptions. They covered construction for educational purposes at all levels except universities at the post-secondary level. The first booklets, available by the end of 1965, were entitled *Physical Education Facilities for Secondary Schools* and *Guidance Centres for Secondary Schools*. Additions in 1966 were *Rehabilitation of Schools*, *Library Materials Centres*, and *Business and Commerce Facilities for Secondary Schools*. The developing colleges of applied arts and technology were an area of major interest during the following year. The publication list was further extended in 1968 with the appearance of *Technical and Occupational Shops*, *Science Laboratories for Secondary Schools*, *Home Economics*, *Library Resource Centres for Elementary Schools*, and *Special Education Facilities for Emotionally Disturbed Children*. Copies of the reports were distributed free of charge to a specific list of recipients, but they proved so attractive and popular that a charge had to be made to others in order to keep the distribution costs within tolerable limits. Other types of publications included articles for periodicals, pamphlets, and leaflets. Wide dispersal of printed material helped the section to establish and maintain contacts in many parts of the world, including almost every country in Europe. Ontario education is in fact known to some countries chiefly through this particular avenue.

Another major contribution of the section was in the area of consultation. Free consultative service was offered to school boards, boards of governors of colleges of applied arts and technology, and those responsible for teachers' colleges, colleges of education, and schools for the deaf and blind. The kind of information the section could supply would be beyond the reach of individual architects if they had to rely on their own unaided research efforts. S.T. Orlowski, who took charge of the section in 1967, believed that the consulting function was of the highest importance.

School design workshops continued to be offered in three different locations around the province each year, attracting trustees, architects, contractors, educators, and administrators. Papers were presented by experts in various fields and discussed by the participants. Consideration was given to such questions as: "Why are costs higher in northern Ontario than in the south?" and "How are practices in southern Ontario influenced by proximity to the United States?" Departmental representatives had an opportunity to present the official point of view on such matters as the need for saving. A mining community might, for example, be advised to construct buildings that were readily transportable rather than solid monuments of brick and stone. The value of the workshops was enhanced by the contributions of speakers from agencies abroad, such as the Educational Facilities Laboratory in New York.

School Plant Approvals unit

The inauguration of a departmental policy of offering grants for school construction in 1944 led to the appointment of a technical adviser to ensure that the funds were spent as intended. A School Plant Approvals unit carried out the functions of this office in the reorganized departmental structure. It had responsibility for scrutinizing all school building projects on behalf of the department and, during the period when federal grants were being paid for vocational school facilities, on behalf of the federal government as well. The whole process of planning and making arrangements for school construction was supervised in detail.

All building plans for post-secondary institutions except universities had to secure the approval of the unit. The huge college of applied arts and technology program absorbed a great deal of the staff's time. The department was determined to avoid the haphazard type of growth that had characterized some of the older universities of the province.

The Personnel Branch

The establishment of the Personnel Branch in 1963 involved fairly detailed specifications of what was expected of its director who, before the reorganization of 1965, reported to the Deputy Minister for Elementary Education. His main function was to serve as personnel management adviser to the heads of other departmental branches and to their senior management, indicating the personnel implications of all their policy and program decisions. In order to discharge this responsibility, he was expected to be present as an observer when such decisions were made so that his advice could be freely sought where it was relevant. In a sense, he was regarded as a kind of watchdog on departmental planning at the branch level.

He was also to make his advisory service on personnel management directly available to other officials with administrative or supervisory responsibilities. This advice and assistance would cover all phases of the staffing process, including the identification and definition of positions, the selection of candidates, orientation, development, evaluation, and retirement. He was to engage in constant analysis and appraisal of the effectiveness of the whole personnel program and, where necessary, recommend improved practices. He thus needed to have continuous contact with the Department of Civil Service to maintain familiarity with revisions in procedures and regulations.

In dealing with personnel problems and grievances, he was to act as a mediator and problem solver, suggesting solutions rather than imposing them. He was supposed to be completely familiar with all grievance activity, whether incipient or at the formal stage. He was not, however, to interfere with the exercise of authority by line officers except in the sense that he was responsible for ensuring the application of personnel procedures and for advising officials which actions might or might not be taken. Since his job emphasized communication, he was to issue to officials complete and comprehensive circulars on all aspects of personnel administration, and to communicate policies to the staff, either directly or through line officers.

The branch was gradually provided with a staff to deal with such matters as classification and pay, organization, systems and methods, selection, training, and development. It processed all personnel transactions and kept detailed personnel records. In 1966, when R. McNeil became director, publication of a *Personnel Bulletin* was begun to inform and guide managers in matters of personnel administration. The branch participated in the establishment and activities of a Staff Development Committee of senior department officials. A full-time staff development officer was not appointed until 1968. During that year, various management development seminars and supervisory courses were offered for departmental officials.

The Information Branch (News and Information Services)

With respect to the reasons for establishing the Information Branch, the minister said:

> With the department responsible for a budget approaching half a billion dollars annually, and with education having become a major concern in all jurisdictions, I am convinced that there is continuing need for a two-way interchange of information on educational activities, policies, and plans between the department on the one side and the public on the other.[47]

Under the direction of C.H. Williams, the branch undertook ambitious programs in four main areas: exhibitions, press services, public inquiries, and publications. The *Report of the Minister, 1965* mentioned participation in the Central Canada Exhibition in Ottawa in August, where emphasis was placed on courses available at the institutes of technology and the teachers' colleges; in the Western Fair in London, where the subject matter was similar; in Canadian Education Showplace and the annual convention of the Ontario Education Association in Toronto, at both of which the reorganization of the Department of Education was the main theme; and in the Canadian National Exhibition, where a display centred on current trends in education at all levels.[48] In 1966 exhibits were provided and staffed at Ottawa, Kitchener, and St Catharines. There was a growing tendency on the part of school boards to organize careers expositions, for which they requested departmental participation. The theme at the Canadian National Exhibition was "Education for Work and Leisure." For the second time, a Student Talent Festival was staged in a theatre next to the exhibit area, involving public performances of dancing and vocal and instrumental music. Similar activities characterized the program in subsequent years.

Press releases on matters of current interest have been distributed in substantial numbers to weekly and daily newspapers, members of the Ontario Legislative Press Gallery, radio and television stations, educational publications, and a considerable number of other individuals and agencies. Newspaper reporters are known to be sceptical about specially prepared handouts, with their implication of managed news. Releases from the branch have, however, stuck largely to brief factual presentations, and the press seems to have found them useful. According to the *Report of the Minister of Education, 1968*, the change in name in the fall of that year from the Information Branch to News and Information Services was intended to signal a new emphasis on service to the news media, reflecting the appointment of Arnold Bruner, who had previously distinguished himself as a reporter, broadcaster, foreign correspondent, and writer, as director of the branch. A press/broadcasting unit was formed with a staff experienced in the news field. After consultation with major newspapers and news services, the branch began the practice of producing feature-length articles on educational developments and events for the news media.[49]

A third function of the branch was to respond to inquiries by telephone or letter on educational matters, whether connected with the work of the department or not. The staff were prepared to make a considerable effort to supply requested information, even to those engaged in graduate studies, who were normally expected to carry out their own research. Press clippings were supplied to other branches of the department to help maintain their sensitivity to public reaction to various developments in education. Responsibility was assumed for organizing tours for Canadian and foreign visitors seeking information about educational facilities and programs.

A fourth, and by no means the least important, function of the branch had to do with publications. Control was exerted over the design and production of a large number of those originating in other parts of the department. The general improvement in their appearance elicited many favourable comments. The branch also made its own contribution to publication. Until October 1967 a newsletter called *Ontario Education News* was issued monthly within the department to keep the staff informed on departmental activities, personalities, and projects. In 1968 the quarterly internal newsletter, *Ontario Department of Education News*, became a monthly publication with similar functions. In earlier years *Ontario Education* was produced quarterly to inform teachers, administrators, and the general public of developments of general interest in education as well of departmental policies and news. Toward the end of 1967 *Dimensions in Education* made its appearance as a monthly publication for departmental staff, teachers, and others. It was expanded the following year to include longer feature articles. Its monthly circulation during 1968 was reported at 100,000.

THE POLICY AND DEVELOPMENT COUNCIL

As created in 1964, the Policy and Development Council was, according to the minister's report for that year, "to conduct a continuing examination of Department policy, to initiate studies where required, and to report its findings and recommendations to the Minister."[50] The idea was reminiscent of that expressed on earlier occasions when attempts were made to establish the chief director as the minister's policy adviser, while the deputy minister was responsible for administration. Early definitions of the council's intended role tended to stress the planning function. In fact, the minister referred to the unit as the "planning and development council" in the Legislature in 1965.[51]

J. Bascom St John, the noted *Globe and Mail* columnist, was persuaded to assume the chairmanship of the council. For approximately six and a half years, St John had produced a daily column in which he had ranged widely over educational topics of current interest. Using a substantial network of contacts, he had brought the kind of informed point of view to bear on the issues of the day that was unique in Canadian newspaper history. While this is not to say that he was always profound, or necessarily always in a position to guarantee the accuracy of the information he received through his contacts, his columns were provocative and written in a pungent style that greatly added to public interest in education. He had found plenty of reasons to criticize the Department of Education, since he began his column at a time when its structural rigidities were becoming most serious and its lack of creative leadership was a matter of considerable concern. Its policy of secretiveness was particularly irritating, and contributed to the sharpness of his criticism.

It was inevitable that charges should be made that St John was "bought off" in the sense that his appointment to head a departmental agency was intended to still a critical voice from outside. Although this opinion continues to be expressed, it is not a valid one. The minister had a genuinely high regard for St John's knowledge and critical powers, and felt that he should be recruited in the band of educational reformers needed to produce constructive educational change. There is no doubt that St John's individual contribution since his appointment has been valuable, although less conspicuous than during his days as a columnist.

By 1967 the four full-time members then on the council were performing a number of worthwhile functions. They participated in policy discussions, brought potential problems to the minister's attention, did editorial work, gave the minister their views on reports, articles, and publications which he submitted to them, represented him on some committees and boards, and reported on policies and programs of interest in other places. The council sponsored or helped to sponsor some fairly important conferences. But it was evident that it was not assuming the major role foreseen at the time of its establishment.

The council has had some distinguished members, including C.A.

Mustard, C.H. Williams, J.F. Kinlin, and R. Bériault. Mustard retired from the department shortly after his appointment, while Williams and Kinlin soon abandoned the council for positions with line responsibilities. There was no evidence of a serious attempt to recruit a competent group of people prepared to make a long-term commitment to policy development. The alternative of building up the council by adding prominent educators from inside or outside the department on a part-time basis was not actively pursued. The council's failure to flourish may have been partly attributable to a misunderstanding about the role proposed for the Department of Educational Planning in the Ontario Institute for Studies in Education, which was established in 1965. It was not as evident to some people as it perhaps should have been that a planning unit in an independent institution with the status of a college could not properly assume the function of policy development for a department of government. Its appropriate role included the development of planning methodology and the conduct of much of the research upon which effective policy making might be based. It might have proved to be a valuable resource and complement to a flourishing Policy and Development Council in the department.

There could be no real question of making a third attempt to split the policy recommending and administrative functions in the fashion that had failed to work in 1906 and 1923. Such an approach raised visions of all the creative thinking being corralled in one part of the organization while the remainder concentrated rather mechanically on the implementation of decisions made by others. But in fact the department was on a path that left decreasing room for purely administrative functions, which were slated to devolve more and more on local systems. As an organism designed to provide creative leadership, it had to be hospitable to innovative ideas throughout. Davis acted in accordance with this implication in his selection of successive deputy ministers. He sought men for the quality of their thinking as well as for their administrative experience and, on finding them, could hardly have expected them to confine themselves to devising techniques for effective policy implementation. Thus if the Policy and Development Council were to have been a functioning part of the structure, it would almost have had to be a service unit, expanding and clarifying ideas proposed by the top administrative officials, sorting out the results of research produced by agencies engaged in that activity and, where necessary, conducting its own research projects. But the council was launched on quite a different basis: first, in that it was supposed to be primarily a source of independent initiative and inspiration, and secondly, in that the Ontario Institute for Studies in Education was expected to fill the department's research needs, and the conduct of research in the department itself was definitely discouraged.

Superficially, there might have appeared to be a further possibility. The council might have been developed as an active, critical agency in a constant state of constructive tension with the remainder of the departmental structure. Such a situation would have demanded the constant vigilance of the minister to maintain an unstable equilibrium, since he would be fighting one of the laws of organizational structures – that they tend to reconcile conflicting or disintegrative internal forces. In a sense, the minister's executive assistant can assume an independent and, if need be, a critical role, but only on the assumption that he lacks permanent security in the organization, and that his role ends with a change of ministers. A council could not be maintained on this basis.

RECENT PROVISION FOR PLANNING

A development during 1969 appears to have ended the possibility that the Policy and Development Council would play a major role in the future. The deputy minister and the assistant deputy ministers began to meet regularly as a Planning Committee, and supporting services were provided by an educational planning and analysis staff headed by T. Campbell. The financial stringencies foreseen for the next few years had made it particularly important that priorities be established and that departmental programs be kept within feasible limits.

The dozen or so people engaged in the work of the new unit were called a task force. They undertook studies relating to program objectives and scheduling dates. Part of the responsibility of the unit was to promote the acceptance of the program budgeting system by departmental management, and to encourage the attainment of its objectives.

CULTURAL EXCHANGE PROGRAMS

The establishment of a cultural exchange program was announced in January 1966, although a co-ordinator, in the person of C.E. Rathé, was not appointed until a year later. The Cultural Exchange Office was responsible for promoting educational and cultural exchange programs between Ontario on the one hand and other provinces (particularly Quebec) and countries on the other, and also for advising and assisting educational institutions in cultural exchange activities. During its first year of operations, it co-operated with the federal government and with private associations in organizing programs for visiting Canadian and foreign students. A large proportion of the visitors came from France.

The office also assisted the Ontario Art Institute in its Centennial Art Purchase Program, which involved the purchase of paintings and sculpture by Ontario and Quebec artists. These creations were displayed in various locations in both provinces over a two-year period, and then placed in local galleries and schools. A grant of over $50,000 was made for a study of the cultural life of Franco-Ontarians by a committee under the chairmanship of R. St Denis.

In the summer of 1969 several young Ontarians went to France as guests of the French government, and thirty young French visitors toured Ontario. Exchange visits also involved camp counsellors and work camp participants. Six theatre directors from Quebec, France, and Germany spent three weeks as guests of the Ontario government at the Shaw and Stratford festivals and at the St Lawrence Centre for the Arts. A French Summer School Scholarship Exchange, begun in 1968, was repeated in 1969. It has provided a considerable number of scholarships for Ontario students to study French in Quebec and in St Pierre and Miquelon. Exchanges of students with Quebec through Visites Interprovinciales have increased steadily in recent years. In 1969, also, over 250 students received assistance for travel abroad in various organized study and work programs.

Through the Cultural Exchange Program, and utilizing the facilities provided through the cultural agreements between Canada and France, the department undertook in 1967–8 to facilitate the recruitment by school boards of language teachers from France. Two categories of teachers were sought: *professeurs détachés* and assistants. The former were fully qualified and experienced teachers at either the elementary or the secondary school level who retained their pension benefits in France while working for an indefinite period abroad. The second were students who had completed part of a university undergraduate course, and who were prepared to serve as part-time instructors under the supervision of qualified teachers. A small number of teachers and assistants came to Ontario under this program.

SPECIAL PROJECTS

Operation School Supplies

Operation School Supplies began in 1965 with an appeal to Davis from a missionary in the Bahamas for assistance in furnishing new schools being built at a rapid rate in those islands. Having established contact with the Bahamian Ministry of Education in order to confirm the need and to ensure appropriate lines of communication, Davis had letters sent to school boards in a large section of southern Ontario around Toronto asking for surplus school supplies. In response, large numbers of used desks and books flooded into storage facilities provided by officials responsible for the Canadian National Exhibition. Students from local high schools volunteered to pack the books during their Easter vacation, and Canadian and American commercial firms provided trucking and shipping services at small cost, or even, in some cases, free of charge. In this way, fifty tons of material reached the Bahamas, and Operation School Supplies was successfully launched. The World Heritage Organization expressed its approval by presenting Davis with its Award of Merit in 1966.

The first project led to requests from other parts of the West Indies for an opportunity to participate. Continuing donations from school boards included pencils, erasers, and rulers contributed by business firms. The

Overseas Book Centre of the Overseas Institute of Canada assumed the responsibility of sorting books into classroom lots according to grade requirements. The Department of National Defence supplied air transport to deliver the materials to Antigua, whence they were distributed among a number of islands. Later in 1966 initiatives on the part of the department resulted in donations of paper from Ontario firms to make possible the continuation of correspondence courses in Jamaica.

More recently there has been a tendency to extend the range of supplies collected and shipped. Of four aircraft flying to Jamaica on March 19, 1969, two carried loads of books, one carried enough small tools and machinery to equip a motor vehicle repair shop and an electrical classroom in a vocational school in Kingston, and one carried hospital beds and medicines for an interdenominational community centre. The vocational school machinery was collected as a result of the efforts of the Eglinton Rotary Club of Toronto.

During the 1969–70 school year a major project undertaken under the Operation School Supplies program involved the replacement of the Grand Turk primary school, which was destroyed by fire on September 10. In November four Canadian Forces Hercules airplanes left Toronto with two tons of textbooks, three thousand exercise books, six thousand pencils, 480 desks, and blackboards to equip the new school. Children at Palmerston Avenue Public School in Whitby, which was twinned with the Grand Turk school in Project School-to-School, sent Christmas gifts to their Caribbean counterparts.

The Co-ordinator of the Special Projects Section, G.J. Mason, was made responsible for promoting good relations between people of different cultural and racial backgrounds, and for encouraging student exchanges between Canada and the West Indies. In March 1969 R.C. Johnston assumed the task of co-ordinating Operation School Supplies. Thus the program was placed on a more or less permanent footing.

Project School-to-School

Project School-to-School involves the twinning of individual schools of Ontario with one or more schools in the Commonwealth Caribbean. The pupils exchange letters, tapes, and class projects as a means of learning about each others' history, geography, and culture. For some fortunate pupils, exchange visits are arranged during the summer. The first such visit was made in 1968 by three pupils from the island of Dominica, who spent three weeks with grade 4 pupils attending Cummer Avenue Public School in North York. The visit was returned by five pupils from the same school during the following month. In 1969 twenty-eight grade 6 pupils made a seven-day visit to a school in Kingston, Jamaica. During the same summer a teacher and seven pupils from Grenada spent fifteen days with their North York counterparts. By the end of 1968 nearly 1,200 Ontario schools were involved in the program. A year later, this number was estimated at more than 2,500, with about a quarter of a million pupils involved.

New ground was broken in 1969 when a grade 6 class in Faucett, Missouri, became involved in the scheme during a two-year study of Canada. As a result of an appeal to the minister by the teacher of the class, the Faucett class was twinned with a grade 6 class at the Pleasantville Government School in Trinidad.

COMMEMORATION OF THE CENTENNIAL CELEBRATION OF CANADA IN 1967

The Legislature of Ontario made certain provisions for the celebration of Canada's Centennial as early as 1962–3, with the passage of Bill 109,[52] which opened the way for full co-operation among the municipalities, the provincial authorities, and the federal government, which had already passed the *National Centennial Act*. The Ontario legislation authorized the minister designated by the government to carry out its provisions to undertake such projects as in his opinion were appropriate for the observance of the Centennial. The official Ontario project was the Ontario Science Centre, described elsewhere, for which the Minister of Tourism and Information assumed the main responsibility. The legislation also enabled municipalities to enter agreements with federal government agencies and to expend funds on their own projects. Many of these had educational implications.

The Department of Education approved and sponsored a considerable variety of activities and projects. Among these was a program of visits to historical sites, Ottawa, and Expo 67. School boards were given permission to include for grant purposes the days on which pupils were away from school on these visits, provided that they were arranged by the boards and supervised by staff members. Legislative grants did not, however, cover transportation costs incurred for such purposes.

In order to facilitate visits to Expo 67, the minister approved a plan devised by the Expo 67 Corporation management to offer education passports to pupils in supervised groups. These passports enabled pupils to gain admission at substantially reduced prices. In order to qualify for them, each group had to consist of at least thirty pupils, with a supervisory adult for every ten pupils.

The Confederation Train and Confederation Caravans were among the main federal projects of a broadly educational character. The train made about twenty stops in Ontario between May 14 and August 25, 1967. The caravans, which were motorized fairs, visited nearly 150 communities in the province not reached by trains. Local Centennial Committees were responsible for scheduling public viewings at each stop. The Department of Education urged municipal directors and superintendents, provincial public and separate school inspectors, and secondary school principals to co-operate in every possible way with these committees so that the maximum educational benefit might be attained from the project.

The Confederation Train undertook the use of novel exhibition techniques to dramatize the various stages of Canada's history. The six exhibit cars combined genuine artifacts and photostats of original documents with living portrayals of history. The visitor to the first car was plunged into the atmosphere of the primeval woods, and then proceeded successively to an animated map showing the geological upheavals that created the country's modern topography, and to a longhouse of the Haida Indian tribe. The second car offered a model of a Viking ship and one of Cartier's, *La petite Hermine*. A subsequent exhibit told the story of the explorations of Champlain and of others who pushed back the country's frontiers. The steerage of an immigrant ship was reconstructed with flickering oil lamps and sound effects. The third car portrayed a French seigneurial home and early military events. The Fathers of Confederation were displayed in graphic form, while Canadians of the time from all walks of life moved around them. Further scenes depicted the highlights of subsequent decades, including the wars of the first half of the twentieth century, the frenetic years of the 1920s, and the depression of the 1930s. The final exhibit was "Canada Today."

Ontario students were encouraged to participate in the Centennial Athletic Awards Program sponsored by the Centennial Commission. The program consisted of three compulsory events and one optional event. The compulsory events, administered in the schools, comprised a standing broad jump, one-minute speed sit-ups, and a three-hundred-yard run. The optional event might be skating, swimming, or cross-country running, and could be administered by a member of a school staff or an outside agency. Awards were given in the form of gold, silver, bronze, and participation crests. Administrators were chosen to co-ordinate the program in the schools of each area. The department distributed school and classroom display posters, standards posters, teachers' manuals, class record sheets, and student achievement cards.

School children were encouraged to plant trees as a particularly suitable form of Centennial celebration. The Department of Lands and Forests offered its co-operation in arranging for pupils to use Crown, Conservation Authority, or other suitable land for this purpose, and also supplied the trees. Presumably this type of activity was of more inspirational than practical value.

OPINIONS ON THE ROLE OF THE CENTRAL AUTHORITY

The situation in the 1920s

This section is intended to indicate certain views about the virtues and faults of the distribution of educational authority in Ontario over the last few decades. These views have all been expressed by observers who have been familiar with, although not necessarily primarily concerned with, the situation in Ontario. A chronological rather than a thematic arrangement has been employed.

When the centralized powers of the Department of Education were at their maximum in the 1920s, E.G. Savage, a visiting inspector, described the system as follows.

Centralisation is complete in Ontario. The Department of Education regulates the subjects to be taken, the length of time for which some of them at least may be studied and the year in which they shall be studied; it issues syllabuses in each subject and prescribes text-books which must be used. Finally it examines the product. Little or nothing is left to the initiative of the principal or of the teachers. All that is necessary is for the teachers, all trained in the same professional school, to follow the syllabus and the text-book, and to see that the facts enshrined therein are known. This is what is, for the most part, done. Pupils of the most ordinary intelligence can then scarcely fail to pass the examiners. Unhappily the adventurer electing to stray afield will receive no credit for his adventures and indeed places himself under a handicap by his wanderings.

There are historical reasons for this high degree of centralisation. It may well have been suited to earlier days when schools were small, and before a tradition of scholarship had been built up. Unhappily it prevents such a tradition from becoming established. It obviously still has its value in the case of small schools with two or three teachers, not perhaps highly qualified in any sense. For these the departmental requirements afford a crutch without which the school would be indeed a lame affair. In this sense the minutely regulated curriculum serves a useful purpose in that it makes possible the establishment of secondary schools in very small places and guarantees that they shall reach a minimum standard. The unfortunate results are that the minimum tends to become the normal and the able teachers in the large Collegiate Institutes in the big cities find the crutch a handicap. It prevents them from going at more than a walking pace, and entirely prevents excursions off the common track. The Collegiate Institutes number on their staffs many teachers of real ability, artists in their various subjects who are capable of creative work, but these find little scope for their abilities and in the course of a few years they tend to become reconciled to the dull round and settle down to become cogs in the machine. There is complete uniformity of method, and at length comes a lack of interest in other methods and in other text-books. The machine works but it has a tendency to get into ruts from which the overworked officers of the department have no time to spare from routine work to get it out.[53]

Views of the Royal Commission

The Report of the Royal Commission on Education in Ontario declared that the Ontario educational system was more centralized than was commonly supposed. It pointed out that local authorities had to exercise their restricted powers within limits established by legislation or by regulations of the central authority. Their power to appoint teachers and to erect school buildings gave an exaggerated idea of the extent to which they exerted control.[54]

The commission observed that the general trend was toward larger units of administration, but that there was no evidence of a corresponding trend toward decentralization of control over such *interna* as curricula, courses of study, textbooks, and the establishment and operation of special services.[55] It recommended that these matters be delegated to local education authorities of such size as to merit responsibility for handling them. It also urged that such *externa* as the business administration of schools, the provision of satisfactory post-elementary education, the provision of enough schools, the enforcement of attendance regulations, the transportation of pupils, the financing of the minimum program, and capital expenditure should remain decentralized, but that they be centralized under the control of local education authorities.[56]

Observations by Frank MacKinnon

In *The Politics of Education*, Frank MacKinnon asserted that educational administrators in Canada, and there is no reason to think that he was not including Ontario, had by far the most power among civil servants in general and within the educational system itself.

Departments of education are the only departments of government in which the deputy minister is called superintendent, chief superintendent, director, or chief director, and in which his subordinates, even in the clerical grades, follow after with equally impressive titles. They are also the only departments which violate a fundamental rule of government that civil servants should be anonymous, for educational officials enjoy the unusual privilege of speaking in public for both the government and the schools. To the public, no teacher, regardless of ability, can command the prestige of an "inspector" or "superintendent." Even the universities pay tribute to the source of power when they automatically bestow on numerous educational officials the honorary doctor's degrees which are rarely given either to outstanding school teachers, or to officials in other government departments.[57]

Reviewing reasons why society permitted strong central control over education, MacKinnon declared that people thought it guaranteed both maximum and equal opportunities for all children. He made a distinction, however, between equal opportunities and the same opportunities. "Standardized curricula, courses, texts, methods, and requirements can ultimately produce the standardized thought, opinion, and habits that result in the mass mind which lives by mass propaganda."[58]

MacKinnon recommended the abolition of provincial departments of education and of the position of minister of education in favour of a provincial authority called the council of education. This council would be headed by a chief adviser, or someone with a similar title, and would avoid titles implying domination, such as "director," "superintendent," and "inspector." The members of the staff would be available for advice, information, research, and consultation. The council would have two main functions. First, it would determine the conditions under which schools would be established as public trusts, and it would arrange for the administration of those schools for which such status would be unsuitable. Once a school became a public trust by act of the legislature, the council would have no control over its management except on its own request or on that of the municipality. The council's second function would be to distribute provincial funds.[59]

MacKinnon made a strong case for settling the responsibility for many of the *interna* and *externa* of education on the school itself rather than on the local school system. Since the focus of interest in this section is on the central apparatus, further discussion of this question is reserved for later treatment.

Views expressed at the Ontario Conference on Education

The Ontario Conference on Education, held at Windsor in 1961, had some politely worded criticism of the Department of Education. Acknowledging that Ontario had a centrally controlled educational system, the group discussing the issue asserted that a considerable measure of constructive leadership might be expected from the department and its officials. Three sources were identified by which educational ideas reached the department: "political influence deriving from public opinion, the wide knowledge from within the Department and from other sources, and constructive proposals from teachers, trustees, parents and other interested groups."[60] It was suggested that the third of these sources had been neglected, and the group accordingly recommended the setting up of an advisory council "to ensure that a wide range of opinions from all possible sources be made available to assist the Department in establishing policies." This recommendation, recalling the Advisory Council on Education that existed between 1906 and 1915, did not evoke any positive response.

No fundamental criticism of centralized control as such emanated from this discussion. The inclination was rather to advocate attempts to make the system operate more effectively. Throughout the period, the teachers' organizations were prepared to respond favourably to the idea of curriculum decentralization, and to express the view that they should have more control over admission to the profession, but there seemed little real hope that departmental authority would be seriously reduced.

Proposals by J.M. Paton

In a study done in preparation for the Canadian Conference on Education in 1962, J.M. Paton outlined a series of recommendations for a partnership between teachers and a provincial department of education.[61] A minister of education and his officials would be responsible for interpreting the opinions of the people about the kind of education they wanted, but these opinions would be defined in very general terms. Authority would be delegated to the teachers' professional organization, or to a joint committee of representatives of the profession and of the universities, to recruit, select, and supervise the preparation of student teachers. The same body would have the power to award certificates, while the department would issue licences to teach. The profession might have the power to suspend and revoke certificates, with provision for appeal to a government-appointed tribunal. Government licences to teach would be issued to those without certificates only in cases of special emergency. The responsibility for maintaining a high standard of professional competence might also be given to the organized teaching profession. Government-appointed inspectors would be restricted to giving advice and making suggestions and to close inspection of probationary teachers and those thought to be near the borderline of professional incompetence. Another aspect of the partnership might be the formation of a provincial curriculum council, consisting of representatives of the universities, the teaching profession, the department of education, and lay bodies such as the school trustees' association. This council would establish guidelines and general suggestions, leaving much of the detail to be worked out by the staffs of individual schools.

Proposals of R.S. Harris for regional councils

R.S. Harris advocated a development in his *Quiet Evolution* that would have implications both for the co-ordination of educational activities and for the centralization-decentralization issue.[62] It would involve the reorganization of education at all levels throughout the province on a regional basis. There would be a series of regional councils with the responsibility of developing a close relationship among the educational institutions of different types, and of co-ordinating the educational services of the region. The councils would make recommendations to the government of Ontario rather than to the Minister of Education, since its terms of reference would involve many government departments. The way in which this aspect of the proposal would work is not altogether clear. Within the government, responsibility must be specifically located if action is to be forthcoming. Presumably the Prime Minister would have to assume a more direct responsibility for guiding educational matters. Suggestions that imply an increase in the burdens of the Prime Minister's office may have a sound basis, but should be made with considerable caution.

Harris anticipated objections to his proposal on the grounds that it would involve a proliferation of meetings of the full council and various sub-groups to elect council members and to hear reports. Answering his own rhetorical question as to whether there were not already enough committee meetings and unread reports, he wrote:

It is a matter of distributing the load. One of the weaknesses of education in Ontario is that in all institutions too few people are involved in the important decisions and too many are in the position where they feel that they are simply employees. The establishment of regional educational councils would necessarily draw many teachers and professors now effectively confined to their classrooms into the corridors of power and influence.[63]

Meetings and committee work do, of course, take time, but there is no substitute for them if effective communication and joint policy making are to be instituted. But it is hard to see how participation in a purely advisory council would draw teachers and professors into "the corridors of power and influence." There is a strong possibility that the responsibility for offering advice without any connection with the process of implementation would produce more frustration than anything else. Everything would depend, of course, on the attitude of the central authority.

Structure suggested by the Provincial Committee on Aims and Objectives

The Provincial Committee on Aims and Objectives of Education in the Schools of Ontario observed that the decentralization of many aspects of educational administration from the department to the local school boards required a new description of the relationship that must exist between the two. The committee expressed the view that the department, "in the interests of the welfare of the children of Ontario,"[64] must retain a certain amount of regulatory power. It went on:

The new autonomy of the larger boards requires ... that the maintenance, "gatekeeper" type of leadership which tends to be associated with the regulatory role, be transformed into other more vital types which must characterize the Department of Education of the immediate future.[65]

It was suggested that the department withdraw from operational functions, retaining policy formation as its only indispensable responsibility.

A rather novel suggestion was that some of the departmental staff should be organized as task force groups who would combine their efforts with those of people from local systems to work on problems and implement the solutions they devised. The report of the committee leaves us a little uncertain about the specific types of problems they would work on. We are told that, under the scheme, the groups would form, dissolve, and re-form according to need, and that they would involve the major portion of the departmental staff. Their work in the task forces would involve frequent contact with children.

The committee considered the departmental bureaucracy to be excessively large, and speculated that a great deal of energy must be spent in perpetuating the organization, at the expense of the needs of children in the schools. "Locking a professional group of this size into a central organization handicaps people who could serve more efficiently at the local level."[66] The salaries paid to departmental personnel were not thought to be high enough to guarantee that the best professional educators would serve in the department. "The creative, dynamic educator is generally found where his worth is recognized financially and a sense of innovative freedom more readily prevails."[67] The recommendation was that the existing staff be pruned and that the resulting savings be used to improve the department's position in its search for talent for the proposed task forces.

The committee was not too enthusiastic about the ten Regional Offices which had been established in the previous three years. These were said to have resulted "in many instances" in an additional layer of administration. Some were commended for having moved toward the function of service centres. Since the new school boards would have less need for consultative help, it was suggested that the offices be reduced in number, and that "those remaining should serve as resource centres, assisting innovation and communicating ideas throughout the Ontario system."[68]

A proposal was made for the creation of the office of educational ombudsman, an idea that is not usually looked upon with favour by official agencies. The case was made as follows:

> The growing complexity of educational systems, the diversity of educational experience, and the emphasis upon equality of educational opportunity, suggest the need for an office in education to which individual problems might be brought. The Committee, therefore, recommends the appointment of an ombudsman in education to act as an independent public officer serving all levels of education in matters of dispute. This is not to suggest a lack of competence or sensitivity on the part of authorities in education. Rather, the recommendation suggests that their responsibilities and prerogatives, as well as the rights of educational consumers, might be better understood and protected through such an office.[69]

The committee recommended a new departmental structure, the diagrammatic representation of which, as presented in the report, breaks no new ground in terms of effective communication. The essential responsibilities of the organization were defined in three categories: legislation; planning, research, and development; and systems evaluation. The bulk of the department's activities would be in the section corresponding to the second of these categories. The section's functions were defined as follows:

> This section is responsible for long-term planning as applied to all activities in education; for short-term research, for the identification of particularly crucial research areas, for long-term study, and the contracting for this research with the *Ontario Institute for Studies in Education*; for the development of demonstration centres in school jurisdictions, the interpretation of new processes and procedures found around the world; and for providing direct aid to school boards where new developmental projects are undertaken.[70]

The three basic sections would be assisted by such supportive services as statistics, grants, data processing, information, and building guidance. A communications section would co-ordinate the work of the department with that of other elements of the provincial structure, receiving external communications initially and channeling them to the appropriate departmental centres. The so-called domain of educational implementation would include local educational authorities, regional authorities, and other educational agencies.

Complementing the formal structure would be an advisory council representing public and professional interests. Its functions would be to evaluate the effectiveness of existing facilities, and to propose the establishment of new institutions or programs and the extension of existing ones in accordance with social and economic trends and the demands of public opinion. "It would also study the numerous proposals emanating from individuals or groups, to bring to bear a broad spectrum of judgment on which to base decisions by government or other bodies."[71] Established by legislation, the council would report to the Legislature through the Minister of Education, and also to the public at large in the manner of the Economic Council of Canada. It would have its own independent budget, appropriated annually. It might conduct investigations on its own initiative or on that of the minister or the government, or commission research by other agencies where appropriate.

The committee suggested that the proposed council might have a full-time chairman and two associates, all appointed for a specified term, possibly seven years, which might be renewable for a further half term. There might be twelve additional part-time members, of whom nine would be citizens with no formal connection with education, and three others with direct experience at different levels of the educational process. These members would be appointed by the government from small lists of names proposed by civic bodies. The committee thought it important that the council not be dominated by partisan appointees or by professional educators. It was suggested that consideration might be given at some time in the future to the possibility of merging the functions of this council with those of the Committee on University Affairs in a fashion that would both ensure the co-ordination of educational policy and preserve university autonomy.

Warnings about decentralization of power

Walter Pitman identified the risks entailed in decentralizing power at the same time that all kinds of new ideas and programs were being pushed from the centre.

The thing which bothers me is this. Along with all these many programmes – one can scarcely describe them all – but along with this, is the concept of decentralization, whereby the Department of Education will be – I think I am paraphrasing the remarks of the Minister – will be the research and planning agency, and also, of course, the agency for distributing funds. Whereas the local boards, the enlarged local boards, which the Minister has provided for in the recent legislation, will have, in essence, the main role for carrying out these programmes.

I think there is something basically dangerous about this concept, and I do want to discuss this for a moment. I am not sure how you can expect people at the local level to carry out the kind of exciting new revolutionary programmes which have been suggested in sections of this report when, indeed, they themselves are only being brought along now to accept some of the implications of the programmes The Department of Education has put into effect in the last five or ten years.

I do not see how you can plan at the centre and leave it to the local community to carry out those plans. Now you can use the carrot, you can use the grant structure, I realize that, but certainly in many many areas, this has not been the case. I am concerned that the planning is going to be entirely at the centre for one thing, because I do not think that the local community will carry out plans that they are not themselves a part of. I really worry about the division which the Minister has indicated is going to take place in the implementation of the plans and the planning that takes place beforehand.

I have a great deal of faith in local autonomy, and I am with the Minister on the fact that you cannot impose progress, you cannot force local authorities to bring in exciting new programmes, exciting new curricula and new administrative procedures and so on. You cannot impose them, but I suggest to him also that you cannot decentralize the power and then expect these local authorities to come up with the same answers which the department wishes.

In many of these areas I think there will have to be a degree of push or pressure, a degree of – well I think almost the use of the "stick" is going to be necessary in some cases to force local authorities to move in some areas. In other areas I realize, and the Minister knows – I have suggested in the past – local authorities have been ahead of The Department of Education in going into new programmes and so on, and I am concerned about this trend. ...

I want to leave that point in the Minister's mind – this problem of the decentralization of authority and control at a time when you are trying to encourage revolutionary change. At a time, indeed, when time itself demands revolutionary change, because the leader of the Opposition commented on the whole problem of the new generation and the generation gap, which is widening and is continuing to widen. The demands of a generation which in many cases can be seen perhaps most effectively at the centre, rather than on the local scene where it appears they may be undermining local authority and the ways that things have been done over the years.[72]

THREE

Principles of local organization and administration

DECENTRALIZATION OF POWERS

J.G. Althouse, renowned Chief Director of Education for Ontario until his death in 1956, spoke enthusiastically in the Quance Lectures of 1949 about local participation in education:

> No satisfactory substitute has yet been found for keen local interest in schools and for local pride in their efficiency. These give body and meaning to sound educational procedures; they identify the school and the community in an inimitable way. With the retention of local interest, educational progress may be slow and spotty; it is almost never temporary. Gains once made are consolidated, for they are indigenous improvements. This is the real reason that Canadian education has seldom gone to the extremes that are seen elsewhere; it is the reason, too, that we have had few ignominious retreats to make. Local interest has provided wholesome, down-to-earth, critical analysis of the experts' enthusiasms. Both factors are necessary, the enthusiasm of the theorist and the hard, practical evaluation of his suggestions.[1]

It is true that Althouse was referring to local interest, and not local control, but he certainly implied more of the latter than existed in Ontario. The firm restraints exercised by a cautious and tradition-oriented department might equally well have been offered as the main reason why education had seldom gone to extremes. The much higher degree of local control exercised in most parts of the United States has commonly been considered to be conducive to innovation and experimentation.

In making the case for the local government in education, Rideout has emphasized the following points. 1 / Local government, as a training ground for democratic practices, is a necessary adjunct of democracy. 2 / Decentralization permits local services to be better attuned to local needs. 3 / The diffusion of power among small units within a province protects education from indoctrination by pressure groups. 4 / The education of children is of such intimate concern to parents that there is need for a much greater face-to-face relationship than in such public facilities as the highway system, the postal service, and national defence.[2]

SIZE AND CHARACTERISTICS OF LOCAL UNITS

The report of the Royal Commission on Education had a great deal to say about the ideal size of local administrative units. It suggested two over-all criteria to determine the basic unit in a decentralized system: 1 / a community of interests within the unit and 2 / a large enough number of pupils to warrant the operation of a modern school system from kindergarten to high school graduation.[3]

Elaborating on the second of these criteria, the report indicated that the system should offer a sufficiently diversified program to meet the needs of each student. The commissioners thought that an enrolment of not fewer than three hundred would be enough to justify the operation of such a program, a number that would be regarded as grossly inadequate by almost any authority today. The report suggested further that, where possible, the unit should be large enough to sustain a junior college, again with an enrolment of at least three hundred. In order to supply this number, the system would need a secondary school enrolment of at least nine hundred. Smaller units might combine to support a single junior college. Further specifications for a unit large enough to operate a modern school system included the following: that it be large enough to constitute a supervisory unit for elementary education; that it be large enough to permit decentralization by delegating to local authorities a measure of freedom with respect to courses of study, textbooks, standards, and school management; that it be large enough to ensure that business administration might be centralized under a full-time business administrator and clerical staff employed by the local education authority; that it be large enough that by the imposition of a uniform tax rate a considerable measure of equalization might be achieved despite local inequalities in financial ability to pay for education; that it be large enough so that special services could be provided efficiently and economically.

On the point of optimum size, the Provincial Committee on Aims and Objectives referred to studies suggesting that, with between ten and fifteen thousand pupils, sufficient teachers and consulting staff could be employed to provide for a school system of high quality. Most estimates were said to indicate that from two hundred to two hundred and fifty teachers constituted the minimum size of staff to enable the best use to be made of subject consultants, librarians, nurses, and attendance counsellors.[4] The difference in attitudes expressed by the two bodies, both consisting of educational leaders of the day, gives some idea of the dimensions of the change in a period of less than twenty years in the concept of what constitutes an adequate education.

In addition to the desirability of maintaining a more specialized staff, there are perhaps two other main reasons why units must be so much larger than formerly in order to provide what is regarded as an adequate educational system. 1 / Special classes for those with unusual handicaps or needs cannot be set up for two or three children; even if the cost could be met, the number of trained specialists would be totally inadequate to satisfy the demand. Effective use of resources demands that the operation be conducted on a reasonable scale. 2 / Present-day education relies heavily on expensive equipment for vocational instruction, television reception, language learning, physical education, and other aspects of the process. Economy requires that this kind of equipment be utilized fully and completely. The false economy of doing without is increasingly being discarded, but extreme waste of resources through under-utilization will hardly be tolerated.

According to the Royal Commission, the community of interests criterion was to be supplemented by attention to topographical features, economic interests, and availability of transportation. Other conditions being satisfied, it would be desirable to have the boundaries correspond to some recognized municipal division. These boundaries should be so drawn that natural attendance areas would not be divided between two or more units. All natural centres, with the exception of cities, should be included. The unit should be large enough so that alterations within it, in both elementary and post-elementary school attendance areas, could be made with ease when changes in population, roads, or means of transportation demanded or permitted.

On the question of the diversity of interests to be brought together in the same unit, the Ontario Committee on Taxation had these comments:

> Participation in government is many things. It is the voter casting his ballot and writing or visiting his representative. It is the effort to persuade an individual to stand for office in the competitive arena of politics. It is the citizen who joins with like-minded fellows in a group or association to press a particular point of view on government. A prime determinant of such activities is every citizen's capacity, either as an individual or as part of a group, actually to influence the political process. This, however, will depend to an important extent on the existence of a reasonable balance among diverse interests within a governmental jurisdiction. A region that is numerically dominated by farmers, or by city dwellers, or by suburbanites, to take a few examples, may engender feelings of defeatism among those left in a hopelessly small minority. The result will be one of political alienation for those so affected, with a consequent lessening of popular participation in government.[5]

The committee traced the conflicting claims for the advantages of large and small units.

> The notion that a unit of government can be too big to function in an efficient and responsible fashion can be traced back to the earliest political thinkers in the history of western civilization. It is precisely to avoid the more vexing problems of bigness that most modern democratic states foster the existence of municipal institutions. Yet there also exists a contrary notion, firmly rooted in practical experience, that a unit of government can be too small in relation to the minimum size necessary for the most efficient discharge of local functions.[6]

The committee observed that there were a large number of municipal units in Ontario that lacked the area, population, and resources needed to function adequately. Their revenue base, unsatisfactory as it was, was further eroded by inefficient assessment and collection procedures. There were strong pressures toward destructive competition for business assessment, to the detriment of sound zoning and planning.

The committee referred to two values that local government is intended to provide: access and service. Access, that is, influence and control on the part of the people, is a fundamental aspect of the democratic system. Service ought to follow as a consequence of access, but it is possible for the two, instead of complementing one another, to come into conflict. To use the committee's example, a maximum provision for access, calling for autonomous government by each city block so that all could participate, would completely preclude economy and efficiency in the discharge of local functions. On the other hand, if only service were to be maximized, each function of government might be separately organized according to its own objectives. Because of the large number of services, efficiency could be maintained only through "a technocracy prepared to function without awaiting direction from a confused and faltering public," thus practically eliminating access.[7]

Since access and service are not automatically compatible, an effort must be made to reconcile them.

> When in proper balance, each value will tend to reinforce the other. The notion of service ... includes not only economy and efficiency in the narrow administrative sense but also full utilization of the latest techniques in order to produce results most in keeping with public needs and expressed wishes. Hence well-developed public access, in terms of widespread popular participation, will help to enhance the serviceability of government. Conversely, the very participation that makes access meaningful can hardly be anticipated on a continuing basis unless government is indeed fulfilling its service objective and constitutes a solid focus of public interest.[8]

In the early days of local government in Ontario, access and service could be readily reconciled. The economy was simple, technology was uncomplicated, and service demands were relatively modest, making it possible for small units to operate with an acceptable degree of efficiency. As far as educational services were concerned, the level of expectation was low and the skills required were rudimentary. These conditions have tended to reverse themselves in the twentieth century. "In the absence of difficult and delicate adjustments, the once happy balance between access and service is collapsing around our heads."[9]

The report of the Royal Commission had some recommendations bearing on the convenience of provincial administration. The 4,532 units of administration in 1948 were considered excessive, and it was urged that the number be greatly reduced. On the other hand, it was thought desirable that provision be made to ensure that some measure of control of education remain with the local community. In this connection, the commissioners found themselves confronted with what they regarded as an unavoidable paradox. In order to give more real control of education to local authorities, it was necessary to take from many small communities powers previously exercised. Nevertheless, since the objective was to create and foster local interest, control must not be removed too far from the people most vitally concerned. The commissioners reasoned that the loss to the small community might be more apparent than real. Local interest in the school had not in the past been noteworthy, and safeguards must in any case be provided against the tendency, resulting from the combination of previously independent small units into larger units, for local initiative to die out.

The Royal Commission's recommendation seemed to imply that the provincial government could produce units of appropriate size simply by passing the necessary legislation. Instead, the government continued to rely on the slow and halting process of persuasion, with some small concessions in the school grant scheme. The question arises whether the failure to use compulsion was attributable to sheer inertia, or whether there were sound political reasons for a course of caution. The stories told by those who inspected schools during the 1940s and 1950s suggest the latter. One man who later achieved a position of considerable prominence tells of being warned that it was as much as his life was worth to go into a certain community and speak in favour of voluntary consolidation. He refused to be intimidated and, of course, survived the experience, but it was evident nonetheless that great popular passion was aroused in favour of the integrity of the traditional unit.

In 1964 there were still 3,200 elementary school boards varying in equalized assessment per classroom unit from $10,000 to over $1,000,000. The introduction of the Ontario Foundation Tax Plan had created new pressures for viable units for financial purposes. With a great many small units, the plan had to be too loaded down with special provisions, and even then could not achieve a uniform minimum standard of services. By this time, the need for better educational opportunities than the small units could provide was becoming so obvious that the opposition to the mandatory reorganization of 1965 was sporadic and ineffective. The major operation that followed in 1969 was, of course, a different story.

THE SCHOOL AS A UNIT OF LOCAL ADMINISTRATION

A major theme of Frank MacKinnon's *The Politics of Education* was that the basic unit should be not some territorial area but the large school or the "unit" of small schools.

"Central Memorial High School" would be created by statute as a publicly owned, body corporate managed by its own individual board of trustees which exercised its powers directly over business matters and which delegated powers over academic matters to a faculty council recognized and constituted by the creating statute. The trustees would have complete control over general policy and the property and finances of the school, all of which would be accounted for by annual audit and report. The faculty council would have full responsibility for the curriculum and services of the school, and would be accountable to the board through the principal. The latter would be responsible to the board of trustees in business matters and to the faculty council in academic matters. All curricular requirements, reports, and diplomas would be issued by, and in the name of, the school.[10]

MacKinnon asserted that public school trusts could be more responsible than legislatures, cabinets, and departments of education because they would be closer to both education and the people, and because they would not be hampered by the weaknesses in the field of education shown by political institutions.[11]

Under MacKinnon's scheme, the school board would look to the government only for general policy and for funds, and to the school through its principal and staff for "initiative, advice, and action." It would not itself maintain officials or an administrative structure. Administrative personnel would be employed by the school and responsible to its officers. Business would be done in the name of the school, with school officials managing the budget, hiring teachers and employees, and doing the housekeeping. Cheques, contracts, and diplomas would carry the school's name. A board member would visit the school, not as "a visiting potentate," but as part of the team. "Like a member of any other board he should concern himself with policy only and not interfere in actual management."[12]

The resemblance between this scheme and the traditional methods of operating universities is clear. And it might well be asked why it could not work as well in one as in the other. There would appear to be at least one basic requirement: that members of the teaching profession be educated to a high level, and that each school or group of schools have a substantial quota of experienced teachers. It would be hard to imagine some of the schools in the more remote regions of the province operating in this manner during the height of the teacher shortage. And yet it would be well if a society could ask itself the really fundamental question: Where it is not safe to permit freedom, can a reasonable substitute be secured by regulation and supervision?

CONTROL OF SCHOOL AFFAIRS BY MUNICIPAL COUNCIL

Elected municipal officials in Ontario have long objected to the requirement that the councils collect school taxes while lacking any control over the rates. Even the implementation of the recommendation of the Ontario

Committee on Taxation that separate tax bills be sent out at different times does not eliminate the sense of irritation. One solution is that adopted in rural Alberta in the 1950s – to abolish school boards and entrust the management of the schools to a committee of the council. This committee carries out all the responsibilities of the former school board except for passing by-laws and approving the school budget.

The main theoretical justification for combining municipal functions under one controlling agency is that it makes possible the consideration of all competing demands for service in relation to one another, and the establishment of a single set of expenditure priorities. Under such a system, those advocating emphasis on education are forced to make their case in the open. There is also a possibility of financial savings through avoidance of wasteful duplication of administrative machinery. It has been suggested, further, that local democracy will function more effectively if the attention of the voters is focused on a single set of candidates. Voter apathy results when the elections call for too many choices.

In the Quance Lectures of 1957 H.P. Moffat made some points in favour of combining education with other municipal functions.

> Supporters of independent school bodies have quoted examples to show the disastrous effects on education that follow municipal control of the school board's budget. All these examples, however, refer to the situation where the school board independently determines the expenditures and then asks the municipality to raise the money.
>
> Would the situation be the same if the municipal body itself was responsible both for determining the costs and for raising the revenues? There is a good deal of evidence that with both authority and responsibility the municipal councils will soon obtain the same perspective as school boards and perhaps be even more sensitive to public demands for better schools.
>
> In Great Britain, since the beginning of the century, the operating authority for public schools has been a committee of the county council. In that country the schools are well supported, and local control is strong. ...
>
> In my own province, where the school boards are semi-independent, the municipal councils have recently been given full authority for the construction of school buildings, on request from the board. Far from shirking this task, most councils have been so zealous in the construction of buildings that a serious bottleneck has developed in the construction and financing of new schools.[13]

Objectors to the Alberta scheme, especially when the government proposed to extend it to urban areas, included the organized educational interests such as the Alberta Teachers' Association and the Alberta School Trustees' Association. They were opposed to the loss of educational autonomy in the management of the schools. Since the council could place any member it wished on the school committee, they claimed that there was no way for the electorate to ensure that their educational interests were in approved hands. Many of those who support a scheme of this kind do so in the hope that it will save money. There is of course a distinct possibility that less money will be spent, which is not necessarily the same thing. But, because of the multiplicity of factors involved, such a claim is difficult to prove.

OPTIMUM SIZE OF SCHOOL BOARDS

Boards of education in Ontario, particularly in the most populous centres, tend to have a relatively large number of members. There seem to be no very satisfactory criteria for determining what the ideal number is. It may be, however, that twenty or more are excessive under almost any conditions. Among the disadvantages sometimes cited with respect to a very large board are that it may be unduly tempted to find work for all members by straying into administrative functions, rather than sticking to policy making, which constitutes its proper responsibility. Furthermore, voters have difficulty obtaining sufficient information to make an intelligent choice where there are large numbers of candidates in the field, even where voting is by wards. Thus it is suggested that a board of better quality might be selected if the maximum number of members were eight or nine.

Bascom St John dealt with this question at the time the Toronto Board of Education had a brief prepared for submission to the Royal Commission on Metropolitan Toronto.[14] In the original version it was suggested that there be only six elected members on a new Metropolitan Board of Education, with a seventh to represent separate school taxpayers in secondary school affairs. St John noted that the small school board principle was common in the United States, and that boards as large as that in Toronto were rare in other parts of Canada. New York managed with an appointed board of nine members, Los Angeles and Detroit each with seven elected trustees, and Chicago with eleven.

SCHOOL BOARD ADMINISTRATION

Unitary versus dual control

Directors or superintendents of education appointed to head the larger local systems before 1969, and all the units established on January 1 of that year, are expected to be educators who also concern themselves with business matters, rather than the reverse. The arrangement is supposed to ensure that the system will have the best possible chance of being operated to the ultimate advantage of the pupils in the classroom. The director is expected to have the background to evaluate needs and demands and to be able to bring to bear the best possible judgment with respect to the priorities that should be assigned to various programs. Having an educator as the administrative head of the system is thought necessary to command the respect of the educational community.

The alternative that has received some attention, and that has been practised in some communities, is not that of putting an official with another type of background in command, but of giving the director or superintendent something considerably less than unequivocal control by appointing a different individual, also reporting directly to the board, as secretary-treasurer. This dual control type of arrangement has had a certain amount of appeal to boards wishing to maintain a maximum of direct involvement in the system, even at the risk of having continuous rivalry and friction between the two chief officials. It has appeared to be a means of keeping the complex administrative bureaucracy under some kind of control. The arrangement has naturally appealed also to many business officials, who may be expected to put up the strongest possible defence of their particular role.

J.W. McPherrin, Secretary-Treasurer of the Board of School Trustees in Nanaimo, BC, made a strong case for dual control.[15] 1 / He regarded the secretary-treasurer as a quasi-trustee, who had a substantial role to play in assisting new trustees to learn more about their tasks. This function was especially important because of the large turnover among such officials. 2 / He looked upon the board and the professional staff as having both common and conflicting interests. When the latter came into play, the secretary-treasurer was a potential ally of the board. 3 / He pointed out that the board had to perform its obligation of setting policy on the basis of the recommendation of its executive staff. If it got advice only from professional educators, it was in danger of becoming a rubber stamp. 4 / The secretary-treasurer was especially well qualified to speak in an executive capacity on behalf of the board. 5 / The superintendent (or director) was free to concentrate on instructional administration, while losing few actual prerogatives, and was relieved of the local politics frequently encountered in a system under unitary control. McPherrin believed that the unitary system would work provided that the board could hire or dismiss the superintendent without any repercussion from the profession. The superintendent must be prepared also to find himself in the public spotlight, especially when something went wrong, and to take full responsibility for all aspects of the operation.

A particularly unconvincing argument sometimes advanced in favour of the system of dual control is that the secretary-treasurer ought to have the thorough background in business methods that an educator must necessarily lack. But there is no reason why the top official cannot have such an individual as an immediate subordinate, and require an efficient performance from him. In fact, a director who failed to discharge his responsibility in this way could hardly expect to be regarded as competent.

Internal administrative organization

The advent of the county board system has led to an examination of principles of internal administrative organization. H.L. Willis, writing as

Deputy Superintendent of the Ottawa Collegiate Institute Board, presented a co-ordinated set of his own and other views about how certain problems might be dealt with.[16] Envisioning a planning committee of a new school board in a position to draw up an organization chart, he posed the question whether it should begin with personnel or with organization, that is, whether it should attempt to fit the chart to the qualities of the people already on the staff, or instead act as if it had a clean sheet, and base its work on organizational principles. A serious disadvantage in the former approach is that it assumes that when people leave they can be replaced by others with the same characteristics, or that the plan can be scrapped and replaced by one that suits new personalities. Neither of these assumptions appears to be tenable. Building an organization on sound principles does not mean, however, that some adaptations cannot be made in order to ensure that various individuals are in a position to do their best.

A basic choice in terms of organizational principles involves a decision whether to adopt a "tall" or a "flat" structure. The first of these involves a relatively large number of levels, with only a small number of officials reporting at the top. Among its other characteristics are that 1 / individual schools have little or no authority; 2 / no single administrator has the entire responsibility for the education of each child; 3 / although there are more line officers, administrative authority lies in the hands of a few; 4 / specialists become the officers responsible for developing a specialized program; and 5 / line officers have narrow spheres of responsibility. This structure is said to be preferred by traditionalists who believe that authority should be concentrated in few hands.

The chief characteristics of the flat organization were presented in the article as follows: 1 / authority levels and line officers are at a minimum; 2 / individual schools have greater autonomy; 3 / the principal is responsible for the total education of each child in his school; 4 / administrative responsibilities are widely shared; 5 / the administrators become generalists with broad areas of responsibility. Presented in this way, the flat structure seems more in keeping with the objective of preparing young people to live in a democracy. When they are at the end of a long line of officials whose chief function seems to be to receive and pass on orders, they can hardly be expected to develop initiative and responsibility.

Willis pointed out the importance of determining the position of the supervisor. If he functions in a line position, as he does in the tall structure, he must be either superior to or responsible to the principal. Experience is said to show that, if he is a line officer exerting authority, he is seldom consulted by those who need assistance. The implication is thus that he should be in a "staff" position.

A further concept dealt with was that of span of control. Willis referred to challenges to the theory that it is impossible for a single individual to supervise the work of more than six people. Recent theories suggest that the number really depends on the nature of the organization: for example, well trained professionals require relatively little supervision, and the maximum of six does not seem to apply. The broad span of control exemplified by this situation is characteristic of the flat organization. As a disadvantage of the broad span of control idea, it has been said that it does not give a superior the time to provide real leadership, and that he is so overburdened that he is not readily accessible. This argument would appear to be valid only if he tried to exert closer supervision than necessary. On the other hand, a supervisor in a tall structure with only three or four subordinates might overload himself by going into excessive detail in performing his functions.

It is not, of course, necessary to think in terms simply of tall and flat structures. By combining these with arrangements for broad and short spans of control, it is possible to get four distinct types, and a great number of variations of these may be devised. Willis offered a scheme providing for flat teams of specialists operating within a tall structure. He ended his article, however, with this warning: "Overemphasis on neat structures and efficient patterns of administration and responsibility may, in the long run, have a disastrous effect on efficiency by blocking natural channels of communication as well as healthy interpersonal relations."

In an article in the *Toronto Education Quarterly* in 1964,[17] G.E. Flower noted the advantages of smaller school systems. He listed four main areas:

(a) The encouragement of precious individual initiative, and a high order of human relations; individual professional workers do not become educational spare parts, anonymous in the maze of a mammoth organization.
(b) Ease of communications and simplicity of co-ordination, mainly because there is less for top administration to co-ordinate.
(c) The point of decision correctly close to the point of action, instead of removed many levels away in an administrative hierarchy.
(d) Greater responsiveness of local officials directly to the expectations and needs of the local community they serve, rather than to a relatively distant "higher authority."

Flower warned that administrators of the future would have to design and reorganize much larger school systems so that these advantages are not sacrificed. His solutions also involved four points:

(a) Adoption of a relatively "flat" organization at all levels, with unfashionably broad span of control, to encourage initiative on the part of subordinates and greater flexibility and adaptability within the larger school system.
(b) A relatively high degree of decentralization within the larger system, probably to a series of sub-divisions, each serving an appropriate geographical and sociological entity.
(c) The staff of the central office to be relatively small, with every effort made

to locate specialized staff for specialized services in the sub-divisions and schools themselves, rather than in the central office.

(d) Each area sub-division to be headed by a senior school administrator, with wide limits of freedom allowed him and his staff, including freedom to differ from other sub-divisions in matters of program and organization. Overall budgetary control must be reserved for the central office, and there would be a single policy-making citizen board of education for the entire larger school system; but surely there is room for far more operational decentralization, to professional staff, than we have ordinarily considered possible. Moreover, wide use could be made of citizen advisory committees within each sub-division.

As an illustration of actual application of administrative principles, *School Progress*[18] described the plan developed by the Burlington Board of Education and recommended by the Interim School Organization Committee for Halton County for adoption in that area. It provided for a high degree of personal leadership and responsibility in the school and community, and for easier communications throughout the educational hierarchy. The plan involved an acceptance by the board of a purely policy-making role. Standing committees were avoided in favour of *ad hoc* committees which dissolved after their specific tasks were completed. Policy was implemented through a hierarchy which included a director of education, four superintendents, and numbers of assistant superintendents, co-ordinators, supervisors, and consultants down to principals, teachers, and students. The plan attempted to outline the roles of officials in such a way as to place the initiative at the community or school level, and to stress delegation of responsibility and authority. Personal leadership, which tended to become increasingly difficult in larger units, was to lie in personal contact and immediate accessibility at all levels of the system. Emphasis was placed on the leadership role of the school principal.

The director of education kept the board and staff up to date on new ideas and on progress in educational research and practice, focused attention on the development of educational goals, and recommended measures to improve the efficiency of the program; he participated in policy making by analysing problems, making recommendations, and preparing detailed policy statements for the consideration of the board; he implemented policy by persuasion, leadership, and regulation; he kept the board informed on the effectiveness of policy and programs; he was responsible for staff hiring, firing, and promoting.

The assistant director's role was less clearly defined, since he had to adapt to the director's style of leadership. If the latter relied heavily on personal contacts, the assistant director might represent him at meetings and maintain direct contacts with teachers. He was expected to co-ordinate the planning process through all parts of the system, and particularly at the school level. He might prepare reports on population movements, subdivision development, enrolments, staff requirements, school boundaries, site locations, and accommodation provisions.

The four superintendents were in charge respectively of program, instruction, special education and services, and business and finance. Assignment of responsibility had to be rather tentative and arbitrary in an integrated system, and varied not only from time to time, but also in accordance with the particular qualifications, interest, and personality of each superintendent.

The scheme provided for an administrative council consisting of the director, the assistant director, the four superintendents, and the assistant superintendent. It was responsible for co-ordination and communication between staff and board. It provided a continuing evaluation of the system and participated in the development and implementation of policy.

The plan gave the principal as much autonomy and responsibility as possible. The largest secondary schools had two vice-principals, one for program and one for instruction, and a business manager, who took over non-educational duties often performed by principals and vice-principals. The principal was encouraged to establish close ties with teachers, parents, and students. He might make contact with parents through existing organizations or by forming special parents' advisory groups. He might invite students to take a more responsible role in school policy-making within a recognized structure. The teacher might be made to feel that he had access to senior officials and to the board itself through a council of senior teaching staff.

SELECTION AND PREPARATION FOR ADMINISTRATIVE POSITIONS

Ostensibly, appointments to administrative positions nearer the top of the hierarchy are made on the basis of demonstrated competence in positions such as that of the school principalship. H.L. Willis claimed that too many school systems were promoting teachers to administrative positions, "not on merit but on seniority and visibility – two pretty thin qualifications for advancement."[19] He pointed out the need for administrators to learn, among other things, to anticipate the needs of militant teaching staffs and to lead teachers to become more professional and less union-oriented. In order to do so, they must develop some perspective on their jobs and rethink the purposes of education. They had difficulty in meeting such challenges because they had learned whatever technical and administrative expertise they had by trial and error and by imitation of those who preceded them. Willis lamented that the superintendency in Canada was sadly lacking in professional preparation, and deplored the fact that there was nowhere in the country outside a few universities where there was a serious effort to identify, train, or select future educational leaders.

Willis proceeded to make specific suggestions for improving the situation. He noted the inconsistency in asking that a teacher have the best kind of professional preparation, including an honours degree, to lead a subject department in a secondary school, but only a summer course or two in addition to a three-year degree to lead an entire staff of professional teachers, and nothing at all to lead an entire community in education. "Apparently the higher one goes in education the less preparation one needs!" Willis advocated the master's degree as a minimum qualification for promotion to administrative rank. He conceded that it would not automatically make a person an educational leader but it would at least ensure that he had more than the minimum aptitude for success in the profession and that he "is visible for more than mere committee work."

In reviewing the kind of educational opportunities available, Willis declared that graduate studies in education were of a much more practical nature than was formerly the case. They were more clinical, providing students with the opportunity to apply theory as well as to study it. He outlined the case method as a study of clinically written descriptions of actual situations in which administrators had been forced to face major problems and to make important decisions. In some of these cases, the student attempted to determine the reasons why the administrator failed. In other cases, the student examined the facts and supplied his own solution, which was then examined by his professor and other students in a dynamic seminar. Field work was exemplified by a project recently conducted at Harvard University, where a team of prospective administrators and professors studied an entire educational system, observing teachers inside and outside the classroom, and interviewed principals, vice-principals, superintendents, nurses, librarians, pupils, and parents. Other activities included attending staff meetings, assemblies, and small group conferences; examining courses of study, equipment, textbooks, building plans, adequacy of school plant, school boundaries, and existing and projected enrolment; and study of the socio-economic structure of the community. The team of prospective administrators had the regular services of a lawyer, a sociologist, an economist, and an architect, and could also call on specialists from the university in almost every field. The final report stimulated an unprecedented interest in education in the particular system involved. The results were not too happy for the superintendent, who retired, and some members of the school board, who were replaced largely as a result of the efforts of an interested citizens' group.

Willis characterized internship as another effective way of preparing administrators. It involved the placement of a student under the auspices of a university in a school system as a special assistant to a principal or a superintendent. He attended lectures and brought problems encountered from the field to be examined objectively in seminar discussion in the light of the latest theory and research findings. As an example of this approach, Willis told how Harvard appointed graduate students as executive secretaries to state committees studying the reorganization of school districts. As a result of their participation, the students felt they had acquired a better appreciation of many problems in education from the point of view of the teacher in the classroom and the official in the department of education as well as from that of the superintendent caught between the two.

Willis listed a number of educative experiences from which Canadian administrators might benefit. These included 1 / courses in human relations, which might give them insights into the behaviour of others as well as of themselves; 2 / exposure to the latest theories of management, including the best in personnel policies and practices; 3 / study of "the fine art of executive decision-making"; 4 / experience of the advantages of constructive conflict; 5 / study of the great systems and theories of education.

The establishment of the Department of Educational Administration in the Ontario Institute for Studies in Education in 1965 marked a serious effort to provide opportunities for the study of the psychological, sociological, economic, and other foundations of educational administration, as well as of techniques of administrative practice. The program is dealt with in volume v, chapter 14, of the present series. Some substantial problems have been faced in terms of reconciling the "practical" and theoretical orientations often exemplified by the active administrator on the one hand and the student of administration on the other. If the latter is to make the impact he desires, he may have to wait until a new generation, suitably prepared, moves into the higher positions. Even then, he cannot be sure that his objectives are met unless he achieves a real meeting of minds at the professor-student stage.

FOUR

The development of local administrative units for public elementary and secondary schools before 1968

ORIGIN OF PUBLIC SCHOOL ADMINISTRATIVE UNITS

Early provisions for a basic unit

When the province was established as a separate entity in 1791, the idea of a publicly supported system of education was totally foreign to the inhabitants. Popular education was considered to be a charity, and not necessarily a completely defensible one at that. The initial small government grants, first to the district grammar schools in 1807, and then to the common schools in 1816, thus represented a fairly radical departure from traditional attitudes and practices. Before 1816 there was no organized form of local administration to take responsibility for the schools. The Common School Act of that year provided for the election by the inhabitants of any "town, township, village or place" of three "fit and discreet persons" as trustees to hire the teachers and prescribe the fees to be paid by parents to supplement government grants.[1] In order to qualify for the grants, the inhabitants had to enrol a minimum of twenty pupils, and to share the cost of the teacher's salary. No property qualification was required for participation in the choice of trustees.

The Common School Act provided for the appointment of district boards of education, consisting of "five discreet persons," with authority to distribute the money voted by the Legislature. The trustees were required to report to the board every three months on the textbooks used, and once a year on the state of the school. They also had to seek its approval to remove a teacher for improper conduct. In 1824 the act was amended to transfer the power of teacher certification from the local boards to the district boards.

The settlements of those days were isolated by slow communication and poor transportation, and necessarily had to develop a great deal of self-reliance. Local improvements such as churches, bridges, roads, and schools involved individual and community effort. The school was regarded with intense proprietary pride. This feeling became so deeply ingrained that it became extremely difficult to move toward the larger units eventually required by a more complex and sophisticated economy. The Royal Commission on Education identified the early half of the nineteenth century as the period of struggle for ascendancy between advocates of two different conceptions of what should constitute a basic unit of school administration.[2] One group believed that this unit should be the attendance area of each school, with a board of trustees to administer the affairs of the school; the other thought that it should be a municipality, whether a city, town, or township, with a single board having jurisdiction over all the schools located there. The Act of 1816 did much to establish the ascendancy of the first group, although efforts were made from time to time to reverse the trend.

The process of surveying land and drawing boundary lines proceeded as settlement advanced. Road allowances were marked, sometimes half a mile, but more commonly a mile or a mile and a quarter apart, and "town lines" were drawn to enclose townships of about one hundred square miles in area. The eight original districts were in the course of time divided into about thirty counties, and the term "district" eventually remained only to describe less organized units further north.[3]

Of considerable importance to the administration of school affairs was the so-called Baldwin Act, passed in 1849. It was a comprehensive piece of legislation giving Upper Canada a full-fledged structure for local self-government. It established the system of local municipalities, cities, towns, villages, townships, police villages, and counties in southern Ontario much as they exist today.[4] It also made provision for the levying of property taxes by the local municipalities and for the requisitioning of tax funds by counties. In assessing the significance of this development for education, C.E. Phillips wrote: "Although the election of school trustees commonly preceded the election of municipal councils for general purposes, the efficacy of the former depended on the latter. Only after the setting up ... of the present system of self-government ... could tax-supported free public education become a real issue."[5]

Attempts to establish the township as a basic unit

A school act passed in 1841 abolished the district boards of education and transferred their functions to the municipal councils of the districts. These councils were given authority to divide the townships of their districts into school sections and to tax the inhabitants of each section up to $200 for the construction of new buildings. In a move toward the enlargement of the basic unit of local control, the act provided for the election of township boards of trustees, to be known as common school commissioners, and to be responsible for all matters affecting the common schools of their respective townships. These township boards were, however, abolished only two years later, when legislation provided for reversion to the system involving a board of three trustees for each attendance area. The Act of 1841 had more lasting consequences in that it provided for the establishment of schools for religious minorities who dissented from the authority of the school commissioners. This provision constituted the first legislative recognition of separate schools.

An act of 1846 designated the attendance area of a single school as a school section, and identified it as the basic unit. The districts were recognized as the intermediate units, and the district councils as the relevant authorities. Provision was made for section trustees to be elected for three-year instead of one-year terms. An amending act in 1847 placed the control of all schools in a city or town under a single board, thus eliminating the board of trustees for each school. This was the first occasion when a distinction was made between schools in urban and those in rural areas. Until 1850 the urban boards were appointed by the city or town council, but, as the method was judged unsatisfactory, provision was made for their election after that date.[6]

Ryerson indicated his view at that time that the system of township units would supersede the school sections, but he was not prepared to press the issue too vigorously. The Act of 1850 continued to recognize the latter as basic units, except in towns and cities, but provision was also made for the voluntary formation of township units. However, since these boards could be formed only by an affirmative vote of the resident householders of each of the school sections of the township, and since an adverse vote in a single section could prevent action, it is hardly surprising that only one such unit had been formed by 1871.

During the course of his long public career, Ryerson gradually became convinced that a more determined effort was required. In 1866 he sought the views of forty county school conventions, and received support from twenty-five. He consequently drafted a bill to provide for the election of township boards when the vote in a majority of the sections was favourable. Although the bill was not presented to the Legislature, the same provision was included in another bill considered during the sessions of 1868 and 1869. This measure was so amended by a committee that Ryerson successfully urged that it be withdrawn. A more drastic bill was drawn up in 1870 that would have given a county council the authority to form any of the townships under its jurisdiction into one school municipality, and to establish a township board of common school trustees. In the form in which it was actually passed, however, township councils were authorized to form township units, but only where at least two-thirds of the ratepayers voted favourably.[7]

Subsequent steps in the direction of reducing or abolishing the school sections were halting. In 1896 the council of any municipality composed of more than one township in territory without county organization was authorized to choose between dividing the municipality into school sections and establishing a single public school board for the whole municipality. In 1921 provision was made for the formation of a township school area of any part of a township lying contiguous to a city or town on the vote of four-fifths of the township council concerned. The following year, this procedure was made subject to the approval of a simple majority of the council. This development was perhaps an indication that inhabitants of areas adjoining the larger centres of population were more readily impressed with the advantages of a larger scale of operations. In 1925–6 the minister, G.H. Ferguson, introduced a bill that would have established the township as the basic unit, with provision for a board of trustees consisting of from three to ten members, each of whom would have had supervisory responsibilities for one of the areas into which the township was divided. Opposition, in large part from trustees in the existing boards, led to the withdrawal of the bill.

The first measure that constituted the basis for real advances was passed in 1932. It gave township councils the power to organize all or part of the township into a school area, and to abolish the constituent sections. The Department of Education began to encourage the practice from 1938 on, and, by the time the Royal Commission reported, more than half the former school sections had been combined in township school areas. Much of the credit for the drive for larger administrative units before 1945 goes to V.K. Greer, who served as Chief Inspector of Public and Separate Schools from 1925 to 1944, and held the new title of Superintendent of Elementary Education from 1944 until his death the following year. Greer's tactics consisted of the use of gentle but steady pressure to bring about reorganization without leaving a residue of bitterness.

The formation of the township school area did not in itself ensure that services would be any better than in the smaller school section. During the 1930s and early 1940s, the changes were not, in fact, very great. But there was a growing interest in the possibility of replacing a number of small one-room schools with a single central school. Post-war prosperity, increased enrolment, the obsolescence of many school buildings, and particularly the rapid improvement in transportation produced a rapid growth in the number of schools of this type. The impossibility of having such schools in the school sections tended to demonstrate the inadequacies of the latter as almost nothing else could have done.

Union school sections

The Act of 1850 made provision for union school sections, which involved the amalgamation of sections in more than one municipality. The merger was to be arranged by the municipal councils and the county superintendent of schools. The arrangement was intended not so much to provide for larger units as to solve certain problems arising from inconvenient municipal boundaries. The first union school section was formed in 1864.

Consolidated school sections

Provision was made in 1919 for the establishment of consolidated school sections. These did not necessarily have to bear a relationship to the township boundaries. Their establishment was difficult because it depended on a favourable vote of the ratepayers in all the sections concerned. Further, the responsibility for initiating a consolidation was not definitely fixed by the act. Only twenty-seven consolidations of seventy-one school sections were arranged before 1925, and in 1940 there were only twenty-eight consolidated schools in the province. McCutcheon deplored the lack of action, despite the fact that consolidation presented rural communities with practically all the advantages of a well-graded urban school, along with the values of a rural setting.[8]

ESTABLISHMENT OF SECONDARY SCHOOL BOARDS

The grammar schools were originally managed by trustees appointed by the Lieutenant-Governor, and were thus in no sense under democratic control. In 1853 they were placed under boards of six trustees appointed by their county council, and the latter was given the right to raise money by taxation for their support. They were also made subject to the regulations of the Council of Public Instruction, which prescribed the course of study and textbooks and appointed a grammar school inspector.[9] One of the reasons given by Phillips for the reluctance to have trustees of secondary schools elected to office was that secondary education was of less general interest than elementary. The academic type was esteemed chiefly by the few who used it professionally, and the vocational type offered later was apparently of benefit only to particular workers and employers.[10]

When the system became established, every city and separated town constituted a high school district, and other high school districts might be established by county councils. High school boards had to consist of at least three trustees appointed by the municipal council. In addition, the public and separate school boards of an urban municipality could each appoint one member to the board. Where a high school was situated in a county in a municipality other than a city or separated town, the county council could appoint three trustees if the majority of the board members favoured such action; otherwise they could appoint only one. In addition to such trustee or trustees, these high school boards were constituted as follows: three trustees appointed by the municipal council in high school districts comprising one municipality; two trustees appointed by each municipal council in districts comprising two municipalities; and one trustee appointed by each municipal council in districts comprising three or more municipalities. Each appointee of a municipal council held office for three years. In the territorial districts, high school boards consisted of six trustees appointed by the municipal councils, with the possible addition of a member appointed by each of the public and separate school boards. Where the high school unit included more than one municipality, the trustees were appointed in equal numbers by the participating councils.[11]

The original grammar schools, which later became high schools, were accessible to students only in the larger communities. The practice therefore developed during the latter part of the nineteenth century of adding fifth or continuation classes to certain of the public and separate elementary schools. The Continuation Schools Act of 1909 provided for the establishment of such schools either by elementary school boards or by county councils. In the former case, the boundaries were coterminous with those of the elementary school district, but in the latter the councils might draw them in any way they saw fit, and in some cases they appeared to be very erratic. Legislation of 1913 recognized the county continuation schools as high schools.[12] The effect was to burden the province with a large number of small high school districts.

Where a continuation school was established by joint action on the part of two or more boards, a committee of not more than two-thirds of the members of the boards concerned constituted the continuation school board. Since county councils contributed to the support of the continuation schools, they were given the right to appoint one member to each continuation school board having jurisdiction within the county.[13]

Early arrangements for vocational schools provided for special areas consisting of two or more municipalities to be constituted a unit, with a vocational school board consisting of members appointed by the school boards of the municipalities included in such a unit. The usual pattern, however, was to have vocational schools and departments managed by vocational advisory committees. These consisted of members of the secondary school board or board of education and others appointed by the board to represent the interests of employers and employees in the area. There might be either eight or twelve members of the committee, of whom half had to be members of the board. Board representatives had to include the chairman and representatives of the county council and the public and separate school boards, if any.[14]

The problem of evolving a suitable system of organization for the secondary schools was never nearly as great as for the elementary schools. Cameron identifies four chief reasons why this was so. 1 / Because the secondary schools evolved out of a system of exclusive grammar schools, all located in the larger urban centres, and never very popular, they were much more amenable to provincial control than were the widely distributed and popularly controlled elementary schools. The fact that the boards continued to be appointed contributed to this situation. 2 / High school inspectors were appointed by the provincial government from 1855 on. 3 / The demand of a large number of groups, including parents, for greater emphasis on vocationally oriented education provided a compelling reason for the enlargement of administrative units. 4 / The obvious inequity of the system of financing secondary education when large areas of the province were excluded from high school districts reached such proportions in the 1930s and early 1940s that some form of reorganization became virtually inevitable.[15]

There was some movement toward relatively minor enlargement of high school districts in the 1920s and 1930s. The initiative was taken by the school boards and county councils rather than by the department. In some cases, pressure came from ratepayers, who found that the "county rate," which was levied on all county property not situated within a high school district, was higher than that paid by residents of such a district. The real movement toward larger units was made possible by legislation passed in 1937, which authorized county councils to establish consultative committees, each consisting of three members appointed by the council, one appointed by the department, and the local public school inspector, who acted as secretary.[16]

When the Department of Education began to press for the formation of larger high school units immediately after the war, it relied on the inspectors to promote the cause. Some of those who were later appointed to leading positions in the department won reputations for initiative and persuasiveness in this field. As one former inspector recounted his experiences, he and his colleagues felt something like competing salesmen, each in his own area. They found a distinctly low-key approach to be the most effective. They gave the local officials a review of the advantages of the new system, along with an estimate of the mill rate that would be required, and hoped that the facts would be convincing, as they often were. There has been criticism of the use of their efforts in this way on the assumption that the change could have been made a great deal more easily by mandatory legislation. But, as was the case with the amalgamation of school sections, such a solution no doubt appears more attractive in retrospect than it did at the time.

The voluntary move toward the establishment of larger units of high school administration was much more successful than that for elementary school units. By the time the Royal Commission reported, a substantial part of the objective in that part of the province organized into counties had been completed. The reorganization continued until 1964, when Davis announced that all sections of Ontario counties would henceforth be part of secondary school districts.[17] The remaining adjustments imposed by this legislation were relatively minor. The situation was less satisfactory, however, in the territorial districts, where there was no counterpart to the county councils in the southern areas. Reorganization there depended on the initiative of local municipal councils and of the provincial government. The former were characterized by a restricted point of view, and the latter was reluctant to use compulsion. Since provincial grants covered nearly all the cost of educating non-resident pupils, there was no counterpart to the public pressure exerted in the south to escape county rates. Furthermore, the sparsity of the population and the problems of transportation made the existence of enlarged units less attractive than in the south. The movement toward reorganization therefore made little headway.

ESTABLISHMENT OF BOARDS OF EDUCATION

In his abortive bill of 1868 Ryerson had proposed a single elected board to control both elementary and secondary schools in all urban municipalities, but no coercion to unite administrative units for the two levels occurred until 1968. The first real progress was made in 1903 when an act was passed authorizing the establishment of a single board of education to administer public elementary and secondary education. At first this privilege was confined to cities with a population of at least 100,000, but in 1904 it was extended to cities, towns, and villages. In 1909 the privilege of adopting a board of education was granted to any urban municipality where the municipal and school district boundaries were coterminous. Legislation in 1911 required the approval of a majority of the ratepayers before such action could be taken. In 1948 county councils were authorized to establish a board of education in any high school district on request of the municipal councils involved, but without the necessity of securing ratepayer approval.[18]

The number of members of a board of education varied with the population of the administrative unit. In a city of fifty thousand or more, such a board consisted of fourteen members, twelve of whom were elected and two appointed by the separate school board of the municipality. Where the ward system was used, however, two members were elected from each ward. In cities with a population under fifty thousand, the board consisted of ten elected members and one representative of the separate school board. In a town or village, there were seven elected members. Trustees elected to a board of education held office for overlapping terms of two years unless the voters decided by referendum to have annual elections.[19]

A union board of education was organized along different lines. It was formed by the union of a public and a high school board as a result of action taken in a high school district composed of a municipality or of two or more municipalities where a municipal board had not been organized and where the boundaries of the high school district and the public school unit were coterminous. The trustees of the public and high schools, who constituted the union board of education, continued to be elected and appointed in the same manner as before its establishment.[20]

Following Toronto's action in 1903, most cities and towns formed boards of education during the subsequent decades. The number of these boards declined substantially after the Second World War, when the creation of district high schools led to the separation of many local high schools from the public elementary schools in the immediate area. This development is not to be interpreted as a policy of deliberate antagonism toward the concept of common administration for schools at the two levels. It is rather an illustration of a lack of positive pressure to secure co-ordination. The Department of Education had elementary and secondary divisions that functioned practically as separate empires until 1965. Teachers were prepared in separate institutions and were organized in different federations, and inspectors who rose from their ranks reflected their distinctive attitudes and interests. County and township councils had their attention focused respectively on secondary and elementary schools. "With no one speaking for an integrated form of government and no overriding authority prescribing the boundaries, it became virtually impossible to establish coterminous public and high school districts."[21] The number of boards of education declined from a high of 125 in 1946 to 52 in 1960, and stood at 53 in 1966.[22]

MANDATORY CONSOLIDATION OF SCHOOL SECTIONS

Between 1938 and 1950 the number of township school areas increased from 30, replacing 154 former rural school sections, to 536, replacing 3,465 former sections. But from this time on, it was evident that the movement toward the voluntary formation of township units had just about reached its limit. There was a very definite decline of initiative on the part of the department during the Dunlop regime. Cameron's report, confirmed by the writer's inquiries, is that Dunlop specifically prohibited any positive steps on the part of the inspectors to encourage consolidation. They were simply to provide information on the request of the local authorities.[23] These instructions were largely effective, although Dunlop was practically alone in his lack of enthusiasm for consolidation. But even a reversal of the ministerial attitude when Robarts succeeded to the position was not sufficient to get the movement started again.

As minister, Robarts does not appear to have contemplated a change toward mandatory amalgamation of the school sections. It thus remained for his successor to formulate the program that represented a fairly drastic change in government policy. Davis had been quickly persuaded that a large part of his contemplated efforts to modernize the school system would be frustrated without the creation of viable administrative units. Local attachment to the school section had of course not disappeared, but its defenders had been reduced to an apologetic group with a case based largely on tradition and sentiment. The way was prepared for the necessary action by widespread consultation with interested groups.

The legislation was introduced in early 1964, just a few months after the previous provincial election. Even if the measure had been proposed as part of the election program, it is hardly likely that it would have been regarded as a fighting issue. Speaking on the matter in the Legislature, Robert Nixon indicated that the Liberal Party intended to support the bill. It would do so even though the compulsory unification of some of the boards would have to be carried out against the wishes of many of the people concerned. Nixon noted also that control of the administration of the local schools would move away from the immediate area, but he agreed with the minister that it would not move so far away that it would be in any sense a removal of local autonomy.[24]

The main legislative provision for the change was contained in an amendment to *The Public Schools Act*. The key clause read: "on and after the 1st day of January, 1965, every township shall be a township school area."[25] The amendment also required that all urban school districts, that is, all village, town, or city districts with populations of less than

1,000 or an average daily attendance of less than 100 must be attached to the adjacent township school area. This measure abolished more than 1,500 rural boards; it reduced the number of rural public school boards in the counties from 1,850 to 423, and in the territorial districts from 233 to 166. The total number of public elementary boards in the entire province was reduced from 2,419 to 1,037.[26] A further provision of the bill enabled townships with a population of 10,000 or more to form two school areas within their boundaries, but only two townships did so.

Davis was able to assert in the Legislature that the process of amalgamation went quite smoothly.

> I think that I can point out to the hon. members of this House that over these past few months many of the boards involved have made representations to the department to endeavour to solve their problems. I think it is obvious that no legislation can be drafted that will adequately meet the individual situations of some 1,500 school boards in this province. But I think I can safely say, Mr. Speaker, that out of the 1,500 that have been consolidated, we have only one or two problem areas left in the province.
>
> This does not mean that everyone is entirely content or satisfied, but it does mean that the proposals have been accepted; that the boards have in fact been elected and the township area is now in fact the smallest unit as far as elementary education is concerned.[27]

One of the problems arose out of the desire of the police village of Baden to become incorporated as a town so as to secure exemption from the act. The government declined to delay implementation of the measure for this purpose.

PROVISION FOR FURTHER VOLUNTARY ENLARGEMENT OF ADMINISTRATIVE UNITS AFTER 1965

The provision for mandatory amalgamation of the school sections was looked upon as a step in a continuous process of enlargement of the administrative units. Another amendment to *The Public Schools Act* in 1964 provided that every county council was to appoint a consultative committee of from three to five ratepayers, with a non-voting school inspector acting as secretary. Provision was also made for similar committees to be established in the territorial districts under somewhat different auspices. There the public school inspector was authorized to call a meeting of representatives of the municipalities and public school boards in any area within a high school district. A public school consultative committee might be, but did not have to be, established at such a meeting. The committees had the responsibility of studying all matters affecting public school education in their respective counties or districts, and of making recommendations to the appropriate authorities. Their particular objective was to facilitate voluntary moves toward the establishment of county school areas. The appropriate by-laws were to be enacted in southern Ontario by the county councils and in northern Ontario by the municipal councils, with the subsequent approval of the minister.

The significance of this development was in part that it moved the responsibility for the organization of local administrative units one step further up. Previously, the townships had had this responsibility with respect to the local sections. Now the county councils had the authority to enlarge the basic township units. There was only one further step in the series: for the province to assume the responsibility for the enlargement or alteration of the county school areas, which became the basic units on January 1, 1969.

In 1965 the terms of reference of the consultative committees were extended to give them the responsibility of investigating and reporting on the desirability of establishing or enlarging county school areas or of altering township school areas. Provision was also made for county school areas for public school purposes to be established in the municipalities that formed a high school district. A county school area would have to be at least as large as a high school district. This provision was in line with what was described as a long-term policy of forming larger units of administration in which both public elementary and secondary schools would be administered by boards of education. The minimum desirable size of a county or district school area was considered to be the area capable of supporting a composite secondary school organization.[28]

The same departmental memorandum that contained these indications of policy gave some specific definition of what were considered to be units of minimum desirable size.

> It is the policy of the Department to encourage the formation of County or District School Areas with enrolments of at least 3,000 pupils or, where, owing to geographic or other factors this is not feasible at present, to encourage the formation of areas which will serve as large a school enrolment as possible. It is also the policy of the Department to encourage the establishment and operation of fully-graded schools with enrolments of at least 300 pupils.[29]

The memorandum proceeded to outline the kind of educational facilities and services that could be provided with enrolments of different sizes.

> (a) A school system with an average daily attendance of 3000 or more pupils is of sufficient size to make efficient use of a permanent staff to inspect and supervise the instructional programme and to administer the building and maintenance programme. Most boards in systems of this size operate some senior public schools with specialist teachers in art, music, physical education, science, history, geography, guidance, auxiliary work, primary reading, kindergarten, industrial arts, home economics, speech correction and library in-

struction. A system of this size will make possible a secondary school of 1000 pupils which is an acceptable minimum for a composite secondary school.
(b) An average daily attendance of from 1000 to 3000 enables a board to provide many of the services that are supplied in a larger system but the board does not operate enough classrooms to justify the employment of a complete supervisory staff.
(c) An average daily attendance of 300 to 1000 makes possible fully-graded elementary schools. A few of the larger systems may have senior schools operated on a part-time rotary basis. Auxiliary classes may be provided for slow learners, and part-time classes in special subjects are possible. It would appear that a system with fewer than 300 pupils cannot provide the quality and variety of education needed in this present age.
(d) Where the average daily attendance is under 300 but over 100 a semi-graded school system may be operated. The principal is not likely to have a university degree and if instruction is given in music, physical education, industrial arts and home economics the board must depend upon part-time teachers. It is not always feasible to provide opportunity classes for slow learners or kindergartens for beginners.
(e) Fewer than one child in five in Ontario is receiving his elementary education in a school system where the average daily attendance is below 100. Every school in this group has at least one classroom with three or more grades. Some classrooms have eight grades. The ungraded one-room school is rapidly disappearing from the educational scene and there is every indication that it will soon be found only in very thinly populated areas.[30]

Each consultative committee was asked to make a thorough over-all study of its county or district, giving consideration to such factors as geographic features, roads, the location of secondary schools and of existing public schools, and the distribution, growth, and probable shifts of population. It was suggested that consultations might be held with school boards, elementary and secondary school inspectors, and municipal councils, and that briefs might be received from various interested groups and individuals. A copy of the recommendations submitted to the county council or, in the districts, to the township councils concerned, was to be sent to the deputy minister.

Cameron reports on the composition of the consultative committees, and makes some observations on the significance of this factor. Among 175 members, there were 89 councillors, who thus constituted 50.9 per cent of the total. In contrast, the public school and secondary school board members made up only 10.9 per cent of the total. In two counties, Grey and Peterborough, where larger units were formed during the first year, it is said that the public school inspector, who acted as a non-voting secretary, was a relatively dominant figure. It seems reasonable to speculate that an inspector's influence, normally exerted in favour of further amalgamation, may have been in inverse relationship to the number of school board members on the committee.[81]

Davis reported the results of the program of voluntary consolidation with obvious satisfaction in May 1967:

The consolidation of school districts is proceeding rapidly. County councils, acting on the recommendations of consultative committees, are enlarging the administrative units in some instances into county school areas. Combined Roman Catholic separate school zones now encompass a great number of former small separate school sections.

The desire for vocational education has brought together in composite high schools many small high schools that were not financially or numerically able alone to attain composite status. I would not have you believe that these changes always occur with the unanimous consent of the ratepayers. But I have yet to find an enlarged area that did not appreciate the educational advantages of larger units, even if the cost was greater than the less-effective education in the small unit. My staff of officials, both in the main office and in the area offices, has been busy considering the educational implications of the larger areas of administration involving many of our cities in cooperation with The Department of Municipal Affairs.[82]

FIVE

The consolidation of local administrative units in 1969

RECOMMENDATIONS OF THE ONTARIO COMMITTEE ON TAXATION

The Ontario Committee on Taxation observed that, as universities, businesses, and trades raised their levels of expectation, secondary education must offer an unprecedented diversity of learning opportunities. The evidence suggested that still larger units than those so far developed were needed to meet contemporary demands. The committee recommended that its twelve proposed county regions constitute those units. The number of high school districts and boards of education contained wholly or partly within these regions ranged from ten to thirty-one. Apart from the single largest one, however, the upper limit was eighteen.

The committee recommended that the process of bringing secondary education under the direct jurisdictions of the county regions should be accomplished gradually. The initial step would be to transfer the power of appointing school board members from the local municipalities and counties to the county regions. From this point, the task of defining coterminous boundaries and enlarging the units could proceed at whatever pace seemed reasonable. From the beginning, the high school districts would be fully dependent on the county regions for approval of their budgets, and would come under the continuing supervision of the education committee of the regional council.[1]

These recommendations are of interest chiefly because of the extent to which they contrast with decisions that were actually made. They perhaps smacked too much of the textbook to appeal to those responsible for appropriate action, or to appear palatable to the voters. Enough of the less important recommendations of the committee were adopted, however, to justify claims that its work had been taken into account.

PREPARATORY STUDIES IN THE DEPARTMENT

Cameron describes the work of a "larger unit committee" established within the Supervision Section of the Department of Education.[2] Consisting of four assistant superintendents, J.R. Thomson, T.H. Houghton, H.K. Fisher, and G.H. Waldrum, it undertook to examine existing research in the area of school district organization, to evaluate such material in the light of the Ontario situation, and to develop draft legislation which would serve as a basis for the eventual consolidation of local units. J.F. Kinlin, later assistant deputy minister, communicated the results of one of his investigations to this group. These results helped to persuade them that any reorganization would have to be based on existing municipal boundaries. They also rejected the possibility of any reorganization based on a two-tier model of regional and local units. They were thus led to the conclusion that the county constituted the most desirable organizational unit, at least in the southern part of the province where counties existed. By the autumn of 1967 the committee had made substantial progress in preparing draft legislation to produce a system of county boards of education for southern Ontario.

OFFICIAL STATEMENTS OF POLICY

Cameron indicates that, although the policy adopted was quite in line with the committee's thinking, its work was not directly connected with the decision to proceed with immediate reorganization. The time and occasion for the official statement came as a surprise to most of the department. The Prime Minister made the crucial announcement in an address at the opening of an addition to a secondary school in Galt. He declared that the government's objective should be to reduce the number of administrative units to approximately one hundred boards of education, which would be responsible for education in the public elementary and secondary schools. He continued:

> It is the intent of the Government of Ontario that these boards of education be established on a county-wide basis in Southern Ontario. These units will include the cities and separated towns within the county. However, there will be a few exceptions. For example, this development will not affect the existing system in Metropolitan Toronto. A few other large cities will have their own boards of education.
>
> In Northern Ontario it is feasible and necessary to establish larger school units and these will be designated.
>
> The possibility of establishing larger units for separate schools is also contemplated.
>
> Legislation is in preparation to be presented to the next session of the Ontario Legislature so that this reorganization of school units can become effective on January 1st, 1969.[3]

Robarts offered detailed reasons for accepting the county as the basic unit for school administration.

1. The county is a recognized and understood unit of administration in Ontario.
2. Present school boundaries for both public and secondary schools are established or altered by County Councils.

3. The Select Committee of the Legislature on The Municipal and Related Acts (The Beckett Committee), suggested in 1965 that, as a practical start towards larger units of local government, the existing counties be adopted as a basic unit.
4. By adopting the larger unit for public and secondary school purposes, the Government is also accepting the suggestion of the Smith Committee on Taxation that efficiency in raising revenue demands that taxes be levied on a base larger than our present small local units. As a basis, many counties have already established assessment departments enabling them to develop a county-wide assessment system.

When he introduced the proposed legislation in March 1968, Davis declared that it was the most significant development in the organizational structure for education in the history of the province. Its major purpose was to create the conditions that would make it possible to realize the goal of equal educational opportunity for all. The legislation was based on several guiding principles.

The first, related to our major and ultimate goal, is that all children regardless of their so-called station in life, the particular nature of their individuality, or the chance of their geographic location have a right to equality of educational opportunity. The second is that the programme of public education should be a continuous and integrated process from kindergarten to grade 13. The third is that all the members of a school board, one of our oldest democratic institutions, should be elected to office by a direct vote of the people. The fourth is that boards of education which are responsible for providing educational facilities, services and personnel, should be fiscally responsible directly to the electorate for the financing of the current and capital costs of education. And the fifth is that The Department of Education, through the legislative grants and the services of its specialized personnel, should be responsible for equalizing the educational and financial differences that may still remain among the boards of education due to variations in population, or geographic, economic and financial considerations.[4]

Efforts to "explain" the government's policy decision need not go further than the case made by the minister. The whole thrust of the Davis years had been in the indicated direction. In particular, Davis's interest in the use of expensive modern media such as educational television and his enthusiasm for the use of data processing techniques had implied the creation of administrative units of which the township areas could constitute only the first stage. The reorganization of the Department of Education was in part designed to produce a more streamlined and efficient organization, but it was also clearly intended to complement strong and active local units. Furthermore, Davis had continuously proclaimed his intentions, and the Robarts government had given clear indications that these were in line with its broader plans.

There are more justifiable grounds for speculating on the reasons why the action was taken so soon after the previous step toward reorganization. It might be supposed that the provisions for further voluntary enlargement of the local units should have been given more time to show results. One convincing reason is that the creation of township areas went so smoothly that the fear of adverse local reaction had been largely dispelled. It was easy to believe that a logical and realistic desire to come to terms with contemporary society had replaced an unreasonable attachment to outdated institutions. In making this assumption, the government was certainly too optimistic.

THE PLAN

A set of so-called guidelines was ready for release on February 1, 1968, filling in details of the new plan as far as southern Ontario was concerned.[5] The document indicated that each of the thirty-eight administrative counties would constitute an administrative unit. There would also be boards of education for Hamilton, London, Ottawa, and Windsor. As Robarts had promised, the six boards in Metropolitan Toronto remained undisturbed. The guidelines also explained the composition of the new boards and the means by which they were to be elected. Steps to be taken by existing boards prior to the consolidation in 1969 were indicated. A supplementary document provided information on the new units to be formed in the territorial districts of northern Ontario.

After the Prime Minister's announcement, the members of the larger unit committee had been given the task of drawing the boundaries of the new units in northern Ontario. They did so in consultation with the regional directors, area superintendents, and business administrators in the northern regions. Draft proposals were drawn up by the committee, submitted to these officials, and subsequently amended on the basis of their criticisms and suggestions.[6] The key factor determining the designation of each unit was the availability of secondary school facilities.

As the legislation was explained by the minister,[7] the new boards would consist of between fourteen and twenty elected trustees, depending on the total population of the county.[8] Trustees would seek election from county subdivisions to be defined by the county councils. The latter were expected to establish these divisions on an existing municipal basis, although in some cases two or more small municipalities would have a single representative. The members representing the separate school supporters were to be elected at large, with provision for wards where there were more than four trustees to be elected. Elections were to be held biennially, with the first one scheduled for December 1968.

The members of the boards of education in those of the defined cities which already had such boards were to continue to be elected in the same manner and in the same number as when the legislation was passed. In addition to these members, however, there would be an additional number of trustees elected by separate school supporters based on the ratio that residential and farm assessment for separate school purposes bore to the corresponding assessment of public school ratepayers; the minimum number of such members would, however, be two. These provisions would of course also apply to Ottawa when its new board was formed.

The unique situation in Ottawa was dealt with by special legislation. The establishment of the Regional Municipality of Ottawa-Carleton provided for a second-tier government over the cities of Ottawa and Eastview, the villages of Richmond, Rockcliffe Park, and Stittsville, and eleven neighbouring townships. Two administrative units were to be established for public elementary and secondary education, one for Ottawa, Eastview, and Rockcliffe Park and the other for the additional municipalities in the region. The implementation of the new educational arrangement was delayed until January 1, 1970. Among reasons for this delay, other than the formation of the regional government, were the special problems caused by 1 / the integration of a number of private high schools into the publicly-supported system and 2 / the need to combine the administrative structure for the elementary and secondary schools in the city into a single unit.

Some rural sections and township school areas in northern Ontario that were too remote to be included in designated school divisions were to remain under local boards. These were to exist for public school purposes only. The minister promised that they would receive expanded service from the department, and would continue to receive special northern assistance and Northern Corps teachers where such action was warranted. Boards operating schools on Crown lands, in hospitals, and under other special circumstances would not be affected by the new scheme.

The boards were to have a more complete responsibility than previously in financial matters. They would be subject only to the Ontario Municipal Board with respect to capital expenditures. Tax bills for education would be distinct from those issued for other municipal services, and would indicate clearly the mill rates for public and secondary school purposes, the amount of tax in each case, and the total amount of tax for education. To avoid unnecessary duplication of expensive equipment and procedures, however, tax bills would continue to be calculated, printed, and issued by the municipalities concerned. The education taxes would be collected by the municipalities and transferred to the board.

Continuing earlier arrangements, each board operating one or more vocational schools or vocational programs in composite schools was to have an advisory vocational committee. Provision was made for similar committees where there were secondary schools using French for instructional purposes and where there were schools for trainable retarded children. These two new types of committees were to consist in part of members appointed by the board. In the case of the French-language advisory committees, the non-board members were to be elected at a meeting of the French-speaking ratepayers. The corresponding members of the advisory committee on schools for trainable retarded children were to be named by a local association affiliated with the Ontario Association for the Mentally Retarded.

The legislation did not establish the attendance areas of the schools, but left such matters in the hands of the boards. There was provision, however, to guarantee certain attendance rights. Where students had attended school before January 1 in a neighbouring county, they were to be permitted to continue to do so. Corresponding provisions were made for the administrative units in northern Ontario.

INITIAL REACTIONS

Initial reactions to the Robarts announcement appeared to be generally favourable. Attention was focused on the desirability of the ultimate objective, and few seemed to realize how difficult the period of transition might be. There were immediate negative reactions, however, from teachers' and trustees' organizations. One of their chief grounds for dissatisfaction was the lack of consultation over the specific plans for the reorganization. The Ontario Teachers' Federation sent a circular to its members containing the following statement.

> He [the Prime Minister] indicated that legislation to implement the plan by January 1, 1969 is in preparation to be presented to the next session of the Legislature. No previous consultation nor subsequent details have been afforded your Federation. Our only source of information to date has been the newspapers and the copy of the speech sent to each school.[9]

There was no question that the leading educational agencies outside the government had not been consulted about the immediate decision to proceed with legislation. Departmental spokesmen insisted, however, that there had been a great deal of broader and more general discussion about policy directions, and that no one who had been paying attention to what was being said need have been surprised. Some of the critics were not prepared to accept this explanation. Walter Pitman put the case as follows.

> The Premier announces it just a few weeks after an election, after a long campaign. We look in vain to the Minister for previous elucidation. I read over a very long and a very detailed and a very excellent account of all the things that The Department of Education was doing in the estimates of last session. I think that one could, indeed, regard this document as a definitive one of all the activities going on in the Minister's department, and in one of his announcements to this House, Mr. Speaker, he indicated that for the last two years his department had been preparing for this piece of legislation. Yet how much is there in that account of the direction in which we are going?

In reply to a question a few weeks ago, the Minister indicated that really the trustees knew that the larger units were coming and they were prepared for them. Well, from the howls that we have received from every corner of the province, the message has not gotten across and I think that communication, in the past, has not been one of the strong points of the Minister and I would suggest, in this particular case, that communication was not only lacking, it was non-existent.[10]

Davis gave his answer the following day by quoting from a brief of the Ontario School Trustees' Council presented to him in October 1967. It referred to the fact that he had indicated at the plenary session of the seminar on policies, purposes, and procedures on county and district educational development held in 1966 that legislation was being considered for the mandatory establishment of larger units of educational administration at the expiration of the first two years of operation of the county consultative committees. The brief expressed opposition to mandatory legislation at that time, and specifically suggested that it not be made effective until at least 1969. What had been done was in fact quite in accord with this resolution.[11] Thus there seemed very little justification for the reputed expressions of shock.

That these explanations were generally considered inadequate was quite obvious. An article in *School Progress* summarized the reactions as follows.

From a pile of Ontario-wide newspaper clippings of editorial comment and interviews with chairmen and superintendents, one sees the psychological "public relations" factor as most significant: opinion is not against the idea of amalgamation, but it *is* sorrowfully against the way it has been handled. The plan may meet opposition which is simply reflecting the irritation, especially of rural boards, of not being "let in" soon enough. Perhaps now some officials know how teachers feel when programs are implemented without full prior consultation and explanation.[12]

If circumstances had enabled Davis to follow his usual approach and consult the major agencies whose interests would be affected before a specific announcement had been made, there is no doubt that a great many misgivings would have been expressed. Under such circumstances, whatever decision followed would have involved overruling the wishes of important groups. Certain antagonism might thus have been intensified. On the other hand, the consultative approach fosters a feeling of partnership, and constitutes a form of recognition of the dignity and worth of those whose views are solicited. Nothing creates alienation so effectively as neglect. Davis's entire political career has demonstrated the keenest awareness of this principle. And, contrary to Pitman's assertion, communication has been one of his strongest points, and has been an important reason why so many potentially thorny problems have been resolved so smoothly.

The Ontario Teachers' Federation had some reservations about the nature of the proposal itself. These were specified in the letter of December 7 to the membership.

1 The Federation questions the advisability of having the new units established on a county basis. It is quite evident, as many studies have indicated, that the counties in many instances no longer are geographic, economic or sociological entities.
2 The Federation questions the further acceleration of consolidation in view of the rapid acceleration between the years 1960 (3,676 school boards) and 1967 (1,490 school boards). Although much consolidation has been accomplished as a result of legislation, many school boards and teachers have worked strenuously to make the consolidations successful.
3 The Federation questions the wisdom of the Premier proceeding with his proposed reorganization before receiving the report of the Committee chaired by Mr Justice Hall which is studying the aims and objectives of education in Ontario. The Federation feels any reorganization should be premised on the aims and objectives of education.
4 The Federation questions the preparation of legislation before the preparation of a white paper which it thinks should outline the reasons for and the details of the proposed reorganization so that all citizens of the province will have an opportunity to examine it and comment on it.
5 The Federation supports the establishment of larger units of administration for the reasons put forward by the Premier. It does feel, however, that any reorganization, locally or provincially, should be examined and discussed thoroughly in consultation with teachers in order to obtain their points of view before implementation.

The Ontario Teachers' Federation asked each of its affiliates to consider the effect of the proposal on the schools in which its members taught. Members were also urged to discuss the proposed plan with their member of the Legislative Assembly so that he would have the advantage of their views when the details of the legislation were being formulated.

The Ontario School Trustees' and Ratepayers' Association similarly questioned the selection of the county as the basic administrative unit. At a meeting on December 2, 1967, it authorized its president, Mrs H. Dorothy Smith, to comment as follows.

This Association acknowledges the need for larger areas of school administration organized as Boards of Education but has serious misgivings about defining areas exclusively along County boundaries, especially as applied to Southern Ontario.

Our investigations lead us to believe that further study is required before legislation is presented to the House.[18]

Misgivings about the choice of the counties as the new school board units centred mainly on 1 / their great range in population and 2 / the wide variety of social and economic interests that some of them included within their boundaries. In September 1968, for example, Haliburton County had a school enrolment to the end of grade 13 of approximately 2,100, and Dufferin and Prince Edward Counties each had between 5,000 and 5,500. Apart from those counties containing the cities of Hamilton, London, Ottawa, Metropolitan Toronto, and Windsor, several had an enrolment in the neighbourhood of 50,000. Waterloo County had a total of over 60,000. In terms of the average assessment per student, Renfrew had about $2,750 and Lambton about $9,600 in 1967–8. In these respects, of course, there were much greater extremes when the school divisions defined in the northern territorial districts were considered.

In defence of the selection of the counties as basic units, the minister reviewed some of the alternatives.

> One that was very definitely considered was to take the map of the province of Ontario and by a very technical analysis just completely redraft the whole structure of the province of Ontario to relate specifically to education, ignoring any municipal boundary lines. This was one approach, Mr. Speaker, that perhaps could have been taken ...
>
> The second approach ... was canvassed carefully, and that is that we use the existing district high school boundaries.[14]

He pointed out, however, that some of the district high school boundaries crossed county boundaries. On the other hand, the elementary school units, which involved the majority of the pupils, were almost without exception confined within county boundaries. It therefore seemed more reasonable to adjust the former to the latter, rather than the other way around.

The selection of the counties had at least a basis for support in the Liberal Party. Davis was able to point to their manifesto used in the election of 1967 in which the Liberals had said that they believed in boards of education, larger units of administration, and the use of the county system. It was a source of considerable satisfaction to point out to them that he felt they had been quite right.[15]

Naturally, much of the opposition resulted from purely local reactions based on specific situations. R.F. Ruston, member of the Legislature for Essex-Kent, reported the results of a meeting of the Essex County Trustees' and Ratepayers' Association. Instead of a single county unit, they recommended four combinations of township areas. They thought that these would be large enough for efficient administration, but small enough to keep down costs and to ensure local control.[16]

Some of the most substantial opposition was expressed in terms of fear that local participation in government was under serious threat. The

Simcoe Reformer published an editorial on July 12, 1968, entitled "County Boards of Education," which contained these paragraphs:

Eventually the County Boards will become Regional Boards with the source of their brainpower and their high-salaried experts in Queen's Park. Local autonomy will become a relic of the past both in educational matters and in the whole range of civic administration.

How the Robarts Government expects to foist this incongruous scheme onto the people of Ontario without courting widespread protest and infinite trouble is more than we can understand. In case of the county school boards plan, Hon. William Davis, the Minister of Education, offers only the one alibi for the new scheme, namely, "that all pupils should have equal opportunity in our school system." Just where do some pupils in Norfolk County's excellent system of public and high schools lack "equal opportunity"? We have yet to hear a sound answer to that question.

Presumably nothing can stop wiseacres at Queen's Park, now that they have embarked on the great scheme of wiping out local autonomy and substituting Queen's Park bureaucracy in all phases of Ontario's administration. Our prediction is that a continuance and enlargement of their present course of action can succeed in bringing down the Conservative administration at Queen's Park, after its long tenure of office, more quickly than could any political ploy by the combined Opposition in the Ontario Legislature.

Near the end of 1967, the Ontario Public School Trustees' Association conducted a survey through its periodical, the *Argus*, to determine the reaction of its 337 member boards to the reorganization plan. Since only fifty-two boards, or a mere 15.4 per cent of the total, responded, the answers might ordinarily be regarded as having very little significance. But these answers are of interest because of the overwhelming trend that was demonstrated. Almost half the boards claimed to be in favour of the principle of larger units of administration. In rather striking contrast, forty-seven, or approximately 90 per cent, were opposed to the idea of county or district boards of education as proposed by the Ontario government. A cynic might observe that it was hardly to be expected that trustees would show an overwhelming enthusiasm for the imminent loss of their own positions. Their traditional attitude had had a good deal to do with the government's resort to mandatory amalgamation.

FINANCIAL IMPLICATIONS OF THE PLAN

The government never made any claim that the new scheme was designed to save money. It acknowledged from the beginning that the provision of a higher level of service would be expensive. Months before the official announcement, Davis said:

I suggest that if the leader of the Opposition feels that we are going to solve the great financial problems involved through consolidation, he should look very carefully at his figures, because while educationally I see great advantages in moving towards integration of elementary and secondary under boards of education, I must warn him that I question whether this in fact will have substantial savings, as far as the investment in education is concerned.[17]

Nixon seemed quite aware of these realities when he spoke of the government's plan nearly a year later. He noted that many of the more expensive services for education were going to be revised, not toward the average, but toward the highest level. Such would certainly be the case as far as teachers' salaries were concerned; it would also be true of kindergartens, which were not currently available in rural areas. People in some communities had been prepared to accept a reduction in bus service as an economy measure, but could hardly be expected to do so when the costs were going to be spread over a large area, including any urban centres contained in the county. There would also be additional expenses for supervision necessitated by larger and more complex organizations. This was what equality of opportunity was all about.[18]

The government's policy, as explained in chapter 8 of the present volume, was to move in regular steps toward the assumption of 60 per cent of the actual cost of education. The Liberals, apparently willing to take their chances on devising means of raising more funds at the provincial level, declared that the percentage should be 80. Apart from the optimum distribution of costs, it is evident that there was a great deal of uncertainty about what the total bill would be, and how it would affect individuals and groups in different parts of the province. Critics said there should have been more careful and thorough prior planning in this respect. There is of course a possibility that substantial benefits would have resulted from such a course of action. But when account is taken of all the intangibles in a complex situation, including the changes of attitude to be expected when people are confronted with drastic organizational changes, the planning process can be very inexact. The hope must be that planning will help, but it cannot be expected to perform miracles. It has one other serious limitation: while it may indicate the need for funds, it is not of much help in raising them. Although there will always be a question as to whether the government would have held up its legislation on the basis of any total cost estimate that the planners might have provided, it does not at this point appear that such a course of action would have been taken.

IMPLICATIONS FOR VARIOUS GROUPS

Elected officials

The new boards of education were certain to be regarded as bodies of some political importance, wielding considerable economic and civic power. Among the very large number of trustees of former boards that were scheduled to disappear, there were numbers of ambitious candidates for the new positions. There were, however, certain factors that tended to discourage some of the most experienced and capable among them. Some would be unwilling or unable to travel the considerable distances involved to attend board meetings, which would be very numerous during the first few months. Also, legislation specified that no trustee could be connected with firms doing business with a board. This restriction was of no great consequence when it was limited to a township, but there were much more serious implications when the principle was extended to an entire county. There had also been many dedicated and effective trustees who had previously served in appointive positions. Some of these were not prepared to face the struggle to try to secure elective office.

Appointed officials

School Administration reported that the imminent arrival of the new legislation had bred "suspicion, fear and general frustration" among professional administrators (as well as trustees) throughout the province.[19] The administrators and their staffs had a nagging fear that they might not have jobs on January 1, 1969. Some may have had doubts that they were really capable of handling positions of greater responsibility. Others were apprehensive, in some cases with good reason, that personal influence and other such factors would carry an undue amount of weight, and that real worth provided no absolute assurance of recognition. Sincere idealism is often manifested among those responsible for carrying out the educational enterprise, but raw greed and selfish ambition are also often close to the surface. Since local administrators were not a direct responsibility of the department, there was no move to guarantee security of tenure, even for a transitional period, comparable to the arrangements made for teachers' college staff moving into universities. In any case, it is hardly reasonable to attempt to provide job security for administrators in the same way as for teachers. Leadership, by its nature, must be constantly on trial.

Teachers

In many respects, the new organization gave members of the teaching profession reasons for a very favourable reaction. They could not but be enthusiastic about the prospect of raising the level of educational opportunity in less prosperous areas. The promise of better facilities and of more programs to meet specialized needs represented the attainment of goals which they had long supported. In terms of their own personal interests, there would be more opportunities to follow specialized lines of professional development. Substantial gains in job satisfaction might be expected.

The teachers have always tended to weigh the prospects for successful salary negotiations in appraising the consequences of the formation of larger administrative units. Although it is possible to argue persuasively that salaries are in the long run largely determined by supply and demand, the teachers' federations have influenced the process in two major respects. 1 / They have kept salaries advancing somewhat more quickly than economic conditions, acting alone, would have dictated, thus ensuring that teacher scarcity would not reach a real disaster point before financial rewards responded, and 2 / they have exerted continuous pressure to keep minimum acceptable qualifications as high as possible to ensure that, in the periods of disequilibrium which have been chronic since the Second World War, it is the salary ceiling that rises and not the quality of teaching that falls. The standard tactic has been to play one board against another, an approach that will work only if the system contains a reasonable number of competing boards. There has been apprehension lest the process of amalgamation go far enough to confront the profession with a monolith differing little in its effects from a single agency with the responsibility of fixing salaries.

There were other reasons for apprehension. These were not, of course, related to retirement benefits, since they were entirely a provincial and federal matter. But there were some aspects of job security and satisfaction that were gained through years of service to a particular board. With the abolition of such a board, assurances were needed that the rights won by service there would not be swept away. Of particular interest was the question whether or not a teacher could be transferred arbitrarily from one end of a county to another. When the administrative units had been small, a transfer had not meant uprooting the teacher from his established home and community. But under the new circumstances the prospects looked quite different.

The real basis for apprehension was the fear that narrow-minded, petty, or irresponsible board members might seize the opportunity to banish an unpopular teacher to a remote part of the county, regardless of the welfare of the pupils, to say nothing of the teacher's wishes. Even the threat of such action might be used to restrict professional freedom to speak openly and frankly or to depart in any way, however healthy, from the conventional modes of behaviour prevalent in a community. At worst, the threat to the integrity of the profession could be as serious as that of arbitrary dismissal.

Robert Nixon dealt with this issue in the Legislature.

> It is possible, as has happened in the past, that the boards, rather than taking a straightforward means of disciplining a teacher or even accomplishing dismissal, will order his transference to another location for teaching which would be tantamount, I suppose, in many cases to the teacher voluntarily withdrawing from employment. I am not saying that this would happen fre-

quently. The Ontario teachers' federation has seen fit to put before the Minister, but not before the standing committee as yet, evidence that it has happened in the past in the township school areas.

No one believes that a competent board would do this, but surely any irresponsible action of this type would be a very serious matter indeed.[20]

Davis responded that he shared some of the views of the leader of the opposition, but yet he also recognized certain problems presented to him by the Trustees' Council. While he was not prepared to change the bill to meet the situation, he hoped for further discussions during the summer and in the early fall. The difficulties might be straightened out before any transfers came into force in the fall of 1969. Representatives of the Ontario Teachers' Federation and of the Ontario School Trustees' Council had been notified that Davis was prepared to meet them in the next few weeks.[21]

During the discussions of the next few months, the federation pressed for the establishment of transfer review boards, which would operate regionally. It was suggested at one stage that the departmental regional directors of education have the responsibility of naming the chairmen of these boards. Certain people felt that the minister himself should perform this duty. The Ontario School Trustees' Council was opposed to having the boards set up at all, asserting that there was no need for them. In fact, perhaps in part, at least, because of the extent to which the issue was publicized, relations were very satisfactory during the first full year (1969–70) under the new boards. Whether there would be a need for conciliation machinery in the future was impossible to foresee.

The department did make one change that was intended to protect teachers against transfers without warning. The standard contract for permanent teaching staff was amended to provide that a teacher who was to be transferred from one municipality to another must be notified of the decision by May 1 preceding the school year when the transfer was to take effect. No such notice was required for transfers from school to school within a municipality. The federation was not at all enthusiastic about this provision, taking the view that it was an inadequate substitute for real protection.

INTERIM SCHOOL ORGANIZATION COMMITTEES

The so-called guidelines distributed in early February of 1968 recommended the establishment by each county council of an interim school organization committee to help prepare the way for the county unit. The membership of the committee was to be drawn from the existing school boards which were partly or wholly located within the new unit, and would consist of one representative from each public school board, high school board, and board of education. The committee was entitled to establish *ad hoc* or other subcommittees to perform specific tasks according to need.

These might be composed of other trustees, officials, teachers, or parents.

The interim school organization committee was to prepare a comprehensive report providing information about the existing school systems to be administered by the new board. This report was intended to serve as an orientation document on which the trustees to be elected for 1969 might base initial decisions and long-range planning. It was also to constitute "an operational guide for administrative and supervisory activities in order to facilitate the smooth transition of essential services."

The following aspects of the organization of each existing board were to be considered.

(1) *Summary of Statements of Board Policies*
general conditions of employment such as salary schedules, sick leave, insurance, educational leave, etc.; after-hours use of school buildings; provision of special education; transportation of pupils; provision of kindergarten classes; extra-curricular activities.

(2) *Summary of Statements of Procedure*
establishing home instruction; preparation of the budget; board meeting procedures; tendering for supplies and equipment, etc.

(3) *Statements of Program Description and Special Services*
Public Schools
- Special Education; Music; Art; Home Economics and Industrial Arts; Physical Education; Rotary System; Library; Audio-Visual Services; Unit System or Non-Graded Program; Other

Secondary Schools
- Arts and Science; Business and Commerce; Science, Technology and Trades; Occupations; Special Education; Library; Audio-Visual Services; Individual Time-Tabling; Other

Special Services
- Psychologist; Guidance; Consultants; Health Services; Other

(4) *Personnel Lists*
A complete directory of supervisory officers, all teaching and other professional personnel, and part-time and supply teachers, as of September, 1968, including type of certificate, years of experience, type of contract and actual salary.
A complete directory of all non-teaching personnel as of September, 1968, including salary and experience:
- secretaries of school boards
- clerical staff working with school board secretaries
- caretakers
- school attendance counsellors
- secretaries of schools
- miscellaneous personnel not included above.

(5) *List of Salaries, Payrolls, Deductions*
A complete payroll list applicable for January, 1969, showing detailed

breakdown for deductions, etc., for all teaching and professional personnel, and all non-teaching personnel; dates of regular salary payments.

(6) *Accommodation*
List of all open schools by boards; location; number of classrooms; special facilities such as library, general purpose room, gymnasium, auditorium, shops, special classes, offices, classrooms not in use, details of heating, water supply, sewage disposal; list of closed schools with similar details; list of schools and additions to schools under construction or planned, with details of accommodation.

(7) *Pupils*
Enrolment of pupils by schools, grades, courses, special classes; non-resident pupils, enrolment projections.

(8) *Pupil Transportation*
List of transportation routes by boards, indicating destination of route, board-owned or contract, contractors, board-employed drivers, number of pupils transported and total daily mileage, contract price where applicable, total approved cost for grant purposes, maps of routes; list of board-owned vehicles with appropriate description.

(9) *Finance*
Current budget of each board; copies of annual financial reports for 1967; estimated expenditures as of December 31, 1968; estimated cash balance as of December 31, 1968; list of insurance policies with pertinent details; contracts and agreements; details of debenture payments; interim financial arrangements concerning building projects.[22]

From its compilation of this material, the committee was to identify problems and outline a series of priorities for the new board to consider.

There were many variations in the way the committees went at their tasks, since they faced a wide variety of circumstances. The following points were made by the chairman of one such committee in presenting its recommendations to the newly elected board in December 1968: 1 / The Davies-Brickell system should become a major element in the structure and business of the new board. Under it, the board could concentrate on its major role of policy formation, leaving administrative duties to the administrators. 2 / To encourage the board in its policy-making and legislative role, standing committees should be virtually, if not entirely, non-existent, with *ad hoc* committees for specific problems being substituted. 3 / The new post of director of education was among the priority items. While the board had to consider the immediate hiring of a strong director, the chairman felt that the decision was so vital that he hoped it would not be made with undue haste. 4 / There were so many changes occurring, and such a relative lack of awareness or, if the voter turnout was any indication, of concern about educational matters that the chairman hoped that a public relations office would soon be established. 5 / A problem of increasing complexity and importance constantly confronting boards everywhere was that of teacher work load. It was suggested that a committee of teachers and trustees look into the hiring of a firm to study this matter thoroughly.

Some of the committees did a great deal of thorough and competent work. In many cases, the reports they presented to the new boards were very important, even vital documents. They tended to be of the greatest value in areas where the new board replaced a number of small ones, with no single one of the latter particularly standing out. Conversely, they received the least attention in areas where small units surrounded a single large urban centre. In such cases, amalgamation tended to be a takeover process, whereby the urban organization was modified and adapted to absorb the additional units. The director of education in one such area characterized the activities of the local committee as "busywork." He conceded that this work had value in giving a large number of officials a feeling that they were making a worthwhile contribution during the transitional period. He did not, however, know of any occasion when the report was consulted for an important purpose.

PROBLEMS OF IMPLEMENTATION IN PARTICULAR AREAS

With the government's decision to accept existing county boundaries, rather than to attempt to juggle innumerable factors in order to produce something like the "community of interest" recommended by the Royal Commission in 1950, it was inevitable that there would be many local anomalies. In response to a message from the minister on January 29, 1968, inviting comments from trustees, teachers, and other interested groups, a number of briefs drew attention to some of these anomalies in the hope that plans existing at the time might be sufficiently flexible to permit them to be eliminated.

Westminster Township shared its largest common boundary with the city of London, and its inhabitants had major social and economic ties with the city. They relied on it entirely for the secondary education of their young people, who were scattered through London schools. Rather than disrupt this pattern, the public school board of the township suggested that it would be desirable if its three elementary schools could be transferred to the control of the London Board of Education. Such a step might also avoid future dislocation, since it appeared probable that London would be expanding in the future to absorb the township.[23]

A similar situation existed in the township of Ameliasburgh. A letter from the council requested that the township be excluded from the Prince Edward County school area and attached instead to the same administrative unit as the city of Belleville. The reasons were largely based on geographical factors. 1 / The township adjoined Belleville, and was very close to Trenton, and its built-up areas were largely suburban sections of both cities. No part of the township had a similar connection with any town or village in Prince Edward County. 2 / Most students of the township had long received their secondary school education in Belleville. 3 / The township had been included in 1951 in the Bay of Quinte District High School Board, which had included Belleville, and still remained a member. 4 / Since the formation of that unit, the public school courses had been designed for students passing into the Bay of Quinte district high school system. 5 / The only secondary school in Prince Edward County was in the relatively remote town of Picton. 6 / School bus routes out of Picton were very lengthy, requiring some students to spend as much as three hours a day in transit. The problem was compounded by the fact that Picton was in the "snow belt." 7 / Ameliasburgh was as close to Belleville and Trenton in terms of other conveniences as it was remote from Picton. A telephone call to Picton involved long distance charges. A variety of other arguments were offered. Among the most telling, perhaps, was that the secondary schools of Belleville had enough accommodation for the immediate future, while Picton did not.[24]

A group of citizens of Kingston and the surrounding townships expressed themselves in favour in principle of the objectives of the proposed plan. In particular, they applauded the goal of improving the educational opportunities of all children within the proposed area. But they were equally strongly opposed to the achievement of such equality by the reduction of standards then existing in any part of the proposed area. The problem as they saw it centred around the shape of Frontenac County and the distribution and character of its population. Like its two neighbours to the west, the county was long and narrow, and very sparsely settled in the area to the north. The problems that had to be overcome in the northern halves of all three counties seemed to bear a close resemblance to those existing in northern Ontario, which were to be dealt with by means of special measures of reorganization. The group therefore suggested that the northern part of Frontenac County, together with similar parts of adjoining counties, be grouped into a special administrative unit of the type proposed for northern Ontario. There would be several advantages for this area. 1 / It would have better representation than that provided by the plan currently contemplated. 2 / Administration would be more efficient in a relatively homogeneous area. 3 / It would be easier to provide for equality of educational opportunity (presumably because of the extra infusion of provincial funds).[25]

The Mayor of the city of Cornwall pointed to unusually heavy financial burdens in 1968 resulting from 1 / the influx into the publicly maintained school system of three hundred students who had previously attended private schools, and 2 / an unusually high rate of unemployment, resulting in extra welfare costs. The mill rate had reached a point where the quest for new industrial assessment was being detrimentally affected. Along with special relief measures, he suggested that the Department of Education give consideration to permitting the secondary school board to join with those of four of the neighbouring townships, Osnabruck, Cornwall,

Charlottenburg, and Lancaster, to form a regional board, leaving the balance of the counties of Stormont, Dundas, and Glengarry to form their own county secondary school boards.[26] Such a measure would have made a maximum contribution to Cornwall's tax base in relation to its educational obligations.

The Peace Bridge District Board of Education drew attention to the wide disparity in sizes of boards under the proposed system. On the basis of taxable assessment and enrolment, the Peace Bridge district board was said to be larger than eight of the thirty-eight proposed county boards, while the proposed Welland County board that would absorb it under the existing plan would have forty-five times the taxable assessment and twenty-five times the enrolment of the proposed Haliburton board. It seemed difficult to understand how the Peace Bridge district board could be considered too small to offer equal educational opportunities under such circumstances. While the board approved the goal of the legislation in providing equal opportunity, it strongly opposed the scheme as outlined.[27]

The Tillsonburg District High School Board faced the prospect of fragmentation, with many of the students having to attend schools in more distant places. Administration of all school affairs would be centred in Woodstock, Simcoe, and St Thomas. A local group therefore proposed the formation of a special area that would recognize the natural routes of travel, trade, and recreation that were considered in the formation of the existing high school district. The case was supported by the municipal council of the town of Tillsonburg, the Tillsonburg District High School Board, and the Tillsonburg Public School Board.[28]

The board of the Kirkland Lake district school area submitted a resolution relating to a proposed distinction between the county units and those in the territorial districts. Whereas the entire county area was to be included in the former, only the organized municipalities and established school sections were to constitute the school division in the latter, thus excluding "vast sources of residential and commercial assessment." The board petitioned the Legislative Assembly to include all of the territorial districts in one or more of the designated school divisions.[29] The basic problem in meeting this request was that, where there was no council or school board, there was no way of providing for elections in the unorganized areas. Once the divisional boards were formed, it was the government's intention to have their areas extended to take in much of this territory.

During the committee stage and in the debate on the bill, the opposition members concentrated considerable effort on trying to persuade the minister to allow himself greater flexibility by providing for ministerial discretion 1 / to modify county boundaries to correct the most obvious anomalies and 2 / to provide for more than one unit, where conditions seemed to demand it, within a single county.[30] He declined to accept the amendment to give himself these powers, declaring that he wanted to allow the scheme as presented a trial for at least two years. This was basically the answer he gave to delegations seeking some special arrangement. It enabled him to combine firmness with his predilection for avoiding a flat negative answer. His opposition critics accused him of seeking a way to hold the Legislature responsible for his refusal to consider any adjustments in boundaries. Robert Nixon said, "It is his responsibility to ask for the power and to wield it in the efforts to get away from the main thing that is wrong with the bill as it is before us now, that is, the inflexibility of the old county boundaries." Walter Pitman suggested that the minister was being forced to cling to the county boundaries, not because they were educationally viable, but because the government had not yet decided what it wanted to do about regional government, and was hanging on to the county as the building block.

Some of the difficulties arose out of tentative provisions of the legislation that had nothing to do with boundaries. The boards of education for the towns of Bracebridge, Gravenhurst, and Huntsville had some apprehensions to express over the possibility that the clerks of the three municipalities with the greatest equalized residential and farm assessment for public school purposes would determine the municipality or municipalities and school sections to be included in each area for which a trustee or trustees were to be elected. Largely because their assessment included many properties owned by the summer or seasonal population, who had little interest in education, the three municipalities answering this description were Medora and Wood, Muskoka, and Monck Townships. But, although among them they had 44 per cent of the assessment, they had only 17 per cent of the year-round residents. On the other hand, the towns of Bracebridge, Gravenhurst, and Huntsville, with a smaller proportion of the assessment, had about 40 per cent of the year-round resident population. The three boards in question recommended that the clerks of the three municipalities with the greatest school population, both elementary and secondary, be added to the three clerks of the municipalities with the greatest equalized residential and farm assessment for public school purposes, and that the committee of six clerks determine the representation from the district. In this way they hoped to have adequate representation from those elements of the population who might be expected to have the greatest interest in providing a superior school system.[31]

The same brief pointed out what was seen as another representation problem. There was only one separate school section in operation in the entire area with less than half of one per cent of the total of the residential and farm assessment in the district. The need for representation from this school section on the Muskoka School Division Board of Education was questioned.

The city of Peterborough also had problems of representation produced in part by the large number of cottage properties in certain parts of the county. As the plan worked out, there were to be seven members on the new board from the city and seven from the county. The city council pointed out that, had membership been on a population basis, the city would have been entitled to ten members and the county four. On the basis of total equalized taxable assessment, the respective numbers would have been nine and five. On the basis of equalized residential and farm assessment for both public and separate school supporters, the respective numbers would have been eight and six. In 1965 official figures had shown that 31.33 per cent of the total assessment of Peterborough county was for residential cottages, and it was suggested that this percentage had probably grown to 40 per cent by 1968. If the cottage assessment were eliminated, the city would get nine representatives and the county five. The cottagers' right to vote was apparently not going to be much use to them in any case, since all school board elections throughout the province were to be held on the same day, and most of the cottagers could not cast votes in both areas where they had residences.[32]

The government was reluctant to use population as the basis for representation on the boards largely because it would have been too difficult to distinguish between public and separate school supporters. To have used undifferentiated population would have produced greater anomalies in some parts of the province than the use of residential and farm assessment in cottage areas. To have used the total residential and farm assessment of public and separate school supporters would have meant that such assessment for the latter group would have been used twice, once to determine public school representatives from the total residential and farm assessment and again in determining separate school representation. If total assessment had been used rather than residential and farm assessment, it would have imposed a severe penalty on dormitory communities.

The township of O'Connor in the Lakehead area had a complaint opposite to that voiced in the Muskoka towns and Peterborough. According to the plan, the Lakehead school division would give Port Arthur and Fort William each six members, the separate school supporters three members, and all other boards in the area three members. The O'Connor council did not feel that this arrangement would provide for sufficient representatives with a knowledge of the operation of rural schools. It urged that a new formula be devised that would take into account the size of the area involved and the number of boards to be amalgamated. Not at all restrained in its demands, the council asked for equal representation between the rural areas and the two cities combined, needless to say without success.[33]

There were complaints from a number of municipalities about the extra costs of elections during an "off year" when municipal councils were not involved. Requests were made to the Department of Education to make special grants to cover these costs. No positive response was forthcoming, at least in part because there appeared to be no way of making an accurate estimate of the costs. There were also objections to the fact that Bill 44, establishing the new boards of education, required the election of boards in 1968 and every second year thereafter. Where the election of municipal councils occurred in alternate years, the two would never coincide. There were strong demands to have this irregularity corrected.

Conferences on larger units

The Ontario School Trustees' Council, the Ontario Institute for Studies in Education, and the Department of Education combined their efforts during the latter part of 1969 to sponsor a series of conferences for trustees, officials, and other interested individuals. The purpose was to help to familiarize them with some of the details of the school district reorganization. Different programs were presented, ranging from discussions of theoretical issues to a treatment of a number of very practical problems. Evaluation of the participants' responses revealed a marked preference for the latter. After the election of the new boards in December, three-day regional conferences were organized by the same three agencies. In these, an attempt was made to assist trustees in their new role, to enable them to identify opportunities for the introduction of new programs, and to help them to provide effective educational leadership. The program of the conferences was handled by experienced trustees, academic and business officials, and representatives of the sponsoring bodies.

Voter response in the elections of 1968

Although there may have been keen interest in the elections on the part of those aspiring to be trustees, the eligible voters showed very little interest in participating in the process. Only about 12 per cent were said to have turned out in the county divisions around Metropolitan Toronto. The *Toronto Daily Star* gave Oakville as an example of voter apathy. At some polls there, no votes were cast, and the 10 per cent overall turnout was the lowest in the town's electoral history.[34] The fact that 1968 was not the regular year for municipal elections was offered as an explanation, but could hardly be regarded as a justification. In view of the great concern being shown by the public over the rising costs of education, it is hard to escape the conclusion that most voters felt themselves helpless to influence the course of events through the school board machinery. The virtues of having the control of education close to the people seemed well on the way to being lost.

SALARIES OF ADMINISTRATORS

Perhaps no issue did more to focus attention on the high costs of the county board system than that of the salaries paid to the newly-appointed directors of education, superintendents, and other officials. Some opposition had been registered on the part of Metropolitan Toronto School Board members to the proposal to pay their director of education $35,000 a year. But in view of the size of the system for which he was responsible, such a salary seemed eminently reasonable in comparison with those of only a few thousand dollars less being offered in county divisions both large and small.

An article in the *Galt Evening Reporter* on March 15, 1969, entitled "Control is Mandatory on Educational Costs," observed:

> If Ontario's Education Minister William Davis, who also holds the role of minister of university affairs, should decide to resign and seek a school superintendent's appointment, the situation would be most understandable.
>
> The transition would provide him with fewer administrative headaches ... and $2,000 more in pay, coupled with longer holidays than he is currently enjoying.

The article referred to the salary of $28,000 a year that a certain county separate school board had agreed to pay its new superintendent. It continued:

> It is fully understandable why there is no dearth of application[s] for key roles in school administration. The two board assistant superintendents for the county separate school board are also in the top pay echelon as they have been offered $21,000.
>
> Following down the financial scale the business administrator receives $15,000, finance controller $12,000, controller of building and maintenance $11,000 and purchasing and transportation supervisor $11,000.

Attention was called to the fact that only a fractional percentage of those who paid the bills were earning salaries within a comparable range. The article ended with an appeal for guidelines and a system of county maximum salaries.

The justification frequently advanced for the high salaries offered was that there was competition for those best qualified for the positions. In some places this claim was perhaps true. There were systems that adopted the policy of seeking fresh points of view and new infusions of talent from outside. But others were partly or completely staffed with officials whose entire previous experience had been in former school divisions of the same county. The new director of education had quite likely been the chief officer of the largest of the component boards. It was difficult to believe that he and his immediate subordinates would have declined positions under the new arrangement had they been offered lesser salary increases. However, once a few boards had established the new salary pattern, others felt pressured to follow suit. Some trustees did not want their boards to appear cheap. There was occasional talk of rewarding "good old Joe," who had only a few more years until retirement. Although the salaries of administrators appeared very high, there were comparatively few individuals involved, and the total was only a small proportion of the entire budget. Thus that item alone did not increase the burden on the taxpayer to any great extent. This kind of reasoning of course ignored the psychological effect of what seemed to be a reckless squandering of the taxpayers' money. When that reaction became evident, the boards often did not hesitate to blame the provincial government.

Davis was not at all pleased about the high salaries. He pointed out, however, that the boards had acted on their own initiative. As he explained in the Legislature, grants were paid on the basis of $900 a month times the number of months the senior administrators were employed, with a maximum of $10,800. A board that received a grant at the rate of 50 per cent would thus get $5,400, and had to raise all the rest by local levies.[35]

When very high salaries are paid only to a few of the most prestigious administrators in the province, there is comparatively little effect on professional priorities. The situation is quite different when such a salary level becomes established for administrators in general. The pressures become almost irresistible for energetic and ambitious teachers, seeking all the accolades our society bestows along with income, to aspire to be administrators, and to compete actively for administrative positions. Those who do not succeed, and remain "mere" teachers, judge themselves, if they are not openly judged by others, to be failures. The effect on teaching is inevitably demeaning. It is a fact of human relations that those in command cannot be exalted without debasing their subordinates. It is pure hypocrisy to speak of the supreme importance of the teacher in the classroom, while at the same time bestowing disproportionate rewards on those whose only defensible role is to facilitate the educative process. And if very large salary differentials are established on the assumption that administration requires a rare combination of talents and skills while classroom teaching is within the capacity of almost anyone, it is indeed time that our educational values received the most careful scrutiny.

The effects of an imbalance in the reward system is creating other serious problems in Ontario. The teachers' colleges, for example, are complaining of losing some of their most valued staff members, not because they are apprehensive about their ability to hold their own under the auspices of the universities, but because they cannot resist the lure of administrative positions. The government is unable to counter the competition, in part because to attempt to do so would arouse further complaints among university faculty members that their prospective new colleagues are already overpaid in terms of their academic qualifications as judged according to university criteria. To try to solve the problem by attempting to bring all university salaries into line, not with the current salaries of teachers' college staff, but with those that would be needed to enable them to compete on equal terms with school systems, would certainly be more than the taxpaying public would tolerate.

Not least among the sufferers is the Department of Education itself. As has been true of so much of the period since the Second World War, its attempt to attract and hold the most capable people has been adversely affected by the very policies it has successfully generated. Some of its leading officials are no doubt attracted by the idea of working near the centre of power. Others who arrived in earlier years are held by sheer inertia. Many more are so motivated by devotion to their work, often rooted in a commitment maintained continuously over a period of many years, that they are prepared to persevere despite financial handicaps. But ultimately the quality of the system is bound to suffer if a reasonable share of the most outstanding recruits cannot be attracted to the central policy-making positions. Even a highly decentralized system cannot function effectively if the departmental staff is reduced to mediocrity.

THE FINANCIAL SITUATION ENCOUNTERED BY THE NEW BOARDS IN 1969

As soon as the new boards began to assess their needs and resources in 1969, it began to be obvious that many areas faced the prospect of substantial tax increases. Long before the exact situation became known, loud protests were heard. Many of these had a factual basis, while others represented pure speculation.

An example of the alarmist type of reaction was an article in the *Globe and Mail* on April 26, 1969. Written by Thomas Claridge, it was headlined "It could cost province more than $50-million to prevent school tax rebellion." Although its estimate of the extra amount that would be needed for legislative grants was not far off the mark, the prediction that Charles MacNaughton's first balanced budget would be a victim turned out to be inaccurate. Circumstances in certain trouble spots were cited to show how serious the situation appeared to be. The warden of traditionally Conservative Dufferin County was said to have suggested the possibility of a tax strike on the part of farmers who could not raise the sort of taxes being demanded. They could quite legally withhold tax payments for a period up to three years before confiscatory action could be taken. If they resorted to such a tactic *en masse*, the municipalities would be bankrupted. The upper limits on their borrowing powers would prevent them from meeting the crisis by taking out loans. Another example of a community in crisis, according to the article, was the village of Shelburne, which had initially been asked by the Dufferin board to raise $155,755 instead of the $62,714 levied in 1968. An increase of these proportions was of course prevented by government action, as explained later.

Even as late as April 24, 1969, the situation remained in many respects obscure, as Davis explained in the Legislature.[36] Because of the great number of former boards, it had not yet been possible in many cases to secure audited financial statements for the previous year's operations. Thus it had been difficult for the new boards to know the costs of the

1968 operations as a basis for determining the increase for 1969. The need to secure other information relating to the proportion of costs among the municipalities, the applicable equalizing factors, the apportionment of local levies, and the establishment of mill rates had all taken more time and effort in the initial year of operation than would be the case in later years. In order to appraise the situation, the department was collecting information from the new school boards through the regional directors of education regarding costs of education in the former units, estimated increases in 1969, budgets for 1969, calculated grants, and local levies.

Davis indicated a certain lack of responsibility on the part of some of the boards that had faced the prospect of extinction at the end of 1968. They reduced the mill rate, spent any surplus left over at the end of 1967, and entered the new administrative set-up either without any balance or, "in quite a number of cases," with a considerable deficit. Funds were spent that, under former conditions, would have been carried forward to the next year. While Davis felt that such expenditure did not represent waste, he suggested that it would have been better to wait until the county board had had a chance to plan on an over-all basis. It was evident that, where the 1967 mill rate had been reduced in 1968, any increase in 1969 would have to be considered in relation to that in the former year.

Davis dealt with some of the accusations that many difficulties could have been dealt with by better prior planning. He said that it would have been impossible to determine in advance some of the possible outcomes in particular areas in the application of the proportion of local levies to mill rates. It was "utter nonsense" to suggest that the results in certain areas could have been foreseen if computers had been utilized, since computers were helpful only to the extent that the data provided and fed into them were accurate and relevant to the cases with which they dealt. The information necessary to meet the situation had not been available and could not have been made available at the time.

Although the information assembled by the department was, as he had indicated, far from complete, certain conclusions were being drawn. It was evident on the one hand that there were many municipalities in almost every administrative division where the increase in the local mill rate was modest and, under existing conditions, quite manageable. For others, however, the impact of reallocation among the municipalities and the assumption of the share of the increased normal costs would create too sharp a rise in 1969. To meet this situation, the government was providing a special grant for any municipality having a population of less than 60,000 to limit the increase in mill rate on provincial equalized assessment to one mill for elementary school purposes and one mill for secondary school purposes over the greater of the 1967 and 1968 mill rates. It was to apply to an expenditure per pupil for 1969 up to 115 per cent of that for the previous year. This limitation was intended to provide an incentive for the boards to try to keep their costs within reasonable bounds.

The department was prepared to assist the boards in their budget review to explore possible methods of bringing about reductions in cost.

The effect of limiting the increase to one mill of provincial equalized assessment would vary from one municipality to another in terms of local mill rates but, on the average, the increase in these latter would probably range from two to five mills. Thus the department would pay a subsidy to the board for the portion of the levy in a municipality above the one mill of provincial equalized assessment or above the three to five mills on local assessment.

There was another anomalous situation requiring a special adjustment. In the territorial districts there were secondary school students now included in the new, larger units for whom the government had formerly met the full costs of education. The proportion of the costs for these students to be borne by local authorities was not offset by a corresponding assessment, with the result that there was an increased liability for the boards and their constituent municipalities. Arrangements were made accordingly whereby the financial burden assumed by the new boards for these students would be entirely compensated for by provincial grants.

Davis announced that it was the intention of the Treasury Department to accelerate the instalment payments on grants to the school boards during 1969. This action would provide them with operating funds and with consequent savings in interest charges. This and the other changes he had announced represented a conscious and deliberate acceleration in the movement toward the assumption by the province of 60 per cent on the average of the total cost of education at the local level. It had been the intention of the government to start this movement in the fiscal year 1970–1 and complete it in 1972–3, but an earlier beginning was now obviously warranted.

SCHOOL BOARD ADVISORY COMMITTEES

Part of Bill 241, an act to amend *The Schools Administration Act*, which was passed in December 1969, authorized boards of education to establish school board advisory committees. These were seen as a device to help keep the new boards in close touch with certain developments in the areas under their control, and as a means of providing a regular channel through which complaints might be heard. Each committee was to consist of three members of the board appointed by the board; the chief education officer of the board or his nominee; six teachers employed by the board, appointed by the teachers in the employ of the board; and four appointees of the board who were neither teachers nor members of the board but who resided within the area under the board's jurisdiction. There was also provision, under specified conditions, for representation of the Federation of Catholic Parent-Teacher Associations of Ontario and of the local Home and School council. The basic function of an advisory committee was to make reports and recommendations to the board on any educational matter pertaining to the schools under the jurisdiction of the board, except salaries of employees and personnel problems and policies.

Some misgivings were expressed over the fact that the establishment of a school board advisory committee was permissive rather than mandatory. It seemed possible that the very boards that appeared to be least sensitive to the desires of parents or teachers might be the most reluctant to establish liaison machinery. After a trial period, it may prove necessary to change the conditions for the establishment of the committees. Much will depend on how effective those established initially prove to be.

REPERCUSSIONS FOR THE MINISTER

Toward the end of 1969, when all the information was in, the minister announced that the extra amount in legislative grants required to meet provincial commitments for the year would be $48.4 million. Robert Nixon based his criticism on this argument: "I think it is generally understood that this is the cost not of implementing county school boards, but the cost of the inadequate provision and planning for the implementation which is the direct responsibility of the Minister."[37] He said that the money would of course be voted, since it had already been spent, and because the county administration had to be saved from complete chaos.

Nixon referred to "many alternatives" to the scheme that was actually carried through, and specified one in particular: that the county boards might have been in operation in only three or four selected county areas during the first year. Full implementation might then have begun in 1970. He did not recognize any disadvantages that might have resulted from thus prolonging the process, nor did he actually present any convincing evidence to show that all or part of the extra amount spent on legislative grants would have been saved if another approach had been used.

On the same occasion, Walter Pitman pointed out that he and his party had been suggesting that a reform in the tax base should have accompanied the educational reform. The two might have been phased over several years and, by the time all the boards had been set up, the province would be paying 80 per cent of the costs of education. The necessary taxes would be raised by progressive forms of taxation such as a capital gains tax or a provincial income tax.[38]

Both Nixon and Pitman speculated on the effect the reorganization had had on the minister's popularity, and neither thought it had been very favourable. Nixon said in this connection:

> There has always been a feeling around the province that Good Old Bill is handling education in such a fine way the Legislature is prepared, after considerable debate, to give him almost any funds he wants to build a modern system of education.
>
> There was always the feeling that, basically, certain concerns for efficiency in the system were there in the front bench of the Cabinet and in the Minister's

mind. But this figure certainly tells a different story. It indicates there was inadequate preparation, that it was a tremendously important programme entered into in a way that is not characteristic of any progressive democratic government, and which is a blot on the record of this government and this Minister.[39]

These words come from the political arena, and must be judged accordingly. From an objective point of view, however, it does appear that Davis emerged from the operation with a definite reduction in his enormous prestige. The reasons, however, are not to be found primarily in an impression that the changes were made in an inefficient or wasteful manner, but rather in the extent to which vested interests were upset, positions abolished and reshuffled, traditional ways of doing things disturbed, and uncertainties about future financial burdens created. There is a human tendency to be much more aware of immediate personal inconveniences than of the possibility of ultimate long-term benefits. Adverse reactions to fundamental reforms are the unavoidable concomitant of vigorous leadership, and history will give Davis high marks for being prepared to take them in his stride.

SIX

The development of the separate school system

ORIGIN

The origin of the separate schools dates from the union of the two Canadas in 1841. Before that time, under pioneer conditions, there had been little thought, and often less practical possibility, of segregating pupils on a religious basis, and in any case, in communities where most residents belonged to one particular denomination, it had been common to find a teacher of the same persuasion. McCutcheon declares that, had Lower and Upper Canada not been placed under the jurisdiction of a single parliament, it is unlikely that separate schools ever would have been established in Ontario.[1] In any case, the Common School Act gave both Roman Catholics and Protestants the right to establish separate elementary schools. Members of a religious order were authorized to teach without examination, thus giving the Roman Catholics a means of supplying their schools with teachers of their own faith. When the Act of 1841 was repealed in 1843, and new legislation substituted, the principle of denominational schools was retained. It was provided that, where the teacher of the existing school happened to be either a Protestant or a Roman Catholic, the members of the other denominations had the right, upon the application of ten or more resident freeholders or householders of the district, to establish a school and hire a teacher of their own persuasion. An application for such a school was to be delivered to the township, town, or city superintendent, and was to contain the names of three trustees. Upon their compliance with the requirements of the act, the school was to receive its share of the public appropriation according to the number of children in attendance. Separate schools were to be subject to the "visitations, conditions, rules and obligations" applying to other common schools.

Egerton Ryerson believed that government should be responsible for education or else have nothing to do with it. He did not think that religion of a sectarian nature had any place in the schools, but felt that Roman Catholics should be able to attend the public schools and find nothing there to bother their conscience.[2] A basic problem of that and later periods was that, although many were willing to declare their opposition to a sectarian approach, very few were prepared to contemplate dispensing with religious teaching altogether. Unfortunately different groups lacked a common concept of sectarianism. For some, even a reading from the scriptures without comment was objectionable if it involved the use of an unacceptable translation. Most people, however, favoured a much more positive approach. For example, thirty-nine of the forty-two groups presenting petitions to parliament when it began consideration of the new School Act of 1841 sought approval for the use of the Bible as a classroom text.[3] As long as all groups wanted the schools to accept some responsibility for religious objectives, and as long as there was disagreement on what the correct version of truth was, there were bound to be problems.

Ryerson's attitude was that the provision for separate schools in a popular system of common education like that in Upper Canada was inexpedient and regrettable. However, since these schools were already in existence, and those concerned attached great importance to them, he advocated their continuance. He hoped, however, that they would eventually die out as a result of the growth of Christian tolerance.

In the early years, separate schools were said to have been set up mainly in areas where the unusual antagonisms between Irish Protestants and Roman Catholics made it impossible to secure their effective co-operation in running a single common school. There was no evidence of a deliberate plan to establish a doctrinally based separate school system. The influence of Pope Pius IX has been considered very important in pushing the movement in that direction. The concept of the total Catholic environment as the ideal educational milieu for the education of the child was by no means new, but it began to be expounded effectively, not before, but some time after the public school system had become well established. As this doctrinal basis for support took hold, it ensured that Ryerson's hope that the separate school system would disappear would not be realized.

Ryerson himself made a powerful, although indirect contribution to the strengthening and solidifying of the support for separate schools. His success in laying the foundations of strong central control over the educational system created the possibility that the whole organization might be oriented in directions that the religious minority considered undesirable or dangerous. The situation was much more threatening than when control was dispersed through a multitude of small communities.

DEVELOPMENT BEFORE CONFEDERATION

No very substantial changes were made with respect to provision for the separate schools in the legislation of 1846 and 1850. In the former year, an advisory Board of Education was formed on the Irish model to bind denominational schools securely into the system. In the latter, the number of petitioners needed to establish a separate school was changed from ten to twelve, the obligation of the town authorities to act on their petition became binding, and average attendance was substituted for enrolment as the basis for government grants.[4] Separate school privileges were extended to coloured people in 1849, and by 1853 there were four schools operating under this provision. The arrangement had long been regarded as an anachronism by the time it was abolished in 1964.

Legislation in 1853 carried matters considerably further. 1 / It relieved the trustees of a separate school from any dependence on the local board of trustees of common schools. 2 / It exempted all supporters of separate schools from taxation for common school purposes if they contributed in rates or subscriptions an amount equal to the tax they would have had to pay for common school purposes had the separate school not existed. They were not, however, exempt from taxation incurred for the building of a common school house if the obligation had been assumed before the establishment of the separate school. 3 / The separate school trustees were required to furnish each year the names and amounts paid by supporters to the local superintendent of schools, who in turn transmitted the list to the clerk of the municipality, to prevent their names from being included on the tax roll.[5] The Roman Catholic bishops proposed that all of their adherents be treated as separate school supporters. Such a measure, which was not accepted, would have removed the individual's freedom of choice.

From 1855 on, separate school supporters no longer had to make contributions at least equal to the taxes they would have had to pay had they remained public school supporters. They were also relieved of the obligation to make an annual declaration of their support for separate schools. A further change during this period provided that a Roman Catholic separate school could be established if five resident Roman Catholic heads of families called a meeting, and if ten Roman Catholic freeholders or householders at that meeting elected three trustees who took appropriate legal action. Although no decisive date appears to be on record, the separate school boards established their right to requisition their funds from the municipalities just as did the public school boards.

A very significant restriction was placed on separate schools in rural areas in that their supporters had to reside within three miles in a direct line from the site of the school house. Subject to this limitation, rural schools, as well as those in towns and cities, were given the right to form union school sections. Not until 1963 was the centre of the three-mile radial zone changed from the school site to a point designated by the separate school board. Thus after that a separate school organization could be established without the necessity of building a school.

When this provision was made in 1963, an enlarged separate school district could still not be created except through the dissolution of the existing school districts. Cameron tells of the extraordinary procedure that was sometimes required for the formation of such an enlarged unit.[6] Separate school supporters had first to go through the process of establishing a series of single units, and then the trustees had to dissolve their units into a larger one. Units created solely to serve as an intermediate step toward the formation of larger units came to be known as "dummy" zones. The exercise of sufficient ingenuity might make possible the organization of a unit that included most of the potential separate school supporters in an area. If there was a gap of more than three miles where it was impossible to initiate the legal procedure to establish a new zone, there was no way of linking the sections on either side. The maintenance of restrictions of this kind was symptomatic of the province's determination to keep the Roman Catholic separate school system from becoming a fully fledged one equal to the public school system. It was widely felt that there must not be enticing precedents to encourage further fragmentation of the public system.

It took some time to settle the question of what area would be included in a separate school division in an incorporated town or city. School sections, to which separate school boards were tied in rural areas, were abolished in these municipal units in 1847. Ryerson tried in vain to have common school boards designate appropriate schools for denominational purposes. Legislative provision was made in 1850 for these boards to prescribe the limits of the separate school divisions, but that arrangement also failed. An amendment authorized the establishment of a separate school in each ward or combination of wards. Dissatisfaction subsided finally in 1863 when provision was made for a single school board for the whole municipality. The only substantial exception to this arrangement until very recently occurred in 1941, when the Toronto and Suburban Separate School board was created with responsibility for the city of Toronto and a large suburban area as well. In 1953 special legislation extended this board's control over nearly all of Metropolitan Toronto under the name "the Metropolitan Toronto Separate School Board."[7]

There were attempts on the part of the Roman Catholic authorities to remove provincial supervision of their separate schools. Ryerson felt that no government could afford to give up this power, and successfully resisted any effort to weaken it. Provision was made for visitation by individuals occupying a number of purely lay positions as well as by religious officials.

SAFEGUARDS PROVIDED BY THE BRITISH NORTH AMERICA ACT

The famous Section 93 of the British North America Act embedded the rights of the Roman Catholic separate school supporters so firmly in the Constitution that they were henceforth for all practical purposes untouchable. The section reads as follows.

93. In and for each Province the Legislature may exclusively make Laws in relation to Education, subject and according to the following Provisions:

(1) Nothing in any such Law shall prejudicially affect any Right or Privilege with respect to Denominational Schools which any Class of Persons have by Law in the Province at the Union:

(2) All the Powers, Privileges, and Duties at the Union by Law conferred

and imposed in Upper Canada on the Separate Schools and School Trustees of the Queen's Roman Catholic Subjects shall be and the same are hereby extended to the Dissentient Schools of the Queen's Protestant and Roman Catholic Subjects in Quebec:

(3) Where in any Province a System of Separate or Dissentient Schools exists by Law at the Union or is thereafter established by the Legislature of the Province, an Appeal shall lie to the Governor General in Council from any Act or Decision of any Provincial Authority affecting any Right or Privilege of the Protestant or Roman Catholic Minority of the Queen's Subjects in relation to Education:

(4) In case any Provincial Law as from Time to Time seems to the Governor General in Council requisite for the due Execution of the Provisions of this Section is not made, or in case any Decision of the Governor General in Council on any Appeal under this Section is not duly executed by the proper Provincial Authority in that behalf, then and in every such Case, and as far only as the Circumstances of each Case require, the Parliament of Canada may make remedial Laws for the due Execution of the Provisions of this Section and of any Decision of the Governor General in Council under this Section.[8]

Endless discussion has centred about the significance of this legislation. Many of those who have had reservations about the desirability of maintaining the Roman Catholic separate school system have refused to accept the permanence of the arrangement. While the majority of the royal commissioners proclaimed their respect for the legislation in 1950, their report contained recommendations that others felt constituted in actual fact a proposal to negate constitutional guarantees. On this point, the majority report of course made a historic blunder, in that controversy over the issue drew attention away from other valuable aspects of the report. Prime Minister Robarts was much more realistic in his lucid review of the issues at the time he presented the Ontario Foundation Tax Plan, which is discussed in chapter 8.

One view of the situation as it emerged from the constitutional arrangements of 1867 is that the right assigned to the separate schools at that time should be regarded as both a minimum and a maximum. Any further "concession" was to be resisted, or at best yielded grudgingly. Those on the other side claimed that the concept of what constitutes an adequate education had grown continuously since pioneer days, and that it was incongruous and unfair to insist that separate schools function as a relic of the past while the rest of the system was adapted to meet new conditions.

It is possible that leaders in educational and other fields who are not directly involved in the support of the separate schools are no more enthusiastic than they were in former days about having to deal with the extra problems created by the existence of a dual system. They may be firmly convinced that Ontario would be better off had the Roman Catholic separate school system never developed in the first place. But the recent period has been characterized by a growing acknowledgment of the fact that feuds over matters of principle must not be allowed to deprive large numbers of children of an adequate education. Government action in the 1960s was characterized by a genuine effort to relieve the relative poverty of the separate schools and to ensure that their pupils were not penalized because of accidents of birth combined with their parents' exercise of a legal right to send them to schools of their own choosing.

POST-CONFEDERATION DEVELOPMENTS

During the period immediately after Confederation, the financial situation became reasonably stabilized. The separate school board could either levy its own taxes or have the municipal council do so on its behalf. In terms of capital financing, a distinct difference in practice emerged between the systems. Municipal councils usually undertook capital borrowing for public schools before 1879, and always did so after that date. The resultant indebtedness was an obligation of the municipal corporation supported by the taxable property assessment of the municipality. Separate school boards, on the other hand, had to undertake their own capital borrowing. Lacking the same financial backing, they have suffered serious handicaps in the capital market.

Further privileges were extended to the separate schools and their supporters by 1879. Among the most important were these. 1 / Provision was made for setting up Roman Catholic model schools for the training of teachers for the Third Class Certificate, and for the appointment from each such school of a representative on the County Board of Examiners. 2 / Permission to vote at separate school elections was extended to supporters who lived outside the municipality in which the separate school was situated, but within three miles of the school. 3 / Permission was granted to an owner of unoccupied land in any municipality to have the land assessed for the support of separate schools, without regard to his place of residence. 4 / The practice of appointing Roman Catholic inspectors for separate schools of their denomination was begun in 1882.

A controversial provision was included in the same act. It permitted the assessor of a municipality to treat a person as a Roman Catholic separate school supporter if he knew personally that he was a Roman Catholic. The onus was placed on the latter to have his name restored to the list of public school supporters if he did not agree with the arrangement. Subsequent legislation considerably limited the assessor's discretion and placed the onus back on the ratepayer to opt to be a separate school supporter. Legislation in force at the time of writing required the clerk of every municipality to keep entered in an index book in alphabetical order "the name of every person who has given to him, or to any former clerk of the municipality, notice in writing that such person is a Roman Catholic and a supporter of a separate school in or contiguous to the municipality." The name stayed on the list until a formal request was received from the person concerned, asking that it be removed. The record book provided for recording such a withdrawal. A further clause said that the assessor "shall be guided by the entries in the index book in ascertaining who have given the prescribed notices."[9] This is a little different from saying that he must be governed by such entries.

Provision was made in 1899 for a separate school to be formed in an area not organized into townships, even though there was no public school in existence there at the time. Under previous arrangements, the first school in the neighboorhood was always a public school, although it might have mainly or exclusively Roman Catholic pupils, trustees, and teachers. Where there was a Protestant minority, those belonging to it could express their desire for segregation by taking appropriate action to set up their own separate school. The new provision emphasized the evolution of the Roman Catholic separate schools into a provincial system, as contrasted with a series of local arrangements designed to give particular communities an alternative to an educational facility which they regarded as distasteful.

During the period when Upper and Lower Canada were united in a single province, the principle was established that certificates obtained in Lower Canada were to be recognized equally with those obtained in the regular manner in Upper Canada. Ontario authorities had considerable difficulty getting rid of this provision in order to gain complete control over provincial certification. Finally, in 1906, the Privy Council overruled the claims of the Grey Nuns and the Christian Brothers and affirmed that separate school teachers should qualify in the same manner as public school teachers. McCutcheon points out that this decision resulted in the gradual elimination of unqualified teachers from the Roman Catholic separate schools.[10]

When provision was made for publicly supported high schools in 1871, all taxpayers, whether supporters of public or of separate elementary schools, were required to contribute to them. During the 1890s, continuation classes began to flourish, as explained elsewhere, as a means of providing some education beyond elementary school for those to whom the high schools were geographically inaccessible. Later legislation limited continuation classes operated by separate school boards to grades 9 and 10, which were treated as elementary grades for grant purposes.

A direct effort was made in the celebrated Tiny case of the 1920s to establish a legal basis for the extension of the separate school system through secondary school. The trustees of the board involved claimed for themselves and other separate school boards the constitutional right to conduct their own secondary schools, to be exempt from municipal taxation for the support of secondary schools other than their own, and to receive government grants on the same basis as that existing at the time of Confederation. The case began as a petition of right, and was appealed to three successive levels, with negative results in each case. The Haldane judgment of 1928 finally established that separate school supporters had no legal claim to financial support for any secondary schools they might erect, or to exemption from support of secondary schools open to the public and operating under public regulation.[11] Efforts to extend the separate school system for some time after that were concentrated on taking advantage of the provision for "Fifth Classes," which could be established under departmental regulations.

ATTITUDE OF THE ROYAL COMMISSION

As has been indicated, the majority report of the royal commissioners was regarded as hostile to the separate school system. Their proposals included what were intended to be looked upon as reassurances. They recommended

(a) that elementary schools under the jurisdiction of the Minister of Education continue to be deemed to include Roman Catholic separate schools as a special form thereof;
(b) that, subject to the qualifications hereinafter set forth, rights and privileges with respect to Roman Catholic separate schools consolidated in the Separate Schools Act of 1863 and subject to Section 93(1) of the British North America Act of 1867 be continued.[12]

The report went back to a very early stage to outline the conditions under which separate schools could be established.

19. ... (1) A class of persons, being Roman Catholics and satisfying certain definite statutory requirements, were to have the right to establish a denominational school under certain specific conditions, and to operate it as a special form of common (elementary) school. (2) The special form of elementary school so established was to be administered by trustees, elected by the persons exercising the right to establish it, who in respect to Roman Catholic separate schools were to have the same powers, perform the same duties, and be subject to the same penalties as trustees of common schools in respect to common schools. (3) Such an elementary school, so established and administered, was to be entitled to support from those Roman Catholics residing within three miles in a direct line of the site of the school-house who had elected to be its supporters, and was also to be entitled to share in the legislative grant apportioned for common school purposes. (4) Supporters of such a Roman Catholic separate school, subject to certain conditions and specific limitations, were to be exempted from the payment of rates for the support of common schools. (5) No similar rights were to be held by Roman Catholic separate school supporters with respect to grammar or other types of secondary schools.[13]

The majority of the commissioners expressed the view, not only that all enactments and regulations relating to Roman Catholic separate schools should be governed by these principles, but also that they should be amended to conform to them.

The elementary schools that the separate system was to control under the Royal Commission's scheme were to cover only the first six grades. Thus grades 7 and 8, and in many cases grades 9 and 10 as well, were to be yielded to public control. The fact that they were to be assigned to secondary schools did not constitute as much of a palliative as the commissioners apparently hoped.

The commission suggested a number of limitations on the separate school system in a move that it presumably looked upon as getting back to basic principles. It emphasized the view that a separate school administrative unit should be regarded not as an area of land but as a group of people living within three miles from the site of the Roman Catholic separate school. It was opposed to the formation of central schools to accommodate all pupils attending the former individual separate schools. It also condemned the department's practice of paying grants for the transportation of pupils to these central schools. The recommendation was

> that a union separate school board be required to maintain and operate schools on the sites of the separate schools which were formerly under the jurisdiction of the boards comprising the union, and that, where such a school has been closed, or is closed, the supporters thereof forfeit their exemption from support of the public school unless they reside within three miles in a direct line of another separate school in actual operation and have elected to support it.[14]

Since the inadequacies of the one-room school were becoming obvious by this time, it is hard to avoid condemning the majority of the commissioners for a blatant disregard of the welfare of the separate school children in their attempt to cut back some of the privileges that the separate school system had won.

Four members of the commission signed a minority report based mainly on their objection to the attitude taken by the majority toward separate schools. Their position was summarized in these words.

> The right of Roman Catholics to establish and operate separate schools cannot be gainsaid, and the desire is expressed in the Majority Report that freedom of action in these regards be not curtailed. But the exercise of this unchallenged right is to be hedged about by many restrictions. The three-mile limit circumscribing freedom to support separate schools is to be retained; additional formalities have been proposed which will render more difficult the exercise of the right of a Roman Catholic to become, and to remain, a separate school supporter and to secure exemption from the payment of taxes for the

support of public schools; limitations for legislative grant purposes are to be imposed on the amount of salary which may be paid to a teacher in a separate school who is a member of a religious order or community; the right to establish separate schools in territory without municipal organization is to be revoked; and the formation of separate school corporations and the establishment and operation of separate schools are to be hampered by the requirement of reference to the Central Advisory Council. Many other examples of a like nature could be cited, but these will suffice to illustrate how the proposals in the Majority Report seek to obstruct the operation of separate schools without directly abolishing them.[15]

FINANCIAL PROBLEMS

When the separate school system made its initial appearance, the financing of schools was largely a matter of obtaining support from individual contributors, first by voluntary or semi-voluntary means, and soon after by compulsory taxation. The complex corporations of the later period were not anticipated when financial arrangements were being worked out. Legislation in 1886 authorized public corporations to direct a municipality to tax their property as Roman Catholic separate school supporters. This property was to be divided between the public and separate schools in the same proportions as Roman Catholic and other owners or shareholders. As the situation developed, however, no satisfactory solution was offered for the problem of how a shareholder's corporate property was to be taxed in favour of the separate school system. Individual ownership was simply too ephemeral, too subject to fluctuating values, and too difficult to identify.

Corporations desiring to assist separate school boards found it somewhat easier to do so after 1913, when new provisions required only that the proportion of property allocated to the support of separate schools must not be greater than the proportion of Roman Catholic owners or shareholders. It was no longer necessary to determine the exact number or proportion, but only that it exceeded a certain figure. An area still out of reach of the separate schools for tax purposes was that of public utilities. Remaining inequalities were a particularly important political issue in the 1930s.

The Hepburn regime grappled unsuccessfully with this problem through legislation passed in 1936. An attempt was made to classify corporations as amenable or not amenable to having a listing of the separate school supporters among their shareholders. Each corporation of the first type was required to report to the clerk of the municipality "the ratio in its assessment which the shares held by such separate school supporters as had filed a notice with the company to that effect might bear to the remainder of the shares."[16] In this case, the separate school supporter had the full responsibility of ensuring that his name was on the list. A corporation assigned to the second classification was to have its assessment and taxes assigned to the two school systems in the same ratio as the assessment roll of individuals supporting separate schools bore to the assessment roll of individuals supporting public schools in the municipality where the corporation owned or occupied taxable property. There was no consideration of the three-mile limit with respect to either type of corporation. The attempt to apply the legislation was a complete failure, and it was consequently repealed the next year.

The possibility of allotting an equitable share of corporate taxes to separate school supporters was made even more remote by the outcome of the Ford Motor Case in 1941. Four years earlier, the Ford Motor Company had diverted 18 per cent of its taxable property assessment toward the support of the Windsor Separate School Board. The Windsor Board of Education sued successfully for the recovery of these funds in the Windsor Court of Revision, also winning a favourable decision from the British Privy Council after successive reversals at the hands of the Ontario Court of Appeal and the Supreme Court of Canada. The grounds for the final verdict were that the company had not met its obligation to establish that at least 18 per cent of its outstanding shares were held by Roman Catholics. Under the circumstances, the principle was fairly firmly established that it was impossible to determine ownership in any conclusive fashion. A satisfactory substitute solution did not become available until government grants assumed large enough proportions and were awarded on a sufficiently sophisticated basis that compensatory payments could be made in lieu of uncollectable corporate taxes.

The taxation base for separate schools has always been much smaller than that for the public schools. It has in fact been traditionally assumed that the former may count on about half the resources of the latter in any given area in relation to the number of pupils to be educated. There have been two basic explanations for this situation. 1 / Those who have supported separate schools have done so on the basis of a conscious choice, which has been more likely to be made, other things being equal, by those who have had children to be educated. This has been particularly true when the separate school tax rate has been higher than that for public schools. 2 / The three-mile limit has excluded many potential supporters. While loss of revenue for this reason has also been accompanied by relief from the necessity of providing for a certain number of pupils, it has often been difficult to achieve economy of operations under conditions of extremely low enrolment. It has been common also to talk about the large size of Roman Catholic families in comparison with their Protestant counterparts. The difference has probably never been as great as many people have assumed, and certainly does not appear to have been an important factor in recent years. There is much more validity in the claim that the average income has been lower among Roman Catholics than among Protestants.

In early years, lack of revenues was balanced to a considerable extent by lesser needs. The main factor was that the separate schools relied heavily on religious teachers, who received very low salaries. Although the number of such teachers rose from 1,728 to 2,085 between 1949 and 1965, the percentage fell from 46.0 to 15.4.[17] The consequence has been that the need for funds for salaries has risen rapidly toward the level applying in the public school system. The cost per unit of sites, buildings, facilities, and services has been comparable, although it has been possible for one system to do without some of the amenities that the other could afford, and perhaps also in some cases to get better value for its money by shrewd business practices.

In 1964 55.5 per cent of the public school boards in Ontario had equalized assessments per classroom of less than $200,000, while 90.6 per cent of the separate school boards were in the same position. The proportion of public school boards having an assessment of $400,000 or more was six times as great as for the separate school boards.[18] Before the introduction of the Ontario Foundation Tax Plan, described in chapter 8, the separate school boards were facing an impossible situation. Under existing conditions, they simply could not have carried on.

With respect to the Ontario Foundation Tax Plan, Bascom St John commented enthusiastically, calling it a masterpiece of political and financial skill. He wrote: "If it works as it is expected to work, it ought to solve the problem almost permanently."[19] Among the particularly complex problems was the constitutional one. St John pointed out that any changes relating to the separate schools must conform to the law or they would be upset by the courts. A scheme, for example, that proposed to transfer local school tax revenues raised for schools in one category to those in the other would be illegal. The so-called foundation plans of the opposition parties, even if otherwise workable, could not collect school taxes in a common pool and then redistribute them.

An unreasonable restriction on the supervisory powers of separate school boards was removed in 1965. Up to that time, the boards were unable, regardless of size, to employ supervisory staff above the rank of senior supervising principal. Boards in places like Toronto, Hamilton, Ottawa, London, and Windsor thus found themselves under a severe handicap. At the same time, even the smallest boards of education were allowed to employ directors of education and as many superintendents and supervisory officials as they required. Beginning in 1965, the establishment of municipal separate school inspectorates was authorized.

THE DRIVE FOR THE UPWARD EXTENSION OF THE SYSTEM

The issue

In the fall of 1962 the Roman Catholic bishops of Ontario sent a brief to the prime minister and to members of the Legislature making a case for a considerable extension of separate school privileges. They requested consideration of four chief concessions: a share in curriculum planning; the right to train their teachers in separate colleges; a revision of the system of financial support for the separate schools; and the extension of support for separate schools through the secondary level on the same basis as for the elementary schools. The Prime Minister responded in terms that were in remarkable accord with those of the leaders of the opposition parties, of nearly all the newspapers, and of other religious groups. They favoured financial relief, but were opposed to the other requests.

Since the bishops' brief was presented, the campaign conducted by many Roman Catholic agencies and individuals for the extension of the separate school system through grade 13 has been sustained and persistent. In an address delivered at the twenty-fifth Annual Catholic Education Conference in Toronto on March 22, 1969, J.E. Brisbois undertook to indicate the dimensions of the movement. He said that the policy had been endorsed by official resolution, and often unanimously, by the following organizations of students, teachers, parents, and trustees: 1 / the Ontario Catholic Students' Federation, representing 32,600 students in seventy-five English Catholic high schools; 2 / the Ontario Catholic Superintendents' and Inspectors' Association, the educational leaders of the new and larger separate school boards; 3 / the Ontario English Catholic Teachers' Association, with a membership of over 14,400 separate school teachers; 4 / the Federation of Catholic Parent-Teacher Associations of Ontario, with 30,000 members; 5 / the Provincial Council of the Catholic Women's League with 72,000 Ontario members; 6 / the Knights of Columbus, with 30,000 members in 136 councils across Ontario; 7 / various diocesan conventions of the Council of Catholic Men; 8 / the Association of Catholic High School Boards of Ontario, representing about 60,000 parents and over 1,700 teachers; the Ontario Separate School Trustees' Association, the elected representatives of all the secondary school ratepayers. Brisbois undertook to refute the accusation that the campaign lacked support from a large proportion of the Roman Catholic population, and that it represented the views only of a particularly voluble group. He said: "Notwithstanding what one may hear to the contrary from editorial writers who have their personal point of view, from well-meaning and sincere critics, and from individual Catholics who tend to be self-appointed spokesmen, the vast majority of the Catholic community intends to maintain and to improve the Catholic Public Schools, and to work for extension and completion of the Separate School System through the remaining secondary grades."

The case for the extension of the separate school system has been presented in innumerable letters, submissions, and other documents. A few points may be cited from a brief presented to the Prime Minister and the Minister of Education in 1966 by the Ontario Separate School Trustees' Association and l'Association des commissions des écoles bilingues d'Ontario.[20] The brief derived support for some of its propositions from a report by Greeley and Rossi on "The Education of Catholic Americans." That report had emphasized the absolute priority of family influence in religious training. It had also found, however, that the efforts of supplementary Christian teaching through Sunday school or religious periods in public schools was no alternative to parish schools. Catholic education at the earlier stages seemed to play the more important role in the formation of general ethical attitudes, as well as attitudes on sexual mores, while the Catholic high school was the more decisive influence in the formation of doctrinal attitudes. Support was offered for the articulation of elementary and secondary school education. The essence of the case for the extension of the separate school system is that it will produce more faithful Roman Catholics who will have a sharper, clearer, and more thorough knowledge of their religion than they could obtain by attendance at the public schools. In making their case among other elements in society, however, it is perhaps not to be expected that Roman Catholics will overemphasize such a point. Members of other religious groups do not usually put the production of good Roman Catholics at the top of their priority list.

Some of the points made in the brief represented a defensive reaction. It was recognized, for example, that ecumenism was being offered as a reason for the abandonment of denominational schools. The answer was said to have been given the previous year by the bishops of Ontario, who had recently taken part in the Vatican Council debates on ecumenism. They had insisted that inter-Christian action and communication required Catholics to be even more firmly rooted in their own faith. They were quoted as saying: "The more open we are in our relations with others, the more necessary it is that we live at the centre of the Church where our faith is nourished by Christ ... We as Catholics and they as members of other Churches do not want confusion." There was an obvious fear that what were regarded as some of the essentials of religion might be lost in a benevolent and somewhat vague effusion of good will.

The brief cited Greeley and Rossi against the argument that Roman Catholic schools were divisive. In the United States, where the study had been conducted, a comparison between Catholic pupils attending denominational schools on the one hand and Catholic and Protestant public school pupils on the other had shown that the former were no more biased than the latter. The brief did not see fit to mention studies conducted to compare standards of ethical behaviour between the respective groups. The results of such investigations have typically failed to identify any difference in this respect. In offering a defence against the accusation of divisiveness, a speaker at one rally referred to many examples of diverse companies offering the same type of product, to different public transit authorities, and to multiple approaches to university education. He said that these and other examples supported the thesis that our society, being pluralistic, thrives on competitive diversity.

The poverty and lack of facilities of the existing Roman Catholic private schools were considered to have unfavourable economic consequences. The brief said that "if separate schools have not the financial support needed to provide equal opportunity in education, *the general level of education in the province will suffer in the long run.*" This situation was said to constitute an economic penalty for religious convictions. Furthermore, the Greeley and Rossi report had shown that Catholics who had obtained all their education in Catholic schools were significantly higher on an occupational prestige index than those who went entirely to public schools. The difference was believed attributable to the friendly environment which stimulated the pupils and gave them security. We are not told whether or not any consideration was given to the possibility that those who attended Catholic schools tended to come from families with higher occupational prestige and that the necessity of paying fees ensured that they were relatively prosperous.

Support was derived from recommendations in the Hall-Dennis report, which criticized artificial boundaries between elementary and secondary school, and advocated that education be regarded as a continuous process of development from kindergarten to grade 13. Supporters of the extension of the separate school system claimed that it was anomalous to force separate school students to switch, not only from one school to another, but from one system to another, at the end of grade 10. The widespread introduction of individualized programs in secondary schools seemed to emphasize the desirability of continuing a program, where possible, in the same school.

An attempt was made to emphasize what was interpreted as the spirit of the guarantees provided in the British North America Act. Since publicly supported secondary schools had not existed in their modern form at the time of Confederation, it had naturally been impossible to cover them specifically. But many were prepared to argue that those who framed the act had expected the terms to be modified or interpreted in the light of changing conditions. There were also some proponents of the cause who, with more enthusiasm than knowledge, proclaimed that the lack of financial support for separate high schools in recent times constituted a violation of constitutional rights. In a legalistic sense, such a claim was, of course, absurd. This kind of thinking is demonstrated in an editorial published in the *Guelph Mercury* on March 6, 1969.

> To limit public support of a Catholic student to grade 10 is to deny the validity of the British North America Act which guaranteed full support for "common" or public secondary classes. These included separate schools at the time of Confederation.

In fact, of course, the extension of support to grade 10 was strictly a post-Confederation phenomenon. Since they had no sound case in prior legislation, the Roman Catholics had to make a convincing case on the basis of equity or social and economic advantages to the rest of society.

On the occasion previously mentioned, Brisbois referred to the fear that, once the regulations had been changed, the separate school authorities would build high schools in every town and village in the province. He claimed that such an apprehension was groundless, and that separate school trustees had established a reputation for conservatism. In view of their recognition of their primary responsibility to provide the best possible education for their children, it might be necessary in some situations to develop compromise solutions, even though these might be regarded as less than ideal.

The nature of the campaign being conducted by the Ontario Catholic Students' Federation is indicated by the program adopted in a certain private high school. It was resolved that the bishops of Ontario be asked to proclaim a Catholic Education Week, which would begin on a Sunday with a student delivering a talk in each of the Ontario parish churches to inform the people of the situation. One paragraph would be carefully composed by the federation for simultaneous delivery to all Catholics throughout Ontario. The speech would contain information about "constitutional rights," "tax injustice," "money paid three ways," and "power of votes." Among the questions to be considered in justifying Catholic education would be the following:

> why should the government have an unquestioned monopoly on the education of youth? why can't there be fair competition? why should we be told to leave God outside the door when we come to school? we want to be taught in a system which at least allows God to come into the picture if we want.[21]

During the remainder of the proposed Catholic Education Week, the information campaign was to continue.

A brief by the Orange Lodge in 1968 stated what is perhaps the essence of the opposing position.

> The Orange Association has strongly supported the principle that public tax dollars are for the Public Schools only and no citizen should have to pay taxes to promote another man's religion. Parents who desire to have their children educated in private or Separate Schools should be prepared to pay for them and not expect the Ontario Government to bail them out when financial difficulties prevail.[22]

Referring to the attempt by the Ontario Separate School Trustees' Association in 1966 to get favourable changes made in the Ontario Foundation Tax Plan, the brief suggested that it was never intended that the separate schools should have parity with the public schools. It pointed out that no mention of such parity was made in the Separate School Act of 1863.

An editorial in the *Kincardine News* on May 22, 1968, which was not highly favourable to the separate school system, demonstrated the weakness in a recently formulated petition that had declared that public funds should be provided only for the schools that were public in character. Centring attention on the word "public," the editor took it to mean that no religious affiliation or discrimination was allowed in these institutions. A local minister, recently questioned on this subject, had asserted that Canada was a Christian country, and could not dissociate itself from the Christian religion. It was time, the editor suggested,

> that some of the thinking members of the Presbyterian Church, along with the United, Baptist and all other Protestant congregations stop and realize that it is the fact that the public school sysem is not public at all, but rather Protestant, that is causing the Catholics to maintain separate schools and in fact giving them the right to separate schools.
>
> How much longer will the province be asked to duplicate the high school system because certain groups insist on religious instruction in the schools?

It would of course be easier to make a case against the granting of separate school privileges if the public schools were completely non-sectarian. But Roman Catholics have made it abundantly clear that they will not be satisfied with "godless" schools whose only virtue in terms of religion is that they are incapable of giving offence. Something of a much more positive nature is wanted.

A statement from the Executive of the General Council of the United Church of Canada has based its opposition to the extension proposal on the values of ecumenism.

> The Executive of the General Council values and wishes to develop the goodwill which presently exists between the United Church of Canada and the Roman Catholic Church. It recognizes the legal right of Roman Catholics to establish and maintain in Ontario a system of separate, elementary schools. It records its regret that a large proportion of the children of Roman Catholic parents are thus segregated from other children of their communities, and its belief that an extension of such separation in secondary schools would be prejudicial to both the ecumenical spirit and Canadian unity.

James B. Conant has offered an extremely strong case for the advantages of a unified high school system in the United States.

> During the past seventy-five years all but a few per cent of the children in the United States have attended public schools. More than one foreign observer has remarked that without these schools we never could have assimilated so rapidly the different cultures which came to North America in the nineteenth century. Our schools have served all creeds and all economic groups within a

given geographic area. I believe it to be of the utmost importance that this pattern be continued. To this end the comprehensive high school deserves the enthusiastic support of the American taxpayer. The greater the proportion of our youth who fail to attend our public schools and who receive their education elsewhere, the greater the threat to our democratic unity. To use taxpayers' money to assist private schools is to suggest that American society use its own hands to destroy itself.[23]

Some proponents of the extension of the separate school system discount the claim that further fragmentation would follow the granting of their demands by claiming that Protestant groups have never shown much interest in using what privileges they have had to establish their own schools. Such an argument overlooks the fact that legislation has given Protestants the right to establish separate schools only at the elementary level and only where the teacher or teachers in the public school or schools in the municipality are Roman Catholics. Anyone who doubts that various groups of Protestants, Jews, or adherents of other religious faiths would be delighted to receive tax relief or tax support for their own denominational schools at the elementary or secondary level or both is obviously not aware of the innumerable briefs and petitions these groups have presented to the government over the years.

In an article which appeared in the *Globe and Mail* on March 17, 1970, Mrs Shirley Gibbon made a plea for aid to Jewish schools. In it she advanced practically all the same reasons for public support for Jewish day schools as are commonly offered by proponents of such support for Roman Catholic separate schools – except that she could not cite a tradition of support in Ontario, nor claim that the Jewish community was as large as the Roman Catholic. She mentioned the importance of the educational environment for the preservation of Jewish culture, the high standards of the Jewish day schools, the relief to the local taxpayer when Jewish parents paid extra amounts to support their schools, the philosophical support provided by the Hall-Dennis report, and precedents in many other countries as well as in Quebec and Alberta. She ended thus: "If we are indeed living in a pluralistic democracy then all segments of that democracy must be treated with equal fairness. And if we really do care about the future citizens of this province then we won't stint on their education now."[24]

Many groups have based their appeal on philosophical, intellectual, or other grounds not strictly related to religion. Who is to say that one basis is not as sound as the other? Thus far, the government's response has been that these groups may establish their own schools, provided that they maintain certain minimum standards, but that they must bear the full cost themselves.

The supporters of the extension of the separate school system through grade 13 are quite right in saying that this action could be carried out in such a way as not to fragment the publicly supported system. But some would avoid fragmentation by ensuring that one group is given a privilege denied to all others. What arguments can be offered for this kind of favoured treatment? That the group in question is somehow more right than all the others? This kind of argument has validity only within the group itself. That it is bigger and more powerful than any other? It is hard to see how this position differs from the slogan "might makes right." If neither of these propositions holds up, we are reduced to the argument that what has already been begun should be completed, even though there was no basic justification for the original fragmentation of the publicly supported elementary school system – whether for Roman Catholics, Protestants, or any other group.

Stand taken by political parties

The Liberal Party

Before 1969 none of the three political parties represented in the Ontario Legislature had taken a stand that could be interpreted as strongly favouring the case for the extension of the Roman Catholic separate school system. During that year the matter assumed political implications as the Liberal and New Democratic Parties declared their support for schemes based on an acceptance of the proposed extension.

In November 1969 it was announced that the twenty-seven member caucus of the Ontario Liberal Party had reached unanimous agreement on a new policy. A crisis was predicted at the annual meeting of the party in February 1970, with a possible challenge to Robert Nixon's leadership. There was said to be considerable criticism from the constituencies, where even a substantial number of Roman Catholics opposed the policy. As it turned out, Nixon fairly easily won reconfirmation of his position, and there seemed little chance of any substantial policy modification, at least until the issue had been tested in an election.

The essence of the Liberal program has been stated on a number of occasions by the party's education critic in the Legislature, Tim Reid. He spoke, for example, to the St Rose of Lima Council of Catholic Men on February 1, 1970. At that meeting, he declared that the Liberals had in mind extending the jurisdiction of the separate school boards to include grades 11 and 12. On winning the next election they proposed to abolish grade 13 altogether. Up to the end of grade 12, they would make available to the separate school boards grants that were much closer to those currently being provided to the public school boards.

Support had been found in the Hall-Dennis report, which the caucus members felt had added a powerful educational argument for giving the separate school boards a continuous jurisdiction from kindergarten to the end of secondary school. In fact, the theory of continuous progress with individualized programs which it had emphasized so strongly had already been introduced into elementary and public secondary schools. In the notes for his address, Reid put the case in this way.

If one regards the school system as a stream where students can move at their own speed in selecting choices relevant to their ability and interests rather than a series of boxes or grades in which each student must be processed, the argument that a break at the end of Grade 10 is illogical and unacceptable has great logical appeal.

He acknowledged the implication that elementary schools should no longer be separated from junior high schools, nor junior from senior high schools.

The Liberals were not proposing to use public funds to support existing Roman Catholic private high schools. They were talking about granting public funds to separate school boards, which they considered to be quite a different matter. While no Roman Catholic private high school would be coerced, they expected that most of those currently being operated would sell their assets to the separate school boards and get out of the education business.

The scheme would call for a considerable increase in co-operation between the public and separate school boards. The Liberals were determined to ensure that there would not be a revolt of the taxpayers because of the impression that funds were not being used efficiently at the elementary or secondary levels. Thus measures would be taken to see that there was no excess structural, classroom, recreational, or transportation space during the period of transition to the new scheme. Population growth would be the main factor providing the needed flexibility. Where, for example, a particular area needed three new secondary schools, one might come under the separate school board. There were further possibilities of saving by co-operative action. Reid suggested that boards of education and separate school boards in certain areas might share the same office. Facilities might also be shared in such areas as transportation, library services, special education, and vocational education. There might be informal arrangements, or even formal arrangements established by legislation, whereby the public and separate school boards, with equal jurisdiction, might have joint organs such as property and building committees.

Reid indicated some of the thinking that lay behind the decision of the caucus. He made it clear at the outset that Roman Catholics had not dominated the proceedings, since they constituted only seven of the total membership. One of the major points that had appealed to the whole group was that, while there had been constitutional provisions for both Roman Catholic and Protestant separate schools, only the Catholics had seriously availed themselves of the opportunity to establish such schools. The evidence lay in the fact that there were over 400,000 children in these schools. As a subsequent point, Reid thought it appropriate to stress that the separate school boards were in many respects very much public school boards.

The New Democratic Party

In December 1969 the council of the New Democratic Party accepted the policy of financial support for the extension of the separate school system through secondary school. Many of the details of the position were derived from a brochure entitled *The Financial Crisis in the Catholic High Schools*,[25] prepared by a committee of the New Democratic Caucus. The brochure made it clear that its contents were tentative:

> The analysis which follows is a summary of the reports prepared by the committee. It does not represent in any sense a final statement of the members of the caucus committee nor has it been considered by the caucus as a whole, but it is published now to help party members and the general public to become familiar with all facets of the problem and to facilitate dialogue with other groups involved.

The brochure dealt with the development of the Roman Catholic separate schools from earliest times. When it came to the contentious issue of how Section 93 of the British North America Act should be interpreted, it referred to the views of many Roman Catholics as follows.

> It is the contention of the Roman Catholic community that the BNA Act protected their rights of administering the education of their children subject to limitations designed to assure proper standards of achievement and that the public support of separate schools was an integral aspect of these rights. Further, some common schools or separate common schools at the time of Confederation prepared young people for the university and could thus be said to have comprehended the total spectrum of pre-university studies. When secondary schools were established and full support was accorded only to separate elementary schools this interpretation of the BNA Act was violated.[26]

After a review of the Tiny case, the brochure concluded that the Roman Catholic authorities could not claim support for grades 11 to 13 on the basis of the latest appeal to the courts for an interpretation of the BNA Act. It proceeded to state, however, that there was no reason why the Ontario government could not use its legislative powers to extend its assistance.

Attention was given to possible threats to the separate school system. The chance that there might be a serious, let alone successful, drive to curtail the legal basis for existing separate school rights was realistically dismissed. A somewhat more credible threat was stated as follows: "It may be that there are those who see an opportunity of undermining the total fabric of separate schools by denying further aid to secondary levels and by so doing, destroying the viability of the entire system."[27] The brochure suggested that a struggle based on this proposition "would set back the many bonds of co-operation and sharing already established between religious groups in Ontario."[28] The NDP would reject it on the basis, also, that the chief sufferers would be Roman Catholic school children.

In considering acceptable ways in which the separate schools might be supported, the brochure asserted that any policy allowing for dipersal of power, whether in terms of local autonomy or of a separate public school system, must comply with the exigencies of financial reality. Thus there must be no wasteful duplication of facilities. "It will be no justice to anyone for the entire educational system to be made less effective in order that the ideals of pluralism and larger involvement are met."[29] The following passage comes close to stating the essence of the position which the NDP adopted as policy.

Although there will be many who do not believe that the religious dimension is a necessary complement to the education of the full man, the fact that a large segment of our society so believes and have sacrificed for this belief, should be taken into account in the provision of justice. The Roman Catholic believes that the common good in the Province of Ontario would be served if support were given to the final grades of the secondary school. Educational practice supports this view. Only two serious considerations call into question the efficiency of a fully completed separate school system – financial realities and the divisive effects on children. If, in the sharing of facilities and human resources, duplication of facilities is avoided and children of both systems play and learn together in a new spirit of co-operation and mutual understanding, these considerations are fully met.[30]

The section of the brochure on "financial considerations" pointed out that, if private Roman Catholic high schools were forced to close because of financial difficulties, there would be a net addition to the cost of the public high schools which absorbed the students. The amount would depend on whether or not there were existing vacancies. "In a sense ... it can be said that the choice is between whether the cost of the Catholic pupils' education is to be met by *additional* grants to public high schools or *new* grants to Catholic high schools. The same amount of public monies will be spent one way or another."[31] Two additional provisos were mentioned. There had to be sufficient Catholic and non-Catholic students to justify secondary schools of both types providing the full range of options and recreational facilities now considered essential to guarantee equality of educational opportunity. This could be done by sharing facilities. In this respect, the position of the NDP did not appear to be distinguishable in any major respect from that of the Liberals. Both parties seemed to emphasize that effective sharing was absolutely essential to the success of the whole scheme. Illustrations of the possibilities of joint planning and sharing were explained in a very effective fashion in the brochure. Unfortunately space does not permit the matter being given full justice in the present context.

The NDP conducted a survey among the seventy-five private Roman Catholic high schools in Ontario to determine how many of them would be willing to turn over their assets for a nominal sum to the separate school boards in their area. Of the fifty-seven responding, thirty-two indicated that they would be prepared to do so. These tended to be the large schools in the major centres of population, and represented 80 per cent of the student population. The NDP, like the Liberals, did not propose to subsidize private schools.

Like the Liberals, members of the NDP found support for a continuous system from kindergarten to the end of grade 12 in the Hall-Dennis report. The brochure added that the acceptance of the continuance concept made a mockery of the existing method of determining the amount of grants by grade. It asked how, for example, it would be possible to decide whether an elementary or a secondary grant should be paid for a student whose work was spread over what were once distinctly grade 8, 10, and 11 levels. Some of the members of the Hall-Dennis Committee did not consider this a valid interpretation of their recommendations. They felt that, if the system were made more flexible and better attuned to individual capacities and interests, students would be able to transfer into it at various points with less difficulty than before.

The Conservative government

The position of the Conservative government has been consistently that equality of opportunity demands that public funds must be used to bring the existing separate school system as close as possible to the public system at the levels which have been traditionally covered. The story of how that objective has been achieved is indicated in part in volume I, chapter 7. As far as the high school level is concerned, the cost of maintaining two systems is considered to involve a financial burden which, at least at present, the province cannot afford. The case made by the opposition parties for avoiding extra costs by joint planning and joint use of facilities is regarded as unconvincing.

THE REORGANIZATION OF LOCAL ADMINISTRATIVE UNITS IN 1969

The reorganization of the separate school administrative units was carried out after the kind of consultation that was lacking in the parallel reorganization of the units for public elementary and secondary school divisions. Organizations such as the Ontario Separate School Trustees' Association and l'Association des commissions des écoles bilingues d'Ontario were asked for their views on how the objective might be achieved. The latter submitted a statement for the minister in May 1968 which may be regarded as illustrative of the feelings of separate school supporters.[32]

The statement reviewed the reasons that Prime Minister Robarts had mentioned in his announcement of November 14, 1967, to justify the establishment of the new boards of education. It observed that these factors were of great importance to the separate as well as the public schools. To leave out the separate schools would automatically place them at a great disadvantage and deprive the pupils of all the benefits received by public school pupils. The association therefore requested the government to establish larger units of administration for separate schools.

In anticipation of adverse reaction to this request, the association had given consideration to certain reasons for possible opposition. It had asked for a legal opinion on whether or not the formation of larger units would contravene the principle of the three-mile limit. The essence of the problem was whether or not the change would prejudicially affect any right or privilege enjoyed by denominational schools. While this matter might require further study, the association felt that legal adjudication would necessarily be made in the context of modern times, when communication was much easier and educational needs much greater than when separate schools were founded and when the British North America Act became law. A second question was whether or not county and divisional boards were the best solution to the regrouping of separate school boards. The association was not apparently prepared to pass unequivocal judgement on this point. It did, however, ask that a flexible approach be adopted.

There were a few objections to the way in which the public and secondary divisions had been established. 1 / The association deplored the fact that another organizational structure had not been adopted which would have permitted separate schools to enjoy a continuous and integrated educational program from kindergarten to grade 13. 2 / It deplored the fact that separate school representation on boards of education was determined by assessment rather than by population. 3 / It deplored the fact that, in regions where the public school supporters were in a minority and must have a set minimum of representatives, the number of separate school supporters' representatives was reduced to provide for this set minimum.

The enactment of Bill 168 provided for the establishment by regulation of combined Roman Catholic separate school zones by uniting the existing zones, and any new ones established in the future, whose centres were in a county or a combination of counties. Provision was made for the later alteration of the boundaries within which a combined Roman Catholic separate school zone might be formed. Cities and separated towns, with the exception of Toronto, Ottawa, and Windsor, were included in the new zones. Like the boards of education, the two zones in Carleton County were defined in *The Regional Municipality of Ottawa-Carleton Act*. Only those parts of a county lying within the three-mile limit of a zone were included in a new combined zone.

The separate school board to be elected in each zone was to consist of eight, ten, twelve, fourteen, or sixteen elected trustees, depending on the total population within the county or combination of counties. In a county zone that included one or more cities or separated towns, the number of trustees to be elected in such places was to be determined by the ratio of their provincial equalized residential and farm assessment for separate school purposes to that of the entire combined zone. The number of trustees to be elected was to be allocated to a municipality or group of municipalities as nearly as practicable on the basis of provincial equalized residential and farm assessment for separate school purposes.

Provision was made for the designation of district-combined separate school zones in the territorial districts, with similar provisions for the election of trustees. A few zones that were too remote to be included in the combined zones were left under the control of local boards.

SEVEN

The development of an educational system for Metropolitan Toronto[1]

THE CRISIS IN URBAN GROWTH

The special problems of providing schooling for the children in Metropolitan Toronto are comprehensible only in terms of the unique pace of urbanization in the area during recent decades. The ways in which this particular conurbation has attempted to deal with the issues involved have attracted national and even world-wide attention. In order to facilitate an understanding of the approach adopted to solve the problems peculiar to education, a brief review of some of the salient aspects of the general situation before 1954 is offered as necessary background.

Mass migration from the countryside, from villages, and from small towns to a few urban centres has of course been a major consequence of the rapidly changing means of production since the beginning of the Industrial Revolution over two centuries ago. In fact, the trend was evident at least a couple of centuries earlier in certain countries in what has often been described as the commercial revolution. And wherever the movement has occurred, organized society has appeared completely incapable of recognizing its significance, of comprehending its dimensions, or of taking any measures beforehand to relieve the consequent suffering and confusion. Social structures have adapted tardily and reluctantly to the new conditions, as if the problems might miraculously disappear by some reversal of the course of history, or as if they could be attributed to some mass aberration on the part of the migrants, who could well be allowed to take the consequences of abandoning their natural habitat if they could not find the means to adapt. Political institutions, especially those evolving over long periods, have tended to maintain a rural orientation. In view of the frequent impoverishment of rural populations, there has frequently been quite sufficient justification for concern about their welfare, but such an attitude has often failed to extend to those who have not shared the wealth concentrated in the cities. Most solutions to the problems of the latter have been in the form of short-term palliatives, while the fundamental sources of the difficulties have remained.

In many political entities, whether nations, states, or provinces, a single centre of population has often exceeded all the others by a wide margin, and at an accelerating rate. For Ontario, the Toronto area is such a centre. With more than two million inhabitants, it claimed somewhere in the neighbourhood of 30 per cent of the population at the end of the 1960s. There is talk of a future megalopolis stretching from Oshawa, thirty-five miles to the east, to Niagara, ninety miles around the point of Lake Ontario, and including Hamilton and many smaller centres along the way. The challenge of devising a plan for orderly growth for this area, or, as the pessimists might put it, of preventing chaos, is as great as any faced by the provincial government.

Population growth in the Toronto area since the end of the Second World War has been almost unparalleled in North America. Nearly all the increase has taken place in what were, until January 1, 1967, the twelve component suburbs: namely, East York, Etobicoke, Forest Hill, Leaside, Long Branch, Mimico, New Toronto, North York, Scarborough, Swansea, Weston, and York. The so-called inner ring, including East York, Forest Hill, Leaside, Swansea, Weston, and York, were at least partly developed as compared with Toronto. Etobicoke, North York, and Scarborough in the outer ring had hardly begun the phenomenal expansion that followed. Before the war, the only formal contact among these municipalities was through their common representation on the county council of York, from which the separated city of Toronto was excluded. The informal contacts that existed were completely inadequate to ensure co-ordinated action.

The city of Toronto entered the period with a reasonable balance of commercial, industrial, and residential development. But it faced many problems traceable to the unfavourable conditions of the preceding years. Like other municipalities, it lacked the funds to extend or even maintain many services during the Great Depression of the 1930s. The funneling of efforts and resources into the subsequent war effort left little for municipal development. There was thus a great backlog of needs to be filled.

The scene was set for the process of urban decay that post-war affluence has typically accelerated in the larger cities of the continent. Previous neglect had contributed to the unattractiveness of living in the central core. The unprecedented availability of the automobile at the same time began to offer the more prosperous a means of escape to the suburbs. As the narrow, inadequate streets became more clogged with traffic, and as public transportation on the same routes became less efficient, suburban residents became increasingly reluctant to travel down town to their work. Thus industrial and commercial enterprises found powerful incentives to follow them beyond the limits of the city proper. A growing proportion of the residents who remained behind were elderly, infirm, and poor, and needed extra welfare services. The flood of immigrants from Europe also required special assistance in the initial stages, but when they began to realize their economic potential they often joined the trek to the suburbs, leaving their places to be filled by newcomers.

The problems of the suburbs, especially those in the outer circle, were of a different order. There was a whole range of municipal services to provide: streets, water supplies, sewers, parks, welfare, and police and fire protection, to say nothing of schools, in what seemed an impossibly brief period of time. The relatively high proportion of residential property in most suburbs left a completely inadequate tax base. A concentration of industry in a municipality such as Leaside tended to keep taxes low, and thus to attract more firms, while the dormitory suburbs had few effective counter-attractions. Needed capital became difficult, and by the early fifties practically impossible, for some municipalities to borrow at reasonable rates because they could not offer adequate security.

Some halting steps were taken toward co-ordination of the disparate components of the area by the provincial government with the establishment of the Toronto and Suburban Planning Board in 1947 and the Toronto and York Planning Board in 1949. The latter recommended the progressive amalgamation of the thirteen municipalities. This solution had lacked any great appeal in Toronto during an earlier period after the process of annexation of areas adjoining the city had been halted. The prevailing feeling at that time was that Toronto had nothing to gain by assuming the burdens of her neighbours. By the early fifties, however, the attitude had changed, and the city council requested the Ontario Municipal Board to take steps to bring about amalgamation. During subsequent hearings, only the municipal authorities of Mimico supported the request; in the other municipalities, local pride or, as many critics suggested, the determination of local politicians to retain their jobs, produced a stand in opposition to the proposal. The attitude of the general public was never accurately gauged. Some years after an alternative had been adopted, Bascom St John was still asserting that "the simple and logical solution was the amalgamation of Toronto and its 12 contiguous suburbs into one municipality."[2]

SCHOOL BOARDS BEFORE 1953[3]

Before 1953 a single board of education administered the entire school system in each of the municipalities of East York, Forest Hill, Lakeshore, Leaside, Toronto, Weston, and York; Etobicoke had a board of education and a union school board; North York had one high school board, two township school area boards, and three rural school boards; Scarborough had one high school board, one continuation school board, three township school area boards, four rural school boards, and one union school board; Swansea had one urban public school board. The range was thus from a unified system to a very strange collection of entities.

The Toronto Board of Education, which dates in its original form from 1850, was responsible for by far the largest school system in the province. It had been noted for good salaries, high quality teachers, including a large proportion of high school specialists, and a wide variety of special services and innovations. The East York Board of Education had been

CHART 7-1
The municipalities of Metropolitan Toronto before 1967

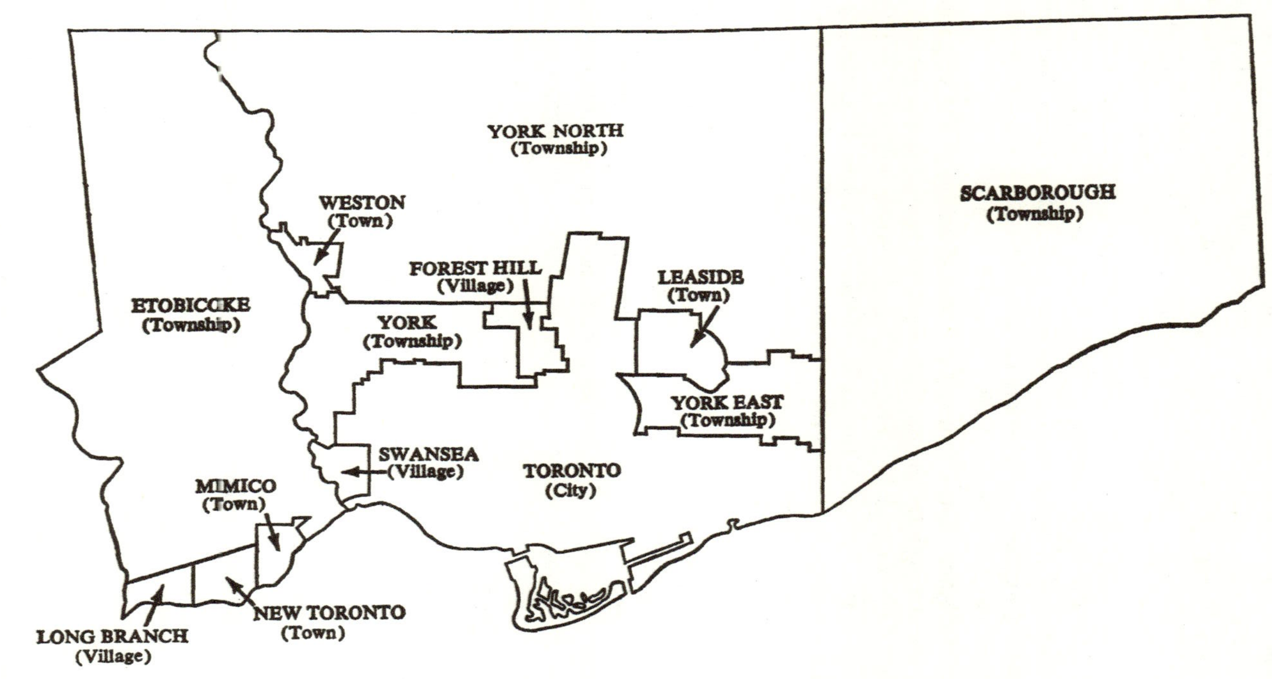

created in 1937 with the consolidation of the rural school sections and the high school area of the township. Since the latter was part of the county system of organization, its board included members appointed by the county council, and its schools were open to fee-paying pupils resident in other parts of the county. The rural school districts of Etobicoke were amalgamated into a board of education in 1949, with the exception of one school section. The board never had any county appointees, although it included a representative of the Toronto and Suburban Separate School Board. The school board in Forest Hill was first established in 1909. It became noted for forward-looking policies reflecting its inhabitants' intensive interest in education and their capacity to finance it at a high level. As it extended the system into the higher grades, it developed a three-level system, ultimately operated on the 6-3-4 plan. The Lakeshore District Board of Education was created by action of the York County Council in 1951 by amalgamation of the school boards of Long Branch, Mimico, and New Toronto. The process of developing an adequate system of secondary education for the three municipalities was thus rationalized. The Public School Board of Leaside was created in 1920, and converted into a board of education in 1945 to provide secondary school education for the town. In North York, schools were organized on a rural basis until 1929. During that year, the process of consolidation into township school areas was begun, and proceeded by major steps in 1945 and 1950. The board of education for North York, like that for Scarborough, was created by *The Municipality of Metropolitan Toronto Act* in 1953. Until 1928 the only secondary school in the township was the continuation school that became a high school in that year, and later gave way to Earl Haig Collegiate Institute. Scarborough moved very slowly toward complete unification of school administration. Before the formation of the first township school area in 1944, there were seventeen rural school sections. As has already been indicated, the situation was still quite complex by 1953. That conditions did not unduly trouble the residents was indicated by a plebiscite in 1952 in which a proposal for a board of education was turned down. They were drawn into the stream of progress by the Metropolitan Act just eight months later. The Swansea Public School Board became a board of education on January 1, 1953, by action of the York County Council, even though the municipality maintained only one elementary school and purchased all its secondary education from adjoining municipalities. Weston's public and high school boards gave way to a board of education in 1916. It provided secondary school accommodation, including vocational courses after 1922, for a much wider area. The York Township Board of Education was established in 1936 to take over the functions of the collegiate institute board and the public school board.

Paralleling the situation in the municipalities, there was little formal co-operation among the school boards of Metropolitan Toronto before 1945. Toronto was so much larger than the other districts and the structure of its system so much more complex than theirs that they seemed to have little in common. But two factors began to change the situation: the possibility of amalgamation and the teacher shortage.[4] In 1945 Toronto's director of education, C.C. Goldring, received authorization from his board to call a meeting of Toronto area boards to discuss the topic of amalgamation. The conference, held in January 1946, led to the formation of the Toronto District and Urban School Trustees' Association. For some years this association carried on an active program of meetings and discussions, the most important topic being salary negotiations. It outlived its usefulness with the establishment of the Metropolitan School Board and was disbanded.

In the early 1950s there was accumulating evidence of the breakdown of the existing system in the metropolitan area. When Township School Area No. 1 in North York requisitioned funds for five new elementary schools, the council approved, but could raise only half the required funds, and the schools erected under these conditions were far below the usual standards.[5] The beginning of a period of rapid increase in teachers' salaries accentuated the penury of the most rapidly developing municipalities. Enrolments were rising in municipalities with a low assessment per capita, but falling in those where taxable assessment per capita was highest.

There were other problems caused or accentuated by the lack of coordination among school systems. Municipal boundaries often seemed capricious and arbitrary, and failed to delineate reasonable attendance areas. Some of the schools built in former periods just inside the borders of the city of Toronto would have made sense had the earlier policy of expansion continued, but were currently incompletely utilized, while those in neighbouring municipalities were overflowing. While Toronto maintained a policy of accepting suburban pupils on a fee-paying basis, suburban boards were not always enthusiastic about such a course of action, partly because the expenditures for this purpose, although not at all unreasonable, were highly visible, and also because the necessity of purchasing services elsewhere was somewhat of a blow to municipal pride.

At this time Toronto was well along in its outstandingly successful campaign to provide special services for the mentally and physically handicapped. Because of their rapid growth and financial difficulties, the suburbs could not begin to match these programs. While here again the Toronto board was prepared to accommodate pupils from other parts of the area in special classes at cost, the process of sharing was not working satisfactorily. The necessary extra expenditure was rather easily eliminated from a suburban budget under pressure of other demands.

THE CUMMING REPORT

School board difficulties in meeting educational needs and the compellingly obvious lack of educational opportunity were perhaps as serious as any of the other problems of Metropolitan Toronto at the time. But they were nevertheless only part of the larger whole, and it was obvious that they would be resolved within the over-all municipal context. The way for change was paved by the studies undertaken by the Ontario Municipal Board as a result of the Toronto request, previously mentioned, for total amalgamation. The outcome was the so-called Cumming Report, named for Lorne R. Cumming, chairman of the board.

The Cumming Report recognized certain virtues in the case for total amalgamation. It would provide a solution to the problems of planning, co-ordinating, and developing water supplies and sewage disposal systems, arterial roads, parks and recreation areas, public transportation, and other facilities. It would offer a means of dealing with the existing inequities in the distribution of taxable resources. It would put the resources of the whole area behind the issuing of debentures, and would make it possible to co-ordinate capital expenditures in the interests of the area as a whole. There were, however, certain overriding disadvantages in the scheme. The change would be so drastic that prolonged and serious administrative confusion would result. An immediate attempt to bring suburban salary scales, working conditions, and services up to city levels would require an unpalatable increase in taxes. There was doubt that a single all-powerful council could deal adequately with both area-wide and local problems. Not least important was the bitter opposition to amalgamation by the political leaders of nearly all the suburban municipalities.

The report thus rejected amalgamation, instead recommending a two-tier form of government, a kind of municipal federal system, reflecting Ontario's experience with a division of powers between county councils and local municipal governments. It called for a metropolitan council, consisting of representatives from the municipal councils of the area, which would continue in existence. The metropolitan council would have responsibility for the administration of justice, health and welfare, the supervision of children's aid homes, assessment, the distribution of water, main trunk sewers and disposal plants, and, significantly, some aspects of education. In terms of school capital costs, it would have these obligations: 1 / to finance capital costs of sites, buildings, and equipment to an adequate standard, 2 / to assume all existing school debentures, 3 / to receive all legislative grants on capital expenditures, and 4 / to select and purchase school sites. In addition, the council would 1 / finance such portion of operational costs as the council might from time to time determine, 2 / receive all legislative grants except those relating to books, milk distribution, and other special expenditures, 3 / require pupils of one municipality to attend schools in another municipality, where it seemed in the general interest, and 4 / provide transportation for such pupils. The report also proposed that the metropolitan council, in consultation with the Department of Education and the eleven boards of education in the area, determine the minimum standard to be financed on an area-wide basis. Cumming hoped that the scheme would leave the local boards largely autonomous in providing education to meet local needs while at the same time ensuring relative equality of opportunity by a more equitable distribution of financial resources.

To have given a municipal council this degree of control over education would have meant a very significant departure from Ontario practice. In view of the long history of protests by municipal councils over the alleged extravagance of school boards, the trustees of the area were not pleased at the prospect of such a change. They were particularly alarmed at the idea of having educational standards determined by the council. By the time Bill 80 was presented to the Legislature on February 23, 1953, their protests, perhaps along with the Frost government's desire to depart as little as possible from past traditions, had brought about the only significant change in the recommendations of the report. Certain educational functions that the metropolitan council was to have performed were to devolve on a parallel body, the Metropolitan School Board.

THE MUNICIPALITY OF METROPOLITAN TORONTO ACT, 1953

The chief educational provisions of the Act of 1953 were as follows. 1 / It provided for boards of education in North York and Scarborough, thus implementing the municipal board recommendation of this form of school board for each area. 2 / It provided for the establishment of a Metropolitan School Board representing the eleven boards of education, and assigned to it certain functions, which, according to one view, "as defined were so vague and so restricted that its activities were confined to major problems of finance and school buildings."[6] 3 / It specified that general legislative grants from the provincial government would go to the Metropolitan School Board, and it directed that in 1954 and 1955 this board pay in maintenance assistance grants to the local boards an amount per pupil, acording to average daily attendance in the preceding year, as specified in the act; in 1956 and annually thereafter the amount of this grant per pupil would be determined by the board. 4 / It gave the board the responsibility of establishing attendance areas where it seemed in the general interest for pupils of one municipality to attend schools in another. 5 / It enabled the board to assume part or all of the cost of operating special classes recognized under the Auxiliary Classes Section of *The Schools Administration Act*. 6 / It gave the board the responsibility of co-ordinating the school building plans of the local boards. The metropolitan board assumed all existing school debentures as of January 1, 1954, became the recipient of provincial grants on capital expenditures, and was made responsible for the repayment of school debt on the portion of the cost of school buildings recognized by the Department of Education for grant purposes.

The Metropolitan School Board consisted of twenty-two members: each of the ten school districts provided one and Toronto, given numerical equality with all the others combined, was represented by ten; the remaining two were appointed by the Metropolitan Separate School Board. The elected chairman of each of the eleven boards would represent the area, with the addition, in Toronto's case, of the trustee in each of the nine wards who polled the higher vote in the municipal elections. One separate school representative came from Toronto and one from the suburbs. It was later arranged that a local board might elect a substitute representative if the chairman did not wish to serve on the metropolitan board. The responsibilities of the board were discharged by three main committees: the Accommodation Committee, the Building and Sites Committee, and the Finance Committee. Their chief responsibilities were respectively 1 / to deal with attendance areas and with special education classes for which the metropolitan board paid the entire cost, and to conduct periodic analyses of current and projected enrolments; 2 / to review capital estimates and to consider individual building applications and proposals for site acquisition; 3 / to co-ordinate the activities of the other two committees, to prepare the board's budget, including the recommendations with respect to maintenance assistance payments, to consider all financial matters, and to deal with personnel problems. A fourth committee, the Legislation and By-laws Committee, met at the call of the chair. Early provision was made by the board for an advisory council as a regular source of professional advice and guidance. It consisted at first of the executive secretary and nine senior officials of the participating boards; the number was later increased. During the first ten years the regular administrative staff, headed by Executive Secretary W.J. McCordic, hardly grew from the original six.

The solution to the whole spectrum of urban problems represented by *The Municipality of Metropolitan Toronto Act* aroused criticism in certain quarters. In retrospect, Bascom St John said of the government of the day that it "did not have the courage to take the supposed political risks involved in this drastic move."[7] He went on to say in its defence, echoing the Cumming Report, that the lack of experienced municipal administrators needed to run a municipality so suddenly created might have been a factor.

Of course, the reasonableness of total amalgamation, whether at one stroke or step by step, was far from obvious to a great many thoughtful people. There was no question that some of the municipalities were too small, even if funds were distributed equally in terms of enrolment, to provide for the range of services that good education was beginning to demand. The subsequent ingenuity with which such services have been devised and the increasing trend to regard them almost as the child's natural right have strongly emphasized this factor. Cynics also point to the habitually small turnout at elections for school trustees as evidence that the public's desire to keep control over education in the local community is greatly exaggerated. Local pride seems to be mainly an attribute of local politicians. On the other hand, there are strong arguments in favour of the view that beyond some point an educational authority is too big. The advantages of being able to attract and hold good administrators are cancelled by the multiplication of bureaucratic levels of authority; personal and informal methods of operation give way to rigid rules of procedure; control of the system is increasingly remote from the supposed beneficiary of the whole process, the learner. Some of the cities in the United States with much larger populations than that of Toronto have demonstrated the disadvantages of size. They have also shown how difficult it is to reverse the process and restore the schools to the surrounding community.

In 1960, Prime Minister Frost justified his choice between the alternatives of outright amalgamation and the development of a metropolitan or federation type of government as follows: "One of the principal reasons, in fact an overwhelming reason, for turning to the metropolitan type of government was to save the city of Toronto from being overwhelmed by being confronted with the combined problems of the 12 surrounding municipalities."[8] In other words, as the Cumming Report had suggested, an attempt to raise the level of services in the suburbs to those existing at that time in Toronto would have increased taxes by an insupportable amount in the latter, no doubt with adverse political consequences for the party in power. Frost went on to point out that extreme inequality between Toronto and the suburbs was the reason why no immediate attempt had been made in 1953 to unify police and fire services, although many had expected them to be included among areas of metropolitan rather than of purely local concern.

An unmentioned factor was the government's continued wariness about letting a single municipal unit grow so large that it would become excessively difficult to control. In some respects, Toronto had given signs of having reached this stage. Whatever the residents of the city may think, the government's apprehension has been reflected in the attitude of a large part of the population of Ontario. They are not at all confident that what is good for Toronto is necessarily good for the province. Such a view, however understandable, has not been too conducive to an understanding of some of Toronto's unique problems.

THE PERIOD OF GROWTH UNDER THE METROPOLITAN SCHOOL BOARD

The first Chairman of the Metropolitan School Board was J.A. Long, at that time Chairman of the Forest Hill Board of Education and Director of the Department of Educational Research at the Ontario College of Education. A number of capable men followed his distinguished lead, and for a time things seemed to be going well. Successive chairmen commented favourably on the ability of the members to work harmoniously together. The advantages of the new arrangements for financing school construction were immediately obvious. During 1954, for example, the board secured the approval of the metropolitan council for twenty-four public schools, thirty-eight additions to public schools, five secondary schools, and nine additions to secondary schools. In his inaugural address in 1955, the new chairman, O. Wainwright, observed: "Trustees have, during the past year, shown an inclination to accept the principle of equality in the extent and nature of new school facilities. They have, through the establishment of a ceiling cost formula, provided a method whereby equality can be achieved without sacrificing individuality." The ceiling cost formula eliminated the extended debates with the executive of the metropolitan council over each new school application.

During the first few years, there was a hint of future trouble in the suggestion that the board members' willingness to view the problems of the entire area from a broad perspective did not necessarily filter down to the members of the local boards. J.C. Van Esterik, chairman for 1957, made these comments in his inaugural address:

> Looking back it is interesting to note that the Municipality of Metropolitan Toronto Act carefully and deliberately sought to preserve the local autonomy of the eleven boards of education in Metropolitan Toronto. The powers of these several boards, in fact, were changed so slightly that the boards tended to proceed on all matters, even on matters with obvious Metropolitan implications, as if there had been no change. Even boards who stood to gain substantially in a financial way tended to accept these bounties without a corresponding recognition of a local obligation to become identified with the work of the Metropolitan School Board.

Van Esterik proceeded to pay the usual tribute to the spirit of trust and co-operation that had developed among the members of the board.

McCordic showed a high degree of enthusiasm for the metropolitan experiment in a lecture delivered to graduate students at the Ontario College of Education during the summer session of 1958.[9] He listed a number of specific achievements of the new organization during its first few years. 1 / Uniform equalized assessment made it possible for the first time to compare the tax burden of metropolitan communities by a direct examination of their tax rates. 2 / The sale of debentures for the whole area had been combined in one department with competent management and a well-trained staff, thus eliminating competition among the thirteen municipalities in the bond market and ensuring the financial soundness of the whole unit. 3 / The procedures for securing building approvals had been greatly improved and streamlined, so that a steady progression of approvals by the Department of Education, the local council, the Metropolitan School Board, and the metropolitan council had replaced the tedious hours of negotiation with local councils and the uncertain, ever-changing procedures characteristic of the former system. 4 / The board had served as an agency for impressing upon the provincial government the special educational needs of Metropolitan Toronto. Its requests for amendments to the Act of 1953 had generally been accepted. 5 /Maintenance assistance payments had been helpful to the districts with lesser resources by spreading the financial burden more equally. 6 / The establishment of attendance areas had contributed to the full utilization of available space. Although shifting children was generally unpopular, there were approximately three thousand attending schools outside their own municipalities. Without the metropolitan system, up to $3 million might conceivably have been spent on new buildings to accommodate them, leaving a comparable amount of space unused elsewhere. 7 / The board had assumed the full cost of all auxiliary classes, and since that time they had been operated on a "first come, first served" basis. A more effective use of existing accommodation had resulted, and the orderly development of special education throughout the area had been ensured.

There were also many informal and intangible benefits. Metropolitan trustees and officials, in their frequent meetings and contacts, had opportunities to exchange information and views about educational matters in their own areas. A large measure of informal co-operation had developed with respect to salary scheduling, staff recruitment, interchange of personnel, and professional in-service training programs. McCordic suggested that these incidental achievements were almost as impressive as the work of the board itself.

In retrospect, as McCordic acknowledged in 1964, a high water mark had been reached. The advantages of the metropolitan system as devised in 1953 were at their most conspicuous, and the difficulties that were to grow rapidly thereafter still seemed manageable. A brief review of certain aspects of the expansion of the system during the period will provide a background against which these difficulties may be evaluated.

During the decade between 1954 and 1964 public elementary school enrolment increased from over 146,000 to over 239,000, or by some 63 per cent, while public secondary school enrolment increased from over 34,465 to over 92,665, or by nearly 169 per cent. In the elementary schools, enrolment increased by 208 per cent in Scarborough, 160 per cent in North York, and 143 per cent in Etobicoke, while there was a decline in Leaside, Forest Hill, East York, and Weston. The secondary school enrolment increased in all municipalities, except of course in Swansea, which had no schools at that level, but the increases were again by far the most spectacular in the three large outer suburbs, where they ranged up to 619 per cent in North York. These three municipalities together accounted for 91.5 per cent of the total increase in public elementary school enrolment and 70 per cent of the increase in secondary school enrolment.[10]

Between 1954 and 1964 the building program had produced 221 new schools, 419 additions, and 506 new sites or extensions to sites acquired, at a capital cost of approximately $372 million. A total of 199,300 new pupil places had been provided. The net increase in schools was 191. Again, the greatest activity had occurred in the three outer suburbs. In North York the number of public elementary schools rose from forty-eight to ninety, in Scarborough from thirty-two to seventy-eight, and in Etobicoke from twenty-one to forty-two. In each of these municipalities, the number of secondary schools was multiplied by six, and North York and Etobicoke had each acquired sixteen intermediate or senior public schools.[11]

In the same decade the number of teachers in the metropolitan area had increased from 6,094 to 12,899. The three outer suburbs accounted for 75 per cent of the increase; in Scarborough, the number rose from 450 to 2,407, in Etobicoke, from 494 to 1,612, and in North York, from 850 to 2,886. The over-all teacher-pupil ratio fell from 29.7 to 25.7, ranging from 27.6 in Etobicoke to 20 in Forest Hill.[12] This reduction did not necessarily reflect smaller classes in general, but rather indicated that more teachers were performing supervisory tasks or offering consultant services, and more classes of a special nature were being established, calling for reduced numbers.

The period saw substantial changes in school organization. The report of the Royal Commission in 1950 had reinforced many people's concern over the sharp division between the elementary and secondary levels, in terms both of the program and of the mode of operation of schools of the respective types. While the commission's recommendation of a tri-level system on the 6-4-3 plan was not officially adopted, individual systems in the Toronto area and elsewhere proceeded to make modifications to suit their needs, prejudices, and financial capacity. This development had actually begun as early as 1932 in Forest Hill, as indicated earlier. East York had followed suit under somewhat different circumstances in 1951, while Toronto and Weston opted for senior public schools, involving a redesignation of existing buildings and a change in attendance patterns, but not necessarily new construction. The Advisory Council of the Metropolitan School Board studied the whole question, and as a result approved the tri-level system, without coming to any agreement on specifics. The municipalities continued to go their own way, following a variety of possible courses of action.

The question of how best to provide for technical-vocational education was of major importance in the 1950s. Up to that time, most suburbs had purchased the necessary services from Toronto and Weston, but this solution was becoming less and less satisfactory. The development of composite schools with a full range of programs was begun in North York, York, Lakeshore, and Scarborough, in contrast to Toronto's pattern of having schools of different types. The need for co-ordinating vocational education and of avoiding costly duplication throughout the area led to the appointment by the Metropolitan School Board in 1959 of a special committee to study the vocational needs of the whole area. The result was an expression of approval of the existing organization in Toronto and of composite schools elsewhere. The whole situation was affected drastically by the Federal-Provincial Vocational School Assistance Program of 1961, and by the subsequent reorganization of the secondary school system by the provincial authorities.

The outstanding pioneering achievements of Toronto in a variety of fields of special education were a considerable source of pride by 1950. The city maintained Sunnyview School for children suffering from orthopaedic handicaps and deafness, three special vocational schools, opportunity classes in a number of elementary schools, and hard-of-hearing, sight-saving, and other remedial classes. Except for some opportunity classes, there was little of a comparable nature in adjoining municipalities. Their practice of purchasing services in Toronto classes when space was available was failing to provide for their needs, and rapid expansion of facilities throughout the area was urgently needed. One of the early achievements of the Metropolitan School Board was to assume all the operating costs of Sunnyview School and of certain types of special classes and to abolish fees for attending them. A period of rapid expansion followed under a variety of schemes which the metropolitan board was unable to standardize because its financial support did not involve direct control.

In his lecture in 1958 McCordic had identified a few clouds on the horizon. 1 / He had noted that the removal of a large part of the responsibility of raising their own funds had created an expansive mood among the local boards, often leading to demands that in sum outran the total resources of the metropolitan area. 2 / With the transfer of responsibility for capital spending to the metropolitan agencies, the local councils had ceased to restrain the school boards in their demand for capital funds, but tended to unite with them in exerting pressure to get as large as possible a share of total available resources. 3 / There was a considerable threat from the local autonomist, who tended to create obstacles to the interchange of pupils and services by letting his enthusiasm for the quality of the educational offerings of his own area overcome his judgment. As McCordic put it, "Irresponsible statements reflecting unreasonable bias constitute a real threat to the one kind of organization which will preserve a large measure of local autonomy."

The serious and growing inequality of representation among the municipalities was a major threat to the system. By 1963 the position was as shown in Table 7-1. The three large outer municipalities of North York, Scarborough, and Etobicoke had experienced by far the greatest increase in both absolute and relative terms. North York's share of the total population had jumped from 9.4 to 18.6 per cent, Scarborough's from 6.7 to 14.5, and Etobicoke's from 6.0 to 10.7. The original inadequacy of their representation on the metropolitan governing agencies had thus become much more pronounced. None of the seven smallest municipalities, Forest Hill, Leaside, Long Branch, Mimico, New Toronto, Swansea, and Weston, had more than 1.3 per cent of the population. At the other end of the scale, Toronto was now also over-represented, its percentage having declined from 56.7 to 38.1.

TABLE 7-1

Metropolitan Toronto Population, 1953 and 1963

MUNICIPALITY	1953		1963	
	Population	Percentage of Metro total	Population	Percentage of Metro total
East York	65,736	5.6	70,176	4.2
Etobicoke	70,209	6.0	177,537	10.7
Forest Hill	17,719	1.5	21,126	1.3
Leaside	15,910	1.3	18,453	1.1
Long Branch	9,140	0.8	11,129	0.7
Mimico	12,301	1.0	18,150	1.1
New Toronto	9,744	0.8	11,785	0.7
North York	110,311	9.4	307,584	18.6
Scarborough	78,803	6.7	240,371	14.5
Swansea	8,344	0.7	9,371	0.6
Toronto	665,502	56.7	630,339	38.1
Weston	8,374	0.7	9,983	0.6
York Township	100,463	8.6	126,311	7.6
Total	1,172,556	100	1,652,315	100

SOURCE: Ontario, *Report of the Royal Commission on Metropolitan Toronto*, H. Carl Goldenberg, commissioner (June 1965), Table 3, p. 11.

McCordic thought at the time that the representation problem could be cleared up within the context of the existing scheme. The matter had, it is true, been considered without any decisive outcome in 1957 by a commission set up by the provincial government to review metropolitan affairs. Speculation involved three possible solutions: 1 / the outright amalgamation of the city and the suburbs, 2 / the voluntary merging of smaller suburbs, either with each other or with larger adjacent municipalities, and 3 / a drastic reorganization of the two-tier system by the provincial government, producing a number of municipal units of approximately equal size. McCordic pointed out that there was still little enthusiasm for the first scheme except among the Toronto representatives. He was also no doubt fully aware of the provincial government's reluctance to nourish the monster that already threatened its own dominant position. He did not think the second solution offered much hope of success, unless perhaps the three Lakeshore municipalities might follow in the steps of their school boards, although such action at this point would be a little different, since it would reduce their voice in the metropolitan agencies which had not existed when the school boards were merged. There was always a willingness on the part of larger and hungrier municipalities to gobble up their small, relatively rich neighbours, but there was little corresponding enthusiasm on the other side. McCordic apparently favoured the third solution, although he seemed to feel that a good deal of pressure would have to be exerted on the government before it would take such a drastic step. Premier Frost suggested another possibility when he mused on a system of multiple votes on important questions, a procedure already familiar in Ontario municipal government.[13]

As McCordic was to indicate later, the incipient problems developed considerably more quickly than he had foreseen. Of major importance were the increasing differences in the financial burden borne by the various municipalities, in contrast to the hope expressed at the time of the passage of *The Metropolitan Toronto Act* in 1953 that these would be progressively reduced. When the act was passed, provision was made for maintenance assistance payments of $150 per elementary school pupil, $250 per academic secondary school student, and $300 per vocational secondary school student. These amounts constituted about 60 per cent of gross expenditure at both levels, to be paid from a uniform levy throughout the area. This percentage was even then regarded as inadequate to meet the Cumming report's objective of an acceptable standard. Yet it continued to decline in succeeding years. The metropolitan board had a considerable majority of members from municipalities that would have lost by the increase in the levy required to augment the payments. By 1963 the amounts they had been persuaded to approve had risen only to $205 per elementary school pupil, and to $335, $380 and $535 per academic, commercial, and technical secondary school student respectively. Since the average unit costs in these respective categories for the whole metropolitan area were $408, $636, $651, and $1,060, the corresponding percentages defrayed by maintenance assistance payments had fallen to 50.2, 52.7, 58.4, and 50.5. Increases of $45, $30, $40, and $40 in the four categories in the same order during 1964 made no substantial difference.

Scarborough's case was presented in the Legislature early in 1964 by G.H. Peck, member for Scarborough South. He claimed that the maintenance assistance payments in 1954 defrayed 82 per cent of the cost of the area's public schools, but only 61 per cent in 1961, with a small rise to 66 per cent in 1962. The corresponding percentages for secondary schools were 87, 52, and 56.[14]

A similar story of a gradual shift of the financial burden back to individual municipalities is evident from an examination of some trends in capital expenditure. As pointed out earlier, the act transferred the responsibility for retiring all existing school debentures from the local boards to the metropolitan board, and required the latter to finance the part of future capital expenditures that was approved for grant purposes by the Department of Education. As of January 1, 1954, the amount approved by the department was $20,000 for both elementary and secondary classrooms. This amount was considered reasonably satisfactory for elementary schools, but completely inadequate for secondary schools. An increase to $25,000 in 1959 for secondary school classrooms still left the grant far below the actual cost, which was rising rapidly for schools at both levels. The provision at the same time of grants for general purpose rooms in elementary schools, for shop and home economics rooms, libraries, and cafeterias in schools at both levels, and for gymnasiums in secondary schools did not solve the problem. The major part of the burden of financing the part of capital projects not covered by the grants fell on the three largest municipalities, which were at or near the bottom of the list in terms of taxable capacity. Between 1954 and 1963, the share of capital costs borne by the local school boards rose from 35 to nearly 57 per cent.

In 1963 the Ontario Municipal Board warned the metropolitan council that the amount of debt being assumed by local municipalities was threatening to get out of hand in view of the demands that continuing expansion was making upon them. It was suggested that the metropolitan council seek a remedy in the legal provision that enabled it to assume a larger share of school debt in an amount recommended by the Metropolitan School Board. As a result, the two agencies established a special committee to consider school finance. This committee recommended that the metropolitan council assume all existing school debt, that is, all debt incurred by the local municipalities on behalf of local school boards since January 1, 1954, and that, as of January 1, 1964, the council assume all new school debt up to a ceiling cost formula prepared by the Metropolitan School Board and approved by the council. The second of these recommendations was adopted, but not the first.

The basic financial problem lay in the wide variation in taxable assessment per pupil from one municipality to another. In 1963 the relative positions of the respective municipalities in terms of elementary and secondary school populations and assessment were as shown in Table 7-2. Scarborough, North York, and East York were in the least favourable position, and Leaside, Forest Hill, and Toronto in the most favourable. During 1962–3 a mill increase in the rate of taxation in Scarborough would yield $9.50 per pupil, while the same increase in Toronto would yield $25.90, in Forest Hill, $38.10, and in Leaside, $43.50, as pointed out in the Metropolitan School Board brief to the Goldenberg Royal Commission.

The consequences of the differences in taxable assessment are shown in Table 7-3. Generally speaking, the municipalities that spent the most per elementary school pupil had the lowest mill rates, and vice versa. For example, Leaside spent $611 per pupil with the fourth lowest rate, and Scarborough spent only $378 per pupil with the highest rate.

The existing situation was difficult also in the light of variations in local needs. It is no discredit to the educational leaders and voters of Toronto who had provided an unusual complement of special services for the disadvantaged and the handicapped to point out that they had responded to

TABLE 7-2

School assessment in Metropolitan Toronto, 1963

MUNICIPALITY	PERCENTAGE OF			
	Public elementary school		Public secondary school	
	Population	*Assessment*	*Population*	*Assessment*
East York	3.30	2.90	4.03	2.96
Etobicoke	12.66	11.89	14.22	11.91
Forest Hill	0.75	1.73	1.69	1.67
Lakeshore	2.05	2.25	2.23	2.30
Leaside	0.71	1.84	1.44	1.80
North York	22.40	17.23	21.82	17.31
Scarborough	20.07	10.43	17.08	10.58
Swansea	0.35	0.55	0.52	0.54
Toronto	30.84	45.50	29.71	45.05
Weston	0.50	0.62	0.70	0.60
York Township	6.37	5.06	6.56	5.28
Total	100	100	100	100

SOURCE: Ontario, *Report of the Royal Commission on Metropolitan Toronto*, H. Carl Goldenberg, commissioner (June 1965), Table 44, p. 139.

TABLE 7-3

School mill rates for residential public school supporters and cost per pupil in Metropolitan Toronto, 1963

MUNICIPALITY	MILL RATE FOR PUBLIC SCHOOL SUPPORTERS	COST PER PUPIL IN DOLLARS			
		Public elementary	Academic secondary	Commercial secondary	Technical secondary
East York	30.61	460	590	677	
Etobicoke	26.69	416	663	818	1,071
Forest Hill	30.09	589	796		
Lakeshore	25.22	413	663	810	957
Leaside	25.42	611	680	586	
North York	31.25	448	650	831	1,078
Scarborough	31.61	378	670	728	1,018
Swansea	25.11	427			
Toronto	29.10	523	768	640	1,212
Weston	24.19	410	562	586	797
York Township	29.99	426	621	618	860
Average		453	684	711	1,111

SOURCE: Ontario, *Report of the Royal Commission on Metropolitan Toronto*, H. Carl Goldenberg, commissioner (June 1965), pp. 132, 134–35, and 138.

an unusually strong set of pressures. They faced the social problems resulting from poverty in the downtown areas and the necessity of preparing immigrant children with language and other difficulties to adapt to a bewildering new environment. Teachers who once regarded the city as a most desirable place to teach became increasingly antipathetic toward traffic congestion, noise, and other disadvantages of teaching in the heart of the metropolitan area, and thus increasingly difficult to attract at the same salaries as those offered by the more attractive suburbs. Another important factor that worked against the developed areas was the increasing age and unsuitability of many of their schools. Although the metropolitan system had made it possible to replace the worst of these, it was easier to make a case for the construction of a bright new suburban school where the children would otherwise be unhoused than for the destruction of an obsolete but still usable building. New sites that had to be purchased near the centre of the city were often inordinately expensive, and the local taxpayer bore the burden. The financial measures open to the Metropolitan School Board simply did not allow differential treatment to take account of such variations.

At the root of the whole problem was the position of those trustees who were expected to serve the best interests both of their own local constituents and of the entire area. These interests too often appeared to be in direct conflict; to do justice to one was to deny the other. And it was hardly surprising that the claims of the municipality the individual trustee represented tended to have the first call. After all, the trustee had been elected on a promise to render service to his own electorate to the best of his ability. There was no point in accusing him of shortsightedness or selfishness under such circumstances. The system might have worked effectively had the component municipalities been of comparable size and wealth, but there was little hope otherwise.

A situation that caused considerable irritation was Etobicoke's independent attitude toward the setting of teachers' salaries. This municipality always seemed to be in the forefront in granting increases, and the others felt compelled, regardless of the virtues of the case, to follow suit. Even more difficult to deal with was Etobicoke's success in out-manoeuvring its rivals by devising special categories of positions and duties with extra remuneration attached. The large number of professional educators on the Board of Education was seen, no doubt with considerable justification, as the reason for such policies, and prepared the way for a clause in Bill 81 designed to eliminate the influence of teacher-trustees. At this time the efforts of the Metropolitan Salary Coordinating Committee, which had no power to enforce its recommendations, were being continually frustrated. But yet it was difficult to blame the people of Etobicoke or their representatives for taking advantage of the situation to get the best possible education for their children.

Recognition of the seriousness of the financial problem led the Metropolitan School Board to establish a committee, headed by McCordic, to study the matter. This committee pointed to some of the anomalies already noted, and reported that certain local boards were compelled to deprive their pupils of recognized educational opportunities because of lack of funds. It identified the maintenance assistance payment scheme as only a partial solution, even if the payments were substantially increased. Other methods of equalization were also rejected in favour of a uniform tax rate throughout the area. In commenting on the proposal, J. Sydney Midanik, chairman of the board in 1962, pointed out that the necessity for some budget control and the resultant loss of some autonomy for the local boards constituted perhaps the most serious drawback.[15] McCordic called the recommendation a giant step for board members to take in view of their deep commitment to the principle of local autonomy. He pointed, however, to the "naïve assumption with which they concluded this first study, namely, that the uniform tax might be applied without any change in the present political organization involving eleven school boards."[16]

The study committee was re-established early in 1962 to look into the implications which a uniform tax rate would have for the relationships among the school boards. Every possible way of distributing the revenues from a uniform levy was given consideration. It was obvious that the local boards could not be permitted to control their own programs and deliver the entire bill to the metropolitan board to collect for them more or less automatically. The situation would require budgetary control by the metropolitan board, and an effective end to local autonomy. If the uniform tax rate were to work, there would have to be either complete amalgamation or a major step toward equalization by the consolidation of the existing municipalities into a limited number of boroughs. The latter solution might permit the continued decentralization of administration and, within limits, of policy making under the co-ordination of a fiscally responsible metropolitan board. Also considered feasible under the borough system was a foundation program plan of financing as an alternative to the uniform tax rate. It would have involved the underwriting by the Metropolitan School Board of a minimum program in terms of such factors as administrative costs, capital expenditure, debt charges, teachers' salaries, maintenance and operation of school plant, and supplies. Local areas would have been permitted to levy taxes for services above this minimum. The scheme would have given the metropolitan board the responsibility of devising a formula, and in many respects would have deprived the local boards, especially those in municipalities that were too poor to consider additional levies, of any real decision-making powers; there would have been little for them to do but follow the formula.

THE GOLDENBERG ROYAL COMMISSION

It was of course recognized that educational problems were not going to be solved in isolation. In many other aspects of its operations, the metropolitan system was breaking down, and demands for reform were becoming more insistent. An active step toward a solution came on June 20, 1963, with the appointment of H. Carl Goldenberg as royal commissioner with the following terms of reference:

to inquire into and report upon

(1)

(a) the structure and organization of the Municipality of Metropolitan Toronto and, more particularly, of the Metropolitan Council and the Metropolitan School Board, their functions and responsibilities and the relations with the area municipalities and the local school boards respectively and with municipalities and planning boards within the Metropolitan Toronto planning area,

(b) the purposes and objectives of the establishment of the Metropolitan Corporation and the Metropolitan School Board, the extent of the accomplishment of such objectives and whether such objectives can be better achieved under a new or revised system of local government, having regard to the past and future development and needs,

(c) the boundaries of the metropolitan area and of the area muncipalities and their suitability in the light of the experience gained through the operations of the metropolitan government, with due regard to probable future urban growth within or beyond the present metropolitan limits and future service requirements,

(d) any related matters affecting the government of the Toronto metropolitan region.

(2) after due study and consideration to make such recommendations with respect to the matters inquired into under the terms set out herein as the Commissioner sees fit to the Prime Minister and the Executive Council of Ontario.[17]

Following Goldenberg's appointment, numerous briefs were prepared and presented to him. In a visit to the Ontario College of Education in 1964,[18] McCordic discussed and appraised some of these. He noted that nine of the ten suburban boards, all but the Forest Hill Board, had instinctively made a case for self-preservation. Of these nine, the smaller ones opted for the status quo, and even those that had suffered serious disadvantages under it were prepared to offer the "success" of the metropolitan organization as the main reason for continuing the system. The four larger suburbs were prepared to absorb their neighbours in the implementation of a borough plan, while Toronto favoured total amalgamation, which really meant that all the other systems would be absorbed by the Toronto system.

The brief presented by the Metropolitan School Board offered the general outlines of a solution in the form of answers to certain questions. Most of these are presented here in summarized form. 1 / It was asserted that, under one central board with regional committees, regional boundaries would have to be coterminous with municipal boundaries if a foundation tax plan were adopted. If they were not coterminous, such a scheme would involve variations in tax rates from region to region, and the preparation of tax bills would be excessively complex. On the other hand, if there were to be a uniform tax for education, and budgetary responsibility vested in the central board, the location of the boundaries would not particularly matter. 2 / Regional committees would perform most of the functions of the existing boards of education. They would engage in local planning, recruit and deploy staff, analyse the need for new school accommodation, select sites and develop initial building plans within an established cost formula, review all plans for repair and maintenance of existing plant, and ensure that board action was being taken on all matters relating to supervision, curriculum, teaching aids, and in-service training. 3 / Representation of the Department of Education on the central board was not thought desirable. A single representative would be little more than an observer unless he had special powers. It was suggested that traditional practice be maintained whereby the board would have substantial autonomy subject to the statutes and departmental regulations. 4 / Opposition was expressed to the idea of municipal council representation on the board. If the intention were to give the council a measure of control over board expenditures, a more drastic solution was required. Again, a single representative from the outside agency would probably be only an observer. In view of past experience with the Metropolitan School Board, support was offered for a board composed of members who also served as local trustees. 5 / While programs would inevitably differ from one area to another, differences in standards should be relatively minor. There seemed to be no good reason why any part of Metropolitan Toronto should be in a specially favourable position to provide buildings, teachers, or curricula. 6 / No enthusiasm was expressed for the idea that the province should be solely responsible for administrative and operational costs, although new sources of municipal revenue would have to be provided. Provincial assumption of school building costs seemed a more likely possibility. 7 / Members of the Metropolitan School Board were unable to offer anything but a variety of individual opinions on how the increasing burden of the property tax should be dealt with.[19]

There were some particular virtues in the brief presented by Forest Hill, the only small suburb that seemed prepared to face the necessity for drastic change. This situation was accepted with certain regrets. The brief pointed out that "the Forest Hill schools over the years have come to be recognized as one of those 'lighthouse' school systems which have enjoyed the leadership and drive and resources needed to pioneer new developments in education and to move well beyond levels of excellence regarded as acceptable elsewhere."[20] Credit was claimed for service to other school systems through example and the provision of staff.

It was recognized that administrative units in an area the size of Metropolitan Toronto had to be larger than Forest Hill to be effective, and that all should share in the available tax resources of the whole area. Despite progress under the Metropolitan School Board, there was documented evidence that inequalities in the distribution of these resources continued to be very serious, and a remedy had to be found. The purpose of the brief was to make constructive suggestions that might assist in planning the new structure so that the existing advantages of the Forest Hill organization might be retained. Among the advantages of the well-structured and well-functioning smaller organization were 1 / the encouragement of individual initiative, 2 / ease of communication and simplicity of co-ordination, 3 / a high order of human relations, 4 / a point of decision close to the point of action, and 5 / responsiveness of local officials and schools to the local community.[21]

Certain disadvantages of highly centralized school systems were pointed out, with Australia as an example. At first glance, it appeared that progress should be rapid, since the central authority had the power to keep laggard schools in line. But, although central planning was facilitated, no change could be brought about until the state authorities were persuaded that it was good enough to justify general adoption, and that the taxpayers of the whole state would accept it. The system made small-scale experimentation in local areas unduly difficult. It was acknowledged that "freedom under decentralization may in fact be freedom to make mistakes and to fail; but it is also freedom to be successful and to show the way beyond an existing general level of operation."[22] The brief stressed that, in a larger system, every effort must be made to decentralize as far as possible.

In specific terms, it was recommended that consideration be given to the establishment of a number of area school divisions within Metropolitan Toronto. Since some of the existing systems were too large to allow for the maximum advantages of small systems, it would be necessary to increase the number of local divisions. Each division would be headed by a director who would "report directly to the office of an official known as the Senior Director of Education."[23] The divisional director would lead and co-ordinate all schools, both elementary and secondary, and would have a staff of specialists in such areas as in-service development, curriculum, psychological services, and other pupil services. The central office would have a co-ordinating and over-all policy role, but would not need a large office staff, since specialist instructional personnel would be attached to the local division office. The organization would be relatively flat at both the central and divisional levels: that is, a large number of officials would report to the director. This plan was considered the best in terms of encouraging local initiative. Emphasis on a team approach was urged, with maximum participation of the staff in decisions affecting their schools.

There would be a single elected board of education for the metropolitan school system. In the light of experience elsewhere, reviewed in the brief, the Forest Hill board questioned whether local boards in the traditional pattern could "usefully be continued as formal sub-level legislating bodies within a larger school system." It appeared that "so little in the way of autonomy could be granted to local boards, in terms of effective policy decisions, especially in the obvious absence of fiscal powers, [that] such vestigial local boards would be a sham and probably a frustration to all concerned."[24] In addition to measures to encourage close relationships between schools and their local communities, and to ensure that employed officials worked effectively with citizens, the brief recommended the establishment of an educational council in each district. Its members would preferably be appointed by the central board, although they might alternatively be elected. They would act as an advisory group, with emphasis on investigation, inquiry, and communication with the local public. Their advice might be offered to the local director, to divisional representatives on the central board, or to the local community.

Against a general background of opposition to its point of view, the Toronto Board of Education, as already indicated, made a case for total amalgamation. McCordic, despite his personal opposition to this solution, acknowledged the virtues of the Toronto case. Toronto had built up a corps of extremely capable administrators, with broad experience and great prestige. It had pioneered in countless areas of educational activity and had been in the vanguard whenever new ideas were mooted. Board members and staff alike shared the view that the metropolitan area was not too large to constitute a sound administrative unit, and that the extension of the procedures they had developed would serve the best interests of the whole area. In view of the certainty that the extension of the benefits of the special services and facilities then enjoyed by Toronto to the suburban municipalities would have increased the burden on Toronto taxpayers, their motives for advocating amalgamation could not be explained in terms of an attempt to gain petty advantage. In recognizing these points, McCordic asserted that "the Toronto statement reflects an honest conviction and merits the same respect extended to the opposite position enunciated almost unanimously by the suburban boards."

Goldenberg had won particular renown as a negotiator and arbitrator in labour disputes, but he had little knowledge of educational administration and organization. The method of procedure he adopted in this area was thus to select a group of experienced advisers to gather the necessary information and work out a set of proposals within his general framework. This group consisted of J.R. Davidson, Toronto school trustee; G.E. Flower, Director of Graduate Studies, Ontario College of Education; D.W. Gilmour, Solicitor, Toronto Board of Education; R.W.B. Jackson, Director, Department of Educational Research, Ontario College of Education; W.J. McCordic, Executive Secretary, Metropolitan School Board; E.B. Rideout, Associate Professor of Education, Ontario College of Education; and D.L. Tough, Superintendent of Secondary Schools, North York Board of Education. Z.S. Phimister, at that time Director of Education for the city of Toronto, was a kind of semi-official member, but attended only one meeting. His position was somewhat delicate in that there was an expectation in some quarters that he would be named the chief official in a reconstituted Metropolitan School Board. His assumption of the position of Deputy Minister of Education in early 1965 of course aborted any such development.

The position of this committee was anomalous throughout. It met Goldenberg only twice, the second time to present him with its proposals. The impression that he left it to operate almost entirely on its own is, however, erroneous, since he kept in touch with its activities through the participation of two members of his staff. The advisers assumed that they were merely offering advice on a confidential basis, and were therefore somewhat taken aback to find their names published in the final report.

Various points of view were expressed by members of the committee as they discussed the issues. The two basic orientations have been described as the formula and the federalist positions. The first of these would have given the Metropolitan School Board relatively limited power, with its principal function that of devising and adjusting a formula for the distribution of funds to the local boards. The second involved greater authority and more flexibility for the metropolitan board, and would depend for its success on close co-operation between the authorities at the two levels in solving their common problems. On the question of how variations in local need should be handled, one view was that these should be regulated by a set of rules, while another was that each board should justify its claim for extra revenues to meet special needs, and the central agency should make a decision on the merits of the case. On the whole, the federalist position prevailed, and was reflected in Goldenberg's proposals, as well as in the subsequent legislation.

According to Goldenberg, the plan offered a middle course between complete centralization and complete decentralization, and was intended to provide flexibility in school administration. There was to be an elected central board with over-all responsibility for school finance and for the development of an acceptable and uniformly high standard of education for the whole area. In the words of the report,

> The administrative responsibilities of this board would be limited to matters related to area-wide policies, to coordination of mutual services, and to the provision of services which can best be provided on a metropolitan basis. Administration and management of the school programme would be decentralized and carried out by a number of local boards to be called District Education Councils. The boundaries of the districts would not be coterminous with municipal boundaries. With centralized finance, the taxable resources of the entire area would be available to all public school districts, while decentralized administration would preserve the initiative of local school staffs and the community interest in the school programme.[25]

Certain criteria were suggested in order to ensure the viability of the eleven proposed school districts. They were to be 1 / approximately equal in size; 2 / small enough so that the district educational council could perform most of the traditional functions of a school board with efficiency and understanding; 3 / within the administrative capacity of a superintendent of schools, supported by appropriate staff; 4 / large enough to provide a full range of services characteristic of urban centres; 5 / large enough to justify a corps of leaders with varied background and experience; 6 / large enough to warrant the use of modern business methods and equipment; 7 / so drawn that each district would manifest specific needs and characteristics to which the educational program could be responsive; 8 / delineated so as to require minimum alteration in existing school attendance areas; 9 / delineated with due regard for ravine valleys, expressways, and railroads that currently tended to separate one district from another.[26] Under the scheme, the metropolitan board would consist of twenty-two trustees, twenty elected by the districts and two appointed by the Metropolitan Separate School Board. The term of office would be three years, the same as for municipal representatives. Board members were to be paid an amount more commensurate with their responsibilities; the existing fixed maximum of $1,800 per year had been regarded as entirely inadequate. The district education councils were to be composed of the two trustees elected to represent the district on the metropolitan board, one appointed by the Metropolitan Separate School Board, and eight elected in the district.

The metropolitan board would set salary scales and policies, and teachers would be under contract to it. A central personnel office would suggest recruitment procedures and maintain staff records. But recruitment, appointment, promotion, and definition of duties would be left to the districts. The actual process of appointment by the central board would be practically automatic, assuming that the recommendation was within the established framework. "Lively competition for the most promising teachers would continue, but it would be based upon factors other than salary gimmicks, availability of parking space, and more lavish buildings, on which the present boards cannot compete on anything like an equal basis."[27] Goldenberg implicitly acknowledged the opposition of the teachers' federations to the idea of uniform salary schedules and policies. But he maintained that the variety of competitive features in existing schedules was not in the best interests of education. He suggested that the teachers were well equipped and organized to negotiate on an area-wide basis, and that the proposals were in their best interests.

Financial policies established by the central board would include salary scales, pupil-teacher ratios, the number of employees allowed for certain functions and services, and the allocation of funds for supplies and equipment. The board would also establish procedures to be followed by the district education councils for the preparation and submission of their budgets. In many respects, this process would be relatively routine. There would, however, be a certain amount of leeway for the provision of special equipment, special services, or experimentation, for which the districts would have discretionary fiscal powers; but these would not cover such items as teachers' salaries, nor would it be possible to exceed the ceiling cost formula for school building.

The proposed administrative arrangements were very much in the spirit of the Forest Hill brief. The chief executive officer of the metropolitan board would be a director of education, supported by a relatively small staff. Each district would have a superintendent responsible for both elementary and secondary education, who would report directly to the director of education. An administrative council, consisting of the director of education, his central staff, and the district superintendents, would advise the metropolitan board on policy. The district staffs would undertake the same range of activities currently required at the local level.

The proposals for education in the Goldenberg report were described as an ideal textbook solution, but they failed to give adequate recognition to the strength of established procedures, ingrained traditions, and vested interests. Furthermore, they overlooked the fundamental principle that if a drastic change is to be made acceptable to a democratic society, it must be simple enough to be grasped by the ordinary individual and appealing enough to overcome his fears of sudden change. The Goldenberg scheme aroused immediate opposition among school officials, not only in the smallest municipalities that were headed for oblivion in any case, but also among the larger ones, where the desire to hold on to established empires was mingled with a genuine conviction that a local sense of identity and local pride in past achievements were in danger of being sacrificed in favour of units that would exist, at least initially, mainly for administrative convenience. The teachers were unhappy for reasons already indicated.

In political terms, the proposals could not be adopted in any recognizable form because the school board arrangement had to correspond with that of the boroughs. The decision with respect to the number and identity of the boroughs involved the crucial issue of whether or not the city of Toronto would be augmented in such a way as to restore it to a position of approximate equality with all the other units combined. In accordance with the policy already referred to of keeping the city in check, the decision was to let it decline. Thus East York kept its identity, with the addition of Leaside, as did York with the addition of Weston, rather than being combined with Toronto. Etobicoke absorbed the Lakeshore municipalities, while North York and Scarborough remained as they were.

THE LEGISLATION OF 1966

The actual preparation of the legislation in 1966 was preceded by a white paper outlining the government's proposals. This document declared that local control of education was to be continued as far as practicable. Local boards were to retain broad powers sufficient to enable them to meet the requirements of an effective educational program. The existing two-tier structure was to continue, with the Metropolitan School Board having the responsibility of controlling and co-ordinating finance.

Several of the leading officials in the local systems decided that the scheme was workable, and expressed their approval in principle. They were accordingly in a favourable position to influence further developments by playing an active part in drafting Bill 81 defining the new set-up. At the time of writing, it would be of doubtful propriety to record the names of these individuals, or to discuss their specific role.

The act provided for a board of education for each of the six boroughs that would exist after the restructuring of the metropolitan area: East York, Etobicoke, North York, Scarborough, Toronto, and York. The members, like their counterparts in the municipal councils, would hold office for a three-year term. No employee of a board of education in the metropolitan area or of the Metropolitan Toronto School Board, as it was now officially called, was eligible to be a member of any board of education in the metropolitan area. This particular clause was a direct result of the antagonism that had resulted among other trustees and school officials from the independent policies with respect to teacher employment practices pursued by the educator-dominated Etobicoke board. Predictably, the teachers' federations protested against the clause. Their case was supported by J.B. Trotter, Liberal member of the Legislature from Parkdale.

> I do not think that teachers should be on a board of education in the borough where they teach; that may be so, but by banning teachers from sitting in the Metro area we are banning one of the most important groups in our society.
>
> They are among the most capable people to be on a board of education; why keep them off? Let us leave it up to the common sense of the public that the board is not loaded with teachers. It would be wrong if the teachers completely ran the board, but with the newspapers looking on, with radio and television, I believe that no group of teachers would gang up to take over any board of education.[28]

In defence of the restrictive provision, T.L. Wells, member of the Legislature for Scarborough North, pointed out that there was nothing new in the bill in that the general legislation of the province had for a considerable number of years provided that no employee of a school board might serve on the board that employed him. At this particular juncture, while a teacher was technically employed by a borough board of education, the financing of something like 95 per cent of that board's expenses was to be through the Metropolitan School Board. Mr Wells

CHART 7-2
School systems of Metropolitan Toronto, 1967

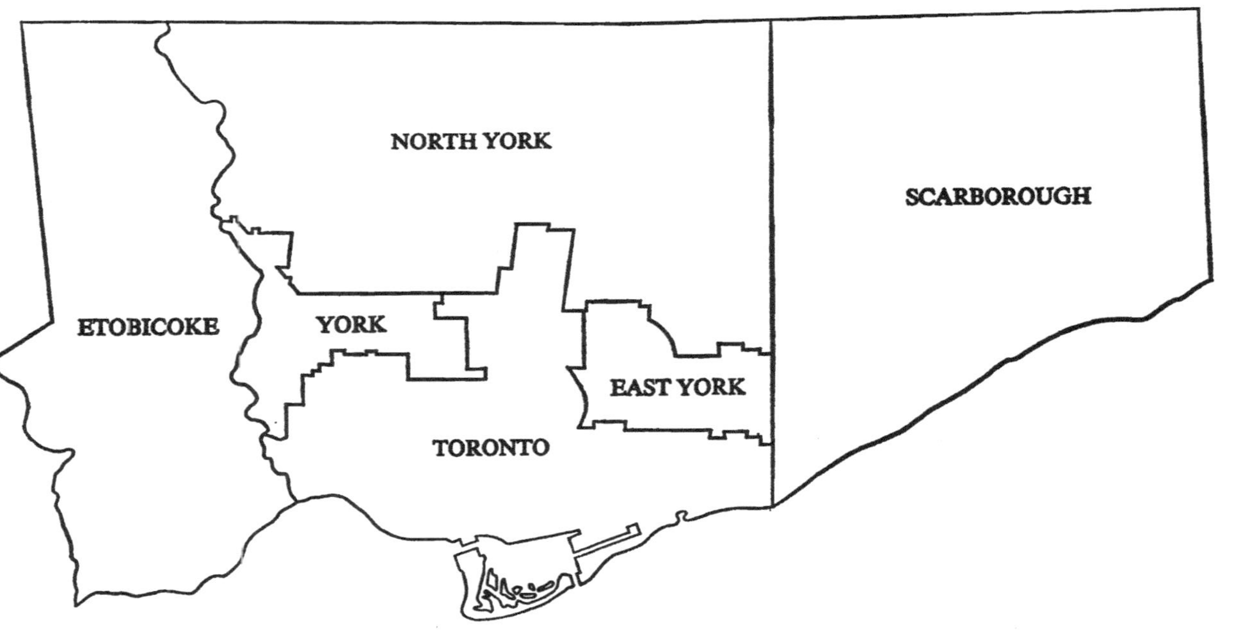

the Metropolitan Separate School Board, who were to get no more than $1,200; 7 / to submit estimates of expenditure for the current year to the metropolitan council. Current funds from a levy not to exceed four mills might be spent on capital projects. As before, legislative grants were to be paid to the Metropolitan School Board, except for those to local boards with respect to expenditures made by the latter for the construction of classrooms and for items eligible for stimulation grants. The local boards were to submit their estimates directly to the Metropolitan Toronto School Board rather than to the local municipal council.

According to the prescribed procedures for budget making, each local board was to prepare estimates separately for public elementary and secondary school purposes by a date and in a form determined by the Metropolitan Toronto School Board. The latter, with the responsibility of providing as effectively as possible for the needs of the whole metropolitan area, was to approve these estimates in whole or in part. Its basic task was to reconcile the demands made by all the local boards within what it regarded as reasonable limits of total expenditure, and to make arrangements for raising the necessary revenue by means of a uniform levy on all ratable property in the metropolitan area. If a local board's estimates were accepted only in part, it might requisition funds from the local municipal council for the unapproved part up to the amount that could be raised in the area by a levy of one and one-half mills on the dollar for public elementary school purposes and one mill on the dollar for secondary school purposes. This provision was designed to give the local boards some flexibility to provide for special needs and experimental programs. A local board that took exception to the metropolitan board's decision regarding its estimates might appeal to the Ontario Municipal Board which, after a public hearing, might dismiss the appeal or sustain it and require the metropolitan board to provide additional funds. It was obvious that there would need to be a reasonable amount of good will among those who reflected conflicting interests if the whole process were to have a chance of working smoothly.

The Metropolitan Toronto School Board assumed all existing school debt, that is, the amount accumulated after January 1, 1954, and was responsible for all future debt. No local board could henceforth discontinue the operation and maintenance of any school under its jurisdiction or dispose of any school site or building or any item of school property, the cost of which had been financed in whole or in part by the issue of debentures, without the approval of the metropolitan board. The proceeds of the sale of such property were to go to the metropolitan board, and must be used for capital expenditure for either public or secondary school purposes, depending on the origin of the funds.

As before, the local boards were to submit their capital budgets to the metropolitan board, which would prepare and submit the composite capital program to the metropolitan council. Individual applications for approval of capital expenditures might be handled in one of two ways. 1 / The existing routine might be followed, in which each application would be scrutinized by the metropolitan board, the Department of Education, and the Ontario Municipal Board. With the approval of these successive agencies, an architect might be appointed, plans might be prepared, and tenders called. The Ontario Municipal Board might then give its consent, if no increase in debenture approval were involved. 2 / The metropolitan council and the Ontario Municipal Board might grant approval of a year's program, thus eliminating the necessity for further consideration of individual applications. The responsibility for approving applications for specific projects within this framework would then be left to the metropolitan board.

There were several other significant provisions with respect to capital expenditure. 1 / The metropolitan board might spend a maximum of four mills in current funds toward the cost of capital projects not financed by debentures. 2 / The metropolitan board could buy land in its own name to provide for schools to serve the needs of pupils from more than one school district, and could have the metropolitan council borrow money to finance such expenditure. The land might subsequently be conveyed to a local board having jurisdiction in part of the area from which the pupils would attend the school when erected. 3 / Local boards might use any part of their local levy, which, as explained earlier, was not to exceed two and one-half mills for public elementary and secondary purposes together, for capital expenditure not approved by the metropolitan board. 4 / Either a local board or the metropolitan board might appeal to the Ontario Municipal Board any decision of the metropolitan council with respect to any individual application. The Ontario Municipal Board, after conducting public hearings, was to dismiss the appeal or require the metropolitan council to raise the necessary funds. 5 / Local boards and councils might enter into financial agreements for the construction and operation of swimming pools constructed as part of a school building.

PROSPECTS OF SUCCESS FOR THE NEW ARRANGEMENT

The act left large areas of responsibility entirely undefined, thus rejecting the definiteness of the Goldenberg recommendations. When the white paper indicated that this was what was coming, McCordic, who was later named Director of Education for the metropolitan board, commented that the government "doesn't even render a verdict on the two most sensitive issues: school building standards and teachers' salaries."[30] The metropolitan school authorities were left to work out a new set of relationships by themselves. They faced a challenge of joint planning involving the six boroughs working through the medium of a fiscally responsible metropolitan school authority. McCordic thought it would be easier to make the scheme succeed if there were a more clearly defined plan to follow.

The legislation did not, of course, fulfill his hope that there would be more definite guidelines than any found in the white paper.

The basic concept behind the new educational plan was not seriously criticized except by those who continued to insist that complete amalgamation was the best solution. But there was adverse reaction to a number of aspects. Some of these were listed in *School Progress*[31]; all those mentioned in the article are presented here for the sake of completeness, even though some have already been referred to. 1 / There was opposition to the idea that the metropolitan board might make value judgments (presumably about school programs). 2 / There would be problems in connection with teachers' salary schedules, even though individual boards had agreed on a uniform schedule. 3 / The Ontario Teachers' Federation was opposed to the barring of teachers receiving salary from one board from serving as trustees on any other board. 4 / One board and other individual critics were against the proposed cabinet of six directors of borough boards and the director of education for the metropolitan board, feeling that such a centralized system was too far removed from parent, teacher, and child. 5 / There was some room for apprehension over capital construction costs and the division of revenues for this purpose.

The same issue of *School Progress* identified concern on the part of members of the Ontario Association of School Business Officials over the clause in Bill 81 specifying that each of the six metropolitan boards of education was to have a director of education who "shall also be the secretary-treasurer of such board."[32] Members of the association were said to feel that this clause represented a change in policy on the appointment of secretary-treasurers that would in time affect the province as a whole. They were prepared to agree that in some cases it was desirable for a board to combine the two functions in one post, but they objected to the elimination of the board's option of separating them. The article attributed to the Department of Education the view that, since the six area directors would be "members of the central board" (presumably referring to the "cabinet"), it seemed desirable that they should be aware of the financial implications of the policies they discussed, and that the best way to achieve that objective was to make the director the secretary-treasurer as well. The response of the OASBO members was apparently that one man could not possibly begin to know everything about educational matters and finances as well, particularly in school systems as large and complex as those in Metro, and that the director would have to rely heavily on a financial aide in any case. The conclusion was that the appointment of a separate secretary-treasurer could accomplish the same thing. There was no mention in the article of the consequence of rivalry between two officials with equal status in relation to the board, which is generally regarded as the real issue in the question of unitary versus dual control.

In his Phi Delta Kappa address, McCordic identified a challenge to several groups whose interests would be vitally involved in the new set-up. Speaking of the teachers, he commented:

Instinctively, I identify with the trustee point of view. Yet I have never had any basic quarrel with the teachers' claim that their employment is with a local board, that it is from this local board they receive their pay, and it is this local board which should set the rates of pay. Indeed, my sabbatical offered me ample opportunity to observe the depressing effect of a nation-wide salary scale upon the level of teacher income. Yet, the nature of the new financial inter-relationship of the six Metro school authorities is such that I cannot imagine the borough boards maintaining a satisfactory relationship with each other if they remain in competition in the matter of teachers' salaries. Moreover, competition may not really be the boon claimed by teachers. There is a real possibility that inter-borough competition will keep salary schedules rigid and unresponsive to the real needs of the time. For instance, the claims of down-town teachers for added salary in proportion to the extra burdens they bear can only be worked out in a Metro-wide scale. Special adjustments to increase the supply of teachers in areas where the supply is inadequate, likewise cannot be fashioned within the present competitive arrangements. I would argue that the new deal for Metro poses a real challenge for teachers. I can only assume that they will not abandon immediately their present insistence that salaries be negotiated locally, but I recognize as one of the basic requisites of an ultimate and lasting solution in Metro that teachers will ultimately agree voluntarily to co-operate in the establishment of Metro-wide salary policies.

The prophecy contained in the last sentence proved quite correct. After a couple of years of unsatisfactory dealings with the local boards, the teachers requested Metro-wide negotiations.

The challenge faced by the administrators and senior personnel was in part to change existing habits and practices. During the first stage of metropolitan government, there had been increasing opportunities for these people to meet and compare notes. But there was always an underlying feeling that co-operation was only one alternative, and that a local board could go its own way if it chose to do so. Now there was a real obligation to work together. McCordic hoped that this inter-involvement of educational leadership would "in the long run strengthen rather than weaken the spirit of enterprise both at the local level and on a Metro-wide basis."

McCordic did not see the metropolitan board exercising an autocratic, overriding authority. Instead, he visualized the chief officers becoming part of an administrative committee acting both as the executive arm of the central authority and as spokesmen for the local boards. He felt that the central staff and officials should be a catalyst rather than a power plant. Indeed, it is hard to visualize the strong-minded leaders who were then in charge of the borough systems acting as anyone's puppets. One can well imagine some vigorous arguments during their weekly meetings in the Advisory Council of Directors, as it became designated, before they hammered out a solution to controversial problems.

The challenge to trustees was that they would have to combine an appreciation of local needs with a greater interest in Metro-wide issues than a number of them had shown in the past. They would have to develop a fuller realization that revenues required to pursue their own programs must come from levies on the whole area. They would have to establish a productive relationship with their colleagues from other areas.

Barry G. Lowes, first chairman of the metropolitan board under the new arrangement, asked his assembled colleagues: "Will it work?"[33] His answer reflected more grim determination than certainty: "I say to you: it can work, it will work, it must work." He went on to review some of the issues and problems that confronted the board. He pointed out that, although the government had not accepted all the recommendations in the Goldenberg report, the basic consideration of this report remained the issue of Bill 81, that is, that the financial resources of the total metropolitan area be made available to all parts of Metro. He referred to the problem of housing the swelling numbers of pupils in the area, amounting to an increase of approximately 17,000 per year. Although half a billion dollars had been invested in 246 new schools, 518 additions, and 563 sites or site extensions since Metro began, they were still losing ground. They simply could not afford to save money by failing to plan and build for known future needs.

Lowes referred to the frustrating fact that the school authorities had no control over the pace of municipal development. While this was as it should be, he felt that there was room for consideration of the financial costs to school boards when housing developments were planned. There was room for closer co-operation with other municipal agencies.

Within the general framework of equal opportunity, Lowes emphasized the importance of providing for the special needs of each particular borough: "It will be our ability to identify, recognize and serve these varying needs that will be the measure of the success of this new Metropolitan Toronto School Board." In elaborating on this point, he mentioned the culturally deprived children, who were mainly concentrated in downtown Toronto, but to some extent also scattered throughout the Metro area. They would need junior kindergartens, smaller, ungraded classes, and special teachers backed up by resource teams if the cycle of poverty and despair was to be broken. Lowes referred to the problems of immigrant children, who also needed special classes and treatment if they were to be integrated into the full life of the community. He expressed the hope that other levels of government would assist in meeting the extra financial burdens of the program. In the area of special education, there was a great deal to be proud of, including, for example, the more than one thousand classes for those with a wide variety of difficulties and handicaps. But the needs of groups such as those with emotional disturbances were still far from being met.

Lowes identified as the board's most immediate problem that of salaries. As a means of ensuring that the best minds went into teaching, he felt that, in co-operation with the teachers, a system had to be devised to reward ability. He advocated a uniform salary scale across Metro that would provide equal pay for equal work under equal conditions. Criteria should be established that would recognize differences in teaching assignments and areas in which it was more difficult to teach. Consideration should be given to the possibility of paying bonuses, reducing class sizes, and hiring lay assistants. These were factors that constituted the basis for the Quality Teaching Study already initiated in 1966. Lowes recognized two opposite points of view with respect to salary negotiations: the first was that they were entirely within the area of responsibility of the local boards, and the metropolitan board must accept any decisions made by these bodies; the other was that the real decisions would be made by the metropolitan board. He suggested a middle course, with the teachers negotiating with the local boards that employed them within limits set by the metropolitan board. The outcome of the effort to operate in this way has already been mentioned.

ADMINISTRATIVE ARRANGEMENTS UNDER THE METROPOLITAN TORONTO SCHOOL BOARD

In the light of the metropolitan board's primary function of preparing the current and capital budgets for the entire area, a complex task extending throughout the year and involving a continuing assessment of the current educational program, the administrative structure was designed to facilitate this process. Reporting to the Director of Education were three officials, the Superintendent of Academic Programs, the Comptroller of Finance, and the Director of Capital Programming and Research. At the time of writing, the positions were held respectively by R.E. Jones, R.I. Thorman, and F.G. Ridge. These officials were respectively responsible for 1 / the assessment of educational programs and the co-ordination of the educational effort of the six local boards, 2 / the current budget and flow of funds to the local boards for their day-to-day operations, and 3 / working with local planning staff in the development of each area's capital requirements. The committee structure of the board, reflecting the same divisions, consisted of the Academic Committee, the Finance Committee, and the Building and Sites Committee.

The functions of the administrative staff were to a large extent informative and advisory. The Superintendent of Capital Programming and

Research and his assistants, for example, reviewed a list of building projects proposed by local boards, and helped to ensure that they were properly designated in terms of relative urgency. The local boards then submitted these to the metropolitan board for formal consideration. The latter, in consultation with local staffs, placed them on one of five levels in terms of priority.

The importance of accurate planning at both the metropolitan and local levels is emphasized by the instability of the school-age population in many parts of the area. A peak load quickly develops in the elementary schools of new subdivisions inhabited mainly by young families. There is a danger that the provision of enough regular school places for the maximum enrolment will leave empty classrooms a few years later. The policy in Metropolitan Toronto has been to provide permanent accommodation for less than the maximum enrolment, and to house the surplus in portable classrooms. In order to make the plan a success, demographic studies must be carefully conducted, taking into account such factors as birth rates, social changes within a community, housing starts and completions, subdivision proposals, and the decisions of various planning authorities.

The work of the Superintendent of Academic Programs involved the development of objective criteria against which area programs would be assessed. This assessment was a necessary step in determining which items were to be included in the composite budget for the whole metropolitan area. The criteria applied to such factors as the pupil-teacher ratio and the provision of junior kindergartens, inner city schools, and special education classes. Consideration was given to long-range goals as well as to arrangements that appeared to be immediately attainable under existing financial and other limitations. Special needs of particular areas were taken into account. For example, junior kindergartens were approved only in schools where the children of the surrounding area were thought to be in particular need of an early introduction to school activity because of social and cultural disadvantages.

The Committee of Board Chairmen became the effective executive of the metropolitan board. Their meetings were attended by the seven directors of education, who did not vote, but whose influence was not noticeably less on that account. It was said that the group's examination of common problems blurred the distinction between elected and appointed officials. They even reached the point where the director of the metropolitan board did not feel any need to withdraw when his salary was being discussed, even though it could by no means be assumed that proposals for large annual increases would automatically be approved.

RECENT DEVELOPMENTS

Even before the changes of January 1967, the metropolitan board had launched certain special research studies in co-operation or consultation with the local boards and various other agencies. One of these projects is the Study of Educational Facilities (SEF) under the technical direction of the well-known architect, R.G. Robbie. It began in 1966 in the hope of devising a scheme for building schools with modular components that would provide the flexibility to meet both current and future needs. The possibility of economizing was foreseen if parts of schools or entire buildings could be moved in accordance with population shifts. The results of this study are producing a revolution in school construction. The findings have helped to bring about a revision of the ceiling cost formula in Metro to provide simply a given number of square feet per pupil, leaving boards free to design schools as they see fit.

The first schools built in accordance with SEF principles were completed in 1970. These provided tangible evidence that buildings could be constructed in much less time and at a lower cost than traditional approaches had called for, while at the same time offering superior accommodation. Roden School, built for the Toronto Board of Education, was the SEF test school. Ten others were started a short time later, and it was expected that a total of thirty-two would be completed by July 1971. Publications from the study were circulated widely throughout Canada and the United States. The first two dealt with elementary and intermediate schools, while the third, published in 1970, recommended facilities for composite secondary schools.

Serious difficulties have been encountered in negotiations with the Metropolitan Toronto council over capital requirements. There have been frequent protests on the part of education officials over the council's power to reduce the board's requests, even though such action cannot occur over the objections of the Ontario Municipal Board. Exercise of this power has been criticized on the ground that it implies a claim to superior knowledge about school affairs on the part of council members. Regret has been expressed that Metropolitan Toronto was not given the same right as the county boards established in January 1969 to issue their own debentures without the necessity of seeking the approval of other municipal authorities. Another way of looking at the matter is that educational needs are seen somewhat differently when considered in relation to capital needs for all services combined, and that it is important that some responsible agency such as the council assess them all in perspective.

In 1967 and 1968 the metropolitan board presented capital budgets to the council totalling approximately $80 million. These were reduced by $6 million and $13 million in the respective years. Lowes commented in his third annual inaugural address in 1969:

> These continuing deferments are like fiscal peristalsis moving wave-like along into the next year's budget, until our 1969 capital program, even after a most diligent review and reduction, totals 109 million dollars. My colleagues and I are convinced that these funds are required, since even those pupil spaces

covered in the budget will have little impact on reducing the 1,119 portable classrooms presently in use, nor make any significant inroads into the replacement of our obsolete schools.

The need for a metropolitan information system was becoming urgent by 1969 in view of the desirability of having up-to-the-minute data. A debenture debt file was in usable form on the computer by the beginning of the year, resulting in a significant reduction in time required in the metro board office and in the Department of Education for the preparation of budgets and the processing of grant claims. The development of a personnel file, a supplies and materials file, and a fixed asset file in subsequent stages was regarded as important. The desirability of standardizing computer languages throughout the seven systems was being recognized.

Metro-wide studies were undertaken in 1968–9 leading to the adoption of a program for French-language secondary schools. At the request of the metro board, the North York board established such a school, L'Ecole secondaire Etienne Brulé, in portable classrooms on the grounds of York Mills Collegiate Institute. The North York board urged that legal arrangements be made to permit the metro board to assume the responsibility for establishing French-language schools in Metro Toronto, thus acting as a divisional board.

In 1969 the metro board became an operating board in another sphere in that it became responsible for the operation of schools for retarded children. One of the first steps taken was to provide for full-time attendance for children of ten and eleven years of age who had hitherto been able to attend for only half a day. As further accommodation became available, it was intended that the same privilege would be extended to younger children. An extensive program of staff training was planned for 1970, and research in co-operation with the University of Toronto and the University of Guelph was being conducted into the characteristics of retarded children and the teaching programs required for them.

The early months of 1970 were marked by a severe struggle between the school boards and the teachers' organizations. Not only were the latter asking for large salary increases, but they were also insisting on negotiating conditions of work. The school boards saw their responsibilities to the electorate threatened, and time passed without any sign that the impasse was being broken. The situation remained obscure at the time of writing. The issues in this contest are dealt with more fully in volume III.

The responses given by Lowes in successive inaugural addresses to his initial question provide an interesting contrast. In 1968 he asked again, "Will it work?" and answered, "I believe that the only honest reply is that we still do not know – but I believe that the accomplishments to date lead one to be optimistic rather than pessimistic about the ultimate outcome." He saw signs that the board was indeed emerging as a co-ordinating, co-operative, encouraging, and stimulating organization. In 1969 the question was repeated, and this time the response was that "on the basis of evidence generated in 1968, the question is no longer relevant – the answer is obviously yes – a resounding yes!" Lowes cited a number of reasons for this verdict. 1 / Communication had improved through the participation of more trustees and officials in the decision-making process. They were involved in numerous *ad hoc* committees, in the Quality Teaching Study, in the Advisory Council of Directors, and in the Committee of Board Chairmen. Reports were being referred to local boards for their reaction prior to a decision by the metro board, and staff were making visits to local boards to explain, to listen, and to confer. 2 / Trustees had demonstrated the capacity to bring complex and difficult budget negotiations to a successful conclusion. 3 / In order to avoid the interminable negotiations with the local boards that had occurred in 1968, the teachers had suggested that a plan be worked out for negotiations on a Metro basis. This approach offered good prospects for success. 4 / The Quality Teaching Study, the Study of Educational Facilities, and other research projects were proceeding well, and promised to produce important results. 5 / Substantial achievements had been registered in the field of special education.

On assuming the chairmanship in 1970, B.C. Bone reaffirmed the verdict of his predecessor. He also paid warm tribute to the contribution Lowes had made by providing the leadership under which members of the previous board had tackled their problems. His review of events during the previous year constituted fairly convincing evidence that real progress was being made.

APPRAISAL AND GENERAL APPLICABILITY OF THE METROPOLITAN TORONTO SYSTEM

To the observer, claims that the Metropolitan Toronto experiment in educational organization is a substantial success do not appear to be exaggerated. If one wishes to be cautious, he need of course only go back to the feeling of satisfaction and relief expressed a few years after the arrangements of 1953 had been put into operation. The situation deteriorated rapidly under changing conditions, and a radical overhaul of the structure soon became necessary. Similarly, the enlargement of problems now only dimly perceived will no doubt call for major adaptations in the future. But in the meantime the citizens of Metropolitan Toronto have a system that, in comparison with those of cities of comparable size in other parts of the world, appears to offer very favourable conditions for meeting their educational needs.

Despite successes achieved by the six metro boards in co-operation with the Metropolitan Toronto School Board, the press has continued to call for amalgamation of educational administration along with other municipal services. On August 30, 1969, the *Globe and Mail* published a response from the seven directors of education in the Metro area entitled "The case against amalgamating the school boards."[34] The article began by dismissing the claim that an amalgamated board was needed to guarantee equal opportunity for all, to spread the cost more evenly, or to provide a strong central body to plan and budget for the area as a whole, since the area already had all these things. On the other hand, the directors felt that such a board would not make the schools more sensitive to public opinion or to local need.

The article disputed the claim that the Metropolitan Toronto School Board was an extra layer of government, on the grounds that its members were locally elected and performed their functions in the metro board as extra duties. The set-up constituted a partnership in which the same people assumed varying roles as the circumstances warranted. At the staff level, the metro board relied on the advice of the six local directors and their associates as well as on that of its own small staff.

As a justification for maintaining a decentralized system of administration, reference was made to the size and complexity of the educational enterprise in the Metro area. There were 544 schools with 19,250 staff members to serve 400,000 children, many of whom required highly specialized services. Enrolment was increasing at an annual rate of between ten and twenty thousand, requiring fifteen or twenty new schools and one thousand new staff members along with two thousand replacements each year. The challenge was expressed in this way:

> Reflect upon the magnitude of this recruitment task – just one of the many responsibilities of a large school system. Each vacancy must be identified, a job specification written, advertisements prepared, applications reviewed, qualifications and experience checked, applicants interviewed, and appointments made ... Is this the kind of painstaking, sensitive task that can be carried out successfully in a central office? Is it a function that can be performed on a mass basis? Can it be done more cheaply? We think not.
>
> Multiply the complexities of such a massive recruitment program by a score of other functions and responsibilities – the planning and acquisition of school sites, the design of new schools, the care and maintenance of buildings, curriculum design, supervision, in-service training of staff, purchasing, personnel problems – the list is staggering.

In essence, the directors' case was that, if the worst disadvantages of a massive bureaucracy were to be avoided, there would have to be a decentralized administration in some form. Since one had already been evolved, and was working reasonably well, there seemed to be no good reason for changing it. The positive side was stated thus:

> In an effort to avoid duplication among the six local boards, the greatest variety of approach has been encouraged in a spirit of healthy competition. All start

with the same bank account, and the competition, therefore, is in terms of originality, effort, and quality. Retention of the community school board has preserved in Metro Toronto a sense of local responsibility.

As part of a general appraisal, it should be pointed out that McCordic himself has not escaped criticism. There are those who have accused him of excessive personal ambition. It has been almost inevitable that such a cry should have been raised in view of the fact that the acceptance of the prescriptions that he has favoured for the metropolitan area have tended to place him in an increasingly influential role. His promotion to the pre-eminent position in the set-up necessarily precluded the selection of any other candidate, no matter how well qualified. Further, he has had to act firmly in order to overcome the effects of extreme local loyalties. Success in this effort could hardly be expected to leave a feeling of pure happiness and harmony. There is general recognition that the development of an effective two-tier organizational structure for Metro has been almost a religion with him. He appears to have worked just as vigorously in that cause when it appeared probable that Phimister would be the first director of education under a strengthened metropolitan board as when he himself seemed headed for the top position. Although this writer has little basis in direct experience for an assessment, he is prepared to predict that history will deal kindly with this man, and that certain qualities that some have seen as faults will in retrospect be judged as virtues.

The question of the possible application of the Metropolitan Toronto solution in other similar circumstances has often been considered. Here again we may refer to McCordic. In attempting to answer this question, he first of all reviews the fundamental principles on which the plan seems to be based.[35] 1 / It is consistent with the belief that public education should be under the supervision of laymen elected from the community. Once elected, the school trustee's first loyalty is considered to be toward the area he serves. Each area is conceded the right to determine its own educational goals, and to meet them in its own way. 2 / In a large metropolitan area, the upper-tier authority must have the responsibility of devising an integrated financial plan in order to guarantee equality of educational opportunity in the face of wide local disparities in the ability to finance education. 3 / To ensure that the upper-tier authority does not drift into too dominant a position, its board should be composed almost entirely of local officials, and local board staff should be meaningfully involved in the staff functions of the central board. 4 / Fiscal unification calls for an integrated system of accounting based on a uniform code of accounts. 5 / The upper-tier authority requires a research and development capacity to integrate the local plans into a rational whole. 6 / The upper tier's fiscal policies must be flexible enough to ensure that the flow of funds is directed according to need, and modified as new priorities develop.

McCordic proceeds to specify certain conditions that must exist in order to make the Metropolitan Toronto system applicable elsewhere. 1 / A higher level of government must be willing and able to impose the system on a municipal unit or units. 2 / Social gulfs created by racial differences and extremes of wealth and poverty must not be so great as to produce a refusal on the part of the more fortunate to pool common resources in the interests of the entire community. 3 / The majority must not be excessively determined to cling to the status quo. It is always a question, however, how much one community's example can help another to solve its own problems. And Toronto must always be aware of its tradition of complacency and self-satisfaction.

EIGHT

Provincial financial assistance to schools

INTRODUCTION

The very rapid expansion of financial activities in the field of education during the post-war period has been traced in volume I, chapter 7. The present account is an attempt to show how financial structures and practices have developed and changed during the same period. The initial review of the major historical landmarks represents a relatively undifferentiated treatment of the topic. For the more recent period, revenue, expenditure, debt, and budgetary practices are dealt with separately. In addition to these dimensions, expenditure may involve the publicly supported school systems, the universities, other tertiary institutions, those parts of the government apparatus responsible for administering or facilitating the operation of the system, and private associations and institutions. Expenditure also involves a distinction between operating funds and those used for capital investment. A review of events and developments in these areas leads into an examination of some of the current problems and of the recommendations for solution offered by responsible observers.

GRANTS FOR OPERATING EXPENDITURE

Early history

Provincial financial support for education began almost with the establishment of the first schools. For many years, however, it was sporadic and meagre. In the early nineteenth century, education was not looked upon as a means of promoting the welfare of society at large, but rather as an amenity with purely local implications. Each community, its economic activity centred mainly on agriculture, was largely self-contained and self-sustaining. Education was one of the services for which it was held basically responsible. The province was prepared only to help stimulate local initiative and to sustain it to a very minor degree.

A private school at Cataraqui received the first government grant to education in Upper Canada in 1796, in the amount of £100. After a lapse of eleven years, the passage of the District Public School Act provided for a legislative grant of the same size to be given to the master of each of the eight district schools.[1] These investments were apparently intended at least in part to help educate young men for the public service. A similar motive was also evidently behind the Royal Land Grant of 1797, by which half a million acres were set aside to form a fund for the establishment and maintenance of four grammar schools and a university. While King's College received an endowment of a little under a quarter of a million acres in 1828, the grammar schools were denied their inheritance until a new act was passed in 1839, although Upper Canada College received 66,000 acres from the university endowment at the time of its founding ten years earlier.

Support for elementary education actually began after these first hesitant steps to assist the grammar schools. In 1816 the Common School Act authorized the annual payment of up to £25 to each common school to help provide the teacher's salary. Apparently the implementation of this provision was at first somewhat erratic and unrelated to local effort. According to Phillips, the latter aspect was attributable in the early years to the fact that "paternalism preferred to give the people anything rather than power."[2]

Toward the middle of the century, provincial interest became more intense and comprehensive. Grants began to be used as a device to pressure local communities into adopting desirable practices and to extend educational services. Ryerson saw them as a means of establishing provincial control so that the community's right to provide for education or not as it saw fit could be effectively challenged.

The first major step toward enforcing a minimum level of local effort came in 1850, when municipalities were given the right to levy rates for the support of the common schools. Three choices were available for defraying school costs: voluntary subscription, a rate-bill for each child attending school, and a property tax. Provision was made for fixing the rate-bill at a maximum of one shilling and threepence per month for each child. This maximum was later reduced as part of the movement toward free schools. Within twenty years, it was obvious that the provision for permissive taxation was inadequate. "Although the schools in a few favoured municipalities were supported generously, the great majority of them were seriously handicapped through the lack of funds."[3] The Act of 1871 established the principle of compulsory local taxation and made the common schools free. Although the high schools could continue the fee system, the municipalities were required by the same act to raise from local sources a sum equal to half the government grant paid to such schools within their jurisdiction, along with certain other funds. High school boards were authorized to make known their requirements to the municipal councils, which were required to provide the necessary funds. This provision replaced that of voluntary municipal aid.

It is perhaps worth noting that not all the common schools were entirely dependent on local taxes and legislative grants after the abolition of fees. A few communities still had a small income from the endowment fund established under the Clergy Reserves project, which was abandoned in 1854. The Roman Catholic Church also made some contributions to the Roman Catholic separate schools.[4]

The attempt to impose compulsory taxation did not by any means go smoothly. People were very much in the habit of regarding education solely as an individual benefit. Those who had no offspring, or who had already raised their families, typically could see no reason why they should pay to educate other people's children. The passage of the Assessment Act in 1866 caused particular cries of outrage. It combined real and personal property, and included personal income as a component of personal property. Despite the criticism, the tax base remained substantially the same for nearly forty years.

Cameron summarizes the process by which the contemporary fiscal base of local school boards developed.

> The main threads, what we might call the warp of the fabric, were woven with regard to the common schools. The basic pattern was formed from five such threads: the adoption of the property tax as one means of raising local revenue, the free school movement, culminating in the use of the property tax as the sole source of local revenue, the battle over the power of school to requisition funds from the municipalities, the right of school boards to borrow for capital purposes, and the periodic expansion and then contraction of the property tax base itself. Interwoven with these five threads are two significant cross, or woof, threads: the support of secondary schools from the proceeds of property taxation, and the gradual removal of barriers to the use of the property tax for the support of separate schools.[5]

Although many adjustments and modifications remained to be made, the outlines had been well established before the end of the century.

Provision was made in 1879 for high school boards, like public school boards, to borrow capital funds only through municipal councils. When the latter would not agree, however, there was recourse to a vote of the ratepayers. Later on, an appeal could be made to the Ontario Municipal Board.

Evidence of attempts by the province to influence the quality of education in the schools appeared in 1850, when average daily attendance replaced population as the basis on which grants were made to the common schools. In 1859 it was stipulated that the same grant was to apply only to the cost of teachers' salaries.[6] Part of the same trend was shown by the much-condemned effort to tie grants to results achieved in the high schools between 1875 and 1882. This episode is further discussed in volume v, chapter 15 of the present series.

Although payment by results failed, the policy of paying stimulation grants to encourage specific kinds of effort became an established feature of the system. The first of these grants were made in 1885 for special high school accommodation units such as libraries, gymnasiums, and laboratories.[7] They were to proliferate in subsequent years, covering a wide variety of objectives.

Early in the nineteenth century, towns in Ontario were few and small, and most of the people lived on farms or in villages. Since they were usually fairly close to the margin of subsistence, there was little variation in the ability to pay for such modest education as could be afforded. There was a kind of equality in poverty for all. As commerce and industry developed, however, and as certain centres of population grew, much greater concentrations of wealth appeared than could have occurred on the basis of a particularly fortunate combination of soil fertility and climate. The concepts of equalization of educational opportunity and of a fair distribution of financial burdens began to emerge. These concepts were, however, easier to applaud than to implement, especially if the principle of substantial local responsibility and initiative was not to be violated. The definition of equality was extremely elusive in the light of innumerable local needs and circumstances. Many of the relevant factors could not be quantified, and the means were lacking to deal even with those that could theoretically be so handled. Furthermore, the situation was always extremely fluid, with predictable and unpredictable shifts in population and wealth continually rendering the most ingenious schemes obsolete. Finally, it was by no means always clear that the province really wanted equality badly enough to pay the price.

The first attempt to take financial capacity into account was made in 1907, when assessment was considered in apportioning grants to rural schools. Since there were no standard criteria for equating assessment, the school boards were classified into groups that were considered, on the basis of certain assumptions, to have equal needs and capacities, and those in the same group received comparable treatment.[8] The same practice was extended to urban elementary schools in 1908. In 1924 legislation provided that any special grants to urban public and separate schools take account of the value of property taxable for school purposes. In 1930 all public elementary and separate school grants to urban and rural boards were made subject to apportionment on the basis of taxable assessment, in addition to average daily attendance and school board expenditure. From 1936 on, grants for secondary school teachers' salaries and those based on secondary school attendance were related inversely to taxable assessment.[9]

For many years before the new system was introduced, grants to the secondary schools were based on a fixed amount ranging from $250 to $300 per school. The amount depended to some extent on the number of teachers employed, the school with fewer than four teachers receiving the highest grant. There was also a grant on teachers' salaries, amounting to 10 per cent of the cost up to a maximum of $1,000, as well as limited grants for school accommodation and equipment. After the change, the percentage of the cost granted by the province varied according to the relation between the amount paid for salaries and the equalized assessment. The attendance grant was awarded according to the same principle. There were also special grants for the support of night school courses and courses in music.[10]

The original grouping immediately after 1907 involved only four rough categories: rural schools and urban schools in counties and rural schools and urban schools in territorial districts. By 1958 there were fifteen basic categories, which lasted until 1963. An elaboration of the scheme developed at that time is left for later discussion.

The equalizing effect of grants was severely limited during the period before the Second World War by the small amounts of money involved. The provincial contribution to total current and capital expenditure never reached one-quarter of the expenditure by boards, and regularly exceeded one-fifth only during the depression of the 1930s.[11] Grants were based on haphazard calculations, and differing assessment practices left room for a large amount of error.

The Ontario Committee on Taxation offered strong support for the principle of equalization in general. It asserted that the principle of local autonomy could hardly be translated into reality if certain municipalities lacked the resources to meet the costs of their basic services. The principle of provincial responsibility, with its strong concomitant of provincial concern for the provision of certain services at stated minimum levels, was said to lend forceful support to the development of equalization in local finance.[12] The argument was becoming particularly strong as education increasingly tended to be regarded as of general benefit to the larger community rather than simply a direct and immediate service to the recipients.

The committee felt it necessary to sound a cautionary note about the danger of producing distortions in the economic allocation of resources. Equalization grants were thought to be least likely to run counter to a rational allocation of resources in the provincial-municipal realm if they conformed to three basic rules.

> First, equalization grants are not a substitute for municipal entities' being of viable size. Second, minimal standards of performance laid down by provincial legislation should not seek levels of services that lie beyond what is socially acceptable at any point in time as a *reasonable* minimum standard. Third, as to those services whose benefits to property owners are unquestionably direct, the need for equalization is precluded in all but the very poorest municipalities.[13]

The first of these points has had particular relevance to Ontario policy in educational finance during most of the recent period. Equalization grants may be said to have constituted the chief means of staving off the inevitable consolidation of innumerable small school areas. Although some boards eventually received 95 per cent of their funds from the province, Rideout comments that grant percentages in the nineties are generally considered to be a clear indication of ineffective local school district organization.[14]

The committee's second principle involves difficulties no matter what the service involved. But education has been a particular problem because of the elusive quality of its outcomes and because of the rapidly changing economic factors that have noticeably affected its importance from year to year. Thus a "reasonable minimum standard" is almost impossible to define, and even if such a standard could be agreed on, it would require continual modification.

The period immediately before 1958

By the late 1930s, school grants amounted to only $8 or $9 million. Then, as in every period before and since, there were complaints that the burden on the local taxpayer was reaching its ultimate limit, and demands for relief were vociferous. But there was no substantial change in the balance of expenditure during the Hepburn regime, which lasted until 1943. Sensing the chance of victory in the election of that year, George Drew included among the twenty-two points of his platform a promise that was worded as follows in the Toronto *Globe and Mail* on July 9, 1943.

> There will be a sweeping revision of our whole system of real estate taxation so that the owning and improving of homes and farm lands, which are the very foundation of our society, will not be discouraged by excessive taxation. As an initial step in that direction, the Provincial Government will assume 50 per cent of the school tax now charged against real estate.

This promise is considered to have struck a particularly responsive note and to have helped the Conservatives win enough seats to form a government. Controversy about what it meant and whether or not it was fulfilled continued for the next twenty years and, in a sense, has not disappeared yet. Taken literally, the last sentence meant that a Conservative government was committed to a provincial grant amounting to half the amount raised from real estate in 1943. Under such conditions, the property tax could skyrocket and the grant remain constant. John Wintermeyer recognized the possibility of that interpretation in 1959:

> If the hon. Prime Minister is saying that what he meant was simply this, in 1943, that if the municipal property burden of taxation was $10 million in that year, he would assume in subsequent years $5 million, certainly he has accomplished the $5 million.[15]

Generally speaking, people would have regarded that interpretation as legalistic trickery. What was generally expected was that the local tax bills would be halved in subsequent years.

When Drew, as Premier, declared that the promise would be implemented, he did so without consulting his lieutenant, Leslie Frost,[16] on whom, as Provincial Treasurer, the responsibility would fall. The latter chose to interpret it as meaning that the government would pay half the costs of education. The task seemed quite formidable, and Frost began to think the Liberals were right in calling the whole scheme ridiculous. He was able, however, to apply what would otherwise have been a surplus of $12.5 million to school grants in 1945, and asserted that he had attained the desired goal. In fact, the provincial government paid only 50 per cent of a somewhat restrictive list of "approved" costs, and even then, the percentage declined in subsequent years. As a response to repeated reminders in the Legislature, Frost would insist that the promise was never meant to cover more than one year, and continually pointed to the huge absolute increase in provincial grants after the Conservatives took office. In relative terms, however, the burden of educational costs continued to fall on property.

Prime Minister Robarts finally made a statement of such fervour and logic that it should have laid the issue to rest except as a matter of historical interest.

> I would like to say, in regard to this hoary old chestnut about some promise made back in 1943, by the leader of the government twice or three times removed from me, it is just completely ridiculous to talk about 50 per cent or 40 per cent of the cost of education in this province in 1943, and the cost of education in this present year of 1967.
>
> Because at that time, just as a very small example, we had, I believe, three universities which were not receiving any support whatsoever from this government. They were receiving, of course, no support from the federal government and, of course, none from the municipality.
>
> We now have 17 or 18 universities which are receiving support from this government. None of this, of course, is counted into these costs we are discussing today; none of the cost of postsecondary education.
>
> When we think in terms of higher education the cost of our institutes of science and technology, junior college programmes, is being borne entirely by this government.
>
> To try and compare 50 per cent of the cost of education in 1943 with 50 per cent of the cost of education in this province in 1967, is a complete exercise in futility.[17]

Grant arrangements in force with minor alterations from 1945 to 1949 were outlined in the appropriate regulations. They were notable for their introduction of the concept of "approved costs" already referred to. This meant that the provincial government would commit itself to the support of certain items of expenditure only up to specified maxima. This was an inevitable development as the amounts of money involved grew rapidly. No government could be expected to refrain from exercising controls over funds turned over to school boards on such a scale. In 1949 approved costs for elementary school boards could not normally exceed $115 multiplied by the average daily attendance for the previous year, although actual average daily attendance below twenty-five was counted as twenty-five. The ceiling could be exceeded, however, by the amount of approved transportation costs or of fees paid to another board.[18]

During this period, urban and rural elementary schools were treated under separate formulas. As far as the former were concerned, the assessment factor was dropped, and funds were apportioned on a percentage basis in inverse relation to population. Percentages of approved costs paid ranged from 60 per cent in municipalities with a population of less than 2,500 to 30 per cent in those of 100,000 or more. Grants to rural school boards still took assessment per classroom into account. There were four categories ranging from an assessment of $30,000 or less per classroom to $80,000 or more, with corresponding percentages of costs paid ranging in 1949 from 89 to 45. As encouragement for the formation of larger school districts, an additional grant was paid to township boards, township area boards, consolidated school sections, improvement districts, and union separate school boards. This grant was equal to the amount raised by one mill on the equalized assessment in counties, and on the assessment of the property ratable for public or separate school purposes, whichever was applicable, in areas without county organization. The grant was not less than $150 or more than $300 for each school section included in the larger unit.[19]

Rural secondary school boards received grants on the same basis as those in urban communities. For academic secondary schools, there was a flat grant of $10 per student of average daily attendance plus a variable percentage of approved cost related to the number of mills required to raise the approved cost on the local taxable assessment. Thirteen successive categories of percentages were defined in 1949, ranging from 15 per cent where the indicated rate was less than four mills to 75 per cent where it was forty mills or higher.[20] The formula for vocational schools was more complex. The province contributed a much smaller proportion of the cost of secondary school than of elementary school expenditure, partly because of the lower ceiling of approved costs.[21] The normal limit for grades A and B continuation schools was $150 multiplied by the average daily attendance for the preceding year, with a figure less than fifty counted as fifty, and for high schools and collegiate institutes, $200 multiplied by the corresponding figure.

The grant system was revised and extended in 1950, and served, with numerous minor modifications, until 1958. The concept of approved costs was retained. For public and separate schools, the list of components in 1950 consisted of 1 / instructional salaries not exceeding $75 for each pupil of average daily attendance, 2 / salaries of night school teachers, 3 / principal, interest, and other charges on debentures and capital loans, 4 / transportation costs where parents or guardians made no direct contribution, 5 / tuition fees paid to another board, 6 / textbooks and library books, 7 / fuel and electricity in the smaller and poorer boards, 8 / rented classrooms, 9 / restoration of destroyed or damaged school property covered by insurance, but not exceeding the amount of insurance proceeds received, and 10 / capital outlays and repairs, but with restrictions on larger boards where the actual expenditure exceeded the approved cost. The total of approved costs as obtained by summing these items was reduced by current receipts from 1 / tuition fees from another board, 2 / amounts transferred to current funds from capital funds, 3 / insurance proceeds, 4 / receipts from the sale of capital assets, and 5 / refunds and reimbursements connected with disbursements previously included in approved cost.[22] For high and continuation schools, the list of components of approved cost consisted of items 3, 4, 5, 8, and 9 above, with the addition of an item corresponding to no. 10 which read as follows: "capital outlays for new buildings, additions to buildings, or for equipment." This was regarded as one of the major features of the new system. From the sum of these amounts was subtracted an amount corresponding to the total from items 2, 3, 4, and 5 in the public and separate school list. For vocational schools, approved cost meant roughly the total of disbursements for new buildings, additions to buildings and equipment.

Flat grants per pupil on the basis of average daily attendance were extended from the secondary to the elementary school level. These amounted in 1950 to $16 per elementary school pupil. In addition, public and separate school boards in cities, towns, and villages with a population of 2,500 or more received a grant based on a percentage of approved cost ranging from 40 in the smallest of seventeen population categories to 16 in the largest. Grants to rural school boards were based on assessment per classroom, ranging from 92 per cent where such assessment was less than $25,000 to 40 per cent where it reached or exceeded $125,000. Special grants were continued to encourage the formation of larger units. The general limitation on grants provided for a maximum of 90 per cent of the operating cost where the assessment per classroom was at least $20,000, and 95 per cent where it was less than that amount.

A continuation school board received 75 per cent of the approved cost where the school was in a territorial district or on an island, and 50 per cent if it was located elsewhere. Those grants to high school boards which constituted a percentage of the approved cost were determined according to two criteria: 1 / population of the municipality and 2 / a category system consisting of four main groups. These latter were defined as follows: a / the board of a city, separated town, or other urban municipality in a county, b / the board of an urban municipality in a territorial district, c / the board of a district not operating a school, and d / the board of a high school district consisting of a township or all or parts of two or more municipalities, not including a city having a population of at least 20,000. In the ten population groupings, the percentage of approved costs constituting the grant for each of these four categories ranged respectively from 15 to 50, 20 to 70, 20 to 65, and 30 to 75. As an illustration, for a board in a city (category 1) where the population was 100,000 or more (the largest population grouping), the percentage paid was 15 per cent; a board in the same category where the population was under 3,000 received 50 per cent. There was also provision for higher rates of payment, up to 85 per cent, in municipalities with a population under 1,500. By 1956 the percentage range in the second and fourth of the above categories had been raised to 20 to 80 and 30 to 85 respectively, while that for the first and third remained the same.

The same provisions applied to vocational schools with certain qualifications. One of these was that the board would receive half of any federal grants made to the provincial government toward the expenses of such schools. There was also a grant for special equipment needed for the schools.

A further grant was paid to each board that operated a school within a high school district. It amounted to $100 for each rural school section included in the district, whether or not it was included in a township school area. This grant was designed to provide an incentive for the formation of larger high school districts.

The second major type of grant paid to boards operating continuation, high, and vocational schools was based on assessment per capita. There were twenty-one categories as the assessment ranged from less than $200 to $1,150 or more. Grants per student in continuation schools ranged from $100 to $60 in these respective categories. Those for high school boards ranged from $120 to $40 where the population was at least 20,000, from $130 to $50 in urban municipalities where the population was between 10,000 and 19,999, from $140 to $60 in urban municipalities where the population was under ten thousand, and from $140 to $100 in rural municipalities where the population was under twenty thousand. Grants for vocational schools ranged from $150 to $70 according to assessment per capita. Where the average daily attendance was under five hundred, these amounts were increased by $20 for each of the first two hundred students. There were special grants for the conduct of night schools based on salaries paid to teachers.

In 1951 approved costs for boards in urban municipalities with a population of less than 2,500 and for those in rural municipalities with a population of less than 20,000 were defined to include costs of structural alterations including new foundations, basements, stairways, roofs, floors, fire escapes, fire doors, heating equipment, lighting, sanitary conveniences, water facilities, fences, blackboards, desks, pianos, and film projectors.[23] Grants awarded public or separate school boards on the basis of population could now range as high as 44 per cent.

There were complaints in the mid-fifties over the fact that the province paid grants for the construction of classrooms only, and not on auditoriums, gymnasiums, cafeterias, shoprooms, and home economics rooms, which Dunlop tagged rather injudiciously as "frills." J.B. Salsberg told his fellow members in the Legislature in 1954 that

many municipalities, despite the financial difficulties they are in, are proceeding with their construction programmes that do provide those facilities that are generally recognized as basic and essential, ... which the hon. Minister calls "frills."

In Toronto, for instance, the Lawrence Park Collegiate required $1 million for additional construction work, and this province contributed to that programme the munificent amount of $24,000. Now, you did not cut out the "frills," Mr. Minister, and I am glad that the Board of Education of Toronto did not cut out those recreational facilities that are so essential for the well-being of our children ... We need more swimming tanks, more assembly rooms, more recreational facilities in every school. We will then have less corner gangs; we will have less truancy, and less delinquency, and fewer tragic experiences.[24]

Dunlop reported to the Legislature that, in 1954, the province paid grants on 81 per cent of the approved cost of secondary school buildings, and on 85 per cent of the cost of elementary school buildings.[25]

On the same point of restricted grants for capital expenditure, F.R. Oliver, leader of the opposition, made some of the same criticisms in 1956. He declared that the types of rooms that Dunlop had implied were frills were regarded as integral parts of school buildings. He also objected that the cost of the site on which the school was built was not included in the approved cost. He pointed out that, in Dunlop's terms, this land was apparently a frill.[26]

A minor change in the 1952 regulations involved a stimulation grant to public and separate school boards that provided milk for the consumption of their pupils. Boards were allowed 50 per cent of the amount so expended.[27] In 1953 special assistance was also extended for the provision of various types of auxiliary classes or units. This was done by allowing the boards to add arbitrary numbers to the average daily attendance according to the category of class as follows: 1 / twenty for each Braille class for the blind, hard-of-hearing class, home instruction class, hospital class, oral class for the deaf, orthopaedic class for physical disabled, and sight-saving class; 2 / eight for each handicraft class, opportunity class, speech-correction and lip-reading class, and partial class of four or more handicapped pupils; 3 / two for each advancement class, discipline class, institutional class, open air class, and partial class of two or three handicapped pupils; 4 / two for each home-instruction and orthopaedic unit; and 5 / one-half for each opportunity, sight-saving, and speech-correction unit. The number of units in the last two categories could not exceed ten.[28]

A similar means was employed in 1953 to assist secondary schools with the maintenance of departments of agriculture. The number to be added to the actual average daily attendance ranged from ten in schools with an attendance of fewer than one hundred to twenty-five where it was three hundred or more. Similarly, where either a public or separate school board or a secondary school board operated industrial arts or home economics classrooms, the numbers to be added ranged from one in schools with an attendance of under fifty to five in those with three hundred or more.

A minor change in 1955 was the recognition under approved costs of the portion of the fees paid to a member association of the Ontario School Trustees' Council which was remitted to the council. In 1957 the recognized allowance for the salaries of elementary school teachers, upon which the grants were calculated, was raised from $75 to $100 per pupil. This was hardly an overly generous provision in view of the extent to which unit costs had risen. In 1958 there was a further increase to $115, where the allowance remained until 1963.

Pressure from those demanding relief from the burden of local property taxes led to the introduction of a very unsophisticated scheme of flat grants. In 1955 these grants amounted to $4 per pupil in both elementary and secondary schools, and in 1956, $6. A distinction was made in 1957 according to type of school, when the payment was set at $11, $20, $25, and $30 per pupil in elementary, continuation, academic high, and vocational high schools respectively. The grants were discontinued in 1958 when a drastically revised plan was introduced.[29]

The flat grants by no means satisfied the critics. In February 1958 Oliver again referred to Drew's famous promise. He mentioned that the provincial contribution to the total cost of education had slipped below 40 per cent in the intervening years, and had barely returned to that point. The grant increases had not kept pace with the increased cost of education at the municipal level. He accused the government of spending only 20 per cent of the provincial budget on education, and demanded that it give its responsibilities in this area a much higher priority.[30]

The 1958 grant plan

The complete revision of the grant structure in 1958 incorporated two changes of major importance. 1 / With the introduction of equalized taxable assessment, it was possible to relate grants to the financial capacity of all school boards. 2 / An attempt was made to deal with rapidly increasing enrolment through a "growth-need" principle related to recognized extraordinary expenditure.

With respect to the first of these factors, there had previously been an incentive for municipalities to under-assess in order to receive as large a school grant as possible. Although the government tackled the problem in 1955, it was not until three years later that a basis was established for equalizing assessment. The Assessment Branch of the Department of Municipal Affairs published a manual to guide assessors and, through assessment of properties on a sampling basis, prepared a set of equalization factors that could be used for grant purposes. In describing this achievement, Premier Frost made no claim that the new procedure was entirely accurate, but he felt that it provided a reasonably satisfactory basis for awarding grants until assessment could be made completely uniform throughout the province.[31]

The introduction of provincially equalized assessment meant a correction of under-assessment, which in some areas was rather extreme. Thus a limitation was placed on the year's increase to prevent very drastic reductions in grants. The maximum increase in assessment per classroom or per capita was 60 per cent. Equalization thereafter was attained in progressive stages. The fact that grants for 1958 were increased by $33 million helped to ensure that not too many boards were disappointed, although the increases were inevitably distributed in a very irregular fashion.

The problem behind the concept of recognized extraordinary expenditure particularly involved rapidly growing suburban communities. In earlier years, people ordinarily lived, attended school, and worked in the same area. A reasonable balance of residential, business, and industrial activity, such as it was, constituted the typical pattern. But the new suburbs tended to be almost entirely residential, and were often largely inhabited by young families with a high proportion of school children. The problem of providing enough new schools and facilities, to say nothing of meeting maintenance costs, seemed overwhelming.

Another factor giving rise to similar problems was the formation, with provincial encouragement, of larger secondary school districts. These often involved extending the services of centrally-located school buildings to students who had to be transported by bus. The extra expenditure for buildings and transportation was relatively slight where a small rural school area was attached to a large urban district. Where an entirely new district was created for a rural area, expensive new building projects and transportation systems were required. Thus the greatest financial burdens tended to be created where the program of school district enlargement had been most effective.[32]

A growth-need factor was thus adopted to assist in such situations. It afforded a higher percentage of assistance to any municipality that was obliged to incur heavy capital costs and other extraordinary expenditures. In municipalities where rapid growth had occurred, the application of the growth-need factor raised the basic percentage of assistance for approved costs as well as the basic per-pupil grant on average daily attendance. For the elementary schools, the grants were adjusted upwards in accordance with the recognized extraordinary expenditure per classroom, and for the secondary schools, in accordance with the recognized extraordinary expenditure per student of average daily attendance.

Recognized extraordinary expenditure per classroom was defined in the regulations as follows: "the quotient obtained by dividing the sum of the amounts recognized for grant purposes for debenture payments, for capital outlays from current funds, and for transportation, by the number of class-rooms recognized for grant purposes, not including the one-half of a class-room referred to in sub-clause i of clause *b* of subregulation 3."[33] The last qualification need not concern us here. Differences in recognized extraordinary expenditure were allowed for in the part of the schedule applying to public elementary and separate schools in urban municipalities with a population of 90,000 or more and in all other municipalities in the metropolitan area: there were three columns applying to boards where the amount of this expenditure was 1 / under $500, 2 / from $500 up to $1,500, and 3 / $1,500 or more. The percentage of recognized cost and the grant per pupil rose successively, other things being equal, from the first to the third category, For smaller urban and for all rural municipalities, there were not three but six recognized extraordinary expenditure categories.

For secondary schools, the relevant term was "recognized extraordinary expenditure per pupil," which was defined as "the quotient obtained by dividing the sum of the amounts recognized for grant purposes for debenture payments, for capital outlays from current funds, and for transportation by the average daily attendance of all pupils that attended the continuation school or high school or schools operated by the board during the preceding year." The procedure for allowing for these amounts was similar to that used for elementary school boards, except that the columns were labelled according to variations in recognized extraordinary expenditure per pupil instead of per classroom. Thus for urban municipalities with a population of 90,000 or more, and for all other municipalities in the metropolitan area, the categories were 1 / under $50, 2 / $50 or more but under $100, and 3 / $100 or more. For other municipalities, there were six categories, allowing for a distinction up to $300 or higher.

Under the new plan, in view of the progress made toward equalization of assessment, greater weight was given to assessment and less to population. However, population was still retained for grouping purposes to ensure a smooth transition from the earlier plan. Thus there were several different tables, each one for boards in a particular type of municipality in a particular population category. Six categories were defined for elementary grant purposes: 1 / boards in urban municipalities with a population of 90,000 or more, 2 / boards in suburban municipalities in Metropolitan Toronto, 3 / boards in urban municipalities with a population between 13,000 and 89,999, 4 / boards in urban municipalities with a population between 6,500 and 12,999, 5 / boards in urban municipalities with a population under 6,500 and in all rural municipalities, and 6 / boards not operating a school. The first three categories were the same for high schools; the additional ones were 4 / boards operating high schools in urban municipalities with a population under 13,000 or in rural municipalities, 5 / boards operating continuation schools, 6 / boards operating vocational schools in urban municipalities with a population of 90,000 or more, 7 / boards operating vocational schools in the suburban municipalities of Metropolitan Toronto, 8 / boards operating vocational schools in urban municipalities with a population under 90,000 or in rural municipalities, and 9 / those not operating a school.

The opposition parties in the Legislature suggested that a few further improvements might have been introduced. For example, Donald MacDonald questioned the reliance on average daily attendance as a basis for payments. He wondered why it was that, when the schools were closed because of a snow storm or the Asian flu, the whole burden of maintaining them had to be borne by the local municipalities. He could see no more reason why grants should be lost under such conditions than when the Prime Minister or the Minister of Education opened a school and, in so doing, declared a holiday.[34]

Revisions between 1958 and 1963

In 1959 a further step was taken toward correcting the former inequities in assessment, but the amount of assessment could rise by no more than 10 per cent. A site grant was instituted amounting to 50 per cent of either the actual cost or the equalized assessment of the value of the property, whichever was less. Approved costs were extended to cover the construction of industrial arts shops, home economics classrooms, cafeterias, gymnasiums, and general purpose rooms or basement rooms used as general purpose rooms. Further, the ceiling of approved cost for secondary school classrooms was increased to $25,000.

In discussing school grants in the Legislature in 1960, J.P. Robarts, then in his first few months as Minister of Education, spoke of some of the problems inherent in the administration of the grant system. It was very difficult to estimate the dollar value of the grant accurately until the Department of Education had received audited figures from each board covering the previous year's costs, approved capital expenditure, statements of assessment, and statements of average daily attendance, all used in computing the grant. Also, the boards were in the habit of asking for each year's grant regulations as early as possible so that they could estimate the grant in establishing their budget, which they had to submit to the local municipal council for inclusion in the over-all mill rate. Thus the department found it necessary to publish the grant regulations and establish the rate of grant on the basis of estimated figures, since the accurate audited figures were often not available until mid-summer.[35]

Cameron[36] discusses the process by which the grant programs were developed over a considerable period of years. As early as 1944, R.W.B. Jackson, as a member of the staff of the Department of Educational Research, established a working relationship with V.K. Greer, who was then acting as Superintendent of Elementary Education and financial adviser to the minister. Upon Greer's death in 1945, Jackson moved into the role of cabinet adviser in the same area. After 1954 he acquired the assistance of E.B. Rideout, whom the Director of the Department, J.A. Long, characterized as the outstanding Canadian expert in educational finance. These two consultants, with Rideout largely in a supporting role, were a major source of ideas and suggestions about how broad policies formulated by the government might be implemented. The research aspect involved various experimental analyses of existing data in order to determine how various schemes would work out and how much they would cost. Robarts depended on them, as did his predecessors and his successor, to produce some of the preliminary estimates that had to provide a temporary substitute for accurate information. In early 1969 Frost was still highly appreciative of Jackson's contribution in this area.

In the early 1960s financial decision-making was a three-way process involving the educational grants committee of the provincial cabinet, a committee of the Department of Education, and the academic consultants already referred to. The first of these consisted of the Prime Minister, the Provincial Treasurer, and the Minister of Education, sometimes supplemented by other ministers if their areas of interest and responsibility happened to be involved. The departmental committee consisted of the Superintendent of Business Administration, the Chief of the Grants Office, and one member from each of the elementary and secondary supervision sections. The names of Paul Cunningham, Floyd Wilson, Gordon Duffin, J.R. Thomson, and others were long associated with this activity. The departmental committee was responsible for translating cabinet decisions into departmental regulations, for overseeing the information needed to calculate the grants, and for supervising the calculation and payment of the grants.

Throughout the period the Department of Education was highly dependent on the resources of the Department of Educational Research, which were at the direct disposal of the consultants, to carry out the experimental work involved in devising new grant plans and in determining how revisions would work out in practice. When a computer was installed in that agency in 1961, it became possible to dispense with many of the manual operations formerly relied upon, to speed up the calculation of the amounts receivable by each board, and to widen the range of experimentation. In view of the unusual or even unique nature of the problems involved, a considerable amount of pioneering work had to be done in computer programming. This activity was a mainstay of the Department of Educational Research in the early 1960s.[37]

The role of extra-governmental consultants is an interesting one. Particularly if they have academic status, they can offer opinions without the same apprehension of the consequences of failure that must concern the upper-echelon civil servant. Promotion is not at stake. If they fall out of favour, they can always direct their energies and activities elsewhere.

Thus they are the most likely source of bold thinking and original ideas, commodities that responsible and constructive governments should welcome. On the other hand, they do not tend to endear themselves to those in the government establishment who have stronger motives for caution. There is the real danger, also, that they may push the civil service into an unduly passive and mechanical role.

The government put strong stress on its promise that no board would receive less in total grant in 1960 than in 1959. But since such a commitment did not necessarily look after increased costs attributable to rising enrolments and other factors, there was still a good deal of dissatisfaction. A more fundamental issue was the widespread feeling that still more relief from the burden of the property tax was required. A Residential and Farm School Tax Assistance Grant was introduced in 1961 in an attempt to satisfy the complaints. During its first year of operation, the scheme involved a payment by the province of $5 per pupil in both elementary and secondary schools. In 1962–3 this amount was raised to $15 for elementary schools, and in 1963–4 to $20, $30, and $40 for elementary and continuation schools, academic secondary schools, and vocational schools respectively. The school board receiving the school tax assistance grant, or the municipal council on its behalf, was required to reduce the tax rate on home owners and farmers by a full 10 per cent below that applicable to commercial properties. This arrangement was justified on the grounds that commercial and industrial property taxes could be deducted from corporate income as a cost of operation. School taxes on farms and homes were not deductible in this way. Cameron observes that this grant, as opposed to the special flat grants of 1955–7, was politically effective because it was plainly visible. By comparing residential and commercial tax rates, a resident taxpayer could see the extent to which his taxes had been reduced.[38]

The "split mill rate" thus established continued after the grants were terminated with the introduction of the new scheme in 1964. In raising the current revenues requisitioned by school boards, municipal councils were still required to maintain a 10 per cent differential between the tax rates applied to the two types of property.

The Federal-Provincial Technical and Vocational Training Agreement had very important implications for school finance in Ontario. The full cost of approved building projects was borne by the federal and provincial governments in a ratio of three to one. An immediate problem was created for the provincial government in that it had to bear the full initial expense and claim reimbursement later. Even its ultimate share of 25 per cent involved fairly large sums of money. The local taxpayers, for their part, were in the unusual position of having to contribute nothing directly. Even though they could tell themselves that the money all came out of the same pockets, there was every incentive for spending as much as they could before someone else anticipated them. Ultimately, the provincial government would have to take a major responsibility for ensuring that such facilities would be maintained. The boards were told that there would be no increase in the maintenance grant for operating vocational courses. They were thus warned that, although the need for the facilities and adequate enrolment would be the major factors in determining justification for approval, assessment of the high school district and ability to maintain the school would also be taken into consideration.[39] Robarts did, nevertheless, announce larger grants for technical education the following year. These were no great burden on the province because the federal government arranged to pay 75 per cent of the provincial grants in this area.

In summarizing developments for the ten-year period between 1953 and 1962, the Ontario Committee on Taxation referred to four outstanding trends. 1 / Percentages of provincial grant contribution increased in urban municipalities for all types of school boards. This phenomenon was attributable to a combination of factors, one of which was the extension to these municipalities of equalization on the basis of assessment from 1958 and, throughout the period, rising enrolments because of a combination of natural population increase, rural-urban population shifts, immigration, and the annexation of suburban areas. 2 / The proportional increase in grant contributions for urban schools was particularly marked among separate school boards after 1958, largely because of the extension in that year of equalization on the basis of assessment. The rise in the provincial grant reflected the scarcity of industrial and commercial properties taxable for separate school purposes. 3 / The proportional contribution to secondary education tended to catch up to that for public schools in urban municipalities, and to decline somewhat elsewhere, reflecting grant formula changes favourable to secondary school enrolment. 4 / The provincial contribution to school finance in small and poor municipalities was high and relatively stable.[40]

Developments leading to the adoption of the Ontario Foundation Tax Plan

The idea of the foundation tax plan began to receive considerable attention in Ontario in the early 1960s. It was given major support at the Ontario Conference on Education in November 1961, followed by the endorsement of the Canadian Conference on Education in 1962. The opposition parties also pressed their particular versions in the election campaign of 1963. The Co-operative Commonwealth Federation (CCF) Party had proposed a type of foundation plan as early as 1954. In preparation for the founding convention that transformed it into the New Democratic Party in 1961, a plan was devised involving six steps: 1 / All property would be re-assessed in relation to current values. 2 / All school taxes on commercial property would be diverted to a central fund for financing secondary education. 3 / A fixed mill rate would be established and applied to all residential property throughout the province. 4 / A "seat-per-pupil" figure would be established representing the cost of providing education for one year for a pupil in an elementary school in a typical medium-sized community. 5 / Weighting factors would be established to adjust the cost per pupil in the districts with a high cost of living, high travel expenses for students, high costs attributable to isolation, and other factors. 6 / Provincial grants would be paid to school boards at a level that would raise the revenue collected through the standard assessments up to the weighted cost-per-pupil figure.[41]

The Liberal Party adopted the foundation plan as official policy in 1962. For a time before that, Wintermeyer, the Liberal leader, had been urging that the total cost of elementary and secondary education be assumed by the provincial government. It is doubtful that the implications of this particular theme were very carefully thought out, or that it had the enthusiastic support of the party's rank and file, although it had a superficial appeal.

Toward the end of 1962 the Ontario Separate School Trustees' Association and l'Association des commissions des écoles bilingues d'Ontario urged the adoption of a foundation plan. Their proposal involved the essential elements of 1 / establishment by the Department of Education of the unit cost of adequate education and 2 / a uniform mill rate on an equalized municipal assessment supplemented by provincial grants to meet the requirements of the foundation level.

The Liberal and New Democratic Party plans bore a considerable resemblance to those worked out by some of the earlier theorists. Cameron[42] outlines a series of these, mentioning the problems and difficulties involved, particularly those centring around the determination of the foundation level. Under a plan adopted in New York State, this level was set approximately at the average per-pupil expenditure for school districts of average revenue-raising ability, or, presumably, at the amount the state government would pay if it were to finance the entire instructional program.

The foundation idea was apparently considered and rejected for Ontario by a number of observers. Inadequacies in assessment procedures and the multitude of small school boards, many of them operating single rural schools, were among the main objections. Maxwell Cameron added another factor in 1936[43] which his namesake did not consider very compelling in 1969[44] – that there were two widely differing cost structures as between the public elementary and separate schools, that the differences were in large measure a result of the low salaries paid to members of religious orders, and that a considerable body of public opinion in the province was averse to a grant system that would divert public funds to the support of religious orders. In 1938 a Committee of Enquiry into the Cost of Education in the Province of Ontario, under the chairmanship of Duncan McArthur, also rejected the foundation concept on grounds of differences in distribution of population, wealth, climatic conditions, and facilities for transportation.[45]

The Royal Commission expressed the view in 1950 that, if the total of specified items of expenditure were to be used as the basis, and the central authority were to bear a share of the cost, the most equitable solution for the distribution of legislative grants was that in which grants were calculated on the basis of the total of the approved expenditures defined according to some appropriate criterion. If the fullest possible equalization of the local burden were to be achieved, the percentages should be graded according to local need expressed in terms of local financial resources available and educational facilities required. But the commission could not identify any easy way to devise a fully satisfactory measure of local need. Population, number of children, number of pupils calculated in terms of average daily attendance, number of teachers, type of municipality, and other bases of a like nature did not take into consideration the wealth of the district, and were thus regarded as unsuitable.[46] The commission did not find full equalization compatible with the decentralization of educational responsibility.

The plan actually put forward by the government represented a smooth transition from the one already in effect. In introducing the new scheme in the Legislature, Prime Minister Robarts reviewed earlier measures to equalize educational opportunity across the province. He commented:

> It is sufficient to point out here that we have poor school areas in our public, separate and secondary school systems. Our school grants have been devised to help equalize opportunity and to rectify these disparities. In many of our public, separate and secondary schools, in recognition of this situation, the Province pays grants up to 95 per cent of the total cost of education. The result of this policy is shown in the growth of fine new schools, elementary and secondary, across the Province and particularly in parts which, from the standpoint of assessment, were the poorer areas. In every part of Ontario the evidence of the policy of equality of opportunity and financial equity may be seen.[47]

Robarts went on to point out that it was a great mistake to believe that separate and public schools had been dealt with in a different way. They had, in fact, received equal treatment. Where either a public or a separate school board had a low assessment, which might result from the absence of corporation taxes or from low residential and farm assessments, it received larger grants. In 1960 the provincial government had provided 58 per cent of separate school costs and 34 per cent of public school costs, while provincial grants per pupil averaged $111.07 for separate schools and $102.36 for public schools.

Robarts reviewed in considerable detail the legal guarantees for the separate school system, beginning with subsections (1), (3), and (4) of Section 93 of the British North America Act. He pointed out that the effect of the legislation was to entrench the rights and privileges of denominational schools as they existed in 1867. Any enactment passed by the Legislature of Ontario could only be valid if it did not prejudicially affect any of these rights or privileges. The Separate Schools Act of 1863 had become unalterable except by amendment of the British North America Act, a step that was out of the question because, even if it were desired by the Roman Catholic minority in Ontario, the fact that the legislation affected minority rights of other groups in different ways in other provinces would make any constitutional change a practical impossibility. Further, the rights and privileges of the Separate Schools Act ran in favour of the individual, and not in favour of the majority of the class of persons referred to as the minority. The basic right of the individual member of such minority to allocate his taxes as he saw fit was inviolate. This constitutional right was one that must be accepted as a fundamental condition of school finance in Ontario, and there was no use in considering grant schemes that were based on any other assumption.

Robarts then referred to the problem of corporate taxes as they applied to separate schools. There had been little difficulty in the implementation of the individual's right to allocate his taxes to either separate or public schools as it had related to personal assessments, whether residential, farm, or commercial. But with the growing industrialization of the province, and the creation of corporate entities at an ever-increasing rate, the matter of corporate assessments had presented very great difficulties. The first effort to deal with the problem, in an amendment to the Separate Schools Act of 1886, had been interpreted to mean that the Roman Catholic shareholder would have the right to allocate the taxes as related to his ownership in a corporation, but the arrangement had never worked satisfactorily. A further attempt was made to improve matters in 1937, with amendments to *The Assessment Act* by the Hepburn government. These had proved to be a failure, and were repealed within a year. However, in recent years assessment per classroom and assessment per capita had tended toward equalization. The lack of corporate assessment had been reflected in need factors, and was compensated for by larger grants.

In introducing his own plan, Robarts referred to other possibilities, including the one involving a central equalization fund. He also described the scheme by which a basic formula would require the province to specify in detail all the elements of an "ideal" or "adequate" school program. Then unit costs per pupil of average daily attendance would be established on the basis of expenditure by one of the "better" school boards. The province would set the mill rate to be levied by every school board, and would pay in grants the amount required to bring the poorer boards up to the foundation level. If any school board spent more than the amount specified by this level, it would have to raise the money itself, if permitted to do so.

In outlining his objections to the equalization fund plan, Robarts mentioned the following points. 1 / It was impossible to assume that the unit cost figure was in all cases a direct measure of the quality of the education; it was a serious mistake to believe that raising the expenditures of all the boards to this minimum level would ensure the raising of the quality of education to the desired level. 2 / No rigid formula of fixed unit cost and fixed local tax rates could possibly work satisfactorily in view of Ontario's wide variations in municipal structure, local conditions, and wealth, and with nearly four thousand school boards operating every conceivable type of school. 3 / While provincially equalized assessment worked reasonably well in a grant system, the situation on a fixed mill rate basis would be chaotic. The only answer would be assessment by the province in every municipality. 4 / If the government undertook to fix the unit cost of the program, to define what it regarded as adequate, and to determine the contribution made through local taxes, local autonomy would be destroyed. The school boards and the province "would be deprived of the good ordinary common sense which runs school boards which are elected and responsible to the people." 5 / There would be a greater centralization of power in the Department of Education. Teachers' salaries would be uniform across the province without regard to the cost of living or other circumstances. 6 / Rapidly growing urban areas had special problems that required special treatment. That municipalities in such areas should pay their taxes into a common fund and then receive a lesser amount on the so-called unit cost basis would be completely impracticable in Ontario. 7 / Constitutional provisions already referred to would preclude the compulsory participation of the separate school supporters in a scheme that would result in the use of their funds for the support of any but their own schools.

These comments were very much in line with the political facts of life. Perhaps the most important fundamental factor was that change had to be evolutionary, especially if introduced by a government already in power, if it was not to cause uncertainty, fear, and adverse reactions at the polls. One of the realities in the situation that no one with any concern for his political future, whether in the government or in the opposition, would care to mention was that a substantial proportion of the population did not at the time genuinely desire equality of educational opportunity. Wealthier communities were simply not willing to give up their favoured positions unless forced to do so. And, as the school board reorganization of 1969 was to show, there were poorer communities that would rather continue with a relatively low quality of education than pay even part of the cost of raising it to what outsiders might regard as an adequate standard. Equality of educational opportunity seems a fine ideal, and only an ignoble society would reject it as an ultimate goal, but it is useless to pretend that it can be achieved easily or quickly.

There are, of course, strong arguments in favour of a continuing measure of inequality. In discussing a number of aspects of educational finance in Saskatoon in 1968,[48] Rideout commented on the soundness of the foundation principle in terms of its provision of a satisfactory standard of educational service throughout an entire province. It met his concern that poor education in one part of a province diminished the productivity and level of living of the whole province. He also expressed the view that very good education in some communities benefited the whole province.

If this is so, and I believe it is, provinces must ensure that the type of foundation program they institute does not discourage willing and able boards from going well beyond the standard provincial program supported by the foundation grants. Every provincial system needs "lighthouse" or "pilot" systems – systems which will experiment with new methods, new curricula, new forms of school organization, new administrative processes, new types of school accommodation, new technological aids to learning, and other adaptations of the educational process to the rapidly changing society in which we live. It is these systems, or even particular schools within these systems, which are the growing edge of educational change. Such systems benefit the whole province, and indeed the whole country in two ways. First, as developments they have pioneered and tested prove themselves, popular demand will cause them to spread to other local systems and finally some of them will be recognized as part of the standard provincial program; thus the existence of "pilot" systems serves to improve the educational level of the whole province in the long run. Second, even without the first benefit, the students educated in the superior system may be assumed to contribute a higher level of social benefits to their province and country, and thus increase the productivity and level of living of the whole province and country.

One of the main reasons why Robarts thought it desirable to preserve local autonomy was that the boards were in a position to attempt to lower the mill rate through economical operation. They should not be encouraged to spend money simply for the sake of uniformity. A foundation program based on uniformity alone would stifle initiative and prevent the steady growth of improvements at the local level.

Further problems in fixing unit costs involved the necessary exclusion of debt charges, transportation costs, and capital outlays from current funds. Some boards in settled communities were completely free of debt and had no other extraordinary charges, while almost all of those in rapidly growing areas were faced with increasing capital outlays and debt charges for new schools.

The Ontario Foundation Tax Plan

Ordinary expenditure

The basic characteristics of the Ontario Foundation Tax Plan as Robarts outlined it were flexibility and adaptability to varying conditions. Each school board was to be provided with sufficient revenue for the adequate financing of the educational program that it considered essential and sufficient to meet the needs of its own community, while at the same time maintaining its responsibility to the ratepayers who elected it. The new plan was to cover a five-year period beginning in 1964. As applied to operating costs, it was designed in three sections, which were independent except for the over-all provision that the total provincial grant was not to exceed 95 per cent of the cost of operation of any school board during the preceding year.

The first section dealt with the basic tax relief grant, which was designed to give general tax relief throughout the province on a common scale. The formula involved a flat grant at the following rates per pupil of average daily attendance: $80 for elementary schools, $120 for continuation schools, $175 for non-vocational courses in secondary schools, and $250 for vocational courses in secondary schools. These amounts incorporated the former Residential and Farm School Tax Assistance Grant. The basic tax relief grant was, of course, quite at variance with the concept of the pure foundation plan. It was politically necessary, however, because without it some of the wealthier boards, unless other special provisions had been made, would have found their grants wiped out completely, and the repercussions can well be imagined.

The second section dealt with special or stimulation grants, some of which had a long prior history. These were designed to encourage the efforts of the boards to provide special services such as textbooks, evening classes, milk, and auxiliary classes, and to move toward such desirable changes as formation of larger units and improved municipal organization.

In 1964 special assistance was provided, after the pattern that had existed for years, for home economics and industrial arts classes operated by a board for a term in the preceding year in a school in which the Science, Technology, and Trades Branch had not been introduced. The procedure involved fictitiously increasing the actual number of classrooms by adding to that number the product obtained by multiplying the number of classrooms devoted to these purposes by a factor of one-half, one, one and one-half, two, or two and one-half, according to whether the school had an average daily attendance of less than 50, between 50 and 99, between 100 and 199, between 200 and 299, or 300 or more. For departments of agriculture in secondary schools, the first two of these categories were combined, and the relevant factors were five, seven and one-half, ten, and twelve and one-half. A single factor was provided for each group of auxiliary classes, units, or teachers as follows: 1 / hard of hearing class, hospital class, orthopaedic class, limited vision class, full-time home instruction teacher – ten; 2 / opportunity class, full-time speech correction teacher – five; 3 / gifted children class, institutional class, health class – one; 4 / school using the services of an approved itinerant auxiliary teacher or teachers, and operated by the board in a municipality with a population under 25,000 – one; 5 / home instruction unit, orthopaedic unit – one; 6 / limited vision unit – one-quarter; 7 / opportunity unit in a school not served by an itinerant auxiliary teacher – one-quarter. By this procedure, a school board got grants based on extra classrooms that did not in actual fact exist, their number being determined by the relative weight given to the service. The number of classes could be translated into the number of pupils by applying the appropriate formula.

The third section was concerned with by far the most complex aspect of the whole structure – equalization grants. These were designed to compensate for differences in local ability to support education by increasing as local wealth decreased, and vice versa, either from one board to another in any one year or, for one board, from year to year as local resources varied. There were three categories of equalization grants: 1 / a corporation tax adjustment grant for elementary schools, 2 / a recognized extraordinary expenditure grant, and 3 / a school tax equalization grant.

The first of these was intended to supplement the revenues of any elementary school board, public or separate, which was receiving a lesser proportion of school tax paid on corporation assessment within the local municipality than the proportion that its residential and farm assessment bore to the total public and separate residential and farm assessment. At the same time, the total assessment of the board receiving such a supplement would be increased by an equivalent amount for the calculation of other equalization grants. According to Robarts, "nothing will be taken away from either a public or a separate school which it is now receiving, nor will any constitutional right or privilege be infringed upon to the slightest degree. I feel that, by the introduction of this provision, the controversy in connection with corporate taxes can be regarded as being finally settled with positive justice to all concerned." Of course the issue was not finally settled. There would have been no problem had the ratio of the taxable property held by the supporters of each system to the total of taxable property corresponded to the respective ratios of children requiring education to the total of all children. But separate school supporters were often less well endowed in terms of taxable property in relation to children to be educated than were public school supporters, and they suffered accordingly. To remedy this grievance, an amendment was made in the 1967 regulations whereby the maximum allocated corporation assessment for an elementary school was determined by multiplying the corporation assessment in a municipality by the ratio of the enrolment of the board's pupils to the total elementary school enrolment.

Recognized extraordinary expenditures, consisting of debt charges, capital outlays from current funds, and costs of transportation, received special treatment, as in the earlier plan. The formula involved the payment of a proportion of the total of such expenditure, varying according to growth-need and to assessment per classroom or per class unit, and running as high as 90 per cent of the total amount for the most needy boards.

The school tax equalization grant was the basic foundation grant which constituted the major element in the whole scheme. At the time of Robarts' announcement, details of how this grant would be administered had not yet been fully worked out. He declared that a fundamental objective would be to retain the flexibility necessary to meet the varying needs and circumstances of schools in different parts of the province. The development of the formula would include classifications which compensated for differences in salaries, maintenance costs, and the like. Robarts hoped that the existing categories based on population and location could be reduced to three. In fact, by 1964, when the plan was ready for implementation, the categorization scheme was dropped in favour of one weighting the pupils of differently situated districts.

The mechanics of the calculations involved can be summarized in the following equation:

> Equalization grant = FLOC × ADA − (BTRG × ADA + ETA × FMR) where FLOC is the foundation level of operating cost, ADA is the number of pupils of average daily attendance, BTRG is the basic tax relief grant, ETA is the equalized taxable assessment, and FMR is the foundation mill rate.

If the result of the calculation was equal to or less than zero, the school board received no equalization grant, although it always got a basic tax relief grant.

Average daily attendance was calculated in different ways where it was used in different parts of the formula. For the basic tax relief grant, it began with the actual average daily attendance of all pupils for whom the board was legally responsible. This basic figure was then modified by adding an allowance for the provision of special services in the manner already explained. The second figure for average daily attendance was calculated as a function of the number of weighted classrooms. This number was determined according to the particular situational category into which the board fell. There were four of these categories: 1 / boards with one thousand or more pupils in average daily attendance in a single school section or separate school zone, 2 / boards with one thousand or more pupils in an enlarged district, 3 / boards with fewer than one thousand pupils in a single section or zone, and 4 / boards with fewer than one thousand pupils in an enlarged district. For boards in the first category, the number of classrooms was the lesser of the number actually operated on the first school day of January in the current year and the number of resident pupils divided by thirty. Boards with fewer than one thousand pupils were treated more leniently in their calculations. Those in enlarged districts were given compensation for amalgamation by a formula that ensured that other small boards would not be dissuaded from following the same course of action. Unlike elementary school boards, secondary school boards were all treated uniformly. The number of classrooms calculated according to these formulas was used also for recognized extraordinary expenditure.[49]

Davis made a major announcement with respect to the operation of the new plans in January 1964.[50] He declared that the local authority was in the best position to determine reasonable levels of expenditure for the community. This was, in fact, probably its major power and duty under the existing school acts and regulations. He thus reiterated that each board retained its freedom to go above or below levels specified for grant purposes.

The principle of the basic equalization grant was that each board would be guaranteed sufficient revenue to meet a satisfactory level in terms of recognized operating costs. The equalizing grant would vary according to the wealth of the board. No board was to be forced to levy in accordance with the maximum number of mills specified, or to pay any amount into a provincial equalization fund. In fact, it could reduce taxes if it so desired, and was willing to bear the consequences. From the point of view of the provincial taxpayer, the plan provided safeguards in that the total amount of aid the province wished to provide was fully controlled.

The foundation levels of operating costs established for 1964 were $210 for each elementary school pupil, $320 for each continuation school student, $420 for each academic high school student, and $550 for each vocational school student. The foundation mill rates were eleven mills for elementary schools and seven mills for secondary schools. When these rates were applied to a school board's equalized taxable assessment, they produced the yield of a standard local effort for the board concerned. The basic idea was that the government undertook to make up the difference between the foundation level of operating cost (less the basic tax relief grant) and the amount raised by a standard local effort.

Cameron[51] asserts, incidentally, that the province was forced to establish a foundation level of expenditure below the actual average expenditure level for two reasons, apart from any considerations of provincial economy. One was that the hundreds of tiny school districts could not have made prudent use of resources equal to the provincial average because they were incapable of employing the necessary personnel or of organizing the necessary programs and services. Support up to the level of expenditure in the wealthiest districts would probably have provided many small boards with substantial surpluses and eliminated local taxation, apart from the statutory limitation on the size of the grant. The second reason Cameron identifies for the establishment of a relatively low foundation level was the disparity in average expenditure levels between the public and separate school systems. In 1962 the average expenditure per pupil of public school boards was $283, and of separate school boards, $178.

"To have attempted to eliminate this disparity of $105 in one year would simply have flooded the coffers of many separate school boards." In fact, the $210 figure actually adopted was about mid-way between the average level of the separate schools and of all elementary schools.

One of the measures provided for the transitional period was a special equalization grant. In 1964 this grant was obtained by multiplying the average daily attendance by figures varying as follows: 1 / for boards where the provincial equalized assessment per classroom was $525,000 or more, $10; 2 / for boards where the assessment was between $300,000 and $524,999, $10 plus 8¢ up to a maximum of $18 for each $1,000 or fraction thereof by which the assessment fell below $525,000; 3 / for boards where the assessment was between $250,000 and $299,999, $28 plus 20¢ up to a maximum of $10 for each $1,000 or fraction thereof by which the assessment fell below $300,000; 4 / for boards where the assessment was under $250,000, $38 plus 10¢ up to a maximum of $19 for each $1,000 or fraction thereof by which the assessment fell below $250,000.[52] It may be seen that this grant was inversely related to the amount of equalized assessment per classroom, but that every board received at least a minimum amount. The provision was designed, along with the basic tax relief grant, to ensure that no board received less under the new scheme than under the old. It cost the government less than the alternative of simply providing a higher basic tax relief grant unrelated to specific need.

To smooth the transition from the previous grant system to the new plan, limits were placed on the increase or reduction applying to any particular board. The effective percentage rate of grant in 1964 could not increase by more than 20 per cent nor be more than 5 percentage points less than in the previous year. The general effect of this provision was to spread unusually large increases or decreases over a period of years; it was also regarded as a safety valve to control possible inaccuracies in the formulas during the first year in which the scheme was in operation.

In introducing the scheme, Davis referred to the limitations placed on the possibility of equalizing educational opportunity by the existence of many small units of school administration. No amount of money poured into the system could compensate for the inefficient utilization of resources under such circumstances. Current plans called for an early reduction in the number of elementary boards particularly. Cameron stresses that "local organizational reform – presumably desirable for non-fiscal reasons as well – was absolutely indispensable to an effective policy of fiscal equalization."[53] He discusses two sets of factors related to the size of school districts. On the one hand, the optimum use of resources is possible only in a fairly large district, where pupil-teacher ratios may be relatively standard, supplies may be purchased centrally, and maximum use may be made of instructional aids. Thus unit costs tend to be greater in some respects in smaller districts. On the other hand, because a much greater division of labour is possible in a large district, resulting in the employment of different kinds of specialists and the provision of special programs to meet particular needs, there is a tendency toward increased unit costs in such districts. In a sense, the two factors are not really contradictory, as Cameron intimates; they simply mean that more services tend to be purchased in a district of reasonable size than in a very small one. As far as the foundation grant plan is concerned, efficiency of utilization of funds is a vital matter.

Cameron comments further on the same point:

With a system of local government characterized by extreme variations in school district size, it is not possible to develop an effective measure of educational need. On the surface, weighting factors appear to compensate for both the increased cost of small teaching units and the increased cost of providing special services, but they do so by reinforcing inefficiency in the first instance and unequal recognition of educational need in the second. Thus, unless all school districts are *capable* of responding in a similar way to the defined needs of the school population, a weighting scheme becomes, in effect, not a corrective for differing needs but a subsidy for differing efforts.[54]

The new plan made drastic changes in the appearance and form of the grant regulations. The former "maze of tables, schedules, and rates," as the Ontario Committee on Taxation called it, was swept away. The committee had high praise for the new formula. Various features were cited to show that the plan exhibited "that quality to which every part of a provincial and local revenue system should aspire – fiscal sophistication in a framework of simplicity."[55] Several examples were selected to demonstrate how readily it could accommodate the changes that future needs or policies might dictate. The level of aid to wealthier school boards could be increased by raising the level of basic tax relief grant. On the other hand, more equalization favouring the poorer boards could be achieved by reducing the foundation mill rates. Equalization could be extended to some of the wealthier boards that just failed to qualify under existing conditions by increasing the foundation level of operating cost. The levels of relative provincial support as between elementary and secondary education could be varied by adjusting the different levels of foundation mill rate, basic tax relief grant, or foundation operating costs. Special instances where specific provincial aid might be considered necessary, as, for example, the provision of education to handicapped children, could be accommodated through variations in the definition of average daily attendance.

The initial reaction to the explanation offered by Davis in the Legislature, and to the publication of the regulations, was by no means as favourable as that expressed by the Ontario Committee on Taxation. T.J. Allen, writing in the *Toronto Daily Star* on February 4, 1964, expressed his exasperation with the complexities of the system. He declared that confusion reigned in every school board in the province, and that a deplorable beginning had been made to a brand-new policy of school finance. Davis dealt with the matter in the Legislature.

While I appreciate that some of us may regard the regulations as being difficult to understand, I think if the hon. members will peruse this document ... they will get some appreciation of the factors that are involved in implementing a plan of this kind. I think, quite frankly, that we should be rather grateful to the gentlemen who worked so hard to draw up the regulations and lay the basic foundation for the new plan. I think if you could compare it, and it is very difficult to do so, with other foundation plans in other jurisdictions, you would find that perhaps more thought and consideration have gone into the development of this plan than perhaps that of any other jurisdiction.[56]

The minister's defence of the departmental experts was undoubtedly heartfelt and justified. In this writer's opinion, however, some improvements could easily be made in providing a series of more intelligible headings for different sections of the regulations to facilitate understanding by the non-expert. A great many problems might be avoided if the regulations were written with a view to ensuring not only the utmost accuracy but also maximum intelligibility. The provision of guides for the assistance of the layman is of course helpful, but does not completely solve the problem.

Cameron reports in detail the immediate effects of the application of the new grant plan.[57] It is possible to mention here only that public elementary school boards responsible for about 70 per cent of the pupils were able to exceed the foundation level of expenditure without the benefit of an equalization grant. The reverse was true of the separate school boards, where boards responsible for only 30 per cent of the pupils exceeded the foundation level.

Extraordinary expenditure

The term "recognized extraordinary expenditure" became familiar, as has been noted, with the grant reforms of 1958. In 1964 it included debt charges, capital expenditure from current revenue, transportation costs, and 15 per cent of tuition fees paid to other school boards. In 1966 expenditure for board, lodging, and weekly transportation of commuting secondary school students was added. The Ontario Foundation Tax Plan initially gave all school boards a basic tax relief grant of 35 per cent of this type of expenditure. In addition, where applicable, elementary school boards received amounts calculated according to whether their provincial equalized assessment per classroom unit was 1 / at or above $230,000 or 2 / below that figure. Those in the first category received 0.1 per cent, up to a maximum of 17 per cent, for each $1,000 or fraction thereof by which their assessment fell below $400,000. Those in the second category received 17 per cent plus 0.1 per cent, up to a maximum of 40 per cent, for each $500 or fraction thereof by which their assessment fell below $230,000. Secondary school boards received 0.1 per cent up to a maximum of 55 per cent for each $2,000 or fraction thereof by which their assessment per classroom unit fell below $1,260,000.[58]

Recognized extraordinary expenditure was also recognized by a growth-need grant. In this case, there was a single category for elementary school boards, as there was for secondary boards. In the case of the former, the percentage was determined by allowing 0.1 per cent for each $50 or fraction thereof by which the recognized extraordinary expenditure per classroom unit exceeded $500. For secondary school boards, the percentage was determined by allowing 0.1 per cent for each $25 or fraction thereof by which the recognized extraordinary expenditure per classroom unit exceeded $1,000. There were maximum percentage limitations for both elementary and secondary school boards to ensure that the grant for recognized extraordinary expenditure could not exceed 95 per cent.[59] The basic expenditure levels of $500 and $1,000 had been identified in 1958 as the average expenditures of boards without extraordinary expenditure requirements.

Changes in the Ontario Foundation Tax Plan after 1964

New basis for equalized assessment

In 1966 the Department of Municipal Affairs revised its procedures for equalizing local assessments. The use of 1940 values was abandoned in favour of full sale value. It was considered that the latter provided a more exact measure of taxable capacity. The change multiplied the dollar value of equalized assessments by approximately 3.5. Thus all formulas involving equalized assessment required a corresponding adjustment. The foundation mill rate was accordingly reduced from eleven to three mills for elementary school boards, and from seven to two mills for secondary school boards. Since the equalized taxable assessment (ETA in the formula) was increased by 3.5 times and the foundation tax rate was reduced by 3.7 times for elementary school boards, the degree of equalization was extended at some extra cost to the government.

The change in assessment values also affected the grant calculations for recognized extraordinary expenditure. A single category for elementary school boards was substituted in 1966 for the two that had been recognized before. The provision was that the rate would be 0.1 per cent, up to a maximum of 57 per cent, for each $2,500 or fraction thereof by which the assessment per classroom unit fell below $1,500,000. For secondary school boards, the rate was 0.1 per cent, up to a maximum of 55 per cent, for each $7,000 or fraction thereof by which the assessment per classroom unit fell below $4,410,000.

Cameron reported that the Department of Education was not involved in the decision to change the equalized assessment scheme, even though the Ontario Foundation Tax Plan represented the chief use to which the scheme was put.[60] Had there been consultation, he did not think there would have been any opposition from the department. He did, however, foresee the possibility of problems arising in the future. If the basis of equalization were to be full value for the current year, the equalizing factors would need annual revision. But not only did the Department of Municipal Affairs fail to keep up consistently with this annual revision, it also neglected to keep the Department of Education informed as to the existing situation. A constantly fluid state in the assessment area promised to add a considerable element of complexity to the administration of the grant system.

Increase in provincial levels of expenditure

The foundation levels of expenditure remained the same in 1965 as they had been in 1964. It was intended that time would be allowed for the grants to find their proper level after the limitations on the first year's increases had ceased to affect the situation. In succeeding years, however, there were substantial upward adjustments. For 1964–5, 1966, 1967, and 1968, the respective amounts per elementary school pupil were $210, $220, $260, and $280. The corresponding amounts per academic school student were $420, $440, $450, and $465. For vocational school students they were $550, $570, $580, and $600.

Enrolment growth grant

Some of the considerations involved in dealing with the problem of extraordinarily rapid increases in enrolment are discussed in the Cameron study.[61] Cameron notes at the beginning of the discussion that, if enrolments were to increase uniformly for all boards, the effective grants would be uniformly lower than the nominal grants since, for example, a grant of $15,000 calculated on the basis of 100 pupils, but paid when the enrolment had increased to 105, represented a nominal grant of $150 per pupil, but an effective grant of $143. This discrepancy would in itself pose no real problem. Where the enrolment increased more rapidly than the average, however, a board was placed in a position of relative disadvantage, since no grant was received for pupils in excess of the average increase. Suburban boards suffered most severely, and exerted pressure on the government to remedy the situation. The departmental committee was not prepared to recommend either a calculation of the grants on the basis of estimates of the current year's enrolment, with a recalculation of the values when the final audited figures were available, or the substitution of the attendance or enrolment of a specific date for the average daily attendance or enrolment for the full year, a procedure that would have made possible the use of a relatively up-to-date figure. The latter solution would not have been entirely satisfactory, since administrative necessity would have required the use of a figure from the January to June period of the year before the grant was to apply, and would thus not have taken into account the increase of the following September.

The solution recommended was a special supplementary provision in the grant program. Cameron attributes the general nature of this provision mainly to E.B. Rideout. Known as the attendance growth grant, it placed the responsibility on any school board anticipating an above-average enrolment increase in the current year to apply for special assistance. To be eligible for it, an elementary school board would have to estimate that its average daily attendance would exceed that of the previous year by at least thirty pupils and 5 per cent. It could thus qualify for a grant of $100 for each pupil, according to the estimate, in excess of the average figure. A secondary school board with an average daily attendance of at least 400 and an estimated increase in attendance of at least 10 per cent over the previous year, could claim a grant of $200 for each student, according to the estimate, in excess of the 10 per cent figure. Any discrepancy between estimated and actual increase would result in the appropriate adjustment in grants the following year. In 1967 the grant was renamed the enrolment growth grant.

Northern assistance grant

Many of the school boards in the northern territorial districts of the province were suffering from special disadvantages of two types. 1 / They had to meet unusual costs for such items as teachers' salaries, transportation, and maintenance and heating of buildings in the severe climate. 2 / Many of the school districts were extremely small, often with fewer than twenty-five pupils, and could support only the most inadequate of educational programs. A departmental study completed in 1966 showed that, of 156 districts with one-room or two-room schools, at least 100 would have been better amalgamated with adjoining districts, while about forty of the remainder, too remote for such a solution, required special assistance.[62]

The special northern assistance grant was established by an amending regulation in 1966.[63] In part, it was designed to provide strong financial incentives for voluntary consolidation. According to the 1967 regulations, a special grant was to be paid 1 / where, in a territorial district, on or after January 1, 1966, the area under the jurisdiction of an elementary school board was enlarged by the addition of an area under the jurisdiction of another such board, 2 / where one or more one-room or two-room schools in the enlarged area were closed, and 3 / where additional classroom accommodation was required by the board of the enlarged area. The amount of the grant would cover the full cost of the construction or acquisition of additional classrooms, not exceeding the number in the abandoned one-room or two-room schools, required during the five-year period after the amalgamation or, alternatively, $20,000 for each constructed or acquired classroom.[64] At the same time, the special stimulation grants for consolidation, involving a single payment of $300 to the board becoming part of the enlarged area, and an annual payment of $500 to the board of the enlarged area for a five-year period after amalgamation, would be applicable.

The second major provision was designed to encourage boards to close the small schools under their control and send their pupils to larger central schools operated by neighbouring boards. The latter would be assisted by a grant covering their expenditure for the construction or acquisition of the classrooms needed to accommodate such pupils up to a maximum of $20,000 per classroom. This provision again covered a five-year period after the arrangement was made. The regulation required that this arrangement be completed during the 1966 calendar year. The board that closed its schools was to receive the full amount of its "supernormal requirement" for tuition fees and transportation or, in other words, the excess of its net requirement over the amount that would be produced by a levy of seven mills on the assessment.[65] This level was approximately double the foundation tax rate defined for normal elementary school boards in the foundation plan formula. Cameron comments on this provision: "The high local tax rate was required, however, to avoid extending an undue advantage to non-educating districts and thus negating the effectiveness of the first category of incentives designed to encourage amalgamation of districts."[66] By the end of 1967, twenty-four agreements had been signed among boards to take advantage of this provision.[67]

As a means of dealing with the difficulty experienced by remote northern districts in attracting and retaining enough competent teachers, the Northern Corps of Teachers was established under the Supervision Section of the Department of Education. Special financial incentives were provided in relation to each teacher's level of qualifications. There were also extra travel allowances. For the 1967–8 school year, there were sixteen teachers in the Northern Corps.[68] A number of isolated districts, identified in a schedule in the grant regulations, were given even further special assistance. This arrangement is referred to later in connection with comments made by the Ontario Committee on Taxation.

Growth-equalization grant

Further study was undertaken to determine the effect of the growth-need grant on boards in different kinds of areas. It was discovered that this grant tended to over-compensate those with a moderate assessment per classroom and a recognized extraordinary expenditure higher than $4,550 per classroom. A similar effect was noticeable for boards with a lower assessment per classroom and an expenditure beyond about $2,500 per classroom. These conditions constituted an invitation to fiscal irresponsibility. The difficulty was attributable to the calculation of the percentage rate for recognized extraordinary expenditure independently of that determined under the equalization formula. With a given growth-need grant, the proportion of the local burden that was relieved by the grant increased as the equalization grant increased. Thus for any given board, a point would be reached beyond which the burden would be reduced at a faster rate than the expenditure increased. Several alternative solutions were considered, including the use of a foundation plan formula for extraordinary expenditures. After long negotiations and modifications in tentative proposals, the equalization and growth-need grants were combined into a single modified foundation-type grant using a variable foundation tax rate. The final version of the plan involved an increase in the normal expenditure level to $1,500 for both elementary and secondary schools.

Cameron describes the background activities leading to the introduction of the new growth-equalization grant in 1968. He has unusual competence for this task because of his own direct responsibility for much of the work. Over two years before the modification in the regulations was actually made, he undertook an investigation into the adequacy of the so-called "normal" levels used as a basis for determining the growth-need grant, at that time defined as $500 per classroom for elementary school boards and $1,000 per classroom for secondary school boards. Among his findings was that there was very little difference in the per-classroom expenditures at the two levels. This conclusion was the basis for the adoption of a single figure for both levels.[69]

Other changes

Certain additional changes were made before 1969 that either were of a minor nature or are treated more fully elsewhere. 1 / In 1967 the concept of average daily enrolment was substituted for that of average daily attendance, thus effectively answering the long-standing criticism that most absences were beyond a school board's control, particularly those attributable to illness or bad weather, and that it was therefore unreasonable that financial support should be reduced on their account. 2 / In 1968 the amounts for special education programs and services eligible for grants were raised, and the number of such programs and services was increased. The abbreviated headings covering these services, as they appeared in the regulations, were as follows: oral class for deaf; emotionally disturbed; neurologically impaired, including perceptually handicapped; Braille; hard of hearing; limited vision; opportunity – primary; orthopaedic; language – for pupils who are from any linguistic cause unable to take proper advantage of the school program; opportunity – intermediate; opportunity – junior; opportunity – no age classification; opportunity – senior; diagnostician – teacher; gifted; hospital, speech; health; institution.[70] Assistance was in the form of payment at a board's stimulation grant rate of part of the salary of each qualified teacher employed for one of these special education programs or services. The salary limits on which the grants were paid differed according to program or service. 3 / Grants for library books were increased. In 1968 a maximum expenditure of $10 per pupil for this purpose was subject to grant at the stimulation percentage rate applying to each board. The increase was provided to offset the federal-provincial special vocational grant for library books, which ceased to be applicable in 1968.

Of special interest, perhaps, was a new stimulation grant introduced in 1968 to deal with the consequences of legislation authorizing secondary school boards to operate French-language schools or classes. It was soon realized that certain private schools in communities such as Ottawa and Welland were likely to turn over their responsibilities to the public system. Such a development would have placed an unexpected burden on the secondary school board. Unless the increase amounted to at least 10 per cent of the total enrolment, qualifying the board for an enrolment-growth grant, no provincial relief would have been forthcoming until the following year. The special provision made available a grant of $200 for each student in excess of twenty that a secondary school board estimated would be added to its enrolment in September 1968 as a result of the closing of a private school. The grant was to be adjusted in 1969 when the actual enrolment data became available.[71] The grant regulations for 1969 swept away all the other course weighting factors except that of 1.1 for a student enrolled in Français in a secondary school.

Grant scheme for 1969

In 1969 the Ontario Foundation Tax Plan gave way without particular fanfare to a new scheme which was regarded as more appropriate for the reorganized school board set-up. According to this scheme, an elementary school board's percentage rate of grant was calculated according to the following formula:

$$100 - 58 \times \frac{\text{PEA/WE}}{\$34{,}000}$$

where PEA/WE was the provincial equalized assessment per resident pupil of weighted enrolment on September 30, 1968 and $34,000 was the average provincial equalized assessment per weighted pupil on the same date for elementary school purposes for the 1969 grant.

Similarly, a secondary school board's percentage rate of grant was calculated thus:

$$100 - 58 \times \frac{\text{PEA/WE}}{\$83{,}000}$$

where $83,000 was the average provincial equalized assessment per weighted pupil on September 30, 1968, for secondary school purposes for the 1969 grant.

There were ceilings of $450 per weighted elementary school pupil and $700 per weighted secondary school pupil on ordinary operating expenditures eligible for grants.

There were two types of weighting factors: location weighting factors and course weighting factors. The former were designed to recognize higher costs in the territorial districts and in the five large urban centres. They involved giving 1 / each pupil residing in a provisional county or in a territorial district a weight of 1.1, 2 / each elementary school pupil in an urban municipality having a population of 190,000 or more a weight of 1.2, and 3 / each secondary school pupil in a municipality with the same minimum population a weight of 1.1. The inclusion of the large urban areas in the category of those requiring extra assistance through this weighting procedure might appear to be rather questionable. Although in these areas costs for certain services were undoubtedly higher than average, their resources seemed more than adequate to provide a higher level of education than smaller communities could afford. A very practical reason for the weighting arrangement from the political point of view was that without it the application of the formula for the percentage rate of grant for ordinary operating expenditure would have given some boards nothing at all. The course weighting factors involved giving 1 / each student enrolled in the regular day classes in the Business and Commerce Branch in a secondary school a weight of 1.05, 2 / each student enrolled in the regular day classes in the Science, Technology, and Trades Branch in a secondary school, or in a special vocational school, or in an occupational program in a secondary school a weight of 1.6, and 3 / each student enrolled in a course in Français in a secondary school a weight of 1.05.

The new scheme involved the continuation of grants for recognized extraordinary expenditure. Capital expenditures from the revenue fund were eligible for inclusion in recognized extraordinary expenditure only up to the sum calculated at one mill in the dollar on the provincial equalized assessment. Other items included were 1 / approved transportation costs, 2 / approved expenditures up to $3.50 a day per pupil for board and lodging and transportation to and from school once a week for pupils not living at home, and 3 / corresponding expenditures for pupils for whom the board was responsible for the payment of fees to attend schools outside its own jurisdiction. The total was to be reduced by 1 / the amount receivable from another board or from the provincial or federal government to defray expenses incurred for pupils for whose fees another board was responsible and 2 / revenues designated by the minister as deductible for grant purposes resulting from the sale or disposal of capital appurtenances and insurance proceeds from capital appurtenances. Most of these items were unchanged from the previous year.

An extraordinary expenditure mill rate was calculated for elementary school boards from the following formula.

$$\frac{0.65 \times \text{REEP to a maximum of \$50 plus } 0.225 \times (\text{REEP} - \$50)}{50}$$

where REEP was the recognized extraordinary expenditure per pupil.

The corresponding formula for a secondary school board was

$$\frac{0.325 \times \text{REEP to a maximum of \$65 plus } 0.112 \times (\text{REEP} - \$65)}{65}$$

The effect was that the mill rate increased in direct proportion to the increase in recognized extraordinary expenditure per weighted pupil up to $50 for an elementary school pupil and $65 for a secondary school pupil, and less than proportionately thereafter. The amount of grant paid was the excess of the recognized extraordinary expenditure over the amount that would have been produced by the extraordinary expenditure mill rate on the assessment. This grant was paid on an estimated basis during the year in which the expenditure was incurred, with appropriate adjustments when actual financial data were available.

There was a special grant to secondary school boards in territorial districts which equalled 67 per cent of secondary school tax levies on assessment that was not previously in a secondary school district. This grant was to be used to reduce the levy on such assessment, and thus ease the shock to the residents of suddenly having to pay taxes to support secondary schools.

Grants to boards operating classes or schools for trainable retarded children were paid both for ordinary and approved extraordinary expenditure. Grants in the first category amounted to 80 per cent of the board's ordinary expenditure, or the sum obtained by applying the board's rate of grant for such expenditure, whichever was greater. Similarly, those in the second category amounted to 50 per cent of recognized extraordinary expenditure, or the sum obtained by applying the board's rate of grant for such expenditure, whichever was greater.

Limits were placed on grants for 1969 which prevented some of the other provisions of the scheme from becoming fully operative. The amount any board received could not be less than 104 per cent nor more than 110 per cent of

$$1969 \text{ ADE} \times \frac{1968 \text{ grant}}{1968 \text{ ADE}}$$

where ADE was the average daily enrolment.

In both parts of the formula, the ADE included resident internal and resident external pupils. The 1968 grant was that before an adjustment was made for the attendance growth grant and after an adjustment for the 1968 enrolment growth grant, and excluded grants for evening courses of study and lump-sum grants.

A very significant provision of the 1969 grant plan was that it eliminated a long list of stimulation grants. The enlarged divisional boards were judged to be capable of establishing their own expenditure priorities without departmental direction. Also worthy of notice was the abolition of the corporation tax adjustment grant which the application of the new scheme would presumably have made largely inoperative in any case.

Effect of the reorganization of local administrative units in 1969

The creation of the new system of divisional boards offered a special set of problems. One of the obligations of each new board was to secure audited financial statements from each of the former constituent boards to show the details of its final year of operations. These tended to come in rather slowly, making it difficult to estimate the increase in costs for 1969. It was reported that the need to secure other information relating to the proportion of costs among the municipalities, the applicable equalizing factors, the apportionment of local levies, and the establishment of mill rates had taken more time and effort in the initial year of operation than would be the case in subsequent years.[72]

There were certain examples of practices on the part of boards going out of existence at the end of 1968 that justifiably led to criticism. Some of them reduced the mill rate, spent any surplus they had at the end of 1967, and entered the new set-up either without any balance or, in some cases, with a considerable deficit. Funds were spent which, under earlier circumstances, would have been carried forward. Although not wasted, they were used for programs that might have been deferred until the new units could establish a priority of needs for the entire area.

Particularly serious political consequences resulted when a board reduced its mill rate in 1968 in comparison with that applying in 1967. The result was generally a spuriously large increase in 1969 when the rate for the larger board was established. Many of the immediate outcries failed completely to distinguish between this particular influence and others that justified more real concern. More genuine problems resulted from the necessity for a gradual integration of employment practices, salaries, fringe benefits, bus routes, and other such factors within the area of the new boards' responsibility. There were differences in the basis of assessment involving difficulties in applying provincial equalizing factors.

Department officials conducted special studies, employing data submitted by the new boards and information supplied by various delegations. It was obvious that the increase in the local mill rate in many municipalities would be modest. In others, the assumption of a regular share of the increased normal costs would cause too sharp a rise in a single year. When the budgets of half the boards in the province had been studied, a procedure was devised to assist the latter type of board. The proposal involved a special grant to boards in municipalities with a population of less than

60,000. Their increase would be limited to one mill of provincial equalized assessment for elementary school purposes and to one mill for secondary school purposes over the greater of the 1967 and 1968 mill rates. This special grant applied to an expenditure per pupil for 1969 up to 115 per cent of the expenditure per pupil for 1968. The latter provision was designed to encourage boards faced with relatively large increases to try to bring their costs down to the 115 per cent level. Departmental assistance was offered to such boards in devising appropriate budgets. It was estimated that the average increase in local mill rates would vary between two and five mills. The department was prepared to pay the special grant to a large number of boards.

There was a special problem in the territorial districts where secondary school students, for whom the province's contribution had long been 100 per cent, were now included in the new and larger units. The proportion of the cost of education for these students was not offset by a corresponding increase in assessment. It was therefore provided that the full cost of educating former non-resident students outside the former board's jurisdiction would be included in the new board's grants.

As an additional measure of assistance, the Treasury Department arranged to accelerate the payment of instalments on grants to boards during 1969. The instalment scheduled for June was paid in advance along with the regular May instalment, and the ones originally scheduled for July and August were paid in June. The consequences included a saving in interest charges.

Grant scheme for 1970[73]

In the calculation of ordinary expenditure for grant purposes for elementary schools in 1970, there was a ceiling of $500 for each resident pupil of weighted average daily enrolment, provided that the increase over the 1969 expenditure per pupil was limited to the greater of $50 and 50 per cent of the excess of $500 over the 1969 expenditure per pupil. For secondary schools, the corresponding ceiling was $1,000, provided that the increase over the 1969 expenditure per student was limited to the greater of $125 and 60 per cent of the excess of $1,000 over the 1969 expenditure per student. The distinction between secondary academic and vocational students was eliminated. In the calculations 1969 expenditure per pupil meant the ordinary expenditure that was eligible for grant in 1969 divided by the average daily enrolment of resident pupils for 1969 adjusted by the 1970 course and location weighting factors. The only course weighting factor that was retained was one of 1.1 for a student enrolled in a course in Français in a secondary school. As in 1969, there was a location weighting factor of 1.1 for a pupil at either the elementary or the secondary level who resided in a provisional county or in a territorial district, and one of 1.2 and 1.1 for elementary and secondary pupils respectively residing in an urban municipality having a population of

190,000 or more as determined by the municipal census of the preceding year.

The formula for determining the percentage rate of grant in 1970 was

$$100 - 46 \times \frac{\text{board's EA/WE}}{\text{S}}$$

where board's EA/WE was the board's equalized assessment per resident pupil of weighted enrolment on September 30, 1969, and S = \$40,500 for elementary schools and \$108,000 for secondary schools.

The grant on ordinary expenditure could not be less than the amount produced by the following formula:

$$\frac{\text{1970 grant}}{\text{WADE}} \times \frac{\text{1969 ordinary grant}}{\text{1969 WADE}} \times \frac{\text{1969 EA/WE}}{\text{T}} \times \frac{\text{S}}{\text{1970 EA/WE}}.$$

In this formula, "1969 ordinary grant" means total provincial assistance, including the education mill rate subsidy, receivable for 1969, less the grant receivable for 1969 for recognized extraordinary expenditure incurred in that year. The education mill rate subsidy limited the increase in the 1970 mill rates in each municipality or part of a municipality for recognized applicable expenditure for elementary and secondary school purposes respectively to the local equivalent of one-half an equalized mill over the 1969 post-subsidy break-even rates.* In the formula, also, "1969 WADE" means the average daily enrolment of resident pupils in 1969 adjusted by the 1970 course and location weighting factors. The term "1969 EA/WE" means the equalized assessment used in the 1969 grant calculation divided by the enrolment of resident pupils on September 30, 1968, adjusted by the 1970 course and location weighting factors. S has the values given above, and T = \$34,250 for elementary schools and \$95,750 for secondary schools.

For a board where the equalized assessment per pupil varied in the same ratio as the provincial average, the formula guaranteed that the minimum ordinary grant per pupil in 1970 could not be less than the

*"Post subsidy break even mill rate for 1969" means the break-even mill rate required in a municipality or part of a municipality in 1969 to provide the amount of the board's requirement apportioned to it as required for that year, less the sum of 1 / the grant payable to the board in a territorial district for the purpose, where applicable, of reducing by 67 per cent the mill rate for secondary school purposes in a municipality or part of a municipality that was not included in a secondary school district in 1968, 2 / the education mill rate subsidy for 1969 payable to the board on behalf of the municipality or part of a municipality, and 3 / revenue of the municipality or part of a municipality resulting from mining revenue payment on behalf of the board. (SOURCE: *Regulation, Apportionment 1970 Requisitions: Divisional Boards of Education*, Ontario Regulation 57/70, 5 February 1970, pp. 3–4.)

ordinary grant per pupil for 1969, including subsidy. Where the assessment per pupil increased at a rate greater than the provincial average, the guaranteed minimum ordinary grant for 1970 was less than the ordinary grant per pupil for 1969, including subsidy; and where the assessment increased at a rate less than the provincial average, the grant was correspondingly greater. The grant for ordinary expenditure could not exceed the portion of the ordinary expenditure recognized for grant purposes. The grant was to be paid on an estimated basis during the year in which the expenditure was incurred, with necessary adjustments to be made when the actual financial data and weighted average daily enrolment were available.

There was no substantial change over the previous year in the definition of recognized extraordinary expenditure. For an elementary school board, the formula for determining the extraordinary expenditure mill rate was

$$\frac{0.45 \times \text{REEP to a maximum of \$50 plus } 0.15 \times (\text{REEP} - \$50)}{50},$$

and for a secondary school board,

$$\frac{0.25 \times \text{REEP to a maximum of \$75 plus } 0.08 \times (\text{REEP} - \$75)}{75},$$

where REEP was the recognized extraordinary expenditure per pupil for 1970.

As in 1969, the amount of the extraordinary expenditure grant was the excess of the recognized extraordinary expenditure over the sum calculated at the extraordinary expenditure mill rate in the dollar upon the assessment.

The purpose of the education mill rate subsidy has already been referred to briefly. The upper limit of subsidizable expenditure was defined as follows. For elementary schools, it was $650 for each resident pupil of weighted average daily enrolment, provided that the increase of the 1969 applicable expenditure per pupil was limited to the greater of $60 and 50 per cent of the excess of $650 over the 1969 applicable expenditure per pupil. The latter term meant the applicable expenditure for 1969 divided by the 1969 average daily enrolment adjusted by the 1970 course and location weighting factors. For secondary schools, the upper limit of subsidizable expenditure was $1,200 for each resident pupil of weighted average daily enrolment, provided that the increase over the 1969 applicable expenditure per pupil was limited to the greater of $80 and 50 per cent of the excess of $1,200 over the 1969 applicable expenditure per pupil.

The grant paid in this category was calculated at the mill rate which was the excess of the presubsidy mill rate for 1970 over the sum of 1 / the quotient obtained by dividing fifty, in the case of residential and farm assessment, or 55.55 in the case of commercial assessment, by the assessment equalization factor for 1969 and 2 / the post-subsidy break-even mill rate for 1969. This mill rate was levied on the total taxable assessment upon which taxes were levied in 1970. An appropriate adjustment was to be made where the general level of assessment on the roll prepared in 1969 was higher than that on the roll prepared in 1968. In rough terms, the grant was a means of subsidizing boards, up to a defined limit, for an increase in expenditure over that of the previous year.

There were special arrangements for isolate boards. An isolate board was defined as an elementary school board in a territorial district which was not a divisional board of education or a district combined separate school board, and had an enrolment of two hundred or fewer resident and non-resident pupils on the first school day of January 1970. If it had one classroom open for a full year, its enrolment was counted as not less than thirty minus the number of non-resident pupils. An isolate board received in grants not less than the excess of its expenditure approved by the minister over the amount produced on its assessment by a mill rate equal to seven or the mill rate set by the district combined Roman Catholic separate school board or that set by the divisional board of education for elementary school purposes in the municipality or district municipality where the isolate board existed, whichever was greatest.

In 1970 commercial assessment, since it yielded additional taxes per unit, was counted as 111.11 per cent of its assessed value. The assessment of concentrators and smelters added to the assessment roll in 1969 was treated as if it had been added to the roll prepared in 1968.

GRANTS FOR CAPITAL EXPENDITURE

Basic considerations with respect to debt

The question of debt incurred by local school boards to help defray current operating expenses is not an issue of any great importance in Ontario. Although a certain amount of such debt was incurred by school boards in the 1930s, and separate school boards have occasionally resorted to the same practice more recently, school debt is almost exclusively the result of borrowing for capital projects.

The underlying principle is reasonably simple. Capital projects can be undertaken only by the immediate withdrawal of labour, equipment, and material from other possible uses. For the time being, the attainment of some alternative objective must be deferred. Someone must do without. In this sense, no part of the cost of the project can be postponed. The relevant questions are, "Who will do without?" and "Under what conditions?" An ordered society must of course reject the arbitrary confiscation of resources, the use of forced labour, and other such methods. The real alternatives are thus either 1 / immediately depriving the whole body of citizens of the requisite resources by means of a tax system, which, it is to be hoped, distributes the burden equitably, or 2 / depriving certain citizens of the resources in question by inducing them to invest some of their disposable income voluntarily in debentures, rather than spending it on goods and services. In return for the postponement of immediate gratification, they are not only repaid the amount of their investment over a period of time, but are also given a reward in the form of interest extracted by the appropriate process from all taxpayers. In the borrowing process thus described, the taxpayer gains the privilege of extending his repayments over a period of time in exchange for the obligation to pay more, by the amount of the interest, than if he made the sacrifice immediately. The lender is compensated for accepting the deferral of immediate gratification by enjoying a greater degree of ultimate indulgence, providing, of course, that he does not choose to continue reinvesting his capital. The argument in favour of borrowing for capital projects is that it is reasonable to spread the cost over most or all of the period during which benefits are received, and to ensure that future generations of beneficiaries share the burden. A very important additional consideration is that borrowing enables a particular community to reach beyond the jurisdiction of the local tax collector to draw temporarily on the surplus resources of neighbouring communities.

In an absolutely stable community, where the rate of capital investment equalled that of capital loss and deterioration, there would be nothing to be said in favour of borrowing. To do so would simply mean the unjustifiable paying of interest. It would be far better to let past generations carry the full burden for facilities enjoyed by the present taxpayers, while the latter would compensate by making a similar contribution to future generations. The case for borrowing must be made on the basis of an acceleration in the demand for capital projects, particularly during a period of unusual demand which may be expected to decline after the immediate crisis has been met. This condition has become almost the normal one in many parts of Ontario.

The Ontario Committee on Taxation felt that there was a strong argument for heavy municipal borrowing in that Ontario had been experiencing sustained and substantial growth over a period of many years. It pointed out that capital investment was most needed in those communities in which the fastest growth was occurring. The projects financed currently through debenture borrowing would be paid for with revenues derived from an ever-broadening tax base. Rapid growth facilitates repayment of debt with little strain, assisted by an element of gradual inflation.[74] The latter of course has its effect by depriving the investor of part of the reward he expected. He tends to compensate by raising his initial price, i.e., by demanding a higher rate of interest. An obvious effect of the high rates of interest characteristic of an inflationary period is to raise the initial cost of borrowing in contrast to a reduction of the real cost in the final stages.

Background of local capital financing

A good deal of information has already been supplied with respect to capital financing arrangements. Some of these may be summarized as follows: 1 / Public elementary and secondary school boards have had to arrange for capital financing through municipal councils in areas where municipal organization exists. In cases of disagreement the issue could be appealed to local taxpayers and, more recently, to the Ontario Municipal Board. 2 / Separate school boards have had the power and the obligation to issue their own debentures, as have other boards in areas without municipal organization. 3 / After 1945 certain expenditures relating to capital were included in approved costs. According to the 1949 scheme, these were defined for public and separate elementary school boards as "principal, interest, and other charges on debentures and capital loans." They did not include amounts transferred to current funds from capital funds or receipts from the sale of capital assets. For secondary schools, the relevant item was "capital outlays for new buildings, additions to buildings, or for equipment." 4 / From 1954 to 1959 the maximum allowance per classroom was $20,000 for both elementary and secondary schools. At the beginning of the period, this figure was not too far out of line for the average board, but it was gradually left behind by rising construction costs. It left large and increasing amounts to be raised locally, particularly in high-cost urban and northern regions. In 1959 the maximum allowance for secondary schools was raised to $25,000 per classroom. 5 / Until 1959 grants were paid only on classroom construction and the most meagre supporting structures. The boards had to take complete financial responsibility for auditoriums, gymnasiums, and general purpose and utility rooms. 6 / The main effect of the grants for recognized extraordinary expenditure beginning in 1958 was to provide extra assistance in the financing of extraordinary capital investment.

Cameron offers a concise analysis of the problems of local school boards and municipalities in financing large capital expenditures.[75] The main outlines of this analysis are as follows. The fundamental problem was that school boards usually lacked sufficient resources to undertake such expenditures except by borrowing. Heavy reliance on borrowing generated pressing problems. 1 / A great many school boards and municipalities were so small and isolated from the centres of business and commerce that institutional markets for capital debentures were virtually non-existent. It might be added that consistent inflationary trends over the years aggravated the difficulty by decreasing the attractiveness of investment in that type of security. 2 / While interest rates on municipal and school board debentures tended to be higher than those of senior governments because of the presumably lower level of security offered, the difficulty was aggravated where the debentures could not be offered to a competitive market. 3 / The Ontario Municipal Board, charged with policing local indebtedness, imposed ceilings which restricted or even prevented the further expansion of total borrowings on the part of certain boards. The position reached by some of the boards in the suburbs of Toronto before the creation of the metropolitan system of two-tier government in 1953 provides an example of what could happen. The developments in that area were reviewed in the preceding chapter.

Cameron offers three possible responses to these problems on the part of the provincial government. 1 / It can increase the revenue capacities of local governments by delegating new taxing powers to them, by improving the use of the existing tax base, or by increasing the proportion of revenue derived from provincial grants. 2 / It can reduce the fiscal demands placed upon local governments, accepting greater responsibility either for the initiation of capital expenditures or for the financing of such expenditures. 3 / It can improve the conditions under which local borrowing is carried out, either by facilitating the access of local governments to the capital market or by interfering with or eliminating the competitive market for school debentures. The response of the Ontario government in the 1960s, as demonstrated particularly by the establishment of the Ontario Education Capital Aid Corporation, has been largely in terms of the third of these choices. Recent adoption of the provincial objective of paying 60 per cent of school board operating costs indicates to some extent an acceptance of the first possibility as well.

Appraisal of debt situation

Figures on Ontario's school board debt position during the post-war period have been presented in volume I. In appraising this situation, the Ontario Committee on Taxation observed that if the municipalities, like the province, were confronted by the continuing prospect of both high and relatively stable levels of annual capital expenditures, or of rising expenditures at relatively stable rates of growth, there would be a defensible case for financing the major proportion of capital projects from current revenue. But this kind of situation was manifestly not in prospect. Given the forecasts of rapidly escalating capital outlays in education and other fields, the committee observed, "not even the early attainment of an 'ideal' provincial-municipal tax system would render feasible their financing on a pay-as-you-go basis, nor indeed would such a policy be defensible in principle."[76] The committee also noted that, in a growing economy, a rise in tax capacity is accompanied by a comparable rise in the ability to carry debt, and that both sources of finance are essential aspects of a sound fiscal policy. It therefore offered the view that a substantial absolute increase in debt at the municipal level was not only inevitable, but also a constructive aspect of public finance. More specifically, it recommended that school board debt, as well as that for other municipal governments, be allowed to attain somewhat higher relative levels than those currently existing, but not the heights they had reached in the late 1930s.[77]

Vocational schools

Note has been taken of the arrangements for financing the construction of vocational schools and vocational extensions to secondary schools under the Federal-Provincial Technical and Vocational Training Agreement. As the agreement was worked out, all expenditures given tentative approval by February 1, 1962, were to be financed in the first instance by the province, with later reimbursement of 75 per cent of the expenditure by the federal government. Also, all expenditures incurred before April 1, 1963, were to be financed in the same way regardless of when the approval had been given. For all other expenditures, the province would assume responsibility for only 75 per cent, leaving the remaining 25 per cent as a responsibility of the school boards.[78] Since the federal grant applied only to provincial expenditure, the federal contribution was reduced to 75 per cent of the provincial grant, or 56.25 per cent of the total cost. When the federal contribution dropped to 50 per cent of the provincial, it accordingly covered only 37.5 per cent of the cost. The reduction in the provincial contribution, despite the disadvantage entailed in the corresponding loss of federal funds, was carried out at least in part in recognition of the desirability of maintaining local fiscal responsibility.

One important form of control was of course that entailed in securing approval for capital proposals. School boards had to submit their plans to the department for scrutiny by a technical adviser before the reorganization of 1965, and thereafter by the School Plant Approvals Section. This procedure was applicable to vocational as well as to all other projects. Assessment of the former, however, involved simultaneous appraisal by the federal Department of Labour. After tentative approval was granted by both agencies, the school board could call for tenders or submit orders for construction, equipment, and machinery. As long as the tendered cost did not greatly exceed the estimate, no further approval was needed from the federal government, and the board was authorized by the province to proceed with the project.[79]

When the 25 per cent contribution was exacted from local boards, they had a choice when considering vocational school construction between an outright contribution of 75 per cent under the vocational grant scheme on the one hand, and, on the other hand, a grant of between 35 and 95 per cent on capital expenditures from current funds and debt charges under the Ontario Foundation Tax Plan. Cameron shows that the effective fiscal treatment of school boards is virtually the same if the same rate of grant – in this case 75 per cent – is applied under either scheme.[80]

Another important change was made in June 1965, when the province assumed the full cost of vocational facilities to be used by two or more secondary school boards on the basis of an agreement between the boards.

The combined enrolment of the two schools had to be at least one thousand before they could take advantage of this provision. This arrangement made possible a wider dissemination of the benefits of vocational education while at the same time ensuring reasonably effective utilization of financial and staff resources.

The Ontario Education Capital Aid Corporation

The creation of the Ontario Education Capital Aid Corporation was made possible by the implementation of what was essentially a federal government policy. It took the form, however, of a provincial action to deal with a matter centred around local needs. It began with negotiations between the federal government and the provinces with a view to establishing a contributory old age pension plan of national scope. The federal government originally proposed a pay-as-you-go scheme that would keep contributions and payments fairly close to an even balance on a permanent basis. Contributions would begin at a low level, and would increase over the years in accordance with the number of beneficiaries and their growing claim on allowances. Full advantage would be taken of the rising capacity of an expanding economy to meet welfare needs. The province of Quebec, however, preferred the funded approach, and in 1964 announced a plan involving a relatively high initial rate of contributions, which would presumably remain fairly constant over the years. The fact that benefits would rise gradually from a low initial level meant that a substantial surplus would be available in the early stages for provincial government use. Quebec won the contest of wills, and Ottawa revised its plan accordingly. The Canada Pension Plan, which came into effect on January 1, 1966, produced surpluses that could be turned over to the other nine provinces in return for provincial securities.

The funds thus made available to Ontario could be used in any way the government saw fit. The decision, which, as Cameron observes,[81] reflected the high priority assigned to education by the cabinet, was to employ them to support the Universities Capital Aid Corporation, and to establish an Ontario Education Capital Aid Corporation. The creation and role of the first of these are described in chapter 12. Funds turned over to the latter were intended for the purchase of debentures issued by municipalities and school boards for the construction of schools.

The estimated contribution to Ontario would be approximately $267 million annually from 1966 to 1976, and a declining amount for the next ten years, when contributions and benefits would be in balance. J.N. Allan, Provincial Treasurer, announced that there would be sufficient funds available to the various municipalities and school boards to provide for the entire school construction program.[82]

Although the Ontario Education Capital Aid Corporation operated under provincial charter, it was administered by senior officials of the Treasury Department as an integral aspect of government activity. Its regular business was conducted by the Municipal Finance Branch of the Department of Municipal Affairs. Financing all or part of a capital project through the corporation entailed a fairly involved process. As a first step, the school board prepared a project plan and submitted it on a very detailed information schedule to the School Plant Approvals Section of the department. The school board prepared a budget of its capital requirements for the ensuing fiscal year, and an estimate of the proportion of these requirements to be financed through the sale of debentures, as opposed to other sources such as accumulated capital reserves or a special levy on local assessment. Public elementary and secondary school boards formerly submitted their capital budgets to the municipal council or councils in municipally-organized territory for approval. After January 1, 1969, school boards, not including those in Metropolitan Toronto, were authorized to issue their own debentures, and the necessity for council approval was eliminated. This change put an end to a good deal of wrangling and frequent appeals to the Ontario Municipal Board.

The next step was the submission of the capital budget to the Ontario Municipal Board. This board reviewed the existing indebtedness of the municipality and authorized the issuing of debentures up to a fixed ceiling. If the board refused its approval, the only alternatives were to reduce the proposed spending to an acceptable level or to appeal to the provincial cabinet. Separate school boards needed to seek the approval of the Ontario Municipal Board for their projects only if they wished to borrow from the Ontario Education Capital Aid Corporation.

It would be hard to improve on Cameron's account of the subsequent procedure. This account is presented here in full, not so much because this amount of detail is needed in the present context, but it demonstrates the complexity of certain government operations. Whether or not every step is needed is a question to which the writer would not venture an answer.

Once the school board or municipal council has received permission from the OMB to borrow up to an accepted limit, the process of applying for funds from the OECAC begins. The treasurer of the municipality or the school board must complete a document entitled "Offer to Sell a Debenture" which outlines the nature of the project or projects being undertaken and the amount and term of the debenture to be offered. This document is then forwarded to the Municipal Finance Branch of the Department of Municipal Affairs.

The Municipal Finance Branch then drafts the necessary local by-law, obtains the OMB's approval of its form, and submits the draft by-law to the local treasurer for transmission to the municipal council or school board. The council or school board must then enact the by-law and the clerk or secretary-treasurer must forward a copy to the Municipal Finance Branch.

The Municipal Finance Branch submits the enacted by-law to the OMB once again, this time obtaining a certificate of validity. This certifies that the by-law conforms to the terms of the borrowing approved by the OMB when the local capital budget was first presented. When the by-law has been validated, the Municipal Finance Branch prints the necessary debenture and forwards it to the local treasurer. The treasurer must then submit the debenture itself to the OMB for validation. Again, the OMB certifies that the terms of its original approval are complied with in the borrowing instrument.

As the final steps in this process, the OMB forwards the validated debenture to the Director of the Securities Branch in the Treasury Department. A cheque in the full amount of the debenture is then issued in the name of the OECAC to the municipality or school boards as final settlement of the transaction.[83]

Before July 1968 the rate of interest to be charged by the corporation was that which prevailed on the day that the validated debenture was delivered to the Treasury Department. This rate was determined by the rate charged for the use of Canada Pension Plan funds, which in turn was prescribed by the federal Minister of Finance on the basis of the average yield on long-term federal securities. Any change in the rate after the debenture was issued by the municipality or school board was compensated for by varying the purchase price of the debenture in inverse relation to the rate change. After the above date, the interest rate was that in effect on the day the original "Offer to Sell a Debenture" was received by the Municipal Finance Branch.

A little contemplation of some of the operations referred to gives an idea of the fertility of the field for more sophisticated computer operations. Here we have the local agency borrowing money from a provincial agency (the corporation), and paying interest on it in part received in the form of grants from another provincial agency (the Department of Education). It should have been possible, and economically desirable, to eliminate purely mechanical transfers of funds from one branch of the government to another in favour of a final balancing of the books, if even that step was indeed necessary. From the point of view of efficiency, one may wonder if the corporation did not represent a rather awkward intervention between the receipt of federal funds and their use for school construction.

Cameron comments that about the only areas remaining under the exclusive responsibility of local government are the decisions to undertake capital projects and the establishment of priorities among projects. He thinks it fairly safe to assume that the province's concern for responsible capital financing is adequately safeguarded by existing supports and controls.[84] Yet, if this is so, it becomes difficult to explain why some boards that were headed for oblivion at the end of 1968 are said to have presented to their communities a fine new school or an extension of the old one as a final gift, regardless of whether or not such construction was likely to be generally advantageous to the new county unit as a whole.

The effect of the corporation's activities has been very favourable. Cameron points out that, in the first fiscal year of its operation, the median advantage in interest rates over municipal debentures was 0.995 percentage points. Assuming that the municipal rate would also have applied to school debentures had it not been for the existence of the corporation, Cameron estimates that the total savings in charges required to service the debt in that single year were approximately $24.5 million. He declares: "If the OECAC maintains a comparable advantage over municipal debentures, and if the school debt increases at a fairly constant rate, then the savings on debt charges will increase proportionately each year."[85]

One is tempted to express surprise that the province did not succeed much earlier in finding a means of placing its complete financial resources behind school board borrowing, so that school boards could obtain money at no higher a rate of interest than that paid on provincial securities. One could argue convincingly that the same should be done for municipal securities issued for other than school purposes. But school boards were obtaining funds from the corporation at interest rates substantially below those paid on provincial securities. Thus capital financing for schools was removed completely from the market. The issue caused some concern on the part of the Ontario Committee on Taxation, which felt that the corporation should be abolished.

Cameron found that the essential weakness in the existing arrangement was its failure to deal with the disparity between local capital need and fiscal capacity. Through a combination of the corporation and departmental grants, school boards had an alternative and less expensive source of borrowed funds than the open market. But school debt was treated as if it were secured only by local taxing capacity, even though the provincial government might supply the funds to repay much the greater share. There was no equalization of local capacities; thus the greater the capacity, the greater the permissible borrowing. Cameron suggested that the payment of capital grants at the time of an expenditure would help to solve this problem.[86] As explained later, this idea was in line with a recommendation by the Ontario Committee on Taxation. Under such a scheme, the part of the total capital requirements to be borrowed by the school board would be equalized in terms of relative taxing capacity, since the grants varied inversely with the latter. Cameron commented also that, if the growth-need concept, as outlined earlier, were embodied in such grants (providing relatively more in grants in cases of unusual requirements) local borrowing would be equalized in terms of fiscal need as well.

If one assumes that it is desirable to make money available for capital expenditure by school boards at a rate of interest below that paid on securities sold by other public agencies, then the corporation plays a useful role, although it is still legitimate to ask if the same objective could not be achieved in a more efficient manner. Apart from this factor, if steps such as those suggested by Cameron were taken to equalize school boards in terms both of relative taxing capacity and of fiscal need, a major justification for the existence of the corporation would disappear. Under the present system of divisional boards, which may be expected to develop the expertise to operate effectively on the open market, there is much less need than formerly to provide a special market for school debentures.

Other recent changes

Some of the grant policies designed to encourage or ease the transition to larger school units have been mentioned from time to time in the section primarily devoted to operating expenditure. Somewhat similar were the measures taken to encourage the abandonment of one-room and two-room structures in favour of larger central schools. In 1966 arrangements were made to ensure the continuation of payment of grants on the approved portion of outstanding debt charges on the abandoned schools. A similar provision applied to school buildings that were sold. The department also arranged for grants to assist boards with the conversion of secondary school buildings to serve as elementary schools.

A new method of calculating approval of capital projects for grant purposes was announced by the minister in February 1967,[87] to apply to those projects for which final departmental approval had been granted on or after January 1 of that year. A few months later the arrangement was extended to include all approvals given in 1965 and 1966.[88] The new scheme was designed to provide substantially greater assistance to boards in meeting building costs, and to do it in a flexible and sophisticated manner so as to take full account of variations in need and cost.

Under the new arrangement, the approved cost was calculated by summing the number of "accommodation units" in the project multiplied by the value per unit. The number of accommodation units depended on the number and size of the "eligible spaces." Tables of accommodation unit factors supplied by the department covered the full range of eligible spaces normally found in elementary and secondary schools. Special consideration could be given to proposals for unusual types of accommodation or room sizes beyond the limits recognized in the tables. Eligible spaces included teaching areas, gymnasiums, libraries, cafeterias, and the like. Swimming pools were not included, although it was possible for a school eligible for two gymnasiums to receive support for one gymnasium and one pool. The remainder of the school, including school offices, staff rooms, furnace rooms, storage space, washrooms, and corridors, was referred to as auxiliary accommodation. The accommodation units assigned to eligible spaces made due allowance for such accommodation. The approved cost was intended to include all items of construction cost, such as site improvements, architects' fees, and necessary furniture and equipment.[89]

The department's tables of accommodation unit values were originally intended to distinguish among four types of schools: elementary, senior elementary, secondary, and secondary-vocational,[90] the last two of which were soon combined. This treatment was designed to reflect the fundamental differences in costs among the three basic types of projects. Each table was further divided into three zones to take account of differences in the cost of construction in different parts of the province. Arrangements were made to provide for a higher value per accommodation unit in smaller projects in the light of market realities. Adaptation to changing costs of construction could be readily provided by changing the values assigned to accommodation units. Such an adjustment was intended to be made annually. The department's intention was that between 80 and 100 per cent of the actual cost of construction would be recognized for grant purposes.

The new plan included the cost of alterations to school buildings, an item not previously recognized except under the arrangements for vocational projects. This feature encouraged boards to effect economies by opting for extensions and conversion of existing structures in contrast to new construction. Since the cost of alterations was not amenable to formula treatment, the approved cost was determined by reducing by 15 per cent the actual cost of alterations as disclosed in bids. Thus the approved cost for both construction and alterations was equated to the over-all provincial average of 85 per cent.

In announcing the retroactive extension of the plan to cover projects approved in 1965 and 1966, Davis indicated that the amount of that approval would be increased by approximately 50 per cent for an elementary school and 100 per cent for a secondary school. Thus if, for example, approval was originally given for a grant of $200,000 for the construction of a ten-room elementary school, the amount would be raised either to the actual cost or to $300,000, whichever was less. If the original approval of a thirty-room secondary school project involved a grant on an approved cost of $750,000, that amount would be raised either to $1,500,000 or to the actual cost, whichever was less. As a means of extending the benefits of the arrangement to boards that sent their students to neighbouring boards, the proportion of the fees paid by the "purchasing" board that was eligible for grants was increased from 15 to 20 per cent.[91]

With reference to vocational school grants, the termination of the technical-vocational agreement between the federal and provincial governments in 1967 posed a problem for the latter. On March 9, 1967, the minister announced that Ontario would continue the capital grants for an additional two-year period.[92] In a further elaboration of the decision in May, he said that the assumption of the 37.5 per cent supplied up to that time by Ottawa would involve the setting aside of roughly $200 million for the two-year period. He promised an assessment of the situation to determine whether the new capital grant formula could be utilized after that period. The boards might thus make their decisions, not on the basis of having incentive grants for technical-vocational education, but on the basis of the actual type of accommodation or educational program they should be developing. The new grants formula was already as acceptable to some boards as the 75/25 formula, although not to those in major urban centres.[93]

RECOMMENDATIONS OF THE ONTARIO COMMITTEE ON TAXATION AS RELATED TO CONTEMPORARY DEVELOPMENTS

Along with its praise for the Ontario Foundation Tax Plan, the Ontario Committee on Taxation suggested that improvements could be made in four aspects of its mechanics: 1 / in its treatment of the calculation of a school board's pupil load, 2 / in its handling of recognized extraordinary expenditure, 3 / in its accommodation of regional and other variations in school costs, and 4 / in its provision for the corporation tax adjustment grant.[94] The advantages of these suggestions were not all overwhelmingly obvious, of course, to officials of the Department of Education.

The committee commented on the critical importance of the calculation of pupil load in determining a board's level of fiscal support. This calculation established the board's basic tax relief grant, its applicable foundation level of operating cost, and its recovery of equalization payments on recognized extraordinary expenditure. The committee was in favour of the shift from attendance to enrolment, since reduced support based on reduced attendance because of illness rightly ought to be eliminated. The original objective of counteracting controllable absence was no longer very relevant. The committee felt, moreover, that a significant defect existed in that a school board's grant, which was paid on a calendar year basis, was calculated on the pupil load of the previous year. The grant thus lagged behind the board's actual enrolment. While the growth need and attendance growth grants helped the situation somewhat, they applied only to those school boards where the enrolment rise was out of the ordinary. The committee noted that a school board's enrolment was particularly weighed down by the January to June enrolment for the previous year, which over the span of the grant year was out of date by one school year until September of the grant year, after which it was out of date by two school years. The situation is shown diagrammatically on page 276. The broken line indicates the attendance period that was two years behind the second half of the year in which the grant was actually paid.

The committee's recommendation on this point was as follows: "So long as school grants are on a calendar year basis, the existing practice of calculating them on the previous calendar year's pupil load [should] be replaced by a system of calculations that reflects school enrolment in the period beginning the first school day of September of the calendar year preceding that in which the grants are paid (20:1)." The Select Committee of the Legislature on the Report of the Ontario Committee on Taxation, which reported in 1968, approved this recommendation, but suggested substituting September 30 for the first school day of the month.[95] While the basic point was apparently sound, serious exception was taken

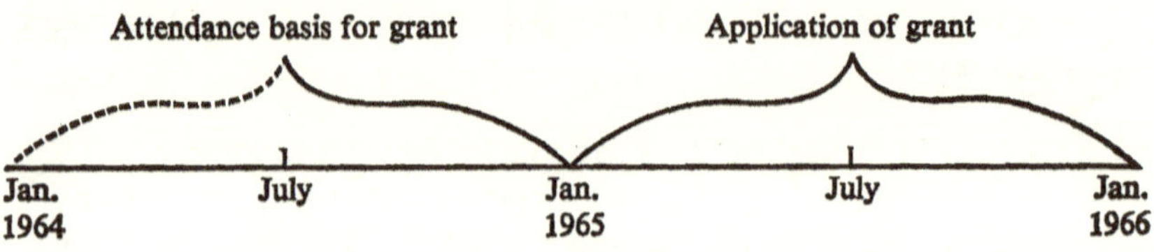

to the proposal to sample attendance on any particular day, since there would be no assurance that it would not be affected by some unusual event.

The department moved in 1968 toward an arrangement that would remove the criticism that the growth need and attendance growth grants applied only to boards where the enrolment rise was out of the ordinary. A revision in the regulations was designed to provide for the payment of the grant wherever the estimated enrolment for the current year exceeded by more than 10 per cent the actual enrolment for the preceding year. This procedure involved a subsequent recalculation using actual figures as soon as they became available. As already indicated, this step was considered unfavourably a short time earlier, and thus represented a reversal of previous policy. Beginning in 1969, grants were paid on an estimated basis on the year in which the expenditure was incurred, and any necessary adjustments were to be made when the actual financial data were available.

A more sweeping recommendation of the Ontario Committee on Taxation, with which the select committee disagreed, was that the fiscal year of local governments be changed from the calendar year basis to one that coincided with the fiscal year of the province. Under such conditions, school grants could be determined for the period extending from April 1 to March 31 of the following year. This practice, the Ontario committee suggested, would make it possible to calculate the grants on the basis of September enrolment in the year in which they were actually paid. The following recommendation related to this point. "In the event that school finances are based on a fiscal year that coincides with that of the Province, the final school grant instalment [should] be based on calculations of pupil load that reflect enrolment in September of the fiscal year in which the grants are paid (20:2)." There were objections to changing the fiscal year of elected boards to a period that would not coincide with their term of office. This was seen as conflicting with the principle that they should have maximum responsibility for their actions. A further aspect of the recommendation that has occasioned objections is that it seems to involve an attempt to match expenditure and enrolment for different periods.

The Ontario committee's recommendation with respect to recognized extraordinary expenditure had to do with the two components relating to capital expenditure: that is, debt charges and capital expenditure out of current revenue. The situation was summarized as follows:

The provincial treatment of capital expenditure for school purposes departs significantly from that of other grant-eligible items of local capital expenditure. For the latter, of which roads and highways are the most important example, the provincial contribution is geared to the entire amount of capital outlay, and is made at the time the work is undertaken. For school capital expenditures, however, the only provincial contribution at the time the work is undertaken is on that part of the outlay that school board finances out of current revenue. The remaining provincial contribution to the work is left to accrue over time in the form of financial relief on debt charges.[96]

Two important consequences of the existing practice were identified. One was an increase in local debt beyond what would result from the application of the policy respecting roads and highways. The second was the degree of uncertainty attached to the status of local school debt. Under the existing grant scheme it was true that provincial relief on debt charge obligations could be anticipated, but future changes in the levels of provincial support could not be forecast. Thus it was impossible to determine what proportion of school debt rested on local assessment and what proportion was backed by the province.

That the situation was unsatisfactory was demonstrated by the fact that the Department of Education had to make substantial exceptions to its regulations in 1967. Because needed school construction would otherwise have meant exceeding the Ontario Municipal Board's ceilings for local debt level, lump-sum contributions had been made on the capital expenditure of eight school boards, three involving secondary schools, and the remainder, public elementary schools. The province was also making lump-sum contributions to the construction of schools in northern Ontario where school areas were being enlarged. In order to regularize and improve the situation, this recommendation was offered: "Provincial treatment of the recognized extraordinary expenditure of school boards [should] be amended so that the grant contribution to capital expenditure is applied at the time the expenditure is incurred (20:3)." This recommendation was supported by the select committee. The Ontario committee recognized the complexity of the problem of dealing with capital expenditure. The other items included in recognized extraordinary expenditure – transportation, board and lodging costs, and tuition fees – were all closely tied in with school construction. The addition of a classroom facility by one board might occasion tuition payments by another board whose students were to be accommodated therein. Conversely, a board acquiring a new facility might be able to discontinue payments to another board. Transportation expenditures were particularly closely related to school construction. For some boards, a new school might reduce costs for this purpose; for others, particularly in rural areas, the construction of a central school might substantially increase them. The committee thus offered the opinion that recognition of the relationship between a board's tuition, transportation, and board and lodging costs on the one hand and its capital outlays on the other should be retained. No specific solution was offered for all the problems involved in making the recommended changes. Recommendation 20:3 was welcomed in the department, which had been urging adoption of the principle for years against the opposition of the Treasury Department.

The committee expressed the view that the Ontario Foundation Tax Plan did not yet attempt to cope systematically with the important variations in operating costs attributable to the geographical and social diversity of the province. It offered as conspicuous examples the higher salaries required to attract teachers to remote areas, the relatively high heating bills of schools in northern Ontario, and the special problem of coping with culturally deprived children in urban slums. The foundation plan, applying uniform rates of basic tax relief grant and foundation levels of operating costs, suffered from the fact that the gross averages used covered a multitude of very different situations. In 1967 it had actually been necessary to devise special operating grant provisions for eleven school boards in northern Ontario, where distress had been particularly acute. The committee expressed grave concern over such a development. "Where any part of a fiscal system, be it a tax or a grant, must incorporate named exceptions to its applications, both fiscal equity and impartial administration are endangered."[97] It was suggested that the proper course of action was to make the formula more discriminating in its application rather than to make exceptions to it. Confidence was expressed that the formula was amenable to the necessary modifications.

As has already been noted, the schemes for 1969 and 1970 in succession simplified the plan by abolishing all course weighting factors except for students enrolled in a course in Français in a secondary school. Trainable retarded children, for example, were treated as secondary school students for grant purposes. Location weighting factors looked after special needs in the northern part of the province and in urban areas of a certain size. The grant scheme was in these respects much more in accord with the committee's recommendations.

Reference was made to the attempt to cope effectively with the fiscal deficiencies of separate schools. As a result of representations by separate school interests and continued study by the department, there had been a series of revisions in the formula. In 1965 provision was made for the mill rate applicable to a separate school board's corporation assessment deficiency to be either the commercial public school rate or eleven mills, whichever was greater, rather than the former alone. As a result of changes in the basis of equalized taxable assessment to full sale value in 1966, the applicable rate was changed to four mills. The committee also took favourable note of the change in 1967 by which a separate school board's corporation assessment deficiency was determined, not with respect to the municipal ratio of corporation assessment to residential and farm assessment, but with respect to the relative corporation assessments per separate school pupil and per public school pupil. The corporation tax adjustment grant thus now registered relative fiscal need rather than the relative fiscal capacity indicated by residential and farm assessment.

What the separate school trustees really asked for was that a fair share of available corporation assessment would be defined as the corporation assessment per pupil of the abler board in the municipality. Thus, to use an example offered by Cameron,[98] if the public school board had access to $10,000 of corporation assessment per pupil, the fair share of the separate school board would also be that amount. The arrangement actually made retained an advantage for the public school boards in that they would lose none of the disproportionate share of corporate assessment that they could tax. The committee was critical of this situation, commenting, "If all publicly supported elementary schools of Ontario are to be treated with complete equity, they should have identical access to local tax resources uninhibited by peculiar defects in the structure of taxation." The relevant recommendation was as follows: "In each municipality, the assessment of corporations that cannot under The Assessment Act direct their taxes for school support [should] be segregated into a distinct allotment taxable by public and separate school boards in exact proportion to the relative pupil enrolment of the boards (20:4)."

Despite the action already taken by the government, the select committee registered its disapproval of the recommended course of action. Its dissent was based on "the belief that, with further adjustment, the Ontario Foundation Tax Plan can provide a satisfactory solution to the problems of constitutional law and equity involved in the distribution of taxes to the public and separate school systems."[99] For the same reason the select committee opposed the recommendation that the elementary school mill rate levied in any given year against the corporation assessment allotment be either the applicable public or the applicable separate school mill rate, whichever was lower.[100]

The assumption behind these recommendations, that is, that the two elementary school systems should be placed on a basis of complete equality, is by no means generally accepted. It conflicts with the idea that public school supporters should be entitled to any advantage corresponding to a balance of the ownership of corporations in their municipality that might be in their favour. Those who hold this point of view are unwilling to assume without evidence that corporation ownership is actually divided between supporters of the two systems in the same ratio as relative pupil enrolments. They are also apprehensive about taking steps that would erode the assessment base of the public school system. Probable political repercussions from any move to reduce the grants to public school boards prohibit such action. The only practical way to improve the position of the separate schools is to increase the relative amounts of funds available to them.

Cameron observes that changes in the corporation tax adjustment grant, coupled with the general extension of equalization, gave reasonable grounds for the expectation that the over-all revenue disparity between the two systems would be reduced. However, as the general level of equalization was improved, the basic inequity of the corporation tax adjustment grant became more obvious. While it contributed to the equalization of public and separate school revenues within the same municipality, it did nothing to equalize revenues from one municipality to another. General equalization would obviate the necessity for the corporation tax adjustment grant, since all boards would have access to the same revenue per pupil with the same effort in taxation.[101] As already noted, the corporation tax adjustment grant was dropped in 1969.

The Ontario committee reviewed eleven "stimulation" grants or individual grants for specific purposes existing in 1967, almost all of which antedated the foundation plan, and a number of which have been referred to in the present account. They were as follows: 1 / the municipal inspectors' grant, which paid between 35 and 92 per cent of salaries to a maximum of $900 per month; 2 / the evening courses grant, which paid between 50 and 92 per cent of teachers' salaries to a maximum of $6 per hour; 3 / a grant for industrial arts and home economics instruction to non-resident pupils, amounting to $7.50 per pupil per term; 4 / a library books grant, which paid either the amount spent for books for kindergarten through grade 13 to a maximum of $2 per pupil per year or 35 to 92 per cent of expenditure up to $9 per pupil; 5 / a textbooks grant, which accounted for the total spent up to variable maxima per pupil according to grade, plus a variable percentage of cost on the amount spent in excess of the maxima to a ceiling of $3 per pupil; 6 / a small secondary schools grant, which paid $10 per resident student up to a $2,000 maximum for academic secondary schools with fewer than 400 students, and $20 per resident student up to a $4,000 maximum for vocational secondary schools with fewer than 500 students; 7 / a television grant, which amounted to the greater of $270 or $1.50 per pupil up to the actual amount spent; 8 / a grant for English, French, and citizenship courses for new Canadians, at 90 per cent of teachers' salaries up to a maximum of $6 per hour; 9 / a free milk grant to elementary schools, which paid either 50 per cent of cost or the net board expenditure after donations, whichever was less; 10 / a grant for Trustees' Council fees, which amounted to 35 to 92 per cent of fees paid to the Ontario School Trustees' Council to a maximum of $30 or 15¢ per pupil. The eleventh of these grants, which was paid on entrance to larger units of administration, had several provisions. For elementary boards, there was a grant of $20 per rural pupil, prior to admission to the larger unit, up to a maximum of $300 per board; this grant was paid only once to the unit absorbed. For elementary boards also, there was an annual grant of $20 per rural pupil, up to a maximum of $500 for each former school section. For secondary school boards, there was a payment of $150 per year for each rural school section or former rural school section within its jurisdiction.

The committee observed that where the grants in question were made for obligatory services, they were not really stimulation grants. Among those that justified the term, the view was offered that they might be merited from time to time as a means of encouraging a board to initiate a new program on an experimental basis, as in the case of educational television. But they should be made for limited periods of time and then phased out when they had had the desired effect on levels and standards of service. If allowed to accumulate, they inevitably led to a grant system marked by unwarranted administrative complexity. Also, if not equalized, they tended to discriminate in favour of wealthy boards and against indigent ones.

The committee noted with satisfaction the incorporation of the grant on school sites into the Ontario Foundation Tax Plan's treatment of recognized extraordinary expenditure. It also approved of the integration of grants for special services into the formula applying to operating costs. With respect to other special grants it recommended that "the grants on behalf of municipal inspectors' salaries, evening courses, industrial arts and home economics instruction to non-resident pupils, library books, textbooks, small secondary schools, and televised instruction be abolished in their present form and incorporated into the basic structure of the Ontario Foundation Tax Plan (20:6)." It was suggested that the first of these, which applied only to certain school boards, might be included either in the grant for operating costs or in a revised treatment of recognized extraordinary expenditure. Evening courses and non-resident students might be accommodated through the plan's pupil load calculations, suitably weighted. Library books might be considered as part of regular school operating expenditures, as should textbooks, which were free of charge as a matter of provincial policy, and did not warrant grant treatment that differed from such items as teachers' salaries. Adjustment on the basis of the calculation of pupil load could take account of the problems of small secondary schools. To the extent that televised instruction continued on an experimental basis only, it could also be looked after by an adjustment of pupil load. As far as the provision of special instruction to new Canadians was concerned, the committee felt that this should not be a financial obligation of school boards at all, and recommended that "the existing grant for English, French and citizenship courses for new Canadians be abolished and that the Province relieve school boards of all costs arising from such courses (20:7)." The committee was unenthusiastic about the free milk grant, the grant for Trustees'

Council fees, and the grants for entering larger units of administration, and recommended that they be terminated. The milk grant was received by relatively few boards, and was an inappropriate field for the school system to be involved in. There was no more reason for subsidizing the Ontario School Trustees' Council than for providing similar support for other organizations such as the Association of Ontario Mayors and Reeves. The grant on entering larger units of administration involved inconsequential sums. The committee believed that boundary reform should be achieved through legislation rather than through incentives. To the extent that a school board's fiscal position was affected by the absorption of another unit, the situation should be reflected in its treatment under the foundation plan.

The select committee supported most of the Ontario committee's recommendations with respect to the existing "multitude" of stimulation grants on the grounds that their implementation would add to administrative simplicity and efficiency. In endorsing the recommendation that the responsibility for the financial support of classes for immigrants be removed from local boards, it suggested that the federal government should assume part of the obligation, since the matter involved more than education. Also, although the select committee favoured the termination of free milk grants, it did not approve of ending the provision of free milk for elementary school children, but rather advocated that the Ontario Foundation Tax Plan include a provision for universal free milk at that level.[102]

The committee's recommendation that special grants for the formation of larger units be repealed obviously became irrelevant with the announcement of mandatory legislation to take effect on January 1, 1969. As to the others, some hesitation on the part of the government was occasioned by the following factors. 1 / Certain grants, such as that for milk, had a strong psychological appeal, and the agency that abolished them could be made to look heartless and inhuman. The fact that they cost very little was an argument for retaining them. 2 / Support for the Ontario School Trustees' Council, again involving small expenditures, had considerable value in maintaining good relations. Its withdrawal might be regarded as an unfriendly act. 3 / There was genuine disagreement as to whose responsibility it was to integrate newcomers into the local community. A case could be made for the assumption by the latter of a substantial part of the obligation. 4 / The Department of Education might legitimately wish to keep fairly definite control over the development of certain programs such as the use of educational television. Generally speaking, this control could be exercised more effectively and precisely through special stimulation grants than by an adjustment of the basic elements of the foundation formula. 5 / As a rule, governments find it desirable to leave existing practices alone unless they cause obvious inconvenience or harm. In short, the committee could be expected to favour a neat and logical formula, and the government to put more weight on human factors, especially those related to political advantage.

Despite all these arguments against abolishing stimulation grants, the Ontario committee's recommendations were adopted almost completely in the 1969 Regulations. The grant plan of that year was swept clear of special grants of all kinds. The move is to be regarded as part of the process of decentralization of responsibility whereby the divisional school boards are expected to establish their own spending priorities.

A final recommendation of the Ontario committee with respect to special grants was that all future grants made by the province for vocational school construction be integrated under the provisions of the Ontario Foundation Tax Plan. The committee noted that since 1965 the province had been discontinuing its practice of absorbing whatever vocational school construction costs were not covered by federal contributions. School boards had themselves been required to finance 25 per cent of the capital outlay, with the senior government contribution limited to 75 per cent. The vocational school construction grant had accordingly been transformed into a flat-rate conditional grant that took no account of the fiscal capacity of school boards. The committee considered this practice unjustified when the equalization provisions of the Ontario Foundation Tax Plan were readily at hand. It noted that the plan could easily accommodate vocational school capital grants if it were amended so as to pay all capital grants at the time these outlays were undertaken.

The select committee endorsed this recommendation. It advocated, however, that new provisions integrated into the Ontario Foundation Tax Plan should recognize the higher costs associated with vocational schools, thus preventing financial distortions in favour of academic schools.[103]

The Ontario committee reviewed and commented on the proportion of the funds the province had contributed over the years to the maintenance and operation of the school system. It recommended that this contribution be raised through deliberate staging to a level of 60 per cent. From the existing average level of about 45 per cent, the sharpest rise should occur at the beginning. Over a three-year cycle, the rate might reach 52, 56, and 60 in successive years.[104] This proposal was accepted as government policy. The government had at last given real evidence of believing that the weight of the local levy on property to support the school system was becoming excessive in comparison with other possible means of raising revenue.

The majority of the select committee agreed that the assumption of a 60 per cent share of school board expenditure on the part of the provincial government over a three-year period was a reasonable short-term objective. The figure was, however, judged to be somewhat arbitrary, and there seemed to be no good reason why 55 per cent, 65 percent, or some higher value should not have been chosen. The majority issued the following warning.

> We do think that with every increase in the proportion of education costs paid by the Province the more likely [is] the possibility of inefficiency at the local school board level or alternatively, the more compelling the need for firmer centralized direction and greater control by the provincial Department of Education. The first prospect is quite obviously not desirable and the second is equally distressing to those of us who have observed diseconomies of scale in growing governmental operations.[105]

While there was no objection in principle to a 60, 70, or 80 per cent provincial share, the majority preferred that the province should seek remedies to the problems of inadequate revenues in a variety of other ways, as suggested in many of the recommendations of the Ontario Committee on Taxation.

The Liberal members of the select committee regarded the 60 per cent figure as "totally inadequate" for several reasons, summarized briefly as follows. 1 / Education was the prime investment that the provincial government could make. 2 / Waste came from a large number of unrelated aid devices rather than from a major single source of aid. 3 / The higher rate of provincial subsidy would bring closer the socially desirable goal of equality of opportunity for all Ontario students. 4 / There were vast new costs in the offing, including action to implement the recommendations of the Provincial Committee on Aims and Objectives, the development of information retrieval systems, and the creation of county boards of education. Many of these costs could be optimized only at the provincial level. They were also difficult to explain in terms associated with local government. 5 / Local alienation from the educational process occurred for reasons other than a lightening of the local financial burden. To ask municipalities to counteract this phenomenon by indulging in regressive local taxation was to attack the problem from the wrong position. 6 / Progressive taxation was always preferable to regressive taxation. With educational costs rising at the predicted rate, a 60 per cent relief would soon be swallowed up in real terms, and the householder would experience little benefit.[106]

In Budget Paper B, attached to Provincial Treasurer Charles MacNaughton's 1969 budget, the government indicated that its primary purpose in assuming an increased share of education financing was to permit some compensating reduction in school board levies. Local boards were warned that the higher provincial grants were to be accompanied by some restraint in school board spending. In the past, increased grants had been translated almost entirely into higher total expenditure. Since enrolments were expected to level off, however, a change was expected in the future. If school boards failed to exercise voluntary restraint, the government would consider establishing machinery, such as a budget review board, to ensure that benefits from increased provincial aid accrued to the local taxpayer.[107]

NINE

Provincial and local revenues

PROVINCIAL REVENUE SOURCES

As has been indicated, revenues from the property tax and provincial grants are the twin pillars of school board support in Ontario, with the balance swinging strongly toward the latter. In order to understand the essentials of the situation, it is thus necessary to give some attention to past, present, and possible future sources of provincial revenue. Given the comprehensive objectives of the present series of volumes, it is impossible to devote more than casual treatment to the topic. The major source of information must again be the report of the Ontario Committee on Taxation, to which general indebtedness is herewith acknowledged in the hope that it will cover any specific instances of unintentional failure to indicate the source. The observations of the select committee of the Legislature on the same report also help to illuminate the situation.[1]

General principles

Two important principles of taxation recognized and discussed by the Ontario Committee on Taxation were the benefit principle and the ability to pay. It was suggested that taxes based on the first of these principles are desirable 1 / when the benefits and beneficiaries of government expenditure programs can be identified relatively clearly, 2 / when a modified distribution of wealth and income is not a policy objective, and 3 / when the imposition of benefit-related charges on the users or beneficiaries of a service will not result in an inefficient use of that service. Examples of impositions following this principle are licences for automobiles, fishing, hunting, the use of parks, and the conduct of certain businesses. The gasoline tax is another important levy in the same category.

The principle of ability to pay is regarded as appropriate for financing the large proportion of government expenditure where it is inappropriate or impossible to assess charges among taxpayers in accordance with benefits received. The application of this principle requires agreement on some generally accepted criterion or criteria by which capacity to pay taxes may be measured, such as income, wealth, or expenditure. The principles of benefits received and ability to pay provide a two-fold categorization scheme that includes all taxes levied or likely in future to be levied by the government of Ontario. The committee defined nine qualities, some based on the paramount consideration of equity, and others on that of efficiency, which should characterize a sound revenue structure. These were adequacy, flexibility, elasticity, balance, neutrality, certainty, simplicity, convenience, and economy of collection and compliance. Particular forms of taxation might be expected to possess some of these qualities, but only the whole composite of tax measures could demonstrate all of them in reasonable measure.

The committee agreed with the usual assumption, as demonstrated in taxation practice, that income should be the chief index of tax-paying. It also felt that wealth and consumption should be taken into account as part of a balanced program. The basis for allocating the tax burden among individuals or families should be the aggregate effect of all taxes taken together. The differential effect of government expenditures on individual incomes, as well as the impact of taxes, must be taken into account in order to produce over-all equity.[2]

Income tax

Certain provinces made an early entry into the field of the personal income tax. British Columbia was the first, with its levy of 0.5 per cent on incomes over $1,500 in 1876. In 1897 the flat rate was abandoned in favour of a graduated percentage ranging from 1.25 to 1.75 per cent. Other provinces gradually followed British Columbia's example, but none exacted a large amount from this source. Ontario was relatively slow to enter the field. In 1936 the first *Income Tax Act* deprived the municipalities of their little-used access to the field and reserved it exclusively to the province. From 1936 to 1942 an agreement was in force by which the federal Department of National Revenue administered and collected the tax and returned the proceeds, after deducting a fee, to Ontario. As a wartime measure, all provincial personal income tax acts were suspended in 1942.

In the post-war period, Ontario settled for an arrangement whereby the federal government continued to collect the entire tax and remitted a specified proportion to the province. Agreements on the proportion to go to the provinces have been by no means easy to reach. The provincial government has consistently pressed for a larger share on the grounds that its need for funds to discharge its obligations has risen more quickly than that of the federal government. The latter, aware that any ground lost would be unlikely to be regained, has been reluctant to vacate a large part of the field. According to the agreement in force in 1969, Ontario, like most other provinces, received a twenty-eight-point abatement on income tax collected in the province.

For any particular province, the alternatives to accepting what it could get through negotiations have not been easy. It could theoretically introduce a higher rate of taxation by collecting a few more percentage points under the federal-provincial agreement, as some provinces have actually done. But by raising its rate much above that of the others, it risks the loss of upper income residents and capital, and the growth of the economy may be slowed. Quebec may have a convincing threat when it declares that it will raise its own revenues and put the blame on Ottawa for forcing it into a position of penury. But Ontario has no assurance that such a course of action will not backfire. Ontario citizens can by no means be counted on to place their provincial loyalties ahead of national ones.

The Ontario Committee on Taxation considered the progressive income tax as a highly desirable means of raising revenue in terms of the criteria it established. This attitude has, of course, come to be widely accepted. The committee gave some attention to the proposition that, since the tax clearly increases the attractiveness of leisure, its inevitable effect must be to reduce labour, and thus production. This argument, however, ignores the fact that, because the tax reduces income available for consumption and investment, it induces many people to increase their labour to restore or protect their standard of living. As the committee noted, "The fact that our enjoyment of the leisure is increasingly tied to our ability to spend, and so to our income, further militates against any significant tendency to substitute leisure for work."[3] The point was also made that work often provides its own incentive, and is relatively unrelated to the level of financial reward.

The committee recommended a continuation of the existing collection agreement between the federal and provincial governments. It had suggestions for improvements, including the following: that the base be broadened to include other elements of income; that all costs of earning income be deductible; that loss carry-over provisions be liberalized; that income averaging be generally available; that husband and wife should be able to file a joint return; and that marginal rates should be reduced.

The select committee expressed the view that a substantial part of the future increased revenue requirements of the province should be met from the personal income tax. Even if the federal government did not, as hoped, provide additional tax room, the relative importance of the tax should not be allowed to decrease. In fact, the committee felt that it should be the first source to be explored when additional tax room was required.[4]

Capital gains tax

Whether or not a capital gains tax should be imposed at either the federal or the provincial level in Canada has long been a matter of controversy. Those who favour it do so in part on the grounds of equity. They can see no reason why financial gains obtained through accretions to the value of property attributable to economic influences entirely beyond the control or influence of its possessor should be less liable to contributions for the public welfare than funds earned as direct income in return for labour. They feel a sense of injustice in observing accumulations of great wealth through speculation when the same result is unobtainable, because of taxation practices, for those whose savings must be accumulated through wages, salaries, or business profits. A case is also made for the practical value of a capital gains tax. It is often suggested that the failure to collect it represents just so much lost revenue. The standard argument on the other side is that the tax would tend to discourage speculative investment that provides a mainstay for a growing economy. Despite the fact that such a tax is levied in the United States and in many other countries, American investors are commonly thought to exert an influence against it, feeling that it would damage the value of their stake in Canadian resources. The Ontario Committee on Taxation recommended against the capital gains tax in these terms: "we must advise that the levying of a capital gains tax by Ontario should be considered only if it is accompanied by a sweeping revision of the entire tax structure of such nature that the addition of capital gains to the tax base should make a clear and indisputable contribution to the equity of the whole revenue system."[5] Perhaps the reason why the *Report of the Royal Commission on Taxation* (the Carter Commission) took a different stand on the issue is simply that just such a sweeping revision of the tax structure was recommended in that document. The Ontario committee's warning that the tax should in no event be imposed by Ontario acting alone may appeal to those who do not share the view that it is undesirable in principle, since such an action might threaten the province's economic position.

Although the select committee believed that the equity of the provincial tax structure would be enhanced by the addition of a capital gains tax, the majority agreed with the Ontario Committee on Taxation that it would be inadvisable for the province to introduce it unilaterally. Some consideration was given to the possibility of levying such a tax on increased land value, on the grounds that a substantial part of the increment was attributable to the provision of social capital and services at public expense. But, although further study of the matter on the part of the government was recommended, the select committee felt that administrative difficulties would be too great to justify such an imposition.[6] The Ontario government declared its intention in 1969 to introduce a capital gains tax as part of a restructured tax system. Such a step would be in accord with Finance Minister Benson's proposal to do the same at the federal level.

Corporate income tax

At the time of the investigation of the Ontario Committee on Taxation, the corporate income tax contributed almost one-fourth of the total revenue of the Canadian government and one-fifth of that of Ontario, where its yield was exceeded only by that of the retail sales tax and the personal income tax, and equalled only by that of the gasoline tax. It therefore had a strong appeal on the basis of the criterion of yield. Like the personal income tax and the sales tax, it was responsive to economic conditions. Given the expectation that Ontario's economy would continue to improve and expand, there seemed a good prospect that the tax would continue to provide a dependable source of revenue. The committee expressed the hope that it would not be overworked as a result of the comparative ease with which it could be collected, and because it made comparatively few voters unhappy. In the long run, because it seemed not to conform to the principle of equity, the committee expressed the hope that it could be reduced. On this point, it could expect more enthusiasm from business interests than, rightly or wrongly, from the average citizen.

The committee recommended that Ontario follow the example of all the other provinces except Quebec by entering into an agreement with the federal government for the collection of corporate taxes. It seemed highly desirable to have a common base and approach to this form of taxation in all Canadian provinces. The select committee agreed on these points, but was not persuaded that there was a convincing case for decreasing the relative importance of the tax in the provincial structure.[7] It concluded that the Ontario committee should have placed more emphasis on it as a source of revenue, even if the assumption was correct that half the burden was shifted to the consumer in the form of higher prices. It noted that there was no agreement among economists on the extent to which corporations were actually able to shift the tax.[8]

Succession duty

The succession duty is a tax of long standing. At the beginning of the present century, rates were low and exemptions high, and it yielded in the neighbourhood of 5 per cent of total provincial revenues. As rates were raised, its importance increased, and by 1930 its contributions had risen to nearly 20 per cent. In 1966–7 this figure had declined again to little more than 3 per cent. Despite such a relative decline, the absolute amount of revenue from it had grown.[9]

The succession duty is of course a form of wealth tax. Its justification rests mainly on the principle of ability to pay. An extreme point of view is that all taxes of this kind represent an unreasonable encroachment on the rights of the deserving in favour of the undeserving. But few people in Ontario today would take such an unequivocal position. It is generally recognized that wealth is earned in an economic and social context defined by legislation and policed by government action. A tax contribution is therefore to be regarded in a sense as a fee for service. Fundamental differences have to do with whether or not the social structure should permit the accumulation of large concentrations of wealth in the hands of private individuals. Whether by conviction or by default, Canadians have obviously opted in favour of providing such opportunities. The relevant questions thus have to do with the ways in which government will compel a sharing of accumulated wealth.

An argument against the succession duty is that, in reducing concentrations of wealth, it hinders capital investment and slows the growth of the economy. It is said to drive wealthier citizens out of the province and to discourage immigration and the influx of foreign capital. Somewhat contradictory is the claim that it encourages the transfer of native industry and resources to foreigners, since it decreases the amount of Canadian capital available for investment. It is probably a safe assumption that these two forces tend to work against one another. The general tendency of the succession duty is, other things being equal, to drive up the rate of return on investment. The Ontario Committee on Taxation expressed itself favourably disposed, with some qualifications, toward this category of taxation, commenting that "a democratic society such as ours, espousing political equality for all its citizens, cannot permit undue concentration of wealth in the hands of a few."[10]

The select committee generally approved the suggestions of the Ontario Committee on Taxation with respect to succession duties, including those designed to make them more equitable and to simplify the method of calculation and payment. Feeling that there was little likelihood that the federal government would help to solve the problems of duplicated administrative apparatus and unnecessarily high compliance costs, it recommended co-ordination of federal and provincial procedures.[11]

Until 1968 succession duties seemed to constitute an unreasonable obstacle for a man with a dependent family in his efforts to accumulate sufficient resources to ensure his heirs a moderately comfortable existence in case of his premature decease. The exemptions permitted were insufficient to prevent a substantial tax contribution from a moderate inheritance. Among measures taken by the federal *Estate Tax Act* in 1968 to rectify the situation was a provision for relief from the imposition when property passed to the surviving spouse. A higher rate than that imposed previously was levied when the estate passed from the immediate family.

In 1969 the Ontario government announced that it would phase out succession duties along with the introduction of a capital gains tax at the time a fundamental restructuring of the tax system was brought about. There still remained a good deal of uncertainty in 1970 as to how changes in the federal estate tax would relate to provincial succession duties. The Ontario government was convinced, however, that immediate relief was needed in this area. It therefore increased the exemption for widows from $75,000 to $125,000, and provided the same exemption for widowers. Under certain conditions, surviving common-law wives and husbands were to be placed on a similar basis. In the event of the death or remarriage of an annuitant within four years of the death of the deceased, revaluation of assets was to be permitted, on application, to take account of the reduced capital value of the annuity.

Sales tax

Up to the present time, the only form of sales tax available to the provinces has been that imposed at the retail level. The Constitution reserves to the federal government the right to levy such a tax at the manufacturer's level. Thus the provinces are entitled to the open, obvious, and politically unpopular form, and the federal government to the safer and, according to a not uncommon view, the more insidious form. In either case, the revenue must come from the tax-paying public.

The retail sales tax may of course be levied at the municipal level. Montreal pioneered this type of impost in 1935 by introducing a tax of 2 per cent on sales of tangible personal property, except for food and certain goods bought by manufacturers. The first province to enter the field was Alberta, which in 1936 chose this means to raise funds to assist the municipalities by contributing more toward education and social costs. It was at first intended that the rate of 2 per cent should apply to almost all goods except bread, milk, and a few other necessities. Before the tax became effective, however, certain other items were added. The measure was so unpopular that it was repealed in a little over a year and not reintroduced. In the face of similar financial difficulties, Saskatchewan introduced a comparable tax in 1937, on what appears to be a permanent basis. The initial rate of 2 per cent was raised to 3 per cent in 1950 and to 5 per cent in 1962. The Liberals took full advantage of the unpopularity of the tax in the election campaign of 1965 and after their success in unseating the CCF government reduced the rate to 4 per cent.

Other provinces followed Saskatchewan's lead in imposing the tax in fairly regular succession. Quebec was the next in 1940, at which time the administration of the Montreal tax was assumed by the province. A number of other municipalities including school municipalities levied the tax on the same basis before 1964, when the province took over the whole field, and a uniform provincial rate of 6 per cent then applied until it was raised to 8 per cent in 1967.[12]

At the time Ontario was ready to take the plunge, British Columbia, New Brunswick, Newfoundland, Nova Scotia, and Prince Edward Island had entered the field. By 1960 it was becoming obvious that the great increase in education costs and the requirements of new hospital services demanded additional sources of revenue. There was a great deal of soul-searching in the government before the decision was announced in the budget address in 1961 that a retail sales tax would be imposed at a rate of 3 per cent. Five years later, the rate was increased to 5 per cent.

In its unadulterated form, the sales tax is highly regressive. Consumption expenditures are not a constant proportion of income throughout the income range, but rather demonstrate an inverse relationship to income level. Those at lower levels cannot escape the tax except by enduring actual hardship. There are two obvious ways of counteracting the regressive feature and relating the tax more closely to ability to pay: 1 / by exempting a wide range of goods defined as "necessities" and 2 / by allowing exemptions against personal income tax liabilities. Because of the complex interrelationship between federal and provincial taxation systems, the first of these was the only practical alternative for Ontario. Under the scheme adopted, the list of exemptions was a long one, including food, children's clothing, materials and equipment used for farm production, services, and the like. The tax credit solution was considered favourably by the Carter Commission as part of a basic reorganization involving the federal and provincial levels of government and different forms of taxation.[13] It was not, however, recommended for immediate implementation because of administrative problems. Some of these were expected to become more amenable to solution as time went on. The commission offered a list of items that should be excluded from the retail sales tax: 1 / all food products, other than restaurant meals over a stated minimum; 2 / fuel, electricity, and eventually building materials entering into the cost of shelter, 3 / goods for which expenditures are made because of ill health or physical handicap, and 4 / magazines, books, and newspapers that could not be taxed without serious difficulty. A longer list of principles guiding the taxation of services was also provided.

There are considerable advantages in the use of the sales tax. It is a relatively stable yielder of revenue, fluctuating somewhat according to economic conditions, but not often going below a fairly high minimum level. It is also very productive. In Ontario, it quickly became one of the best revenue producers, and reached a position comparable to that of the personal income tax. The Ontario committee recommended that, while food should continue to be exempt, and the exemption for consumer goods should be broadened wherever administratively possible, the list should otherwise be shortened. The committee strongly urged the inclusion in the tax base of as many as possible of the consumer services that do not enter into the costs of taxable goods.[14] This approach was anathema to the New Democratic Party in particular, which tended to deplore any measure that enhanced the regressive features of the tax.

The Carter Commission recommended a drastic readjustment of sales tax arrangements affecting the federal and provincial governments. It advised a transfer of sales tax room to the provinces in exchange for more federal direct tax room. If the federal tax were at the retail level, such an exchange would be greatly facilitated. The commission labeled the sales tax at the manufacturer's level a bad tax that should be eliminated because of the numerous inequities resulting from its application.[15]

The select committee agreed that the inclusion of consumer services would make the tax more equitable, and that the exemption of all food products would remove most of the regressiveness that would otherwise be present. The majority of the committee suggested, however, that the same gain in equity could be obtained by an alternative device at a lower cost in lost revenue. The proposed device was the retail sales credit, which could be balanced against the provincial income tax. When the amount of the credit exceeded the income tax liability, a refund would be paid as a form of negative income tax.

Other taxes
Space will not be taken up here to review the role of the many other forms of taxes that are available to the Ontario government, nor to discuss their virtues and defects. In total, they contribute a substantial proportion of provincial revenues. They fall, in general, into the category of consumer benefit taxes, with certain built-in limitations, such as that 1 / they must appear reasonable to those who pay them or, as is true of other taxes, they will produce seriously adverse public reactions; 2 / they must not go beyond what the traffic will bear if maximum yield is to be maintained; 3 / the cost of administration must not be excessive.

PROVINCIAL DEBT
The possibility of meeting part of the current crisis through a substantial increase in the provincial debt is often placed in the category of the unthinkable. The Ontario Committee on Taxation observed that "the balanced-budget tradition has remained strong, even at the highest levels of government, and for much of the post-war period Canadian fiscal policy was significantly impaired by the view, apparently shared by successive ministers of finance, that deficits are a curse and only to be suffered most unwillingly."[16] In part, this attitude is attributed to defensiveness resulting from the public's tendency to equate budgetary deficits with the failure of government policy. The committee pointed out, however, that, "If pursued rigidly by all levels of government, regardless of changes in underlying economic conditions, the policy of the annually balanced budget would bring higher taxes and decreased government expenditures in recession, lower taxes and increased expenditures in inflation, and accordingly could lead only to the aggravation of economic instability and eventually to economic disruption."[17] To the extent that it has been followed, this policy has been at variance with commonly accepted current fiscal theories. Obviously, however, even though Ontario's economy is a very large and influential component of the national economy, it does not constitute the kind of unit that by itself could be manipulated in such a way as to maintain a continuously high level of economic activity. That task must be primarily the task of the federal government but, to be really effective, calls for co-ordinated action on the part of the two senior levels of government. The balanced-budget-at-all-costs tradition in Ontario is only one bit of evidence that such co-ordination has been somewhat deficient in the past.

As a brief digression at this point, it may be observed that, in the ultimate interests of the people of Ontario, as of all Canadian citizens, demands made on the federal government must not be pushed to the point where they seriously threaten the ability of the latter to play its dominant role in regulating the economy. Unfortunately, it seems impossible to tell how much taxing capacity in the personal income and corporation tax fields can be yielded to the provinces before such an eventuality occurs. Ontario government leaders, including Provincial Treasurer MacNaughton, have expressed the view that this point is still far off. In 1968 MacNaughton claimed that the federal government could well abate up to 60 per cent of the personal income tax and 33 per cent of the corporation income tax while still retaining adequate leverage for fiscal control.[18]

The Ontario Committee on Taxation reviewed the possible means of determining a reasonable and bearable level of public debt. Among the recognized indices are 1 / gross debt in relation to provincial domestic product, 2 / gross debt in relation to provincial personal income, 3 / net interest costs in relation to provincial domestic product, and 4 / net interest costs in relation to ordinary revenue.[19] No matter what index is applied to Ontario's post-war public debt, the results give cause for reasonable satisfaction. The ratio of capital debt to domestic product stood at the relatively low level of 8 per cent in the late 1920s, rose to an all-time peak of almost 30 per cent in the 1930s, and then declined to about 7 per cent in 1956. By 1965, it had risen to 8 per cent. The committee observed that "by historical standards, the present burden of provincial debt is near its lowest point."[20] This verdict was confirmed in 1965 by the Hon. J.N. Allan, then Provincial Treasurer, who declared in his budget address for that year:

> The net capital debt at March 31, 1965 is estimated at $1,423 million. In relation to the wealth and resources of this province, the level of the net debt is well within reason. It approximates the 1964 increase in the gross provincial product, and is equivalent to the provincial net revenue for 14 months.[21]

The select committee concurred with the recommendation that provincial debt might justifiably be allowed to grow somewhat more rapidly than provincial domestic product. It felt, however, that the province's credit must be maintained intact, and that increased taxation revenues must be fully utilized in preference to an excessive expansion of debt.[22]

In the light of these facts and opinions, it appears quite reasonable to assume that part of the present burdens arising from new educational programs can be financed not only by an absolute, but also by a relative increase in the public debt. Such a course of action would be particularly justified on the grounds that capital expenditure for new buildings and facilities for universities and colleges of applied arts and technology in particular is reaching a peak. As the proportion of young people seeking education at these institutions tends to level out, and as the population increase slows, the situation may be expected to stabilize somewhat in a few years. The case for spreading capital costs over future generations of taxpayers appears to be particularly convincing and valid at the present time.

APPRAISAL OF FINANCIAL PROSPECTS

In its study of the financial problems confronting the Ontario government during subsequent years, the appraisal by the Ontario Committee on Taxation in 1967 was extremely sobering. In one of its most pessimistic statements it observed:

Our projections lead us to the clear and inescapable conclusion that in the absence of remedial measures, the present unsatisfactory revenue and spending positions of the provincial and local governments of Ontario will deteriorate sharply and continuously within the coming decade ... The concrete problem that emerges is that of determining the most appropriate means of financing a combined provincial-local expenditure-revenue gap which will have grown to some $600 million annually by 1969 and to more than $1,300 million by 1975, just to finance existing programs. To the extent that major new programs are introduced, the projected gap will be correspondingly increased.[23]

A great deal of attention was given to these problems as the Legislature opened in the fall of 1968. Terrance Wills wrote in the *Globe and Mail*: "The horizon holds big financial problems for the Government, and the tax solutions the Government comes up with ... probably will determine its survival at the next election."[24] He quoted the Prime Minister in the same article:

"Our forecasts indicate that under the present tax system total revenues collected by the provincial Government will grow by only 40 per cent between now and 1973. On the other side of the ledger, our forecasts indicate that, when we project present spending patterns, the total expenditures by the Government will increase by 74 per cent in the same period of time. These results of our forecasts add up to what the Treasurer of Ontario has warned will be a financial nightmare."

Provincial Treasurer MacNaughton was quoted as saying that the government must cut $300 million from the estimates for the ensuing year if the line were to be held at existing tax rates, along with reasonable borrowing. Although his subsequent budget made this statement sound more pessimistic than necessary, no one pretended that the long-term problem was likely to disappear.

A team of *Toronto Daily Star* writers dramatized the situation. The government, they said,

can only get the money it needs – about $300 million to balance the budget – by higher taxes or a merciless slashing of present provincial programs including such sacred cows as education and highway construction.

In order to produce $300 million of additional revenue Queen's Park would

> have to collect an additional 12 percentage points of personal income tax, thus raising the provincial income tax from 28 to 44 per cent [*sic*]; or increase the present 12 per cent corporation tax to 26 per cent; or raise the retail sales tax from 5 to 8 per cent; or increase the gasoline tax to 33 cents per gallon from 18 cents; or simultaneously tap all of these major tax sources for lesser amounts ...
>
> To save the $300 million through austerity measures, the government would have to eliminate, for example, all provincial subsidies to municipalities for road construction, plus all grants and subsidies for health units and community health facilities, plus all provincial grants to children's aid societies, urban renewal projects, forest protection, and its total capital investment in housing.
>
> Or it could fire all of its 50,000 civil servants.[25]

This assessment of the situation indicated the prospect of major tax increases. The Ontario Committee on Taxation, from its vantage point in 1966–7, recommended increases in three revenue fields: the personal income tax, the sales tax, and the gasoline tax, with the last of these playing a relatively minor role. From the brief discussion of the virtues and faults of these taxes in earlier pages, with numerous references to the committee's views, the justifications for this recommendation should be reasonably clear. The personal income tax is lucrative and progressive, and, provided that it can be levied with the full co-operation of the federal government, easily administered. The sales tax is also lucrative and, if the right exemptions are provided, need not be too regressive. The committee, in fact, assessed its impact under existing circumstances as neutral or mildly progressive. The recommended increase was one percentage point to bring it to 6 per cent. The gasoline tax is closely tied to road benefits, and increases in Ontario would begin from a reasonably modest level in comparison with the rate imposed in many other places. Another consumption tax that the government in fact found amenable to an increase was that on alcoholic beverages. Although the great majority of Ontario residents are consumers of alcohol, they defend their status very apologetically. It is practically impossible to mount an effective campaign against a further rise in liquor tax, even though by far the major part of the cost to the consumer is accounted for by tax from one source or another. A prudent government will simply make sure that a single rise is not so sharp that it prompts a compensating reduction in the consumption of the product.

As might be expected from earlier observations, the committee felt that a reduction in the property tax was justified even under conditions of financial stringency. The main advantage would be in terms of a gain in equity. It was suggested also that there be no immediate recourse to further succession duties or to the mining profits tax short of far-reaching structural changes. The uncertain incidence and capricious economic effects of the corporation income tax were said to mark it as a decidedly inferior source of additional revenue.[26]

PROVINCIAL TAXATION POLICIES AS OUTLINED IN 1969

The budget for 1969–70 was worked out on the basis of the recommendations of the Ontario Committee on Taxation and of the select committee as evaluated by a task force in the Department of Treasury and Economics in co-operation with the staffs of the Departments of Revenue and Municipal Affairs. A comprehensive plan of policy options was thus provided for the government.[27] In his introductory statement, MacNaughton observed that, up to that time, it had been possible to raise revenues at the provincial level without serious economic and social effects, but that the pressure to provide essential services at the municipal level had led to disturbing increases and distortions in property taxation. A co-ordinated fiscal framework was needed for the future, in the light of the growing demand for revenues, to avoid overloading the tax system and making it economically punitive and socially burdensome. The 1969–70 budget was described as "a two-part plan to lay the foundations for a modernization of the public finance system in Ontario."[28] The first part, dealing with the actual budgetary year, emphasized the continuation of essential public services and municipal aid within the existing framework. The second part included Budget Paper B, a white paper which indicated the government's long-term intentions.

MacNaughton was able to report a more favourable situation for 1968–9 than had been forecast. The performance of the economy had surpassed expectation. On the basis of estimates rather than of complete data for the latter part of the year, it appeared that total net revenues would be somewhat higher than had been anticipated. The budgetary deficit for the year was expected to amount to approximately $267 million. Allowing for a surplus on non-budgetary transactions, the net cash deficit would be about $149 million as compared with the forecast of $252 million.[29]

A policy of rigid financial restraints had made it possible to hold net general expenditure estimates for 1969–70 to $2,996 million. Existing revenue sources were expected to yield $2,817 million, including some delayed payments from the federal government, leaving a budgetary deficit of $179 million. The non-budgetary surplus was estimated at $75 million, while net requirements for debt retirement would be almost $65 million. Thus the over-all cash requirement to be financed would be about $169 million. Obviously the threatened financial nightmare was still at least a year away.

Policy for the year was to aim for a balanced budget or a small surplus to avoid the need for borrowing in the public capital market. Two reasons were given for the selection of this particular option: 1 / the need to avoid inflationary demands on the capital market and 2 / the determination not to resort to borrowing, which would be an ineffective substitute for the steps that had to be taken to strengthen the province's fundamental fiscal position.[30] As a consequence of the decision to try to balance the budget, the government had to impose additional taxes.

The possibility of an immediate increase in the income tax was rejected for two main reasons. The first was that the federal government had already stepped in with its 2 per cent Social Development Tax, which meant that Ontario taxpayers would have to pay an additional $225 million. The federal government had also imposed a temporary surtax of 3 per cent for the 1968 and 1969 tax years. Considerable bitterness was expressed in provincial circles that extra levies had been imposed in such a way that the provinces got no share in them. MacNaughton's second reason for avoiding an immediate increase was that it was better not to make rate changes when significant reforms were in prospect.[31]

For similar reasons, no major changes were made in corporation taxes. A greater contribution from the corporate sector was, however, required by three adjustments. 1 / An acceleration of instalment payments of income tax by corporations was expected to increase revenues by about $42 million. 2 / The rate of capital tax was raised from 0.05 per cent to 0.1 per cent, with a minimum of $50 per year. At the same time, place-of-business taxes were abolished. 3 / Adjustments in the sales tax meant increased payments.

Despite general expectations to the contrary, there was no increase in the general rate of the sales tax. The idea of removing the exemption for food purchases had been considered and rejected. Such a change would have required offsetting credits to remove the regressive features that would otherwise have resulted, and it was thought best not to try to arrange for such credits until a provincial personal income tax system was in operation. Four categories of adjustments were made in sales tax procedures. 1 / Differential rates were extended by incorporating the 10 per cent hospitals tax relating to amusements and entertainment, and by imposing the same rate on liquor sales and on meals costing over $2.50. 2 / The exemption was removed on machinery and equipment used in the production of goods and the provision of taxable services, except for machinery used in farm production. 3 / The 5 per cent tax was imposed on hotel and motel accommodation, but not on other services. 4 / Smaller changes included the levying of the tax on the rental of motion picture films and video tapes.

Among miscellaneous impositions, an increase of 2¢ per package of cigarettes was expected to yield $16.5 million. There was no general change in the gasoline tax, but the exemption allowed for the operation of boats and snowmobiles was removed. The only other area in which changes were made had to do with mining. Processing operations of mines became subject to assessment and property taxation for the benefit of mining municipalities in 1970. Properties used mainly for obtaining minerals from the ground remained exempt. Also, since the government felt that the existing rates of mining tax, varying up to 12 per cent, provided the province with an inadequate return for the consumption of irreplaceable resources, a flat rate of 15 per cent was substituted, with a total exemption if profits were less than $50,000.[32]

Long-term provincial revenue policies

In Budget Paper B, MacNaughton declared that the government intended to establish its own personal income tax system within the next two years. He claimed that the move to an independent tax was necessary to preserve the province's fiscal integrity and to achieve meaningful tax reform in Ontario. The first reason he offered for the proposal to abandon the existing federal-provincial agreement was that the federal government had effectively pre-empted any significantly increased provincial effort by its own heavy use of the field. It is somewhat difficult to see how this fact justifies separate taxation systems, which could hardly impose a lighter over-all burden on the population. MacNaughton's second reason was more convincing. He pointed out that the agreement restricted the provinces to across-the-board rate increases when they wanted to obtain more income tax revenues, since the federal government reserved to itself the right to change the tax base and the progressive rate structure. The Ontario government felt that it must have the opportunity to improve the equity and simplicity of the existing system. The features that the proposed system would have were stated as follows:

- it will aim for greater simplicity and greater progressivity than the present system;
- it will be structured to produce significantly increased revenues and thereby improve the growth potential and the progressivity of Ontario's overall tax mix;
- it will be designed as an integrated personal income tax-tax credit system which coordinates provincial and municipal taxes and allows control over the level and distribution of overall tax burdens;
- it will be both a collection and a payments mechanism, which could eventually be adapted to replace income maintenance programs.[33]

Budget Paper B indicated that the Ontario government intended to tax capital gains when it introduced its provincial income tax. MacNaughton asserted the government view that such a tax must be brought into the system to achieve greater equity between taxpayers with equal incomes and among taxpayers at different income levels. The positive gains would far outweigh any disadvantages in terms of the reduction of private savings and a slowing of economic growth. The government was hopeful that a uniform capital gains tax could be levied all across Canada, and was prepared to co-operate with the federal government to achieve this end. If the latter was not prepared to tax capital gains, either in concert with the provinces or on behalf of the provinces as well as in its own right, Ontario was prepared to go ahead on its own.[34] The federal government, of course, demonstrated its interest in the field within the year.

The paper indicated in 1969 that the Ontario government proposed to accept the urgings of the Carter Commission, the Ontario Committee on Taxation, and the select committee that the administration and collection of the corporation income tax be turned over to the federal government. Before doing so, however, it would have to ensure that the interests of the corporate taxpayers and its own revenues would not suffer.[35]

With respect to the succession duty, the paper expressed the Ontario government's irritation at Ottawa's unilateral action in changing the basis of the duty. It indicated, however, that Ontario would attempt to bring its own practices into harmony with those of the federal government or, as perhaps a more desirable alternative, would relinquish the field in exchange for a federal rebate of 75 per cent of the revenues that would accrue to Ontario from full application of the new federal *Estate Tax Act*.[36] MacNaughton did not assess the prospects of federal agreement to the latter proposal.

Policies indicated in 1970

In certain fundamental respects, MacNaughton's budget address in 1970 had a considerably subdued tone. The Provincial Treasurer stated flatly that the government was not contemplating any major changes in the areas of personal and corporate income tax until federal-provincial tax structure negotiations were concluded. It was prepared to explore fully with the federal government potential ways of achieving Ontario's reform objectives within the framework of the national income tax system.[37] The release of the federal government's White Paper on Taxation, with its proposals for drastic change in the whole structure, was of course sufficient reason for the Ontario government to stop talking about launching its own provincial income tax scheme – at least in the immediate future. So also was the realization that radical changes had a decidedly irritating effect on the voters, as demonstrated by reactions to the establishment of the divisional boards of education.

MacNaughton did not appear to be any better pleased with federal actions and proposals than he had been the year before.

> Notwithstanding the widespread recognition of the totally unsatisfactory distribution of revenue sources, I must report, with regret, that the recent Tax Structure Committee exercise has left us no closer to resolution of the problem of federal-provincial fiscal imbalance ... In my last budget I set out the Government's proposals for achieving comprehensive and co-ordinated tax reform, both in the provincial-municipal sphere and the federal-provincial shared-tax fields ... In recent weeks, we have asserted our fundamental disagreement

with the federal approach to tax reform. We will continue to make proposals for a more acceptable tax system and to suggest means of achieving that goal.[38]

The Ontario government agreed with some of the federal government objectives, such as tax relief for low-income families, fairer treatment of wage and salary earners, child care allowances for working mothers, and a fair and equitable form of taxation of capital gains. It took exception, however, to the federal approach to tax reform on three major grounds: 1 / federal taxes would be increased rather than maintained or reduced; 2 / changes were being made on a piecemeal rather than a comprehensive basis; and 3 / adverse economic effects would be produced.

MacNaughton was able to report a much more favourable financial situation than he had foreseen the year before. In fact, it was so much different from his forecasts that there were grounds for calling his judgment into question or for accusing him of having engaged in scare tactics. Instead of increasing by slightly less than 8 per cent in 1969, the gross provincial product rose by 9.6 per cent. Personal income taxes produced $50 million more than predicted. A series of other revenue sources had proved more lucrative than expected. Net general revenues for 1969–70 would be about $3,292 million, compared with the original forecast of $2,998 million. Thus there would be a small surplus even though net general expenditure would amount to $3,206 million. Despite this situation, MacNaughton insisted that the longer-term trend was still unfavourable because of the unsatisfactory balance between federal and provincial revenue sources.

In addition to changes in the succession duty mentioned earlier, there were some adjustments in the sales tax for 1970. The 5 per cent levy was removed from a number of production tools that were subject to extraordinarily rapid replacement from wear and tear, or had a very short economic life. A similar provision applied to certain materials used directly in the manufacturing process.

A third area in which changes were made had to do with pollution control equipment. The government extended to the end of 1973 the accelerated capital cost write-off provisions for such equipment used for the control of water pollution under the provincial corporation income tax system. The joint effect of federal and provincial measures would allow firms to depreciate the cost of water and air pollution control equipment in two years.

Effect of provincial financial prospects on education

The overwhelming commitment to education of the Ontario government, which has done so much to increase recent financial problems, involves both quantitative and qualitative expansion. The most expensive of the programs may be summarized as follows: 1 / a general upgrading of the publicly supported school system, particularly with respect to improved facilities and high levels of teachers' salaries; 2 / the geographical extension of high quality facilities beyond the minority of privileged areas to which they have heretofore been confined; 3 / the provision of services to those with special handicaps and needs beyond the privileged minority to which they have heretofore been confined; 4 / a revolutionary expansion of university education with the objective of providing the traditional quality of instruction for all who desire it and can meet reasonable standards for admission; 5 / the creation of almost a whole new system of tertiary education for those not bound for university. The creation of county boards of education is not mentioned here because it is to be regarded as an intermediate device for the achievement of some of the other objectives. No mention is made, furthermore, of any major program in the adult education area, where the most conspicuous advance is attributable to the federal government, although the success of its initiatives in the manpower area owes much to provincial assistance and co-operation.

A major source of security for these programs is the powerful conviction Ontario's citizens have developed that in education lies their salvation and that of their children. They are frequently vague about the process by which educational values are realized; they are not at all confident that they can identify the desired outcomes; they are often unprepared to defend a specific practice or policy. But there seems no doubt that they have supported the high priority assigned to educational development in the 1960s. This is not to say that they will not favour a shift in emphasis to another area, such as health services, in the 1970s. But their willingness to see such a priority shift is based on the feeling that the educational system has attained a high level of development, and that it will continue to be maintained at this level.

General support for education has not, of course, precluded some severe criticisms in general or in detail about educational spending. For an example of one extreme, we may go to an editorial printed in the *Free Press* of Acton, Ontario, on February 26, 1969.

Like a voice in the wilderness, we mention frequently in our editorials about government spending, deficit budgeting and the seeming inability of our senior governments to use even the simplest rules of business in conducting our public affairs.

Last week Premier Robarts sounded off in a speech that Ontario must be given a larger share of tax money collected by Ottawa, or he will be forced to levy more taxes himself ...

Wouldn't it be better for Mr. Robarts to take a look at what some of his ambitious young cabinet ministers are doing with our tax-money – education minister Bill Davis, for one, who must take the blame for today's astronomical education costs.

While Mr. Robarts expresses concern about deficits out of one corner of his mouth, out of the other he talks about bilingual schools – He sets up pay scales for elected officials of municipalities and school boards which are completely absurd.

Isn't it time our provincial government took a long, hard look back to the days before we had a 5 per cent sales tax on top of an 11 per cent sales tax. It might be refreshing, for a change, to be able to announce a tax reduction.

An editorial in the Hamilton *Spectator* on March 30, 1968, began with the same concern with costs, but suggested somewhat more constructive remedies:

Queen's Park has increased Hamilton's 1968 school grant by $707,600, relieving local taxpayers of just over one mill in education expenses; they still face a school tax rise of seven mills – $35 on a $5,000 property assessment.

The small measure of relief patches only one hole in Ontario's education tax sieve. Even with the province's weird assortment of grants, local taxes for education have grown dangerously high. The latest grant adjustment is, at most, a temporary stopgap ... Drastic changes in school financing ... must be implemented quickly or education costs will tax people right out of their homes.

More important, the costs themselves will have to be held within the province's ability to pay. A top-to-bottom examination of education administration and practices is as urgent as tax reforms.

Several possibilities should be explored. A provincial teacher-hiring system, with Ontario-wide pay scales based on qualifications and regional cost-of-living differentials, would eliminate the inflationary competitions among school boards which try to outbid each other for teachers.

Greater use of teachers' aids and closed-circuit television could reduce the need for highly-paid teachers and the pyramids of non-teaching supervisors built on large teaching staffs.

Innovations in building design might produce better, more economical use of school space; current school designs are expensive but not necessarily the best taxpayers could get for their money.

Shift systems for high school classes should not be rejected automatically; most Ontario schoolrooms stand empty most of the time.

New concepts in school financing and in education itself are the only alternative to intolerable taxation or a decline in Ontario educational standards.

A second important reason why, despite the expression of sentiments of this kind, education's high priority is not likely to be seriously impaired is that an extremely large and growing percentage of the population have some direct involvement in education, whether as learners, parents of learners, teachers, officials, or administrators. These groups constitute a powerful interest block. While certain elements among them may disapprove of what they regard as extravagance or the pursuit of useless goals at some level or in some area other than the one in which they are involved, it is unlikely that firm support for a drastic reduction of any educational program can be won from any part of the educational establishment. There would be too much fear of unfavourable precedents.

The Provincial Treasury is requiring increasingly convincing evidence of the worth of educational programs before they receive government authorization. Long-term cost forecasts and the definition and valuation of educational outputs are being demanded. The latter concept is causing considerable concern among educators, fearful of the fate of some of the intangibles that cannot be assessed in terms of dollars and cents. It is, however, a highly salutory experience for many of them to contemplate the cost of these intangibles. Nor does it seem unreasonable that educational objectives, no matter how elusive, should be defensible to reasonable men endowed with the responsibility of making them financially feasible. The mystique that has traditionally surrounded education is not an adequate defence when the latter has become the largest of social enterprises.

In dealing with its financial problems in future years, there is little chance of a "merciless slashing of present provincial programs including such sacred cows as education" indicated as one possibility in the *Toronto Star* article. Some measures of austerity there certainly can and will be. That financial stringency has been felt is shown by the fact that institutions at the tertiary level have had to accept drastic revisions in their plans for new and adequate buildings, facilities, and equipment to accommodate existing student loads. Operating expenses have been reduced to the point where it is questionable whether all qualified applicants can gain admission to a program in any part of the province that is even minimally acceptable in terms of their desires and needs. As with all austerity programs, it is unrealistic to think that the present one can be managed in such a way that only the least deserving claims will be denied. But there is no evidence of any basic damage done to any of the major new programs.

At a conference of school board chairmen and directors of education called New Patterns for a New Decade, held in September 1969, Robarts, Davis, and MacNaughton combined forces to indicate how important it would be to curb expenditures during the next few years. MacNaughton declared that the provincial government's forecasts showed an increase from the $1.5 billion school bill for the current year to $3.4 billion by 1973–4. This increase constituted the total amount of the anticipated increase in provincial revenue during the four-year period. Obviously an increase of these dimensions could not be allowed to occur.

LOCAL REVENUES

Establishment of modern pattern of revenue collection

Passing reference has already been made to the transition in the mid-1800s from financing schools by voluntary contributions to compulsory taxation of the local community. Before 1841 the rate-bill was the chief source of revenue. In that year, the newly established municipal councils of the provincial districts were required to raise by means of a general tax on property an amount equal to the provincial school grant allotted to the district. Two years later, the councils of incorporated cities and police towns were permitted to raise the full amount of the municipality's share of the cost of common schools by a general property tax. The rural areas of the province were given the same right in 1847. There the district council made the decision to abolish rate-bills, either for the whole district, or for one or more townships only, or for one or more school sections only. In 1850 the annual school section meeting in the rural areas and the school boards in urban areas were given the responsibility for choosing the means of raising local school revenue. Within twenty years, most of the common schools were, by option of their boards, supported by compulsory local taxation. The Act of 1871 made this system of support mandatory.[39]

The counties had a relatively small part to play in the financing of common schools. They did, however, continue to contribute to the cost of local public elementary education until 1945. Their role has been more important in the area of secondary education. From 1865 on, they acted as intermediate financial units for schools at this level. Until 1947–51, when most of the large high school districts were formed, they had the responsibility of meeting the local share of the cost of educating "county" pupils, that is, those not residing in a high school district.[40]

As indicated earlier, the School Act of 1847 established all cities and towns as common school districts and provided for the election of boards of trustees by the municipal councils. Whether the boards had a right to requisition funds from the councils, or could merely throw themselves on the generosity of the latter, was not at once evident. After the Toronto city council refused to raise the funds in 1848, and consequently left the schools closed for an entire year, arrangements were again made for the election of the trustees, and there was provision for the raising of revenue through rate-bills. After 1850 those rural school sections that chose to raise their current revenues by a local levy could ask that the tax be levied and collected by the township council. If the latter declined the honour, apparently a very common event, the board could perform the task for itself. In 1853 the boards were given complete authority to levy their own taxes. Since this procedure struck many as an unnecessary and wasteful duplication of effort, common school boards were authorized in 1869 to requisition their operating funds from the municipalities. In 1885 they lost their own largely unused tax-levying rights, except in municipally unorganized townships, where such rights were obviously needed.

In this way an enduring pattern for the raising of current revenues was established. It was not a popular measure with municipal councils. The years since the arrangement was solidified have been marked by innumerable disagreeable sessions in which council members have asserted that they are not errand boys with voter opprobrium their only reward, and that they surely have some right to curb the wanton extravagance of the school board. Members of the board have replied by standing on their legal rights and proclaiming their own direct responsibility to the electors. From time to time, councils have resorted to litigation to make their point, but without success. There has been little appeal in Ontario for resolving the problem by resorting to the Alberta solution of scrapping the school boards and putting educational affairs in the hands of a committee of the municipal council. The Royal Commission on Education in Ontario supported the fiscal independence of local boards as far as current expenditures were concerned. This position was strengthened by the recommendation that all local education authorities be elected.[41]

The financing of capital expenditures was not a serious problem before the middle of the nineteenth century. The costs of school buildings were met in the same way as were operating expenses, supplemented by general subscriptions. A more formal arrangement began to develop with the District Municipal Act of 1841, which required the district councils to levy a tax of up to £50 in every school district not having a school. The Common School Act of 1850 allowed both urban and rural school boards to request the municipal council to levy taxes to meet capital as well as current requirements. Provision was also made for the borrowing of funds by the council, or by the school board on the council's approval, to meet capital requirements. Only the council could, however, impose taxes to pay the debt. From 1879 on, all public school boards were required to borrow only through municipal councils. In urban centres, if the council refused the request, the issue could be arbitrated by a vote of those ratepayers entitled to vote on a money question.

The final stage in the establishment of the modern pattern occurred in 1932, with the creation of the Ontario Municipal Board. This agency must approve all municipal borrowing. It bases its decisions on an appraisal, made by formula, of the municipality's ability to support the proposed debt level. Its activities have fairly effectively superseded the appeal to the ratepayers as a means of breaking a deadlock between the school board and the council.

The taxes to which the municipalities and school boards had access around the middle of the nineteenth century were ill-defined property taxes. Assessment was extremely inexact and erratic. Both the definition and valuation of property were aspects of the legislative process. Arbitrary values were placed on various items of real and personal property without regard to variations in size, quality, and sale value. In 1850 a drastic revision of the system identified taxable items and gave local assessors the responsibility of valuing each item. The base of the tax was extended in 1853 to include all goods, chattels, shares in incorporated companies, money, notes, accounts, and debts at their full value.[42] The tax, had it been effectively administered, would have constituted a comprehensive levy on income and wealth. But many rural and small urban areas disregarded their obligation to assess the income of their residents.

> Many people with large incomes were quick to avail themselves of these lax conditions once they became known, with the result that many colonies of the relatively rich sprang up in these tax-haven jurisdictions. In many municipalities where income tax assessment was practised, it virtually became a tax on wage and salary earners, most recipients of investment income or professional fees being almost entirely exempt or grossly under-assessed. Frequently, misdirected economy prevented efficient tax administration and collection, while in many smaller municipalities local politics were responsible for the poor results.[43]

In 1890 the municipalities were given the option of substituting a special business tax for taxation of the personal property of businesses. The tax was to be applied to the so-called annual value of the business premises, a term defined as 7 per cent of the capital value of the premises. The maximum tax rate was fixed at 7.5 per cent of the annual value. Since the option did not attract anyone, the tax was made compulsory in 1904.[44] The Assessment Act of that year eliminated the personal property tax and required the levying of a municipal personal income tax on all residents. The act provided a definition of income for the first time. As the Ontario Committee on Taxation comments, it followed the United Kingdom pattern by taxing annual accretions but leaving personal capital intact.[45] It exempted income from farming and real estate, except interest on mortgages and dividends from taxable corporations, including dividends from shares in toll-road companies. Personal exemptions, applicable to employment income only, gave the greatest deduction to a householder living in a city or town, and diminishing graduated deductions to householders living in other municipalities, non-householders living in cities or towns, and non-householders living in other municipalities. Municipal income taxes continued to be levied until 1936 but, because the base was narrow and local administration ineffective, they produced comparatively little revenue.

The compulsory business tax of 1904 was somewhat different from its earlier counterpart. The base was a flat percentage of the real property assessment, this percentage varying with the nature of the business. Cameron calls it a rather crude substitute for the taxation of personal property,[46] and reiterates the regrets expressed by the Ontario Committee on Taxation that the municipalities lost "a key source of potential revenue capable of yielding large amounts of money, broadening greatly the base for local taxation and materially improving its over-all equity."[47] It may have been a matter of regret that such lucrative sources of revenue were lost, but it is hardly realistic to suppose that municipalities were the appropriate political agencies to collect personal property taxes. At any rate, by the beginning of the Second World War, the local authorities, including school boards, had no means of raising their own revenue except by taxing real property and business assessment.

The situation with respect to local revenue during the period after the Second World War has been summarized effectively by Cameron.

> The tax base has developed through an evolutionary historical process from a comprehensive measure of income and wealth (and consumption if the purchase of shelter is considered as such) to a limited measure of the ownership and use of real property, supplemented by an arbitrary measure of the value of business conducted in or on real property. This tax base is distributed very unevenly throughout the province, resulting in an inequitable tax-rate structure. Furthermore, the taxation of property has been called upon to provide an amount of revenue which is increasing considerably more rapidly than the tax base. Taxation for educational purposes has increased more rapidly than taxation for other local functions. The result has been both a persistent and general increase in the rates of taxation and an increase in reliance on borrowing. All of this has led to increased provincial involvement in the financing of education and to a growing conviction that even this involvement has been insufficient.[48]

Particularly because of the influence of the Ontario Municipal Board, borrowing has been confined largely to funds for capital purposes, although separate school boards have been free to make their own decisions in this respect.

Appraisal of the property tax

The Ontario Committee on Taxation defined seven attributes of an ideal tax source for local governments.

(1) It must be possible for local authorities to impose rates of tax that differ significantly from area to area without engendering widespread evasion or massive shifts of resources from high to low tax rate areas.
(2) Changes in local tax rates from year to year by small amounts must not result in great delays or confusion or impose heavy administrative costs.
(3) In all but the poorest areas, local governments should be able to finance the provision of public goods and services that would satisfy the residents' most exacting demands if they are willing to pay high local tax rates.
(4) The tax should not provide a means whereby the residents of one area can tax the residents of another in order to finance more collective goods for themselves.
(5) Administration and compliance costs must be moderate.
(6) Local residents and their representatives must be able to determine the

cost, in terms of higher tax rates, of a proposed increase in local government expenditures.

(7) Most of the constituents of most local governments must accept the tax as a generally fair method of allocating the costs of local government.[49]

The property tax is considered a particularly suitable and convenient one for municipal authorities to levy. Noting in 1968 that 50 per cent of the expenditure for elementary and secondary education in Canada was raised from this source, Rideout proceeded to indicate some of the reasons for the heavy reliance placed on it.[50] An important consideration was that the tax was convenient to administer. It was difficult for a local resident to avoid paying and "alone of major taxes, a change in its rate places no major compliance burdens on local businesses." Its chief justification was, however, the stability and thus the predictability of its yield. The Ontario Committee on Taxation recognized these virtues, and referred to others.

First, there is no question but that the high visibility of this tax enhances that essential component of effective local autonomy, public accountability, even though on occasion this may lead to false economies. And second, the property tax, although imperfectly reflecting benefits received, can be a useful if rough index for gauging the propriety of existing provincial-municipal divisions of spending responsibilities. It can translate the often vague idea of a service that is "primarily local" into the somewhat more concrete notion of a service that is of benefit to persons as owners or occupants of real property and hence one that should be provided locally.[51]

With reference to the first of these two points, it is interesting to speculate on the general effect of complaints about rising levels of property tax on the actual performance of school trustees. Recent Ontario history fails to offer examples of concerted and effective campaigns on the part of ratepayers to force their elected representatives to hold tax rates at existing levels. There is a pervasive acceptance of the idea that annual increases are to be expected. In larger urban districts, the position of particular trustees tends to be reinforced as their names become more and more familiar to the public. If they wish to continue to be re-elected for one term after another, the main thing they must avoid is becoming identified with some illogical extravagance such as going to too many conferences that can be justified only on the most tenuous grounds. They can help to create the impression that they are on the side of the voters by complaining at the appropriate times about the pressures that tend to force them to support increased expenditure against their better judgment, such as the department's inducements for the extension of certain services or the insatiable demands of the teachers' federations for higher salaries. There are, perhaps, broad limits beyond which they could not go without so arousing the ire of the voters that something more than the usual insignificant proportion would turn out to elect a whole new slate of trustees pledged to effect a real cut-back in expenditure. But traditional practice makes this kind of action unlikely.

As far as the committee's second point is concerned, it is easier to see its application to some other municipal services than to education. The benefits rendered to property by education are, as has been noted, particularly difficult to define. The committee offered the view, however, that there was strong justification for applying the property tax to services that were indirectly related to property, since the distinction between direct and indirect benefits was highly tenuous, and since a theory of direct benefits, even if workable, would be unduly confining, and thus injurious to the principle of local autonomy.

The property tax is, of course, a regressive one. That is, its burden does not fall on people in direct relation to their ability to pay. For those at the lower income levels, residential units tend to reach a minimum of assessed value that demands a rather high proportion of personal income to maintain. At the upper income levels, ostentatious accommodation is relatively uncommon. The spread in average assessed value per residential unit is much less than that of income. As a means of reducing the regressivity of the tax, the Ontario Committee on Taxation proposed a flat exemption that would reduce the taxable assessment of every self-contained dwelling unit, whether a detached, single-family dwelling or a unit within an apartment house or other multiple-family structure.[52]

The committee commented in some detail on the disadvantages of the property tax as a means of raising revenue.[53] Rather than being accepted enthusiastically, it had to be tolerated in spite of its shortcomings. Its most serious weakness was considered to be that few if any residents believed that it provided a fair method of allocating the costs of local government. Two conflicting points of view might be identified. Some felt that it was not closely enough related to the ability to pay. They believed that those at the upper end of the income scale should bear a greater proportion of the burden, and that those at the lower end should receive more benefits. Others, on the contrary, felt that the property tax did not achieve a close enough relationship between contributions and benefits. If those who received the benefits had to make a greater contribution toward them, they would reduce their demands for more public expenditure.

The second disadvantage identified by the committee was that there was too much temptation to tax non-residents through the real property tax. The committee asserted that local governments must not be allowed to tax natural resource properties or they might well capture all of the profit in excess of that necessary to keep the properties active. The solution recommended was that they be forced to adopt a fixed relation between the tax rates on residential and on business properties. A further illustration of the practice of taxing non-residents involves the rapidly growing numbers of summer cottagers with property in certain areas of the province. These people often have legitimate complaints about the lack of normal municipal services, such as roads, water, and garbage collection, in relation to their taxes. But education offers the most contentious issue. Genuine summer cottagers have no direct use for these services, and normally pay their share of property taxes in the area where they regularly reside. The only real argument in favour of their contributing on behalf of their cottage property is that the ownership of such real estate presumably indicates a high level of income and thus a greater than average ability to pay.

The committee's third point had to do with certain constraints on local governments forced to rely almost exclusively on real property taxes to finance their discretionary expenditures. They must take account of the danger that large increases in the tax rate on residential property will seriously reduce new construction in the short run and raise rents in the long run. Also, if local rates on business properties differ too much from those in other areas, some businesses will die or stagnate and others will leave. This particular weakness, the committee suggested, could be countered by enlarging local government areas to encompass whole regions.

The committee's recommendation, as noted elsewhere, was that provincial grants should rise to the point where they contribute 60 per cent of the cost of public education. It has been observed that this recommendation was incorporated in government policy, to be fully implemented in the early 1970s. The committee had three reasons for not urging a higher percentage of provincial grant. 1 / Public education is particularly well suited to local government, whether the criterion is a reasonably open market for teachers' services, diversity and experimentation in education, or the need for programs accommodated to regional peculiarities. "If it is to be more than an illusion, such local authority must be marked by a genuine degree of autonomy. And to be genuine, governmental autonomy must have a basis in the revenue system."[54] 2 / On the question of cost control, responsibility in government spending must be assumed by one agency or another. At the stage when taxes are imposed, this control is exerted by the taxpayer himself. When revenues are derived from a higher level of government, it is exerted by that level. To reduce reliance on either one merely shifts the task to that extent to the other. The committee referred to what it considered a fallacious argument: that since the province financed over 90 per cent of the expenditure of certain needy boards without exercising almost complete control over them, it could assume the same level of spending for all boards without reducing their autonomy. The point was that the boards that paid a large proportion of their own expenses provided efficiency yardsticks under existing conditions that enabled the province to countenance comparable autonomy for the boards it had to finance more heavily. 3 / The balance among different taxes should be a contribution to equity. The committee warned, in this connection, that equity required much more than the improvement of one particular tax, but could be achieved only in the context of the over-all manner in which the total fiscal system distributed burdens and benefits.

The committee had a good deal to say on how the property tax should be distributed. It looked with no favour on the tax differential between residential and farm property on the one hand and industrial and commercial property on the other, as instituted with the Residential and Farm School Tax Assistance Grant in 1961 and continued under the Ontario Foundation Tax Plan. The committee regarded split mill rates as an inefficient and inequitable means of distributing a tax burden. The case made for this proposition has appeared to a number of observers as rather weak. It has been said by certain critics of a different political orientation to reflect an undue concern for the interests of private capital. The committee did, however, assert its desire to ensure that the abolition of the offending provision was accomplished without hardship for residential and farm school taxpayers.[55]

The property tax base

The major reliance placed by school boards, as well as other municipal authorities, on the property tax emphasizes the importance of its being levied efficiently and equitably. The general impression, mentioned earlier, that it is not imposed fairly ought to be a matter of serious concern. The Ontario Committee on Taxation devoted a great deal of attention to this question. The subsequent material is largely a review of its observations and recommendations.[56]

Assessment

Before 1940 there was a great deal of inter-municipality variation in assessment. In that year, legislation permitted the appointment of county assessors to supervise and assist local officials and to produce a greater degree of uniformity. Additional responsibility was given to county assessors in 1944 to work toward county equalization. In 1961 county assessment departments were authorized under the direction of a county commissioner. These could be established only with the unanimous consent of the local municipalities but, once they were set up, the independent assessment operations of all the constituent municipalities were eliminated. Further legislation in subsequent years removed some of the remaining barriers to the formation of larger assessment units.

An important step was taken in 1947 to improve the provincial assessment machinery with the establishment of an Assessment Branch in the Department of Municipal Affairs. By 1950 this branch had produced a *Manual of Assessment* as a guide to municipal assessors. When the province began to make payments in lieu of municipal taxes on Crown properties in 1952, the Assessment Branch became directly involved in the work in the field. Eight regional offices were established in 1957 as base points from which the assessment of Crown properties and the equalization of assessment for school grant purposes were undertaken.[57]

The analysis of the Ontario Committee on Taxation, which of course occurred before a number of recent developments to correct the situation, indicated that extreme inequalities in property assessment had been concealed by the prevalence of gross under-assessment. These had inevitably resulted in serious inequities in taxation. Despite the statutory requirement that a fresh assessment be carried out annually, and that assessed value be calculated at full actual value, most assessments in Ontario represented less than half current market value. The 1966 assessment equalization factors issued by the Assessment Branch of the Department of Municipal Affairs had placed assessment levels in 921 of 935 municipalities at less than 50 per cent of market value. A number of other statistics told a similar story.

The procedure for the equalization of local assessments introduced in 1958 failed to correct the defects in certain assessment practices. Nothing was done to ensure comparable treatment of all properties within municipalities. There were some serious departures from standard practice that required correction. For example, two out of five municipalities were either greatly under-assessing or greatly over-assessing their local industries by comparison with all or most properties of other types. It was also common to assess apartments at a considerably higher level than other residential properties in the same municipality, according to the Ontario Committee on Taxation. "From the evidence of our own survey, reinforced by the Department's equalization data, it is hard to avoid the conclusion that certain places have been deliberately discriminating against industrial and commercial properties and apartment buildings in favour of the remaining residential properties. Metropolitan Toronto and the city of Hamilton are among such municipalities."[58] With respect to variations in assessment, Bascom St John commented: "The tricks that an imaginative official working under the Ontario Assessment Act may play on the tax-paying victim are astonishing, and few can resist the temptation."[59] The effects of past variations could have been remedied only by complete re-assessment.

A second weakness in the equalized assessment procedure was that the factor produced for each municipality was a composite of four factors, based on the ratio of assessed value to equalized value of four categories of property: residential, farm, commercial, and industrial. Cameron points out that the use of a single aggregate factor produced an inequity when applied to the assessments of public and separate school boards having jurisdiction in the same municipality, since the proportion of each type of property supporting each board might be quite different. He suggests that this weakness could have been corrected by the use of distinct factors either for each type of property or for each type of school board.[60]

The committee's recommendation was that all real property, whether taxable or not, be assessed each year at 100 per cent of actual current value. As indicated earlier, the provincial government undertook in 1967 to achieve this objective, with some initial difficulties, and with certain awkward consequences for the Department of Education. The eventual provincial decision was to take over the assessment function completely. This decision appears to remove nothing of any particular value from the area of local responsibility, and to promise substantial increases in efficiency in raising revenue.

Weight of taxation on different types of property

Both the Ontario Committee on Taxation and the select committee of the Legislature felt that mill rates for commercial and industrial taxpayers should be uniform with those for residential and farm taxpayers. That is, they disapproved of the split mill rate, in part because of its instability. The alternative offered was to tax different classes of property on the basis of different percentages of their actual assessed value.

In this connection, the Ontario Committee on Taxation made the following specific proposals:

(b) Residential properties, recreational properties and wasteland be subject to property tax on a taxable assessment of 70 per cent of assessed value;

(c) Business properties other than transportation and communications properties, but including working farms and taxable mining properties, be subject to property tax on a taxable assessment of 50 per cent of the assessed value;

(d) Occupants of business properties other than working farms and transportation and communications properties, but including taxable mining properties, be subject to business occupancy tax on a taxable assessment of 50 per cent of the assessed value of the occupied property at the same mill rate as the property tax; and

(e) Roadways and rights-of-way over land used by transportation and communications businesses be exempt from property and business occupancy taxes, and other properties of such businesses be subject to property tax and the occupants thereof be subject to business occupancy tax on a basis to be determined when the assessment of the properties has been completed.[61]

In accepting the same general approach, the select committee included the following in a somewhat more lengthy set of principles. 1 / The percentage factor applied to the actual value of residential properties to determine taxable assessment should be less than the factors applied to commercial and industrial properties. 2 / The percentage factor applied to working farm properties should be still lower. 3 / The variety of percentages currently used to determine business assessment by type of enterprise should be eliminated. The select committee thus disagreed with the Ontario Committee on Taxation on the relative weight of taxation to be borne by different classifications of property. It objected to the proposed

70 per cent factor for residential property on the grounds that it would produce a shift of the municipal tax burden from commercial and industrial to residential taxpayers. The proposed 50 per cent factor for working farm properties also seemed to threaten to place an increased burden on the farm community. Measures were also thought necessary to ensure that the rate of business taxes to be paid by small businesses did not result in a shift of the tax burden to this section of the business community.[62]

The scheme suggested by the select committee as an alternative to that of the Ontario Committee on Taxation involved the application of a 60 per cent factor to actual assessed value to determine the basis of taxation for both residential and business property, and also for recreational properties, wasteland, non-working farms, and taxable mining properties. The corresponding factor for working farms would be 40 per cent. A graduated business tax increment would be applied, ranging from 10 to 40 per cent of the assessed value of the real property. In order to introduce progressivity to business taxes by relation to the value of the real property assessment, a business tax would be levied on 10 per cent of the first $10,000 of assessment, 20 per cent of the second $10,000, 30 per cent of the third $10,000, and 40 per cent of any amount in excess of $30,000.[63] Two members of the select committee expressed doubt that this approach would avoid shifting some of the tax burden to residential property owners, and suggested that studies of its effects be made before implementation.[64]

Special provisions for farms

The select committee disagreed with a recommendation by the Ontario Committee on Taxation for the repeal of the provision of *The Assessment Act* requiring that the actual value of farm lands and buildings be determined on a special basis, and of the provisions of *The Assessment Act* and *The Police Act* providing for exemption of farm lands from taxation for certain expenditures. The implementation of the first of these recommendations seemed likely to drive a significant number of farmers from the land. The select committee thought that farm land should be assessed at its actual value in agricultural use. Also, there seemed no justification for requiring a farmer to pay for services not available to him. The two committees agreed that the farm dwelling and other parts of the farm holding not qualifying as working farm be classified as residential property. The select committee dissented, however, from the proposal that only those parts of a farm in full utilization be classified as working farm.[65] In order to retain land in proximity to urban centres for land use, the two committees agreed that an appropriate land-use policy would be needed in addition to favourable taxation arrangements.

It was difficult to find an arrangement that satisfied the farming community. Referring to an Ontario Farmers' Union Brief presented on February 12, 1968, the Minister of Education noted the recommendation "that the provincial government enact legislation providing that farm land only be taxed for services to property." In response, he wrote:

If this is a suggestion that farm land be exempted from education taxes, it has been raised many times in the past and the answer is well known.

Services to "property" and services to "people" cannot be separated. Services such as roads, fire protection and education are all services to people and at the same time enhance the value of property.[66]

Special provisions for residential property

As a means of making taxation on residential property more progressive, the Ontario Committee on Taxation recommended a basic shelter exemption for each self-contained dwelling unit. This exemption would be based on either 1 / $2,000 of taxable assessment multiplied by the provincial equalization factor for the municipality or 2 / 50 per cent of the residential taxable assessment applicable to the unit, whichever was less. The provincial government implemented the first part of this recommendation in 1968, but not the second part. The majority of the select committee indicated approval of the legislation, but suggested means of achieving in another way what the rejected 50 per cent limitation had been intended to do – prevent owners of second residences of low value from benefiting unduly. The proposal was that the basic shelter exemption be an additional credit recoverable by means of a decrease in personal income tax, whether it was a positive or a negative amount.[67]

Two dissenting members of the committee contended that the basic shelter credit for municipal taxes did not offer a real solution to the problem of unequal municipal tax burdens. They also questioned the logic of repaying the taxpayers' money to them instead of restructuring the tax system to collect the needed amounts on the basis of the ability to pay. They regarded the exemption as a political expedient to hand out favours to the electorate. As an alternative, they recommended the establishment of a municipal foundation program which would put a ceiling on the regressive property tax and provide local governments with needed funds for a basic standard of services without having to resort to an above-average level of taxation.[68] MacNaughton seemed to agree with this view in Budget Paper B in 1969 when he said that this measure did not constitute adequate long-term support.[69] He declared that the exemption payments would be replaced by some form of tax credits and refunds under the provincial personal income tax.

Realty-based business tax

The schemes put forward by both committees, upon which comments have already been made, had an important place for a realty-based business tax. In expressing cautious approval of such a tax, the Ontario Committee on

Taxation observed that it was much simpler and much to be preferred to business taxes in most other places, which required the calculation of a separate tax base. The committee warned that the tax must not be pushed so high that business would cease to be competitive with that in other provinces. As imposed at the time, its cardinal weakness was the indefensible structure of its rates of assessment.

The Ontario Committee on Taxation made several further suggestions, of which limitations of space do not make possible more than passing mention. 1 / The idea of a home-improvement exemption was rejected on the grounds that it merely increased the burden on all other local taxpayers. 2 / It was considered unwise to think of assessing and taxing sites only, as an alternative to the existing practice. Reasons for this conclusion were that, by narrowing the tax base, such an approach would depart from the existing and accepted relationship of taxation to the value of the accommodation provided. It would increase the weight of taxes on farming operations, and compress urban construction on to more crowded sites, but would not eliminate the land speculator. Whatever the validity of this recommendation, there are certainly many people who feel that there should be some feasible taxation policy that would help to counter the social ills arising from inordinate increases in land values in urban and suburban areas. If a site value tax is not the answer, and it may not be, it seems not unreasonable to demand an alternative solution from the government. 3 / It was recommended that fixed assessments and fixed taxation agreements not be made in the future, and that steps be taken to solve the problems created by those already in force.

The exemption of mining properties from normal assessment and taxation in Ontario has long been a matter of controversy. The Ontario Committee on Taxation declared that it had considered sympathetically the possibility of treating them in the same manner as other properties, but had concluded that this approach was not immediately practicable. Thus no change should be made in the principle of exempting mine structures and plant and the mineral content of mining lands and making provincial payments in lieu of local taxes. Certain procedural improvements were suggested, however. As already noted, the provincial budget for 1969 did actually make more substantial changes than the committee recommended.

Tax exemptions on real estate

There have been several major categories of property that have been exempted from ordinary procedures of assessment and taxation, in addition to mining properties, which have constituted a particular type of business operation. The former have included 1 / property owned by the federal government and by Crown corporations and agencies, 2 / comparable property owned by the provincial government, 3 / most property owned by local municipal authorities, including school boards, 4 / private schools and universities, 5 / charitable institutions, and 6 / religious institutions. The federal and provincial governments have made payments to municipal councils in lieu of the taxes that they would have paid if they had been assessed in the usual way. Agencies and institutions in the last three of the above categories have paid nothing at all.

The Ontario Committee on Taxation reviewed the situation in order to determine the implications of these exemptions. In summary, it reported, "We regard it as a safe presumption that under-assessment of exempt properties remains common and that the total of tax-exempt assessment understates the loss of potential tax revenues."[70] Not only was a substantial proportion of potentially taxable property out of reach of the tax collector, but the distribution of such property among municipalities was also very uneven. The city of Kingston was in a particularly difficult position in this regard, with its unusual concentration of public institutions and its paucity of industry.

On February 9, 1969, Syl Apps, member of the Legislature for Kingston and the Islands, described Kingston's plight with a quotation from a brief presented to the select committee by the city of Kingston as follows:

> The Kingston tax base has been struck a nearly mortal blow by the staggering amount of tax-exempted property. For the year 1967, $46,100,000 assessment was tax exempt out of a total assessment of $132,800,000 – in other words, 34 per cent.
>
> Included in this tax exempt figure are land and buildings owned by the city of Kingston, the board of education, federal government property, in which grants in lieu of taxes are paid, and some provincial property on which the non-educational portion of taxes are paid, but there still remains $30,500,000 of tax-exempt property to which no taxes are paid, except garbage taxes.[71]

The committee considered certain arguments in favour of tax exemptions. They placed the beneficiaries in a position where they did not have to appeal continually for public support, and could avoid the controversy that might be occasioned by an annual appeal for a grant. They produced "a stabilized allocation of community benefits to good causes." But the committee found the contrary arguments more compelling.

(1) Exemptions narrow the tax base, thereby increasing the tax load on owners of taxable property.
(2) A tax exemption is an indirect subsidy, the cost of which is not generally apparent, and is subject to less control than a grant, which ordinarily is renewable annually.
(3) Tax exemption may not distribute a government subsidy in the most equitable or desirable manner.

(4) The proportion of all properties in the community that are exempt varies from one municipality to another, thereby creating disproportionate burdens among local communities.
(5) Exemptions are for the most part legislated by the province but their burden falls on municipalities and local school boards.
(6) Exemptions, once established, are not readily terminated. Thus they tend to perpetuate community wishes of an earlier day. In addition, the range and extent of exemptions can grow well beyond justifiable limits.[72]

The federal government was commended for the adequacy of its payments in lieu of taxes in comparison with those made by Ontario or any other province. In 1968 these were an estimated 75 per cent of the full payment had the properties been subject to municipal taxation. The validity of such a comparison must, however, be appraised in the light of the fact that the provincial governments have a more direct responsibility for making up any deficit caused by one particular aspect of their policy. For example, if they starve school boards by depriving them of certain sources of funds, they have the opportunity of paying compensating grants. As far as the federal government was concerned, the committee found a serious shortcoming in that federal Crown agencies did not necessarily match the standard set by the government on its own properties. The committee recommended that grants by the provincial government first be put on a sound basis, and that the province then petition the federal government to make parallel arrangements. The exemptions of Indian reserves would, however, be continued. Also, the federal government would retain the right to determine the basis of grants for school purposes, the existing method of assessing federal properties for grants in lieu of taxes would be continued, and all matters relating to federal grants in lieu of taxes would continue to be referred to the Minister of Finance for a final decision.

Provincial government payments authorized by *The Municipal Tax Assistance Act* were regarded as a genuine advance. But the committee found a number of unsatisfactory aspects to the existing situation. Objection was taken to the exclusion of major forms of provincial property such as provincial hospitals, educational institutions, penal reform institutions, experimental farms, and fish hatcheries. It was also pointed out that provincial payments in lieu of taxes, except those on behalf of the Hydro-Electric Power Commission, were made only to municipal councils, and that nothing was provided for school boards. Furthermore, provincial operations that were akin to businesses were not subject to full payments in lieu of business tax. The relevant recommendation was as follows:

The Province make payments in lieu of school taxes on its properties, in addition to those now made in lieu of municipal taxes, and to the extent that they apply to elementary schools, such payments, as well as those now made by the Hydro-Electric Power Commission of Ontario, be computed at the lower of the public or separate school mill rate applicable where each property is situated and be distributed to the school boards on the basis of pupil enrolment.[73]

The select committee agreed with this recommendation, with the observation that the equalization features of the Ontario Foundation Tax Plan could reduce the existing deficiency in the payments in lieu of taxes, but could not eliminate them. Having adopted a uniform practice with respect to municipal and school taxes, the province could then attempt to persuade the federal government to do the same.[74]

The Ontario committee suggested certain exceptions to the proposed obligation of the provincial government and all its agencies to make full payment in lieu of municipal, school, business occupancy, and local improvement levies on their properties: 1 / public highways, 2 / land betterment works, to the extent that they conveyed an unrestricted community benefit, 3 / recognized historic sites, monuments, and memorials not being exploited commercially, and 4 / remote or undeveloped Crown lands not under lease or subject to mining or timber rights, and not benefiting from local government services.[75] The select committee approved of the approach and the contents of the list, with the addition of provincial parks.[76]

The tax-exempt status of real estate held by local authorities is provided for by *The Assessment Act*. Separate rights of exemption cover publicly owned or controlled elementary and high schools when used and occupied for school purposes, as well as public squares, highways, lanes, and other public communications. Municipal utilities make payments on a basis prescribed by *The Assessment Act*. Exemption does not extend to tenant-occupied municipal property.

In some cases the argument that property owned by local authorities should be subject to taxation seems illogical, since it would mean that the agency would be taxing itself. In other cases, a transfer of funds from one agency to another would be involved. While wasteful accounting operations should not be encouraged, there is thought to be some advantage in maintaining an awareness of the full financial implications of property ownership by local government. While the Ontario Committee on Taxation did not recommend that taxes be levied on such property, it was in favour of assessing and taxing municipal utilities according to existing practice, since it seemed desirable to maintain a basis for comparing costs between municipal and private enterprises of a comparable nature, whether or not the utilities were required to be self-sustaining. Both committees agreed that the same types of property should be exempt from municipal as from provincial taxes.

For an illustration of the consequences of maintaining the tax-free status of universities, it is instructive to continue our review of the particular problems of the city of Kingston. Syl Apps elaborated further on the case in 1968.

Kingston is fortunate in having a great university located within its borders ... The contribution it has made to the people of Ontario in almost every field of education has been tremendous ...

Located, as it is, in the centre of a fine old residential area of the city, its expansion has been made possible only by the purchase of many of these residences. Being a tax exempt organization, every new acquisition by the university has resulted in a reduction in the assessment, and consequently in tax revenue available to the city. This has increased the tax burden being shouldered by the remaining property owners who feel, and rightly so, that the providing of existing and future services for the university, should not be reflected in their tax bills ...

These municipalities must be given the right to tax university property. In return, this money should be reimbursed to the university as an addition to the operating grants now being provided by the Department of University Affairs.[77]

The argument has been particularly strong with respect to Queen's University because of the extraordinarily small percentage of its student enrolment coming from the immediate area and, conversely, the unusual degree to which service has been rendered to the province, the nation, and other countries. Queen's is the biggest university in Ontario in relation to the size of the community in which it is situated. Thus there appears to be the most compelling case for expecting all citizens of the province to contribute to the cost of the service which the municipality has been providing for the university. The issue has not been basically a difference between "town and gown," despite some expressions of irritation over the difficult situation in which both sides have been placed. Successive principals, Corry and Deutsch, have expressed unequivocal support for the city's case, although they have been powerless to offer any satisfactory solution. Queen's, of course, provides only an extreme example of a general problem. Even in the larger cities, university encroachment on previously taxable property has been regarded with considerable disquiet.

The Ontario Committee on Taxation recommended that all exemptions from property taxation be removed from institutions of higher learning. In the future, grant support would be provided to compensate for such taxation only for those institutions recognized for acceptable educational purposes by the Department of University Affairs or the Department of Education. Much the same arrangement would apply to private schools, which would receive compensatory support only if they provided approved education at the elementary or secondary level. The select committee unequivocally endorsed these recommendations.

The provincial budget for 1970–1 included the first step to permit municipal taxation of university properties, with compensatory provincial grants. During that year, cities in which universities were located were empowered to tax university properties to the extent of $25 per full-time student. The estimated cost to the Provincial Treasury was $2.5 million for the year. The treasurer identified the measure as a start toward the goal of broadening the tax base by removing exemptions. It was intended that the interim formula would be changed to the normal method of taxation once university properties had been properly assessed.[78]

Since all the universities but Waterloo Lutheran are already publicly assisted, and even that institution receives provincial payments in lieu of former federal subsidies, there is no question that they offer a program that is acceptable to the province. They are not, however, enthusiastic about any step that increases their already overwhelming dependence on provincial financing. The question of private schools is more difficult. The Department of Education has consistently avoided helping such schools to finance any aspect of their operations, fearing the consequences of compromising precedents. There is no great eagerness to assume the responsibility for assessing their programs beyond the supervisory functions now exercised. The schools, for their part, could hardly be expected to welcome a mere substitution of a provincial subsidy for tax-exempt status, provided there is no net gain, and would have reason to fear a weakening of their position if they had to justify their existence at frequent intervals to a public agency.

Public hospitals may be considered along with utilities in terms of the principles of property taxation. The committee recommended that these be made subject to full realty taxes and, where applicable, local business taxes. They would recover these amounts through the Hospital Care Insurance Plan, with funds ultimately coming from the provincial, and, if possible, federal governments. There are at least two obstacles to the implementation of this recommendation. 1 / The psychological impact of removing any kind of privilege from hospitals would be unfavourable, even if full compensation were provided in some other way. Popular sentiment might lead to a focusing of attention on the first of these aspects, with the second ignored. 2 / Any step that appeared to inflate medical costs, whether or not it simply reflected a change in financing procedures, would produce an adverse reaction at a time when such costs have been rising at an extremely rapid rate.

The majority of the select committee approved without qualification the recommendation of the Ontario committee with respect to taxation of public hospitals. Two dissenters, while agreeing with the principle that most exemptions from municipal taxation should be eliminated, questioned the proposal that municipal taxes should be charged to the Ontario Hospital Care Insurance Plan. Such a change, in their view, would relieve one regressive tax with an even more regressive one, the hospital insurance premium. They supported the recommendation only if it were made clear that the added cost to the hospitals would come entirely out of an increased provincial grant.[79]

The problems raised in connection with religious agencies are somewhat similar. At present, *The Assessment Act* and the Provincial Land Tax exempt places of worship and the accompanying land, and the former provides in the same way for religious seminaries. Except for such seminaries, however, land and buildings owned and used by religious bodies for their administrative, charitable, welfare, social service and educational purposes are subject to taxation. Places of worship must also pay local improvement charges under *The Local Improvement Act*. But property used for recreational purposes may be exempted by local by-law.

Arguments in favour of the general benefits conferred on the community by the activities of religious bodies were considered by the committee. There were said to be indirect contributions to the welfare of those who did not make a practice of attending church. It was claimed that the continued teaching of a code of morality was beneficial to all members of society. Values were also seen in the active concern and constructive criticisms that churches express on contemporary social issues. The committee did not express the scepticism about the validity of these assumptions that certain critics are prepared to voice. But it found little to justify burdening all property owners with the cost of tax relief given to places of worship. In one important sense, however, they could not be treated in the same way as charitable institutions. The direct subsidization of places of worship is not part of Ontario's heritage, and would be difficult to establish. Thus there was no realistic way of compensating them for the withdrawal of existing privileges, which were deeply embedded in the history of the province. The solution offered was a concession to sentiment rather than a manifestation of logic. It involved assessment of church property at full value, but taxation at reduced rates, beginning at 5 per cent and rising gradually to 35 per cent.

The select committee had particular difficulty with this recommendation. A majority accepted it, with the modification that the maximum of taxable assessment should be 20 per cent, and that the tax should be introduced at the rate of two additional percentage points a year over a period of ten years. Other members took the view that places of worship should remain completely exempt from taxation. One thought that only the land, but not the structure, should be taxed.[80]

Consistently following its opposition to tax exemptions in general, the Ontario Committee on Taxation, supported in general by the select committee, also recommended their abolition with respect to charitable organizations, social and community service groups, and similar bodies. As in the case of universities and private educational institutions, support by governmental agencies at one level or another might be substituted. Legislation would be required to permit each municipality to make annual grants to charitable organizations that, in the opinion of the council, were for the general advantage of the inhabitants of the area. Such a recommendation raises questions of the most fundamental kind about the nature of the democratic state. Is it legitimate to place private agencies in a reasonably secure and stable position to work out their own ideas of what constitutes a social benefit? Or must they justify their operations continually to a publicly elected body? Can the latter be expected to display a sensitive understanding of relatively intangible objectives? Will it be prepared to support activities that make a contribution to the welfare of the wider community rather than exclusively to its own constituents? It must of course be recognized that the committee did not recommend that charitable agencies be made completely dependent on public funds, but merely that an automatic and hidden contribution be made deliberately and openly. These agencies could always escape control by appealing for further private donations. But any steps in the direction of public intervention should be taken with full awareness of their ultimate implications.

Tax exemptions for population categories

A substantial case has been made for the exemption of only one category of the population, those aged sixty-five or over. A major argument advanced is the extremely pragmatic one that people in this age group are very often dependent on small incomes from pensions or savings. Continued and substantial increases in taxes often pose a serious threat to their ability to maintain their homes. Even on utilitarian economic grounds, it is desirable to take steps to keep them from becoming a public charge. A second argument involves the vexatious issue of distinguishing between direct and indirect social benefits. From the most immediate point of view, old age pensioners have little direct use for education, either for themselves or for anyone directly dependent on them. It is not easy to make a convincing case for their dependence on a society which rests on education as one of its essential pillars.

In 1967 Ontario municipalities and school boards in territory without municipal organization were authorized to allow an annual credit or refund equivalent to one-half of the taxes imposed on property owned and occupied by those sixty-five years of age and over, up to a maximum of $150. The amount so allowed could be reimbursed to the municipal agency by the province, and become a lien on the property, becoming payable on its sale other than to an immediate relative also qualified to receive the credit or refund. In other words, a person in this category could defer the payment of his taxes for the rest of his life, or at least up to the value of the property, and leave the amount involved to be deducted from the estate he left to his heirs. This arrangement did not have as wide an appeal as some may have expected. Many old people place great value on the possession of unencumbered property, whether or not there are ever likely to be direct financial implications from liens. Also, not a few feel an obligation to do as well as possible by their heirs.

The opposition in the Legislature saw a certain amount of political capital in the provisions of this legislation. J. Renwick, member for Riverdale, put the case as follows:

There is no basis whatsoever, on any equitable principle, why a person 65 years of age or older should, because they happen to be a ratepayer, be subjected to the education tax.

In most cases, those persons have paid the education tax for many, many years. In most cases, none of those families have anyone within the education system. To suggest in a specious way that, in some way or other, if there was a total relief up to the $150 as is provided in the bill for a person who owns his home and who is an elderly person, it would be a subsidizing of that person, is consistent only with the Tory view that they will not subsidize or assist anyone in this society, without making them, at some point, pay the price.[81]

The Ontario Committee on Taxation was not enthusiastic about tax relief to specific groups in the community, whether by tax deferral or outright tax reductions. There was apprehension about establishing awkward precedents that would make it difficult to deny similar concessions to other apparently deserving claimants such as young families with school-age children and people with income deficiencies, including recipients of mothers' allowances. Furthermore, establishing broad categories such as "persons sixty-five years of age or over" meant extending aid to those who did not require it, while the alternative of a means test meant a burden on the administrative agency and an annoyance to the taxpayer. R.F. Nixon expressed some of the same sentiments in discussing the bill in the Legislature. He mentioned various groups for whom a good case for relief could be made, including citizens in agricultural communities whose operations as farmers did not enable them to sustain their burden of municipal taxes.[82] He and his party did, however, support the principle of the bill, accepting the desirability of providing some kind of assistance to older people. But they took exception, as did the members of the New Democratic Party, to the provisions for a lien on the property of the recipients of relief. According to the rules of the political game, it is difficult to see how they could have stood anywhere except on the side of public generosity.

Distribution of local revenue

Frequent reference was made in the treatment of provincial assistance to school boards in earlier sections to the unequal distribution of real property assessment in different parts of the province. A review of some of

Cameron's findings in this area is of particular relevance. In one of his most dramatic statements, he writes: "Again adjusting the 1965 tax base to full value, the district with the largest relative taxable assessment could have provided the average elementary educational programme with a tax levy of .58 mills in the dollar. The district with the smallest relative assessment would have required 116.04 mills, two hundred times the former."[83]

In another analysis, Cameron examined variations in assessment per classroom unit in 1964, the last year before the mandatory consolidation of school sections into township school districts. The assessment data available for that period were based on 1940 values, with indeterminate effects on the relative distribution of assessments among school districts. Of all the elementary school boards existing at that time, 7.5 per cent had tax bases of less than $50,000 per classroom, 25.2 per cent less than $100,000, and 64.0 per cent less than $200,000. At the other extreme, 0.5 per cent had tax bases of $1 million or more. The secondary school boards showed much less extreme variation, although the wealthiest group had five times as much taxing capacity per classroom as the poorest. It must be kept in mind, of course, that the low assessments for the separate schools were somewhat offset by allocated corporation assessment provided in the form of a grant. In any case, the figures demonstrate the extreme difficulty of devising effective equalization formulas. The situation has certainly been simplified successively in 1965 and 1969 in the two major steps toward consolidation. No exact figures can be offered here to show the distribution of assessment after these developments, but variations are still great.

Reactions to local tax burden

That the burden on real estate has been approaching some kind of limit has been a persistent theme over the years. Farquhar R. Oliver, leader of the opposition, remarked in the Legislature in 1957,

> On the subject of education I want to say this, that I doubt if there is any matter in which the provincial government is concerned in a financial sense that has caused more unrest and more distress to taxpayers in this province than the weight of taxation for education. As has been evidenced by the briefs presented by the mayors and reeves, and other associations, the tax for education is becoming more than the people of the province can bear.[84]

As leader of the provincial Liberal Party, John Wintermeyer for a time advocated the complete abandonment of the property tax in favour of the assumption by the provincial government of 100 per cent of the cost of education. His argument was based mainly on the unduly heavy burden in relation to the size of the tax base. He asserted that "the simple fact is that the municipal opportunity of taxation is just not broad enough, and not equitable enough, to provide equality of education in Ontario."[85] To demonstrate the lack of balance between the two levels, he claimed that in

Ontario provincial taxes were among the lightest in Canada, while municipal taxes were exceeded only by those in Saskatchewan. He went on: "the basic cost of expansion in this province is borne by the property owners. I suggest to you that 100 years ago, property was the basic source of revenue, the basic source of wealth. That is not the case today."[86]

One of the recommendations made by the Ontario Conference on Education in 1961 reads: "If the present trend of increasing costs of education continues in the future, it is the opinion of this group that most of this additional financing will have to be borne by sources other than real estate." The actual producer of the recommendation was the same group that advocated a foundation tax plan. R.F. Nixon observed in 1964, "All of us are aware of the fact that the financial burden of education at the local level has reached the point beyond which it cannot be increased."[87] And in a letter to the minister in late 1968, the Clerk-Comptroller of the Corporation of the City of Kingston wrote:

> The following resolution was passed at the meeting of City Council held on October 15th 1968:
> "... that it is the unanimous opinion of this Board that property taxation is an inadequate and inequitable means of raising the money needed for education and that the burden on the residential taxpayer, especially those retired and on fixed incomes, is intolerable;
> "that it is imperative some supplementary means of taxation to meet the increased and increasing costs of education be speedily found."[88]

While devoting considerable attention to possible improvements in the real estate tax, the Ontario Committee on Taxation generally took the view that the amount of such taxes was not intolerable. Its proposal, subsequently adopted by the government, that the average level of education grants be raised to 60 per cent of school board expenditure over a three-year period, thus involved other considerations. The majority of the select committee, in endorsing the proposed course of action, and the Liberal minority, in pressing for provincial assumption of 80 per cent of school board costs, avoided a direct claim that higher property taxes could not be borne, but rather condemned them on the basis of inequity.

Range of school board revenues

During the past thirty years the property tax and provincial grants have accounted for all but a small proportion of school board revenues. In 1939 sources other than these constituted 17.5 per cent of the total, according to the Ontario Committee on Taxation, but, by the time the latter made its report, this figure had declined to less than 4 per cent.[89] In fact, most of such revenues came in a roundabout way from the same sources as other funds, since they consisted mainly of tuition fees paid to school boards by other local authorities, including school boards. The gradual amalgamation of smaller units reduced the number of non-resident pupils and fees.

Fees

Under ordinary circumstances, children have long been eligible to attend a designated elementary or secondary school without paying fees. But there have been special circumstances under which fees have been required, in many cases payable by the board having the responsibility for the child's education. In some instances, the parent or guardian has been liable for payment for special privileges.

Section 5 of *The Public Schools Act* specifies that a child who has attained the age of five years on or before December 31 in any year has the right to attend a school in the area in which he resides, or in another area where his board has made appropriate provision. Where the board operates a kindergarten, the age of eligibility is reduced by one year, and where it operates a junior kindergarten, by two years. The board may, however, admit a child to one of these classes below the age of ordinary eligibility, and may charge a fee for the privilege.

Where a child resides at too great a distance from the school in his own area to make attendance practical, he may attend a school under the jurisdiction of another board, provided there is sufficient accommodation. Under such circumstances, his parent or guardian is liable for a fee. The board where he resides must refund the amount of taxes the latter has paid each year up to the amount of the fee. If the parent or guardian wants the child to attend a school in an area other than the one where he is entitled to attend, and if the child does not meet the distance requirement, such reimbursement cannot be claimed. If the parent or guardian owns property in the other area, and is assessed for an amount at least equal to the total assessment for public school purposes divided by the average daily attendance during the previous year, he is not liable for the fee.

A child who is a ward of a children's aid society may attend, without payment of a fee, a school operated by a board that was supported by the assessment of the residence where he lived with his parent or guardian in the year in which he became a ward. He may also be admitted without fee to a school administered by a board supported by the assessment on a residence where he has been placed for adoption on a temporary basis. Under other conditions, a child who is in the custody of a "corporation, society, or person" is liable for payment of a fee for attendance at a school in the section where he resides. This provision applies both to elementary and secondary schools.

Fees are paid on behalf of a child who resides on land that is exempt from taxation for school purposes. Such a child is entitled to attend a school that is accessible to him provided the appropriate supervisory official has certified that there is sufficient accommodation.

One school board can purchase education from another for the children for whom it has responsibility. Under such an arrangement, the purchasing board pays fees determined by a somewhat involved calculation that has the effect of distributing net maintenance costs between the two boards according to the proportion of children under the jurisdiction of each. Due allowance is made for variations in cost for different courses. Fees may be paid on a similar basis by the federal or provincial government where either acts as the purchaser.

In 1963 Bascom St John was constrained to comment on the provision that he quoted as follows from subsection 6 of section 70 of *The Secondary Schools and Boards of Education Act.*[90]

(6) ... where a pupil
(a) has completed Grade 8; and
(b) has attended one or more secondary schools for a total of six or more years, he shall not be admitted to a secondary school except upon payment of such fees as the board that operates the school may prescribe, but such fees shall not exceed the average cost per pupil in the schools maintained by the board for the preceding calendar year as provided ...[91]

St John noted that the term "shall" in legal terminology means "must." Thus school boards were legally obligated to exact fees of all students who enrolled in a secondary school beyond their sixth year. They would have been quite within their rights in insisting on a payment of several hundred dollars, representing the actual cost of a year's education, although there seemed to be no reason why a token fee of one cent would not have met the requirements equally well.

The boards were not actually fulfilling their technical obligation. But St John did not think it right that students ought to have the threat implied in the legislation hanging over them. He was particularly critical of the practice of refusing admission to grade 13 to students who had passed grade 12 with an average of less than 60 per cent. They were ostensibly held back for their own good, since it was said that their chance of obtaining credit for grade 13 subjects was too poor to justify the attempt. In fact, there was great concern for maintaining the school's record of success on the examinations, a record that might be spoiled by the presence of too many questionable candidates. As St John pointed out, a genuine failure in one year and a forced repetition of grade 12, even despite success at that level, would be sufficient grounds for a school to use the fee clause as a weapon to get rid of unwanted students.

The subsection to which St John objected has been modified, and now reads as follows:

(6) Notwithstanding subsection 1, 2 and 3 and section 68, where a pupil
(a) has completed grade 8; and

(b) has attended one or more secondary schools for a total of seven or more years, he shall not be admitted to a secondary school except upon the payment of a fee as provided in subsection 4 of section 100a of *The Schools Administration Act*. 1966, e. 141, s. 8 (2).

Personal property tax

Although the attempt to tax personal property was abandoned in Ontario in 1904, the possibility of resorting to such a source of revenue is not completely a dead issue. The Ontario Committee on Taxation noted the inclusion of personal property in the tax base in several other provinces. The trend of current recommendations was, however, toward its elimination. On the other hand, such property, broadly or narrowly defined, remained subject to taxation in most parts of the United States. The committee thus felt it necessary to devote brief discussion to this form of taxation.[92] It noted the particular difficulty of discovering and valuing all forms of personal property. Where efforts had been made to collect the tax, the tendency had been to reduce the list to a very few readily indentifiable items such as the stock-in-trade of businesses and motor vehicles. Another step in the retreat from full utilization had been the definition of the value of personal property as an arbitrary percentage of realty assessment. A realty tax differential would serve the same purpose without the pretence that personal property was being taxed. A more serious fault, perhaps, was that the assessor was usually unable to check the completeness or accuracy of the taxpayer's declaration of his holdings. Thus the tax became, in effect, a contribution on the part of the most compliant. Because of such factors, the committee rejected the personal property tax as a potential source of revenue.

Some consideration was also given to the poll tax as a source of municipal revenue. Like the personal property tax, it has some indirect implications for school board revenues. Ontario municipalities were entitled to levy it on male inhabitants from twenty-one to sixty years of age who were not otherwise taxed locally or whose local property or business taxes were less than the poll tax. The tax was levied at a flat rate, and ranged from $1 to $10. Certain categories of citizens within the defined age range were exempt. Because the committee found the tax unfair, regressive, expensive to administer, and widely evaded, its abolition was recommended. This recommendation was implemented by the Legislature, an action which received the approval of the select committee.

The Ontario Committee on Taxation also considered and dismissed other possible sources of municipal tax revenue. 1 / The introduction of a municipal income tax under existing conditions would be folly because of difficulties and expense of administration and because of its potentially adverse influence on patterns of residence and economic development. 2 / The sales tax was also thought to be more appropriate for administration at higher levels of government. 3 / A tax on transient accommodation would be arbitrary and discriminatory unless administered as part of a general tax on services within the broader spectrum of a retail sales tax.

Mechanics of tax collection

In connection with the mechanics of tax collection, the Ontario Committee on Taxation took account of the perennial complaint of municipal councils that they were held responsible, at least by uninformed members of the public, for the rapid increase in educational costs, because they had to issue the tax bills. Separate statements about the educational mill rate and the amount of the tax attributable to education did not overcome the false impression. Accordingly, the committee recommended that

> The requisitioning powers of public school boards, separate school boards and boards of education be terminated, and that these boards levy their taxes to be collected through bills issued for the purpose by municipalities and payable at times distinct from those at which municipal tax bills are payable. (20:10)

A policy change in accordance with this recommendation was announced by Prime Minister Robarts. It had been instituted for high school district boards, and was extended to the county boards of education when they were created in 1969. Whether the councils would be relieved from all blame for unpopular financial decisions was debatable as long as regular municipal machinery for collection was still used. To construct special machinery, however, would have entailed an unjustifiable waste.

Current changes and future prospects

In Budget Paper B, attached to the 1969 provincial budget, the government provided a considerable amount of information on its intentions with respect to the reform of local taxation. The need for action and the general plan for reform were indicated as follows.

> Property taxation in Ontario stands in need of fundamental reform, perhaps more so than any other area. As the Smith Committee and the Select Committee so clearly showed, the present property tax is grossly unfair and inefficient. The proposed provincial actions to reduce the burden of financing that falls on the property tax and to offset its regressivity via personal income tax credits will substantially ameliorate these shortcomings. But reform of property taxation is still necessary and desirable, both in its own right and in order to facilitate and complement reforms in government structure and provincial grants. Therefore, the Government is determined to overhaul the entire system of property taxation and make it as equitable and efficient as possible.[93]

According to the paper, the plan for reform involved four main aspects: 1 / the reassessment of all real property at current value, 2 / the broadening of the local tax base by the removal of exemptions, 3 / the imposition of a more neutral business assessment rate, and 4 / the determination of an appropriate distribution of tax burdens among different classes of real property. The reform of assessment was identified as the most crucial of these reforms, since it provided the basis for all the others.[94]

As justification for the government's decision to take over full responsibility for assessment on January 1, 1970, the paper pointed out that current property assessment was full of inconsistencies. Many properties were said to be under-assessed, some over-assessed, and some not assessed at all. Similar properties were assessed at different values within the same municipality and between municipalities. Different municipalities were inconsistent in their assessment treatment of particular classes of property. The government doubted the adequacy of the solution recommended by the Ontario Committee on Taxation – that municipalities be given more aid and incentives to improve their assessment practices. This approach seemed to call for a complete change in management practices.[95]

It was estimated that the changeover would save the municipalities about $15 million a year, allowing a corresponding reduction in provincial grants. The assessment reform would add to the rolls many properties that, under existing conditions, were not paying any taxes, and would raise the amount contributed by others that were not paying their fair share. Thus the municipalities stood to gain substantial revenues. The government proposed to consider measures to cushion the impact of the reform, although certain hardships would eventually have to be borne if equity was to be achieved.[96]

The government's plan to broaden the tax base was expected to have three beneficial results. 1 / It would increase the revenue-raising capacity of the local government sector as a whole. 2 / It would reduce disparities among municipalities, which varied greatly in terms of their proportion of tax-exempt properties. 3 / It would shift the tax burden within each municipality. The government had already announced that it did not intend to remove the exemption enjoyed by churches. Although the status of other private properties was under review, the government did not plan to eliminate exemptions in general until proper assessment had been completed. In the long run, full local taxes would be paid on all property owned by the province and the agencies and institutions which it supported. A modest beginning in that direction had already been made.[97]

Reflecting the comments of the Ontario Committee on Taxation and the select committee, the paper condemned the existing practice of applying different rates of business assessment to different categories of business, thus penalizing some and favouring others. The current schedule of rates was said to be full of categories and definitions that might have been relevant fifty years before, but had become inappropriate and obsolete. Again, reassessment at current value was a necessary preliminary to any fundamental reform. Only after such a process had been completed would the government be able to measure and evaluate the impact of business assessment rates on different businesses, on different municipalities, and on municipal revenues in total. As an interim measure, the government was considering a reduction in the existing number of business assessment rates, a narrowing of the existing range of rates, and a general modernization of business tax legislation.[98]

Among measures already taken or scheduled for the future that would tend to affect property tax burdens, the paper mentioned the following: 1 / Mining processing facilities would begin to pay property taxes. 2 / Increased provincial grants for education would reduce the tax burden on all properties. 3 / Regional school boards and regional governments would tend to even out property tax burdens within their boundaries. 4 / Personal income tax credits or refunds for property taxes paid would tend to reduce the ultimate burden of residential property taxes on those least able to pay.[99]

In principle, the government agreed with the adverse views of the Ontario Committee on Taxation and the select committee with respect to the split mill rate. No change was contemplated, however, until reassessment had been completed and the impact on municipal finances carefully examined. As to the recommendations of each of the committees for new ratios of taxable assessment to total assessment for various classes of property, the government felt that such a course of action would be premature and inappropriate. Once more, reassessment was seen as an essential prerequisite to any drastic action. Consideration was being given to appropriate tax treatment for transportation and communication properties. As to working farms, the government's attitude was that they should be subjected to a considerably lower property tax than non-farm properties because of their limited ability to pay taxes out of current revenue. If reassessment should threaten them with any significant increase, the government was prepared to apply interim measures to hold the line on their tax burdens.[100]

TEN

Budgetary practices

PROVINCIAL

The Ontario government, including the Department of Education, has been introducing a modern approach to budgeting during the last few years. A review of procedures followed at the beginning of the period of reform will help to indicate the nature of the changes.

Procedures followed in 1967

The first step toward the preparation of the estimates for 1968–9 was taken on April 28, 1967, when branch directors and other officials responsible for budget preparation were presented with a memorandum specifying the timetable and explaining how the estimates material was to be submitted. In May the preparation of estimates got under way in all sections of the organization. As compared with the previous year, officials were asked to make three changes in procedure: to prepare more fully developed written justifications for their requests, including identification of the primary criteria, current and projected levels of activity, and relevant performance data; to make a more detailed breakdown of salary requirements, with particular reference to those in the "unclassified category," and to identify training and staff development costs separately from other travelling expenses. Estimates were prepared under three program categories: 1 / existing program, 2 / expansion of an existing program, and 3 / extension to an existing program.

An existing program was one being carried out currently in which no change was expected in the standards of service or the size of the workload. The only permissible increases in expenditure were for merit increases and salary revisions for the approved staff complement, an increase in unit costs, increases due to approved additions to the budget during the previous year, and increases resulting from the placing of orders for periods of longer than a year. Program contractions, as well as increases in unit costs, had to be explained.

Expansion of an existing program meant the increase necessary to maintain at existing standards a larger number of units of work because of uncontrollable factors such as increases in the population, in the number of applicants, or in enrolment. Increases in the 1968–9 budget might arise from additional positions, travel expenses, maintenance supplies, and equipment resulting from increased enrolment; an increase in the number of individuals or agencies eligible by legislation for an existing service, grant, or benefit; an increase in the number of requests for an existing service; an increase in workload in services branches attributable to increased activity in other areas of the department; provision for second or third years of courses already under way in institutions; and additional travel by existing staff in order to maintain a service at its current level.

An extension to an existing program involved the increase that resulted from a proposal to improve the standards of service offered, to broaden the coverage of a service or program, or to add new programs or activities. Increases in the 1968–9 budget might be attributable to new courses in new subjects; the improvement of a course by adding more years of instruction; an improvement in the method of providing a service through new procedures and new types of equipment; an improvement in the level of a service, grant, or benefit; and increases resulting from changes in organization, such as decentralization to the areas (regions). Program expansion and extension were shown in "packages," that is, the various elements were grouped and shown separately in terms of salary, travel, maintenance, and other expenditures.

Preparation of initial estimates entailed the use of a series of forms. 1 / TB1 – *Summary for Department and Branch* was used to summarize the expenditure data for each branch, section, institution, and area (region) by item or object of expenditure, that is, salary, travelling expenses, maintenance, and other expenditure. This form was completed at the end of the operation. 2 / TR2 – *Analysis of Programs* was used to present written information and cost detail relating to existing programs and program expansion and extension. All changes in existing programs had to be supported by written narratives indicating the factors that had a bearing on budget preparation, the extent to which they could be measured or counted, and their relationship to the financial and staff resources and administrative arrangements proposed for the subsequent fiscal year as compared with the current budget. Examples of the type of data included were number of students enrolled, average cost per student, comparative course costs, number of plans to be checked, number of requisitions to be processed, average number of postings per day per operator, floor areas to be maintained, current and projected student-teacher ratios, number of schools to be visited, and average annual travel cost per field position. 3 / TB3 – *Summary of Programs* was used to summarize expenditures by program, and listed program expenditure by total. Like TB1, it was completed in the final stages of the process. 4 / FA4 – *Details of Salary Provision for 1968–69* provided detailed information on the total salary request. 5 / TB5 – *Details of Travel Expense Provision* was used to indicate detail on regular, conference, staff training, and related travel requirements. 6 / TB6 – *Detail of Maintenance Provision* was used to indicate information on new equipment to be purchased, showing item, cost, and replacement policies; cost of maintenance contracts; items to be rented, with costs; printing needs, including kind of form, number, and cost; advertising needs, with a breakdown by kind, purpose, and cost; use of telephones and telegrams, with detail on the cost of each type of service; rental of accommodation, with an explanation of the need, a description of the lease, a statement of the number and classification of the occupants, and a specification of the rental cost; moving expenses; and miscellaneous items. 7 / TB7 – *Detail of Other Provision* was used to provide detail on all items other than salary, travelling expenses, and maintenance. One item coming under this heading was data processing.

By June 1 officials below the level of branch director were expected to have forwarded their budgets to the latter. During June these directors met with the deputy minister and the assistant deputy ministers to consider program proposals. They then reviewed and co-ordinated the estimates submissions for their respective branches, incorporating program proposals that were tentatively approved for inclusion at such meetings. The branch estimates were subsequently reviewed by the responsible assistant deputy ministers and submitted, by July 15, to the Budget Office. Between the middle of July and the middle of August, these branch estimates were analysed in the Budget Office. During the latter part of August departmental budget review meetings were held at which the branch directors presented their estimates to a committee consisting of the deputy minister and the three assistant deputy ministers. During September final departmental decisions on policy matters were made and the estimates were co-ordinated and typed and made ready for submission to the Treasury Board Secretariat on October 2.

Early steps to implement program budgeting

A major initial step toward the introduction of program budgeting was taken by the Treasury Board in 1967, when it requested of the Department of Education, as well as of other departments, a forecast of programs, revenue, and expenditure required to cover the five-year period between 1968–9 and 1972–3. Two reasons were offered for this request: 1 / it would help the department to crystallize and cost its plans and objectives over the forecast period; 2 / it would inform the government of the extent and nature of future revenues and expenditures, including those arising from existing responsibilities and those associated with proposed new and extended programs and activities. This information was regarded as essential both for the assessment of requests for funds to meet immediate needs and for the selection of appropriate fiscal policies and the determination of program priorities. The information submitted cut across branch and division organizational boundaries. Plans were made for an annual updating of the five-year forecast.

Planning-programming-budgeting

The principles of planning-programming-budgeting, or simply "program budgeting," were outlined in a guide issued for use in the government service by the Treasury Board in 1969 under the title *Effective Management through P.P.B.S.* The justification for the new approach was set forth there:

For an entire government, for a single department, or for an organizational unit within a department, the range of problems, the possible range of responses to these problems, and the chronic shortage of funds to fulfil all demands, calls into question old methods of establishing priorities, designing appropriate programs, managing operations and controlling budgets.[1]

The weaknesses in traditional methods were identified as follows: 1 / vagueness of objectives; 2 / limited analysis of alternatives; 3 / partial costing of programs; 4 / inadequate consideration of implications of present decisions for future years; 5 / short review and decision period; 6 / emphasis on expenditure control instead of performance; and 7 / gaps between planning, budgeting, and control.

Stated in a positive form, somewhat as the converse to these weaknesses, the objectives of a program budgeting system were given as follows.

(1) To define departmental Objectives clearly and to relate them to defined provincial needs and goals;
(2) To stimulate the in-depth analysis of all existing and proposed new programs in terms of their costs and benefits;
(3) To link the planning and budgeting process through the annual review of Multi-Year Plans;
(4) To measure actual and planned performance;
(5) To provide a systematic way of integrating all of these elements in order to arrive at a more effective system for the allocation and management of resources.[2]

The main purpose of the guide was said to be to illustrate the effect of a program budgeting system on the management process. Management tasks were defined as setting objectives; organizing, motivating and communicating; measuring; and developing people.

Determining an appropriate course of action was said to depend on 1 / the analysis of issues, 2 / the identification of objectives and alternatives, and 3 / program analysis or benefit-cost analysis. The first two of these were to be based on background studies undertaken by specialized staff. For the Department of Education, a research group of substantial size would seem to be needed to perform these functions. To depend on the uncertain interests of the professors at the Ontario Institute for Studies in Education would appear to risk building in a serious weakness.

Once the objectives were defined, management's task would be that of establishing a program structure, which involved the systematic listing of all programs being undertaken or proposed, along with related activities. The structure would make possible the identification of gaps and overlaps in the programs designed to fulfill stated objectives, and would provide the framework for examining the effect of changes in priority and emphasis among programs. It would evolve over a period of time as new alternatives were examined and implemented. The process of identifying the alternative ways of achieving an objective would be followed by a decision as to which ones justified technical study and benefit/cost analysis. The results of such study and analysis would be a technical assessment of the relative merits of the alternatives considered, which management would use as a basis for recommending a course of action. If this recommendation implied a change in departmental policy or spending levels, it would have to be considered by the central agencies or by the cabinet.

Programming was defined as the process of laying out work programs, along with the scheduling of resources, space, manpower, and results. The guide indicated that the traditional budgeting process in the Ontario government had involved an isolation of the budgeting function, with little or no programming except what was carried out by individual departments. Two undesirable consequences were 1 / that decisions on spending levels and other policy matters were not made until December, with the result that departments had very little time to modify or implement new programs for the next year, and 2 / budgeting decisions were made in the light of projections covering only one year of operations. In order to counter these weaknesses, the program budgeting system used a multi-year plan, usually prepared in the first half of the year. This plan would give departmental management and the cabinet the means of studying one or more alternative sets of five-year integrated programs for departments and the government as a whole. In the light of this information, financial requirements could be estimated for several years into the future, and tentative decisions could be made with respect to the introduction or modification of programs to be begun later. Departments would be made aware of basic policy decisions early enough to prepare their estimates more realistically and to organize their future operations more effectively.

Since short-term changes in operating programs were often wasteful or impossible to make, there would have to be a fairly firm commitment to the first year of a multi-year plan. Such a commitment would not preclude adjustments in priorities or in levels of activity even at an early stage. For later years, substantial formal revisions would have to be allowed for, as well as gradual revision due to changes in policy. With relatively little leeway for modifications in the first year, however, it would be possible to define guidelines for budgeting that reduced the process almost to a matter of routine. The department's creative energies would be concentrated on the production and justification of the multi-year plan, and in its modification as the need arose. As the guide expressed it, the estimates would be superseded by the multi-year plan as the basic vehicle for soliciting policy decisions.

Sections of the guide elaborated on various aspects of program budgeting touched upon in the introduction. It was stated that the objective should be defined in terms of the intended impact on society of the product or service which the program provided. An illustration of a possible objective of an urban transportation program was that of reducing the average commuter travel time in a particular metropolitan area. It is rather easy to see how studies might be designed to determine the various means of attaining such an objective, and the advantages and disadvantages of each method, including the costs involved. It is also easy to say that the objective of eliminating lung cancer in two years is unrealistic because of the lack of the necessary knowledge and technique. The educators, however, have had difficulty defining objectives that can be handled so readily. If they offered something vague, such as to improve the quality of the next generation of citizens, they might find themselves without any solid basis for producing or evaluating relevant programs, and thus of persuading the hard-headed members of the Treasury Board, that a specific number of dollars should be spent to attain such an objective. If they turned to the researchers for support, they would probably get years of investigation leading only to inconclusive results. On the other hand, they might make more immediate headway with the objective of producing a certain number of graduates of a specified program in a given number of years. The researchers could tell them with some degree of certainty what facilities and manpower would be required, and what the approximate cost would be. But there might well be no effective answer to questions about the value of the accepted training program to prepare its graduates for successful social adaptation over a long period of time. An efficient procedure might be devised to attain an unproductive goal.

There is no doubt of a growing feeling in government circles that education has long been able to command a high and growing proportion of available financial resources merely on the basis of a general assumption that education is self-justifying, and that its outputs are not measurable in any case. A concerned society would seem entitled to better evidence than it has often had that education really justifies the high priority it has been given. On the other hand, it is to be hoped that the "benefit" side of benefit/cost analyses will not be interpreted in too mechanical a fashion.

The view was expressed in the guide that the process of defining objectives should ideally begin at the top with a statement of over-all provincial objectives. However, since the analysis required in such a process was so great, and since there was a risk of unnecessarily restricting the initiative of departments, it was proposed that the process take place at the departmental and over-all government levels simultaneously. This distribution of responsibility was related to differences in levels of objectives. These were defined as 1 / the activity level, where they would be quite precise, and might require redefinition each year, 2 / the program level, where they would still be fairly precise, but might not need redefinition for several years, and 3 / the functional level, where they had to do with long-term goals. Obviously the contribution required from the top would increase as one proceeded from the first of these levels to the third.

In a separate chapter dealing with evaluation criteria, the guide identified four levels of such criteria, ranging from simple to complex. 1 / Volume indicators might indicate the quantity of goods and services produced by the program or the number of beneficiaries. An example from education might be the number of students in a school system. 2 / Performance indicators assess the efficiency of a program by comparisons with, for example, results achieved in previous years, results anticipated in the multi-year plan, or results achieved by others in similar operations. They may also relate results to unit costs or to staff input. The guide warned that, although more than one performance indicator might be needed, too many might simply confuse the analysis. 3 / Measures of effectiveness indicate achievement in terms of the contribution to the program objective. 4 / Measures of benefit are somewhat similar, except that they are usually expressed in monetary terms, and may also include indirect benefits not included in the program objective. These last two criteria are of course the ones that educators have difficulty applying to programs designed to attain their intangible goals. The guide noted that many decisions cannot and should not be made solely on the grounds of economic desirability as expressed in a benefit/cost ratio, although such a ratio was claimed to be a valuable screening and measuring device when used with care.

Preparation of estimates and budget on the basis of the multi-year plan

The guide indicated a rough timetable, shown on page 341, for the preparation, review, and final approval of the estimates for the budgetary year beginning in April 1971.

Departments were assured that the basic request for them to prepare their multi-year plan, issued in December, would provide guidance on format and detail required, as well as guidelines provided by the Department of Treasury and Economics on the basic assumptions to be followed in the preparation of the plan, such as population growth and wage and price trends. In the early stages of the application of the new approach, departments could obtain policy guidance from sources such as the record of significant issues raised in the Legislature, expressions of policy and priorities revealed during the review of estimates of earlier years, and

December, 1969	– Instructions issued for preparation of departmental multi-year plans.
January–March, 1970	– Departmental preparation of multi-year plan; preparation of economic and fiscal guidelines for multi-year plan.
April–May, 1970	– Review of departmental plans and development of alternative government-wide multi-year plans.
June–July, 1970	– Review of multi-year plan by Cabinet Committee on Policy Development. Recommendations to Cabinet on operating policies. Issuance of general guidelines for 1971–2 Budget and Estimates preparation.
July, 1970	– Issuance of more specific guidelines to departments and technical instructions for preparation of 1971–2 Estimates.
October 1, 1970	– Submission of departmental Estimates for 1971–2 to Treasury Board.
October–December, 1970	– Review and final approval of Estimates and preparation of Budget.

miscellaneous individual policy statements. As time went on, provincial objectives would become more clearly established, and there would be an increasing amount of assistance from previous multi-year plans and from cabinet responses to program memoranda. Most of the data for programing operations would come within individual departments. Proposals for new or changed programs and activities would require an analysis providing the data necessary for projecting both costs and output. Where no change in the service level was planned, the data from the previous multi-year plan would suffice, except for an allowance for changes in the basic assumptions about wage and price increases and increases in load.

Each department was expected to make a list of programs reflecting a descending order of attractiveness in terms of benefit/cost ratio or cost/effectiveness ratio. This list would depend on a priority list of objectives, the order of which would take account of government policy and departmental preference. The ideal was said to be to have a program to achieve each objective. The priority list would be revised each year. One sort of program which might be postponed, although highly attractive according to the criteria applied, would be one requiring more resources than would be available under current over-all financing policy. It might seem preferable not to introduce it at a far less than optimum level, but instead to upgrade a more modest program.

In devising the multi-year plan, departmental management was expected to match priorities to the funds and other resources likely to be available. This process would involve a study of different combinations and levels of programs and activities. A departmental submission would include a Plan A and a Plan B. Plan A, which would assume the maintenance of the same level of service in all programs and activities as in the previous year's budget, would provide the "base case," involving a projection of funds and other resources and an indication of anticipated output over the five-year period. It would not include any extensions of, or improvements in, service, but only the changes attributable to projected population growth and estimated changes in cost. Plan B would outline new programs, as well as program and activity extensions and deletions. A combination of the two plans would constitute an ideal course of action and level of activity. The department would submit a priority list of additions, and of deletions, as outlined in Plan B. This list would constitute a basis for discussion between the departments and the central agencies if only part of Plan B could be included in the over-all multi-year plan of the government as a whole.

As a means of ensuring the ultimate availability of adequate information, each department was urged to undertake an in-depth analysis of at least one on-going program each year. It was said to be desirable to analyse the entire program, even when only part of it was being changed, in order to make sure of its continued desirability as a whole. There was a suggestion, however, that such an undertaking might be excessively burdensome over the short term.

Documentation requested for the multi-year plan submission was to include the following items: 1 / general information, covering departmental objectives, specific programs designed to meet objectives, program priorities, and other comments; 2 / a summary of each program on one page or less; 3 / a table of inputs by program/activity; 4 / tables of resource requirements, including funds by program/activity, manpower by program/activity, and space by program; 5 / program memoranda for new programs and activities. The multi-year plan was to include information on eight years, ranging from the year before the current one to the fifth year after the one for which the budget was being prepared.

The process by which the cabinet committee would consolidate the plans from individual departments need not, for the most part, concern us here. It is sufficient to note that the committee might request additional brief submissions or oral presentations from specific departments when major policy issues reflecting them were raised.

Under the program budgeting system, the instructions regarding standards and the format of the estimates submission issued by the Treasury Board would be accompanied by general expenditure and program guidelines established by the Cabinet Committee on Policy Development on the basis of the review of the multi-year plan. Each department would examine its own multi-year plan in the light of these guidelines in order to determine to what extent the two were compatible. If there proved to be any significant discrepancy, the department was expected to adjust its priorities and change its plans accordingly. After this step had been taken, the manager of each organizational unit with responsibility for a portion of the total departmental budget would determine the resources required to carry out his functions. The estimates of all these organizational units would then be assembled by activity, program, and department, and the manager at each level of responsibility would review the submissions of organizational units reporting to him. Total departmental estimates were to be reviewed by the deputy minister assisted by senior managers of the department. The approval of the minister would be sought for at least the highlights before the submission went to the Treasury Board.

Since the program budgeting system was designed to permit the Legislature, the cabinet and its committees, and departmental management to make decisions on the basis of objective-oriented programs and activities rather than the traditional objects of expenditures, such as salaries, travel, and maintenance, the estimates had to be changed in format from the traditional organization/line item basis to a program/activity basis. The transition was planned so that it would take place over a three-year period, beginning with the preparation of the estimates for 1969–70.

Implications for education

The rapid rise in expenditure on education in relation to that in other departments of government was demonstrated in volume I, chapter 7. This development was in line with the priority system established at the beginning of the Robarts regime, and thus presumably would have occurred to some extent under any reasonably effective minister of education. But Davis's unusual skill and persuasiveness in bargaining with his colleagues has undoubtedly obtained for education considerably more than it might have got with a less effective proponent. It would appear that, by introducing objective and rational procedures wherever possible as a basis for determining for what purposes and in what quantities money will be spent, the system of program budgeting will reduce the personal element in decision making. It may be overly dramatic to suggest that the gate is being barred behind Davis, but there certainly seems little doubt that another minister, no matter what his department, will find it extremely difficult to duplicate Davis's performance.

LOCAL

Traditional school board budgeting practices

Anything in the nature of a complete description of school board budgetary practices would be entirely beyond the scope of the present work. Only a few comments are thus offered, mostly having to do with recent problems and trends.

As a first step in the preparation of a school board's budget, the one or more individuals with the responsibility for part or all of the operation have traditionally provided a statement of the amount of money needed for each specified purpose. In some cases the entry has been a purely mechnical one requiring the repetition of the previous year's item and amount. Hardly less mechanical has been the calculation of decreases, or more likely of increases, determined purely by board policy, as for example, those having to do with the teachers' salaries. Where changes of policy have been required to justify an expenditure item, a statement of the reason has been supplied for the board's consideration. A second major aspect of the preparatory work has been the assembly of information about non-discretionary items of income, such as school grants. Among the smaller school boards, the whole operation has been in the hands of the secretary-treasurer. Larger boards have required a coordinated effort of varying degrees of complexity. One of the major responsibilities of the local school inspector was, until recently, to offer information and assistance in the preparation of budgets. In many cases he might have to refer to points of law in order to indicate whether a proposed use of funds was permissible. Qualified accountants are now attached to departmental Regional Centres in order to provide this consultative service.

Each year's preparations have also commonly involved a building program. If properly designed, it has been phased to facilitate the issuing of debentures or otherwise raising capital funds. There are also problems of ensuring completion at the time of the accommodation is needed. Proposals for new buildings or for extensions of existing ones have had to satisfy quite exacting criteria established by the Department of Education.

The trustees' basic functions have been to appraise and approve the budget and the building program, and to agree on the amount of money to be raised by local taxation and by the issuing of debentures. Until 1969 the latter was, of course, contingent on the acquiescence of the local municipal council or councils and of the Ontario Municipal Board, except in the case of separate school boards. Since January 1, 1969, the divisional boards have been responsible for issuing their own debentures, and no longer need council approval. In discharging their responsibilities, trustees of less prosperous boards with a high degree of dependence on provincial grants often used to wonder how much discretionary power they really had, at least as far as operating expenditures were concerned, since there often seemed to be no alternative to a recommended course of action. Trustees of larger boards have tended to exercise power, not only in relation to the proportion of discretionary items in the budget, but also according to the degree of their knowledge and understanding of the programs presented to them by their appointed officials. A purely negative position is extremely difficult to assume and maintain. To a considerable degree, a trustee exercises power only if he can offer credible alternatives to the proposals made by officials.

Small school boards have often experienced considerable difficulty in discharging their budgetary responsibilites. An interesting vignette is offered by a memorandum sent to departmental inspectors by the Superintendent of Elementary Education in 1960. It announced that a study of the 1958 financial reports of the elementary school boards of the province had revealed that a number of school boards had ended the year with deficits on their current accounts of more than 10 per cent of their 1958 current operating costs. It was apparent that the 1959 figures would reveal a worsening situation. Each inspector was asked to study the financial reports of the boards in his inspectorate and, where it was evident that a particular board's position was deteriorating from year to year, he was asked to arrange a meeting and assist in the preparation of a budget that would reverse the trend and eliminate the deficit within a reasonable number of years. The seriousness of the problem was such that the inspectors were asked to give it priority over all but the most urgent matters.[3]

The traditional annual budget and building programs may have been adequate for the purpose of raising money, but they had a number of deficiencies. Some of these were pointed out by R.G. Ferguson in an article in *School Administration* in 1967.[4] His chief points may be summarized as follows. 1 / The annual budget was inadequate for operating budgetary control because it covered a calendar year, which included parts of two different academic years, whereas the logical basis for control was the academic year, which began in September. The annual budget was not intended to be more than a vehicle for raising operating funds from external sources. 2 / Forward planning for capital funds, generally carried out under the building program, was not sufficiently integrated with planning for operating funds, which constituted a possible source of some capital funds. 3 / Virtually no forward financial planning was carried out for operating funds beyond the period of one year. The future consequences of current decisions were not considered. 4 / There was inadequate attention to cash flow planning, which involves projecting the amounts of cash inflows and outflows for each month, week, and sometimes even day, in order to determine cash balances. Cash flow forecasting could be used by the school system to co-ordinate its payments and receipts in order to minimize the cost of short-term financing and to maximize the income from investment of excess funds.

Proposed improvements

To indicate faults is to imply remedies. Ferguson emphasized the value of long-term enrolment forecasts for planning of capital funds, building, and teacher recruitment. According to his suggested procedure, development of these forecasts should begin as soon as reliable September enrolment figures were available. By the end of the calendar year, a building program should be ready for review and approval in principle. With approval secured, the development of a detailed building program could be undertaken and financing requirements could be specified. Simultaneously with the process of enrolment forecasting, policy and program plans should be prepared. These would indicate the types of academic programs, the types of equipment and supplies, pupil-teacher ratios, and other such matters. Policies would be reviewed and settled early in the new year. The program for the following school year should then be established on the basis of approved policies. Cost estimates for running the program would constitute the preliminary operating budget. The annual budget to be submitted for board approval could then be prepared. Since it is based on the calendar year, the cost for the first eight months would be known from the operating budget settled the previous September. Most of the items that are subject to the discretions of the board in any particular year are those applying to the first four months of the school year; that is, to the last four months of its financial year. After board approval of the budget, the detailed planning for this four-month period could be undertaken. Enrolment forecasts could be re-estimated as the end of the school year approached. On this basis, the program could be reviewed and the cost estimates refined. The individual costs of the program could be summarized and approved.

Ferguson pressed the case for proper operating budgetary control to ensure that the objectives of the school system are achieved within budgetary limitations. The procedures involve breaking down the over-all operating budget, based on the calendar year, into budgets for each key official responsible for spending money. Actual spending is compared with the budgetary allocation each month. In cases of substantial divergence between the two figures, the official is called to account. The cause may be either irresponsible spending or erroneous planning of the program in the first place. One of the main advantages of the procedure is that control of operations is achieved with minimum effort on the part of senior administrators.

Increasingly sophisticated procedures are being advocated with respect to the evaluation of proposed programs. There is more insistence on comparisons with existing programs in terms of costs and results. Where budgetary decisions are to be made, these are more likely to be based on the consideration of alternative courses of action rather than on an affirmative or negative response to a proposal.

Special problems in 1969

Budgeting for the 1969 calendar year posed very difficult problems for the newly-elected trustees of county boards. Elections were held on December 2, 1968, and budget requisitions had to be ready for the following year by March 1, 1969. The accounting systems and business procedures of all the former boards merged into the new one had to be appraised and co-ordinated, with whatever assistance could be provided by the preliminary work done by the interim school organization committees. Strong pressure to improve accounting procedures was seen as a result of the boards' new responsibility for raising their own capital funds. Overshadowing the technical details was the responsibility of equalizing educational facilities within the larger area, which meant increasing contributions from the wealthier sections of each county area. Most school boards were not yet in the position to rely on modern data processing techniques to help them solve their problems. Making one fairly safe prediction about the consequences of the formation of the county boards, Webb wrote in his *School Administration* article:

Unquestionably, more full-time purchasing agents will be hired by the boards. More accountants may be added to administrative staffs. And budgeting, which might have been a somewhat hit-and-miss affair in some sections of the province, will undoubtedly command more professional attention.[5]

Proposals for discretionary powers within schools

Most principles of local budgeting seem to involve the introduction of business-like efficiency and the centralization of financial controls within the board structure. Frank MacKinnon enters a strong plea for discretionary powers on the part of the school staff.

The school boards and staffs which do the work should handle detailed policy and the actual spending of money. Our school would receive its allotment of funds on the basis of a formula with sufficient flexibility in its budget to permit it to do some things in its own way. There is no reason why its personnel cannot spend this money just as well as, and better than, government. There is every reason why school personnel should then be in a position to provide the library, pianos, instruments, communications equipment, films, and other things which its students, that is its customers, who are an important segment of the public, may show that they need. I believe that the main claim for increasing financial responsibility in the schools today is the need to permit the schools to respond readily to rapidly changing situations and to the opinions and needs of young people. These opinions and needs cannot be registered on government quickly enough, and governmental response to them must be ponderous. Relevance, therefore, must be determined and promoted in the school.[6]

Whatever their virtues, MacKinnon's proposals did not promise at the end of the 1960s to be the wave of the future.

ELEVEN

Federal financial assistance for provincial non-university programs

THE EARLY STAGES OF FEDERAL-PROVINCIAL CO-OPERATION

Financial assistance by the federal government for school construction or the operation of school programs was not an issue in the nineteenth century, even though education had for some time been regarded as a matter of fundamental national concern and worthy of national subsidy in other countries. However, as Phillips points out, keen competition for world markets at the beginning of the twentieth century began to arouse Canada to the need for subsidizing vocational training to improve the efficiency of production.[1] Through the *Agricultural Aid Act* of 1912 and the *Agricultural Instruction Act* of 1913, the federal government made available to the provinces sums of money amounting by 1924 to a total of $11,400,000. The *Technical Education Act* of 1919 provided $10 million over a period of ten years for any form of vocational or technical education of employees in industry and mechanical trades. Grants under this act had to be matched by provincial expenditures on vocational education. Since only Ontario had used its full allotment by 1929, an extension of time was provided. The operation of the *Vocational Education Act* of 1931, which promised a subsidy of $750,000 a year for fifteen years, was postponed by the depression of the 1930s.

These early federal activities conformed fairly well to the proposition that the federal interest was confined to such measures as would improve the economy or the economic welfare of individuals. In some cases, however, objectives like the promotion of good citizenship were included. It was clearly federal government policy to avoid direct entry into the field of education, but rather to influence certain developments in the provinces through financial incentives.

Through the *Unemployment and Agricultural Assistance Act* of 1937, the federal government made $1 million available for the whole of Canada for the training of unemployed young men and women registered with the Employment Service of Canada. Grants were made, not on the basis of population, but for acceptable projects proposed by the provinces, for which the latter would pay half the cost. Agreements under the act provided for federal assistance for such items as living allowances for trainees; travel expenses for trainees, instructors, and supervisors; salaries of supervisors, placement officers, vocational guidance officers, and instructors;

compensation for accidents; medical aid; equipment and supplies; printing and publicity; and rentals. The *Youth Training Act*, passed in 1939, provided $1.5 million in federal funds for a three-year period. Except for the fact that the provinces did not have to spend matching amounts, the grants were made under conditions similar to those specified by the *Unemployment and Agricultural Assistance Act*. Agreements were signed under this act to provide for training that would contribute to the successful prosecution of the war.

WARTIME MEASURES

From 1940 on, a war emergency training program was carried on, at federal expense, in technical schools, industrial firms, universities, and other convenient places, for men and women employed in, or seeking employment in, war industries. Federal funds covered the cost of salaries of instructors, living allowances and travel expenses of trainees, equipment, supplies, and other items. Approximately $24 million was spent in all provinces under the War Emergency Training Program.

The *Vocational Training Co-ordination Act* of 1942[2] had substantial financial implications. It was designed to prepare individuals for employment that would contribute to the efficient prosecution of the war, either in industry or in the armed forces; to provde assistance for veterans of the armed forces to prepare for employment after discharge; to provide training to fit the unemployed for gainful employment; and to fit individuals for employment contributing to the conservation or development of natural resources under federal control. It authorized the Minister of Labour to enter into agreements with the provinces to provide financial assistance for projects that would help to realize the objectives of the act, and for training projects being carried out under the *Youth Training Act* of 1939.

The *Vocational Training Co-ordination Act* provided for the appointment by the Governor-in-Council of a Vocational Training Advisory Council, to include equal representation from employers and employees, as well as representatives of other groups. According to the act, the Minister of Labour could refer to the council for consideration and advice such matters relating to the implementation of the act as he saw fit. As first constituted, the council consisted of sixteen members representing, not only the required groups, but technical education, women's organizations, agriculture, war veterans, and adult education as well.[3]

REHABILITATION OF VETERANS

Under re-establishment training agreements drawn up between the federal government and the provinces in 1945, the former paid the entire cost of training programs for men and women discharged from the services. The Department of Veterans Affairs also provided counselling and supervision. The special agreements ended in 1948, and training of veterans was continued under Schedule L of the regular vocational training program.

YOUTH PROGRAMS

In 1945 the federal government appropriated $500,000 for youth training to be allotted among the provinces during the fiscal year 1945–6.[4] Ontario received $75,000 of this amount. The federal share, which could not exceed that of the province, covered such items as salaries of full-time instructors for classes authorized under the agreement, and salaries of supervisors, school principals, and other staff whose services were needed for some aspect of training projects; travelling expenses; living allowances for trainees; the cost of board and lodging supplied to trainees in residences or boarding camps operated under the agreement; tuition fees at rates usually charged non-resident pupils by provincially or municipally controlled schools; and expenditures on a variety of types of equipment and facilities.

THE OPERATION OF VOCATIONAL PROGRAMS IN THE IMMEDIATE POST-WAR PERIOD

In 1946 an agreement was signed on behalf of their respective governments by the Acting Minister of Labour and the Ontario Minister of Education providing for financial assistance by the federal government for certain vocational programs. Specifically excluded were 1 / vocational courses in grade 9, unless at least 50 per cent of the time was spent on vocational and related subjects, and in all lower grades, 2 / vocational courses of "university grade," although not those offered at provincial technical institutes, and 3 / manual training. The federal government agreed to pay to the province 1 / an annual grant of $10,000; 2 / an annual grant equal to an amount expended by the province not exceeding the proportion of $1,910,000 equal to the proportion of the country's population between fifteen and nineteen years of age resident in the province at the time of the previous census (Ontario's share was $579,-000); and 3 / a grant for capital purposes over a three-year period between 1945 and 1948 up to the province's share of $10 million as determined by the calculation prescribed in 2 / above (amounting to a maximum of $3,031,500).[5]

Under the agreement, the province was to submit information on the projects for which it wanted federal subsidies, stating the nature and purpose of each project, the method by which it was to be carried out, and the details of expenditures involved. While the Minister of Labour could reject any particular project, he could not impose any amendments or alterations. The province was to maintain full records of all expenditures and commitments made under the agreement, keeping such records separate from the provincal account books, and making them available at the minister's request for full examination or audit.

CAPITAL EXPENDITURE

In 1951 an amendment to the Vocational Schools Assistance Agreement provided for federal assistance for capital projects involving the purchase, alteration, construction, and equipping of centres for the training of apprentices and other types of co-operative training financed jointly by the provincial and federal governments. The way was thus open for federal contributions to the construction of facilities for institutions such as the new Provincial Institute of Trades, just as they had been available for Ryerson Institute of Technology and the Lakehead Technical Institute.

TECHNICAL AND VOCATIONAL TRAINING IN THE 1950s

On April 14, 1950, a Vocational Training Agreement consolidated the various separate arrangements that had been made under the *Vocational Training Co-ordination Act* of 1942. The federal government was concerned with the following aspects of vocational training: Divison A – training of approved veterans according to Schedule L; Division B – training of the unemployed according to Schedule M; Division C – training of young people according to Schedule O; Division D – training of foremen and supervisors according to Schedule Q; Division E – training of service tradesmen according to Schedule K. For the time being, the agreement with Ontario related only to Divisions A, B, C, and E. For the first year in which the agreement was in force, the limits of the federal contribution were set at $14,000 in Division A, $60,000 in Division C, and $5,000 in Division E. The federal contribution was not to exceed the provincial contribution except in Division A, where the federal government assumed the entire cost. The agreement authorized the Minister of Labour, after consultation with the province, to appoint a regional director to supervise and co-ordinate training programs undertaken by the province under the terms of the agreement.

Provision was made in 1953 for the inclusion in Ontario's agreement with the federal government of Division D, involving training of supervisors and foremen as provided in Schedule Q. The federal government was to share equally with the province in meeting 1 / the costs of salaries and travelling expenses of instructors, supervisory personnel, and clerical staff, subject to all appointments, salaries, and terms of employment receiving the approval of the Dominion Director of Training, and 2 / the costs of approved printed matter and films used for instructional or publicity purposes. The province had to meet the costs of office space, office furniture and supplies, and telephone charges. Any payments by industries for participation in training sessions reduced the federal and provincial contributions by an equal amount.

Vocational and Technical Training Agreement No. 2, covering a five-year period after March 31, 1957, involved the setting aside by the federal government of $40 million for the entire country. Of this total, $25 million was allocated for capital expenditures, and the remainder, in annual allotments ranging from $2.5 million to $3.5 million, for maintenance of programs. Each province received an initial sum of $30,000, and the Northwest Territories and the Yukon $20,000 each. The rest, paid on the basis of equal sharing of costs with the provinces, was distributed in relation to each province's proportion of the population in the fifteen-to-nineteen year age group. The agreement specified minimum and maximum amounts to be spent for various items such as buildings and equipment, the operation of vocational or composite high schools, the maintenance of programs of advanced technical or trade and occupational training, and the training of teachers for trades and technical programs. Between 1957 and 1961 Ontario received over $7 million under this agreement.

VOCATIONAL CORRESPONDENCE COURSES

An agreement was signed on June 6, 1950, covering a five-year period, by which the federal government made available up to $125,000 for all provinces to assist in the preparation of vocational correspondence courses. As was true of other agreements, the federal share could not exceed that of the province. A course qualifying under the agreement had to be one recommended by the committee of provincial representatives on vocational correspondence courses and approved by the federal Minister of Labour. No specific share of the grant was allotted to any one province. Each province receiving financial assistance had to agree to make any of its vocational correspondence courses available to residents of any other province at the same price charged to its own residents.

APPRENTICESHIP TRAINING

Federal-provincial agreements with respect to apprenticeship training were made for the first time under the terms of an order-in-council approved in 1944.[6] Apprenticeship was recognized as being normally under the constitutional jurisdiction of the provinces. At that time, however, a number of provinces had no apprenticeship act, and others had acts applying only to a limited number of occupations. The order-in-council was designed to stimulate positive action to fill the gaps.

While the federal-provincial agreements specified the basic principles under which federal assistance was provided, the provinces were left with a good deal of discretion to determine the details in consultation with the trade unions and employers in various industries. Certain standards had to be met with respect to wages, length of apprenticeship, conditions under which an apprenticeship agreement could be cancelled, conditions under which an apprentice might transfer to another employer, the length of a probationary period, representation on apprenticeship committees, programs of instruction, inspection by provincial authorities, the administration of tests and examinations, the ratio of apprentices to journeymen in a given trade, and the minimum age for entry to apprenticeship. The federal government assumed the entire cost of training for ex-members of the armed forces whose apprenticeship had been approved by the Minister of Pensions and National Health, and half the cost for civilians.

THE TECHNICAL AND VOCATIONAL TRAINING ASSISTANCE ACT, 1960

The passage of the *Technical and Vocational Training Assistance Act*[7] on December 20, 1960, was a major landmark in the evolution of federal-provincial relations and in the development of technical and vocational education in the province. At this point the focus of interest is on financial provisions of the act. Other aspects are dealt with in various parts of the present series of volumes.

The act authorized the Minister of Labour to enter into an agreement with any province, for a period not exceeding six years, to provide for federal contributions toward the costs of provincial programs of technical and vocational training involving any of the following groups: the unemployed; students in technical or vocational courses given as part of the normal program in regular secondary schools; those preparing to carry out technical or vocational training programs as teachers, supervisors, and administrators; those past the regular school leaving age who had left school and required training to develop or increase occupational skill; apprentices; supervisors in industry; those acquiring skills in science or technology, except where university credit was involved; the disabled; those serving in the armed forces or in any other agency under the control of the federal government.

The federal government's contribution ranged from a maximum of 50 per cent of the cost of certain programs, provided that it was matched by provincial payments, to 100 per cent of those of purely federal concern. Most of the basic principles were similar to those behind previous legislation and agreements. The scope of the programs and the extent of assistance, however, were much enlarged. New ground was broken in terms of assistance for capital projects.

The act also provided for agreements for periods up to six years by which the federal government would maintain its financial support for training originating under the *Youth Training Act* of 1939 and continued under the *Vocational Training Co-ordination Act.* A further section of the act authorized the Minister of Labour to undertake and direct research in the area of technical and vocational training. Where he considered it appropriate, such research could be undertaken in co-operation with one or more of the provinces.

THE AGREEMENT WITH ONTARIO, 1961

Federal contributions to operating costs

An agreement under the terms of the act was signed by representatives of the federal and Ontario governments on June 26, 1961, by which the province, in consultation with the federal government, would "develop, organize and carry out training programs for the development of skilled manpower."[8] The provincial government agreed to establish an appropriate administrative organization under a qualified provincial official to co-ordinate the training programs provided under the agreement. This official might also be designated by the Minister of Labour, with the approval of the province, to act as regional director to provide liaison with the federal Director of Training for the purposes of the agreement. This arrangement indicates how completely the federal government was prepared to work through the provincial machinery. There was also provision for the provincial government to establish an advisory or consultative committee on the technical or vocational training of manpower, to include representation from employers, labour, the Department of Education, youth, the National Employment Service, the regional co-ordinator, and other federal or provincial departments or agencies.

The agreement with Ontario specified that, under Program 1 (the vocational high school training program), assistance would be given for those courses in which at least one-half of the school time was devoted to "technical, commercial and other vocational subjects or courses designed to prepare students for entry into employment by developing occupational qualifications." Courses providing students with an essential basis for further training after they left high school might also be included. The federal government's assistance for this program would amount to a maximum of $15 million for all provinces and territories up to March 31, 1967, with an annual contribution not exceeding $3 million. Ontario would, like other provinces, receive an initial allotment of $30,000, plus an amount, up to that contributed by the province, equal to its proportion of the Canadian population between fifteen and nineteen years of age residing within its borders. The province could use the subsidy, at its own discretion, either to meet actual provincial costs or for authorized provincial grants for operating costs of approved technical and vocational secondary school programs and courses. No part of the funds could, however, be used for capital expenditures.

Under Program 2 (the technician training program), training was to be provided at the post-secondary school level "to an agreed standard of qualification in the principles of science or technology and other fields with emphasis on the application thereof, except where such training is designed for university credit." The federal government agreed to pay 50 per cent of provincial costs of approved projects or programs. The same conditions of assistance applied to Program 3, for trade and other occupational training. This program was intended to offer pre-employment training, upgrading, or retraining for individuals over the age of compulsory school attendance who required increased occupational competence.

Program 4, a training program in co-operation with industry, was designed to provide training, retraining, and upgrading for industrial employees, including management. The federal government agreed to contribute 50 per cent of provincial costs of approved training programs. After February 1, 1964, it would pay 75 per cent of the provincial contribution to industry's expenditures for approved programs in these categories: 1 / basic training for skill development in such subjects as mathematics, science, and communcation skills, 2 / apprenticeship, and 3 / retraining of employees who would otherwise be displaced because of technological or other industrial changes.

Program 5, for training the unemployed, was designed to improve employment opportunities and to increase trade or occupational competence. Apart from training allowances, the federal government agreed to pay 75 per cent of approved provincial costs. It would contribute to training allowances as follows: 1 / basic allowance of $35 per week; 2 / 90 per cent of any supplementary allowances for dependents, amounting to a minimum of $20, $30, and $40 a week for one, two, and three or more dependents respectively, and 3 / 90 per cent of any supplementary allowance up to a maximum of $15 a week to compensate for the necessity of living away from home in order to take the course. In addition the federal government would pay 90 per cent of the provincial contribution to wages paid to those being trained under an approved training-in-industry project.

The federal contribution was 50 per cent of provincial costs for Program 6, designed for the technical-vocational training, retraining, or vocational assessment of any disabled person who, because of a continuing disability, required assistance to fit him for employment in a suitable occupation. The same rate applied to Program 7, which provided "training for occupationally competent persons in the art or science of teaching, supervising, or in the administration of technical or vocational training programs at all levels whether in industry, in vocational schools or in institutes." The federal government was to contribute 100 per cent of the cost of Program 8, designed for training provided by the province in skilled or semi-skilled or other occupations for members of the armed services or for those employed or to be employed by other federally administered agencies. The 50 per cent rate of assistance applied to Program 9, for assistance to university students and nurses-in-training according to provisions of the *Youth Training Act* of 1939, which were continued under the *Vocational Training Co-ordination Act.* The same rate of assistance applied to Program 10, which was intended to stimulate and encourage research projects relating to technical and vocational training and manpower requirements. The federal government was also to continue its support for the preparation, revision, printing, and servicing of provincial technical and vocational correspondence courses.

Federal contributions to capital costs

The federal government agreed to contribute to capital expenditure for approved training facilities for all programs covered by the agreement, as well as by the Apprenticeship Training Agreement. Capital expenditure was defined to include grants made by the provincial government to municipalities or other public bodies for such facilities. Federal contributions amounted to the sum of the following items: 1 / 50 per cent of the capital expenditure incurred by the province; 2 / 25 per cent of the same expenditure up to $480 per person in the fifteen-to-nineteen age group residing in Ontario as determined by the 1961 census; 3 / 25 per cent of expenditure incurred for the alteration of premises and the purchase of machinery for training and equipment under Program 5 after the additional payments under item 2 reached their limit. The provincial government was required to secure prior approval from the Minister of Labour for each project for which a request for a federal contibution was to be made. The minister could reject a proposal, but could not impose alterations or amendments. Excluded from federal assistance were the following items: 1 / purchase of land; 2 / costs of financing capital projects; 3 / property taxes; 4 / legal, advisory, or consulting fees and salaries, except architects' and engineering fees related to capital projects; 5 / general shops or facilities used for industrial arts classes; and 6 / costs resulting from damage to real or personal property or from loss of personal property.

Appraisal of the effects of the agreement

The Provincial Committee on Aims and Objectives of Education in the Schools of Ontario declared that the agreement of 1961 had resulted in a massive program of technical and commercial school building which had increased the accommodation in such schools from about 90,000 in 1961 to a total of approximately 230,000 at the time the report was made. It is not, of course, possible to say how much building would have occurred without federal assistance. The committee hazarded the opinion that "it had the desirable effect of making it possible to provide greater opportunities for students in an area in which the various provinces had not shown initiative prior to federal involvement."[9]

In its *Third Annual Review*, released in November 1966, the Economic Council of Canada gave no grounds for complacency, or even for satisfaction, with the adequacy of existing measures for manpower development. Despite the improvement in the employment situation after 1963, it felt the necessity of issuing a warning:

> Recent experience thus reinforces the need for the development of much more effective supporting policies – especially for improving productivity, strengthening competitiveness, facilitating adjustments to change, and increasing manpower training and mobility – if high employment is to be consistently achieved and maintained with other basic economic and social goals.[10]

THE ADULT OCCUPATIONAL TRAINING ACT, 1967

Terms of the act

When the six-year agreement made in 1961 expired in 1967, the new Department of Manpower and Immigration embarked on policies that differed substantially from those adhered to earlier. The *Adult Occupational Training Act*,[11] which received royal assent on May 8, 1967, involved the repeal of the *Technical and Vocational Training Assistance Act*. It was designed to provide assistance, directly or through provincial machinery, for occupational training, which was defined as "any form of instruction, other than instruction designed for university credit, the purpose of which is to provide a person with the skills required for an occupation or to increase his skill or proficiency therein." An occupational course was one involving not more than fifty-two weeks of full-time or 1,820 hours of part-time instruction.

The act defined an adult as a person at least one year older than the regular school leaving age in the province in which he resided. He was eligible for a training allowance under the act if he had been a member of the labour force without substantial interruption for at least three years or if he had one or more persons wholly or substantially dependent on him for support. Under the procedures outlined in the act, an adult who had not attended school on a regular basis for at least a year might request of a federally-appointed manpower officer the opportunity to undertake occupational training. The latter might arrange for any occupational training course that would, in his opinion, increase the applicant's earning capacity or opportunities for employment. The course could only be one operated by the province in which the applicant resided, or by a provincial or municipal authority in the province, unless there was no suitable course being offered at or near his place of residence. In making his decision, the manpower officer was to take into account any reports received from a joint committee established by the Minister of Manpower and Immigration and the provincial government to assess manpower needs in the province.

Provision was made for the Minister of Manpower and Immigration to enter into a contract with any province to provide for federal payment of costs incurred by the latter or by a provincial or municipal authority for the operation of an occupational training course, or for a training course for apprentices, where enrolment was arranged by a manpower officer. Payment of tuition or other charges might also be made to institutions not operated by provincial or municipal authorities, provided that the course offered had the approval of the province.

The federal authorities might make contracts with employers to operate occupational training courses. These were not to cover training on the job or in skills useful only to the employer unless such training was necessary because of technological or economic changes affecting the latter that would otherwise result in loss of employment by the trainee. Agreements might also cover compensation to the employer for costs incurred in providing training for his employees in courses offered by outside agencies. Again, provincial sensibilities received consideration through the provision that the courses offered inside or outside the industrial firm in question had to have the approval of provincial authorities.

For adult trainees approved under the program, the federal government was to pay a training allowance of between $35 and $90 a week, the exact amount for each individual determined by regulation, up to June 30, 1968. There were arrangements for subsequent increases in accordance with changes in the average hourly earnings in industry. Payments might also be made to employers offering the training up to 1 / the average amount of earnings of a regular employee for the same number of hours as the training covered, or 2 / the maximum training allowance paid to the individual, whichever was less.

Federal authorities were authorized by the act to enter into agreements with the provinces to contribute toward capital expenditures by the latter for occupational training facilities. The sum contributed under such an agreement could not exceed either 1 / 75 per cent of the capital expenditures incurred by the province on occupational training facilities after March 31, 1967, or 2 / $480 for every member of the youth population of the province in 1961 minus the total federal contributions to capital expenditures under the *Technical and Vocational Training Assistance Act*, whichever was less. In addition, after funds available under the above conditions had all been paid, the federal government might agree to pay 1 / 50 per cent of capital expenditures or 2 / $320 for every member of the youth population of the province in 1961 minus the total federal contributions to capital expenditure under the *Technical and Vocational Training Assistance Act*, whichever was less. As before, the youth population of the province meant the number of young people between fifteen and nineteen years of age.

Implementation of the act

Under the agreements with the provinces made in accordance with the act, the federal government emphasized its intention of referring to training in suitable provincial or municipal courses all adults who wished to take occupational training and who had a good chance of having their lifetime earnings substantially increased as a result. They might be referred to occupational training courses in vocational high schools, trade schools, institutes of technology, or non-credit courses in universities. Although no full-time course could be more than one year in length, an adult might first take a course of up to one year in basic training for skill development, and another of up to a year in a skill.

The federal government assured the provinces that it would not abandon the program without notice, and thus force them in effect to pay the full cost. It guaranteed that any future reduction in its contributions would be limited to a maximum of 10 per cent a year.

The act represented a greater degree of direct federal intervention than had been possible under earlier acts and agreements. The attitude of the federal government was apparently that it would still work through provincial institutions and facilities wherever possible, but that it would no longer leave the welfare of those requiring retraining so completely to provincial initiative. One of the effects of the *Technical and Vocational Training Assistance Act* had been that the provinces, such as Ontario, which had been most capable of providing help for residents who needed it, also received the most federal assistance. It was hoped that the new act would succeed in providing a better balance throughout the country.

CONCLUDING STATEMENT

The purpose of this chapter has been to indicate the financial involvement of the federal government in various educational and training programs of concern to the province. While the purpose and nature of these programs has necessarily been touched on, they are more fully explored in volume IV, chapter 19 under the heading "Adult Training and Retraining." Federal financial assistance to universities and, in recent years, to other institutions of post-secondary education is discussed in chapter 12 on university finance. Federal financial responsibility for educational programs entirely within its own areas of responsibility has also been excluded from the present chapter.

TWELVE

University finance

INTRODUCTION

It was shown in volume I how the universities of Ontario have grown in the period since the Second World War from a handful of institutions making insignificant demands on government revenue to a substantial group of enterprises with budgets requiring a major public effort to meet. In the present chapter attention is given to the development of a need for heavy reliance on government assistance, to the form in which such assistance has been given, and to the implication of the consequent relationship for the universities, the provincial government, and the supporting public.

PROVINCIAL GOVERNMENT ASSISTANCE FOR OPERATING COSTS

Early history

Government grants to universities in Ontario have a long history; in a sense they antedate the existence of the universities themselves. The Royal Land Grant of 1797, which was intended to assist in the establishment of a series of district grammar schools, was also supposed to provide for a provincial university. While the authorization thus given was for the setting aside of half a million acres for schools and university, the ultimate amount was approximately 548,000 acres. Although King's College received its charter in 1827, it did not get its share of rather less than half that total until 1828. When it began operations some years later, the income from this grant, along with other private sources of revenue such as tuition fees, was sufficient to enable it to meet its needs.

Other institutions received support from small legislative grants. In 1867 these included Queen's, Victoria, Trinity, Ottawa, Regiopolis, and St Michael's. Toronto was not included, apparently because of its land endowment, which the others would gladly have shared. Harris describes their grants as consolation prizes or as sops to the legislative conscience.[1] It is curious to observe that the Legislature, in support of the principle that denominational institutions must assume full responsibility for their own maintenance, could not bring itself to provide them with land grants, but yet could justify giving them public funds, however meagre. But the anomaly was removed when, as the *Globe*, with its Free Church editor and voluntaryist policy, was pleased to announce on December 2, 1867, all the grants to the colleges were to be terminated as of July 1, 1868.[2]

The government's policy until nearly the end of the century was one of unadulterated non-sectarianism. It supported only what became known as the Ontario Agricultural College and the School of Practical Science, which it established and controlled.[3] During that interval continued pressure was exerted by the colleges and universities for a reversal of this policy, but to no avail. Principal Grant of Queen's was a particularly strong advocate of the alternative position. In 1893 he succeeded in working out a compromise whereby Queen's received a grant of $6,000 for the School of Mining and Agriculture established in Kingston the previous year. It was in accordance with the same policy that a grant was made to Queen's in 1909 for the Faculty of Education, which it established at the government's request. Similarly, the denominational University of Ottawa received assistance in 1947 in establishing its Faculty of Medicine.

During the period of financial drought, even the provincial University of Toronto received no direct grants, although it seemed to have a strong case in that its acceptance of the federation plan involved the assumption of substantial costs for the expansion of its operations. In 1901, however, a small measure of financial support was introduced; after 1907 it could be described as substantial.[4] Annual maintenance grants were paid to Queen's beginning in 1907–8 and to the University of Western Ontario beginning in 1910–11. By the early 1940s the total of the annual grants to these three institutions was in the neighbourhood of $3 million.

Thus were the precedents for government assistance to non-denominational universities established. The amounts were small, and determined on an entirely arbitrary basis. The subsequent story revolves around two main points: 1 / the transformation of such grants to the point where they became the major source of university revenue and 2 / the devising of rational and equitable bases for their award. The government's position toward the support of denominational institutions has remained substantially the same throughout the period.

Factors in changing government attitude

The present-day attitude toward government responsibility for financing higher education is mainly a phenomenon of post-war growth. It represents not the emergence of any new concept, but rather the intensification of ideas of long standing to the point where they have transformed the entire character of the enterprise. The first of these ideas is that of equity; in fairness to the talented individual, the opportunities and privileges of higher education should be unrestricted by financial obstacles. This proposition has not, of course, been carried to its ultimate conclusion. Three further stages may be differentiated: 1 / removal of, or compensation for, all fees; 2 / provision for living costs contingent upon attendance; and, what is by far the most expensive item, 3 / compensation for lost income during the period of educational preparation. To mention these potential steps is not, of course, to express the opinion that they should be implemented. It may be suggested at this point that a society that bestows privileges of his order on a category of its members is almost certain to demand a much greater degree of specific recompense than Canada, or any other Western nation, has yet seen fit to exact of its students.

The second major influence transforming the degree of responsibility for financing higher education accepted by post-war governments has been the conviction that the resultant economic, and to a lesser extent social, benefits demand such an investment. This familiar point has been reviewed in volume I. It was given authoritative support when the Economic Council of Canada defined the return on such investment at between 14 and 17 per cent per annum. During the period in question, we have heard less and less of the truism that any young person with the requisite intellectual capacities and sufficient determination could get a university education. Governments have reflected the growing conviction that if a person, because of an immature lack of determination, or an understandable ignorance of the consequences of failing to overcome forbidding financial obstacles, does not reach the highest possible levels of educational attainment, the whole community, and not he alone, must bear the unfavourable consequences. Measures for the direct assistance of students are discussed in volume IV. By far the most expensive aspect of the problem has been the provision of the educational facilities themselves.

The impact of the Berlin airlift and the Korean War was very strong during the 1950s. A report of the Industrial Foundation on Education in 1957[5] asserted that immediate action was required to make a maximum contribution to a united effort on the part of the free world to meet the threat to our freedom and to compete successfully in foreign markets. The keynote was contained in the recommendation that an immediate effort be made to achieve the following purposes:

1. Determine more definitely the aims and objectives of our society as a basis of forecasting the performance required of our educational system. This should involve a policy statement of the attitude of our society as a whole towards the present Communist challenge as well as the economic challenge to Canada inherent in the rapid development of other industrial nations.
2. Based upon these policy statements and objectives, measure the number and kind of university trained personnel required to enable us to remain progressive and to make the most effective contribution towards the defence of freedom.

It is not certain to what extent these sentiments, expressed by S.H. Deeks, the Executive-Director of the foundation, represented the views of the hard-headed business men he was reputed to represent. A number of influential voices were raised, however, to offer the hope that our educational system could pursue some more worthy objectives than simply that of beating the Russians.

The developing crisis in the 1950s

In observing in his annual report that a number of powerful agencies had addressed themselves to the problem of financing higher education, C.T. Bissell, then President of Carleton University, expressed the view that only a respectable start had been made. He wrote, "The problem before Canadian universities is of such gargantuan dimensions that it will take the combined resources and ingenuity of government, business, and individuals to solve it."[6] He mentioned that at the conference of the previous November he had presented a statistical analysis of the capital needs of Canadian universities during the period 1955–65. He had estimated that they would need approximately $285 million to carry out essential projects. After an additional year of experience with Carleton's problems, he was now convinced that the original estimate should be doubled. The estimate of Carleton's own needs had risen from $5 million to $11 million.

While details of government grants to universities have been largely confined to volume I, it is appropriate to mention a few figures from Dana Porter's 1957 budget in order to show how far Bissell's estimates were removed from current practice. During the previous five years, grants for new buildings and facilities had amounted to $17.6 million, and a further $9.7 million was to be added, making a total of $27.3 million for the six-year period. An additional $1 million also being provided for the Faculty of Dentistry at the University of Toronto. For the succeeding year, operating grants would reach $9.4 million.[7]

The Industrial Foundation on Education performed a valuable service by analysing the various possible sources of income open to the universities during the late 1950s. The report already mentioned noted the shifting of great private fortunes to the public coffers through taxation, thus diverting large amounts that would otherwise have gone into the endowment funds of the universities. Canadian university income from this source had increased in absolute terms; between 1920–1 and 1955–6, it had risen from $1.5 million to $3.5 million. But the failure of endowment funds to keep pace with the increase in university operating costs over this period was shown by the fact that they had met 16.5 per cent of operating costs in the earlier year and less than 6 per cent in the later.[8] This decline was mentioned more as an irremediable fact than as a basis for any positive action.

Assumption of provincial responsibility in the early 1960s

The year 1960–1 constituted a kind of watershed in the provision of funds to finance the universities. At that time, their sources of revenue were as follows: students' fees, 29 per cent; provincial government, 28 per cent; federal government, 16 per cent; assisted research funds, 14 per cent; gifts and grants, 3 per cent; endowment income, 3 per cent; miscellaneous, 7 per cent. From that time on, funds from provincial sources tended to become more dominant, and the problem of working out an acceptable relationship with the provincial government became paramount.

The procedure for determining the amount of the grant to particular universities was highly informal. In effect, each university had to make its own special plea for the funds it needed or thought it would like to have. The method by which the government sought expert advice is discussed in volume IV, chapter 2, where an account is given to the origins and evolution of the Advisory Committee on University Affairs, later called more simply the Committee on University Affairs. The procedure was indisputably wide open to abuse. Whether there was such abuse would be difficult to establish, but there were certain to be suspicions. Officials in Carleton University were apparently not sure whether their particular problems were solely a result of the difficulty of raising needed private funds in a city largely occupied by impecunious civil servants, with a conspicuous absence of industry, or whether the institution bore the consequences of its reputed Liberal orientation. After the system had been changed, President Dunton wrote in his annual report for 1966–7: "Until this year Provincial grants have been decided on some unknown basis in what appeared to be a rather arbitrary way, and Carleton had felt strongly for several years that it was not receiving a fair share in relation to other universities, to the work it was carrying on and to the rate of its growth."[9] On the whole, the system worked in such a way as to constitute a reasonable tribute to the probity of the government of the day. But as the amount of funds involved continued to multiply, a more satisfactory method of distribution was obviously needed.

Pleas for the systematization of university grants

The University of Toronto President's report for 1960 contained some suggestions. What was needed was a scheme of grants made according to formulas that would ensure an equitable and flexible distribution, and that would give the universities the security they needed for intelligent planning. Such formulas were not to be found in a per capita grant, but rather in a scale of student costs. It was pointed out that the cost of teaching a student in an engineering course or an honour arts and science course was almost twice that for a student in a general course, and that the cost for a student working for a PhD or a degree in medicine or dentistry was even greater. In addition to a recognition of these financial levels in a system of grants, there would have to be special consideration given to new institutions with small student bodies but heavy initial cost.[10]

The Ontario Council of University Faculty Associations made a very effective case for the systematization of university grants in a brief to the Prime Minister in 1963.[11] It pointed out the closeness of the financial relationship between the government and the universities. Because the former was paying not only more, but an increasing proportion of the total cost of operating and developing the universities, the provincial grant had become the major determinant of the development of each university. It had thus become a matter of critical importance that the method of distributing grants be an equitable one that would produce the right kind of higher education "without generating resentments, difficulties and inefficiencies."

The council was convinced that the government should treat the universities in somewhat the same way that it did the secondary schools, by drafting a more exact and comprehensive statement on the way in which grants were allocated. It criticized past practice:

> There has never been any announcement of the factors which determine the relative size of grants, what areas of academic effort are given the highest value, or whether there is any fixed relationship between such considerations as enrolment, faculties, and functions, on the one hand, and capital and maintenance grants on the other. The statistical tables in this report disclose no clear pattern, nor does any analysis of the grants made over a period of years. In any given fiscal year, institutions in apparently comparable circumstances seem to receive quite different treatment, and individual institutions seem to receive different treatment in different years.

The council urged the establishment of a policy, based on consultation with university spokesmen, that would guarantee both capital and maintenance grants for a reasonable period of time. Such a policy should be stated publicly and be subjected to discussion. Once established, it would enable the universities to engage in activities with long-term implications such as planning new facilities, organizing new projects, building up research potential, and recruiting the right kind of staff. Without some reasonable assurance about their future financial position, universities could not undertake reasonable long-range planning.

As Bissell had done in his 1960 report, the council emphasized the differences in the cost of educating different categories of university students. Up to that point, it seemed that the only recognition of such differences had been in terms of special grants for graduate students, and even these appeared to be of an emergency nature, possibly to be discontinued as soon as the urgent need for university teachers had been met.[12] The council mentioned four factors that should be taken into account in a grant formula: "(1) the basic cost of education per student,

(2) the difference in costs between different kinds of university education, (3) the special costs of expansion, and (4) the cost of such special aspects of university work as research and other vital and traditional university activities which cannot be easily allocated on a per student basis." The words after "research" in the fourth point certainly pose difficult problems for anyone attempting to produce the desired formula. The council suggested that it would be undesirable to tie all grants to specific purposes, since such a procedure would involve the government to an unacceptable degree in the internal academic policies of the universities. The formula should provide for a general unconditional grant related to the number and kind of students, which would be supplemented by specific grants for a limited number of special courses or facilities which the government wished to encourage for some particular reason.

The council had some definite views about the appropriate method of administering university grants. It recommended the university grants committees as they functioned in the United Kingdom and Australia. Such committees were composed of people with long and successful experience in university work, usually as teachers and as administrators. They were commissioned to deal directly with the various universities, to receive their budget submissions, to examine them as part of a national university pattern, and then to arrive at an assessment of the total higher education requirements for an ensuing period of at least three years. On the basis of their assessment, the committees dealt directly with their respective governments. Three advantages were seen in this system: 1 / it ensured that the necessary decisions were made by knowledgeable people; 2 / it guaranteed freedom from direct governmental interference; and 3 / it made it publicly clear that such guarantees had been given.

The council stepped on controversial ground when it asserted that, without such an independent body, the decisions about the allocation of funds, which would necessarily be made by the government, would inevitably be suspect. A reasonable alternative actually being pursued by the present government is to devise, with the co-operation of the universities, and with necessary expert advice, a formula that so effectively covers all eventualities that there is minimum room left for arbitrary decisions. This approach has the advantage that it eliminates the possibility that the independent commission itself might be subject to bias, a not inconceivable eventuality. On the other hand, a truly comprehensive and all-inclusive formula may develop rigidities that could act as obstacles to innovation and progress. Whether an independent commission or the government would be in the better position to counteract such rigidities is an open question.

Bascom St John expressed strong approval of the council's brief. He was particularly pleased with its recommendation that a university grants committee be established, since he had been advocating such an intermediary for some years. He deplored the lack of university support for the proposal up to this time.

The Council of Faculty Associations is absolutely right when it insists that universities ought to be autonomous. It is wrong for the political authority to make direct grants to universities, picking and choosing, adding and subtracting, without explanation and without making all the facts known ...

The existing Advisory Committee on University Affairs has wholly failed to do the job required of it, and might well be courteously retired. To take its place, there ought to be a small body of highly qualified citizens, completely divorced from politics, past or present. It ought also to have a strong staff to do independent research on university needs.

A proper university grants committee ought to be separate from the universities too, and be able to judge from an impartial viewpoint whether university plans were adequate or too grandiose. It ought also to be able to take into account the possible private donations to university support which have been traditional in this country.

It ought to make independent reports on all aspects of post-secondary education, and on the specific amounts of money that would be needed, year by year, for the maintenance and extension of this vital social need. We who pay the bills ought to know whether our governments are falling short of their duty.[13]

With reference to the last sentence, one might ask whether it is reasonable to expect governments to set up agencies with the specific task of determining how well they are spending the taxpayers' money. The opposition in the Legislature might also legitimately claim this functon. The question of which agency or agencies should conduct research into university problems and needs has been a difficult one to settle under existing arrangements.

Some of the recommendations of the Robbins Report in England (1963) may be noted in this connection. It advocated, as a linear successor to the University Grants Committee, a grants commission with oversight over the entire body of autonomous institutions, including the universities, their associated schools of education, and the schools of advanced technology. The commission's duty would be to advise the government on the size of grants, to distribute the money, and to assess the correct allocations to the different institutions concerned. A new ministry called the Ministry of Arts and Science would be responsible for this and other intermediaries. The functions of the Minister of Education would remain separate. These recommendations had considerable influence on subsequent developments in Britain.[14]

St John elaborated in a later column on some of the questions needing research. There had, for example, been a number of communities in

Ontario where a sudden and vigorous interest had developed over the prospect of a new university. Local enthusiasm had been almost entirely emotional. Some of the reasons why the new institutions were being promoted required a searching look. Among the problems that had been investigated by the British University Grants Committee were 1 / the cost of providing a new university place, both in existing and in new institutions; 2 / the amounts needed for different faculties; 3 / the average unit cost for student residences; 4 / the cost of university research; 5 / the cost of introducing new types of courses. St John saw research being done into such problems either by an independent grants commission or by the newly-announced Department of University Affairs.[15]

The Ontario Council of University Faculty Associations revealed its naïvety in its observation that the University Grants Committee "makes a formal assessment, based on its own peculiar competence to do so, and then submits to the government a formal recommendation on a total budget. The government may, of course, in extraordinary circumstances, refuse to accept this total budget, but it must justify its refusal before the legislature and before public opinion." To the present writer, such an assessment of the situation appears to be downright unrealistic. It seems almost inevitable that the government would determine the total to be allotted to universities in any given year on the basis of broad policies, and that the onus would be on the commission to justify its estimate of the universities' total needs, rather than the other way around. Furthermore, it seems most unlikely that the public would tend to side with the grants commission if the amount the government were prepared to make available fell substantially short of its estimate of need. The public reaction to very large increases in annual expenditures is usually one of scepticism. Even those who are convinced of the necessity of a major expansion of provisions for higher education are inclined to wonder if substantial economics could not be effected without serious damage to the program.

On the other side of the argument, it may be pointed out that opposition members in the Legislature have often believed there was political capital to be gained in criticizing the government for failing to grant the full amount that the universities claimed would meet their "minimum" needs. A.E. Thompson, Liberal leader at the time, claimed that the $63 million budgeted for operating and special grants in 1965–6 was at least 15 per cent short of what the universities had expressed an absolute need for. He quoted a number of presidents as expressing dissatisfaction that they had not received more, and drew unfavourable comparisons between the operating grants and the $100 million being invested in buildings and facilities, which he referred to contemptuously as "bricks and mortar." He implied that there were classrooms standing empty for lack of funds to employ the faculty to use them. On this point, Robarts drew him up with a request for proof, which he made no move to provide.[16]

Some of the complexities of interpretation were evident in Davis's answer to Thompson a few days later.

The hon. leader of the Opposition, Mr. Chairman, suggests that the universities have been cut back 15 per cent. This, Mr. Chairman, is inaccurate. In fact, the universities received 91 – I am using total figures – 91 per cent, perhaps a shade more, of the totals that they requested, not the demonstrated need.[17]

What the universities asked for and what the government thought they needed were thus clearly distinguished.

A similar situation occurred in 1968, when the following exchange was recorded in the Legislature.

Mr. MacDonald: The Minister described it as minimal and the reduction was, as I understand it, from $340 million requested by the presidents to $220 million – that strikes me as being a bit more minimal.

Hon. Mr. Davis: Well, Mr. Chairman, as I recall it, the amount that the university affairs committee recommended to the government, which was discussed by the government and returned to the university affairs committee – and I think I am right in this – that the request for a reduction was in the neighbourhood of $4.5 million in the total budget – $4.5 million – and I think this, in the total context, is a minimum reduction in budget. $4.5 million that was the total reduction [*sic*].

You cannot compare, Mr. Chairman, what the university presidents in total are asking for with the initial recommendation of the committee on university affairs. They made a recommendation to the government and this amount was reduced by $4.5 million.[18]

A university president may be ever so competent, moderate, and responsible, combining a profound loyalty to his own institution with a sympathetic understanding of the needs and interests of the broader community, in the best traditions of Canadian university administration. But to ask him to assume the role that was expected of him in Ontario in the early 1960s was to put him in a position where his case for funds simply could not be accepted at face value. What president, for example, could opt to wait for new buildings and faculty until the needs of a neighbouring institution, appraised as more urgent according to someone's subjective criterion, had been met? What president of a great and prestigious institution could view complacently the prospect of restraints on its drive for excellence? What president could look with equanimity on the possibility that students might have to be turned away? Dare one also ask what president could steel himself to ask his faculty to subject some of their endearing but possibly wasteful practices to critical examinations for the ultimate benefit of the public treasury?

Donald MacDonald, in urging the use of a formula as a means of ensuring the independence of the universities, quoted Principal Corry of Queen's University on this point.

University presidents are not as different from other men as they sometimes encourage people to think. This, by the way, is a strictly impartial judgment I made of them long before I became one ...

In the kind of situation I am speaking of they face a standing temptation to indulge their worst instincts. More than that, their staffs will abet and push them to do so. Even if they resist the grosser temptations, there will always be scores of things that will be worth doing if resources could be found. I know of several projects that are very good, and I am aching to try. The Queen's staff has many such that I have not even heard of yet.

Am I to reject the possibility of mounting a number of these and disappoint the staff or am I to try it on? If there is money to be had why don't we get our share of it if we can?[19]

Macdonald went on with Corry's arguments to show how the situation could develop if adequate solutions were not found. If a university accumulated a deficit, the government would be forced, in the discharge of its legal responsibilities, to ask how such a deficit had been accumulated. That step would involve it directly in university administration, which neither it nor the universities wanted. If it was unprepared to meet the total demands of all universities combined, either because it judged the amount beyond the capacity of the economy to meet, or because it thought the estimates of need were inflated, it could hardly reduce each university's request by a uniform amount. To protect the taxpayer, and to be fair to all suppliants, the details of each budget would have to be examined. The government would be forced into the position of having to decide which specific program to support. Furthermore, since universities would inevitably find that they received less than they thought they needed, they would be driven to lobbying in search of better terms. It was wrong that government should be harassed by such importunities. This development would not occur immediately, but would happen bit by bit as the circumstances required one inescapable decision after another. Against its will, the government would be driven by the insidious logic of the situation.

The crucial problem of the time was to devise, by the creation of an intermediate structure, a means of appraising the needs of each university in relation to all the others, and of distributing the available funds in an objective and defensible manner. The provincial government could not afford to weaken its prerogative of determining the total amount of money it was prepared to allot to the universities as compared with competing interests. While there was also an underlying obligation to the community to ensure that government money was not spent on frivolous or unproductive purposes, the government took the view, for the time being at least, that the best results would be obtained if the university authorities were largely left to decide on the internal distribution of funds. The policy could not be one of complete non-intervention, since in some areas, such as the health sciences, it was necessary to provide special incentives to ensure that urgent social needs were met. What was particularly to be avoided was a detailed specification of the objectives that were to be pursued, and the methods and procedures to be used.

The minister's comments about university grants in February 1965 made it quite evident that the development of an appropriate formula was accepted government policy. Davis pointed out, however, that the problem was a very complicated one. The task of administering the grants would be very simple if the universities needed only to calculate the number of students in each faculty and apply for a fixed amount of money for each student, but a much more difficult calculation was needed. The government was moving in the right direction, with a number of very competent people working on the problem. But time would be needed for its solution.

The report on university government in Canada by Duff and Berdahl had some comments on the subject of grants. It was suggested that the establishment and periodic re-evaluation of grant formulas should be undertaken by the provincial advisory committees so that the latter "would always retain certain discretionary powers." Given the function of advisory committees, it might have been more appropriate to refer to influence rather than power. In any case, the commissioners urged academics who were concerned about the maintenance of university autonomy to strive for an advisory committee with members of high quality, and to co-operate with it in producing a master plan that would reflect university values.[20]

The commissioners referred to the five-year grants that seemed to operate successfully in Britain. While these were considered impractical for Canada in view of the rapidity with which changes were occurring, they urged that serious consideration be given to three-year, or at least two-year, grants. They saw no reason why capital grants at least could not be planned this far ahead. Under such a scheme, universities could work out their budgets more slowly and carefully, with more flexibility for planning ahead. The result would be an improvement in the quality of internal university government. The commissioners may not have known what a radical departure from Canadian provincial practice it would be to abandon the principle of annual appropriations, although something of the kind soon proved possible with the fixing of the basic income unit.

An account of some the background work that went into the development of a formula is provided in *From the Sixties to the Seventies*, an important report prepared by the Presidents' Research Committee.[21] From the time of its reconstitution in 1963, this committee had been urged by R.W.B. Jackson to work out a formula as the only alternative to the gradual imposition of complete and rigorous government control. He is said to have called the existing situation a "morass of indecision and misunderstanding." Members of the Advisory Committee on University Affairs discussed the topic with university delegations in December 1963. Principal Corry's address at Dalhousie University, which has already been referred to, generated intense interest in the question. The Research Committee devoted considerable attention to the topic at its meeting in January 1964 and commissioned a study and a working paper for the presidents in March of the same year. Subsequent action involved the preparation of a proposal by the combined efforts of B. Trotter of Queen's, T.L. Batke of the University of Waterloo, R.B. Willis of Western, C.C. Gotlieb of Toronto, and H.G. Conn of Queen's. An interim report was ready for the Committee of Presidents in June 1965.

The development of an operating grants formula

In the meantime D.T. Wright of the Committee on University Affairs had been named chairman of one of that body's sub-committees to work on the same problem. The two groups combined their efforts to produce a proposal for an operating grants formula that would be acceptable to the government and the universities. They submitted a report to the Committee of Presidents, which approved it in principle, and to the Committee on University Affairs, which recommended it for adoption and for use in determining operating grants for 1967–8. The joint subcommittee continued developmental work, including the improvement of definitions and interpretations, the consideration of amendments, and a study of the problem of extra-formula support for newer institutions.[22]

The formula and its initial application

An operating formula was finally put in effect in 1967. Some of the possible courses of action considered during the preliminary work are described in the *Report of the Committee on University Affairs for 1967*. At one extreme, it might have been possible to establish faculty-student ratios, ratios of non-academic to academic staffs, average "approved" salaries, average teaching loads, class sizes, the number of research students per professor, and other such factors. These could have been varied from one faculty to another according to need. Comparable norms could have been developed for administrative functions. An approved total level of expenditure could thus have been structured as a necessary function of the defined factors. The result would have been an entirely unfamiliar type of strait-jacket for the universities. As the report indicated,

> Provincial grants have not, in general, been earmarked in the past, nor has there been any effort to establish line-by-line budget control. It would certainly not have been consistent with the sincere espousals of support from all quarters for effective university autonomy in Ontario to develop a new approach to financing which itself would be the agent for the erosion of autonomy.[23]

The formula that was actually devised was much simpler and, in a sense, consistent with the approach advocated earlier by the Ontario Council of University Faculty Associations. The factors taken into account were 1 / enrolments in various categories, 2 / weighting numbers reflecting average costs, faculty by faculty, and 3 / a dollar multiplier, or unit value which, once fixed, would determine all grants and expenditures. Formula income covered all maintenance costs, the purchase of books for libraries, the purchase of all equipment except that required for the initial equipping of buildings, and all ordinary costs of operation. An aspect of major importance was that, although grants were based on average costs of performing various functions, the universities could actually apportion the funds to faculties and departments in any way they chose.

The unit value for 1967–8 was set at $1,320, which represented the grant for one student in each of the following categories: general arts, general science, pre-medicine, pre-business administration, pre-commerce, journalism, secretarial science, social work, first year honours arts and science, technology (at Lakehead University), and undergraduate diploma courses. The unit value was multiplied by various weights for more expensive courses and programs. Category 2, with a weight of 1.5, included upper years honours arts, commerce, physical education, law, library science, fine and applied arts, physical and occupational therapy, medical internship and residence, and art as applied to medicine. Category 3, with a weight of 2, included the upper years of honours science, the upper years of honours psychology, geography, and mathematics, nursing, engineering, food and household science, pharmacy, architecture, forestry, agriculture, hygiene and public health, degree and diploma courses in music, dental hygiene, and public health nursing. Category 4, with a weight of 3, included medicine, dentistry, and veterinary medicine. Category 5, with a weight of 2, included master's level work and first-year PhD work direct from the bachelor's degree in commerce and business administration, social work, hospital administration, public administration, and journalism. Category 6, with a weight of 3, included work at the same level as in category 5 in the humanities, the social sciences, mathematics, law, fine and applied arts, library science, physical and health education, and physical and occupational therapy, as well as MPhil work and all other graduate courses. Category 7, with a weight of 4, included work at the same level as in categories 5 and 6 in psychology, geography, engineering, science, medicine, agriculture, architecture, forestry, food and household science, hygiene and public health, music, nursing, pharmacy, child study, dentistry, veterinary medicine, and urban and regional planning. Category 8, with a weight of 6, included PhD work except the first year direct from the bachelor's degree. Part-time undergraduate students were given one-sixth the weight of full-time students working toward the same degree. Part-time graduate students doing course work were given one-fifth the weight of the full-time equivalent in the same category, while those doing dissertations under supervision were given a weight of 1. Preliminary year students were given a weight of .7. There were special arrangements for weighting attendance in trimester courses.

One of the initial problems was caused by a decision to count graduate enrolment on a semester-by-semester basis as a matter of administrative convenience. It was discovered, however, that this practice significantly reduced the income produced by graduate students under the formula. Further study by the Ontario Council on Graduate Studies and the Subcommittee on Operating Grants led to recommendations for procedural revisions. Additional measures were also required to ensure that enrolment figures were accurately calculated and classified. The Committee of Presidents adopted a resolution favouring the institution for each university of an audit of enrolment certified by an independent auditor.[24]

For the most part, the formula weights worked reasonably well in practice. Adjustments were made, however, in 1969–70 to give medical internship and residence a weight of 2.5 rather than 1.5; medicine, dentistry, and veterinary medicine a weight of 5 instead of 3; and part-time graduate course work a weight of one-third that of the full-time equivalent. A problem was posed by the implementation of the recommendations of the Macpherson report at the University of Toronto, which had the effect of blurring the former distinction between general and honours courses. It was considered undersirable for the formula to penalize changes in the program. The Committee on University Affairs thus took the view that a procedure should be worked out whereby Toronto would receive total support of the same order as if the previous program had been maintained. How this problem would be solved remained uncertain at the time of writing.

The report of the Committee on University Affairs for 1967–8 claimed six advantages for the formula. 1 / The resulting grants were clearly equitable. 2 / University autonomy was clearly preserved. 3 / The government was provided with a means of consistently foreseeing and controlling the general magnitude of university and college grants. 4 / There was a maximum incentive for university efficiency, since there was no basis for the apprehension that improved management would lead to a corresponding reduction in support. Long-range planning of university operations was greatly facilitated. 5 / The formula system gave freedom to the individual institution to order priorities and exert initiative. 6 / Private donors were assured that gifts for operating purposes were an added resource for the university and not a substitute for public support.

Appraisal of formula approach

Donald MacDonald expressed himself as favourably impressed by the formula arrangement. He agreed with the minister that in theory a step forward had been made. To some extent, however, he felt that judgment should be reserved until it was clearer what was going to happen in connection with "special considerations." Interestingly, he was at this stage not very enthusiastic about the independent grants commission.

I have talked to people who are thoroughly familiar with the British university set-up and who contended, rightly or wrongly, that behind the façade of this buffer between government and the universities, you still had an impact of politics. So that, while the buffer group, so to speak, was making the decisions in the mysterious ways in which political influences sometimes operate, that influence had its impact and the decision was made as a result of the impact of political influence, even though it was being made by the university grants commission.[25]

He seems to have realized that the system actually worked out in Ontario had certain advantages of openness to public scrutiny that an independent commission might not offer.

Value of the basic unit

Much of the research work of the Committee on University Affairs centres around the preparation of a recommendation for the value of the basic income unit for each successive year. The committe has had to consider, not only the usual inflationary pressures, but also such factors as the need to ensure that academic salary levels remain competitive with those in other places, the rapidly escalating costs and rates of obsolescence of library materials and laboratory equipment, and the general expense of maintaining the current rapid rate of expansion of undergraduate and graduate work. Maximum effort is made to finance the development of new programs through the ordinary formula rather than with special grants, but such a course of action has not always proved possible.[26]

The universities were not too happy about the value of the basic unit in 1967–8 which, as already mentioned, was set at $1,320. President Dunton of Carleton declared that all the universities of the province thought it was too low, and would handicap them.[27]

In meetings with the Committee on University Affairs in August 1967 and January 1968, the presidents presented a case for a rise of at least 15 per cent in the value of the basic income unit to make up for what they considered the excessively low value established for it in 1967–8. They made a particular case for the need to build up library collections and to pay faculty salaries that would sustain Ontario's position in the international market. When it was announced that the value of the unit would be $1,450, representing a rise of only 10 per cent over the previous year, they decided to resort to the public forum. While commending the government's policy of giving education the highest spending priority, and recognizing the need to keep the costs of education in line with the province's resources, they suggested that there would ultimately be unfavourable social and economic consequences if sufficient sums were not invested to keep the universities operating at an appropriate level. The amount of grants announced was insufficient, in the light of an expected increase in enrolment of about 12 per cent, to keep classes from growing larger and opportunities for enriching contact between faculty and students from being reduced. Despite their failure to influence the decision respecting the budget for 1968–9, the presidents decided to renew their efforts for the subsequent year. With the financial strings tightening, however, they were again forced to accept a good deal less than they requested.[28]

The presidents are obviously a powerful pressure group. There are two aspects to their efforts to secure the maximum financial support that demand particular emphasis. On the one hand, it is their inescapable obligation to defend the optimum conditions of work load, research support, staff assistance, and facilities required by the university community in order to carry out those functions for which it is fitted. Provided these conditions are really essential, and do not involve a clutter of wasteful practices and traditional privileges bearing no relation to productive intellectual effort, the university community may expect the most strenuous exertions on the part of its presidential representatives to protect its position. If the economy of the province is insufficient to offer a reasonable quality of higher education to all comers, then it would appear that the necessity of some further restrictions on admission must be faced. In such an eventuality, the presidents can ensure that the issues are confronted squarely rather than permitting a gradual erosion of the quality of university offerings. On the other hand, the presidents, as the representatives of a particular interest group, have no privilege of determining what absolute amounts, or what proportion of the province's economic effort, will go into higher education. When their case is made, it is the government's obligation to make a binding decision. The verdict of the voting public is supposed to deal with any mishandling of this responsibility. The debates in the Legislature would be more enlightening if they centred around a discussion of economic and social priorities, based on a recognition of the limitations of the province's admittedly rich resources, rather than around the apparent assumption by the opposition that any tendency to restrict the presidents' requests represents the action of a miserly government sitting on a private gold mine.

It became the practice to establish the value of the basic income unit, at least tentatively, for more than one future year at a time. The value of the unit was $1,556 for 1969–70, including $26 per unit for computer equipment. It was subsequently established on a two-year basis, amounting to $1,650 for 1970–1 and $1,730 for 1971–2. The total increase for this two-year period was a little over 11 per cent.

Extra-formula support

The formula did not provide for all university requirements. A particular problem was that small classes in newer institutions and new programs in general required extra support before they reached the stage of viability. While efforts were continuing to develop a supplement to the formula to look after such needs, extra-formula support was continued. It was hoped that this type of assistance would be provided only for a limited period. Somewhat exceptional was the case of Laurentian University and the University of Ottawa, where it was recommended that a 7 per cent premium over ordinary formula income be paid to offset the higher costs of bilingual operation. For 1967–8 extra-formula allowances, expressed as percentages of formula operating income, were paid as follows: Brock University, 125 per cent; Erindale College, 250 per cent; Lakehead University, 40 per cent; Laurentian University, 40 per cent; Scarborough College, 85 per cent; Trent University, 125 per cent; York University, 15 per cent.[29]

In 1967 the Committee on University Affairs asked for five-year projections of extra-formula cost requirements from individual universities. The results were anything but satisfactory from the over-all provincial point of view. Although the percentage allowances requested showed some decrease over the period, the reduction was less than the anticipated enrolment increase. Thus the absolute amount of money requested followed an upward trend. After a series of meetings with representatives of the universities concerned, the committee made recommendations that would have phased out the extra-formula grants within a specified period of time. After the government accepted this recommendation, the Committee of Presidents objected that the proposed grants would be too small. As a result, the minister asked that a special study of the matter be undertaken. The study committee charged with this task was headed by M. Elizabeth Arthur; as a result of its efforts, recommendations were made that produced a greater degree of satisfaction. The transition to regular status under the formula was eased for Lakehead, Brock, and Trent Universities.[30]

In discharging its task, the special study committee reviewed within each emerging university the scope of program development, details of courses offered, enrolment in individual courses, teaching loads, and "other aspects of academic and non-academic costs which necessarily involved a scrutiny of academic programs of a sort which had never been undertaken before."[31] A model of a hypothetical university was made to indicate how it would develop on the basis of certain assumptions about class size, scope of program, teaching loads, and cost factors. There was considerable criticism of the inadequate planning on which the claims of some of the universities for special support during the emergent period had been based. Some had not even undertaken studies to project their operations on the basis of ordinary formula support. The committee recommended that the universities in question place severe limitations on the growth of new courses and the addition of staff for undergraduate teaching; that they weed out some of their existing courses; that they expand their student numbers so as to increase student-faculty ratios and the average size of course sections, thus reducing their costs per student. A lack of innovation was also identified. It was claimed that, by an excessive copying of the older universities, the newer ones would not only produce needless duplication and continued gaps in offerings, but would also perpetuate high-cost, small-scale operations.

Extra-formula support for special programs

Extra-formula support has been provided for a variety of special programs. In 1968–9 these included the following: the trimester system and veterinary medicine at Guelph; a biology station at Lakehead; bilingualism and nursing at Laurentian; health sciences at McMaster; bilingualism and medicine at Ottawa; medicine and dentistry at Toronto; optometry and Purdue scheduling models at Waterloo; dentistry and information and library school at Western; and law at Windsor. From work begun in 1967, the Committee on University Affairs established a basis for phasing out all extra-formula support over a period of a few years.

Recent restraints on spending

The Committee on University Affairs conducted a long-term review of the general aspects of university operation and development up to 1974–5 as a basis for its budgetary recommendations for 1969–70. Its analysis indicated a need for $272,500,000 for operating and $130,000,000 for capital expenditures. In accordance with cabinet guidelines, the Treasury Board requested that the operating estimates be reduced by $5 million, or somewhat less than 2 per cent. A more restrictive approach was taken, however, toward capital expenditure. The board asked that capital support be restricted to those projects for which final commitments had been made, and to other projects only if they could be defended as absolutely essential. The committee's estimates, revised on this basis, were then found acceptable.

Financial decisions for 1969–70 involved substantial restraints on university development, particularly in the area of graduate studies. It is notable that such restraints involve the judgment of the university community itself, as opposed to specific government decisions. In accordance with this approach, financial assistance is given for students in PHD programs established after January 1, 1967, and in masters' programs established after July 1, 1967, only if they have been approved by the Ontario Council on Graduate Studies. Pressure has been exerted to confine graduate work in new universities, during the period of emergence, to masters' programs in specified areas approved under the appraisal system. The universities are being encouraged to co-ordinate their efforts in order to allow each one to participate actively in part of an over-all graduate program. Some apprehension has been expressed by the committee lest projected enrolment in graduate studies prove to be inflated. In some cases, the proportion of non-Canadian students in graduate schools has grown so large that more than a hint has been expressed that financial constraints may be imposed. The cautious opinion is offered in some quarters that rapid expansion based on a high proportion of non-Canadian students represents a certain type of empire building. This form of ambition would not be objectionable if it provided a solid base for meeting real future needs. It is this premise that is being questioned.

Warnings against unjustified expansion have included reference to areas other than graduate studies. Support for any new academic programs will be forthcoming only after they have been reviewed by the Committee on University Affairs and secured its approval.

According to the *Report of the Committee on University Affairs* for 1968–9, the result of a general planning review for the five-year period from 1969–70 to 1974–5 was gratifying. Development was proceeding in an orderly and disciplined fashion. The operating grants formula was inhibiting program development where adequate enrolment could not be forecast. For the succeeding five years, there was a prospect of a much more limited growth in the number of programs than there had been between 1964–5 and 1968–9, while continued rapid growth in enrolment promised significant economies of scale.

The report discussed some of the changes effected by the formula method of support on internal university budgeting procedures and on the relationships among different elements of the university community. Academic bodies were assuming more responsibility for resource allocation, and there were more critical and realistic internal reviews of proposals for new programs. Faculty and administrators were developing different attitudes toward one another. "Where, previously, the administration was seen as functioning to win support for ever-increasing academic aspirations, administrative officials and academic staffs now seem to be drawn together to wring the maximum benefit out of the resources allocated."[32] Individually universities were, quite appropriately, allocating their resources in different ways.

A certain amount of disquiet existed because the formula did not provide for an upper limit on government grants for any one year. In 1968–9, for example, actual enrolment exceeded projections by a substantial number. For this reason an extra $12.7 million in government grants was required to meet operating costs. While such a development was the inevitable result of the government's policy of providing university places for all those who were qualified and wished to attend, the report indicated that some means might have to be found to evade unanticipated costs or to soften their impact.

Future prospects

Looking into the future, the Ontario Committee on Taxation foresaw some very serious challenges. It estimated that, on the basis of the 6 per cent rise after 1963–4 in the "operating cost per year per equivalent undergraduate student," a figure obtained by assigning a weight of three to each graduate student, the figure would reach $3,500 by 1974–5. On this basis, the total operating cost of provincially assisted universities in Ontario would reach $602 million in the same year. The committee assumed that fees would rise at the same rate as per capita income, or by about 4 per cent per annum. They would thus constitute a declining percentage of total income, amounting to only about 15 per cent by 1974–5. Predictions about the level of federal support were made before the present system was introduced, and thus were rather far off the mark. So also were estimates of the amount that the province would need to provide in operating grants for provincially assisted institutions. The committee's figures showed such grants reaching $153 million in 1969–70.[33] In actual fact the estimated provincial grant to colleges and universities for that year, as indicated in the 1970–1 budget estimates, was $314.9 million. This figure, of course, included the amounts required to compensate for grants formerly paid by the federal government.

The report of the Committee on University Affairs for 1968–9 indicated that, because of cost increases attributable to rising enrolment, increases to compensate for fixed fees, inflation, and any increase in real costs, there might be annual cost increases of 20 per cent over the next few years. There was considerable doubt that grants could be expected to rise at a comparable rate. Several possible ways of reducing the rate of cost increase were suggested. 1 / The universities might economize by rationalizing their efforts and terminating programs that had outlived their usefulness. The results of such efforts, already being made, could not be expected to have spectacular effects. 2 / Productivity might be improved by filling empty places in programs where enrolment was inadequate, and by using technology. Again, the hope of producing substantial savings had not thus far been realized. 3 / Entry might be restricted to a smaller proportion of the relevant age group. 4 / Other sources of income might be sought, possibly including increased fees, with appropriate loans enabling the student to draw on prospective future earnings. 5 / The character of university study might be changed, with a possible major shift to part-time study. 6 / A significant deterioration in quality might be permitted. The report indicated that the solution or combination of solutions chosen would require a substantial amount of research and debate.

PROVINCIAL GOVERNMENT ASSISTANCE FOR CAPITAL COSTS

Introduction

The present discussion is confined to some of the changes in principle and procedure with respect to provincial assistance for capital costs that have characterized the recent period. Three developments have unusual significance: 1 / the assumption by the provincial government of the responsibility for meeting most of the cost; 2 / the development of the

Ontario Universities Capital Aid Corporation as a means of making the necessary funds available on a reliable basis; and 3 / the search for an acceptable formula in order to ensure the distribution of capital funds to individual institutions in an equitable fashion.

Until fairly recent years, funds for the renovation and expansion of buildings and facilities were typically sought from private sources. In some cases, large single donations were obtained for specific projects, often involving appropriate recognition of the donor. Benefactions from the Massey family to the University of Toronto have provided notable examples. In other cases, campaigns for the building fund have involved appeals to a large number of individuals, corporations, municipal governments, charitable foundations, and other agencies for somewhat more generalized purposes, although specific future additions to capital stock have normally been assigned a position in a list of priorities.

Growing need for assistance before 1964

The extent of capital needs by 1962 was indicated by a report of the Committee of Presidents.[34] There was some evidence of the increasing cost of providing additional student places. The committee observed that the Department of Economics had forecast a figure of $5,000 per student. This estimate was, however, being greatly exceeded. McMaster's expansion program, exclusive of residences and the purchase of land, was expected to cost $42,500,000 for an additional 5,800 students, thus averaging $7,350 per student. Taking account of the factors omitted in McMaster's estimate, Toronto's expenditure to provide for more than double its existing enrolment was estimated at over $8,000 per student. Waterloo thought it could provide places at $5,000 per student, but allowance for a library, residences, and such items as a students' union could easily bring the figure to $7,000. Taking increasing costs into consideration, the committee suggested that total capital investment might have to reach $150 million, or even $175 million, by 1965.

The Ontario Universities Capital Aid Corporation

The provincial government announced the creation of the Department of University Affairs and of the Ontario Universities Capital Aid Corporation, with, of course, interrelated functions. Robarts explained the purpose of the corporation in the legislature in May 1964.[35] Its first purpose was the obvious one of spreading the capital cost of the universities over a number of years. During a period requiring the rapid expenditure of very large amounts of money, it did not seem reasonable to attempt to meet all costs from current revenue. The familiar case for spreading the burden over future beneficiaries was presented. The second point was that the corporation would be able to provide funds as they were required without any relation to any particular agency's fiscal year. Planning on a long-term basis would thus be facilitated. This arrangement would help to correct an awkward situation in which the universities received an allotment of funds out of current revenue, and an appeal for a new allotment had to be made in each successive year.

As Robarts explained it on another occasion, the specific functions of the corporation were to purchase from the universities the bonds and debentures they issued for capital construction projects that had been approved and processed through the Department of University Affairs. Also, subject to government approval, the corporation was empowered to borrow funds needed to carry out its purposes. The government would provide funds in its annual operating grants for the universities to pay interest on their loans from the corporation. The corporation consisted of five members appointed by the Lieutenant-Governor-in-Council, who would be responsible for its management and control under the oversight of the Provincial Treasurer.[36] In reacting to the announcement, Bascom St John described the machinery of the new corporation as surprisingly complex. He wrote: "As the sole purpose of the corporation is to lend money to universities for construction projects only, it would appear that such a simple function could be adequately carried out by one man and a stenographer."[37] He noted that the corporation had no authority to determine the amounts to be lent, or the borrowers, or the projects. He acknowledged the value, however, in making grants in some way other than directly from Provincial Treasury revenues. He wrote that, because of the legal requirement that revenues not spent during the government's fiscal year had to be returned to the Provincial Treasury, there had been continual complaints that the government had provided less than the universities had asked for.

St John saw a threat to the universities' autonomy in the fact that the government would perform an act of interference every time it refused to approve a request from a university. This, of course, was an aspect of the situation that the search for a capital grants formula has recently attempted to deal with. St John's solution, which he also proposed for operating grants, was to establish an independent grants commission. Such a commission might also have performed the functions of the Ontario Universities Capital Aid Corporation by receiving and holding funds without regard to the restrictions imposed by the limits of the fiscal year.

There was some initial misunderstanding about the way in which the corporation functioned. Davis undertook to clear this up in early 1965.

> There will be no repayment by the universities in 1970 or 1971 for the capital moneys borrowed, either principal or interest ... I notice in two or three press releases that some concern is being evidenced by the question of how the universities are going to pay this back ... They will receive special operating grants with which they will pay off the debentures. There is no capital obligation on the university whatsoever.[38]

Problems of capital financing in the mid-1960s

The Committee of Presidents reviewed the capital development situation in the report *From the Sixties to the Seventies*, published in 1966, and found a number of causes for concern. These centred around 1 / the growing dependence on the provincial government as funds from other sources declined, 2 / the increasing size of the program, 3 / the lack of evidence of over-all co-ordination of capital development, 4 / certain insensitivities in the way in which provincial assistance was given, and, in connection with this point, 5 / the tendency to neglect students' residences, lounges, lunchrooms, athletic facilities, and other such amenities lacking an immediate and obvious academic purpose.[39]

It was acknowledged in the report that much careful planning had been done by individual institutions. As long as Canada Council funds and proceeds of public campaigns were making a substantial contribution, and the government was making capital grants without too many restrictions, building programs proceeded fairly smoothly. But difficulties were growing along with the increasing assumption by the province of responsibility for capital development. Costs of construction were increasing, as was public resistance to the traditional basis of compensation for expropriated property. Since the Department of University Affairs had taken over the program of capital support, the Committee on University Affairs had been left out of the picture, except for atypical projects, and had thus not been in a position to take an overview of the whole situation.

Different universities had had varied experiences under the current arangement. In some cases there had been nothing worse than delays; "in others the planned and phased construction schedules [had] been interrupted or even stalled without adequate explanation and without any apparent consideration of the academic consequences."[40] These frustrations were evidence of the lack of consistent and co-ordinated planning. Student facilities always seemed to get eliminated from the list of accepted projects. While there was no evidence that there was a deliberate intention of being hard on students, they suffered from the absence of a policy. Bureaucratic decisions under pressure from the Provincial Treasury produced a situation where some universities could not afford any expenditures for their students outside of class.

The policy at this stage was that the universities themselves must raise 15 per cent of the capital cost of academic facilities and 50 per cent of the cost of other projects. The proceeds from fund-raising campaigns were nearly exhausted, and the difficulty of raising money from private sources was increasing. It seemed ironical that the greater the share of capital costs underwritten by the government, the more difficult it became for the universities to raise their reduced share. There was a growing impression that the heavy government commitment in this area eliminated the need for the private donor's contribution.[41]

The report of the President of Carleton University for 1966–7 reflected that type of difficulty in particularly acute form. Most universities in the province were said to have reached the point during the previous year at which it was quite impossible to raise enough private funds to cover the required proportion of total costs. Although Carleton had received help from thousands of individual givers, the main local employer, the federal government, made no contributions to Ottawa universtities. In other areas, business concerns with anything like the same number of employees were giving a great deal of support to local institutions.[42]

The minister commented on the problem in the Legislature in June 1967. He recognized that the universities were finding that it was physically impossible to raise their 15 per cent share of costs, and declared that he was looking forward to the development of a formula comparable to that already worked out for operating costs. It had to provide for equality of distribution and for some method of control. He speculated on the possibility of calculating a provincial average square foot cost, with the Department of University Affairs paying 100 per cent up to a certain amount per square foot. Or perhaps the basis might be numbers of students. In any case, whatever formula was developed must be flexible if it was to have any chance of working.[43]

In November 1966 the Committee of Presidents summoned a meeting of university officials concerned with capital finance and planning. As a result of this meeting, the government was urged to support comprehensive planning by the universities, making available the funds necessary for the performance of this function. A revision of the existing procedure for capital support was advocated. The Committee of Presidents was urged to set up a committee of university officials to study capital financing and planning. As a result the Subcommittee on Capital Financing was appointed in January 1967 under the chairmanship of D.M. Hedden of McMaster University. This group subsequently worked with the Committee on University Affairs and the Department of University Affairs to outline an attack on the problem in three phases. For the short term, lasting up to June 30, 1969, it was hoped that interim procedural improvements could be devised so that existing plans for expansion could be carried out as effectively as possible. The second phase, overlapping the first, and covering the period from 1967 to 1972, would involve studies of each university's requirements leading to standards acceptable to all and, if possible, to a realistic financing formula. In the third phase, covering the period from 1970 to 1975, a more sophisticated formula would be devised and applied against more adequate province-wide and regional enrolment projections.[44]

Further structure for these activities was provided by the appointment of a joint steering committee consisting of equal numbers of representatives from the Committee on University Affairs and from the universities, under the chairmanship of D.T. Wright. At its first meeting in June 1967 it arranged for studies in several areas: enrolment; a space inventory of Ontario universities; system resources such as libraries, computers, television, and residences; policies and practices for control of capital planning elsewhere; and the structure of the building industry.[45]

The *Report of the Committee on University Affairs* for 1967 elaborated on the need for and the techniques employed in conducting these studies. The inventory and space utilization study was necessary in order to determine the resources of each member of the system as a basis for establishing its future needs. Since the inventory would require continuous updating, it seemed necessary that it be computer-based. The services of a qualified private firm were therefore obtained. With reference to the study of building practices, traditional methods of employing architects and consulting engineers and open tendering by general contractors needed examination. Consideration must be given to such concepts as package deals, design/execute tenders, construction management, negotiated contracts, and system building. It was suggested also that radical re-thinking of design criteria was required to provide for more flexibility of use. Ways must also be found to respond to the increasing rate of technical obsolescence. The report suggested that space management in a large university with many kinds of undergraduate and graduate teaching and research programs presented a more difficult problem than that found in almost any other kind of organization or institution.[46]

Increased provincial assistance in 1968

As a result of various studies, the Committee on University Affairs recommended a change in capital grants policy for projects undertaken during the 1964–9 period. Under this scheme, the province was to pay 85 per cent of the first $10 million for approved capital projects and 95 per cent of the cost of the remainder. A most important aspect of the recommendation was that the scheme should cover not only academic buildings and essential services, but also student unions, cafeterias, gymnasia, and other such buildings. The recommendation was accepted and put into practice in 1968. At the same time a change was made in the procedure for approving capital projects. Previously, plans for these had been submitted to the Department of University Affairs and appraised individually with reference to various criteria. The new policy authorized the Committee on University Affairs to review each university's plans as a whole and to assign priorities to its different projects.[47]

The arrangement for increased grants met with all-round approval. The *Kitchener-Waterloo Record*, however, expressed editorial criticism of one exception: there was no support for the construction of stadia and related playing fields. Some rather dark motives were suggested for the omission. It was seen as implying "that the physical activities are a secondary part of university life, a belief in keeping with the general Canadian tendency to regard athletes and physical exercises as slightly suspect and lowbrow." Nevertheless, the Department of University Affairs seemed to be well on the way to a "permanent, sensible, workable grants system." With the polite but firm insistence of university representatives, the departmental educators might be educated to the realities of modern university operation.[48]

The development of a capital grants formula

The result of the efforts of the Joint Capital Studies Committee was the production of an interim capital formula using the general approach and format to be incorporated in the final scheme. The essential information, although imperfect, was available at this stage. The formula was, however, offered with a warning that considerable further study would be necessary. An outline of the concepts, principles, and methodology used in devising the formula was summarized as follows:

(1) The critical quantitative parameters for the formula were (i) the space standard, 130 net assignable square feet/eligible full-time students and (ii) a cost standard (in 1968 dollars) of $55.00 per square foot of additional space required for capital projects and their related equipment.

(2) The above space standard was used in arriving at total space entitlement for all of the provincially-assisted universities combined, in each year of a five-year capital planning period 1st April, 1969 to 31st March, 1974. Funding within this period is intended to provide for university enrolments in the 1974–75 academic session.

(3) A share of the total provincial space goal for each year was assigned pro-rata to individual universities by means of a scheme for assigning "weights" to the various categories of enrolment so as to reflect their differing space requirements.

(4) The formula does not encompass Health Science facilities. Also excluded from capital formula considerations as such are projects representing replacements and renovations, land acquisitions, and general services and site development. Such projects, since they are not linear-related to the general development of capital facilities, must, of necessity, be recognized by providing for them under special funds established for this purpose.

(5) Projected enrolment data and "base inventories" of space were obtained from each university. The former permitted the calculation of space requirements and together with the latter information, it was possible to derive incremental space needs and to express these results in terms of dollars of assistance.[49]

Planning for future expenditure

As indicated previously, capital grants for 1969–70 were restricted to an amount sufficient to meet commitments for projects already under construction, to carry out required planning, and to undertake new construction where it was judged to be absolutely necessary. Projects under way reflected decisions on priorities established by each university and submitted to the Department of University Affairs in 1968. Urgent requirements for new construction were identified from information available from the space inventory and an assessment of need based on an over-all average of 130 net assignable square feet per student.

Subsequent work involved the creation of a comprehensive outline for a five-year development program, indicating the degree of support each university might expect, not only for new construction, but also for repairs and renovations, land purchase, and site development. Efforts were also devoted to meeting the special needs of emergent universities and those universities with unique problems. The guiding principle of the whole approach was that, while total resources must be restricted, each university would have the maximum possible scope in ordering priorities.

This attitude is elaborated in background material accompanying the document from which the preceding quotation was obtained.

> While it is clear that many distinct kinds of space, including teaching space, laboratory space, office space, research space, libraries, administration buildings, dining facilities, recreational facilities and the like must be provided for a university, it seems to be appropriate to attempt to find global or total measures of need on a combined basis for all kinds of space required. It would, of course, be possible to determine space allowances for each such individual category of function, but this would seem only to lead to homogeneous stereotypes and to inhibit necessary flexibility. The tendency to mixed-function space, and such problems as arise in determining library requirements when it is seen that in some universities there are single central facilities whilst in others there are varied patterns of departmental libraries and dispersed reading rooms, indicate that no simple uniform measures could be readily developed for standardization of provisions for distinct categories of space. Moreover, the prospect of fairly radical changes and teaching methods involving, on the one hand, the use of large lectures and on the other further development of individual instruction through such contrasting means as tutorials and television, suggest that there is good reason to encourage the greatest flexibility in space use and assignment. Certainly, if an effective control of the total can be established, it should not be necessary to control the pieces as well.

Between early 1969 and early 1970 there was little apparent progress in revising the interim formula. The Joint Committee had been relatively inactive, ostensibly waiting for further information from the consultants. The capital funds required for each university for the two-year period between 1970–1 and 1971–2 were determined by a calculation of new space required, which was the difference between available space (actual areas as of September 1969 plus the areas added for additional projects given approval before April 1, 1969, minus any proposed deletions scheduled to occur before September 1972) and space required by the interim formula for full-time students (determined on the basis of ninety-six net assignable square feet per weighted unit of enrolment for 1972–3) increased by 1 / additional space required for part-time and trimester students, 2 / additional space required by emergence, and 3 / additional space required because of structures over forty years of age. Amounts of funds were specified for each year of the two-year period.

Assistance for residences

No provincial assistance was offered for the building of residences before 1964. By that time it was evident that enrolment, particularly at universities in smaller cities, was exceeding the capacity of private lodgings. The government therefore accepted a recommendation of the Committee on University Affairs whereby capital grants were made available for residences at the rate of $1,400 a bed, provided that mortgage financing did not exceed $4,200 a bed, nor the total cost, $7,000 a bed. Because actual costs tended to rise above the ceiling, universities were forced to make contributions that they could ill afford in the light of other obligations. In 1966 the Ontario Student Housing Corporation was therefore established as an adjunct to the Ontario Housing Corporation; it proved able, through businesslike management and large-scale operations, to provide residences at considerably reduced costs. The principle followed throughout the period has been that residences should be supported on a self-amortizing basis, since only a certain proportion of the students are able to live in residence, and these should not therefore enjoy special subsidies.[50]

FEDERAL ASSISTANCE

Background

The federal government entered the field of grants to institutions of higher education in 1917, when the National Research Council first began to assist the universities with scientific research. This practice was continued and expanded during the Second World War. At the end of the war, a new element was introduced with the massive problem of looking after veterans, for many of whom a university career had been delayed, and for some of whom it would have been denied under earlier circumstances. Large amounts of money were provided by the federal government for the assistance of such veterans. The strains placed on university facilities, moreover, led to a federal policy of assistance to the institutions themselves.

The case for federal support was presented in strong terms to the Massey Royal Commission on National Development in the Arts, Letters and Sciences by the National Conference of Canadian Universities. The amount of the suggested grants would vary from $100 to $200 per student according to the program in which he was enrolled. Describing the financial crisis faced by the universities as "so grave as to threaten their future usefulness," the commission pressed for federal assistance, in addition to the help already being given for research and other purposes, but on a population basis. It recommended that the contributions be distributed to each university in proportion to the student enrolment. It also advocated an extensive system of post-graduate scholarships and an enlargement of the system of bursaries and loans to undergraduates under the existing federal-provincial plan.[51]

Establishment of policy on operating grants, 1951–2

As a response to these recommendations, the federal government began in 1951–2 to make unconditional operating grants to the universities. These were made at the initial rate of 50 cents per head. In introducing them, Prime Minister St Laurent said that they were primarily designed to assist the universities to maintain the highly qualified staffs and working conditions that were essential for the proper performance of their functions rather than to increase existing facilities.[52] The funds were divided among degree-granting institutions according to their full-time student enrolment. The per capita rate was raised to $1.00 in 1957, to $1.50 in 1958, and to $2.00 in 1962. By 1962–3 the total amount granted in this way to all the provinces participating in the scheme, that is, all except Quebec, was $34 million.

In the first year of the plan, the grant was accepted in all Canadian provinces. But the federal government thereafter encountered difficulty with the province of Quebec, which was determined to resist any precedent that might weaken its financial responsibility for institutions within its own borders. Prime Minister St Laurent outlined the federal position at the National Conference on Canada's Crisis in Higher Education at Ottawa on November 12, 1956.

> The Federal Government has the absolute right to levy indirect taxes for any purpose, and the power to impose direct taxes provided they are intended for the Consolidated Revenue Fund of Canada. Out of these moneys it can then, with Parliament's approval, offer gifts or grants to individuals, institutions, Provincial governments or even to foreign governments. This is a royal prerogative which is not in any way restricted by our constitution.[53]

As a means of ensuring that federal grants would be completely free of influence for political purposes, the government arranged to have them distributed through the National Council of Canadian Universities. Despite these arrangements, the Quebec government induced its universities to leave the grants untouched under the implied threat of losing all provincial support. Ontario, like the other provinces, had no inhibitions of this type. The approval of the provincial government was perhaps exceeded only by that of the universities themselves, which welcomed not only the funds, but also the prospect of avoiding too great a reliance on a single source of public revenue. The federal government's disagreement with Quebec was finally settled in 1959 by the promise of an arrangement, made effective in 1960–61, whereby the latter received a tax abatement approximately equivalent to the amount that would have been available under the formula.

There were some objections to the basis used by the federal government to distribute its grants on the grounds that it provided relatively less to the provinces that were best endowed with institutions, which in some cases provided substantial services to neighbouring provinces by accommodating their students. Nova Scotia offered a prime example. An opposing argument was that it would be desirable in the long run to encourage each province to develop its own facilities. There was a certain amount of dissatisfaction expressed in the universities because no allowance was made for part-time students. Thus the scheme worked to the disadvantage of institutions with large extension programs.

Increasing role of federal government

At the time the operating grant was doubled in 1956, the sum of $50 million was placed at the disposal of the Canada Council to assist universities with their building programs. This sum was distributed according to a precise mathematical formula which took into account both provincial population and full-time student enrolment. At this stage, the Ontario government was embarking on a program of what seemed to be, by the standards of the day, large-scale assistance for both maintenance and capital purposes.

In its submission to the Commission on the Financing of Higher Education in 1965,[54] the Ontario Council of University Faculty Associations had a few comments on the division between federal and provincial financing of higher education, even though it disclaimed any particular competence to advise in this area. It suggested that research was outside a strict definition of education, although any actual separation between teaching and research within the university would be undesirable. If its interpretation were acceptable, federal funds could be appropriately used for research equipment, supplies, and assistants in the sciences, and for whatever proportion of library costs could be attributed to research in the humanities and social sciences. One-third to one-half of professors' time, and therefore salaries, might also be designated for research. The submission indicated further that the federal government could legitimately be expected to provide some general grants on a per-student basis, and substantial grants for graduate work and certain kinds of professional training. The rationale for federal involvement was that recognition should be given to population mobility, differences in needs and resources among the provinces, and the greater national interest in some aspects of university work. It was suggested also that the federal government should contribute substantial grants for construction and equipment of medical and research facilities.

In early 1966 the federal government announced an increase in its per capita grant from $2 to $5. Grants were related to actual student enrolment on the basis of a weighted formula. One of the changes that had lasting consequences was the provision for grants on the basis of enrolment of part-time students in degree programs. This development had particular significance for Atkinson College, which thus became eligible for financial support from the general budget of York University on a basis similar to that of other academic divisions. The subsequent adoption of a formula for provincial grants provided for the same category of students by allocating one-sixth of a basic operating unit for each course registration by an undergraduate student engaged in part-time degree studies. McCormack Smyth, Dean of the College, claimed that this allotment was inadequate to cover the relatively large administrative costs involved, and suggested that the relevant course registration should count for at least one-third of a unit.

The federal government's new scheme was short-lived. Later in the year, it was abandoned in favour of a plan for direct fiscal transfer to the provinces. The program involved a reimbursement of either $15.00 per capita of the population or 50 per cent of the operating costs of all post-secondary institutions, including universities, colleges of applied arts and technology, teachers' colleges, and colleges of education. Allowance was also made for grade 13 classes, since this level was considered post-secondary in other provinces. Debenture charges paid by the universities for capital construction costs were not included, since these were not classed as operating costs.

The federal government's move out of the field of direct grants put both denominational institutions and the provincial government in an awkward position. The former were in danger of losing their direct support without the prospect of compensating grants from the provincial government, which was unenthusiastic about modifying its historic policy of assisting only non-denominational institutions. It yielded, however, to the point of offering 50 per cent of formula income as compensation for the lost funds. Grants to colleges affiliated to provincially assisted universities have been made through the parent university according to the recommendation of the Committee of Presidents. Grants go directly to Waterloo Lutheran University, which remains the only independent church-related university in the province.

The minister elaborated on the arrangement in the Legislature on June 5, 1967. The grants would be paid on the basis of enrolment statistics provided to the Department of University Affairs in December of the current year. The application of weights for enrolment would be exactly like those used for the provincially assisted institutions. Since the formula made no provision for theology and pre-theology, however, students at all levels in these courses would be given a weight of one. Every effort would be made to treat the institutions fairly. If for any reason the grant resulting from the application of the formula at the 50 per cent level did not equal the federal grant paid in 1966–7, the institution concerned might request an amount equal to the latter sum.

Davis asserted that the new arrangement was not to be regarded as a change in the provincial policy of support to higher education. It was to be seen only as an appropriate and equitable means of compensating for federal grants previously received. Grants were to be paid only to those institutions and operations that were in existence during the 1966–7 academic year, and for which federal grants were paid.[55]

PRIVATE DONATIONS

According to a report produced by the Industrial Foundation on Education in 1957, university endowment income in Canada rose from $1.5 million in 1920–1 to $3.5 million in 1955–6. The increase had not, however, come close to keeping pace with the rise in university operating costs. While endowment income had met 16.5 per cent of these costs in the former year, it contributed less than 6 per cent in the latter. The report suggested that, since the greater part of the national wealth was in the coffers of business and government, they were the only sources that could be tapped for any substantial increases.[56]

The establishment of the Industrial Foundation on Education itself represented a hope that corporate aid might provide an important source of revenue. The same report outlined the reasons why such aid should be forthcoming. It began by asking why corporations should support education financially on a voluntary basis. The alternative was to increase taxes and thus ensure the equitable sharing of educational costs. The chief answer offered in the report was that the autonomy of institutions of higher education must be protected and preserved. Then followed an argument involving a somewhat questionable definition of terms: "Free enterprise in education is a natural corollary of free enterprise in industry and commerce and ... the greatest insurance to its preservation is to provide university income from as many sources as possible."[57]

It is difficult to assess the results of the foundation's campaign. Certainly the amount of corporate giving did increase substantially in the five-year period after 1956. From $739,093 given to seven institutions in that year, it rose to $2,629,714 in 1959 and to $4,844,712 in 1961.[58] The reasons for this development would be difficult to establish, apart from the vigour with which the campaigns of certain universities were conducted. In any case, the trend was not sustained. Although the lists of available scholarships in the calendars of universities and colleges of applied arts and technology attest to the frequency with which contributions have been made for this purpose, and though substantial individual contributions have continued to be made, the corporations have by and large opted in favour of compulsory donations through taxes. Thus they have delivered the universities into government hands. Given the extent of the higher educational enterprise, they could hardly have done anything else. In any case, corporate giving is a highly regulated activity. Unless carried out in response to effective tax incentives, it tends to place a corporation at a disadvantage in relation to its competitors. The shareholders can also reasonably take the attitude that they should have the privilege of determining the identity of the recipients and the amounts to be donated, rather than having it done for them before the distribution of profits. Tax incentives that facilitate corporate giving amount to an indirect device for allocating government funds.

Bascom St John expressed his views on the question some years later.

> One of the still unsolved issues is what proportion of university costs ought to be borne by industry. Unquestionably some responsibility exists, because increasingly university trained talent is necessary and is being used in business and industry. In fact, without this source of trained ability modern business could not exist.
>
> It is not enough to say that since businesses are being so heavily taxed they might as well leave university financing to the Government. Governments have many other responsibilities, and it would be healthier from every point of view if the universities had several sources of income and support.[59]

The important place held by private donations was indicated in the report of the President of the University of Toronto for 1960. In May of that year, it had been announced that the university fund had reached a total of $15 million, some $2,400,000 in excess of the projected goal. The sum was the more impressive because it did not include certain large benefactions received during the year for specific purposes, including a grant of more than $2 million from the Corporation of Metropolitan Toronto for a building to house the School of Social Work and the School of Business. A celebration in May marked the conclusion of two years of intensive work, one devoted largely to planning and preparation, and the other to the solicitation of funds. The campaign involved approximately six thousand active workers organized in committees and groups headed by Wallace McCutcheon and Neil McKinnon acting as co-chairmen. It had been considered essential to establish the necessity of private gifts to a university that had been traditionally the recipient of generous government aid. The report asserted that this point had been made. Yet, in order to see the results of the campaign in perspective, it must be noted that the total of capital funds required for the ensuing five years was approximately $50 million. In other words, major reliance had to be placed on government support.[60] The importance of private benefactions was not, however, to be judged simply by their size. They gave the university a large margin for acting entirely according to its own set of priorities, and thus for maintaining its self-defined character.

The Association of Universities and Colleges of Canada reported some university points of view in 1965 on the current and future role of corporate and private giving. The prevailing opinion was that the amounts of capital funds needed were so large that contributions from this source would inevitably constitute a declining proportion of the total. Representatives of some universities suggested that private giving should supply "imaginative venture capital" rather than providing basic academic facilities. Corporate giving was said to be most meaningful when it was applied to the areas for which it was most difficult to secure government support. Donors were often interested in the welfare of particular institutions, but many feared that their contributions to building campaigns would only relieve governments of their proper responsibility and enable them to reduce their contributions by the amount donated. There was a danger that the universities might be penalized for their success and be less able to acquire private funds for special projects and facilities. However, the success of some university campaigns had been recognized in certain provinces as a form of endorsation of the university expansion program, and had encouraged the provincial government to increase its contributions.[61]

FEES

The reaction of some of the unhappy presidents to their failure to get as much money as they had requested from the provincial government in 1965 was to suggest that a general rise in fees would be necessary. Whether or not it was a perfectly legitimate response to the responsibility of meeting their financial obligations, this proposal was seen as an embarrassment to the government, if not, indeed, a means of subjecting it to pressure. Donald MacDonald attacked Robarts for a remark made some time earlier to the effect that he did not believe that free education jibed with free enterprise. He had also gone on record with the flat assertion that there was no immediate chance that his government was going to provide free college education for everyone.[62] He would nevertheless hardly have wished to be in the position of being held responsible for any substantial increase in fees.

In its "Submission to the Commission on the Financing of Higher Education" in 1965, the Ontario Council of University Faculty Associations considered the question of fees. It noted, first of all, that this source accounted for between a fifth and a third of university revenue. It then explored advantages and disadvantages of two contradictory courses of action: 1 / to increase fees towards or to an amount that would cover the whole operating cost and 2 / to reduce them towards or to zero, or even to pay each student a stipend in lieu of what he would otherwise earn.[63]

The case for the first alternative was based on the assumption that in a market economy it is better to offer everything at its full cost rather than to have any concealed subsidies. This view may be consistent with an acceptance of the contribution of higher education to the welfare of the whole of society. If it is accordingly proper for the state to subsidize higher education, the subsidies should be given to the student. Such a policy would free the universities from the most obvious threats of direct control by the state, but would no doubt force them to be responsive to students' demands. The council did not see any great likelihood that Ontario would move in the direction suggested. Since the economy seemed already to be a network of concealed subsidies, there was no strong case for removing higher education from this pattern.

Some inequity was seen in the way the existing subsidy operated. A student who could raise the annual fee, and could also afford to forego a year's earnings, got the indirect subsidy represented by government contributions to the operation of the university. If fees were raised to $1,500, for example, and direct subsidies were paid, averaging $1,000 but scaled to a means test, the inequity would be reduced. It would require elaborate new administrative machinery to apply the means test. But the council saw merit in higher fees with offsetting direct subsidies:

> This would in principle allot university places more nearly in relation to student merit than is now the case. As university teachers we favour any change which would transfer university places *from* those who fill them merely because their parents can afford it and because they value the social cachet, *to* those who could intellectually get more from and give more to the university but cannot now afford to come. This would improve university standards and increase the social usefulness of the university.

The council assumed that there was a reservoir of potentially good students who could not currently afford to enrol. It assumed also that what they could not afford was not merely the fees but the loss of the earnings they would have to forego.

But the same problem could be taken care of by the opposite proposal, which was to a considerable extent in effect in the United Kingdom, Western Europe, and the Soviet Union. The council did not, however, think it realistic to envision a society so affluent that higher education could be made entirely free, especially in view of the expected steeply rising total cost of higher education in relation to the national income. But it did assert a belief that fees should not be raised. Concern was expressed that governments, taken aback by the size of the bill they must expect in the next few costly decades, might reverse the trend toward higher education for all those who were intellectually capable of it by allowing or procuring a fee increase with no offsetting direct subsidies to students.

APPRAISAL

There has obviously been a revolution in university finance in Ontario in little more than a decade. Entirely new practices and relationships have had to be worked out. The foregoing account has perhaps inevitably tended to dwell on difficulties, problems, and frustrations – even of fears about the ultimate outcome. There has been evidence of illogical and shortsighted practices. Fatuous views have been held and expressed, and justified courses of action have had to be defended against foolish criticism. The story has nevertheless been an inspiring one. The universities have accepted their new role conscientiously and courageously, and have undertaken the search for a solution to their financial problems with a clear concept of the essentials of the autonomy they must maintain. The government has shown an equal perception of the issues at stake, and just as firm a determination to discharge only its essential functions, without encroaching on the prerogatives of the academic community. Both sides have shown a willingness to attack problems on the basis of thorough, objective analysis and reasoned argument. There is little evidence of pride in positions taken or dogged adherence to outmoded policies. The effect of temporary lapses has been overcome by overriding adherence to a policy of co-operation.

The basic problem seems to have been substantially solved. The dangers that Corry outlined so perceptively have been averted. That is not to say, of course, that security is ever absolute, or that vigilance can be relaxed. But a pattern has been established that should enable the universities to grow and flourish and perform their functions with the essence of their traditional position intact. The widespread interest in Ontario's solution to its problems which has been shown in other provinces is sufficient evidence of that.

The question of how successfully the province can reconcile its demands for higher education with its willingness to pay the necessary price is of course one for the future. But if the prospects look excessively difficult, one need only visit the numerous campuses and observe their unique collection of magnificent buildings, largely constructed in little more than a decade, to realize that the achievements of the people of Ontario have been, in that typical Canadian expression, "not too bad."

THIRTEEN

Educational activities of provincial government departments other than Education and University Affairs

THE DEPARTMENT OF THE PROVINCIAL SECRETARY AND CITIZENSHIP

General educational role at end of 1960s

Particularly since 1961, when it assumed certain responsibilities formerly discharged by the Community Programs Branch of the Department of Education, the Department of the Provincial Secretary and Citizenship has been one of the most active of provincial government departments in the field of education. A major area of its responsibility is that of providing language and citizenship training for adult newcomers. As of 1969–70, it conducted classes for this group, administered summer courses in teaching English as a second language, distributed teaching materials, conducted tests in English and in knowledge of Canada for applicants for citizenship and others, and conducted research into areas of its special concern. Up to this time, it had also produced over twenty teacher-training films, the first of their kind in Canada, and had conducted hundreds of teacher-training seminars in addition to summer courses. The minister responsible for the department at the time of writing was Robert Welch.

Organizational arrangements to provide for the needs of immigrants

Premier George Drew made the first post-war provision for language and citizenship training in 1947. An Adult Education Advisory Board was established to determine what kinds of programs would be appropriate. In 1948 this board was transferred to the Community Programs Branch, within which a Citizenship Office henceforth concerned itself with language and citizenship.

In 1959 the Citizenship Division was established in the Department of the Provincial Secretary. Among its duties were the translation of documents into the language of immigrants and the provision of information to the immigrants and to the government about their needs. The problem of overlap in having two government agencies involved with immigrants was solved two years later by incorporating the relevant functions of the Community Programs Branch in the Department of the Provincial Secretary and Citizenship.

Direct provision of classes

In the early days of the program, refugees who had served in the Polish army constituted one of the main groups requiring assistance. A large proportion of the classes at that time were conducted in Hydro construction, mining, railway construction, and bush camps. Most instruction, however, came to be given in secondary school evening classes. The Community Programs Branch occasionally organized classes in communities where the school boards were not prepared to do so. Its responsibility for direct service gradually shifted toward the provision of institutional classes in hospitals, sanatoria, and mental institutions.

Classes were also held at the headquarters of or in conjunction with certain voluntary agencies. After 1958 year-round daytime classes were operated five days a week at the International Institute of Metropolitan Toronto; these were designed for the unemployed, shift workers, women, and others unable to attend in the evening. Such classes were extended into the YMCA and the Italian Education Centre (COSTI) in Toronto, and were also held in co-operation with the International Services at London, the Workmen's Compensation Board Rehabilitation Centre at Downsview, the University Women's Club at Sudbury, and the Italian Education Centre in Hamilton.

Beginning in 1948, intensive summer school courses were provided, originally in co-operation with the University of Toronto and, after 1956, with the assistance of the Toronto Board of Education, which supplied free accommodation. From 1958 on, summer classes provided a laboratory for teacher training.

About 1960 an experiment with "kitchen classes" was undertaken as a joint project with the Social Planning Council of Metropolitan Toronto. These classes involved the assembly of groups of learners in someone's house. The scheme broke down because of the inability of the provincial authorities to assume the task of local organization. They were prepared to assist only to the extent of supplying the teachers.

In 1964–5 the Citizenship Division (of the Department of the Provincial Secretary and Citizenship) co-operated with the Provincial Institute of Trades and with COSTI to establish language training classes in a trades training program. Bilingual instructors were used in the initial stages of trades training. When the students had sufficient proficiency with the language, instruction was given in English.

An experiment was undertaken in 1964 in co-operation with the Toronto Board of Education involving a ten-week intensive course of classes offered four nights a week. Seven classes with about 140 students were held at the International Institute and at the Italian Education Centre. Attendance proved to be good, and progress was adjudged to be equal to or slightly greater than that achieved by students attending classes two nights a week for a full year. As a result of this success, the Toronto and North York Boards began to offer such classes on a regular basis.

In 1965 the Citizenship Division departed from its usual terms of reference in responding to the application of a number of school-age children for admission to classes given at the International Institute of Metropolitan Toronto. Although the cost-sharing agreement with what was then the federal Department of Citizenship and Immigration applied only to the provision of adult classes, the children were admitted on condition that they were at least twelve years of age and had obtained a release from regular school classes signed by the appropriate school authorities. Special classes of five hours a day were set up to expedite the early return of the children to regular classes. The program was designed as a special supplement to the efforts of the school boards to meet the needs of immigrant children, but was not intended to relieve the boards of this responsibility.

In 1964 the Citizenship Division, the federal Department of Citizenship and Immigration, and the Toronto Board of Education recognized the need for special classes for those approaching the time for their appearance in court for citizenship examinations. Some of these people had become hazy on what they had learned in classes taken two or more years earlier, and needed refresher and up-dating courses, while others who had come from English-speaking countries needed only to study citizenship subjects. A twelve-week course was set up on a revolving basis, operated during the school year by the Toronto Board of Education and by the Citizenship Division during the summer months. Similar classes were also established in Hamilton, London, and Windsor.

In the middle and late sixties, classes were operated in industries where the hours of work or the location prevented attendance at classes offered by school boards or voluntary associations. The Citizenship Branch (Division) provided the teachers while the industry provided the classrooms and paid the wages of the employees who attended. The industry usually benefited in terms of improved communication resulting in increased production and in the reduction of accidents. In some cases, however, the employees took advantage of their improved qualifications to seek better employment elsewhere.

In 1965–6 a pilot project, undertaken in co-operation with a Toronto Community Committee on Immigrant Children, involved the provision of classes for immigrant women with pre-school children. The mothers received language instruction from volunteer teachers while their children were cared for by volunteer workers who introduced language patterns into play activities. The voluntary agency located the participants and the volunteer workers, while the Citizenship Branch supplied technical advisers to the volunteers. The experiment involved follow-up work to determine the success of the children when they entered school. By 1969 five such programs were being conducted in Toronto and one in Windsor, with another planned for Hamilton.

Among the most recent services offered was a special daytime class for the professionally trained immigrant. It represented an effort to investigate the possibility of developing language skills more quickly in those with considerable formal schooling than in those without it. The result would appear to be rather predictable. Classes were also offered for those with speech difficulties or emotional problems.

Financial arrangements

According to the terms of an agreement in 1953, the federal government agreed to pay half the provincial expenditure for the salaries of teachers involved in the programs. The provincial authority paid rental fees, where necessary, when the courses were provided in co-operation with private agencies. School boards operating evening classes for adult newcomers might, if they obtained the prior approval of the Deputy Minister of Education, recover 90 per cent of the direct teaching costs based on a rate of $6.00 per hour for the services of the teacher. This 90 per cent was shared equally between the federal and provincial governments. When language classes were given approval under Program 5 in 1965, school boards could, if they secured the prior approval of both the federal Citizenship Branch and the Technology and Trades Training Branch of the Department of Education, recover the cost from federal and provincial sources. Some underemployed adults were also accommodated under Program 3.

Teacher training

A summer course for teachers of English as a second language was first offered by the Department of Education in 1958. At that time the idea was rather novel, and there was some scepticism about the need for such a course. Since there was only a short time available in which to cover the ground, it appeared necessary to emphasize the practical approach and concentrate on teaching methods and problems. Attention was also given, however, to the structure, syntax, morphology, and phonology of the English language, with some comparative phonology and an introduction to phonetic transcription. Theory was supplemented by practice teaching under observation. Participants attended seminars and, on alternate days, classes in a foreign language radically different from English in order to gain sensitivity to the students' problems.

The Department of Education continued to sponsor the course after the language and citizenship programs were placed under the Department of the Provincial Secretary and Citizenship. The former paid the salaries of the required specialists and issued certificates to the successful candidates, while the latter organized the course, specified the content, and provided for co-ordination with the night school. Originally intended for night school teachers in Ontario, the course was extended at the request of the Citizenship Branch in Ottawa to include teachers from other provinces and, at the request of External Affairs, to include those going out as teachers or teacher trainers to Africa and Asia under the technical assistance program.

From the time responsibility for citizenship education was first assumed, the Community Programs Branch concerned itself with helping teachers devise and use appropriate techniques. Before the formal course was available, the work was done mostly through seminars and advisory visits. After 1948 five or six seminars were held on the average each season in different parts of the province. They usually extended over a whole day and an evening or parts of two days, and consisted of general discussions of language problems, demonstrations of actual teaching at different levels, and an examination of resource materials available to teachers. In Toronto and a few of the larger centres, special seminars were held with teachers employed by groups such as churches and settlement houses. Advisory visits were made to teachers in more remote communities where there was not a large enough group for a seminar.

A contribution to language teaching in the 1960s was the development of a linguistic library from which teachers interested in linguistic theory or instructional techniques could borrow books. Another contribution to the same cause was the acquisition of a series of language training films for the use of the liaison staff in seminars. The five titles were 1 / "The Nature of Language and How It Is Learned," 2 / "The Sounds of Language," 3 / "The Organization of Language," 4 / "Words and Their Meaning," and 5 / "Modern Techniques in Language Teaching." The branch purchased another set of twelve films from the BBC in 1965 dealing with problems encountered in the classroom. They were considered particularly valuable for the new teacher as a means of drawing attention to the advantages and pitfalls of different approaches. Additions to the stock of films continued to be made in subsequent years.

The first provincial conference for teachers of English as a second language was sponsored by the Citizenship Branch in 1967 as a means of enabling teachers to exchange ideas and keep up with the latest developments. At the suggestion of many of the participating teachers, who numbered more than one thousand, the conference was repeated the following year, and promised to become an annual event.

Distribution of materials

Resource material has been supplied to language and citizenship classes from the beginning. The responsibility was assumed at first by the Community Programs Branch and, from 1951 on, by the federal Department of Citizenship and Immigration. Even after that date, the branch continued to purchase supplementary material, primarily for the use of instructors.

Citizenship resource materials prepared and published by the federal agency consisted of the series *Canadian Scene*, *Our Land*, *Our History*, *Our Government*, and *Our Resources*. The series selected for language training was *Learning the English Language*, written in an adaptation of Basic English. There were thought to be two main reasons for the choice: 1 / that the material offered an adequate and inexpensive way of teaching enough English for immigrant purposes and 2 / that it was well organized, and enabled even relatively untrained teachers to achieve satisfactory results. The staff of the Community Programs Branch, and later of the Citizenship Division, were increasingly aware, however, of the deficiencies of the material. Their main objection to Basic English was that it was a sub-language, and gave the student a false impression of the English language. Negotiations were therefore conducted with the federal authorities to permit a more satisfactory alternative.

Under a new agreement reached in 1963, the Citizenship Division was authorized to purchase or produce a variety of language textbooks and to offer a choice of these materials for language classes. The Department of Citizenship and Immigration agreed to provide reimbursement based on the average expenditure for textbooks during the previous five years. The division thereupon proceeded to canvass the views of members of school boards, night school principals, and language teachers across the province on the suitability of items on a list prepared by a prominent group of linguists. A selection was made on the basis of these views and of the cost factors involved, and the new materials were made available.

There remained a problem in that, although most of the newer materials had attractive features, they were not Canadian in their content or in the general impression they created. Publications that might have been appropriately revised would have been too expensive for general distribution. Thus it was evident that Canadian-produced material was needed. C.W. Martin was accordingly employed to write the desired textbooks on the elementary and intermediate levels. Martin's background included the teaching of second languages at the secondary and adult levels and the devising of English language courses for use in other circumstances. His *Introduction to Canadian English*, in the original and revised forms, got an enthusiastic reception. As it developed, the series consisted of Book 1 for students at the elementary level, Book 1 for teachers at the same level, Supplementary Book 1 for the latter group, Book 2 for students at the advanced level, and Book 2 for teachers at the same level. They were adopted, not only in a large proportion of Ontario classes, but also in other provinces and abroad.

Testing and certification

From 1947 on, the regulations under the *Citizenship Act* provided that the courts might accept a certificate of proficiency in English and citizenship issued by a provincial Department of Education as evidence of fitness for naturalization. The Community Programs Branch and its successor agency in this area of responsibility accordingly arranged to provide examinations and to issue certificates of proficiency to successful candidates. During the decade after 1951, an estimated 20 per cent of the students attending classes tried the examinations, and approximately 15 per cent were successful. In some citizenship courts, judges have insisted that applicants for citizenship produce the certificate. In certain communities, voluntary agencies have offered encouragement by sponsoring ceremonies for those successfully completing the examinations, or even awarded prizes to those receiving the highest marks.

Special projects

As early as 1948, thirteen half-hour programs were broadcast from nine stations in Polish and Ukrainian, giving newcomers information on Canada's past, and telling how others had established themselves. Later uses of the media involved the co-operation of the Citizenship Division with the Metropolitan Educational Television Association in the production of the television course "Let's Speak English." The course consisted of seventy-eight half-hour programs broadcast in Toronto three times a week between October 1961 and April 1962. It was later offered by stations in other parts of Canada. At the Ohio State Awards, it received Honorable Mention, with flattering comments on several of its features. Arrangements were made to evaluate the results of the broadcasts, leading to the tentative conclusions that 1 / the program aroused interest in language learning, 2 / it tended to improve the achievement of those attending classes, and 3 / it could not replace class instruction in which corrections could be made on the spot. On the whole, the approach was judged to be of limited value.

After 1956 the Community Programs Branch and the Citizenship Branch undertook in succession to conduct various forms of research into language training. Activities undertaken included the production and evaluation of instructional material, and experimentation with various approaches to teaching at the elementary level using different textbooks, as well as no textbooks at all, in order to identify the crucial factor in the early stages of learning English. In the summer school of 1962 a research project was undertaken to determine the amount of learning that could take place at different levels in a short period of intensive training.

Mention has already been made of the experimental provision of periods of full-time instruction for children of at least twelve years of age. It was determined in a follow-up study of such children that over half of them successfully completed their academic year despite an absence of three months from their regular classrooms. As a result of this finding, a recommendation was made to the Select Committee on Youth that special English language instruction be provided for the immigrant child in school. Subsequently, a number of school boards, with supporting grants from the Department of Education, implemented this recommendation.

Other services

In addition to language and citizenship training, the Department of the Provincial Secretary and Citizenship has provided information services, translation services, community services, and public relations facilities. Most of these could be classified as educative in the broad sense. Information services have been provided both for groups and for individuals through English and foreign language publications, seminars, exhibitions, and a directory of ethnic organizations. Translation services are provided for individuals and for other departments of government. Documents dealt with include trade certificates, trade testimonials, proof of age documents, educational certificates, professional certificates, and correspondence. Community services have involved co-operation with voluntary organizations providing assistance to newcomers and with such agencies as the Social Planning Council of Metropolitan Toronto. Contact has been maintained with the ethnic press and with any association involved in promoting citizenship or the economic adjustment of newcomers. Members of the staff have been prepared to speak to interested groups on any aspect of citizenship and immigrant adjustment. Public relations have involved the preparation of press releases for the ethnic and English language press designed to inform the public about available government services. Messages are also sent to ethnic organizations on the occasion of significant events or commemorations.

THE DEPARTMENT OF LABOUR

The Department of Labour has been concerned with industrial training in two major respects. 1 / It has facilitated and promoted occupational and trades training in an effort to improve the quality of the labour force. 2 / It has been responsible for the certification of tradesmen, in the process of which it has established certain minimum levels of competence. To a considerable extent, certification has been designed in the interests of public safety.

Apprenticeship

Originally the department's only instrument for discharging its responsibility for the improvement of the labour force was apprenticeship. The role of the department was defined in *The Apprenticeship Act* of 1928. The original version of the act had an attached schedule, listing as "designated trades" bricklayer, mason, carpenter, painter and decorator, and plasterer. Provision was made for the Lieutenant-Governor-in-Council, on the recommendation of the Minister of Labour, to make additions to this list. An inquiry leading to the designation of a particular trade might be initiated on the receipt by the minister of a petition signed by at least twenty-five employers. In 1964 designated trades included barbering, bricklaying, carpentry, electric wiring and installation, hairdressing, painting and decorating, plastering, plumbing, refrigeration and air conditioning, sheet metal work, steamfitting, motor vehicle repair, and body and fender work.

The Act of 1928 gave the Minister of Labour the responsibility of regulating the conditions of apprenticeship in designated trades. No minor could be employed in such a trade for longer than three months except under the prescribed contract, which had to be signed by the prospective apprentice, by his father, mother, guardian, or a judge of the local county or district court, and by the employer. Provision was made for the appointment of a Provincial Apprenticeship Committee composed of equal numbers of employers and employees to advise the minister on conditions governing apprenticeship. The Lieutenant-Governor-in-Council could also appoint an Inspector of Apprenticeship (later called director) responsible to the minister, to register apprenticeship contracts, to ensure that the conditions were complied with, to arouse and promote interest in the adoption of the apprenticeship system, to assist in the establishment of apprenticeship training programs, to co-operate with educational authorities in providing apprenticeship training, and to deal with other similar matters.[1] The inspector could refuse to register any contract of apprenticeship that was not in his opinion for the benefit of the apprentice.

Regulations might be made under the act, including

> prescribing the powers, duties and functions of apprenticeship committees relative to the designation of any trade, the period or periods of apprenticeship, the qualifications upon which apprenticeship may commence in any designated trade, the standard of education for the apprentice, the nature and number of educational classes to be attended by the apprentice, the course of training to be given an apprentice in a designated trade, the number of apprentices that may be employed by an employer in a designated trade, the issuance of a certificate to an apprentice who has completed his term of service, fixing the hours of labour and rates of wages for apprentices, recommending such methods of assessment of employers as may be deemed necessary to maintain a system of apprenticeship in any industry or designated trade.

The act underwent a number of revisions during succeeding years. In 1964 it was superseded by *The Apprenticeship and Tradesmen's Qualification Act*, which followed the same lines as its predecessor. Arrangements were continued for the Minister of Labour to appoint a provincial advisory committee in any trade or group of trades to advise him on the establishment and operation of apprenticeship training programs and tradesmen's qualifications. The Director of Apprenticeship could also appoint local apprenticeship committees to perform functions comparable to those of provincial committees. The director's powers to enforce the act were specified in some detail. In general, during and since 1964 there have been attempts to make the apprenticeship system more flexible and more in tune with modern educational ideas. The program offers more choice, a larger amount of educational content, and less arbitrary time serving.

The formal part of the apprenticeship training program was offered during the 1950s in the Provincial Institute of Trades, which began operations in 1952, and in the 1960s in other provincial institutes and vocational centres. Their educational offerings are discussed in volume IV, chapter 14. In 1967–8 and 1968–9 the colleges of applied arts and technology took over their responsibilities, as indicated in the subsequent three chapters of the same volume.

Federal financial involvement in apprenticeship training began with the federal-provincial agreement worked out in 1944. As has already been indicated in chapter 11 of the present volume, Ontario's apprenticeship act met the conditions under which the federal government was willing to share equally in the instructional, administrative, and supervisory costs of apprenticeship programs.

In June 1969 there were about 17,500 active apprentices in over one hundred designated trades, with the total increasing by 10 to 15 per cent a year. Most of them were receiving three eight-week periods of formal education at the colleges of applied arts and technology, with which the Department of Labour made yearly contracts. The department was increasing its efforts to keep the formal educational and on-the-job components relevant by conducting individual trade surveys and analyses. The development of research was tending to reduce reliance on the advisory committees.

On-the-job training

In 1965 the Department of Labour added a new dimension to its activities by going into on-the-job training on a substantial scale. A new Industrial Training Branch was established with a training staff which had grown by the spring of 1966 to about 180.[2] Three divisions of the branch were responsible for program development and promotion, field services, and administration. A large-scale promotion campaign was undertaken to sell the advantages of on-the-job training to employers and prospective employees. The favourable response was attributed to the acute shortage of skilled workers in many trades and occupations and to the financial and technical assistance that the department was prepared to provide.

The nature of some of his department's activities was explained by the minister, Honourable H.L. Rowntree, in the Legislature in March 1966.

> One of the new ingredients of our industrial training programme is short-term skill development. We recognize that not all jobs call for fully trained craftsmen or journeymen. Often the need is for workers who possess several specific skills. Short-term training provides a method of teaching these specific skills on-the-job where complete trades training is not required.

Under this system, training is carried out in periods ranging from two weeks to two years. The trainees learn under qualified instructors and, in some instances, depending on the complexity of the skills involved, on-the-job instruction is supplemented by classroom work carried out by The Ontario Department of Education.[8]

Departmental staff concentrate on developing expertise in analysing the needs of particular industries, in co-operating with them in drawing up a training schedule, and in devising a program. Instructors have been sought and given assistance in developing teaching techniques. Research has been conducted to determine whether the programs are successful on a cost/benefit basis.

In 1969 financial assistance for the programs was given on an individual basis, depending on need. On the whole, the federal and provincial governments together contributed between 10 and 25 per cent, although assistance in specific cases might go as high as 50 per cent. Attention was being focused increasingly on disadvantaged groups, including certain immigrants and Indians.

An idea being introduced from Europe, but still in experimental form in Ontario, was that of modular block programming. It is a method of linking industrial and institutional training, involving the design of programs in small blocks that may be added to over an extended period – even a lifetime. The successful development of the approach will depend on closer co-operation between industry and formal education than has existed in the past.

THE DEPARTMENT OF CORRECTIONAL SERVICES

Issues

Multitudes of humanitarians have advocated rehabilitative treatment for adult and juvenile offenders confined to correctional institutions on the grounds of society's obligation to promote the dignity and personal fulfilment of all of its members. On the practical level, there has been massive evidence of the cost of releasing embittered and vocationally incompetent men and women to repeat their transgressions and continue the dreary cycle of conviction and incarceration. The case for an effective educational program during the period of detention appears to be overwhelming. It is reinforced by the relatively low educational status evidenced by the average offender. It would be a denial of some of the most fundamental educational assumptions to accept the claim made by certain recent investigators that education does not reduce crime, but merely produces smarter criminals. One would need to make sure that what was designated as education was not simply a kind of mechanically administered skill training, lacking a major component of human sympathy and compassion manifested without any suggestion of condescension.

The correctional institutions face some very serious difficulties in carrying out their educative functions. A fundamental problem is revealed in a statement of purpose contained in the 1968 annual report of the Minister of Correctional Services.

The main purposes of the Department of Correctional Services are 1 / to hold in custody, for prescribed periods, those persons sentenced by the courts to its jurisdiction and 2 / to attempt to modify the attitudes of those in its care, whether children or adults, to such an extent that their actions upon release will be essentially law-abiding rather than law-breaking, and to provide them with the kind of training and treatment that will afford them better opportunities for successful personal and social adjustment.[4]

However skilfully the writer of the statement may have tried to word the first of his two points, it unavoidably reflects society's insistence that the offender be punished by detention. And there is no use trying to escape the fact that popular support for punishment is based only partly on the belief that punishment is in itself corrective; there is a large element of sheer vengeance in society's attitude toward the convict. Any hope that the latter, however, insensitive, will not be aware of this attitude is naïve in the extreme. Thus it is extremely important that there be no complacency about the problem inherent in the statement that follows the above quotation: "Any program within the Department must be designed with prime emphasis on these two purposes and carried out in such a way that they are in consonance with each other."

It is of course possible that the convicted law-breaker will conclude that punishment is not only inconvenient and unpleasant, but sufficiently certain that he should, in his own best interests, avoid making himself liable to it in the future. Although his rehabilitation may not go very deep, there is a reasonable chance that it can be sustained provided that he has marketable skills and, even more important, that society will give him a fair chance to use them rather than holding his past transgressions against him to the point where he has no real option except to repeat them. The type of individual who is retrievable in this way represents a common stereotype in the public mind, and has a great deal to do with the form and structure of the Ontario judicial and detention system. But there are far fewer transgressors of this type than most people think. Among other categories, many of whom do not return to the institution, are those whose rehabilitation may have progressed very far before detention, or even been practically completed, through contemplation of the offense and its implications and consequences, through the traumatic experience of arrest, trial, and conviction, and through the sense of alienation from society resulting from self-identification as a criminal. Those who commit crimes of passion often fall into this category. Another major group consists of those who attribute their state to bad luck, to what they see as the malign nature of social institutions, and to the ill-will of their fellow citizens. They have no personal sense of remorse, and perhaps not even any great feeling of regret for having been apprehended, since it is quite possible to learn to enjoy life in modern reform institutions. To change their attitude in any fundamental sense is a monumental task. And it is completely unrealistic to overlook the fact that there are incorrigibles who are unreachable by any known techniques. The institutional function in their case is reduced to protecting the rest of society from their depredations. Society cannot be blamed for depriving them of their freedom in defence of its own best interests; in fairness, and again in its own best interests, it should not be too ready to consign anyone to the incorrigible category. In the Canadian penal system, the most serious offenders are of course detained in the federal penitentiaries, and are not the direct responsibilty of the province.

It is only to be expected that the inmates of a prison will resent involuntary detention, and that their resentment will be directed against those whose responsibility it is to detain them. Thus there is almost inevitable tension between the custodial staff on the one hand and those in charge of education and rehabilitation on the other. If the latter are as successful as they would like to be in persuading the inmates that they are motivated by genuine interest and sympathy, that, in a sense, they are "on their side," a clash between the two staff groups can be quite serious.

A particularly difficult problem in institutions of detention is the development of a destructive sub-culture. It is characterized by bullying, fear, group loyalty, admiration for undesirable models of behaviour, and a common hostility toward all categories of staff. Newcomers may be absorbed quickly into this sub-culture, and progress rapidly in the school of crime. They emerge from the institution as much more of a menace than when they went in. Where such an atmosphere dominates the institution, it is exceedingly difficult to eliminate. Under the circumstances, the educational program may impart skills, but has little chance of achieving any truly rehabilitative objectives.

Juveniles are sent to training schools as a result of behaviour that in an adult would result in conviction and incarceration. They are typically the product of unfavourable home conditions, quite often of broken homes. Working mothers have probably been blamed for far more of the trouble than they have caused. It is not the fact that the mother is out of the home a considerable part of the day that creates the problem, but rather the attitude she displays toward the child during the time she is at home. Delinquent children have usually learned to think of the world as a cold, unsympathetic, unfriendly place. Their teachers have failed, as have their parents, to demonstrate a convincing interest in them, and they have learned to dislike school. Their behaviour ranges from the completely withdrawn to the highly offensive and irritating. They may suffer from serious emotional disturbances. John Brown, MPP for Beaches-Woodbine, has objected strenuously to the presence of emotionally disturbed children in training schools, making a strong case for regarding emotional disturbance as the primary consideration, rather than the commission of an offence, in determining appropriate treatment.

Role of the department

The Department of Reform Institutions, established twenty-two years earlier, was renamed the Department of Correctional Services in 1968, presumably to indicate a more enlightened attitude toward adult and juvenile transgressors. At the same time, the existing jails, reformatories, industrial farms, and regional detention centres were labeled "correctional institutions." The department is responsible for 1 / children up to sixteen years of age who are assigned to training schools by the juvenile and family courts under *The Training Schools Act* and 2 / all adult offenders in the province with sentences up to two years less a day. Education is a major aspect of the treatment of both groups.

Early objectives and program

There have been very substantial improvements in educational programs in the correctional institutions in recent years. This is not to say, however, that the existence of good intentions is a recently developed phenomenon. Immediately after the Second World War, the so-called Ontario Plan was proclaimed as the basis for the custody, care, education, and rehabilitation of prisoners. Its substance was as follows:

(1) Considerable extension of the classification of prisoners, with smaller Institutions and for special groups.
(2) Replacement of the Common Gaols by modern Industrial Farms. This, as it progressively evolved, would help to remedy the classification problem and, at the same time, reduce the size of the inmate population at the Ontario Reformatory, Guelph, and the Industrial Farm, Burwash.
(3) Rapid expansion of the academic study programmes in the Reformatories and Industrial Farms to the effective limit.
(4) Inauguration of formal vocational training and expansion of it to the effective limit in conjunction with the present industrial and other work.
(5) Physical drill for all inmates likely to benefit by it, with an up-to-date recreation programme, physical and mental, for all inmates.
(6) Permanent employment of specialists to apply the best penological and scientific methods.
(7) Increased care in the selection of suitable officers and employees. Formal, as well as practical, training of Guards, and special courses for other personnel as conditions require it. Selection of faculty to give the technical and formal training on a broad perspective.
(8) Systematic and intensive efforts by very carefully selected personnel to rehabilitate ex-prisoners.[5]

At the same time, the objective of the training schools was to provide the best possible rehabilitative treatment for each child. The program included the prescribed academic courses given in the regular public and separate schools, along with as much practice as possible in various handicrafts.

During this period, the opportunity of enrolling in academic and vocational education classes in the reformatories appears to have been regarded very much as a privilege to be granted rather than as a matter of course. A major proportion of the inmates had not completed elementary school, and some were illiterate. The Ontario course of study was followed as closely as possible. At the Ontario Reformatory at Brampton, there were six academic classes with small enrolment to provide for the large amount of individual instruction required. A policy of individual promotion was followed, with each student urged to progress as quickly as possible. The local inspector of public schools provided supervision. The vocational program consisted of courses in sheet metal, radio, welding, machine shop, motor mechanics, and cooking. It was claimed that a student who had had six months of training was on the level of a second-year apprentice.

By the mid-1950s the educational programs in the adult institutions had assumed greater importance, and more active steps were taken to encourage inmates to enrol in them. Illiterates and near-illiterates could attend classes for half of each day, and many were reported to be attaining grade 4 standing. Academic instruction for those at a stage between grade 4 and grade 10 was provided only in evening classes at Guelph, but daytime classes were held at the Ontario Training Centre in Brampton and at the Andrew Mercer Reformatory for Females. The correspondence courses of the Department of Education were available in all institutions. Vocational classes were provided in a considerably enlarged group of trades and crafts as compared with the 1940s. An effort was being made to employ psychometric tests in order to ensure that each individual chose an area of vocational specialization in line with his own particular aptitudes and inclinations. A program of training for custodial officers was being offered at Guelph, with some claim of success.

The Training Schools Advisory Board has been an element of major importance in the administrative structure for the training schools during the period under review. The members of this agency have advised the minister on the state of the training schools and on the welfare of the children admitted to them. They have maintained a continuous examination of the program at each school and suggested appropriate modifications. Since the establishment of the aftercare system, they have considered all recommendations of aftercare officers with respect to the placement of wards. They have also made recommendations to the minister on the termination of wardship, which may continue until the individual concerned is eighteen years of age.

The annual report of the minister for 1955 contains the twenty-fourth annual report of the Training Schools Advisory Board. Some of the sentiments it contained have a stern, old-fashioned sound.

> Parents who are delinquent in their duty are the chief cause of juvenile delinquency. Children cannot be allowed to do as they please following their own desires. They must be counselled, corrected and directed in accordance with right, reason and in the light of the Ten Commandments of God and inspired to do right.[6]

At this time, it was being recognized in the training schools that pupils in the primary and junior divisions benefited from being separated from adolescents. An attempt was being made to prepare students to fit into classes in the regular school system without loss of time when they emerged from the training schools.

Academic programs were being increasingly differentiated from one school to another to provide for groups of children with varied capacities and needs. The Bowmanville school offered auxiliary classes up to grade 10, with a high school commercial course and a vocational program including woodwork, machine shop, horticulture, auto mechanics, sheet metal, leather craft, laundry, barbering, farming, and cooking. An attached farm offered a variety of practical experiences. At Guelph, the academic program covered grades 1 to 8, with an auxiliary class and a manual training shop. Educative activities included communal activities in the school residence, a recreation program featuring sports and crafts, and participation in cubs and scout camps.

The annual report of 1959 contains an assessment by the deputy minister, Hedley Basher, of the situation as it existed at the time. He referred to the policy adopted when the department was founded – a policy aimed at the rehabilitation of the offender through a treatment and training program. He mentioned the disappointment of some people that such a policy had not shown immediate results. The difficulties in implementing it had involved obtaining the necessary physical plant, recruiting professional trained personnel such as psychiatrists, doctors, psychologists, social workers, and rehabilitation officers, and encouraging the custodial officer to become treatment-oriented and to promote a constructive rather than a repressive atmosphere so as to give the offender cause for hope rather than despair. Basher claimed credit for a reasonable amount of progress in all these areas, but also acknowledged that a great deal needed to be done.[7]

The annual report for 1960 gives an account of programs of staff training. Regular courses were offered at the Staff Training School at Guelph. In-service courses were also provided in various institutions to give all members of staff the over-all picture of policy and methods in their own particular institutions. An attempt was made to acquaint custodial staff with the aims of treatment and to develop in treatment staff an appreciation of the problems faced by the custodial staff. The department also assisted in a university extension course on correctional problems. As a means of augmenting the interest created by the course, staff libraries were being improved.[8]

The opening of the minimum security Ontario Training School for Girls at Trelawney House in Port Bolster was a significant development at the beginning of the 1960s. It was a self-contained unit, adapted from a former residence, and designed to accommodate about twenty girls. Although it was recognized that small units were relatively expensive to administer, they offered a more home-like atmosphere than did the larger institutions. The girls were soon participating successfully in certain community activities, and some were attending the local high school.

In a number of respects the early 1960s constituted a period of progress. In particular, there were improvements in buildings and facilities. But many of the staff members that the reform institutions were able to recruit were mediocre. Teachers were being offered far better salaries and working conditions in the regular school systems. Those who chose to work in the training schools had to accept the twelve-month working year required by the civil service. The courses they offered were criticized as often being poorly structured and uninspired. They were not well equipped to offer that special measure of interest and sympathy needed to overcome the hostility manifested by many of the students in their charge.

Changes in staffing procedures with respect to teachers since 1965

A very substantial change was brought about by an arrangement made in 1965 under the direction of the Honourable Allan Grossman, minister since 1963, to enable teachers to work on a ten-month contract parallel to that employed by school boards. They were subsequently paid according to a scale equal to that of the larger school systems, with an additional bonus of $500 a year. They taught classes of about fifteen in the academic and twelve in the vocational program. As a result of the favourable welfare and working conditions being offered, it was possible to select among a surplus of applicants for positions in the schools, and to insist on a high level of preparation as well as evidence of special personal characteristics. It became reasonable to expect that the strongly antipathetic attitude that many of the children brought to the schools could be broken down, and that they could return to the regular system with at least a moderate prospect of success.

By 1969 the department had about 120 fully qualified teachers and about 35 trade instructors. The latter were all in the civil service category, and not generally as well qualified as the graduates from the College of Education programs. The work of the schools continued to be inspected by Department of Education superintendents, and visits were made by program consultants. Stress was being placed on the use of instructional technology including educational television. Innovations such as team teaching had been encouraged by the Director of Education, Douglas Mackey, who was appointed to the new position in 1965. He had also initiated research studies into such questions as where the students went and how well they succeeded after they left the schools.

Staff training and development

The department provided an impressive program of staff training and development in order to produce attitudes, knowledge, and skills in harmony with enlightened correctional practices. The program included courses, seminars, and conferences at the departmental Staff Training School; programs offered within the government service; seminars and courses offered by outside agencies; and continuous programs conducted by individual correctional institutions. Appointment to the regular staff was preceded by a five-week basic course at the Staff Training School. Conferences, seminars, and workshops were offered continuously to keep staff members aware of new trends and developments in the field of corrections as well as to give them an opportunity to discuss matters of particular interest with specialists. Training at more advanced levels was intended to meet the particular needs of individual groups such as superintendents, assistant superintendents, jail governors, chief supervisors, recreation supervisors, teachers, and others. The extension programs of various universities provided considerable help in meeting certain needs.

The department offered fellowships to assist graduate students working in the social sciences. Three of these were awarded in 1967 and six in 1968. The recipients were expected to serve the department for a period of time equal to the years of support. Many of them continued their association as permanent members of the professional staff.

Recent educational provisions for adult offenders

Education of necessity continued to be offered to adults only on a voluntary basis; any other approach would be a contradiction in terms. Special efforts were concentrated on younger offenders who were most amenable to training and most able to benefit from it. There were five training centres for young men where they attended school full time. The program was equally divided between academic and vocational classes. The federal Department of Manpower had co-operated in setting up a special course at the Brampton Training Centre, which was intended as a prototype for other institutions. It was possible to establish eligibility for apprenticeship programs which might be entered on after release. The libraries were considered an important element in the educational program, and reported a high turnover of books. Recreational activities were receiving increasing emphasis, and the program was already benefiting from the availability of graduates of the recreation courses offered by the colleges of applied arts and technology.

Increasing demands for educational facilities resulted from the provincial assumption of responsibility for the county jails in 1968. Many of these were notoriously lacking in rehabilitative amenities and services. Important recent developments have included arrangements with Sheridan College of Applied Arts and Technology whereby inmates may be released under certain conditions to attend courses there and instructors from the College may visit the institutions to assist with educational activities. The prospects of improving the constructive aspects of the instructional program have been improved by the passage of the so-called Omnibus Bill by the Parliament of Canada, removing certain restrictions on the release of inmates for educational purposes, home visits, and other privileges.

The training school program

As of 1969 boys assigned to a training school by the courts were sent to a Reception and Assessment Centre at Bowmanville, where their needs were diagnosed by a team consisting of a medical doctor, a psychiatrist, a social worker, a psychologist, a chaplain, and a guidance teacher. They then went to a classification committee consisting of the superintendents of a number of schools along with a psychologist, a social worker, and a guidance teacher. Here a choice of the appropriate school was made on the basis of their intelligence, interests, and other characteristics. The schools differed somewhat in terms of the age groups they dealt with and the instructional program they offered. In all of them there was a basic program consisting of 1 / social aspects, including participation in community activities, 2 / spiritual aspects, including classroom instruction in religious education, chapel services, weekly church services, and counselling, 3 / recreational aspects, including sports, hobbies, crafts, camping, scouts, cubs, cadet corps, and musical activities, and 4 / certain common academic offerings. The different schools also provided individual academic programs at the beginning of 1969 as follows. Coldsprings Forestry Camp at Ganaraska, for boys aged thirteen to sixteen, offered part-time classroom instruction in basic academic subjects and vocational training in such areas as reforestation, road and park improvement, and fire fighting. Pine Ridge School at Bowmanville, for boys in the same age range, offered an occupational training program for grades 9 and 10, with academic, vocational, and senior opportunity classes; its vocational courses included welding, carpentry, building construction, painting and decorating, sheet metal, auto servicing, horticulture, and agriculture. Brookside School at Cobourg, for boys of twelve and thirteen, offered opportunity classes for special education and remedial teaching and also industrial arts. White Oaks Village at Hagersville, for boys aged eight to twelve, offered classroom instruction at each boy's individual grade level, with remedial instruction. Sprucedale School, for boys of fourteen to sixteen, also located at Hagersville, offered the secondary school Science, Technology, and Trades course and one and two-year occupational training programs, with vocational work in machine shop, welding, carpentry and building construction, auto mechanics, and mechanical drafting. Glendale School at Simcoe offered the Five-year and Four-year Arts and Science and Business and Commerce Courses as well as industrial arts and mechanical drafting. Hillcrest School at Guelph, for boys of fourteen to sixteen, offered the Department of Education correspondence courses beyond grade 10, programmed learning for slow learners, and vocational courses in sheet metal, carpentry, and machine shop. Accommodation in these schools ranged from 40 to 190.

After commitment by the courts, girls were sent to the Reception and Diagnostic Centre at Galt, where diagnostic procedures were handled by a medical doctor, a psychiatrist, a psychologist, a social worker, and a teacher. Like the boys, they then proceeded to a Classification Committee, from which they were sent to one of three schools. The girls' schools also had a basic social, spiritual, recreational, and academic program, but varied in their school offerings. In 1969 Grand View School at Galt, for girls aged thirteen to sixteen, provided one and two-year occupational training courses and music instruction as well as vocational courses in home economics, serving, cooking, commercial work, business machines, beauty culture, and practical nursing. Kawartha Lakes School at Lindsay, for girls of the same age range, provided courses in the Arts and Science and Business and Commerce programs, with vocational courses in home economics and sewing. Trelawney House at Port Bolster, for girls from ten to thirteen, provided remedial teaching.

There were also three private training schools for Roman Catholic children: St John's at Uxbridge for boys up to sixteen from the western part of the province, St Joseph's at Alfred for boys in the same age range from the eastern part of the province, and St Euphrasia's in Toronto for girls. A school in a special category for boys of all faiths was built at Sudbury in 1968. The operational expenses of the private schools were fully met by provincial funds.

There was a periodic evaluation of students by a committee of the senior staff in each group of training schools. The Advisory Board, as mentioned earlier, received recommendations for placement. Through the recommendations of this board, students might be assigned to their own home, a foster home, or a boarding home until the period of wardship was terminated. The guidance and support of the department's aftercare officers, numbering approximately one hundred in 1969, were particularly important during the first few weeks after discharge, when the child faced the most serious adjustment problems.

THE DEPARTMENT OF JUSTICE

The Office of the Fire Marshal

The Office of the Ontario Fire Marshal, under the direction of M.S. Hurst, operated in 1969 as part of the Department of Justice. It was involved in two major educative activities: the training of fire fighters and the production and dissemination of information on fire prevention. The first of these involved training municipal fire fighters in the basic skills of firemanship, and fire department officers in the broader aspects of fire protection technology. Fire fighters were given short courses on an itinerant basis and in three regional fire training schools a year conducted in different parts of the province. Fire department officers were trained at the Ontario Fire College at Gravenhurst.

Training of fire fighters

The fire training program began in 1939, when a two-day course in fire fighting was given to fire chiefs and firemen from all over Ontario with the co-operation of the University of Toronto Extension Department. University faculty members lectured and, not for the first or last time, had difficulty in selecting appropriate material and in communicating effectively. A lecture on hydraulics was regarded as distinctly unsuitable. A more successful aspect of the program involved demonstrations of fire fighting equipment at the headquarters of the fire department.

In the early stages of the program, regional firemen's training schools were established at St Catharines and Kirkland Lake under the auspices of the University of Toronto, at London under the University of Western Ontario, and at Kingston under Queen's University. Emphasis was placed on training for candidates from the north because of the prevalence of frame buildings in that region. Courses were for municipal fire fighters, since the Department of Lands and Forests was mainly responsible for dealing with forest fires.

During the Second World War the Air Raid Precaution Services were organized, and various forms of training were provided. In over a hundred municipalities, between five and six thousand auxiliary firemen completed thirty weeks of part-time training. The Fire Marshal's Office produced a training manual and a large amount of literature on fire protection and anti-sabotage measures. Assistance was provided with training of members of the armed forces in methods of fire fighting. During the Korean War, there was increased emphasis on such activities, including preparation for dealing with an atomic attack, a possibility which members of the public and education officials were often reluctant to face.

Training was provided by travelling instructors, who went around establishing programs in the headquarters of fire departments. These programs involved a few weeks of three-hour evening sessions in which basic skills of firemanship, such as the use of equipment, were taught. Since many of the participants were volunteers, they did not always face the long sessions with enthusiasm.

The Ontario Fire College

In 1949 *The Fire Departments Act* was amended to provide for the establishment of a fire college for fire officer training. It was some time, however, before the college materialized. A forward step was taken in 1956, when the Attorney-General of the day, the Honourable Kelso Roberts, had $100,000 placed in his budget to begin the implementation of the scheme. It was hoped that the proposed college might be associated with the Ontario Agricultural College at Guelph, but there was no great enthusiasm at that institution. The excuse given was that the smoke produced by fire-fighting activities might damage the seed-beds used in agricultural experiments. In fact, none of the universities was particularly interested in sponsoring the college.

Finally the local municipal authorities in Muskoka offered a site near Gravenhurst on which some useful buildings were located. The Ontario government proceeded to purchase these in 1957, and renovations were completed in time for an official opening on August 22, 1958, under the principalship of D.E. Barrett. From that time on, all specialized and advanced training were held at the new college, the first of its kind in the country.

The construction of additional buildings was begun immediately, and equipment and training facilities were increased. Some of the early structures provided were a four-storey drill tower, a general purpose building, and a test fire building. By 1969 the total complement of buildings had risen to thirteen, with residential accommodation increased from thirty to forty students. The college was advertised as one of the best equipped fire training establishments on the continent.

The number of students enrolled at any particular time was completely determined by the residential accommodation. Thus a succession of courses was offered, with groups of trainees continually coming and going. During its first full year of operation, the college offered twelve courses between early May and late October. The calendar for 1969 listed 22 courses given during an academic year extending from February 24 to November 28.[9] A small group in the new fire protection technology course attended from the beginning of the academic year until the first of August. Other courses were arranged in sequence, mostly of two weeks' duration, but some lasting only a week.

The program for 1959 included courses in the following areas: radiological monitoring, basic fire inspection practice, atomic fire hazards in industry, advanced fire inspection practice. Courses were directed at such groups as Fire Marshal's Office staff, volunteer fire officers, company officers, senior fire officers, fire department instructors, and county fire co-ordinators. A large part of the program consisted of practical work dealing with such matters as flammable liquids and gas hazards, heating equipment and air conditioning, gas appliances and propane gas systems, electrical hazards, and detection and alarm systems. Considerable attention was paid to the use of the most up-to-date equipment. Where appropriate, courses also covered problems of organization and administration of fire departments.

The students paid no fees, since the college was maintained entirely by the provincial government. Those who came from Ontario municipal fire departments were provided with free board and lodging as well as instructional materials, and were reimbursed for their travelling expenses. Students from industrial and institutional fire brigades in Ontario and all those from outside Ontario were responsible for such expenses themselves.

A new departure in the program began in 1967 with the introduction of the fire protection technology course designed to provide a combination of academic study and practical experience under a co-operative scheme. Comparable in course content to many of the technology courses offered at Ryerson Polytechnical Institute and at the colleges of applied arts and technology, it represented a recognition of the need to emphasize the development of adaptability and flexibility in the face of the increasing complexities of modern society, with an assumption that such qualities could be produced by longer programs with a larger component of general education. The new course consisted of a fire prevention unit of 320 hours, a fire fighting operations unit of 320 hours, and a fire department administration unit of 240 hours, making a total of 880 hours of study to extend over a three-year period. A practice period of at least two months was recommended after each unit. Some of the components of the program of studies were English, including report writing, science, mathematics, principles of fire prevention and fire protection, features of building design, the preparation and interpretation of building plans, design of fire detection and fire protection equipment, functions of testing laboratories, preparation of fire prevention by-laws, and development of fire prevention programs.

There was some speculation about the possibility of bringing the type of fire-fighting program offered by the Ontario Fire College into the colleges of applied arts and technology, and some discussions had been held on the matter, but without a definite outcome. From the Fire Marshal's vantage point, the benefits from such a development appeared to be somewhat doubtful. The existing concentration of resources in one institution made a superior program easier to maintain than if the offerings were fragmented. Furthermore, the practice of paying all expenses for the major proportion of students would have been difficult to continue in the colleges of applied arts and technology.

Regional fire schools

During 1968 over one hundred fire fighters were given courses in regional fire training schools at Chatham, Barrie, and Sudbury. Each course consisted of forty hours of study and practice during a five-day period. Lectures were presented in the classroom, and practical training was provided on the fire training ground, using the facilities of the local municipalities and the equipment supplied by the Office of the Fire Marshal. Among the problems of offering such courses was the difficulty in getting men released from their regular duties, since municipal units were often understaffed.

Information services

The purpose of the program of information services was to create a public awareness of the danger of fire and of the best methods of dealing with it. Publicity and technical information were provided through the municipal fire departments and the news media. In 1968 the office's film loan library consisted of 303 titles and 894 films having to do with such matters as fire prevention, fire department training, civil defence, and life-saving techniques. Borrowers included municipal fire departments, industry, insurance and service organizations, hospitals, schools, and government institutions. A publication entitled *Fire Marshal's Quarterly News* was produced four times a year to inform fire chiefs and their staffs of the latest developments in relation to their responsibilities. A great deal of material written for specific purposes was offered to the general public and to special groups. The publicity program also involved contact with the newspapers and with radio and television stations.

The Ontario Police College

The Ontario Police College at Aylmer was formally opened in January 1963, while the Honourable F.M. Cass was Attorney-General. It remained under the supervision of the Ontario Police Commission, and was directed from the beginning by J.L. Mennill. Its primary purpose was to provide training at all levels for police personnel, including officers of the Ontario Provincial Police and municipal police departments, as well as personnel from other departments and commissions of the Ontario government having duties in relation to law enforcement. The director was also authorized to admit railway and harbour police to utilize excess accommodation. Recently provision has been made for the acceptance of a maximum of two students from outside Ontario in any one course.

The college began operations in buildings formerly utilized for training purposes by the RCAF. They were remodelled where necessary, redecorated, and furnished in an appropriate manner. By 1969 the facilities consisted of an administration and classroom building, a drill hall with recreation facilities, dormitories accommodating 350 men, a dining hall and kitchen building, a health centre, an outdoor range, a building housing a library, study room, lounge, and snack bar, a staff residence, and various maintenance buildings.

In the initial stages the program consisted of twelve-week courses for recruits and refresher courses of varying lengths. More advanced courses were soon added. The program for 1964 consisted of three recruit courses, each of twelve weeks' duration; three general police training courses, each of ten weeks' duration; a supervisory and command training course and a detectives' course, each of five weeks' duration; and a shorter chiefs' course and a chief constables' seminar. There has been increasing emphasis recently on a police administration course. A traffic enforcement course and a traffic control course have been offered for several years in co-operation with the Ontario Traffic Conference.

The courses were all highly utilitarian in content. The recruit course was designed to provide constables at the probationary level with the basic knowledge of law and procedure required to perform normal duties. It was split into two parts to enable the student to take field training in the interval. The subject matter included law in general, traffic law and traffic accident investigation, courts and evidence, physical activities, police methods, and such miscellaneous topics as first aid and public relations. The general training course offered basic training for officers with a minimum of three years' experience. It was originally established to meet the needs of older, experienced officers who, before the college existed, had no opportunity to attend a formal course at a training school, but relied only on in-service training. It was intended to be phased out as increasing numbers of officers qualified at a recruit course. As offered in 1969, it was similar in content to the recruit course, with the addition of English, which took twenty-three of the four hundred instructional periods. The two-week supervisory course was for officers who had completed earlier training and either were in a supervisory position or were being considered for promotion to such a position. It included an introduction to the principles of management; elements of supervision; human relations in supervision; planning, evaluating, improving, and directing; reporting; effective communications; field supervision; and case studies. The criminal investigation course involved a study of law, investigative procedures, weapons training, and miscellaneous topics. The traffic enforcement course was designed to provide special training for officers responsible for the supervision and planning of traffic programs. The content included accident investigation, enforcement procedures, safety programming, and a review of the laws of evidence. The traffic law and accident investigation course dealt with the law and procedure of accident investigation rather than policy or methods of controlling traffic. The police administration course was for chief constables, deputy chief constables, and inspectors. It included such topics as the historical evolution of the police;

basic concepts in police action and police attitudes toward the criminal law, the courts, the legal profession, the public, and the accused; the historical background and development of the Criminal Code; basic principles of criminal procedure in the criminal courts; the process of setting, clarifying, and redefining organization objectives; principles of organization; and many others.

Successful candidates were granted appropriate diplomas. Recruits had to pass not only the formal course examinations, but also a personal assessment by the staff of the college. Success in the program of studies alone was not regarded as sufficient to ensure an effective police officer.

There were no fees for the basic groups for whom the college program was primarily intended. The costs of travel, board and lodging, supplies, and textbooks were defrayed by the Ontario government. Students not in these basic groups were charged for board and lodging, and had to look after their own travel expenses. Officers from outside the province were charged $50 a week in 1969 to cover all expenses except travel. The traffic law enforcement course provided in co-operation with the Ontario Traffic Conference involved a small fee for books and supplies. Fees for the traffic control course were set by the conference.

The courses provided by the college proved highly popular, and enrolment expanded rapidly from year to year. The number of student weeks of training rose from 5,565 in 1963 to 9,939 in 1965, and to 12,033 in 1968. During the latter year the newly established Metro Toronto Branch of the college also accounted for approximately 3,100 training weeks. This branch was opened mainly because the facilities at Aylmer did not provide enough space to accommodate recruits from Metropolitan Toronto. Staff were seconded from the Metropolitan Toronto Police Department to act as instructors. They were somewhat handicapped by inadequate facilities. Those available at Aylmer were also proving too limited.

In planning the future development and expansion of the program, emphasis has been placed on the need for refresher courses. The director of the college has urged a series of these courses, involving not only specialized content directly related to police duties, but also a considerable element of social sciences, including psychology, sociology, and political science. A trend toward more liberal studies, along with more advanced courses, will probably be characteristic of the future program of the college.

THE DEPARTMENT OF TOURISM AND INFORMATION AND THE DEPARTMENT OF PUBLIC RECORDS AND ARCHIVES

As of 1970 the Department of Tourism and Information and the Department of Public Records and Archives were supervised by the same minister, the Honourable J.A.C. Auld. In some respects, the activities of the two departments were co-ordinated for convenience and efficiency: for example, their operations were covered in the same annual report, and they co-operated in the production of certain publications and in the development of historical sites. In other respects, their work was not closely related.

The Department of Tourism and Information

Scope of educational program

The Department of Tourism and Information was involved in a number of areas of broadly defined educative activity. The most important of these were 1 / the production and dissemination of information, including brochures, pamphlets, posters, maps, photographs, and films; 2 / the development and maintenance of historic sites, from the erection of commemorative plaques to the full-scale restoration of earlier communities; 3 / providing support for museums; 4 / offering assistance in training adults and young people to deal courteously with visitors while serving in permanent positions or in temporary summer jobs in the tourist industry. Also, 5 / as a project that will call for continued maintenance and expansion, the Ontario Science Centre was planned and constructed to celebrate the Centennial of Confederation, although it was not officially opened until September 1969. There was a very comprehensive program of Centennial events in 1967, in which the department was involved in varying degrees. These included the Confederation Train, which visited fifteen Ontario municipalities and was inspected by 925,000 people; a voyageur canoe pageant, in which teams from most of the provinces competed in a race across the country; and a subsidy program for many cultural and educational activities.

Pamphlets, booklets, and brochures were prepared for distribution in order to describe and extol the attractions of Ontario, both natural and man-made. While there may be no direct implications for education in the attempt to improve the economy by luring foreign tourists to the province to spend their money, it is perhaps not inappropriate to point out that the income so generated has played a considerable part in the ability of the people to pay the local and provincial taxes on which the maintenance of an expensive educational system has been based. As the Ontario Economic Council has indicated, tourism is the largest single element of international trade, and receipts from foreign visitors to Canada have been rising twice as fast as our merchandise exports.[10] The same report recognized that an interest in history, traditions, and cultural attainments resulting from rising levels of education had an important influence on people's decision to travel. The publications of the department have represented an attempt to capitalize on this interest.

At one extreme, with a maximum emphasis on illustration and a minimum on words, is a brochure with no title other than *Ontario, friendly, familiar, foreign and near*[11] interspersing a series of brightly coloured photographs on the cover, and filled with similar attractive illustrations of a wide variety of emblems and scenes. Another, entitled *Rocks and Minerals, Ontario*, again most attractively illustrated, provides a brief course in geology and mineralogy for the tourist who wishes to travel with the maximum of informed preparation and with a definite purpose in mind. He may be interested in collecting specimens, semi-precious or otherwise, or merely in observing interesting rock formations. A brochure labelled *Ontario Fishing* not only informs the enthusiast about this activity, but also offers vistas of the scenic grandeur of the province.

Another type of publication has involved the co-operation of the archives staff in supplying historical material and sometimes in doing the actual writing. An unusually informative booklet, written by the archivist, D.F. McOuat, is entitled *Historic Ontario*. It draws attention to many of the historical landmarks of the province, gives information about the origins and early development of many communities, and refers to the contributions of individual pioneers. The Department of Education purchased large quantities for distribution in order to stimulate an interest in local history. The production of another brochure with the bilingual title *Sur la route des pionniers/Heritage Highways* involved co-operation between Ontario and Quebec; it illustrates the routes of the original explorers of parts of the two provinces, and presents a substantial amount of historical background.

These publications have value for the stay-at-home as well as for the traveller. Many a teacher has discovered their usefulness as stimulators of interest in provincial and local geography and history, and many a pupil has taken advantage of them as project material. For school purposes, whether or not they contribute to informed travel may be merely incidental. But they may also have considerable educational value as inspiration for excursions to interesting sites, an activity that has become increasingly common in recent years.

The production and distribution of promotional literature has been pursued with a considerable degree of energy throughout the 1960s. For 1960 the Department of Travel and Publicity, as it was then called, reported the distribution of over five million items, from booklets and brochures to road maps and post cards.[12] Recent reports do not provide exactly comparable information, but the number has increased greatly.

Plaques and historic sites

The reconstruction and maintenance of plaques and historic sites is an enterprise with considerable educational potential. The annual report for 1960 indicated that fifty-one plaques were put up in that year, making a total of 228 since the beginning of the program. The department acted on the recommendations of the Archaeological and Historic Sites Advisory Board of Ontario. Decisions were made on the basis of extensive research carried out in archives, libraries, registry offices, and early newspapers. This program was continued actively throughout the 1960s.

An important milestone was the passage of *The Archaeological and Historic Sites Protection Act* of Ontario in 1953. It prevented the Minister of Education, for a stated period of time, from excavating or altering an archaeological site or removing objects therefrom.

Among the most interesting examples of the development of historic sites was the restoration of the early Huron settlements in the Midland area. In 1960 archaeologists were employed to explore the area with a view to possible reconstruction of the original buildings and fortifications. On March 19, 1964, the Prime Minister announced the formation of the Huronia Historical Development Council to restore Ste Marie among the Hurons, a Jesuit mission abandoned in 1649, and the naval and military establishments at Penetanguishene, maintained for nearly half a century after the War of 1812. An expanded museum was to be built on Nancy Island to house the hull of the schooner *Nancy* and to tell the story of the naval war of 1812 on the Upper Great Lakes.

As restored, Ste Marie was provided with replicas of the ancient buildings and fortifications, all supplied with tools, utensils, and furnishings as in the original settlement. The timber palisades, longhouses, food storage pits, and drying scaffolds helped to restore an authentic seventeenth-century atmosphere as it existed in the Huron village.

Another of the many sites with important educational values for both children and adults is Upper Canada Village in eastern Ontario. There a visitor may observe a replica of life as it was lived in the settlements of the area in the early part of the nineteenth century. Wool is carded and spun, butter is churned, candles are made, blacksmiths ply their trade; these and many other activities provide the most vivid of history lessons. The archives people played their usual role in researching the earlier period and ensuring authenticity in the restorative work.

The Department of Public Records and Archives

First established in 1903, the Bureau of Archives became the Department of Public Records and Archives of Ontario by an act of the provincial Legislature twenty years later. The act defined its functions, which were summarized by D.F. McOuat:

(1) To collect, preserve, and make available the non-current records of enduring value of the Government of Ontario;

(2) To collect, preserve, and make available other unpublished material dealing with the history of Ontario.
(It should be noted that, while the Archives is not primarily the custodian of published works, this line of demarcation is somewhat indistinct.)[13]

There has been little change in the act or in the basic purposes of the archives throughout the years, although there has been a great increase in activity, along with corresponding modifications in structure and additions to staff.

On April 1, 1959, the department was transferred from the area of responsibility of the Minister of Education to that of the Minister of Travel and Publicity, at that time the Honourable B.L. Cathcart. The annual report for the same year indicated an active program of acquisition, analysis, indexing, and storage of material.[14] Documents received were classified as 1 / government records, 2 / municipal, legal, and land records, and 3 / non-government records. Some of those in the first category included sixty-five volumes of timber records obtained from the Department of Lands and Forests. Dealing mainly with lumbering operations in the Ottawa and Belleville areas between 1845 and 1900, they consisted of letter books, licence registers, records of timber and ground rent dues, cash and day-books, and scrap-books containing memoranda, printed circulars, posters, regulations, and other official directives. Of great interest also were the background materials used by J.G. Hodgins in the preparation of his twenty-eight volume *Documentary History of Education in Upper Canada.* Documents in the second category included municipal records such as council minutes, accounts, by-laws, and collectors' and assessors' rolls; land and property records such as deeds, mortgages, and wills; and church records, such as marriage, birth, and death registers. In the third category were such items as a letter from a resident of Government House, Toronto, during the Rebellion of 1837, in which he described events of that time, and the diary of an officer in the British Army during the Napoleonic Wars, in which he described the burning of Washington.

The report included references to the augmentation of the newspaper collection, the main type of published material of concern to the archives. An attempt is made to obtain complete sets of local papers, many of them extinct, from earlier periods, and to preserve them on microfilm. Other types of material acquired include maps and pictures.

The department's activities expanded rapidly during the 1960s. By 1969 the total number of staff members had risen to nearly sixty. The organizational structure had also been adapted to provide a more ambitious program and to satisfy more numerous and more varied demands. The Historical Branch was established under the new ministerial regime, and in 1967 the Record Services Branch was added. Along with the Archives Branch, these constituted the main organizational components of the department.

As of 1969 the Archives Branch was engaged in the identification and preservation of records. No government document was supposed to be destroyed without the approval of the Provincial Archivist. While it would be absurd to think that such a rule could be enforced to the letter, it is important for the archivist to be able to exert some control over procedures employed in dealing with different categories of documents. Apart from government papers, the department could not of course command material, but had to acquire it through contact and liaison with many agencies such as historical societies, women's institutes, and the like, as well as from private sources. Many items were donated, while others were purchased with the limited funds available. Increasing competition was being felt from book publishers, universities, local libraries, and other agencies ambitious to establish their own collections. When material was received, it had to be analysed, related to other historical documents, arranged in series, catalogued, and stored. Much of it was microfilmed or reproduced in other forms. Often the most extreme care was required to ensure that fragile items were not damaged in handling, and that they were stored in such a way as to prevent further deterioration.

Highest on the priority list of those served by the archivist's staff were people in government departments who needed information in deciding on a particular course of action. One type of assistance sometimes made it possible to avoid unnecessary duplication of research. If a study appeared to be needed as a basis for a certain policy decision, the records might reveal that a similar or related investigation was conducted twenty years earlier and the results shelved. Sometimes a study of historical documents helped to clear up the question of ownership rights to property or rights-of-way. Pension claims might be established by consulting early church or municipal records. A conservation authority might need to know the maximum flood levels in a certain area over a period of years. Reforestation policies might be determined on the basis of whether or not trees of a certain type were ever grown in a particular area.

Services to another major group constituted a contribution to education in a very fundamental sense. This group consisted of the students and staff of universities, particularly in departments of history, but to a lesser extent also in departments of political science, sociology, geography, and other social sciences. A very substantial service was offered in locating, reproducing, and making available material required by researchers in such disciplines. Many inquiries were also received from school children working on projects, but these could be dealt with only to a limited extent. As a general rule, those who inquired had not exhausted the material available from secondary sources in any case. A certain number of original documents were lent at cost to teachers wishing to put them on display. Material was also provided for the construction of the historical kits that were being found useful in some schools.

Various groups and individuals sought information for a number of purposes. In recent years, the study of genealogy has greatly increased in popularity, and inquiries relating to family trees have multiplied. Activities arising out of Centennial celebrations and projects vastly increased the demands on the staff. The latter did their best for the genealogists, but they were not always able to invest the large amount of time required to track down specific items which were of interest to only a very few people.

To some extent, the Historical Branch was concerned with the "exploitation" of history in that it increased the province's interest for tourists. The staff assisted with the program of erecting plaques by going into the background of the person or event concerned in great detail to ensure accuracy. The unveiling ceremonies helped to give local people a knowledge of history and a sense of pride in their community, as well as attract tourists. Similar contributions of this branch to the development of historical sites have already been mentioned. Assistance was also given to some 180 local historical museums scattered throughout the province, both municipally owned and private, in the form of advice on the selection of materials and displays. Matching grants up to $1,000 a year were also available for institutions in the former category.

Mention has been made of publications of the Department of Tourism and Information produced wholly or partly by the archives staff. In fact, any publication that involved historical references produced by any branch of the government was checked, if not entirely written, by the same group. They also carried out or assisted with a variety of special projects; for example, they constructed an exhibit on the evolution of parliamentary government for display in the provincial Parliament Buildings. They also co-operated with the School of Architecture at the University of Toronto and with the Ontario Heritage Foundation in the conduct of research on old buildings.

The recently established Record Services Branch was concerned with the handling, organization, storage, and maintenance of papers in all the departments of the provincial government. These functions had become very important in recent years, and the rapid accumulation of records entailed an expensive and burdensome storage problem. The branch attempted to establish procedures that would ensure the selection of documents of potential value, the destruction of the remainder at the appropriate time, and the provision of low cost storage for what was considered essential. A process of successive screenings was supposed to result in the ultimate arrival in the archives building of material of real importance.

THE DEPARTMENT OF LANDS AND FORESTS

The educational activities of the Department of Lands and Forests as of 1969 might be grouped under four main headings: 1 / informational assistance to the public, 2 / training at the technician level for prospective employees and others, 3 / in-service training and development programs for employees, and 4 / a Junior Forest Ranger program. The first of these involved the production of hundreds of booklets, brochures, pamphlets, reports, maps, and other materials. It also included park interpretive services designed to promote in park visitors an appreciation of the environment and an enjoyment of historical and natural phenomena. The techniques and devices used in these services consisted of museums, exhibits, publications, labeled trails, conducted trips, illustrated talks, and special group programs. The second function was carried out at the Ontario Forest Ranger School near Dorset until 1968, when it was turned over to certain colleges of applied arts and technology. In terms of the third, the department had one of the most comprehensive programs in the provincial government.

Promotional literature

Like the Department of Tourism and Information, the Department of Lands and Forests produced a great deal of interesting material on the natural attractions of Ontario. The immediate purposes of the two departments were, however, somewhat different. The former was primarily concerned with attracting native and foreign visitors for economic advantage, while the latter concentrated on the conservation and effective long-term utilization of natural resources. Seen in perspective, these interests might be considered identical.

One type of publication offers scientifically valid information about a particular type of animal or plant life. One of the most popular of these is entitled *Ontario Snakes.*[15] It provides an illustration of each type of snake found in Ontario, describes its characteristics and habitat, and explains its role in the natural scheme of things. One of the purposes of the publication is obviously to dispel some common misconceptions about snakes and to counteract the prevalent fear of them. Another booklet, *The Ecology of the Timber Wolf,*[16] tells about research into the numbers, range, and habits of wolves in the Algonquin Park area. One purpose of the investigation was apparently to provide sound information upon which a policy with respect to bounties might be based. Conservation officers generally seem to feel that the wolf bounty is at best a complete waste of money, but find it difficult to counteract the pressure to continue it. On the subject of wolves, a brochure entitled *Wolves and Coyotes in Ontario*[17] involves much the same treatment and purpose as *Ontario Snakes.* A booklet called *Fifty Years of Reforestation in Ontario*[18] presents a kind of historical treatment of the topic with a collection of reports made over the years showing how steps have been taken to repair the destruction caused by the cutting of the best timber in Ontario during the nineteenth century. *Your Forests* is a periodical introduced in 1968 containing informative articles about different kinds of trees, conservation and utilization of forests, and related subjects. A bulletin called *The Farm Woodlot*[19] is concerned mainly with the management of hardwoods on private lands in southern Ontario. A brief booklet entitled *Fur in Ontario*[20] is designed to be of assistance to the commercial trapper.

These and many other publications are of great potential value in increasing knowledge, understanding, and appreciation of Ontario's natural resources on the part of young people and adults. Teachers and students can use them profitably in a variety of science and geography projects, especially those directed toward conservation. Unfortunately at the time of writing there was a feeling among some people in the Department of Lands and Forests that the educational system was not excessively receptive to the causes they promoted.

The Ontario Forest Ranger School

The Ontario Forest Ranger School was established at Dorset in 1945. In the early stages, efforts were concentrated on meeting the in-service needs of the department's own staff. When the backlog had been dealt with, the technician-type course was introduced for high school students. The enrolment had reached about 160 a year by 1968 when a decision had to be faced on whether to continue the course or abandon it in favour of the colleges of applied arts and technology. The responsibility was assumed by Sir Sandford Fleming College, the Sault Ste Marie campus of Cambrian College, and Lakehead University.

In the early 1960s the technician-type course covered one calendar year, and could be entered with grade 10 standing or higher. It was intended for those who were interested in a career in forestry or other allied occupations. It qualified a person for a position between that of the average woodsman and the professional forester and biologist. Graduates were employable by the government or private industry as cruisers, scalers, woods foremen, photo technicians, conservation officers, wildlife managers and technicians, fisheries managers and technicians, research assistants, land assessors, survey assistants, parks officers, and forest protection officers, and, of course, forest rangers.[21]

By 1965 the admission requirement was the Ontario Secondary School Graduation Diploma or equivalent standing. Applicants were also given a learning capacity test, and additional tests might be required as well. The cost of each of the three terms of the course, including residence, was approximately $250.

In-service training for departmental employees

Some idea of the need for a very comprehensive training program may be gained by considering the department's mode of operating. The normal staff complement in 1969 was somewhat over 3,200, but swelled to about 10,000 during the summer, many of the extra number being new to the job. The increase was part of a seasonal pattern. The temporary employees stocked streams, planted trees, banded birds and animals, acted as park attendants, and performed many other functions. They were in obvious need of intensive, short-term training. For this purpose, every one of the twenty-one districts of the province offered courses lasting from two days to two weeks. The district forester was the main official responsible for the program.

One illustration of the reasons for the increased training needs of regular staff has to do with the growing complexity of law enforcement. It is no longer sufficient to expect a woodsman with a uniform and a book of rules to protect the province's natural resources in the field or in the law courts. In-service courses are provided for conservation officers and for officers whose responsibilities involve law enforcement in forest protection, parks, and accident control. Included are two-week courses at the Forest Ranger School and participation in the program of the Ontario Police College at Aylmer.

Some of the objectives of the in-service training program as it has been operated in recent years include 1 / orienting new employees, 2 / improving employee morale, 3 / teaching safety and good housekeeping, 4 / teaching methods of fire prevention, 5 / providing refresher training in methods and techniques, 6 / providing training in new methods and techniques, 7 / increasing employees' opportunities for promotion and salary increases, 8 / providing training in the optimum use of new and existing equipment, 9 / familiarizing employees with management skills and aids, 10 / teaching cost budgeting and control, and 11 / teaching effective verbal and written communications. One of the orientation courses introduced a few years ago was intended to present new employees with an overall picture of the Ontario Government Service, with special reference to the Department of Lands and Forests. In all-day sessions held once a month or oftener, it covered historical background, basic policies and objectives, personnel policies and information concerning organization of personnel, facilities, opportunities for self-development, and employee organizations, activities, and benefits. The course was given co-operatively by district officers and members of the Personnel Branch at the head office.

The task of preparing suitable instructors for in-service courses is a major one, since the number required had reached about sixty by 1969. Courses for instructors were held at the Forest Ranger School, but these were expected to be dispersed regionally. An example of an instructors' course of one week's duration was described by P.F. Suessmith and M. Stengels. It was designed to give participants a unique opportunity for self-criticism by having their successive performances recorded on video tape. Their perception of their own presentations was said to reinforce the criticisms made by other members of the class and the instructor.

Reliance was placed on outside agencies for certain types of training. In order to remedy an acute shortage of administrators, an arrangement was made for the University of Toronto Extension Department to offer a two-year certificate course as early as 1940. In 1960 a similar arrangement was made to provide a one-year Resource Management course for university graduates, preferably with about five years of prior experience. In recent years, the University of Toronto has also provided a graduate course in ecological land use of several weeks' duration. As of 1969 the department reimbursed approved employees for a major part of the expense involved in taking outside courses. In certain instances, where it could be shown that the existing qualifications were unavailable on the market, leave of absence might be granted for as long as two years for advanced study.

The Junior Forest Ranger program

The Junior Forest Ranger program provided eight weeks of practice in resource management techniques for seventeen-year-old boys during the summer. When it began in the 1940s it involved attaching boys to individual forestry officials in a rather casual arrangement. In 1969 the program was highly structured, consisting of about equal parts of work and learning. Boys could at one time attend year after year, but were later restricted to a single summer. They received remuneration at the rate of $5 per day. The cost of financing the participation of about 1,850 boys in 1969 was over $1,200,000.

THE DEPARTMENT OF MUNICIPAL AFFAIRS

In 1969 the Department of Municipal Affairs was involved in a variety of promotional and educational activities, many of them under the direction of a Chief of Information and Education Services. At the time of writing, the incumbent was J.M. Main. The principal types of activity were 1 / personnel training within the department, 2 / training of municipal assessors, 3 / training of municipal clerks and treasurers, 4 / assistance to the Ontario Conference on Local Government in providing courses for elected and appointed municipal officials, 5 / the conduct of workshops for locally appointed officials, and 6 / the production and distribution of informational material.

Personnel training within the department included an initiation course for new employees to enable them to become familiar with the aims, operations, and structure of the organization. At one time this course extended over ten half days, but it was later condensed into five full days. Some consideration had been given to the provision of more advanced courses on a department-wide basis, but in 1969 these were given only by specific branches such as the Community Planning Branch and the Municipal Assessment Branch.

The latter branch has been responsible for the training of municipal assessors, an activity that will increase in importance since the recent assumption of the assessment function by the province. Formal training, sponsored by the Institute of Municipal Assessors, has been available since 1954 through the Extension Department of Queen's University. By 1969 778 students had graduated from this program. Between 1967 and 1969 diploma courses for municipal assessors became available at five colleges of applied arts and technology: Cambrian, Fanshawe, Loyalist, St Lawrence, and Seneca. The staff of the Municipal Assessment Branch worked closely with these colleges in developing course content for the two-year program. They also assisted in an instructional capacity, at a considerable cost to the branch in terms of its own personnel resources. The first year of the program involved an intensive study of economics, political science, English, mathematics, statistics, and principles of public administration; the second consisted of a further study of economics, the non-valuation aspects of assessment, land-use planning, sociology, valuation, English, and other liberal studies. The student had also to devote four months of his training to practical field work. An important contribution to training as well as to the work of the assessors is a publication produced by the Department of Municipal Affairs entitled *Appraisal Notes for the Assessor.*

The Association of Municipal Clerks and Treasurers of Ontario, in co-operation with Queen's University, developed a syllabus for use in its three-year training course. The Municipal Accounting Branch of the Department of Municipal Affairs was represented on the Education Committee of the association, and thus assisted in the work of course revision. A course for municipal clerks and treasurers was first offered in the extension program at Queen's University in 1958. A municipal accounting trainee program, begun on a very modest scale in 1968 with two recruits, was designed to provide the experience and qualifications required by a municipal accounting adviser.

The Information and Education Services Branch has been closely involved in the expanding program for actual and potential elected or appointed municipal officials and other interested individuals operated by the Ontario Conference on Local Government. This program began to take shape in 1965 in response to a desire on the part of thoughtful people to ensure that campaigns conducted by such associations as the Junior Chamber of Commerce not only would succeed in "getting out the vote" at election time, but would also get out an intelligent, informed vote. The first trial course was held at Barry's Bay in January 1965 on the initiative of St Joseph's Apostolate at Combermere. This agency had attempted to alleviate the cultural inadequacies of the area by offering short courses in arts, crafts, and other fields. In response to its appeal, the Information and Education Services Branch helped to prepare a syllabus for a course on municipal affairs involving eleven weekly evening sessions, at a nominal fee of $5 per person. It also assisted in making contacts with newspapers, radio stations, churches, school boards, school principals, Home and School associations, and other agencies in order to build up interest and ensure an adequate attendance. The resulting enrolment of around seventy exceeded all expectations.

In the early experimental stages, a course held at the University of Waterloo attracted about 170 people, including an excellent representation from senior appointed and elected officials, and a wide variety of occupations. The fee was $20 for a single adult, $30 for a couple, and a token amount for students. To a considerable extent as a result of an initiative taken by the Municipal Relations Committee of the Ontario Chamber of Commerce, and with the co-operation of the Department of Municipal Affairs, the Ontario Conference on Local Government was established in November 1965. Additional participating groups were the Ontario Junior Chamber of Commerce, the Ontario Municipal Association, the City Engineers' Association, the Ontario Association of Rural Municipalities, the Community Planning Association of Canada (Ontario Division), the Association of Ontario Counties, the Association of Ontario Mayors and Reeves, the Regional Development Service, and the Department of Economics and Development.

In the fall of 1966, the conference sponsored a six-seminar pilot course in municipal affairs at Peter Robinson College in Peterborough in co-operation with Trent University and the Peterborough Chamber of Commerce. The course was expected to appeal particularly to citizens seeking election and re-election. The topics covered were Brief History of Local Government, Forms of Municipal Government in Ontario, Structure of Municipal Government and How Council Operates, Relationships to Boards and other Authorities in the Community, Municipal Finance, Province-Municipality Direct Relationships, Functions of the Municipality, the Difference between Business and Government Decision Making, the Responsibility of Elected and Appointed Members of Municipal Government, and Why the Individual Should Take an Active Interest or Participate in Local Government.

In 1969 the OCLG offered four courses in the spring and four in the fall in centres in different parts of the province. These centres included Kingston, Owen Sound, Oakville, Toronto, Sault Ste Marie, and Chatham. The objective was an attendance of between sixty and one hundred, although there was difficulty in practice in keeping it below the desired maximum. Each course extended over six evenings, and involved presentations of twenty to twenty-five minutes by each of two speakers, followed by discussion. Graduating students were presented with certificates signed by the minister. There had been about 2,400 graduates from these courses by mid-1969, and they had been considered very successful. Strong pressure was developing for more advanced offerings on specialized phases of municipal affairs. Whether this demand could be met would depend on the availability of staff and other resources.

There was no active campaign to sell the Ontario Conference on Local Government courses, but indications of local interest produced a ready response. The conference acknowledged a request, and provided information outlining the responsibilities of the local groups. If the interest was serious, and the local members of the conference were agreeable, plans were made and preparations were set in motion. Particular efforts were made to ensure adequate publicity. The conference co-ordinated the necessary activities at every stage, while the Department of Municipal Affairs selected suitable speakers and made contact with them.

In expounding the values of the course, Mrs V. Thorne, Supervisor of Information and Education in the Department of Municipal Affairs, referred to the apathy that is "currently being cited as one of the greatest dangers in the struggle to retain local autonomy."[22] She considered much of this apparent indifference a defence mechanism to hide lack of knowledge and fear of the unknown. She saw the courses as a sign of citizens' hunger for knowledge and understanding.

The courses had a considerable appeal to housewives, who often enrolled to keep up with the interests of their husbands and growing children, and ended up by seeking and gaining office themselves. Graduates of the program had a remarkable record of election to office, although it was impossible to tell whether the course had had a profound influence on their appeal to the voters, or whether they were the kind of active, energetic people who would have tended to attract support in any case. The benefits for a great many participants were simply an increased knowledge of municipal affairs, with an excellent prospect that their new-found concern would be reflected at the polls.

The courses were self-sustaining, with fees set to cover costs. A certain proportion of the proceeds was contributed to the conference to defray its expenses. The financial aspects of the program apparently offered a less serious problem than the availability of good speakers. Mrs Thorne paid tribute, however, to the co-operation received from university lecturers and municipal officials in offering their services.

The Municipal Organization and Administration Branch of the Department of Municipal Affairs operated a general municipal advisory service. During 1968 the staff participated by invitation in over fifty municipal workshops, seminars, and other meetings as observers, panel members, or speakers. The school board consolidation of January 1, 1969, focused an unusual amount of attention on municipal and school board election procedures. Instructional material was also developed in the form of a *Provincial Grants Handbook* which was updated frequently. It was designed to make municipal officials aware of the grants and subsidies available to municipalities through the various government departments and agencies.

THE DEPARTMENT OF HEALTH

As of 1970 the involvement of the Department of Health in education and training included the following activities. 1 / Training in technical, supervisory, and managerial skills involved a substantial proportion of the department's employees who, in 1969–70, numbered approximately twenty thousand, the majority of whom were engaged in hospital service. 2 / Financial assistance was provided under certain conditions to students in health science programs in educational institutions. 3 / Financial assistance was provided to such institutions for the development of health science programs. 4 / Research activities in universities, as well as in other institutions, received financial support.

Training

Organizational structure

The department established a Professional Education Committee in 1958 with responsibilities in areas such as in-service professional education; conferences, conventions, and technical visits; the selection of bursary candidates; departmental conferences. During the early 1960s there were various other organizations and committees operating at the hospital and central office levels, such as the Bursary Selection Committee in Public Health, the Bursary Selection Committee in Mental Health, the Committee on Sanitary Inspectors, the Committee on Laboratory Technicians, the Committee on Public Health Nursing, the Committee on Nursing Education and Registered Nurses, various hospital management committees, and the Training and Development Section of the Personnel Branch. In 1964 the Professional Education Committee was replaced by an Education Committee, which, among other functions, continued the work of its predecessor in determining training and development needs.

In May 1966 a Departmental Professional Training Committee was formed to make recommendations to the deputy minister on the administration of a training fund approved by the Legislature for 1966–7. This fund was to be allocated among people outside the Civil Service who were training within the professional disciplines which were of concern to the Department of Health. Among these were physicians training to be psychiatrists, as well as students engaging in graduate studies with the intention of teaching in Ontario universities.

A Public Health Bursary Committee was established to award bursaries according to the schedule established by the Departmental Professional Training Committee. It originally had representation from medicine and dentistry, public health laboratories, public health nursing and nursing service, public health inspection, and public health education. A Professional Services Bursary Committee awarded bursaries to students in psychiatry, psychology, bacteriology, speech pathology, physiotherapy, and other disciplines.

Programs offered in 1964–5

Training programs in which the department has been involved may be divided into three categories: 1 / intra-department programs, which may involve outside agencies to some extent, 2 / inter-department programs, and 3 / training and development outside the service. A brief review of the situation in 1964–5 will indicate the nature and scope of these activities.

Among courses offered in the intra-department category, the following fell in the category of skills training. 1 / A course of two years' duration for child care workers was offered at Thistletown Hospital, a provincial psychiatric centre for children. It consisted of lectures and practice, and led to a certificate in child care work. 2 / Also of two year's duration was a course for hospital aides and attendants conducted at individual Ontario Hospitals and designed to prepare such personnel to assist in nursing care of patients under the direction of registered nurses or physicians. The course was divided into introductory and advanced parts. 3 / The first year of a two-year course for medical laboratory technologists was given at the Ryerson Polytechnical Institute and the last year at the central laboratory of the Technical Training Centre. Successful sudents received a certificate in medical laboratory technology. Bursary assistance was provided by the Department of Health. 4 / A course of five months' duration was given at the Ontario Hospital at Kingston for occupational therapy assistants. Candidates could be either from the Civil Service or from outside. On graduation, they might be employed in Ontario Hospitals or in public hospitals. 5 / Some members of the Department of Health participated in short courses for pest control officers conducted annually by the Industrial Hygiene Branch of what was then the Ontario Agricultural College. 6 / Departmental staff participated in a four-year graduate training program in psychiatry, the university phase of which was offered at Queen's University, the University of Ottawa, the University of Toronto, and the University of Western Ontario. 7 / Courses consisting of fifteen weeks of instruction and six or seven months of hospital practice were offered for registered nursing assistants in forty-two training centres. The Department of Health operated five of these and provided assistance and instruction in the operation of the others. Successful candidates were eligible for registration as registered nursing assistants. The department provided bursary assistance. 8 / Courses consisting of six weeks of instruction and one week of field service were held periodically for rehabilitation officers employed in the Rehabilitation Branch of the department. 9 / The department supplied the major proportion of the teaching for a course for sanitary inspectors conducted at Ryerson, as well as providing bursary assistance for students. Of one academic year in duration, the course led to a Certificate in Sanitary Inspection (Canada).

Less formal in-service training was provided in the following forms. 1 / A two-week course in environmental sanitation was offered for summer camp inspectors employed on a casual basis during the summer months. Refresher courses were also conducted for sanitary inspectors employed by the department and by local municipalities. Instructors were supplied for courses in environmental sanitation put on by other agencies such as Ryerson, the Civil Defence College at Arnprior, the Ontario Agricultural College, and the School of Hygiene at the University of Toronto. 2 / Plans were being made for the development of training courses for local air pollution staff, involving both lectures and field training. 3 / The Laboratory Branch conducted annual refresher courses lasting between one and two weeks for representatives of regional laboratories. There was also provision for the appointment of two fellows-in-training to the central laboratory, who were working toward certification by the Royal College of Physicians and Surgeons. 4 / Staff educational conferences in public health nursing were held at least three times annually. Annual worker conferences were also conducted for local nursing personnel in administrative, supervisory, and staff positions.

No formal courses were given by the department to develop clerical, stenographic, or secretarial skills, which were expected to be acquired on the job. The same applied at that time to supervisory and managerial training.

In the category of inter-departmental training, two members of the Department of Health attended a senior officers' conference of three weeks' duration in May 1964. About twenty members were enrolled in a personnel officers' course. Five individuals were enrolled in the first year of a certificate course in public administration. At various times, staff members were sent to courses on data processing machines conducted by IBM. Varying numbers of people also attended the following: a course in public administration at Ryerson, a course in personnel and business administration operated in conjunction with Organization & Methods Services, a course in supervisory training conducted by the Department of Civil Service, and courses in specification writing conducted by the same department.

Training and development outside the services included 1 / a correspondence course in hospital organization and management involving two years of study and attendance for four weeks in each year at the University of Manitoba. It was taken, with bursary assistance, by a number of hospital business administrators and senior hospital business staff. 2 / Some staff members attended evening extension courses given at the University of Toronto and at Ryerson. An evening course for registered nursing assistants was conducted at the Toronto Registered Nursing Assistant Centre. 3 / Medical staff, social workers, psychologists, and members of other professional groups attended a long list of trade and professional seminars and conferences. Of particular importance among these was an annual conference in the form of a refresher course for nurses sponsored by the Registered Nurses' Association of Ontario, and held at Honey Harbour. 4 / There was provision for educational leave for employees of the department to improve their qualifications, particularly for members of professional groups proceeding toward higher degrees. 5 / Professional staff combined employment in the department with post-graduate training at the School of Hygiene of the University of Toronto, leading to the Diploma in Public Health, the Certificate in Public Health, the Diploma in Veterinary Public Health, and other qualifications. They attended lectures during the day and made up the time off by overtime duties. 6/ The School of Hygiene conducted an annual refresher course in the Division of Post-graduate Medical Education in the University of Toronto in co-operation with the Department of Health. The latter also provided a large number of delegates. The course covered a wide range of public health and associated topics of interest to medical staff, public health nurses, and social workers. 7 / Annual area conferences were conducted in several parts of the province. 8 / Senior members of the staff of the Department of Health assisted in giving an annual one-week course for public health inspectors sponsored by the Ontario Branch of the Canadian Institute of Public Health Inspectors and the Department of Extension Education of the Ontario Agricultural College. Other members of the staff of the department participated in the course. 9 / Staff of the department played a large part in organizing the annual meeting of the Ontario Public Health Association, in developing the program, and in conducting the meeting. Presentations were made on current public health problems of interest to medical officers of health. 10 / Many departmental staff attended short courses of three days' to two weeks' duration throughout the continent; these covered such topics as mental health, tuberculosis, maternal and child health, and alcoholism and drug addiction.

Subsequent program development

By 1967 the Child Care Worker Training course was being offered, not only at Thistletown Hospital, but also at the Children's Psychiatric Research Institute at London and the Lakeshore Psychiatric Hospital at Toronto. A Mental Retardation Certificate course was developed in 1967 as a basic qualification for new classes of employees being established in the Mental Retardation Branch, such as counsellors, instructors, and medical assistants. The course consisted of one year of supervised ward experience and lecture periods, and had to be completed within two years of the date of employment. The second part offered training in three specialties: those of medical assistant, residential counsellor, and occupational instructor.

A course was developed at Ryerson leading to a certificate in public health inspection. Guest speakers from the Department of Health lectured in their particular specialties as required by the course curriculum. Bursary assistance and the hope of future employment were offered by the department.

Among the evening classes attended by one or more staff members during 1967, with departmental support, were the following: certificate courses in business, in personnel and industrial relations, and in public administration at the University of Toronto; BSc courses at Trent University; courses in haemotology and histology given by the Ontario Society of Medical Technology; a BA computer science course at York University; courses in correspondence and report writing, in front office procedures, in public relations, and in electronic fundamentals and circuits, and certificate courses in secretarial science, in public administration, in systems and procedures, in purchasing, and in business administration, all at Ryerson; and BScN courses at various universities.

Departmental staff were participating in management courses put on by the Department of Civil Service up to the limit of the department's allotment. In 1967, 367 members attended supervisory training courses. In addition, 115 attended position administration and classification courses, three attended the training course for statistical personnel, nine attended the training program for systems and procedures officers, and four attended the course in establishment and maintenance of filing systems.

The Training Section of the Personnel Branch also developed its own one-week basic management development course, which was based on the responses to a questionnaire administered to several hundred staff members by the Department of Civil Service in March 1967. The course was offered on twenty different occasions in 1969 for the benefit of 480 participants. It covered such topics as the supervisor's responsibilities, supervisory problems experienced by group members, blocks to communication, one-way versus two-way communication, position specification writing, motivation to work, performance appraisal, non-directive interviewing, leadership, and problem solving and decision making. Methods employed included lecture-discussion periods, film viewing, case studies, role playing, and practical exercises. When it was observed that a number of senior people were attending, an advanced management course was developed. After being offered four or five times, however, it was abandoned because of poor attendance. The participants often felt that they should continue to carry out their regular responsibilities while the course was going on.

The Training Section also put on a position analysis course designed to develop skills in writing job specifications. Among topics covered were the position administration system, concepts of organization and their application to the department, position analysis techniques, and review of model specifications in a position analysis guide. A considerable part of the three-day period was devoted to the writing of practice exercises.

Research grants

Grants from provincial funds

Administration of research grants was the responsibility of the Research and Planning Branch of the Department after it was established in 1966. The Ontario Council of Health, also set up in the same year, had a Health Research Committee which, after appraisal by independent referees, made recommendations with respect to grant approval.

The Province of Ontario Health Research Grants, amounting to $1,084,000 in the fiscal year 1968–9, supported projects carried out by competent investigators at universities, hospitals, nursing schools, and clinics, as well as those conducted in private medical practice. Assistance was provided for research directed at problems from the whole field of health in its widest aspects. Emphasis was placed on areas not already supported by existing agencies, particularly the following: 1 / operational, epidemiological, and developmental studies, and 2 / health research projects involving education, training, or service. For the most part, responsibility for supporting basic research was left to the Medical Research Council, although grants might be given for mixed projects and for those on the borderline between the basic and applied types.

Sponsors of the projects were normally expected to provide research and office space, office furniture, equipment, and routine secretarial services. The grants might cover salaries (other than that of the applicant), supplies, special equipment, travel funds, employer contributions to fringe benefits, and publication costs. A request for a renewal of a grant was expected to be accompanied by a progress report, with a brief summary of the work done. A final report on the findings was also required. Control over the expenditure of the funds was not usually regarded as excessively restrictive or burdensome.

Federal contributions

A National Health Grants Program was established in 1948 to provide for federal grants-in-aid to the provinces and territories of Canada to promote health care and service programs. Amounts awarded increased greatly after that time. Support was usually accorded to scientific research oriented toward health, with special relation to health needs and to provincial and federal health services. Acceptable forms included studies leading to the prevention of disease, disability, or death, particularly when the results were immediately applicable; epidemiological studies of diseases and conditions which were of general importance to public health; hospital-based studies, particularly those aimed at improving patient care through new administrative and organizational techniques; community-based studies in the delivery and utilization of medicare services, as well as studies in community health care programs such as those sponsored by health units; operational or administrative research on health programs and services, and including the evaluation of services provided by public health laboratories, various levels of government, community agencies, medical care insurance, and dental practitioners; research on the problems of occupational health, air pollution, sanitation, public health engineering, and water pollution; and studies on the training and utilization of health manpower resources. The grants were channelled through the provincial government to universities or to non-teaching institutions or agencies. In the fiscal year 1968–9 they amounted to $1,516,000 for the province of Ontario as a whole.

Grants to foundations

The Department of Health supported four research foundations in 1969–70: the Alcoholism and Drug Addiction Research Foundation, the Ontario Cancer Treatment and Research Foundation, the Ontario Mental Health Foundation, and the Ontario Heart Foundation. These agencies received $3,309,700 for specific research purposes in the 1969–70 fiscal year. Since the role of such foundations involved the promotion of worthwhile causes, the funds might be regarded as in part an educational contribution.

Seed money for university programs

Another form of financial support for educational institutions involves short-term funding of new university programs. While the grants may in exceptional cases be paid over a period of five years, they are expected to cover from one to three years, after which the institutions are supposed to provide for maintenance through their regular budgets. Examples of grants made in 1969–70 were the following: $42,000 to Queen's University for a child health program; $150,000 to the School of Hygiene at the University of Toronto for the training of electron microscopists and for advanced graduate courses; $99,000 to McMaster University for the development of family practice; $52,000 to the University of Ottawa for a family practice unit; $304,000 to McMaster University for a field unit pilot project; $85,000 to York University for graduate training in psychology; $32,000 to the University of Western Ontario for the development of a course for physio-occupational therapists; and $42,000 to the University of Toronto for the development of an audio-visual program.

Bursaries and scholarships

The department has offered a wide range of bursaries for students in nursing, dental hygiene, social work, psychology, and public health, as well as fellowships in academic medicine and psychiatry. The amounts spent on these forms of assistance ranged from $200,000 in 1950–1, two years after the program began, to $1,850,000 in 1969–70. The value of individual awards for a year of study ranged in 1969–70 from $8,000 for post-doctoral work to $1,400 for undergraduate degree, diploma, or certificate courses. In each case, the recipient was expected to return specified service after completion of the course, or to return the funds. An undergraduate medical and dental bursary agreement involved a commitment to enter or set up a practice in an area designated by the Minister of Health as an under-serviced area of the province where medical or dental services were inadequate, and to maintain such practice for a period of twelve months for each academic year of study for which bursary assistance was received.

THE DEPARTMENT OF SOCIAL AND FAMILY SERVICES

The Department of Social and Family Services or, as it was called until 1967, the Department of Public Welfare, first began to offer in-service training courses for welfare field workers in Toronto in 1949. As developed in subsequent years, these courses were of six weeks' duration, each involving from six to eight individuals from secretarial, bookkeeping, nursing, selling, and welfare occupations. Instruction was informal, and included problem-solving activities. The course also involved a study of legislation relating to old age assistance, blind persons' allowances, disabled persons' allowances, mothers' and dependent children's allowances, and other such matters. A preliminary examination was given for admission, and a final over-all evaluation at the end.

At a later stage, the department began to provide courses for employees of municipal welfare departments. These were supervised by a Committee of the Ontario Welfare Officers' Association, and were devoted to offering precise information about welfare statutes and programs which municipal welfare employees had to administer at the local level. Again, classes were informal, and mutual exchange between instructors and students was encouraged. The department realized that morale in certain municipal welfare offices was low, and hoped to improve it through the courses.

In 1961 the federal government, through the Department of National Health and Welfare, offered training grants to the provinces. The provincial departments of welfare were expected to use most of the money for bursaries for students in schools of social work. There was also a suggestion that a course in public welfare might be developed to provide trained personnel at the intermediate level for service in the government welfare field.

J.W. Monteith, Minister of National Health and Welfare, spoke of the shortage of trained social workers in the House of Commons on May 30, 1961.[23] He had to extrapolate from figures produced in a survey conducted ten years earlier. At that time, there were 4,500 welfare positions in Canada, of which approximately 30 per cent were filled by people with graduate degrees in social work, as opposed to the 60 to 85 per cent that welfare agencies thought desirable. It was estimated that there were 7,000 welfare positions in 1961, of which only about 2,500 were filled by graduates. On the basis of the agencies' expressed preference in 1951, there appeared to be a shortage of between 1,700 and 3,500 social workers.

On the initiative of the Ontario Department of Public Welfare, an Advisory Council for Public Welfare Training was established on February 9, 1961, under the chairmanship of C.E. Hendry, Director of the School of Social Work of the University of Toronto, and consisting also of J.S. Band, Deputy Minister of Public Welfare, Rev. S. Bowers, Director of the School of Social Welfare at St Patrick's College, Miss B. Touzel, Executive Director of the Ontario Welfare Council, Miss R. Morris, Commissioner of Public Welfare for Toronto, and S. Legge of Massey Ferguson Limited. The council's terms of reference were to

(1) consider ways and means of continuing the recruitment of suitable persons for training and placement in the public welfare services throughout Ontario;
(2) consider and recommend measures in the advanced training of personnel for service in the public welfare field in Ontario; and
(3) consider and recommend measures that may encourage and contribute to the further development of the present programs and facilities for the education and training of social workers with specific reference to the public welfare services in Ontario.[24]

The council addressed itself to a variety of tasks such as estimating the costs of expanding existing schools of social work and of establishing new ones, publicizing the attractions of careers in social work, studying social welfare salaries in government service, and estimating personnel requirements in provincial and municipal offices. In 1963 measures were taken to offer a public welfare training course for people employed by the municipalities and by the Ontario Department of Public Welfare. The federal and provincial governments assumed equal shares of the cost for instructors and equipment, and met the students' expenses in the same way.

In June 1963 the Sub-Committee on In-Service Training of the Advisory Council recommended that the following courses be offered: 1 / a one-week course, held several times a year in central localities in various parts of Ontario for full-time administrators of welfare in middle-sized and small municipalities; 2 / a six-week lecture course, held either in Metropolitan Toronto or in each large city, and tailored to the specific requirements of the area, for subordinate welfare workers; 3 / a course leading to upgrading to the position of field work supervisor for selected workers from the Department of Welfare; and 4 / short seminar and discussion courses for Department of Welfare senior field staff to review new legislation, policy, and procedures and to encourage such staff to help and advise the small municipalities in administration.

The system of bursaries established to attract students to the School of Social Work at the University of Toronto and the School of Social Welfare at St Patrick's College provided for payments of $150 a month for single students and $200 a month for those with dependents for the period of enrolment. Fees and travel expenses were also covered. The federal government contributed half the cost up to $125 a month for single students, or $1,500 for the calendar year, and $166 a month for married students, or $2,000 for the year, as well as half of some travel expenses. The recipient could accept other non-committing awards up to $1,000 a year. Income from any source above $1,000 during the academic year was deducted from the bursary. In return for the assistance provided, the recipient committed himself to work in a public organization for a period of time equivalent to that for which he received bursary assistance. If he did not meet this commitment, or failed the course because of lack of reasonable effort, he was obligated to repay the allowance.

Although it is impossible to say how much the bursaries had to do with it, and to what extent other influences were responsible, the two schools found that the number of applicants for their courses increased very rapidly. It soon became realistic to press for the establishment of facilities at other institutions.

Dealing with the need for training at the intermediate level, the council urged the establishment of a course at the Ryerson Institute of Technology. Students would be recruited from grade 12 or higher, and would take some academic work, such as theoretical psychology, history, and the principles of welfare, along with technical work in administration, interviewing, assessing need, and techniques of service, and would do practical work involving field experience. This initiative helped to get the very successful Ryerson Welfare Services course in operation in 1964, and provided a pattern that was later followed by the colleges of applied arts and technology.

When the courses in the colleges were established, the advisory council played an important role in determining the occupations for which they would prepare candidates, and in studying the question of suitable course content. The council was also consulted by universities considering the establishment of undergraduate programs. It tried to provide leadership to ensure co-ordinated consultation and planning of the many educational ventures that got under way.

As of 1969, the aims of the Training and Staff Development Branch of the Department of Social and Family Services were as follows: 1 / to develop internal training programs and to utilize educational institutions to ensure that staff were equipped for the responsibilities and tasks assigned to them; 2 / to collaborate with the educational system in developing the manpower necessary to fulfill the requirements of the department; and 3 / to participate in departmental planning to ensure that staff were equipped to deal with changes in legislation and policies.[25]

Internal staff training activities included orientation, in-service training, staff development, and educational leave. Orientation was designed to ensure that each new employee was made aware of the structure of the department and the services it provided, and that he appreciated the relationship of his own and other government departments to the Legislature. Orientation to the department was separated for the first time in 1968–9 from training in skills for specific jobs.

The department itself provided in-service courses where educational institutions could not meet its needs. These included short courses for staff of various branches as well as for related agencies such as the children's aid societies. Procedural and training manuals were made available for family benefits, municipal welfare administration, and homes for the aged. A basic training course for field services consisted of a first and third phase, each involving two weeks of study in a classroom setting, and a second phase of from twelve to fifteen weeks in field practice. Staff development consisted of meetings, conferences, workshops, institutes, and short courses sponsored both by the department and by other social and educational agencies. There was a program of educational leave with pay so that selected individuals could attend schools of social work or Ryerson Polytechnical Institute on a full-time basis on full salary. Assistance was also given for enrolment in extension courses involving evening or summer school attendance.

The department tried to avoid duplicating educational programs offered, or potentially offered, by educational institutions. It attempted to work with these in order to ensure that appropriate courses were planned. Field instruction was provided for students in schools of social work, Ryerson Polytechnical Institute, and colleges of applied arts and technology. This service was given by regular staff as part of their assignments, as well as by a few full-time instructors. The bursary program mentioned earlier also continued in 1969–70.

THE DEPARTMENT OF AGRICULTURE AND FOOD

The Department of Agriculture and Food has been involved in the following educational activities: 1 / the early development of the Ontario Agricultural College, the Ontario Veterinary College, and Macdonald Institute, and control of these institutions until they became part of the newly created University of Guelph in 1964; 2 / continued contractual relationships with that university for the conduct of research and the provision of a diploma course in agriculture, which may be taken in attendance or by correspondence; 3 / control and maintenance of the four colleges of agricultural technology at Centralia, Kemptville, New Liskeard, and Ridgetown; 4 / a special arrangement with Fanshawe College of Applied Arts and Technology to provide a course in agricultural technology; and 5 / short courses offered in all the institutions referred to. The University of Guelph and the colleges of agricultural technology are dealt with at some length in volume IV.

The establishment of the University of Guelph, with the removal of control over its constituent institutions by the Department of Agriculture and Food, did not end its close association with the latter. The transition to the new status was made quite smoothly, with no noticeable evidence of ill-feeling. The research program continued to be supported by direct grants from the department, since it was not in the tradition of Ontario universities to finance large-scale experimental programs out of their regular budgets. The need to carry out agricultural research has been a major reason why the University of Guelph has been relatively well endowed with staff, buildings, and facilities. It has been government policy to ensure that it has the means to carry out certain important functions related to agriculture.

The continuing education programs offered at the University of Guelph and the colleges of agricultural technology in 1969 varied in length from one-day sessions to extended correspondence courses. In depth, they ranged from a very elementary approach to one suited to the post-diploma level specifically designed to assist diploma graduates in keeping abreast of changing trends in agriculture.

THE DEPARTMENT OF ENERGY AND RESOURCES MANAGEMENT

The educational concerns of the Department of Energy and Resources Management have been most evident in the activities of the Conservation Authorities Branch. Education has been considered an essential means of achieving the objectives of this branch. A very brief review of the conservation program will provide the necessary background.

The main responsibility of the branch in 1969 was to organize and supervise conservation authorities in various parts of Ontario. These authorities were corporate bodies representing municipalities located within the watersheds of rivers and streams. Between 1946 and 1969, thirty-eight of them were established on a voluntary basis. The initiative might come from municipal officials, service clubs, or other individuals or agencies. An authority might be established on a favourable vote of two-thirds of the representatives present at a meeting, provided that two-thirds of the municipalities within the watershed were represented.

The need for some specific conservation measure, such as flood control, often provided the immediate motivating force behind the decision to organize an authority. A wide range of conservation measures might be undertaken with funds raised by local levies with the assistance of government grants. The Conservation Authorities Branch also provided technical advice and administrative assistance, often supplemented by contributions from the staff of such departments as Lands and Forests and Agriculture and Food. Among the projects and programs undertaken by conservation authorities were the following: 1 / the construction of large flood control dams and reservoirs and small water supply reservoirs, the formation of community ponds, and stream channelization and improvement; 2 / the acquisition of conservation lands, including flood plain lands and reservoir sites, stream bank erosion control, soil conservation measures, assistance to landowners for grass waterways, and tile drainage; 3 / large-scale public forest land acquisition, assistance with reforestation on private lands by the provision of tree planting equipment and labour, and windbreak planting; 4 / the improvement of stream habitat, the development of wildlife habitat, and the provision of shrubs and trees suitable for wildlife; 5 / the development of recreational facilities on conservation lands, including those for picnics, swimming, boating, winter sports, and nature study.

There are perhaps two salient reasons for the emphasis on education in the work of the officials of the Conservation Authorities Branch. One of these is a general feeling that increasing urbanization should be balanced by conscious efforts to provide children with opportunities for direct contact with natural phenomena. Whether the belief is valid or not, many people still hold the view that moral and spiritual strength is to be gained through an intimate acquaintance with the works of nature. The other reason for concern with education is that conservation measures are not likely to be completely or permanently effective unless children grow up with an awareness of their importance. The Honourable J.R. Simonett, Minister of Energy and Resources Management, stressed this point in an address at the official sod turning ceremonies for the Claremont Conservation Field Centre on May 28, 1969.

> All our citizens, but particularly our young people, must have some sense of responsibility and obligation towards our natural resources. It is only through education that they will appreciate how fully the economy of this Province and nation really depends on the products of our farms, forests, minerals and waters.

The educational efforts of the department have been undertaken in part through co-operation with other agencies, particularly school boards, and in part through direct measures. In the first of these areas there have been opportunities to assist with the recent drive to establish facilities for outdoor or conservation education. In the address referred to, Simonett declared that it made economic sense to use some of the investment in open spaces, forests, streams, ponds, and wildlife for outdoor education. The school boards could assume the responsibility for acquiring or constructing the necessary buildings.

The establishment of the Albion Hills Conservation School in 1963 by the Metropolitan Toronto and Region Conservation Authority with funds provided by the Metropolitan Toronto and Region Conservation Foundation offers an example of pioneering educational initiative on the part of one particular authority. The school has offered five-day, weekend, and summer programs. Among the groups involved have been school students from Metropolitan Toronto and the surrounding region, Girl Guides, 4-H Clubs, Junior Farmers, Junior Conservationists' Associations, Resource Rangers, and teachers' college groups.

The same authority established a conservation field centre at the Cold Creek conservation area in King Township. It consisted of a building containing classroom and laboratory facilities to serve as a base for students to undertake one-day field studies of renewable natural resources such as soil, water, wildlife, and forest, and to develop outdoor recreational skills. The centre was open for classes five days a week from September to June. Operational costs were borne by school boards and other users on a per-student basis. An additional development of the same type was the Claremont Conservation Field Centre, completed in 1969. The building contained a laboratory, lounge, kitchen, cafeteria. washrooms, and field equipment storage areas. The four-hundred-acre Claremont conservation area itself constituted the classroom. The facilities were expected to be kept open seven days a week the year round.

Arbor days and, in 1967, Centennial forest plantings have been used by some of the conservation authorities to demonstrate conservation practices to school children. In some cases, the latter have planted windbreaks for their own schools. Soil judging contests have also been used to teach aspects of soil conservation. Certain authorities have sponsored 4-H conservation clubs.

As of 1969 the Metropolitan Toronto and Region Conservation Authority maintained a highly educational enterprise in Black Creek Pioneer Village at Steeles Avenue and Jane Street. Twenty buildings had been restored and furnished as a typical crossroads community of the 1830 era. Included were a harness shop, a general store, a blacksmith's shop, a fire house, a shoemaker's shop, a school, a church, an artisan's house, a gentleman's house, an inn, and a flour mill. During a large part of the year, appropriately dressed staff carried out the activities of pioneer village life, including the tending of farm animals and poultry. A barn museum contained a large collection of nineteenth century toys and displays of a sugar bush, flax processing, a woodworking shop, and a cooper's shop.

The Department of Energy and Resources Management maintained a Junior Conservationist Award Program designed to give boys between the ages of sixteen and nineteen a worthwhile educational experience during a period of seven weeks in July and August while they made a useful contribution to conservation work. They took part in projects such as stream bank erosion studies, soil sampling, and birdhouse building, and made visits to municipal and industrial operations. They lived in camp, and received remuneration at the rate of $5 per day in addition to meals and lodging. Recreation was provided in the form of trap-shooting, archery, swimming, and fishing.

THE DEPARTMENT OF MINES

The Department of Mines has given a basic course in mineral exploration of about a week's duration in various parts of the province. In 1968 seven of these courses were offered in the established form, along with four specifically for Indians and one advanced course in Toronto. The program consisted of lectures, and, where possible, field trips and visits to museums. Films might be shown, and discussions held on minerals, rocks, geological maps, claim staking assessment work requirements, and other such matters. At Madoc the subjects taught were drilling, handling explosives and blasting, claim staking, geological mapping on cut lines, magnetic surveys, the use of air photos, and cross country travel.

The department maintained a reference library for the use of the staff, people in the mining industry, and those engaged in research or study. It contained nearly fifty thousand publications and more than nine thousand maps. Among the publications were scientific periodicals, engineering journals, mining newspapers and magazines, and government publications.

The department's large staff of cartographers produced work that was highly rated and served educational as well as other purposes. Publications of various kinds were also issued. Those of one type, which give an account of the origin and development of particular mining communities, are of considerable historical interest. An example, entitled *The Golden Porcupine*, tells how various mineral deposits were first discovered, and pays tribute to the prospectors whose efforts opened up the area. A dramatic account is given of some of the difficulties faced in earlier days, including the destruction caused by forest fires. Other booklets, done in similar style and with comparable content, are *Cobalt, the Town with a Silver Lining*; *Elliot Lake, the World's Uranium Capital*; *Manitouwadge, Cave of the Great Spirit*; and *The Red Lake Gold Field.* These publications, all written by L. Carson Brown, Director of Public Relations of the Department of Mines, are of potential value for students working on social studies projects.

Another booklet, *The Pellet Makers*, by W. Treadwell, concentrates on the story of the development of Ontario's resources of iron ore. It combines historical, geographical, statistical, and other information in a compact account that makes interesting reading, not only for the student, but also for the reader with less serious purposes. Of the same type is *Ontario's Mineral Heritage*, again by L. Carson Brown.

A publication of a somewhat different type is called *A Career for You in Canada's Mineral Industry*, prepared by the Canadian Institute of Mining and Metallurgy. It is addressed to graduates in physics, chemistry, mathematics, geology, mining, metallurgy, engineering, and related subjects. It discusses the importance of the "mineral industry," its growth potential, its scope for scientific research, the question of the relative danger of working in a mine, the types of activity involved in the practice of various specialties in the field, and other such matters. Such a publication may be considered an appropriate item for the stocks of a vocational guidance counsellor.

THE DEPARTMENT OF HIGHWAYS

In terms of educational activity, the Department of Highways has been notable for the extent of its internal staff training program. In 1967–8, according to official reports, a total of 6,654 employees, constituting over half the department's staff, took part in some form of training. A training centre was maintained where forty-one courses, totalling eighty-six weeks of training, were held. Mostly technical in content, these courses led to qualifying examinations. Some employees took courses offered by the Department of Civil Service. In addition, nearly two hundred were assisted to enrol in courses offered by other agencies.

The types of courses taken depended on the specific functions of the branch and section to which the employees were assigned. The branches were Services, Operations, Planning, Design, Administration, and Personnel. In the Equipment Section of the Services Branch, courses listed were Mechanic 2 Trades Tests, Bodyman Mechanic Test, and Draftsman 1–2, all leading to an examination. A course in automatic transmissions and a highway equipment instructors' conference did not involve an examination. In the Property Section of the same branch an examination course was given for probationary property agents. The Land Surveys Section was involved with courses for survey technicians and draftsmen, and the Special Services Section with courses on oil fired heating units and public health inspection.

Courses for employees of the Operations Branch included those for survey technicians, construction technicians, highway inspection assistants, and engineering office supervisors. There were also courses in materials and contract administration and in municipal surveying. Employees involved with materials and testing took courses for advanced concrete inspectors, advanced grade inspectors, or advanced asphalt inspectors, or, among others, a course in photo interpretation. Senior accounting and supply clerk courses were given for those involved in accounting operations. Those involved in maintenance took landscape crewman and sign painter courses.

In the Planning Branch, highway capacity seminars were offered in the executive category, traffic technician courses in the Traffic and Planning Studies Division, and draftsman and junior draftsman courses under functional planning. The courses for those in the Engineering Surveys Division, the Bridge Division, and the Road Design Division of the Design Branch were for junior draftsmen, draftsmen, and survey technicians, with a seminar also for highway design supervisors. For the Administration Branch, there were estimator and survey technician courses. For different sections of the Personnel Branch, courses were provided for engineers-in-training, senior engineers-in-training, and administrative trainees, as well as a shorthand course, a management seminar, supervisory training courses, and courses in industrial safety and motor vehicle safety.

Department employers sought a great variety of educational services from outside agencies, largely in the form of evening classes or seminars lasting from one to five days. A sample of the topics will give some impression of their scope and range: public administration, civil technology, RIA course, computer programming and analysis, calculus, public relations, concrete paving and soil cement, adult learning and teaching, real estate, probability theory and mathematical statistics, highway technology, diesel engines, hydrology, colour printing, and first aid. Among the agencies providing the courses in these areas were the extension departments of various universities, Ryerson Polytechnical Institute, school boards, the Society of Industrial and Cost Accountants, and a number of industrial corporations.

THE DEPARTMENT OF TRANSPORT

The Department of Transport has assumed a substantial responsibility for promoting traffic safety through education. It has prepared and supplied numerous pamphlets, leaflets, and guides for motorists, pedestrians, school children, teachers, driving instructors, and other groups.

In a booklet entitled *Teaching Traffic Safety*, a guide for teachers in elementary schools, a message from the Minister of Transport, Irwin Haskett, urges teachers to remedy the deficiencies of many parents by moulding children's attitudes towards permanent and positive safety habits. Safety discussion, it is suggested, can fit into art, arithmetic, health, science, and social study lessons, as well as into a formal safety program. The booklet begins by presenting some statistics on traffic accidents in Ontario in recent years. Instructional content is provided for different grade levels: for example, in grades 1 to 3, suggestions are made for the safe crossing of streets, walking, playing, and using the school bus. A list of instructional procedures follows. For pupils in grades 4 to 6, the objectives are to strengthen safety habits already learned, to give the pupils a sense of responsibility for their own and others' safety, to inculcate an understanding of the reason for the rules of the road, and to teach safe cycling. Teachers are urged to promote "Elmer, the Safety Elephant Who Never Forgets," the symbol of traffic safety for children in primary grades, using kits of material supplied by the Ontario Safety League.

A manual for teachers entitled *Traffic Safety for Nursery Schools and Kindergartens* outlines a course for four- and five-year-olds. Materials supplied include a set of five posters, a safety chart listing and illustrating the five basic safety rules for children, and a letter to parents explaining the course and asking for their co-operation. A new rule is presented each week, with related stories, games, and songs.

Among the materials provided to enable teachers to explain the rules of safe cycling to the children in their charge is a full-colour film strip. It attempts to stress the responsible attitude that prevents accidents. Posters, folders, and book covers also contribute to the "Fun on Wheels" theme which is the title of the film.

Children's fondness for joining clubs has been capitalized upon in the Crusader Cycle Club program, designed not only to produce safe cyclists, but also to develop the habits and attitudes that will lead to safe driving later. In 1969 a three-part course was offered, consisting of instruction, inspection, and examination. In a minimum of three indoor instruction meetings, the members were taught group manual signals, traffic signs, lane markings, and rules of the road. The inspection phase involved a safety check of the bicycles used for taking part in the tests. Each child who passed the tests was given a membership card, a pin, and the title "Knight Rider." Concerned adults were urged to sponsor the clubs, either on their own or, if the operation was to be on a large scale, with the assistance of the police, the local safety council, a service club, or a Home and School association.

A *Teachers' Guide for the Driver Instruction Programme in Ontario Secondary Schools* is provided jointly by the Department of Transport and the Department of Education. The first part of the manual outlines aims, objectives, and policies, and indicates some of the conditions under which a program of driver education may be conducted in schools. The second part, entitled "getting the course started," includes information on such matters as creating interest, getting permission for the course, securing equipment, obtaining the consent of the parent or guardian, applying for an instruction permit, scheduling the program, keeping individual driving records, and many other relevant topics. The third part deals with general and special qualifications of instructors and essentials for effective instruction. The fourth and fifth parts present the actual course outline, suggesting what should be taught in the classroom and behind the wheel. Finally, appropriate tests and records are suggested and teaching aids and resources are indicated.

In view of the fact that a disproportionate number of pedestrian accidents involve older people, the Department of Transport has devised a program to impress members of this group with the dangers they face as pedestrians, and to suggest safe ways to cope with traffic. The program may be used by organizations prepared to assist "senior citizens' " groups in the community. Of one and one-half hour's duration, it consists of four items: 1 / a pamphlet entitled *The Lost Art of Walking*, 2 / a set of three posters, 3 / a set of twenty-six coloured slides, and 4 / a manual explaining the program, and containing information about traffic problems of older pedestrians, statistics on traffic accidents of older people, and a reading script to accompany the slides. Instructions are provided for making arrangements and for organizing groups to which the program may be presented.

THE DEPARTMENT OF CIVIL SERVICE

The Department of Civil Service has developed a substantial training program in recent years in response to a shift in the government approach to staffing. Rather than relying on the purchase of fully developed skills, it has increasingly sought candidates with an appropriate background and desirable personal qualities, and has then attempted to provide the kind of training needed. If no outside agency offers exactly what is wanted, an internal program is set up. In addition to improving skills, this procedure tends to boost morale. Employees who are caught up in a large and increasingly complex organization feel that the government is showing an interest in them.

In May 1958 the department began to operate a staff development centre on Kempenfelt Bay on Lake Simcoe, where in-residence courses and seminars were held. The land and buildings were acquired from the Department of Lands and Forests, which purchased them earlier in the same year. There was sleeping, dining, and classroom space sufficient to accommodate thirty-five people. Operations were conducted between April and November of each year. While the Staff Development and Research Branch had first claim on the facilities, time was also made available for other departments to conduct their own training programs and staff conferences.

Courses and programs offered by the department have covered a wide range of skills on a number of different levels. Those for management have been receiving increasing emphasis in recent years. Reasons for this emphasis were given in a leaflet entitled "The Senior Officers' Conference and Seminar."

> Vast social, political, technological and educational changes in Canadian culture are giving rise to major innovations in administration within the Government of Ontario. Unprecedented growth in variety of services, rapidly increasing size, changing inter-governmental and government-community relationships, growing numbers of specialists entering government service, emergence of collective bargaining, computerization of many routine clerical and accounting operations, and application of new knowledge and skills in management, represent some of the more obvious changes taking place.[26]

The leaflet went on to assert that the senior executive needed to engage in a continuous review of the social philosophy on which the government was founded, and to understand its implications. He was said to need to be sophisticated in the use of new knowledge and to be ever receptive to new developments in public administration.

The senior officers' conference outlined in the leaflet was for branch directors or others at an equivalent level who were nominated by their deputy minister and accepted by a group of their peers. A high degree of homogeneity was assumed to be conducive to effective communication. During the three-week period of the conference, participants were expected to live in residence, to disentangle themselves completely from departmental business, and to discourage members of their families from paying visits. Course content was continually revised in the light of research and evaluation. It typically covered the following areas: 1 / structure, processes, and relationships of government, including such topics as growth of positive government, federal-provincial relations, municipal government, administrative discretion, taxation, financial administration, personnel management, and management-labour relations; 2 / the impact of cultural, economic, sociological, and psychological forces on public administration; 3 / the latest advances in administrative practices, such as management science, organization theory, decision making, and information processing technology; and 4 / administrative behaviour in terms of such topics as motivation, personality theory, perception, influence processes and leadership behaviour, group and inter-group behaviour, and role theory.

Another course of two weeks' duration was designed for line managers between first-line supervisors and top management: that is, for those who were responsible for the work of their departments and who supervised a significant number of employees engaged in relatively standardized work. The general purpose of the course was to enable participants to examine and discuss concepts that might prove useful in organizing and planning work, bringing about change, and coping with human needs. The content was divided into three parts: 1 / organizational planning, devoted to the examination and discussion of such concepts as departmentation, line-staff authority, centralization versus decentralization, unity of command, span of control, use of committees, and "assistant to" positions; 2 / human relations, covering the growth of management concepts over recent decades, the development of sound human relations under stable work conditions, the effects of technological change on human relations, leadership, motivation, communication, and labour-management relations; and 3 / systems and procedures, including systems analysis, records management, management of systems, management information requirements, decision making, and problem solving. The course provided an opportunity for small group discussions and case studies.

A supervisory course was intended for first- and second-line supervisors who were responsible for directing the work of others in the basic work unit. It consisted of four parts: personnel management, human relations, communication, and administrative techniques. 1 / The personnel management part included an outline of the government of Ontario, with particular attention to the relationship between the Treasury Board on the one hand and the Civil Service Commission and the Department of Civil Service on the other. The job classification scheme, recruitment procedures, job description, and work allocation were discussed, with reference to particular problems the supervisor might encounter. 2 / The human relations part attempted to improve the supervisor's insight into his own behaviour as well as that of others. Recent theories and research findings of behavioural science were related to problems in the work setting. 3 / The importance of establishing and maintaining satisfactory lines of communication was emphasized in the light of the trend toward geographical decentralization and departmental specialization. The purpose, effects, distortions, and manipulation of two-way communication were examined. 4 / Administrative techniques studied included systems and procedures methods, data processing methods and uses, organizational analysis, and records management. The course, like the others, provided opportunities for the discussion of specific cases and for the exchange of personal views.

A "power play" seminar was described in the staff development calendar for 1970 as a new learning game designed specifically for public officials, politicians, managers, and professionals or specialists to enable them to acquire rapidly "a high degree of skill in recognizing various forms of common but not easily identified techniques of influence." They were supposed to learn more about the tactics used by lobbyists, special interest groups, peers, subordinates, representatives from other political spheres and private organizations, consultants, union representatives, salesmen, and others. The game involved a competition between participating groups. No use was made of lectures, films, textbooks, or other traditional teaching techniques during the week over which the seminar extended.

In addition to management development programs, the calendar listed ten administrative skills programs, seven systems, data processing, and computer technology programs, three skills training programs, seven communications skills programs, two human relations programs, a French language training program, two "additional services," and three future programs. Most courses lasted for a period ranging from one day to three weeks. It is impossible to supply further details in the present context because of limitations of space.

The program of management training was in general characterized by an experimental and undogmatic approach. The opinions of participants were sought on the value of the course, its particular strengths and weaknesses, and the performance of the instructors. There was also some attempt to determine whether or not courses produced any perceptible change in the behaviour of the participants.

With the expansion of the colleges of applied arts and technology, it is to be expected that those being recruited by the Civil Service at the technician level will have more satisfactory basic qualifications than in the past. Cartographic technicians, for example, may already be familiar with geological and cartographic terms, map symbols, and methods of depicting roads, towns, geological boundaries, and rivers – things that they formerly had to be taught after they were hired. Initial training in such cases may need to involve only the process of becoming familiar with the specifics of the job. On the other hand, the need for upgrading may be expected to increase at this level, as at all others.

THE DEPARTMENT OF PUBLIC WORKS

The educational contribution of the Department of Public Works has consisted in the construction of buildings for institutions of a variety of types under the direct control of the Department of Education. No facilities were provided during the emergency period of the Second World War. In fact, the buildings occupied by the normal schools at Toronto and Ottawa and the Ontario School for the Deaf were turned over to the Department of National Defence for the duration of hostilities. At the end of the war, these buildings were returned to the province. The construction program reached a high level in the 1950s, and continued to accelerate during the 1960s.

Among the major projects involving the Department of Public Works were the construction, renovation, or extension of buildings for the following institutions, with the dates of completion indicated: the Ontario School for the Deaf, Belleville (1959); the Ontario School for the Deaf, Milton (1967); the Ontario School for the Blind, Brantford (1961); Ryerson Polytechnical Institute (1958, 1959, 1963); the Provincial Institute of Trades (1962, 1968); Toronto Teachers' College (1955); Hamilton Teachers' College (1957, 1961); Lakeshore Teachers' College (1959); London Teachers' College (1958); Port Arthur Teachers' College (1961); the Provincial Institute of Mining, Haileybury (1960); the Hamilton Technical Centre – later the Mohawk College of Applied Arts and Technology (1969); the Northern Ontario Institute of Technology, Kirkland Lake (1963); the Ontario Vocational Centre, London (1964); the Althouse College of Education, London (1967); the Eastern Ontario Institute of Technology, Ottawa (1964); the Lakehead Institute of Arts, Science, and Technology (1957); the Ontario Vocational Centre, Sault Ste Marie (1965); the Western Ontario Institute of Technology, Windsor (1959); Windsor Teachers' College (1962); the Nightingale School of Nursing, Toronto (1962); the Clarke Institute of Psychiatry, Toronto (1966); the University of Guelph (buildings completed at various dates).

INTERDEPARTMENTAL CO-OPERATION

In view of the involvement of so many departments of the provincial government in one or more aspects of education, the question of co-ordination is one of considerable importance. Observers over the years have persistently called for improvement in this area. In 1950 the royal commissioners saw enough departments concerned with education, even if narrowly defined in terms of the affairs of the publicly supported schools, to make the following recommendations.

(a) that an "Inter-departmental Committee on Education" be established, and that it be composed of at least one senior official of each department of government concerned with publicly supported education;
(b) that the Committee be empowered and required to study the existing division among the departments of powers and duties relating to education and the relevant departmental activities conducted by them, and to make recommendations as to any re-allocation of these found necessary to secure better co-ordination of those activities which affect publicly supported education;
(c) that the Committee be constituted as a standing committee, with functions as follows:
(i) to discuss ways and means of co-ordinating activities conducted by two or more departments in the field of publicly supported education;
(ii) to discuss changes in legislation proposed by another department which may affect the activities of the Department of Education;
(iii) upon request, to advise the Legislative Committee on Education with reference to private Bills and Bills submitted by a department of government, relating to publicly supported education;
(iv) to discuss matters relating to education which concern the Department of Education and one or more other departments.[27]

There was no move to implement the Royal Commission's recommendation, and the departments continued to go their own way. From time to time criticisms continued to be voiced. In April 1962 M. Belanger, member of the Legislature for Windsor Sandwich, cited the lack of liaison between the Apprenticeship Branch of the Department of Labour and the Department of Education. He declared that the principals of elementary and secondary schools did not know the branch's requirements for entrance to apprenticeship courses. Rather than getting the information as a matter of course, they had to write for it to the Department of Labour. Belanger asserted that a similar situation existed with respect to the Department of Lands and Forests – that the principals were not regularly informed of the requirements for junior forest rangers, or of how students could continue their courses to become forest rangers.[28]

A.E. Thompson, as Leader of the Liberal Opposition, touched on the same theme during the debate on the Speech from the Throne in 1965. He sought support from a brief from the Ontario Federation of Agriculture to the provincial government, in which it had been claimed that most government departments displayed a singular lack of interest in what other departments were doing. Even branches within departments had erected barriers instead of bridges, and a competitive rather than a co-operative spirit was said to prevail.[29]

R.S. Harris devoted considerable attention to the question of interdepartmental liaison in *Quiet Evolution*,[30] and offered his over-all view of the situation.

There neither is nor ever has been much in the way of a formal relationship between the Department of Education and the other government departments – no interlocking directorates, few standing committees, and only occasional official conferences. This is not to say that the departments have been working at cross-purposes or that there either has been or is a lack of co-operation on matters of mutual concern. The relationship has usually been close, but it has been informal rather than official and based on contact between individuals rather than on recognized procedures which follow automatically. It is an arrangement which is better geared to the solution of particular problems than to the consideration of over-all policy.

Harris went on to review specific contacts as he observed them. The closest relationship seemed to involve the Departments of the Provincial Secretary and Citizenship, Labour, and Reform Institutions (later Correctional Services), all of which depended on the Department of Education to provide instruction for their educational programs. In these cases, there was day-to-day contact. He referred to an interdepartmental committee established by the Departments of Education and Labour in March 1966, which he called a new departure. This committee, at the time the present volume was written, pursued two main objectives: 1 / to co-ordinate the activities of the two departments in technical training programs for industry and 2 / to co-ordinate activities relating to federal government agreements on manpower training. The membership consisted of three appointees from each department, with a rotating chairmanship. The committee held meetings four times a year. Harris indicated that the only other committee involving the same departments and, incidentally, Health, was the School Management Committee, which arranged salary contracts for teachers in schools operated directly by government departments.

Harris found considerably more tenuous relationships between the Department of Education and the other departments which conducted or supervised their own schools. Almost the sole link between the former and the Department of Lands and Forests was the membership of a senior Education official on the Advisory Council of the Forest Ranger School. A similar situation existed with respect to Health; another senior Education official was a member of the Educational Advisory Committee of the College of Nurses, and there was a representative of the Department of Education on the Planning Council on Nursing Education and Related Matters, established by the Minister of Health in 1965. On a less formal level, members of the Department of Health served on the Department of Education's curriculum committees. Before the establishment of the University of Guelph, the Chief Director of Education had been a member of the Board of Governors of the Ontario Agricultural College, but that tie had disappeared. Informal liaison was maintained by secondary school inspectors with the agricultural schools.

It seemed to Harris that what was needed was "the systematic development of a network of standing interdepartmental committees which meet regularly and whose terms of reference are sufficiently general to permit the members to consider over-all policy."[31] The Senior Co-ordinating Committee established a short time previously by the Departments of Health and University Affairs seemed to provide the model. In February 1966 the ministers of these two departments had held a joint meeting with representatives of McMaster, Ottawa, Queen's, Toronto, and Western, the five universities involved with the health sciences, to acquaint them with the government's plans for the development of health resources and manpower in Ontario. One of the results was the establishment of a Senior Co-ordinating Committee, consisting of the Deputy Ministers of the Departments of Health and University Affairs and the Chairman of the Ontario Hospital Services Commission, and charged with the responsibility of reviewing the plans and needs of each university and of producing a co-ordinated plan for the development of the health sciences. A second consequence of the meeting was the establishment of the Ontario Council of Health, set up in April 1966 by the Minister of Health, to act as his senior advisory body on health matters.[32]

There seems to be considerable merit in Harris's recommendation that there be committees patterned on the Health and Education Senior Co-ordinating Committee for Education and University Affairs, Education and Agriculture, Education and Health, Education and Labour, and Education, University Affairs, and Labour. One may perhaps be permitted some scepticism about his further proposal that there also be a committee involving all departments of the government on which each would be represented either by the minister or by the deputy minister. He suggested that such a committee would serve two main purposes. 1 / It would use the development of the educational system as a whole to determine what proportion of the provincial budget would be allocated to education, and what proportion of that figure would be allocated to each department. 2 / Negotiations with the federal government over financial support for education could be based on a co-ordinated plan for the development of the entire educational system.[33]

If all departments were represented by their respective ministers, it is hard to see how the proposed committee would differ from the cabinet. To suggest that the latter body should be the vehicle for the development of a co-ordinated educational plan is perhaps unrealistic in view of the weight of its existing responsibilities. Also, although the earlier review of the educational and training concerns of a number of departments has shown that these are quite important, they do not begin to cover the range of interests and responsibilities of the Departments of Education and University Affairs. Thus on a large proportion of the agenda, most ministers would take a relatively passive part, and might find the proceedings extremely tiresome. They might well be inclined to suggest that the Ministers of Education and University Affairs (whether a single individual or two) look after their duties within their own departments. Much the same might be said of a committee consisting of deputy ministers. Participation would be meaningful largely in terms of their own rather restricted interests.

It would be theoretically possible to co-ordinate educational activity by placing everything coming under the broadest definition of the term under the jurisdiction of a single minister. The objection that the job would be too big for one individual could be met by limiting his responsibility to matters of major concern and ensuring that the administrative structure of his department provided for adequate delegation of powers. There would, however, be some other very serious drawbacks. 1 / Education has come to be such an important government function that a minister who had the sole responsibility for all its ramifications would carry disproportionate weight in the government, and make it difficult for the cabinet system to work in its traditional form. While portfolios differ substantially in importance under existing conditions without making the system unworkable, there is no doubt a point beyond which an imbalance should not be pushed. 2 / Education in the sense of providing information and influencing public attitudes is a fundamental and inseparable aspect of the work of some departments. For example, promoting safety is basic to the work of the Department of Transport, encouraging a healthy and constructive attitude toward the conservation of natural resources is of vital concern to the Departments of Lands and Forests and of Energy and Resources Management, and spreading the word about the scenic and other attractions of the province is a central responsibility of the Department of Tourism and Information. There are obviously some educational functions that could not be concentrated exclusively in any single government department. Thus a serious effort at devising effective means of ensuring interdepartmental co-operation seems to provide the only solution.

The development of the system of colleges of applied arts and technology has acted as a co-ordinating influence as far as post-secondary educational institutions are concerned. Forestry technician training has already been taken over from the Department of Lands and Forests, and formal training for fire fighters may well follow. The training of health services personnel at certain levels, including the training of nurses, is likely to be an increasing responsibility of the colleges. The gathering in of various fragments of post-secondary training is justified on several assumptions: 1 / that the colleges have high prestige, 2 / that assembling various forms of training in a single institution ensures the fullest utilization of expensive equipment and facilities, and 3 / that the variety of educational offerings in the colleges provides an optimum educational experience. Against the forces of integration, it would be a difficult struggle for a particular department to maintain its own separate institutions.

There have been other evidences of increasingly effective co-ordination. In May 1967 Davis asserted that co-operative effort between the Department of Education and other provincial government departments had greatly increased. Most of the officials in the main office served on one or more liaison committees with the Departments of Health, Labour, Social and Family Services, the Attorney General, Transport, and Economics and Development.[34] A short time later, he commented on the success of the Senior Co-ordinating Committee involving Education and Health, and cited similar efforts involving Social and Family Services and the Ontario Student Housing Corporation.[35]

Despite this trend, one still hears echoes of Harris's verdict that there is not sufficient high level co-ordination to ensure a coherent policy in such areas as industrial training. People speak with satisfaction of pleasant and productive interchanges of views and information through informal associations and in committees, but often add that something more is needed. It is to be hoped that the suggestion that the matter should be given continued serious study will not seem unduly trite.

FOURTEEN

Interprovincial co-operation

RATIONALE

It is relatively common among countries organized on a federal basis to have the major responsibility for education assigned to the component provinces or states. The degree of local responsibility varies from nominal to almost complete. In nearly every case, however, there are official agencies to co-ordinate at least some aspects of the national effort in this field. Canada has been conspicuous, or even unique, in the absence of such organs. It has a close counterpart in the Federal Republic of Germany, but even there state autonomy has been more effectively modified by the development of informal co-ordinating structures.

It is commonly believed in most countries of the world that education provides an essential cement to hold disparate interests together. The school is held responsible for developing and sustaining a sense of common purpose and for fostering a feeling of national pride. In this cause, it is often encouraged to perpetuate historical myths and distorted versions of past events. At best, it is expected to identify and extol the peculiar virtues of the national culture or cultures and to ensure that they are looked upon with affection and respect.

Many Canadians hold these views on the function of the school, but they have had little effect on actual practice. To a large extent for historical reasons, the provinces have been left with the responsibility of determining whether or not education will be administered to serve national purposes. For the most part they have not assigned a high priority to this function, as A.B. Hodgetts has demonstrated so dramatically in *What Culture? What Heritage?* It may not be an exaggeration to suggest that the country may yet pay the price of such a policy by dissolution into fragments.

Co-ordination of educational systems in Canada could make a contribution to unity, not only by encouraging the development of national sentiment and a sense of common purpose and destiny, but also by facilitating population mobility. No one knows how many families have been discouraged from moving from one province to another because of the prospect that the children might be put back a grade, not necessarily because of real academic deficiency, but more probably because they could not meet some technical requirement. Adjoining provinces have typically been able to persuade themselves of the superiority of their own programs and practices, and the records are full of restrictions and requirements designed to ensure that ill-prepared newcomers are not given any undeserved advantage. The most important objective has often seemed to be that of protecting the province's standards rather than that of accommodating the pupils. Barriers to the movement of teachers across provincial boundaries have made their own major contribution to the perpetuation of a parochial attitude.

There have been numerous advocates of uniformity as the obvious solution to the problem. They would standardize major aspects of school systems right across the country: structure, curriculum, textbooks, certificates and diplomas, and, where applicable, admission requirements to various institutions. The result would be that a pupil could resume his studies after transferring from province to province with no more difficulty than if he moved to an adjoining school district within a single province. Such a solution would unfortunately mean a rejection of most of the constructive innovations of recent years. Uniformity could be maintained only by imposing a system of rigid regulations. Teacher initiative would have to be suppressed because variations in the common curriculum could not be tolerated. Textbooks and other instructional materials could be changed only through the operation of ponderous machinery. Desirable regional and local variations in educational need and interest would have to be ignored. Not least serious, the co-ordinating function would have to be carried out by a massive bureaucracy operating at a maximum distance from the local community.

The move to break down the grade barriers, the emphasis on the interests and needs of the individual, the progress in devising more flexible programs, the decline in importance assigned to certificates and diplomas, and other related developments offer a superior alternative to standardization and uniformity. When the migrating pupil is assured of being evaluated in terms of his real capacities and achievement, and is placed accordingly, the most serious barriers will have disappeared. Davis held out this possibility in an exchange with Bernard Newman in the Legislature on May 25, 1967.

Mr. Newman: May I ask the Minister how far we have progressed toward uniformity in recognized education standards across Canada?
Hon. Mr. Davis: ... The concept, I think, of education today is such that we are not really looking for standardization. ... The question of transfer from one jurisdiction to another, whether it is inside the province or interprovincial, ... will not relate necessarily to specific curriculum or subject matter.[1]

During the debates in the Canadian House of Commons in October 1968, Mark Rose, member for Fraser Valley West, spoke of the dangers in the pursuit of uniformity.

Uniformity, you see, can only go so far, because an overdose can be stifling and deadly, whether it is within one school, within one province or across a whole nation. Public education historically has been preoccupied with group learning and the supposed efficiency intended to result from improved class or mass methods and techniques. But the results of such preoccupation have been almost uniformly disappointing. That groups learn anything is a misconception, and within this misconception lies the root of the problem. Groups learn nothing. Only individuals are capable of learning, and he, the individual, has often been overlooked by the education industry.

It would be much too optimistic to think that the continuation of current trends would in time solve all the problems created by differences in educational approach from one province to another. In the area of information, in particular, the need for co-operation and co-ordination will continue to grow. On the higher administrative levels, the exchange of many types of data offers the hope of substantial benefits for the country as a whole, as well as for individual provinces. At the level of the pupil himself, a transfer to another province may be greatly facilitated if he can be accompanied by records of his previous achievement and other types of information in readily recognizable form. Going beyond the exchange of information, certain enterprises would seem to promise superior quality and possibly financial savings if undertaken with a broader base of support than a single province can provide. The production of television programs and the development of tests and programmed texts constitute obvious examples.

The desirability of co-ordinating provincial effort has been regularly and freely recognized. Many English-speaking Canadians have advocated what has appeared to be the obvious solution – increased federal power. At conference after conference, national associations having a direct or indirect concern with education have passed resolutions advocating federal involvement in some aspect of educational affairs. While many of these resolutions have been merely requests for financial assistance, the possibility of supervision and control has loomed in the background.

If there is any obvious fact of political life today, it is that the province of Quebec will not accept a federal co-ordinating role. Provincial control of education is regarded as essential for the preservation of French-Canadian culture, which must flourish in Quebec if it is to survive anywhere. Those who advocate the extension of federal control are either implying that the departure of that province should be expedited, or else are making a completely unrealistic evaluation of the possibilities. The solution must be sought elsewhere: specifically, in voluntary interprovincial co-operation. The decade of the sixties saw very substantial moves in that direction.

INFORMAL INITIATIVES

The Canadian Education Association had long provided a forum for the exchange of information and views among departmental officials and other educators in the various provinces. A discussion of the development and contributions of that association is reserved for volume VII of the present series. It was at its annual meeting in September 1960 that J.P. Robarts, as Minister of Education for Ontario, took the initiative in forming a Standing Committee of Ministers of Education, and was named its chairman. This was one of the first significant actions among those which established his reputation as an active and effective proponent of interprovincial co-operation.

EARLY ACTIVITIES

One of the first important initiatives of the standing committee was taken in 1964, when an *ad hoc* subcommittee was appointed to investigate the possibility of establishing an educational information system for Canada. There was talk at that time of having an educational information service, with a data-processing centre located in Toronto or Montreal, into which statistical data would flow and from which tabulated material would be returned to suppliers and other authorized users at the federal, provincial, and municipal levels. It was hoped that day-to-day operations and long-term planning could thus be based on up-to-date and comparable data. The Ministers' Information Systems Committee was placed under the chairmanship of R.W.B. Jackson of the Department of Educational Research of the Ontario College of Education, and included representatives of the provinces and of the Dominion Bureau of Statistics. Initial proposals were approved by the ministers, subject to further consideration on the basis of a report to be submitted to them.

During the same year, the ministers put a damper on the drive to establish a Canadian council on admission to college and university by withholding their approval of a proposal of the National Conference of Canadian Universities and Colleges and the Fédération des collèges classiques. The ministers felt that they needed more time to study the implications of the scheme.

STEPS TOWARD THE FORMATION OF A SECRETARIAT

Discussion of the possibility of establishing a secretariat for the ministers' committee, which would constitute an interprovincial office of education, extended over a considerable period of time. There were questions about how such a secretariat or office would relate to the secretariat of the CEA. At one time, some people thought that most of the activities of the latter organization would be absorbed, along with its permanent staff, into the new structure. This development did not occur, and the CEA continued its independent existence with the assurance that provincial support would be maintained.

A good deal of speculation preceded and accompanied the holding of a conference on education and the development of human resources in Montreal in September 1966, shortly before the annual meeting of the

CEA. Specifically designed to consider the implications of the second annual report of the Economic Council of Canada, it was sponsored by the ten provincial Ministers of Education, and was attended by delegates from provincial departments of education, business, industry, and educational institutions, as well as by members of the Economic Council. An announcement that an interprovincial office would be formed was expected, either at that conference or at the meeting of the CEA which followed in Vancouver, but the ministers contented themselves with the much more modest step of setting up an *ad hoc* committee to study ways of improving interprovincial co-operation. As an incidental sidelight, some rather overblown apprehensions were expressed that the conference represented a scheme by a group labeled the "Pussycats" to dominate Canadian education for utilitarian purposes. This group, which was said to include W.G. Davis, J.J. Deutsch, then chairman of the Economic Council of Canada, F.W. Minkler, Director of Education for North York, R.W.B. Jackson, Director of the Department of Educational Research of the Ontario College of Education, and D.H. MacLaren of Air Canada were supposed to be working together to bridge the gap between Canadian education and the technological revolution, in part by bringing pressure to bear for the establishment of a Canadian office of education. The notion that they were working together on any coherent or consistent plan was in fact a figment of a newspaper reporter's imagination.

The delay was obviously attributable to certain questions about the form, status, and role of the proposed organization. There were differences in opinion about its relationship to the CEA. It appeared doubtful that the political concerns of the ministers could be comfortably accommodated within an association such as the CEA. Yet many were unhappy at the possibility of fragmenting the effort toward a unified national approach to education. For a time it appeared that, while the organizations would be distinct, an enlarged secretariat of some forty would serve the needs of both. The final decision was made in favour of complete separation, with the hope that a relationship of close co-operation could be maintained.

Members of the *ad hoc* committee were R.L. Stanfield, Nova Scotia, J.-J. Bertrand, Quebec, W.G. Davis, Ontario, G.J. Trapp, Saskatchewan, and L.R. Peterson, British Columbia. They met on January 20, 1967, and recommended that a Council of Ministers be established to collect and exchange information on matters of mutual concern and to facilitate effective consultation with the federal government. Preliminary planning in preparation for policy decisions involving the federal government might include instructional media, manpower programs, and forms of assistance to post-secondary school students. Other interprovincial concerns would include educational planning, tests for university admission, and educational information systems, in which the ministers had for some years taken an interest. The *ad hoc* committee emphasized that each provincial department of education would remain autonomous, and that no recommendations or decisions of the council would be binding on them with respect to their own areas of responsibility.

ORGANIZATION OF THE COUNCIL OF MINISTERS OF EDUCATION

After ratification of the agreement by all the provincial governments, the council came into formal existence at a meeting of the ministers in Regina on September 26, 1967, with Davis as the first chairman. In a memorandum approved at that meeting, the purposes of the council were defined as follows:

1. To enable the Ministers to consult on matters of common concern.
2. To provide a means for the fullest possible co-operation among Provincial Governments in areas of mutual interest in education.
3. To co-operate with other educational organizations in such ways as to promote the development of education in Canada.[2]

The membership of the council consisted, of course, of the ten Ministers of Education, with provision for the annual election of a chairman from among them. Provision was made, however, for a minister to be represented at a meeting by a deputy minister or other official, who would have the right to vote. A minister might also be accompanied at meetings by such officials and advisers as he considered appropriate. The normal schedule consisted of an annual meeting of two days in late September, a meeting of two days in early December, and a meeting of three days in late May.

Despite the small size of the council itself, it was thought necessary to have an executive committee of five members, consisting of the chairman, the vice-chairman, the immediate past chairman, and two other members elected annually, with assurance of representation from each of British Columbia, the Prairie provinces, Ontario, Quebec, and the Atlantic provinces. The executive committee was expected to deal with administrative matters and to act as a finance committee.

The main activities of the council were expected to be carried out by interprovincial committees composed of experienced personnel from the provincial departments of education. These were to be set up as the need arose. A member of the secretariat would serve as secretary of each committee in order to record the minutes and assist in other ways. The committees were authorized to form subcommittees and to employ research assistants to conduct studies as needed.

An early decision was made to establish three main committees: an Instructional Media Committee, a Post-Secondary Education Committee, and a Manpower Programs Committee. The first of these was responsible for recommending action with respect to developments in the media field which were of concern to all the provinces. It also dealt with such federal government organizations as the National Film Board and the Canadian Broadcasting Corporation. A Sub-Committee on School Broadcasting, consisting of French and English sections, had the task of working with the CBC in program planning as well as performing certain liaison functions. An *ad hoc* Sub-Committee on Educational Television was requested to submit recommendations by September 1, 1969, with respect to 1 / the foundation level of support for educational television broadcasting, 2 / interprovincial exchange of programs, and 3 / the development of suitable technical standards for television equipment for educational purposes.

The Post-Secondary Education Committee was expected to study such aspects of post-secondary education as testing and student assistance, and to recommend action by the council in dealing with the federal authorities responsible for financial assistance to post-secondary education. A Sub-Committee on Student Assistance was formed to work in that specific area. The Manpower Programs Committee, the third of the group, was to study problems related to the implementation of the federal *Adult Occupational Training Act*.

The primary responsibility of the secretariat was to assist the council and its committees by providing central office research, co-ordination, administration, and distribution of materials. The secretary-general was identified as the council's chief officer, with responsibilities for acting as treasurer, preparing budget estimates, disbursing funds, supervising the secretariat staff, acting as an *ex officio* member of all committees and subcommittees, and other such functions. E.J. Quick, an official of the Ontario Department of Education, was seconded to act as secretary-general from early 1968 until September 1969, pending a permanent appointment. He was succeeded by Maurice Richer. Toronto was selected as the headquarters of the secretariat.

ACTIVITIES OF THE COUNCIL

To outside observers, it seemed that the council was very slow in beginning operations. An article by Ralph Mitchener in the *Canadian Annual Review for 1967* included the following statements.

> One official of a national education association commented that it seemed to take the Council of Ministers six months to make one breast stroke. While in 1967 there was some truth in this statement, it must be recalled that for many years the ministers did not even get their feet wet.[3]

A reason offered for the council's apparent torpor was that national concerns had to be second in importance to individual or regional policies and priorities related to them. The reviewer foresaw that, once the council was ready to assert itself, the federal government "would need to co-ordinate its views on education and on the policies of the many federal departments with responsibilities for education assistance."[4]

A very practical reason why no very ambitious projects could be undertaken was that funds were not available until the new financial year beginning in April 1968. Until that time, only makeshift arrangements could be made. The council was to be financed through provincial payments on a per capita basis.

It is probable that the outsider will always tend to underestimate the significance and value of the council simply because of the methods by which it operates. Its members have shown a determination to conciliate and compromise wherever possible, both among themselves and with the federal government. For their part, the federal authorities are also eager to avoid noisy confrontations such as occurred in the Gabon affair. Thus information is exchanged on a confidential basis and care is taken to ensure that the atmosphere of trust is not broken.

Davis was by no means prepared to concede that nothing of importance had been accomplished during the early part of the first year's operations. Information he provided in connection with the departmental estimates for 1968–9 included the following statement.

> The improved communications resulting from our discussions have already paid substantial dividends. Because the Provinces were able to consult effectively together to formulate ... solidly documented proposals, the recent changes in federal manpower and retraining programs were considerably more workable than they otherwise would have been, to the advantage of the entire country.

In a summary of the achievements of the council, Davis mentioned the following decisions made at the first annual meeting held in September 1968. 1 / Financial support was approved for the Canadian Council for Research in Education to enable it to continue as a co-ordinating agency for Canada-wide research. 2 / The council accepted the recommendation of the Ministers' Information Systems Committee to co-operate with the Dominion Bureau of Statistics in the compilation of educational data. (The ambitious objectives of the committee had shrunk rather drastically since its original formation.) 3 / The council agreed to continue a study of the usefulness of the Service for Admission to College and University. 4 / There would be co-operation with the Ontario Institute for Studies in Education in its Canadian Studies Project. 5 / There would be continued support for the French-English Teacher Exchange Program of the Canadian Education Association.

Davis indicated that most of the council's activities had been carried out through committees composed of experienced officials from the provincial departments of education. He saw several advantages in this method of operating. 1 / It avoided duplication of facilities already existing at the provincial level. 2 / It ensured the most efficient use of the scarce supply of specialized staff. 3 / It ensured that the continuing work of the council was closely co-ordinated with provincial programs. 4 / It developed a climate of mutual confidence among the staffs from all provinces through close working relationships. 5 / It ensured continuity and co-ordination of programs and made quick and concerted action possible when events required it. The council and its committees made a practice of holding their meetings in different parts of the country in order to secure maximum involvement of all provinces. Davis declared: "In many respects the council is one of the first practical steps toward the implementation of a new federalism based upon meaningful consultation and cooperation." Even a recent air strike had been unsuccessful in breaking communication; a telephone conference involving participants in ten provincial centres had been conducted on a matter of urgent common concern.

The council operated in 1968–9 under the chairmanship of J.-G. Cardinal, Minister of Education for Quebec. During that time, most of its activities were in the fields of international, federal, and interprovincial co-operation. Reports on these were given at the annual meeting in September 1969.

Participation in international activities was carried out in co-operation with the appropriate federal authorities. Among the achievements of the year were the following. 1 / Reports were prepared on education within Canada for intergovernmental organizations and their international conferences. 2 / Delegates were selected to attend international conferences on education. 3 / There was consultation with provincial authorities to ensure continuity and rotation in the naming of delegates as representatives. 4 / Delegates were given briefing sessions to provide appropriate background information. 5 / There was co-operation with federal authorities in registering, transporting, and accommodating delegates. 6 / Reports on the proceedings of conferences at which the council was represented were prepared and distributed. 7 / International visits of education officials at the intergovernmental level were co-ordinated. 8 / Liaison was maintained between departments of education and international organizations concerned with education.

The Post-Secondary Education Committee, which had been co-ordinated by Y. Martin, reported that it had prepared a questionnaire designed to study the different aspects of participation in the work of the Service for Admission to College and University by the provinces and by institutions of post-secondary education. The committee indicated that the organization seemed to have moved to more solid ground in that it had made satisfactory arrangements with respect to funding and test development. A further area of study was that of provincial assistance to post-secondary education. A questionnaire survey had, despite deficiencies arising from inconsistencies in reporting techniques, provided the basis for the exchange of useful information among provincial departments of education. The survey, with appropriate modifications and improvements, was to be repeated the following year. A study had also been made of federal-provincial arrangements for financing post-secondary education. Statistical studies of eligible students and expenditures were being analysed to provide guidelines for future developments.

The committee identified as the area of its major concern that of student assistance. At the meeting of the council in 1968, it had been agreed that there were serious flaws in the existing arrangements, and that modifications were urgently needed. As a result, an *ad hoc* subcommittee had been appointed under the chairmanship of A.P. Gordon, Assistant Deputy Minister of University Affairs for Ontario, to study the question. Its specific terms of reference were 1 / to collect and analyse data and policies on student aid programs in post-secondary education, 2 / to project requirements in student aid for 1970 to 1990, and 3 / to recommend practices and policies that could be applied during this period. It undertook to conduct a comprehensive survey of existing schemes in Canada and abroad, and to develop projections for the period up to 1985 of the costs of various types of assistance programs.

The Manpower Programs Committee, co-ordinated by E.B. Angood, submitted to the ministers in August 1968 the results of a study of problems encountered in the implementation of the *Adult Occupational Training Act*. As a consequence of this study, the ministers consulted the Minister of Manpower and Immigration and members of his department. The federal minister agreed to consider specific recommendations, and to co-operate to study the possibility of further revisions of the legislation.

The report of the Instructional Media Committee, co-ordinated by C.H. Williams, indicated that it had engaged in discussions with the federal Task Force on Educational Broadcasting over the proposed *Act to Establish the Canadian Educational Broadcasting Agency*. As a result, the second reading of the bill was postponed to give the Council of Ministers an opportunity to discuss the matter and bring their point of view to the attention of the Secretary of State. The committee had also made arrangements for a survey of instructional media in Canada. There had been meetings with representatives of the National Film Board to consider methods of liaison with the departments of education as well as problems of equipment testing.

An *ad hoc* Sub-Committee on Educational Television had been set up under the chairmanship of T.R. Ide to consider the following matters: 1 / the foundation level of educational television programming that the federal government should be asked to ensure for each province; 2 / the procedures that should be adopted to facilitate interprovincial exchange of programs, in the light of such factors as the legal and other problems related to copyright, residual payments, and compatibility of equipment; and 3 / the development of technical standards for television receivers, video tape recorders, MATV systems, cable systems, and 2500 megahertz systems. A report on these matters was submitted in September 1969.

Generally speaking, the Council of Ministers of Education has attempted to focus its attention on a fairly restricted number of areas in the hope of attaining some tangible successes. It appears to have made a promising beginning, and offers prospects of making an important contribution to Canadian understanding and unity at a time when disintegrative tendencies are strong.

ONTARIO-QUEBEC AGREEMENT ON EDUCATIONAL AND CULTURAL MATTERS

An important forward step was taken in the field of interprovincial relations with the signing of "An Agreement for Co-operation and Exchange in Educational Matters between the Government of Ontario and the Government of Quebec" by Prime Ministers Robarts and Bertrand on June 4, 1969. The preamble of the brief document recognized the historic and linguistic heritage of Canada which had developed from the English-speaking and French-speaking communities. It mentioned also the contribution of other ethnic groups in moulding the character of the country. Carefully avoiding controversial designations, it called English and French the two "working" languages of Canada. In view of the signatories' declared conviction that increased co-operation between the two provinces was essential to the continued strength of the country, they agreed to a program of exchanges in the educational and cultural fields.

The basic document was divided into five parts entitled respectively 1 / Languages, 2 / Government Administration, 3 / Education, 4 / Cultural Affairs, and 5 / Implementation of the Agreement. Under the first heading, the two governments promised to provide "wherever feasible" public services in English and French, and education for the linguistic minority in each province in its own language, with the means also for the latter to acquire a good knowledge of the language of the majority. The articles under the second heading, dealing with the production and exchange of information, mutual assistance in translation and interpretation, and other inter-governmental contacts, had a less direct bearing on education, except for the promise of co-operation in the training of civil servants, notably translators and interpreters. The third part calls for more specific examination:

Article 7
We will exchange information on the methods of teaching English and French and encourage exchanges of specialists in these fields.

Article 8
We will encourage exchanges among teachers, administrators and students at all levels and in all fields of our educational systems.

Article 9
We will co-operate in establishing exchange programmes for the development of language teachers.

Article 10
We will co-operate in establishing standards for recognition of teacher training programmes undertaken in each other's province.
Article 11
We will encourage agreements among educational institutions at all levels for granting recognition for studies undertaken in each other's province.
Article 12
In co-operation with the many private non-profit organizations now engaged in student exchanges, we will encourage summer employment exchanges to enable our young people to become better acquainted with each other and with each other's customs.
Article 13
We will exchange technical information and programmes in the field of educational broadcasting and television.

In the area of cultural affairs, co-operation and exchanges were promised in literature, music, theatre, dance, visual arts, libraries, archives, museums, and folk arts, with due recognition of the contributions of many ethnic groups.

Although the areas of co-operation were defined specifically enough, comparatively little was said about the intended means of implementation. These were to be worked out by a Permanent Commission for Ontario-Quebec Co-operation, consisting of five representatives from each government. Meetings would alternate between Quebec City and Toronto. Each government promised to allocate at least $150,000 annually for the implementation of the agreement.

The agreement was the culmination of a long period of discussions between the Robarts Government and successively with the Liberal Lesage régime and those of Union Nationale leaders Johnson and Bertrand. For Ontario, it was part of a continuous process of accommodating the French-speaking minority so that their culture might have a realistic chance of survival in the province. It was very much in the spirit of the reports of the Royal Commission on Bilingualism and Biculturalism and the St Denis report. For Bertrand, it was an assertion of his intention to work for the maintenance of Confederation and for the preservation of the historic rights of the English-speaking inhabitants of Quebec. Some saw in it a strategy on his part for making the point that had eluded him a few months earlier when members of his own party, under the leadership of Education Minister Cardinal, had forced him to shelve legislation that would have reinforced the right of the minority to instruction in the language of their choice. An agreement entered into voluntarily with a sister province lacked the overtones that would undoubtedly have aroused protests from Quebec extremists had Ottawa been a participant.

FIFTEEN

Educational concerns of the federal government

EXTENT OF FEDERAL GOVERNMENT INVOLVEMENT IN EDUCATION

Federal involvement in education may be considered under two headings: 1 / educational activities that are carried on by its various branches and agencies in order to further their own organizational objectives and 2 / education as a service to the Canadian people. There is no basis for controversy about the first. Just as the majority of provincial departments could not perform their functions without supplying information to the public and to some extent influencing public attitudes, so also are federal departments bound by the same realities. Effectiveness in their work demands that they utilize the available media to the best advantage.

Again paralleling provincial departments, they must be concerned about the capacities of their own employees if they are to operate efficiently. While they may quite justifiably be urged to rely on the facilities of formal educational institutions operated by provincial governments, they must also be prepared to supplement the training provided there by maintaining their own programs, particularly to fill specific training needs.

Educational service to the people may be divided into three categories: 1 / the management of schools or other educational institutions; 2 / the exertion of influence or pressure to ensure that certain kinds of services are provided, such as apprenticeship and manpower training; and 3 / the general financial support of educational enterprises designed and operated entirely by the provinces. There have been differences of opinion between strong federalists and provincial autonomists with respect to all three of these.

Direct federal maintenance of educational institutions arises mainly from the responsibility of that level of government for Indians and Eskimos and for the armed forces. In recent years, there has been an increased trend toward the purchase of provincial services for Indian children, and the relative importance of the armed forces has been declining. As a result, it is unlikely that federal schools will play a significant part in the educational set-up in the immediate future.

Instead of being a relatively minor matter that can be relegated to childhood and early youth, education is coming to be seen as a fundamental aspect of the totality of life. Any level of government that expects to maintain a genuine *raison d'être* can therefore be expected to involve itself in educational concerns. The real issue is not whether provincial governments can legitimately claim complete and absolute control over all educative activities, which would be quite incompatible with membership in a federal union, but where the dividing line between federal and provincial jurisdiction should be. Past experience should have persuaded Canadians that there is no hope of reaching firm, final, and decisive agreement on the matter. The continuation of federal government therefore implies an unending state of tension between the two levels.

The federal government has staked its chief claim in the field of educational service to occupational training and retraining in order to discharge its responsibility for the economic welfare of the individual and the country. In order to dampen controversy, its spokesmen have used ingenious arguments to try to dichotomize education and training. While there may be practical advantages in this approach, it perpetuates a concept of man as a collection of separable abstractions. He cannot in fact develop as a cultural or a spiritual being apart from the way in which he earns his living. The kind of job training he receives will inevitably have a profound influence on whether or not he is and remains an effective participant in and perpetuator of, for example, French Canadian culture.

The hope for the survival of the federal system in a culturally divided nation lies not only in a sincere desire on all sides to co-operate, but also in a federal policy of working wherever possible through provincial institutions and programs and of avoiding any steps that will bring the federal government into open and direct conflict with provincial objectives that are compatible with the welfare of the nation. The record of the federal government, regardless of which party has been in control, has been good. That provincial apprehensions have not been dispelled is a result not of examples of blatant federal interference, but rather of the fear that inadequate revenues might make it impossible for the provinces to carry out their educational responsibilities, thus leaving a vacuum for the federal government to fill.

The federal government's provision of financial assistance to the provinces, in particular for post-secondary education, is justified in terms of the desirability of ironing out some of the grossest inequalities among provinces in the distribution of economic resources. If this objective were not valid, there would be no defensible reason why the federal government should not completely vacate enough tax room to enable the provinces to assume full financial responsibility. It is perhaps inevitable that the richer provinces will question whether the process of equalization is not being carried too far, and will complain that their inhabitants are being unduly penalized for initiative and good management. Such views have been heard in Ontario, which contributes most toward the subsidization of services in other provinces. There is, however, an evident acceptance of the principle that some sharing of the wealth is the price of unity.

On this point, the Provincial Committee on Aims and Objectives (the Hall-Dennis Committee) commented:

We are fully aware that education in Canada is first and foremost a provincial responsibility. That does not mean or imply that the Federal Government has no interest or responsibility in the field. It has a vital interest in co-operation with the provinces to see that adequate resources are available in all provincial areas. Only by so doing will educational opportunity be equalized throughout the nation.[1]

Another type of objection to federal subsidies may come even from provinces that stand to benefit from some redistribution of national wealth. There is an apprehension that funds from any level of government cannot continue indefinitely to be handed over to another without some kind of restrictions being imposed. The freedom to reject the funds in order to avoid the restrictions is not always possible to maintain in the face of political pressures. The Ontario government was forced into a medicare scheme at a time and under conditions not of its own choosing. Successive Quebec governments have feared that something comparable might be attempted in some field of education.

The contrary position is that, at least as far as higher education is concerned, there indeed should be some strings attached to federal aid. In 1968 the Association of Universities and Colleges of Canada advocated a Canada-wide system of higher education. It was claimed that universities could not successfully pursue their objectives only in a provincial context, but must operate concurrently in provincial, regional, federal, and national contexts. An editorial in the *Globe and Mail* emphasized the point.

It is simply impossible for universities to live wholly within provinces and meet the costly demands of research and technology or produce graduates capable of dealing with all the multiplicity of Canadian problems that admit to no provincial boundaries.

Only on one of these problems have the provinces welcomed federal initiatives – the financial problem. Yet the accomplishment of national goals in almost every area, from the equality of opportunity available to the individual Canadian child to the establishment of centres for training foreign aid specialists, requires the co-operation of the whole. The parts can do the job only in part, and often badly and wastefully; and the Constitution and regional jealousies say that it shall continue so.[2]

Information about the involvement of the federal government's educational role is dispersed widely through *Ontario's Educative Society*. Chapters 11 and 12 of the present volume offer particular concentrations of such information. Another example is chapter 20 of volume IV, which deals with adult training and retraining. The present chapter does not aim at a comprehensive treatment, but rather deals with certain activities in representative departments and agencies that are particularly federal in their focus. The activities of the Department of Labour and the Department of Manpower and Immigration are not dealt with in the present chapter, since they are considered to be adequately covered under other headings.

THE DEPARTMENT OF NATIONAL HEALTH AND WELFARE

Along with the establishment of the Department of Health in 1919, a publicity service was created to provide health information to the press, professional journals, and the public. Since then, materials have been prepared and distributed for use in adult education programs dealing with prenatal and child care, mental health, dental health, and other areas of concern to parents, professional health workers, and school children. One of the earliest publications to achieve widespread popularity was *The Canadian Mother's Book*, which appeared in 1925. The department has also undertaken, in co-operation with provincial departments of public health, to prepare and supply informative materials for teachers.

One booklet for use in schools is entitled *Resource Guide on Smoking and Health for Canadian Teachers – Grades 5-13*, produced in co-operation with the Canadian Education Association and the Canadian Teachers' Federation. Its purpose is to assist educators to convince young people during their formative years to become or remain non-smokers in order to avoid the hazards of lung cancer, chronic bronchitis and emphysema, and coronary heart disease. The booklet emphasizes a factual approach to the subject, and suggests ways to relate it to physical education, social studies, the language arts, mathematics, general science, art, the library, and extracurricular activities. Another booklet provided for general and school use is a *Dental Health Manual*. It has sections on the teeth and gums, the foundation teeth, the permanent teeth, structure of the teeth, functions of teeth, tooth decay, how to prevent tooth decay, treatment of tooth decay, irregular teeth, diseases of the supporting structures of the teeth, taking the child to the dentist, and tumours and cancer of the mouth.

A number of training films have been produced for teachers, particularly in the area of child development. Television programs on smoking and health have been tested and telecast in schools in Metropolitan Toronto. For several years a bi-monthly bulletin called *Health Education* has been published and distributed free of charge to teachers and public health personnel. In the area of consumer education, the Food and Drug Directorate's Educational Division has produced information on consumer affairs, drugs and cosmetics, and drug abuse.

Research has been conducted into various health questions in order to support the department's educational programs. One of these studies, entitled "Teachers' Habits and Attitudes toward Smoking," was completed by Vera Pezer in 1964 in the University of Saskatchewan. Based on the responses of sixty-four smokers, seventy-seven non-smokers, and twenty-two ex-smokers, it was of interest chiefly because of the light it threw on the attitudes of these groups toward student smokers.

The work of this department illustrates how much more effectively a single national agency can produce a certain type of educational material than could the individual provinces working in isolation. Health information is "neutral" in the sense that it is relatively unrelated to provincial variations in outlook or culture. Thus provincial departments have had no reluctance to co-operate fully in the use and distribution of the material.

THE DEPARTMENT OF INDIAN AFFAIRS AND NORTHERN DEVELOPMENT

The federal government has been responsible for the education of Indians living on reserves. In 1968 there were fifty thousand of these people living on 169 reserves. Their children were being educated at the elementary level in federal, residential, and provincial schools. Most of the federal schools, which had an enrolment of about 7,500 children, were on reserves some distance from urban centres or in isolated northern communities. Provincial schools, attended by about 4,200 children, were proving increasingly attractive to Indian parents. In effect, the federal government bought services in these schools for those who attended. In 1968 there were about 1,200 children enrolled in residential schools as boarders. Only 680 of these, however, attended classes in federal classrooms; the others were enrolled as day pupils in nearby provincial schools.

The federal schools in Ontario were located in three areas. 1 / Those in the southern area were in the vicinity of Sarnia, Wallaceburg, London, Brantford, Cornwall, Belleville, and the Muskoka District. 2 / The central area included isolated communities between Sudbury and Kenora, all accessible from the outside by road. 3 / The northern area included communities beyond the CNR line running from Sudbury to Nakina, Sioux Lookout, and Winnipeg. They were almost all accessible only by plane. The government faced a considerable problem in attracting suitable teachers to these locations.

Federal schools ranged in size from one to twenty-five classrooms, with the majority having between three and eight. The multi-classroom schools offered instruction in grades 1 to 8, but, as a result of the high attrition rate, most of the children tended to be concentrated in the primary grades. The curriculum and textbooks of the Ontario Department of Education were employed. Teachers had to have certificates recognized by the Ontario Department of Education or, if they came from outside the province, departmental Letters of Standing.

Concern about the high rates of failure and withdrawal in the primary and elementary years in federal schools has led the Indian Affairs Branch to undertake research into these questions. Children having difficulties have too often been assumed to have below average potential for learning. The importance of language problems has not always been recognized. The whole question of the relevance of the cultural milieu from which the child has come appears to call for thorough investigation.

A recognition of the special educational needs of Indian children led to the offering of a teacher aide's course and a kindergarten teacher's course at Centennial College in 1969, the former lasting from August 6 to 29 and the latter from August 25 to 29. The participants, all Indians, were selected by band councils or school committees and approved by the Department of Indian Affairs and Northern Development. The department defrayed all costs, including board and lodging. The primary purpose of the teacher aide's course was to produce an understanding of the developing child and to create an awareness of the techniques used in the learning process. The course included practical activities in the Centennial College demonstration nursery school and observation in other schools. The kindergarten teacher's course was intended for teachers already teaching in the far north and for those about to assume positions in that area. It was designed to develop an understanding of the role and value of the teacher's aide.

THE CANADIAN PENITENTIARY SERVICE

According to J.D. Weir, Assistant Director, Inmate Training (Education), the Canadian Penitentiary Service, the educational program in Canadian penitentiaries began in 1851 with the appointment of a teacher at Kingston Penitentiary to offer instruction at the elementary school level to individual inmates in their cells during the evening. For seven decades after Confederation, progress was extremely slow. The punitive and retributive approach was dominant, and there was little understanding of or faith in rehabilitation as a goal of the prison program.

An important milestone was reached in 1936 with the appointment of a royal commission to inquire into the Canadian penal system. The resulting report, which appeared two years later, recommended drastic changes in penal practice, including a reorganization of the educational system. The commission advocated a well-rounded program of adult education to meet the needs, abilities, and interests of the inmates, most of whom were found to be academically under-educated, vocationally unskilled, and culturally deprived. The curriculum was to include academic, cultural, recreational, and physical components. The necessity of recruiting competent and concerned teachers was also stressed. The implementation of many of the recommendations was delayed by the Second World War.

A serious effort was begun in 1946 to improve educational services along the lines suggested by the royal commission's report. Action was further encouraged by additional inquiries and reports. In 1960 the Correctional Planning Committee of the Department of Justice made a thorough study of provincial institutions and of selected correctional systems in other countries. The report indicated in detail how correctional educational services might be improved. Emphasizing the importance of occupational training, it recommended that training programs meet standards leading to provincial and union recognition and certification, and that training provide the skills required in a particular region.

The Canadian Penitentiary Service undertook a ten-year plan of institutional development for the period between 1963 and 1973, with the purpose of making optimum use of existing facilities and of constructing new institutions. Implementation of the early part of the plan involved the opening of several new medium security institutions, a maximum security complex, and a treatment centre for drug addicts. Included were facilities designed for the operation of a new educational program.

The average educational level of inmates arriving at federal penitentiaries in Canada in the late 1960s was grade 6. About 15 per cent were considered to be functional or semi-functional illiterates. Thus a major emphasis had to be placed on elementary education. Efforts were made to devise an adult approach, employing programmed learning, individual instruction, and audio-visual aids. In 1967–8 an estimated 950 inmates out of a total population of 7,000 participated at this level, either as full-time or as part-time students. A further 1,196 were involved at the secondary school level, with an opportunity of proceeding as far as the senior matriculation level. A considerable number of inmates attended classes in the basic academic subjects, English, mathematics, and science in order to be able to take vocational or occupational training. The further education program included socio-cultural activities in drama clubs, choral groups, art classes, current events groups, and great books seminars. Provision began to be made for a few inmates to be released during the day to attend classes in universities and technical schools.

Substantial use was made of correspondence courses offered by provincial departments of education. In 1967–8, 861 of these were completed, ranging from the elementary school level to senior matriculation. Heavy reliance was also placed on university extension courses.

Like provincial departments such as the Ontario Department of Correctional Services, the Canadian Penitentiary Service has found that lack of motivation presents a very serious problem. Many of the inmates have a level of verbal ability that is considerably below that of their performance ability. Frequently education at earlier stages in their lives has been an unproductive and distasteful experience. Progress is usually slow during the first stages of prison life. The authorities usually try initially to concentrate on small primary group relationships with an informal structure, and to use learning to relieve boredom.

THE DEPARTMENT OF FISHERIES AND FORESTRY

A section of what became the Forestry Branch of the Department of

Fisheries and Forestry was formed in 1962 with specific responsibility for information and education. The basic objectives were to increase the public's understanding and appreciation of the values of forest resources and to enhance awareness of public responsibility for optimum use of such resources. To further these objectives, educational aids, brochures, publications, and films relating to the forests and resource conservation were made available to the schools and other agencies.

Examples of publications are *Forest Conservation*, *Forestry Lessons*, *Conservation Activities*, *Forest Enemies*, and *Canada's Forests*. Among those which have been used as references and textbooks are *Native Trees of Canada*, *Forest Flora of Canada*, *Canadian Woods*, and *Forest Regions of Canada*. Information wall charts have been produced entitled 1 / "These Products Come from Canada's Trees," 2 / "Canada's Six Leading Commercial Softwood Trees," and 3 / "Canada's Most Important Hardwoods." These posters have been distributed to schools throughout the country by provincial departments of education. In 1968 alone, over 3,000 Ontario schools requested copies of the second of the three charts.

Films have been produced by the National Film Board for the Forestry Branch as a means of providing information about Canada's forests and about careers in forestry. These have been supplied to the Ontario Department of Education and have been made available for free loan to schools from the Forestry Information Service and other agencies. In 1969, at the instigation of the Forestry Branch, the National Film Board produced a series of educational filmstrips on the forest regions of Canada designed specifically for school use.

Among the films produced to impart information about the forests is one called "Leaves of Green," which describes leaf structure and arrangement, showing the biological and aesthetic importance of leaves. It is designed to produce an enhanced appreciation of nature and to motivate further study among elementary and junior high school audiences. Another called "The Boreal Forest" shows how living things relate to one another in the boreal or northern coniferous forest, and identifies the plant and animal life found there. It is intended for use in general science and biology classes in high schools and colleges, and in museums and organizations concerned with conservation. "The Changing River," aimed at the middle grades of school, deals with the ecology of a river system, emphasizing the biological relationships between plants, birds, mammals, fish, and insects and their environment. A more technical film entitled "The Mechanism of Moisture Movement in Wood" is designed for specialists in wood technology, engineering, architecture, and others who use wood as a material. Using animation and time-lapse photography, it shows the mechanism by which moisture moves through and out of the structure of wood during drying, and demonstrates such effects of drying as shrinkage, collapse, checking, and case-hardening. A film called simply "The Forest" gives a historical account of the forest industry in Canada, showing how wholesale cutting devastated large areas of forest in earlier days, and contrasting these with modern methods and equipment. It is considered suitable for both school and adult audiences.

Certain films are produced as a means of advocating forest fire prevention and of demonstrating methods of dealing with forest fires. One called "Right to Burn" illustrates how easily a fire can occur, and presents modern methods of forest fire fighting, including co-operative efforts of ground and air crews. It is intended for woodlot owners and potential forest rangers. Another entitled "Research on Survival in Bushfires" is primarily for the use of men engaged in firefighting. It shows how scientists test survival tents made of laminated fiberglass and aluminum.

Research activities of the Forestry Branch are conducted in association with the universities. Scientific and technical papers produced as a result of branch activity are supplied to university libraries.

Educational or promotional efforts in the fisheries area are designed 1 / to assist fishermen, fish handlers, and others who depend on the industry for a living, 2 / to encourage the consumption of fish, and 3 / to emphasize the importance of conservation measures. Many of the approaches used are similar to those employed by the Forestry Branch. Training programs of varying duration have been held in a number of locations in the Maritime provinces, Quebec, and British Columbia, covering such matters as engine overhaul and maintenance, navigation, nets, and gear and equipment. This type of activity has not been of great direct concern to Ontario. In the area of consumer education, the former Department of Fisheries has a long history of involvement in displays, demonstrations, and test kitchens. Regional offices have mantained contact with radio and televison stations, educational and consumer groups and institutions, and the fishing industry. Publications on handling, preparing, and cooking fish have been widely distributed. A special effort has been made to provide materials that will be used by home economics teachers in educational institutions.

Among films recently produced by the National Film Board for the promotion of the fishing industry is one entitled "Trawler Fisherman," which depicts life on a stern trawler on the offshore grounds of the North Atlantic. It is intended to indicate the opportunities for young Canadians in commercial fisheries. An older film, directed toward the problems of conservation, is called "The Salmon's Struggle for Survival." It shows how various technological innovations have been developed to assist the salmon to survive in the face of industrial development along the Fraser and other British Columbia rivers.

THE DEPARTMENT OF TRANSPORT

Some of the most important responsibilities of the federal Department of Transport are the management of airports, flying training, aeronautical engineering, aviation planning, research and development, radio communications and aids to navigation, air traffic control, marine regulations, ship inspection, and the Canadian Coast Guard. Most of these require specialists with specialized training, which is provided through departmental courses given at the Air Services Training School in Ottawa or obtained from outside sources such as universities or technical colleges or institutes.

The Air Services Training School was established in 1959 at Ottawa International Airport to consolidate several smaller government courses previously given in various parts of the country. It has classrooms for lectures and workshops where on-the-job conditions are simulated. Most of the students are preparing to begin careers in aviation, although a considerable number of others are Department of Transport employees seeking more advanced knowledge to keep up with new and increasingly complex types of equipment continually coming into use.

As of 1967, three main groups of courses were given at the school: air traffic control, meteorology, and telecommunications and electronics. One of the longest, of twenty weeks' duration, was for air traffic controllers. The students, who had to be high school graduates to qualify for admission, studied air regulations, meteorology, radio aids to air navigation, aircraft performance, air navigation, and air traffic control procedures. They spent about half their training time in classrooms and the rest in practice under simulated conditions. After graduation they were given three months of practical training in a control tower before receiving their air traffic controller's licence. In addition to this preliminary course, the school offered a one-week radio course for qualified air controllers without radar experience and a three-week advanced technical course for supervisors.

A three-month basic weather course was offered to train meteorological technicians to make weather observations required for the preparation of weather forecasts. These technicians were also trained as weather map plotters and as teletype operators. Among the more advanced courses in meteorology was one of sixteen weeks' duration designed to teach technicians how to provide weather information to pilots and others. A more recent course was for empolyees selected to work on research programs in meteorology.

Telecommunications and electronics courses were for three main groups: radio operators, electronic technicians, and radio regulations personnel. In one of these, an eight-month course for radio operators, students learned Department of Transport procedures in air and marine services, and the use of departmental equipment required for both. They received special training to increase their typing and Morse code speeds, and learned the intricacies of teletype circuits and international communications procedures. A considerable proportion of the time was spent in training in making meteorological observations. Courses for radio technicians involved the use of aviation, weather, and marine radar.

Others, varying in length from a week to two months, dealt with other aids to air navigation. Training was offered in the operation and maintenance of automatic error-correcting and channelizing equipment used in keeping departmental communications systems running efficiently. Certain courses dealt with transistor and miniature techniques, marine radio beacon training for lightkeepers, and radio training for Department of Northern Affairs personnel assigned to isolated posts. Training for radio inspectors and operators covered such topics as the enforcement of international regulations, the assignment of frequencies to radio stations, and the detection and remedying of radio interference. Monitoring operators were trained to police the radio spectrum to ensure that all users remained on their assigned frequencies and conducted communications in accordance with international regulations.[3]

An educational contribution of the Meteorological Service has been the provision of materials for study in schools, either as an aspect of general science or as a means of interesting students in meteorology as a subject in its own right. Sets of weather maps have been prepared and distributed, with sufficient explanatory information to make possible their intelligent use. Exercises have also been provided, enabling the student to make simple forecasts.

THE CANADIAN GOVERNMENT TRAVEL BUREAU

The Canadian Government Travel Bureau has had as a primary objective the promotion of travel to Canada. It has maintained travel counselling facilities in Ottawa and travel promotion offices in such countries as France, the Federal Republic of Germany, Japan, Mexico, the Netherlands, the United Kingdom, and the United States. It has had an important informational role both at home and abroad.

Certain kinds of assistance have been provided to schools, students, and teachers. 1 / One of the bureau's publications, called *Summer Courses in Canada*,[4] has listed the different summer courses offered in Canadian universities each year, has indicated the dates on which they begin and end, and has provided other useful information. It has been widely distributed in Canada and the United States, and to some extent in other countries. 2 / Reference sets of materials have been made available on request to schools, teachers, and senior students to assist in geographical studies. There has been a special "Teachers' Package" for this purpose. 3 / Assistance has been given to university students in the form of information and advice to help them write theses on subjects related to the tourist industry. 4 / Groups of students have been encouraged to tour the bureau, with senior personnel making themselves available to answer questions. 5 / Senior officers, including the director of the bureau, have addressed university and other student gatherings on request. 6 / Career advice has been offered through personal interviews to students who show an interest in tourism or related fields.

As a second form of educational involvement, the bureau has co-operated with other tourist organizations in sponsoring, helping to organize, and participating in programs designed to improve the reception and care of visitors to Canada. These programs have taken the form of educating tourist personnel to improve tourist services. An example is "Project Hospitality," a program financed by the Office of Tourism, of which the Canadian Government Travel Bureau is a branch, and operated by the Canadian Tourist Association. The first stage has consisted of a series of community leader conferences in ten or twelve areas in each province. The second stage has been a series of follow-up owner-operator seminars in the same areas within a month or six weeks. In the third stage, the various organizations in these respective areas have been encouraged to hold staff clinics, with the ultimate objective of reaching and involving tourist service staff such as restaurant and hotel employees, gas station attendants, taxicab drivers, store clerks, and others. By 1968 the project had encouraged the formation of over one hundred new clinics for service establishment staffs and a similar number of technical training courses. In 1967 training sessions were begun with the purpose of enabling people to organize their own hospitality training seminars for employees.

The bureau has also had certain programs to further the education of its own employees. 1 / It has paid half the registration fee for those who have enrolled in correspondence training courses offered by the International Union of Official Travel Organizations. 2 / It has arranged for internal and exchange training programs with provincial tourist bureaus. 3 / It has allotted time for employees to take special French-language courses offered in the Public Service of Canada. In addition, training programs have sometimes been offered for employees of other organizations, such as the Canadian Automobile Association. Training courses in tourism have also been arranged for trainees sent from foreign countries under the auspices of the Colombo Plan.

ATOMIC ENERGY OF CANADA LIMITED

The atomic energy program developed in Canada during the Second World War was at first under the direction of the National Research Council. In response to the growth of the Chalk River enterprise and the extension of the commercial aspects of its program, Atomic Energy of Canada Limited was established as a Crown company in 1952. In addition to a major program of nuclear power development, it undertook extensive research into fundamental and applied fields of atomic energy.

Having assembled a strong group of experts, AECL has assumed a major responsibility for the training of scientists, engineers, and technical personnel. Senior undergraduates, graduates, and university faculty members have been engaged for summer projects. The latter have been able to continue research on their return to the university on the basis of techniques or problems with which they have become acquainted during their stay. Experience with the company has provided part of the background of a considerable number of university faculty members. In 1968 it was reported that sixty former AECL staff members occupied university posts, many of them as heads of departments.

Other contributions to education have included encouraging visits and arranging tours for groups, including high school students. Talks and lectures have been given to various organizations as part of a program of general public education in atomic energy. Publications and scientific equipment have been exchanged with other countries.

THE DEPARTMENT OF NATIONAL DEFENCE

The Department of National Defence has been concerned with an extensive training program in connection with the Canadian Armed Services. Some of the relevant activities are dealt with in volume IV in connection with the Royal Military College of Canada. Attempts to secure additional information from the department for the purposes of the present volume did not meet with a positive response. It would appear that such matters, in the view of at least some of the officials concerned, were a military secret.

In 1969–70 there were schools for dependents of members of the armed services operating in the various provinces in the following numbers: British Columbia, three; Alberta, ten; Saskatchewan, five; Manitoba, seven; Ontario, twenty-three; Quebec, twelve; New Brunswick, two; Nova Scotia, six; and Prince Edward Island, one. A number of these were actually administered by the provincial department of education or by local school boards. Most schools covered only some of the grades between kindergarten and grade 13. The enrolment of all schools in Canada combined was 11,873, and the total number of teachers, 570. The program in Ontario was the standard one for Ontario schools.

Schools for the dependents of the armed forces overseas were also in operation at bases in Belgium, Holland, Sardinia, and the Federal Republic of Germany. All schools were under the administration of a director of education with headquarters in Germany. From kindergarten to grade 6, the schools used a composite curriculum designed to minimize the difficulties involved in the movement of pupils from different provinces to the schools and their re-adaptation on their return to Canada. Most schools provided conversational French in the elementary grades. Between grades 7 and 13 the curriculum was that leading to the certificates and diplomas granted by the Ontario Department of Education. Options in commercial courses, industrial arts, and home economics were provided at the secondary level.

Staff for the overseas schools were employed on the basis of a two-year agreement involving the teacher, the Department of National Defence, and the Canadian school board employing the teacher. Thus the latter could continue to maintain superannuation and other benefits. His salary continued to be paid by the board in accordance with existing schedules, and the Department of National Defence reimbursed the board. Single teachers were preferred, in part because of housing difficulties.

There has been a certain amount of controversy about the provision of schools for dependents. While it appears creditable to try to ensure that children's progress through school is interrupted as little as possible because of a sojourn in a foreign country, the segregation of Canadian children in a kind of ghetto is hardly the equivalent of providing them with the kind of educational experience they would gain in a Canadian environment. At the same time, they miss the opportunity to acquire the direct knowledge of a foreign language and culture which is denied to their compatriots at home. Fears that they will have difficulty adapting to foreign schools or of making the transition back again are no doubt in many cases exaggerated. Even if the process involved the loss of a year on the way to advanced education or employment, it may be that the sacrifice, if it can be called that, would be well worth while.

THE DEFENCE RESEARCH BOARD

The Defence Research Board, which was established in 1947, is a civilian service within the Department of National Defence which concentrates on the conduct of research for the Canadian armed forces. As of 1969 military problems of both an immediate and a long-term type were investigated, many of them under conditions of secrecy. Also, through a system of grants, the Board supported unclassified basic research in universities and affiliated institutions with the following objectives: "to acquire new scientific knowledge of interest to defence science, to maintain a link with the academic community of the universities, and to assist in securing the services of competent younger scientists for its own laboratory operations."[5] While the university program was said to be broadly based in the physical and biosciences, emphasis was placed on work that was likely to support the defence research program.

THE DEPARTMENT OF VETERANS AFFAIRS

The programs carried out as a means of implementing the *Veterans Rehabilitation Act* of 1945 were largely completed nearly two decades ago. Their influence on the lives of those who benefited from them and their implications for federal involvement in education have nevertheless been of lasting importance. For this reason, they are given brief treatment in the present context. Much of the information offered is from *Rehabilitation*, by Walter S. Woods, published by the Queen's Printer, Ottawa, in 1953.

The idea behind rehabilitation training was that a discharged person was entitled to assistance to attain the status in civilian life that he probably would have attained had there been no interruption because of military service. The help he received was related to his period of service and the benefits he needed to achieve satisfactory rehabilitation. He was given assistance by counsellors to plan and complete a program that might, but did not necessarily always, involve training or other benefits provided by the act. The general attitude was that rehabilitation was a good investment, both for the veteran and for the country. While it was not considered in the public interest to try to train those of inferior ability for the highly skilled trades or the learned professions, it was regarded as highly desirable to develop leadership and to prepare those with the requisite capacities and personal qualities for responsible posts in various fields.

There were early plans for two sections of the rehabilitation training program under the general headings of vocational training and "interrupted education." The first was to be made available to a veteran who needed help to resume a former occupation or to prepare for a new one better suited to his physical and mental capacities and to his economic needs. It was assumed that such training would be a safeguard against unemployment if an economic depression should occur. Interrupted education included all types of academic and professional education given in an accredited university, as well as pre-university courses for those who lacked university admission requirements or who would benefit by brief refresher courses. The term was somewhat inappropriate in that university opportunities were not restricted to those whose formal education had actually been interrupted, but included also those who had discontinued the process for economic or other reasons. The number who chose university work as a means of rehabilitation was actually twice as great as had been anticipated. This development was of great significance in demonstrating that the pool of talent for the universities was much greater than had been realized.

Measures taken in 1942 turned out to be of value in facilitating post-war rehabilitation. At that time, because of urgent long-range requirements for professionally trained men in the armed services and war industry, physically fit men who were making good progress in their university courses were urged to remain until graduation, and bursaries were provided to enable suitable candidates to enter university in the scientific and technical fields. This meant that the universities were regarded as an integral part of the war effort, and were thus reasonably well prepared to absorb the veterans at the end of the war, most of whom were entering for the first time. Their number, which reached something like 55,000 was also lower than it would have been had the universities completely broken off operations.

One of the effects of training and experience provided in the armed services was that many men and women whom the depression of the 1930s had deprived of a high school education developed the ambition to qualify for university. Many were given assistance by the Canadian Legion Educational Services to catch up while still on active service. At the end of the war the Training Branch of the Department of Labour co-operated with the provincial departments of education to organize pre-matriculation classes. Retired teachers were recruited, and arrangements were made for special examinations. Some veterans were able to qualify for university admission in from six to twelve months, as compared with the two-to-four-year period required by the average adolescent. The result was a considerable increase in the number of university-trained people whose skills were to be so much needed in the post-war period.

The success of the veterans in academic work was a matter of surprise to some and of comment by many. They were generally found to be at least as good as, and often better than, their younger civilian counterparts. Explanations were found in their greater maturity and experience, and in the definiteness of their goals. Many had family responsibilities, and all of them were anxious to earn a living as soon as possible. Many of them valued the opportunity, which they would not otherwise have had, of attending university with DVA benefits. On the whole, their record was of lasting significance for the cause of adult education, since it tended to minimize the handicap to learning of being out of school for several years, and to emphasize the importance of motivating influences in adult life.

The vocational training program was operated by the Canadian Vocational Training Branch of the Department of Labour in co-operation with provincial departments of education. Use was made of all available training facilities and, where these were inadequate, special courses were set up. They were normally operated by the provincial authorities, with the costs met from federal funds. Courses varied in duration from a few months to several years. They included academic courses below university level to provide the qualifications for such occupations as banking and accountancy, trade training in schools and on the job, technical courses, and advanced occupational and professional courses in nursing, art, accountancy, business management, and other areas. In some cases, there were arrangements for subsidizing on-the-job training.

The Department of Veterans Affairs program represented a massive federal involvement in educational affairs to meet an emergency that could not conceivably have been dealt with by the provinces alone. It had the full co-operation of the latter, and little objection was heard over federal interference. In part, this was because assistance was being offered primarily to individuals as such through whatever facilities the provinces could provide. There was no obvious pressure for substantial permanent changes in the educational structures maintained by the provinces, although the program did give a new impetus to the development of technical and trades training.

THE PUBLIC SERVICE COMMISSION OF CANADA

Major efforts in the area of training and staff development in the federal public service are of comparatively recent vintage. As recently as 1962, the Glassco Commission commented unfavourably on the situation.

> Training and development have not, in general, received anything like appropriate attention in the public service. In many departments training needs and possibilities have not been recognized. Where they have been recognized, training specialists of the proper quality have often not been used. There has been, in general, no development of a common policy on training or a common approach to it for the public service as a whole. Such training activity as there is, therefore, tends to be fragmented, uncoordinated, and tied to no very clear conception of objectives and how to achieve them ...
>
> Lack of knowledge of outside developments in training techniques and development techniques is widespread. Training specialists tend to talk in terms of methods and techniques which, while common in industry and the universities years ago, are no longer representative of the best thinking and practice. There is little evidence that training courses or development programs are measured against the real results they produce.

During the subsequent period there was a great increase in training and development activity in an attempt to remedy these deficiencies. The problems of lack of co-ordination and fragmentation were difficult to deal with in an organization that in 1968 had about 200,000 employees in some fifty semi-autonomous departments and agencies scattered across the country.

Responsibility for training and staff development, according to the arrangement that existed in 1969, rested with the Treasury Board and the Public Service Commission. The former was concerned with the development and regulation of policy, and the latter with the operation of central programs and with the provision of advice on departmental programs. More specifically, the Treasury Board was interested in the following matters: 1 / the contribution that training should make toward the achievement of departmental program objectives; 2 / the costs of training programs being operated by departments and standards of reasonable training costs; 3 / the ways in which departments were determining their training needs and evaluating their training programs; 4 / desirable standards for determining the effectiveness of programs; and 5 / the adequacy, in terms of quantity and quality, of training resources available to departments.

The Bureau of Staff Development and Training of the Public Service Commission had four main roles, with an organizational structure to match: consultative, operational, evaluative, and resource.

1 The Consultative Division provided direct services to departments and agencies on their own request. These included assisting them in develop-

ing effective training programs for their staff; helping them with the design, implementation, and evaluation of their training programs; and advising them on training techniques, learning theory, and the use of outside institutional and consultative resources. The division also, on request, provided support and consultation to Treasury Board Staff on departmental, inter-departmental, and service-wide programs.

2 In its operational role, the bureau designed, implemented, and evaluated development programs in the following areas: executive development; administrative trainee development; centrally operated programs in areas where departments lacked economic capacity to offer training programs for particular professional, managerial, or occupational groups, or where central operation of such courses would be more effective; programs operated by universities, private institutions, and other agencies.

3 The evaluative and research function involved developing a clear understanding of training objectives and of the behaviour to be expected from their attainment. More specifically, it was concerned with measuring results against training objectives of centrally operated programs and, on request, of departmental programs; conducting research into and evaluating new developments in adult education and training; adapting techniques, methods, and processes developed elsewhere to the needs of the public service; producing and maintaining an inventory of staff resources to meet the requirements of the public service.

4 The bureau functioned as a resource and information centre for development and training purposes. Its inventory of resources included its own staff, qualified people in other departments, and outsiders qualified in particular fields. It assumed a responsibility for training professional trainers as well as resource personnel for special training assignments.

J.J. Carson, Chairman of the Public Service Commission of Canada, described the Career Assignment Program (CAP) in an address to the Industrial Relations Management Association of British Columbia in March 1968, later published in the *Canadian Personnel and Industrial Relations Journal* under the title "Executive Development: a Necessity, Not a Luxury."[6] This program had been announced a short time before by himself and E.J. Benson in his capacity as President of the Treasury Board. It was designed to deal with a number of problems that made executive development a necessity. The first of these was that the age group from which executives would have to be drawn during the next decade was particularly small, reflecting the low birth rates of the 1930s. The matter was particularly serious because of the large number of new ventures and programs that would have to be undertaken and led to accommodate the increasing work force of young people emerging from the schools and universities. The second problem was that the executive function was becoming more sophisticated, and called for new skills and knowledge. "The home-grown executive who has been plodding along his corporate route and assimilating its conventional wisdom is finding himself at an increasing disadvantage in a society that is rapidly changing its concepts, its yardsticks *and its values*."[7] A third problem was that, just when competent leadership was very much in demand, there were clearly defined and widely circulated anti-leadership sentiments in the modern world. Carson asserted that leadership served the individual human goals that society valued highly, and that these goals would not be attained without it.

The Career Assignment Program involved the early identification of those judged to have executive potential, attendance of the trainees at a unique in-residence management training course, and rotational assignment between departments, occupational specialties, other levels of government, universities, and, if possible, industry. The three-month in-service course was designed to achieve the following objectives:

(1) create an understanding of the aims and objectives of the Canadian Government; its political, sociological and economic setting; form of organization; methods of management; and relationship to current management theory and practice;
(2) increase each participant's ability to analyze, think through and resolve management problems;
(3) provide insight into the characteristics required for effective leadership;
(4) foster values and attitudes essential for identification with and commitment to, the goals of the Public Service.[8]

The course was to be given by senior government executives and by guest lecturers from business, industry, and the universities.

The typical candidate was to be about thirty years of age with five or six years of work experience and the intellectual capacity to do graduate work. Increasing emphasis was to be placed on bilingual skills. He would have to prove that he could operate in either a managerial or an advisory role, and in specialties outside his basic professional training and experience. Having demonstrated his capacity for leadership, he would be given opportunities for rapid promotion. The success of the program would depend on the effective breaking of traditional career patterns that operated along occupational and departmental lines. While acknowledging that such a change would be difficult to bring about, Carson emphasized his belief that it was a dire necessity.

Courses other than the Career Assignment Program listed in the *Calendar of Courses* for 1969–70 included the following: a general management development course, an orientation course in staff relations, an introductory course in staff relations, an introductory generalist course, an introductory course in staff relations and pay, a financial management course, an advanced financial management course, a materiel management course (general level), an advanced materiel management course, a development course for managers and assistant managers of support services, a course in communication for managers, and a records management course.

The programs and courses offered by the bureau have been overwhelmingly popular. In 1968, even though as many as five were being offered each week, only one out of five applicants could be accommodated. There was a tendency to focus efforts on giving model courses that might provide examples for departments interested in offering their own.

THE CANADIAN INTERNATIONAL DEVELOPMENT AGENCY

The nature of external aid

Canadian assistance for educational development in other countries has had two chief implications for education in Ontario: 1 / it has involved the sponsorship of foreign students enrolled in universities and other institutions and 2 / it has provided Ontario educators with opportunities for service abroad. The presence of foreign students has meant that extra facilities have had to be provided and that efforts have had to be made to ensure that the visitors have enjoyed a productive educational experience. A period of teaching or advisory activity in another country has helped to produce a broader and more mature outlook among those who have served.

Canada became involved in international development assistance in 1950 when the Colombo Plan was launched. Initially involving Commonwealth countries, both as donors and as recipients, it was later enlarged to include other countries in the area as well as the United States. For several years after it began, this plan represented Canada's only bilateral aid program, and the countries of the area have continued to receive the major proportion of Canadian assistance. In the years following 1958, however, the aid program was extended to include the Caribbean area, Africa, and Latin America.

In 1951 two advisers and one teacher served on overseas assignments, and fifty-nine foreign students were brought to Canada. By 1966–7 the numbers of advisers and teachers had risen to 342 and 824 respectively, and almost three thousand students received training in Canadian institutions. The shift toward assistance with educational activities, in contrast to other forms of aid, occurred in the 1960s. This change reflected a shift in priorities among the recipient countries themselves, where it was increasingly realized that adequate supplies of trained manpower offered the best hope of creating wealth.

Canada's policy has been to provide educational and technical assistance as a means of establishing, expanding, and improving local facilities so that most of the training required by the recipient countries can ultimately be carried out at home. Maurice Strong, Director-General of what was then the External Aid Office, outlined the nature of the approach in 1968.

Canadian educational assistance, like that of other donors, is responsive in nature. This means that we provide help in response to official requests received from the recipient government. We do however play a role in the formulation of the requests. In close cooperation with other donor countries and international agencies we have attempted to provide assistance to projects in which the most effective use will be made of Canadian resources. In the negotiations of our teacher and university programmes and the related capital assistance, we have indicated that we give priority to those positions and projects where we can best make a contribution commensurate with our experience and capabilities. We now concentrate on filling teacher training positions and senior positions in secondary schools and in supplying educational advisers. It must always be remembered that we cannot effect just a direct transfer of our experience and our institutions to a newly developing country; our efforts must be directed to their need to use new techniques and new technology within the framework of their educational systems and institutions.

Although the educational needs of the developing countries are vast, there are certain limitations on their capacity to absorb overseas personnel, particularly of the highly qualified type. We are therefore careful to relate increases in our supply of teachers and university professors to the availability of local resources required for the support of educational facilities. All of our development programmes are cooperative undertakings with the local authorities because, if the success of the project is to be ensured, local authorities must make their own contribution and must be able, after a period of time, to accept the full responsibility for them.

Among the educational institutions in which teachers and advisers were engaged in 1967–8 was the Dar-es-Salaam Technical College in Tanzania, which also received Canadian equipment. Training in Canada was provided for the Tanzanian counterparts of the Canadian educators. Two Canadian teachers of agriculture and mechanical engineering served at the Hardy Technical Institute at Amparai in Ceylon. A Canadian adviser undertook a survey of technical education in Zambia. A Canadian principal and eight teachers served in the Bonaberi school in Cameroun. A study was conducted on the feasibility of establishing a Canadian educational assistance program for secondary teachers training in Ethiopia. Five teacher training specialists were engaged in the improvement of in-service training in Kenya. A team of advisers undertook to establish a curriculum development unit in the Ghanaian Ministry of Education, while a comparable number of Ghanaians undertook study in Canada.[9]

In the address referred to, Strong spoke of the increasing need for assistance in establishing and expanding university facilities in certain countries. Canada had to be particularly selective in meeting these requests because of her own acute shortage of university instructors. It had nevertheless been possible to undertake a number of team projects. The first of these involved a commitment by the University of British Columbia in 1961 to help the Universities of Malaya and Singapore establish courses in accounting and business administration. Later the University of Toronto had entered into contracts to set up a regional engineering college in India and a department of anaesthesia in the Faculty of Medicine at the University of Lagos, Nigeria. Similar projects had been undertaken by other universities across the country.

An important form of assistance has involved the construction and equipping of school buildings. An example is the Accra Trades Training Centre in Ghana. Canadian educators recommended the facilities to be included, advised on preliminary and working drawings, and suggested the equipment that Canada should supply. They also helped recruit a Canadian staff, one of whose tasks was the training of Ghanian counterparts to take over their functions in due course. Some of the latter were sent to Canada for training. In Malaysia, Canada has equipped fifty-three vocational training centres. Schools have also been constructed in Dominica, Grenada, Antigua, and other Caribbean islands.

Canadian supervisors of aid projects in various countries have conducted on-the-job training programs. Hydroelectric and other large-scale projects have required the development of skilled manpower for their continued operation. Profound effects on the need for education and the ability to finance it have resulted from the exploitation of primary resources, the growth of new industries and markets, increased specialization of effort, and higher standards of living.

The external aid program has provided for training awards for study in Canadian universities or other educational institutions and for observation and study in non-academic settings. The practice has been to make training awards on the basis of a bilateral agreement between the Canadian and nominating governments. Academic education has been sponsored only at the university undergraduate level or higher, and only when the equivalent is not available in the student's own country. In some cases, special programs have been devised to meet particular needs. As examples of these, Strong cited a course in public administration at Carleton University and in community development at the Coady Institute at St Francis Xavier University. Particular emphasis has been placed on types of training that are most likely to produce indigenous instructors.

Training in trade and sub-professional programs of one and two years' duration were first offered in 1963. Students have taken courses in engineering, business administration, agriculture, and health in Canadian institutes of technology. An additional year of teacher training has also been offered to follow technical training.

Organizational structure

The management of the external aid program was entrusted to what was known until the latter part of 1968 as the External Aid Office, and was then renamed the Canadian International Development Agency. It reported to the Secretary of State for External Affairs. Its Planning and Policy Co-ordinating Division were responsible for the operation and administration of bilateral agreements. The Education Division maintained contacts with provincial governments, with the Canadian National Commission for UNESCO, and with Canadian educational and professional organizations. It was responsible for the recruitment and training of individuals for overseas service. The Technical Assistance Division undertook to locate and provide Canadian facilities for academic, technical, and commercial training. It had the task of screening requests for technical assistance from overseas countries.

In 1967 a Voluntary Agencies Division was established to assist voluntary organizations in undertaking and maintaining international development activities. The Canadian government provided $5 million for 1968–9 to be used in supporting projects that were compatible with the policies governing the Canadian aid program. Support was based on the principle of matching the agencies' efforts. A list produced by the External Aid Office in 1967 showed 111 Canadian voluntary groups operating in the field of overseas development, and making an annual contribution of $35 million. The Canadian University Service Overseas (CUSO) alone had about nine hundred volunteers in forty-two countries.

THE NATIONAL FILM BOARD

The National Film Board of Canada was created in 1939 as a successor to the Canadian Government Motion Picture Bureau, founded in 1921. Its purpose has been to produce films and other visual material designed to interpret Canada to Canadians and to people abroad. As constituted in 1969, the board itself consisted of nine members, four of whom were from the federal civil service, including the Government Film Commissioner, who acted as chairman, and five of whom were prominent citizens representing the five major geographical regions of Canada. The board reported to the Secretary of State.

In an article in the *Toronto Daily Star* on October 4, 1969, entitled "A life-or-death drama at the National Film Board," staff writer Marci McDonald appraised the board's record in this way.

> In its 30-year history, the grand old dame of Canadian cultural institutions has been all things to all people. Educator. Social conscience. Newsreel eye. Feature film mogul. Experimental utopia. A Canadian travel poster on wheels.
>
> It was, and still is, our best public relations agent. Its trophies and triumphs dazzle the eye as you enter the Cote de Liesse plant lobby.[10]

During the first decade of its existence, the board's contribution to the production of educational films was a disappointment to many educators. A.S.R. Tweedie estimated that, in 1950, fewer than 10 per cent of the films and filmstrips used in Canadian classrooms were of Canadian origin.[11] The first attempts to induce the board to make a greater effort in this area led the Canadian Education Association to establish a National Advisory Committee on Educational Films, with little immediate result. A more serious effort was made to provide a basis for fruitful co-operation in 1950 when a CEA/NFB Advisory Committee was set up. Originally it included one representative from the Atlantic provinces, one from Quebec and Ontario, one from Manitoba and Saskatchewan, one from Alberta and British Columbia, one from Toronto and Montreal (alternating), one from the CEA, one from the Canadian Home and School and Parent-Teacher Federation, and a chairman. In 1954 a second delegate was added from the Atlantic provinces, and in 1956 arrangements were made for representation from each province.

At first the provincial departments of education met the expenses of those of its members who served on the committee, but the board itself began to assume this responsibility in 1953. After long discussion of the advisability of co-ordination, reciprocal representation was arranged between the CEA/NFB Committee and the Committee on School Broadcasting. The existence of machinery for co-operation resulted in a substantial shift toward the production of educational materials by the board.

In January 1969 Hans Möller, supervising producer of the board, indicated the dimensions of the latter's involvement in education.

More and more of our funds and facilities have in the last ten years been devoted to classroom material oriented at the special requirements of teachers and students in school. Since the provinces, by Canada's constitution, have full and exclusive jurisdiction in education, we as federal servants must work very closely, and tactfully, with provincial governments and the teachers active in classrooms. In fact we work with dozens and dozens of classroom teachers and planners of curricula in all parts of Canada. This is a truly co-operative effort by which the educators do not just give advice here and there, or "rubber-stamp" our products, after they are completed, but they become directly and actively involved with the media, they write scripts, direct photography on location, shoot photographs themselves or prepare artwork, edit visuals, all in accordance with their own particular talents and all in intimate collaboration with us. At the same time, and this is equally important, we get involved in the learning process as much as possible. This intimate work with teachers has brought us closer to the learning situation than most producers of classroom materials. It also gives us unique opportunities to try out material in classrooms, in informal situations, before we release it for general distribution.[12]

The National Film Board held its first Summer Institute for the Study of Film and Television in the summer of 1966. The effects of this institute were seen in various activities subsequently undertaken by the educators who attended. Programs of film screening and criticism were carried out in schools; two hundred teachers in the Montreal area assembled for a day's session on the communication arts; the Policy and Development Council of the Ontario Department of Education held a conference of teachers and administrators to discuss means whereby the department and practising teachers might best assist each other in media study. The program was continued the next two years under the title "Summer Research Institute of Screen Study" under the joint sponsorship of the National Film Board and McGill University. A fourth annual institute was held in Vancouver in 1969.

Other types of educational activity by the Board have included the following examples. 1 / A multi-media kit called "Toronto: City in Transition" was prepared with the help of four or five classroom teachers and a curriculum officer from the Ontario Department of Education. 2 / Films entitled "A Search for Learning" and "Knowing to Learn" have been used in courses for the preparation of teachers. Such filmstrips as "Children Learn from Filmstrips" have also been employed for the same purpose. 3 / Members of the staff of the board have given lectures at teacher training institutions on the production and use of media in the classroom. 4 / A slide series has been prepared on Indian schools for internal distribution in the Department of Indian Affairs and Northern Development. 5 / The board has been involved in a graduate studies program at Sir George Williams University.

The future of the National Film Board was in some doubt in 1969 and 1970. Budgetary restrictions curtailed many of its projects, and forced the dismissal of a considerable number of its employees. Private film makers were taking over an increasing part of its former activities. The provinces were assuming more and more responsibility for information and education. In the *Toronto Daily Star* article previously referred to, a number of possible future roles for the board were suggested. 1 / Although the federal government had not seemed enthusiastic, it might become a training ground along the lines of the National Theatre School. 2 / It might assist with community development by enabling people in depressed areas to define and record their problems on film, in the process coming to grips with them and perhaps finding a solution. 3 / It might become a giant film research laboratory. At the time of writing, the situation was still hazy.

THE CANADA COUNCIL

Origin and purposes

The establishment of the Canada Council for the Encouragement of the Arts, Humanities and Social Sciences was inspired by the work of the Royal Commission on National Development in the Arts, Letters and Science, commonly referred to as the Massey Commission. The commission had declared in its report of 1951 that a great increase in financial assistance to individuals and organizations would be needed if the arts, humanities, and sciences were to flourish in Canada. It emphasized the need to balance support being provided for the natural sciences with corresponding encouragement for the arts and letters. The Canadian Parliament passed the legislation establishing the council in March 1957.

According to the legislation, the council reported annually to Parliament through the Secretary of State. It enjoyed independence of action, however, in establishing its policies, managing its investments, and controlling its expenditures and grants. It had a governing council, consisting of a chairman, a vice-chairman, and up to nineteen other members, as well as a staff headed by a director and an associate director. Members of the council were appointed by the government for three-year terms, except for the chairman and vice-chairman, whose appointments might be for up to five years.

Funds

Two funds of $50 million each were originally placed at the disposal of the council. It has also had responsibility for the management of funds received by gift or bequest. The Endowment Fund was invested in various forms of securities. The policy adopted by the council was to use income from these to finance its programs, while attempting also to achieve moderate capital gains over the long term. The University Capital Grants Fund was invested in short term Government of Canada securities to facilitate its expenditure in large part over a short period of time. By the end of the 1963–4 financial year, over $54 million in principal and interest had been used, leaving a balance of $11,499,000. Among private donations during the early years, two of unusual size were placed in a Special Fund and invested in the same way as the Endowment Fund. The largest contribution, from an anonymous donor, provided income for research fellowships in engineering, medicine, and science. It amounted to a total of over $4 million. The other, of $600,000, was from the Molson Foundation, and provided two annual prizes of $15,000.

Activities supported in 1963–4

In its report for 1963–4 the council indicated that the Endowment Fund had provided it with an operating budget of $3,170,000, which was used to provide support for the arts, humanities, and social sciences, for the Canadian National Commission for UNESCO, and for the management of the Endowment and University Capital Grants Funds. Grants and awards had amounted to $2,585,000, support for the Canadian National Commission for UNESCO to $82,000, and administrative and other expenses to $419,000, leaving a reserve of $82,000 to be carried over to the next year. Scholarships and fellowships accounted for $1,141,000 of the amount spent on awards and grants, of which $55,000 was used for the exchange of scholars. Also, $45,000 went for special projects and grants to individuals, and $1,399,000 for assistance to organizations in the arts, humanities, and social sciences. Among arts organizations were agencies concerned with music, theatre, ballet and opera, the visual arts, and arts publications. A considerably smaller amount went to humanities organizations, including libraries, and to activities in the same field such as conferences, creative writing, and scholarly publications. Social science activities were supported by grants for research, conferences, and publications. While the arts got most of the grants to organizations, the major proportion of the scholarships and fellowships went to the humanities and the social sciences.

Assistance for publication took the form of grants-in-aid to established publishers. Writers were eligible to compete for scholarships. A large part of the program of aid to publication was concentrated on scholarly books and articles as a means of stimulating scholarship and research. Most of the funds thus expended were channeled through the Humanities Research Council and the Social Science Research Council. Grants in the area of literature were designed to encourage creative writing and to make Canadian writers known abroad. Translation grants were made to help overcome language difficulties and to make important works in French and English accessible to both linguistic groups.

The council initiated programs from time to time to meet specific needs or to provide incentives for programs that showed some prospect of ultimately becoming self-sustaining. Travel assistance and matching purchase grants enabled art gallery directors to travel around the country and buy works of contemporary Canadian artists. Canadian universities were given assistance to hire a resident artist for a year or two in the hope that they would continue the practice on a permanent basis. Young musicians were invited, through council initiative, to perform with symphony orchestras or to participate in recitals across the country.

The council performed the function of making awards to Canadians for outstanding achievement in the arts, humanities, or social sciences. The Canada Council Medal, inaugurated in 1961, was designed to recognize such achievement over an extended period. It was accompanied by a cash award of $2,000, except when awarded posthumously. The Molson Prizes were reserved for Canadian citizens between the ages of thirty-five and seventy who had given at least ten years of service, were recognized as outstanding authorities in their field, had authored or created a work, and had made an outstanding contribution in the arts, humanities, or social sciences that would enrich the cultural or intellectual heritage of the nation or make a noteworthy contribution to understanding and amity among French- and English-speaking Canadians. The Canada Council also administered the Governor General's Literary Prizes.

Activities in 1967–8

In 1965 the Canadian government gave the council an unconditional grant of $10 million, and in 1967–8 began making annual grants. For the 1968–9 fiscal year, this grant amounted to $20,580,000, greatly overshadowing the income from the Endowment Fund. The largest private bequest up to that time was one of several million dollars from the estate of Dorothy J. Killam, received in 1967.

The expansion of the council's activities between 1963–4 and 1967–8 is shown by the fact that in the latter year approximately $11,324,000 was spent on aid to the humanities and social sciences and $7,125,000 on aid to the arts. In the first two of these fields, the emphasis was still on fellowships, which claimed $7,513,000, while $3,811,000 was used for grants-in-aid for research, university libraries, meetings of scholars and artists, visiting lecturers, publication of scholarly works, and other forms of assistance. In the arts, $917,000 was spent on bursaries and awards and $6,208,000 on grants.

Basis for making awards

The twelfth annual report of the council, for 1968–9, provided an account of the way in which policies were developed. At the head of the assessment process was the Advisory Arts Panel, consisting of sixteen members who met approximately four times a year for periods of two or three days. Five members changed each year, so that the panel renewed itself effectively each year. Qualifications for membership were described as follows.

> They must be old enough in years to bring a mature judgment to bear, but young enough in spirit to risk their reputation on what is new and uncertain. They must be able to distinguish the valid in what is new from the decorative periphery of the arts. Each member of the Panel must be eminent in his particular field, and sitting together they must represent all the major art forms so that any persons whose concerns are brought before them will be judged by their peers or their betters. And the members must also represent the various regions of the country so that they can bring a sensitivity to particular needs.[13]

In order to deal with the assessment of individuals, the panel was subdivided into small review committees on the basis of each art form. These committees reviewed the decisions made previously by juries of equally distinguished members in order to discover any weaknesses in the system, such as evidence of bias. The juries, consisting of from three to six people, found the task of recommending awards to senior artists relatively manageable, since they could expect to find a fairly substantial record of achievement to evaluate. In the bursary competition, there were much greater difficulties, since the element of uncertainty was larger. The juries sometimes had to travel from one end of the country to another, or even to New York, to evaluate performances in the visual arts or in music. There were special problems with short-term and travel grants, which were designed to meet urgent needs, and thus had to be made promptly and to be available at any time. Since the necessity for prompt action precluded consideration by a jury, reliance had to be placed on consultation with two or three assessors working individually.

The council found that the assessment of institutions devoted to the arts, while occasionally entailing extraordinary difficulty, did not ordinarily present the continuing problems that had to be faced in dealing with individuals. A large store of information was accumulated over the years about all the major organizations receiving subsidies, and once their operating standards had been established, only a normal rate of improvement or, at worst, a slow deterioration, was anticipated. A sudden change in either direction called for a reassessment. The prospects of an entirely new organization could often be judged by the people involved, who were likely to be well known to the council's consultants. Assessment of theatres, ballets, and orchestras was facilitated by attention to the critical comments of the media, by continual correspondence, and by frequent conversations with informed people.

Scholarships and fellowships were being granted in the humanities and social sciences with an eye to meeting the needs of university teaching and research. More and more of the limited resources of the council were being concentrated on the senior levels above the master's degree, where it was felt that they could be most effective. Apart from awards for academic study in the arts, assistance to individuals in that area was channeled through two competitions, one for senior artists with established reputations, and the other for younger people giving evidence of exceptional promise. Awards were based on the candidate's qualifications and on a proposed program of work or study. There was also a limited number of special, non-competitive awards. There were, in addition, a few special post-graduate fellowships in engineering, medicine, and science derived from special funds given to the council for the purpose. A number of scholarships were administered on behalf of the Canadian government under a cultural exchange program with France, Belgium, and Switzerland to enable senior French-speaking students, scholars, researchers, lecturers, and artists from these countries to visit Canada.

Many different facets of the organizations' budgetary operations had to be taken into consideration. The council agreed that artistic directors sometimes launched their organizations on new ventures without adequate consideration of the costs and benefits involved. It was often true, however, that relatively high risks produced the greatest artistic benefits. Thus the virtues of prudent financial management were not to be exaggerated. The council predictably pointed out that, although there had been very considerable increases in the resources provided to arts councils and other government bodies for the subsidy of the arts, funds had not kept pace with the demand.

The process of determining the needs of various organizations called for a close scrutiny of the estimated figures for the year for which a grant was requested, and a comparison of these with the figures in the financial statement of the year just completed. There was a detailed analysis of the proposed program, involving a consideration of the realism of the anticipated box office receipts and of private donations. Other arts councils and government agencies were consulted as part of the process of determining an appropriate level of grants. Comparisons were made among different organizations in a specific art discipline, although a uniform approach was rendered impossible by a variety of factors. Consideration was given to differences in the level of provincial and municipal subsidies and in private grants, and allowances were made accordingly.

Survey of achievements of recipients of awards

The council's annual report for 1968–9 gave the results of a fairly detailed investigation which had been conducted into the achievements and characteristics of the 455 young artists who had held bursaries at some time between 1958 and 1965. They had to their credit a long list of individual successes too numerous to mention in the present context. They had studied and performed in a number of different countries, particularly in Europe, in addition to Canada. The facts revealed about the income they were earning hardly suggest that the arts are a very lucrative occupational field. The council found reason for satisfaction, however, in the discovery that the great majority had continued their careers without interruption after receiving their bursaries.

Activities supported in 1968–9

Between 1965–6 and 1968–9 the council's total arts subsidy increased from $3,441,000 to $8,766,000. In the separate arts fields, the comparable figures for the same two respective years were as follows: music, $865,000 and $2,093,000; opera, $196,000 and $515,000; dance, $455,000 and $1,060,000; theatre, $1,023,000 and $2,060,000; festivals, $249,000 and $545,000; visual arts $436,000 and $1,872,000; and writing, $150,000 and $544,000. Expenditures for consultants rose very modestly from $67,000 to $77,000.

In the area of the social sciences and the humanities, the council's total grants increased from $3,117,000 to $16,601,000. The breakdown for the same years was as follows: doctoral fellowships, $1,181,000 and $9,298,000; post-doctoral fellowships, nothing and $280,000; leave fellowships, $305,000 and $1,262,000; research grants, $412,000 and $2,899,000; Killam grants, nothing and $493,000; publication grants, $138,000 and $303,000; meetings and exchanges, $150,000 and $413,000; research collections, $565,000 and $1,000,000; special awards and grants, $89,000 and $158,000; adjudicators' fees and expenses, $32,000 and $152,000; and aid to foreign students and scholars, $245,000 and $343,000.

The doctoral fellowships program provided aid to Canadians and landed immigrants for study in Ontario or abroad. In 1968–9 the number of potential candidates was estimated at 5,590, approximately 68 per cent of whom were studying in Canada. The 2,183 recipients of fellowships constituted roughly 39 per cent of the eligible population. Although there was a large increase in the amount of assistance, however, the proportion of applicants receiving awards declined in comparision with the previous year.

In 1968–9 leave fellowships were awarded to 170 university staff members and research grants to 817 researchers, almost all of whom were career scholars. On the basis of a new and reduced list of educational institutions, and a more limited count of career scholars, the recipients of research awards constituted 9.4 per cent of the over-all population of career scholars in the humanities and social sciences. In comparision, more than 60 per cent coverage was available in the natural sciences. The average Canada Council grant for work in the humanities and social sciences was $4,200, as compared with $7,700 in the natural sciences. The council naturally suggested that the grants in the former fields were disproportionately low.

During the same year, the cultural exchange program, which had for a number of years involved France, Belgium, and Switzerland, was extended to Italy, the Netherlands, and the Federal Republic of Germany. With respect to the first three countries, there were two aspects to the program: 1 / grants to Canadian universities and cultural organizations to enable them to invite distinguished professors, scholars, or artists to visit Canada, and 2 / a program of fellowships and scholarships for citizens of these countries for graduate studies or research in Canada. The second aspect also applied to the last three countries mentioned above. Of the twenty-two foreign scholars subsidized, sixteen came from France, five from Belgium, and one from Switzerland. There were 190 fellowships awarded – 136 in France, fifteen in Belgium, fifteen in Switzerland, eleven in Germany, five in the Netherlands, and eight in Italy. Twelve outstanding artists were also invited to Canada by the National Theatre School and the Jeunesses Musicales du Canada, including eight from France, one from Belgium, and three from Switzerland. As a result of a cultural agreement between Canada and Italy, the Canadian Cultural Institute was created in Rome. In 1968–9 this institute offered two senior fellowships to enable outstanding Canadian artists to spend a year in Italy with their families.

THE NATIONAL RESEARCH COUNCIL

The National Research Council, a body corporate established in 1916, has engaged in a variety of activities, most of them concerned either directly or indirectly with education. It has awarded grants-in-aid and fellowships for research in universities; supported seminars and conferences for research scientists; co-ordinated research; operated research laboratories; published scientific journals and other materials; maintained a library and documentation centre; and exchanged information with other countries on scientific research.

The council was set up to co-ordinate and promote scientific and industrial research. It was given charge of all matters in these areas that might be assigned to it by the Privy Council Committee on Scientific and Industrial Research, and also advised the latter on scientific and technological developments affecting the expansion of Canadian industries and the utilization of Canadian natural resources. Of the twenty-one members of which it consisted in 1969, eleven were drawn from Canadian university faculties and four from industry.[14]

The encouragement and support of research in Canadian universities has been a responsibility of the council since it was founded. Beginning in 1950, grants and scholarships were administered by an awards committee established for this and related purposes. In 1969 graduate scholarships were available to promising students for research in science and engineering. While most were tenable only at Canadian universities, a few were granted each year for study abroad. A certain number of post-doctoral fellowships were awarded, some tenable in the council's laboratories and some in the laboratories of other agencies and departments of the federal government. The award of graduate dental fellowships was begun in 1950. The 1967 science scholarships were established for graduate studies leading to the doctorate in science and engineering in universities other than those where the holders obtained their first degrees. One of their purposes was to encourage interchanges among cultural and geographical regions of Canada.

Research grants were made to individual members of science faculties on the basis of projects devised by the latter. The funds might be used to purchase special equipment and supplies or to employ assistants. Since many of these assistants were graduate students, the grants were an indirect form of student subsidy. The role of granting agencies in financing university research is dealt with further in volume IV, chapter 8, entitled "University Research."

Since the council's first laboratory building was opened in 1932, laboratory activity has expanded greatly. In 1969 the laboratories were organized in twelve divisions, each with a director, and research was conducted in the following areas: biosciences, pure and applied chemistry, pure and applied physics, mechanical engineering, aeronautics, radio and electrical engineering, building research, and radiation biology. The council maintained the Prairie Regional Laboratory in Saskatoon and the Atlantic Regional Laboratory in Halifax.

The National Research Council has published the annual *NRC Review*, summarizing the work of the laboratories; the *NRC Research News*, which appears five times a year; and an annual report to Parliament, containing a brief description of the council's activities and a financial statement. Eight scientific journals published in 1969 were as follows: *Canadian Journal of Chemistry, Canadian Journal of Physics, Canadian Journal of Biochemistry, Canadian Journal of Botany, Canadian Journal of Zoology, Canadian Journal of Microbiology, Canadian Journal of Physiology and Pharmacology*, and *Canadian Journal of Earth Sciences.*

THE MEDICAL RESEARCH COUNCIL

The Medical Research Council was established in 1960, after which it operated virtually as an autonomous body within the administrative framework of the National Research Council. Its members were selected from faculties of medicine and pharmacy on the basis of their competence and interest in research. Its main concern was the development of medical research and the support of medical researchers in Canadian universities.[15]

In 1969 assistance to researchers in the medical and pharmaceutical sciences working in universities and their affiliated hospitals and institutes was provided in a number of forms. Operating grants were awarded on an annual or term basis to meet normal operating costs; major equipment grants were for the purchase of special equipment costing $5,000 or more; general research grants were placed at the disposal of the deans of the sixteen Canadian medical schools and the eight schools of pharmacy to be used at their discretion for the development of research.

The 1969 program of support for individuals included medical research associateships involving long-term salary support for a small number of independent university researchers. Medical research scholarships covered the salaries, for periods of up to five years, of young investigators who had completed their formal studies and showed promise of becoming independent scientists. Medical research fellowships were designed to facilitate advanced training in research. In 1968 studentships were first awarded to enable highly qualified graduates at the bachelor's level to undertake further study. All Canadian schools of medicine and pharmacy were provided with limited funds for summer undergraduate awards to the value of $1,200 each.

Additional support programs included awards to research groups of two or more senior investigators and negotiated development grants to stimulate local initiative and to assist the medical schools to build up new research programs. Visiting scientists and professors were sponsored to promote international co-operation and the exchange of scientific information. Support was provided for research symposia organized by Canadian medical schools, and some travel grants were made to enable delegates to attend international conferences.

THE NATIONAL LIBRARY OF CANADA

The National Library is a depository for books, government documents, and periodicals published in Canada, and of books relating to Canada published in other countries. It also purchases many books and periodicals published outside Canada in the fields of the humanities and social sciences, including literature, history, economics, religion, philosophy, and art. Some foreign government documents are collected on a selective basis. A collection of Canadian recordings is maintained.

The most important of its contributions to education has been its location service, which has constituted the basis for much interlibrary lending in Canada. This service was made possible by the National Union Catalogue which in 1969 included the holdings of 262 libraries across Canada. The catalogue enabled the National Library to indicate the location of books, serials, and documents in answer to multitudes of requests. Materials were also lent to university libraries.

THE NATIONAL MUSEUMS OF CANADA

As of 1969 the National Museums of Canada were the National Museum of Man, the National Museum of Natural Sciences, the National Museum of Science and Technology, and the National Gallery. The Canadian War Museum operated under the National Museum of Man, and the National Aeronautical Collection was the responsibility of the National Museum of Science and Technology. The museums had three main functions: collection and preservation, research, and education. Emphasis shifted during the late 1960s from the first two to the last of these functions. The education function was accomplished through exhibits, publications, and programs.

In the fiscal year 1968–9 there were five exhibit locations, excluding the National Gallery, which attracted over 1,200,000 visitors. There were 1,560 group visits to the Victoria Memorial Museum Building, which housed the National Museum of Man and the National Museum of Natural Sciences. The groups were conducted on guided tours by specially trained staff.

An adult lecture series, presented during the winter months, consisted in 1968–9 of thirteen programs, four of which were Audubon lectures. In the same year, forty-seven programs were produced for the Saturday morning lecture series. These programs, which had been presented for over half a century, were specially designed for children. During the summer for the past several years there has been a program of Indian Days for children aged eight to twelve. Trained university students have provided the supervision and offered some craft instruction, although the main emphasis has been on acquainting the children with the history and traditions of the Indians.

The National Museums have offered an answering service to deal with inquiries from teachers and pupils across the country. Information has been requested on mammals, fish, birds, Indians, Eskimos, and other topics. Sometimes material has been sent in for identification. Certain publications have been kept on hand for free distribution in response to inquiries.

THE CANADIAN NATIONAL COMMISSION FOR UNESCO

Origin and objectives

The Canadian National Commission for UNESCO is a semi-official body, with many of the characteristics of a voluntary agency. It was established in accordance with Article VII of the UNESCO Constitution.

1 Each Member State shall make such arrangements as suit its particular conditions for the purpose of associating its principal bodies interested in educational, scientific and cultural matters with the work of the Organization, preferably by the formation of a National Commission broadly representative of the Government and such bodies.
2 National Commissions shall act in an advisory capacity to their respective delegations to the General Conference and to their Governments in matters relating to the Organization and shall function as agencies of liaison in all matters of interest to it.

The commission was established through the initiative of the Canada Council in accordance with legal authorization by the Canadian government. The council drew up the constitution, appointed the chairman, the vice-chairman, and the secretariat, and provided the budget. The terms of reference of the commission were given in the constitution:

(a) to service as an agency of liaison between organizations, institutions and individuals in Canada interested in the activities of Unesco, the Unesco Secretariat, and the National Commissions or other co-operating agencies of Member States;
(b) to promote an understanding of the objectives of Unesco on the part of the people of Canada and facilitate Canadian participation in Unesco affairs;
(c) to carry out activities in Canada in support of Unesco objectives and programmes;
(d) to assist The Canada Council in advising the Department of External Affairs on matters relating to Unesco;
(e) to assist The Canada Council in the execution of its external relations programme.

Structure

As of 1969 the membership of the commission was as follows: two persons selected by the Canada Council from among its members to serve as president and vice-president; representatives of about seventy non-governmental organizations interested in education, natural sciences, social sciences, culture, and communications; two representatives of the Canadian Education Association; members-at-large appointed by the Canada Council on the advice of the commission's executive committee because of their knowledge, experience, and ability to make a special contribution to the work of the commission; a representative of the Department of External Affairs; a representative from each of such federal government agencies concerned with aspects of the UNESCO program as might be designated by the executive committee; the Director or Associate Director of the Canada Council; the Secretary-General of the Commission. Management of the commission's affairs was in the hands of an executive committee of a dozen members. The secretariat was provided by the Canada Council as a branch of its own staff.

Activities

The Associated Schools Project was initiated in 1952; the following year, the member states were invited to nominate a few selected secondary schools to participate in a program of education for international understanding. The purpose was to further UNESCO's objectives of fostering respect for justice, the rule of law, human rights, and fundamental freedoms. Fifteen member states responded with the nomination of thirty-three schools willing to participate for a minimum of two years. It was agreed that each school would work on a project from the following list: 1 / the rights of women, 2 / the study of other countries, and 3 / the Universal Declaration of Human Rights. The UNESCO secretariat provided documentation, practical advice, liaison services, and a series of tests for evaluating the effect on students of participation in the project.

As time went on, the number of participants increased, and new features were added. Regional and national seminars were organized to discuss and appraise results, to share results, and to consider future possibilities. Efforts were made to integrate the program into national educational systems by securing approval for curricular adaptations and for recognition of the topics covered in formal examinations.

As a result of several years of urging, the Canadian National Commission appointed an advisory committee under the Chairmanship of A.E. Hobbs, Principal of Oakwood Collegiate Institute in Toronto, a pioneer Canadian participant in the project, with J.H. Stewart as secretary. During 1965–6 Stewart conducted an active promotional campaign among provincial departments of education and in schools across Canada. The number of participating schools representing both language groups rose to twenty-six. Stewart continued to provide service by interviewing interested teachers and officials, preparing newsletters and reports, assembling useful information, making regular visits to the schools, organizing conferences and seminars, and maintaining contacts with headquarters in Paris and with participating schools in other countries.

A progress report published in 1968 indicated the approach that a participating school was expected to take.

> The basis of the project must be experimental classroom teaching in the area of education for international understanding. Of course, this is not to say that other aspects, such as club activities, extra-curricular projects and fund-raising do not have important rôles to play; it is just that, by their very nature, such projects will surely limit the number of students who become involved. Ideally, a UNESCO Associated School, by a total approach to all pupils, by materials used, and by the way in which these materials are handled, will attempt to effect certain attitude changes and to promote a deeper understanding amongst today's youth of the common dignity of man. Above all, it has to seem to students, teachers, education authorities and the community in general that education of this sort is a legitimate function of the school.
>
> History and geography are the two subject areas which immediately come to mind when one thinks of teaching for international understanding; and, indeed, it is these two departments which, in most cases, have played the key rôle in co-ordinating the studies of Canadian UNESCO Associated Schools.

The progress report gave examples of how the teaching of history and geography was adapted to fit the purposes of the program. In one school, ancient history was taught in grade 10 with an emphasis on human rights in the ancient world, and on the difficulties of the ancients in bringing about international understanding. It is to be hoped that modern attitudes and aspirations were not in the process fictitiously attributed to the ancients. At other schools, emphasis in ancient and medieval history was placed on the development of the world's great religions. A Toronto school introduced a unit on prejudice. Others concentrated on the problems of Negroes in America and Indians and Eskimos in Canada. One unit on Indians involved the purchase of fifty or sixty new books for the library, the use of library facilities for displays of Indian artifacts and pictures, and visits to a nearby reservation. Geography tended to be taught with an emphasis on the human aspects. In some cases, a term or even an entire year was spent on the study of a single country.

Although history and geography have been the main vehicles for attaining the objectives of the project, other subjects have played a part. Foreign languages have emphasized the cultural point of view. Letter writing has been encouraged among those from different language groups. Certain schools have given courses in world art, and some have undertaken art exchanges with students in other countries. Different kinds of musical contributions from various countries have often been the subject of study. International themes have been selected for study in English literature. Home economics has dealt with world nutrition, cultural and domestic differences among nations, the rights of women, and varieties of family life and relationships.

Extra-curricular activities have constituted an important part of the project. All participating schools have had UNESCO clubs or committees, in some cases meeting in regular study sessions and in others co-ordinating the work of various groups in the school. There have also been United Nations clubs, current affairs clubs, Red Cross clubs, and others whose activities can be centered around the international theme. Students from many schools have attended conferences in different parts of their own country or abroad. There have been fund-raising drives to support philanthropic causes including literacy programs and famine relief. Twinning programs with schools in other countries involve the exchange of letters, scrapbooks, slides, and tapes.

The Canadian National Commission has recognized a major responsibility for adult education. It has regarded many of its informational activities as falling in this category. The report of the secretary-general in 1969 mentions a number of other concerns in the same area.[16] It was felt that some way should be found to mobilize Canadian resources and skills for effective participation in adult literacy programs supported in various parts of the world by UNESCO and the United Nations Development Program. Not only might a contribution be made, but Canada might also obtain useful experience that could be applied at home. In this area, the commission had not been able to define a role that was realistic in terms of its position and resources.

The commission has undertaken to sponsor or support meetings and conferences. One of these, on educational research, was held on August 26–30, 1968, in co-operation with the Ontario Institute for Studies in Education. Another, which took place in Montreal in September of the same year, dealt with the cultural role of modern mass communications in contemporary society. An attempt was made to analyse the interrelationships between artistic creativity, communications technology, and social change. The Canadian Broadcasting Corporation acted as co-sponsor.

The commission has co-operated with the United Nations Association, the Canada Branch of the International Labour Organization, the Canadian Hunger Foundation, and the National UNICEF Committee to establish a Canadian International Publications Service. This service has offered through regular mailings to school libraries selected publications of the United Nations and specialized agencies. The service has resulted in reduced costs as compared with the separate retail prices of the publications.

An activity which the commission regarded as of great importance during 1968–9 was the preparation of the Canadian chapter for the eighteenth edition of *Study Abroad*, an authoritative international directory of scholarships and fellowships. This directory was the only source of such information except that available from the country in which awards were held.

Among publications distributed in 1968–9 were the *Source Book for Science Teaching, New Trends of Mathematics Teaching, Biology Teaching, Physics Teaching,* and *Chemistry Teaching.* The secretary-general's report indicated an intention of expanding the commission's promotional campaign and of eventually providing publication information to all schools in the country. The direct mailing list of the previous year had included universities and major libraries.[17]

The commission, although not primarily a grant-awarding agency, has had a modest amount of funds available for this purpose. Grant proposals have been assessed in terms of whether or not they have appeared to be the best way of carying out the organization's responsibilities. Some of the specific types of awards available in 1969 were 1 / grants for projects that directly support the commission's program; 2 / grants to provide for Canadian representation at international meetings consistent with UNESCO interests; 3 / grants to organizations to enable their representatives to accept executive office or appointment to important committees in their international affiliates; 4 / grants for the direct support of the UNESCO program. Assistance was also provided for certain projects that fell outside these categories.

Notes

CHAPTER 1

1 Charles E. Phillips, *The Development of Education in Canada* (Toronto: W.J. Gage, 1957), pp. 235–6.

2 Factual material in this section follows the *Report of the Royal Commission on Education in Ontario, 1950*, J.A. Hope, chairman (Toronto: King's Printer, 1950), pp. 183–6.

3 Robin S. Harris, *Quiet Evolution: A Study of the Educational System of Ontario* (Toronto: University of Toronto Press, 1967), pp. 109–10.

4 Ontario, Department of Education, *Report of the Minister, 1947*, p. 4.

5 Ontario Department of Education, Memorandum re Duties, Powers and Responsibilities of the Chief Director and the Deputy Minister of Education, Toronto, 27 November 1944, G.A. Drew.

6 John Scott, "Davis Sees Two Athletic Camps, Wants More," *Globe and Mail*, Toronto, 29 July 1969.

7 *Report of the Royal Commission on Education in Ontario, 1950*, p. 352.

8 Ontario, *Report of the Minister of Education, 1963*, p. xii.

9 *Ibid., 1965*, p. 33.

10 Ontario, Legislative Assembly, *Debates*, 27th leg., 2nd sess., 28 April 1964, p. 2557.

11 William G. Davis to J.N. Allan, 21 May 1963.

12 H.R. Beattie, interview held 9 May 1969.

13 This was, and remains, a confidential document.

14 Information papers provided by the Honourable William G. Davis, Minister of Education, to the Legislative Assembly of Ontario in connection with the Departmental Estimates 1969–70, November 1969, p. 15.

15 *Ibid.*, pp. 15–16.

CHAPTER 2

1 J.M. McCutcheon, *Public Education in Ontario* (Toronto: T.H. Best, 1941), p. 31.

2 Frank MacKinnon, *The Politics of Education: A Study of the Political Administration of the Public Schools* (Toronto: University of Toronto Press, 1960), pp. 18–19.

3 Ontario, Department of Education, *Report of the Minister, 1965*, p. 4.

4 J.F. Kinlin, "Eight Years in Mathematics with the Department of Education," *Ontario*

Mathematics Gazette, IV, 2, March 1966.

5 *Ibid.*, p. 5.

6 Northrop Frye, ed., *Design for Learning*. Reports submitted to the Joint Committee of the Toronto Board of Education and the University of Toronto (Toronto: University of Toronto Press, 1962), p. 84.

7 Ontario Association for Curriculum Development, J.R. McCarthy, "Curriculum Crossroads," report of the Ontario Conference on Education held in Windsor, Ontario, November 1961, p. 90.

8 According to the peculiar terminology developed in Ontario, "Français" is French taught to French-speaking students.

9 Ontario, Legislative Assembly, *Debates*, 27th leg., 2nd sess., 29 April 1964, p. 2595.

10 *Ibid.*, 27th leg., 5th sess., 17 May 1967, p. 3536.

11 Ontario, *Report of the Minister of Education, 1964*, p. 11.

12 *Ibid., 1967*, p. 5.

13 *Centennial Story: The Board of Education for the City of Toronto 1850–1950* (Toronto: Thomas Nelson & Sons, 1950).

14 *Report of the Royal Commission on Education in Ontario, 1950*, J.A. Hope, chairman (Toronto: King's Printer, 1950), p. 331.

15 *Ibid.*, p. 330.

16 Ontario, *Report of the Minister of Education, 1952*, p. 5.

17 Ontario, Department of Education, Memorandum to Inspectors re Duties of Inspectors, No. 2(j) January 1963, G.A. Pearson, Superintendent of Elementary Education.

18 Ontario, Department of Education, Memorandum to the Secondary School Inspectors re Unsatisfactory Certificated Teachers, 15 February 1960, S.D. Rendall, Superintendent of Secondary Education.

19 Ontario, Department of Education, Memorandum to Elementary School Inspectors re Teacher Ratings, 10:1964–65, G.L. Duffin, Superintendent of Elementary Education.

20 James M. Paton, *The Professional Status of Teachers*, Conference Study no. 2., p. 39.

21 W.W. Worth, "Can Administrators Rate Teachers?" *Bulletin*, XLII, 4, 28 September 1962, 283–4, 313–15. Reprinted from the *Canadian Administrator.*

22 Ontario, Legislative Assembly, *Debates*, 28th leg., 1st sess., 5 June 1968, p. 3974.

23 G.P. Wilkinson, "The Old Order Changeth," *Bulletin*, XLVIII, 4, October 1968, 211.

24 Ontario, *Report of the Minister of Education, 1966*, p. 10.

25 Ontario, Legislative Assembly, *Debates*, 27th leg., 5th sess., 17 May 1967, pp. 3539–40.

26 Louise Rachlis, "Northern Success Opens New Doors for Remedial Reading," *New Dimensions in Education*, IV, 1, April 1969, 10–11.

27 Ontario, Legislative Assembly, *Debate*s, 28th leg., 1st sess., 17 May 1967, pp. 3539–40.

28 Ontario, Department of Education, *Educational Television,*

January 1968.

29 19 Eliz. 2, 1970, Bill 43, 3rd sess., 28th leg., Ontario, An Act to Establish The Ontario Educational Communications Authority.

30 Ontario, *Report of the Minister of Education, 1965*, p. 26.

31 *Ibid., 1968*, p. 26.

32 *Ibid., 1965*, pp. 27–8.

33 *Regulation, Municipal Recreation Directors' Certificates,* Ontario Regulation 20/66, pp. 1–2.

34 *Regulation, Arena Managers' Certificates and Arena Programmes,* Ontario Regulation 68/67, as amended by O. Reg. 368/67, pp. 3–4.

35 Ontario, Legislative Assembly, *Debates*, 27th leg., 2nd sess., 28 April 1964, p. 2538.

36 *Ibid.*, 30 April 1964, p. 2681.

37 *Ibid.*, 27th leg., 3rd sess., 1 February 1965, pp. 170–1.

38 Ontario, *Report of the Minister of Education, 1965*, p. 37.

39 Ontario, Legislative Assembly, *Debates*, 28th leg., 2nd sess., 25 February 1969, p. 1548.

40 *Ibid.*, 28th leg., 3rd sess., 24 February 1970, p. 4.

41 Francis R. St John Library Consultants Inc., *A Survey of Libraries in the Province of Ontario 1965* (Toronto: Ontario Library Association through the co-operation of the Ontario Department of Education, 1965).

42 *Ibid.*, p. 11.

43 Ontario, *Report of the Minister of Education, 1951*, p. 18.

44 Ontario, Legislative Assembly, *Debates*, 27th leg., 5th sess., 17 May 1967, pp. 3542–3.

45 Ontario, *Report of the Minister of Education, 1968*, pp. 30–1.

46 Ontario, Department of Education, *School Design Forum.* An Account of a Series of Workshops Sponsored by the Division of School Planning and Building Research, p. 1.

47 Ontario, Legislative Assembly, *Debates*, 27th leg., 3rd sess., 2 June 1965, p. 3575.

48 Ontario, *Report of the Minister of Education, 1965*, p. 35.

49 *Ibid., 1968*, p. 39.

50 *Ibid., 1964.*, p xiii.

51 Ontario, Legislative Assembly, *Debates*, 27th leg., 3rd sess., 3 June 1965, p. 3638.

52 Ontario, *Statutes*, 11–12 Eliz. 2, 1962–3, chap. 19.

53 H.H. Mosey, "The Philosophy and Operation of the Grade 13 Year," *Headmaster*, Spring 1968, p. 3.

54 *Report of the Royal Commission on Education in Ontario, 1950*, p. 183.

55 *Ibid.*, p. 266.

56 *Ibid.*, p. 198.

57 MacKinnon, *Politics of Education*, p. 30.

58 *Ibid.*, p. 56.

59 *Ibid.*, p. 141.

60 Ontario Association for Curriculum Development, "Leadership in Education," report of the Ontario Conference on Education held in Windsor, Ontario, November 1961, p. 66.

61 Paton, *Professional Status of Teachers*, pp 66–7.

62 Robin Harris, *Quiet Evolution: A Study of the Educational System of Ontario* (Toronto:

University of Toronto Press, 1967), p. 133.

63 *Ibid.*, p. 147.

64 Ontario, Provincial Committee on Aims and Objectives of Education in the Schools of Ontario, *Living and Learning* (Toronto: Newton Publishing Company, 1968), p. 154.

65 *Ibid.*, p. 154.

66 *Ibid.*, p. 155.

67 *Ibid.*, p. 155.

68 *Ibid.*, p. 155.

69 *Ibid.*, p. 155.

70 *Ibid.*, p. 157.

71 *Ibid.*, p. 166.

72 Ontario, Legislative Assembly, *Debates*, 28th leg., 1st sess., 4 June 1968, pp. 3903–4.

CHAPTER 3

1 J.G. Althouse, *Structure and Aims of Canadian Education*, lectures delivered under the Quance Lectures in Canadian Education (Toronto: W.J. Gage, 1949), p. 29.

2 E.B. Rideout, "The Financial Support of Education," *Canadian Education and Research Digest*, VIII, 2, June 1968, 93. (Paper presented at the Saskatchewan School Trustees Association invitational conference on "Emerging Trends in Education," Saskatoon, Saskatchewan, 29 February 1968.)

3 *Report of the Royal Commission on Education in Ontario, 1950*, J.A. Hope, chairman (Toronto: King's Printer, 1950), p. 268.

4 Ontario, Provincial Committee on Aims and Objectives of Education in the Schools of Ontario, *Living and Learning* (Toronto: Newton Publishing Company, 1968), p. 153.

5 Ontario, Committee on Taxation, *Report of the Ontario Committee on Taxation*, II: *The Local Revenue System* (Toronto: Queen's Printer, 1967), 508.

6 Ontario Committee on Taxation, *Report*, I: *Approach, Background and Conclusions*, 51.

7 Ontario Committee on Taxation, *Report*, II, 504.

8 *Ibid.*, p. 506.

9 *Ibid.*, p. 505.

10 Frank MacKinnon, *The Politics of Education: A Study of the Political Administration of the Public Schools* (Toronto: University of Toronto Press, 1960), p. 138.

11 *Ibid.*, p. 148.

12 Frank MacKinnon, *Relevance and Responsibility in Education*, lectures delivered under the Quance Lectures in Canadian Education (Toronto: W.J. Gage, 1968), p. 82.

13 H.P. Moffatt, *Educational Finance in Canada*, lectures delivered under the Quance Lectures in Canadian Education (Toronto: W.J. Gage, 1957), pp. 83–4.

14 J. Bascom St John, "How Many Seats on School Board?" *Globe and Mail*, Toronto, 28 January 1964.

15 "Case Made for Dual Control," *School Progress*, XXXVII, 6, June 1968, 11. (The numbering of points here does not correspond to that in the

original article.)

16 H.L. Willis, "Reorganizing for Effective Administration," *School Progress*, XXXVII, 10, October 1968, 44–5, 85.

17 G.E. Flower, "The Best of Two Worlds," *Toronto Education Quarterly*, III, 3, spring 1964, 8–9. Published by the Toronto Board of Education.

18 "Planning for Larger Units," *School Progress*, XXXVII, 12, December 1968, 42.

19 H.L. Willis, "Is the Canadian Superintendent a Leader or Paper-Shuffler?" *School Administration*, January 1968, p. 17.

CHAPTER 4

1 C.B. Sissons, *Church & State in Canadian Education* (Toronto: Ryerson Press, 1959), pp. 6–7.

2 *Report of the Royal Commission on Education in Ontario, 1950*, J.A. Hope, chairman (Toronto: King's Printer, 1950), pp. 204–5.

3 Sissons, *Church & State in Canadian Education*, p. 4.

4 Ontario, Committee on Taxation, *Report of the Ontario Committee on Taxation*, III: *The Local Revenue System* (Toronto: Queen's Printer, 1967), p. 31.

5 Charles E. Phillips, *The Development of Education in Canada* (Toronto: W.J. Gage, 1957), p. 175.

6 *Report of the Royal Commission on Education in Ontario, 1950*, pp. 206–7.

7 *Ibid.*, pp. 207–8.

8 J.M. McCutcheon, *Public Education in Ontario* (Toronto: T.H. Best, 1941), p. 112.

9 Phillips, *Development of Education in Canada*, p. 199.

10 *Ibid.*, p. 268.

11 McCutcheon, *Public Education in Ontario*, pp 44–5.

12 David M. Cameron, "The Politics of Education in Ontario, with Special Reference to the Financial Structure" (PhD thesis, University of Toronto, 1969), p. 42.

13 McCutcheon, *Public Education in Ontario*, p. 45.

14 *Ibid.*, pp. 46–7.

15 Cameron, "Politics of Education in Ontario," pp. 40–1.

16 *Ibid.*, p. 44.

17 Ontario, *Statutes*, 12–13 Eliz. 2, 1964, chap. 106, sec. 3 (1a).

18 Cameron, "Politics of Education in Ontario," pp. 47–8.

19 McCutcheon, *Public Education in Ontario*, pp. 45–6.

20 *Ibid.*, p. 46.

21 Cameron, "Politics of Education in Ontario," p. 48.

22 *Ibid.*, p. 49.

23 *Ibid.*, p. 398.

24 Ontario, Legislative Assembly, *Debates*, 27th leg., 2nd sess., 27 February 1964, p. 489.

25 Ontario, *Statutes*, 12–13 Eliz. 2, 1964, chap. 95, sec. 6(1).

26 Cameron, "Politics of Education in Ontario," pp. 403–4.

27 Ontario, Legislative Assembly, *Debates*, 27th leg., 3rd sess., 26 January 1965, p. 48.

28 Ontario, Department of Education, Memorandum to Public School Consultative Committees re Larger Units of Administration, 28 December

1964, William G. Davis, Minister of Education, p. 1.
29 *Ibid.*
30 *Ibid.*, p. 2.
31 Cameron, "Politics of Education in Ontario," p. 415.
32 Ontario, Legislative Assembly, *Debates*, 27th leg., 5th sess., 17 May 1967, p. 3541.

CHAPTER 5

1 Ontario, Committee on Taxation, *Report of the Ontario Committee on Taxation*, II: *The Local Revenue System* (Toronto: Queen's Printer, 1967), 528.
2 David M. Cameron, "The Politics of Education in Ontario, with Special Reference to the Financial Structure" (PhD thesis, University of Toronto, 1969), pp. 462–3.
3 John P. Robarts, address given at the dedication of an addition to Southwood Secondary School, Galt, Ont., 14 November 1967.
4 Ontario, Legislative Assembly, *Debates*, 28th leg., 1st sess., 15 March 1968, p. 833.
5 Ontario, Department of Education, *The Reorganization of School Jurisdictions in the Province of Ontario: A Guide for Southern Ontario*, January 1968.
6 Cameron, "Politics of Education in Ontario," p. 464.
7 Ontario, Legislative Assembly, *Debates*, 28th leg., 1st sess., 15 March 1968, pp. 833–7.
8 Some of the smaller northern units would have only ten trustees.
9 H.A. Wilson, President, Ontario Teachers' Federation, to members of the Ontario Teachers' Federation, 7 December 1967.
10 Ontario, Legislative Assembly, *Debates*, 28th leg., 1st sess., 2 April 1968, p. 1518.
11 *Ibid.*, 3 April 1968, p. 1595.
12 Margaret Gayfer, "Amalgamation Is Coming! Amalgamation Is Coming! Get the PR Guys Ready!" *School Progress*, XXXVII, 3, March 1968, 35.
13 Ontario Urban and Rural School Trustees' Association Incorporated, Press Release to Canadian Press, 5 December, 1967.
14 Ontario, Legislative Assembly, *Debates*, 28th leg., 1st sess., 3 April 1968, p. 1595.
15 *Ibid.*, pp. 1593–4.
16 *Ibid.*, 12 March 1968, p. 674.
17 *Ibid.*, 27th leg., 5th sess., 9 March 1967, p. 1212.
18 *Ibid.*, 28th leg., 1st sess., 2 April 1968, p. 1511.
19 Robert Webb, "Ontario's Bill 44 Is Now Law – What Are the Interim Pains?" *School Administration*, June 1968, p. 17.
20 Ontario, Legislative Assembly, *Debates*, 28th leg., 1st sess., 10 July 1968, p. 5429.
21 *Ibid.*, p. 5432.
22 Ontario, Department of Education, *The Reorganization of School Jurisdictions in the Province of Ontario: A Guide for Southern Ontario*, January 1968, pp. 17–19.
23 Public School Board of the Township School Area of Westminster, "Brief to the Honourable William G. Davis, Minister of Education, re resolution passed by the Public School

Board of the Township School Area of Westminster, 6 December 1967," London, 28 February 1968.

24 Reeve of the Corporation of the Township of Ameliasburgh to the Honourable William G. Davis, Minister of Education, 14 March 1968.

25 Some citizens of Kingston, "Brief on the Re-organization of School Jurisdictions in the Province of Ontario," Kingston, 15 March 1968.

26 N. Kaneb, Mayor of the City of Cornwall, to the Honourable William G. Davis, Minister of Education, 25 March 1968.

27 E.H. Maskell, chairman, J.H. Yeo, secretary-treasurer, and members, Peace Bridge District Board of Education, Fort Erie, to the Honourable William G. Davis, Minister of Education, 12 March 1968.

28 "Submission to the Ontario Department of Education from a Committee of Interested Persons Residing in the Vicinity of the Town of Tillsonburg, Concerning the Proposed County Boards of Education," Tillsonburg, 6 December 1967.

29 The Public School Board, Kirkland Lake District School Area, to the Honourable John P. Robarts, Prime Minister of Ontario, 18 April 1968.

30 Ontario, Legislative Assembly, *Debates*, 28th leg., 1st sess., 16 July 1968, pp. 5505–7.

31 Boards of Education for the Towns of Bracebridge, Gravenhurst, and Huntsville, "Brief to the Honourable William G. Davis, Minister of Education," 1 March 1968.

32 E. A. Outram, City Clerk, Peterborough, "Brief Recommending Re-consideration of the Ratio of City and County Representation on the New School Board Under Bill 44," 1 May 1968.

33 Council of the Township of O'Connor, "To Whom It May Concern," 2 April 1968, citing a resolution passed by the Oliver Municipal Council, 13 March 1968.

34 "Only 12% of Metro-area Voters Elect School Super-boards," *Toronto Daily Star*, 3 December 1968.

35 Ontario, Legislative Assembly, *Debates*, 28th leg., 2nd sess., 13 February 1969, pp. 1244–5.

36 *Ibid.*, 24 April 1969, p. 3505.

37 *Ibid.*, 5 December 1969, p. 9404.

38 *Ibid.*, p. 9405.

39 *Ibid.*

CHAPTER 6

1 J.M. McCutcheon, *Public Education in Ontario* (Toronto: T.H. Best, 1941), pp. 68–9.

2 E.C. Guillet, *In the Cause of Education* (Toronto: University of Toronto Press, 1960), p. 72.

3 D.M. Cameron, "The Politics of Education in Ontario, with Special Reference to the Financial Structure" (PhD thesis, University of Toronto, 1969), p. 29.

4 C.B. Sissons, *Church & State in Canadian Education* (Toronto: Ryerson Press, 1959), pp. 21, 24–5.

5 *Ibid.*, p. 33.
6 Cameron, "Politics of Education in Ontario," pp. 55–6.
7 *Ibid.*, pp. 32–6.
8 *A Consolidation of the British North America Acts 1867 to 1965*, consolidated as of 1 January 1967 (Ottawa: Queen's Printer, 1967), pp. 28–9.
9 Ontario, *Revised Statutes*, 1960, vol. 4, chap. 368, sec. 54(5).
10 McCutcheon, *Public Education in Ontario*, p. 73.
11 Sissons, *Church & State in Canadian Education*, pp. 97–100.
12 *Report of the Royal Commission on Education in Ontario, 1950*, J.A. Hope, chairman (Toronto: King's Printer, 1950), p. 502.
13 *Ibid.*, pp. 502–3.
14 *Ibid.*, p. 519.
15 *Ibid.*, E.F. Henderson, Arthur Kelly, J.M. Pigott, Henri Saint-Jacques, Minority Report, p. 790.
16 Sissons, *Church & State in Canadian Education*, p. 105.
17 Cameron, "Politics of Education in Ontario," p. 133.
18 *Ibid.*, p. 134.
19 J. Bascom St John, "The World of Learning," *Globe and Mail*, Toronto, 25 February 1963.
20 Ontario Separate School Trustees' Association and l'Association des commissions des écoles bilingues d'Ontario, Brief to the Prime Minister and the Minister of Education of the Province of Ontario, October 1966, p. 6.
21 The origin of this quotation is being withheld to avoid possible embarrassment to the group responsible.
22 Provincial Grand Orange Lodge of Ontario West and the Provincial Grand Orange Lodge of Ontario East, Brief to the Honourable John P. Robarts, Premier of Ontario, and Members of the Cabinet, April 1968.
23 J.B. Conant, "Free School for All," in *The Teacher and the Taught*, ed. Ronald Gross (New York: Dell Publishing, 1963), p. 242.
24 Shirley Giblon, "A Plea for Aid to Jewish Schools," *Globe and Mail*, Toronto, 17 March 1970.
25 Ontario, New Democratic Party, Caucus Committee, *The Financial Crisis in the Catholic High Schools: A Basis for Discussion*, Walter Pitman, chairman (Toronto, 1969), p. 2.
26 *Ibid.*, p. 5.
27 *Ibid.*, p. 7.
28 *Ibid.*, p. 8.
29 *Ibid.*, p. 9.
30 *Ibid.*
31 *Ibid.*, p. 10.
32 L'Association des commissions des écoles bilingues d'Ontario, Statement to the Minister of Education of Ontario and to the Deputy Minister of Education of Ontario, 9 May 1968.

CHAPTER 7

1 The writer wishes to acknowledge an unusual degree of indebtedness for the information in the presentation that follows to Mr W.J. McCordic, Executive Secretary and later Director

of Education for the Metropolitan School Board during the entire period of its existence. Specific references are made from time to time to some of his more personal views and ideas, but these by no means do full justice to his contribution to the section.

2 J. Bascom St John, "Local Education Authorities," *Globe and Mail*, Toronto, 18 September 1962.

3 Much of the material in this sub-section is found in *Historical and Statistical Submission Regarding Public Education in Metropolitan Toronto*, a survey covering the period 1953–63, requested by H. Carl Goldenberg, commissioner, Royal Commission on Metropolitan Toronto, and prepared by the Staff of the Metropolitan School Board at the direction of a Special Committee of the Metropolitan School Board.

4 *Ibid.*, p. 25

5 *Ibid.*, pp. 26–7.

6 *Ibid.*, p. 35.

7 J. Bascom St John, "Local Education Authorities – Toronto Board," *Globe and Mail*, Toronto, 18 September 1962.

8 Ontario, Legislative Assembly, *Debates*, 26th leg., 1st sess., 4 February 1960, p. 151.

9 Reprinted as "An Experiment in Metropolitan Government," *Canadian Education*, XIV, 2, March 1959, 3–15.

10 Ontario, *Report of the Royal Commission on Metropolitan Toronto*, H. Carl Goldenberg, commissioner, (Toronto: Queen's Printer, June 1965), pp. 121–2.

11 *Ibid.*, p. 123.

12 *Ibid.*, pp. 123–4.

13 Ontario, Legislative Assembly, *Debates*, 26th leg., 1st sess., 2 February 1960, p. 152.

14 *Ibid.*, 27th leg., 2nd sess., 27 January 1964, p. 418.

15 J. Sydney Midanik, Chairman, Metro Toronto School Board, inaugural address, 1962.

16 W. J. McCordic, "Metro's Dilemma in Public Education," lecture delivered before School of Graduate Studies, Ontario College of Education, July 1964.

17 *Report of the Royal Commission on Metropolitan Toronto*, p. xi.

18 McCordic, "Metro's Dilemma in Public Education."

19 *Historical and Statistical Review of Public Education in Metropolitan Toronto*, 1953–63, pp. 89–92.

20 Village of Forest Hill, Board of Education, "Brief to the Goldenberg Commission," p. 3.

21 *Ibid.*, p. 17.

22 *Ibid.*, p. 20.

23 *Ibid.*, p. 25.

24 *Ibid.*, p. 32.

25 *Report of the Royal Commission on Metropolitan Toronto*, p. 145.

26 *Ibid.*, p. 146.

27 *Ibid.*, p. 152.

28 Ontario, Legislative Assembly, *Debates*, 27th leg., 4th sess., 22 April 1966, p. 2577.

29 *Ibid.*, p. 2582.

30 W.J. McCordic, "The New Challenge for Metro," address

delivered at a meeting of the Ontario College of Education Chapter of Phi Delta Kappa, 28 January 1966.

31 "Criticism Is Symptom of General Dissatisfaction with Bill 81," *School Progress*, XXXV, 6, June 1966, 8.

32 James Nuttall, "Metro Toronto Bill 81 Draws Business Officials' Ire over Role of Secretary-Treasurer," *School Progress*, XXXV, 6, June 1966, 10.

33 Barry G. Lowes, Chairman, Metropolitan Toronto School Board, inaugural address, 10 January 1967.

34 "The Case against Amalgamating the School Boards," *Globe and Mail*, Toronto, 30 August 1969.

35 "W.J. McCordic, "Urban Education: An Experiment in Two-Tiered Administration," in *Politics in Government of Urban Canada: Selected Readings*, L.D. Feldman and M.D. Goldrich, eds. (Toronto: Methuen, 1969).

CHAPTER 8

1 J.M. McCutcheon, *Public Education in Ontario* (Toronto: T. H. Best, 1941), p. 52.

2 Charles E. Phillips, *The Development of Education in Canada* (Toronto: W.J. Gage, 1957), p. 291.

3 McCutcheon, *Public Education in Ontario*, p. 56.

4 *Ibid.*, p. 60.

5 David M. Cameron, "The Politics of Education in Ontario, with Special Reference to the Financial Structure," (PH D thesis, University of Toronto, 1969), p. 66. The writer wishes to acknowledge a general and very profound debt to Dr Cameron, whose entire volume has been extremely helpful.

6 *Ibid.*, p. 88.

7 *Ibid.*, pp. 80–1.

8 *Ibid.*, p. 92.

9 Ontario, Committee on Taxation, *Report of the Ontario Committee on Taxation*, II: *The Local Revenue System* (Toronto: Queen's Printer, 1967), 384.

10 McCutcheon, *Public Education in Ontario*, p. 64.

11 Ontario Committee on Taxation, *Report*, II, 384.

12 *Ibid.*, I, 48.

13 *Ibid.*, p. 49.

14 E.B. Rideout, "Memorandum on the County as an Intermediate Unit for School Finance," Department of Educational Research, Ontario College of Education, University of Toronto, July 1962. Mimeographed.

15 Ontario, Legislative Assembly, *Debates*, 25th leg., 5th sess., 3 February 1959, p. 112.

16 According to Frost's statement to the writer, 17 January 1969.

17 Ontario, Legislative Assembly, *Debates*, 27th leg., 5th sess., 9 March 1967, p. 1232.

18 *Regulations, General Legislative Grants: Public and Separate Schools*, Ontario Regulation 64/49, May 1949, pp. 4–5.

19 *Ibid.*, p. 3.

20 *Ibid.*, p. 5.

21 Ontario Committee on Taxation, *Report*, II, 385.

22 *Regulations, General Legislative Grants: Public and Separate Schools, High Schools, Continuation Schools and Vocational Schools*, Ontario Regulation 134/50, July 1950, pp. 2–3.
23 *Ibid.*, Ontario Regulation 159/51, August 1951, p. 3.
24 Ontario, Legislative Assembly, *Debates*, 24th leg., 4th sess., 23 March 1954, p. 738.
25 *Ibid.*, 24th leg., 5th sess., 16 March 1955, p. 833.
26 *Ibid.*, 25th leg., 1st sess., 14 March 1956, p. 1025.
27 *Regulations, General Legislative Grants: Public and Separate Schools, High Schools, Continuation Schools, and Vocational Schools*, Ontario Regulation 262/52, August 1952, p. 9.
28 *Ibid.*, Ontario Regulation 30/53, March 1953, p. 6.
29 Cameron, "Politics of Education in Ontario," p. 100.
30 Ontario, Legislative Assembly, *Debates*, 25th leg., 4th sess., 11 February 1958, p. 85.
31 *Ibid.*, 26 February 1958, p. 395.
32 Cameron, "Politics of Education in Ontario," pp. 94–5.
33 *Regulations, General Legislative Grants: Public and Separate Schools, High Schools, Continuation Schools, and Vocational Schools*, Ontario Regulation 49/58, 1954, p. 4.
34 Ontario, Legislative Assembly, *Debates*, 25th leg., 4th sess., 12 March 1958, p. 760.
35 *Ibid.*, 26th leg., 1st sess., 28 March 1960, p. 1832.
36 Cameron, "Politics of Education in Ontario," pp. 191–8.
37 See further discussion in volume 5, chapter 12.
38 Cameron, "Politics of Education in Ontario," pp. 100–1.
39 Ontario Department of Education, "Memorandum to Principals of Secondary Schools and Secretaries of Secondary School Boards re Financial Assistance to School Boards for the Construction of Vocational Accommodation, 1960–61: 51," Toronto, 27 March 1961, John P. Robarts, Minister of Education.
40 Ontario Committee on Taxation, *Report*, II, 387.
41 New Democratic Party of Ontario, Report of the Committee on Financing Education in Ontario, 1961. Mimeographed. Acknowledgments to Cameron, "Politics of Education in Ontario," p. 213.
42 Cameron, "Politics of Education in Ontario," pp. 198–201.
43 M.A. Cameron, "The Financing of Education in Ontario," (D PAED thesis, University of Toronto, 1936), p. 167.
44 Cameron, "Politics of Education in Ontario," pp. 202–3.
45 *Ibid.*, p. 203.
46 *Report of the Royal Commission on Education in Ontario, 1950*, J.A. Hope, chairman (Toronto: King's Printer, 1950), p. 724.
47 Ontario, Legislative Assembly, *Debates*, 26th leg., 4th sess., 21 February 1963, p. 914.
48 E. Brock Rideout, "The Financial Support of Education," *Canadian Education and Re-*

search Digest, VIII (2), June 1968, 92–3. (Paper presented at the Saskatchewan School Trustees Association invitational conference on "Emerging Trends in Education," Saskatoon, Saskatchewan, 29 February 1968.)

49 *Regulations, General Legislative Grants: Public and Separate Schools, High Schools, Continuation Schools and Vocational Schools*, Ontario Regulation 16/64, pp. 5–7.

50 Ontario, Legislative Assembly, *Debates*, 27th leg., 2nd sess., 27 January 1964, pp. 217–20.

51 Cameron, "Politics of Education in Ontario," pp. 221–3.

52 Ontario Regulation 16/64, p. 8.

53 Cameron, "Politics of Education in Ontario," p. 207.

54 *Ibid.*, pp. 208–9.

55 Ontario Committee on Taxation, *Report*, II, 389.

56 Ontario, Legislative Assembly, *Debates*, 27th leg., 2nd sess., 29 April 1964, p. 2579.

57 Cameron, "Politics of Education in Ontario," pp. 230–6.

58 Ontario Regulation 16/64, p. 8.

59 *Ibid.*

60 Cameron, "Politics of Education in Ontario," p. 269.

61 *Ibid.*, pp. 281–6.

62 *Ibid.*, pp. 287–8.

63 Ontario Regulation 351/66, cited in Cameron, "Politics of Education in Ontario," p. 288.

64 Ontario Regulation 24/67, General Legislative Grants, *Elementary and Secondary Schools*, January 1967, p. 14.

65 *Ibid.*, p. 15.

66 Cameron, "Politics of Education in Ontario," p. 290.

67 Ontario, Department of Education, *Report of the Minister, 1967*, p. 10.

68 *Ibid.*

69 Cameron, "Politics of Education in Ontario," pp. 294–306.

70 Ontario Regulation 43/68, p. 10.

71 Cameron, "Politics of Education in Ontario," pp. 313–14.

72 "Taxes and Grants Explained," *New Dimensions in Education*, IV, 3, June 1969, 8.

73 *Regulations, General Legislative Grants: Elementary and Secondary School Boards*, Ontario Regulation 58/70, 5 February 1970, pp. 5–6.

74 Ontario Committee on Taxation, *Report*, II, 147.

75 Cameron, "Politics of Education in Ontario," pp. 370–2.

76 Ontario Committee on Taxation, *Report*, I, 75.

77 *Ibid.*, p. 184.

78 Cameron, "Politics of Education in Ontario," p. 352.

79 *Ibid.*, pp. 343–4.

80 *Ibid.*, p. 353.

81 *Ibid.*, p. 369.

82 Ontario, Legislative Assembly, *Debates*, 27th leg., 4th sess., 23 March 1966, p. 1821.

83 Cameron, "Politics of Education in Ontario," pp. 375–6.

84 *Ibid.*, pp. 379–80.

85 *Ibid.*, p. 384.

86 *Ibid.*, p. 392.

87 Ontario, Legislative Assembly, *Debates*, 27th leg., 5th sess., 20 February 1967, p. 666.

88 *Ibid.*, 5 May 1967, p. 3086.

89 Information offered in this and subsequent paragraphs is largely

derived from an article entitled "Here's Some Guidelines for Your Better Understanding of New School Building Grants," in *School Progress*, XXXVII, 2, February 1968, 44–7, by R.E. Mitchell, who himself is said to have designed the plan.

90 Ontario Department of Education, "Memorandum to Directors and Superintendents, School Inspectors, Secretaries of School Boards re Approval of School Buildings and Additions for Grant Purposes, 1966:67:65," 1 February 1967, J.R. McCarthy, Deputy Minister of Education.

91 Ontario, Legislative Assembly, *Debates*, 27th leg., 5th sess., 5 May 1967, p. 3087.

92 *Ibid.*, 9 March 1967, p. 1214.

93 *Ibid.*, 29 May 1967, p. 3949.

94 Ontario Committee on Taxation, *Report*, II, 392–9.

95 *Taxation in Ontario: A Program for Reform*, The Report of the Select Committee of the Legislature on the Report of the Ontario Committee on Taxation, John H. White, chairman (Toronto, 16 September 1968), p. 115.

96 Ontario Committee on Taxation, *Report*, II, 394.

97 *Ibid.*, p. 396.

98 Cameron, "Politics of Education in Ontario," p. 278.

99 *Taxation in Ontario: A Program for Reform*, p. 116.

100 *Ibid.*

101 Cameron, "Politics of Education in Ontario," p. 280.

102 *Taxation in Ontario: A Program for Reform*, p. 117.

103 *Ibid.*, p. 118.

104 Ontario Committee on Taxation, *Report*, I, 278.

105 *Taxation in Ontario: A Program for Reform*, p. 12.

106 *Ibid.*, pp. 16–17.

107 Ontario, Department of Treasury and Economics, Taxation and Fiscal Policy Branch, *1969 Ontario Budget*, presented by the Honourable Charles MacNaughton, Treasurer of Ontario and Minister of Economics (Toronto, 4 March 1969), pp. 61–2.

CHAPTER 9

1 *Taxation in Ontario: A Program for Reform*, The Report of the Select Committee of the Legislature on the Report of the Ontario Committee on Taxation, John H. White, chairman (Toronto, 16 September 1968).

2 Ontario Committee on Taxation, *Report of the Ontario Committee on Taxation.* I: *Approach, Background and Conclusions* (Toronto: Queen's Printer, 1967), 12–13.

3 Ontario Committee on Taxation, *Report*, III: *The Provincial Revenue System*, 25–6.

4 *Taxation in Ontario: A Program for Reform*, p. 170.

5 Ontario Committee on Taxation, *Report*, III, 80.

6 *Taxation in Ontario: A Program for Reform*, p. 171.

7 *Ibid.*, p. 178.

8 *Ibid.*, pp. 10–11.

9 Ontario Committee on Taxation, *Report*, III, 147.

10 *Ibid.*, p. 132.

11 *Taxation in Ontario: A Program for Reform*, pp. 184–5.
12 Ontario Committee on Taxation, *Report*, III, 212–13.
13 *Report of the Royal Commission on Taxation*, V: *Sales Taxes and General Tax Administration* (Ottawa: Queen's Printer, 1966), 78.
14 Ontario Committee on Taxation, *Report*, III, 246.
15 *Report of the Royal Commission on Taxation*, V, 6.
16 Ontario Committee on Taxation, *Report*, I, 61.
17 *Ibid.*
18 Ontario, Legislative Assembly, *Debates*, 28th leg., 1st sess., 12 March 1968, p. 662.
19 Ontario Committee on Taxation, *Report*, I, 115.
20 *Ibid.*, p. 116.
21 Ontario, Legislative Assembly, *Debates*, 27th leg., 3rd sess., 10 February 1965, p. 415.
22 *Taxation in Ontario: A Program for Reform*, p. 308.
23 Ontario Committee on Taxation, *Report*, I, 205.
24 Terrance Wills, "The Tax Nightmare Awaiting Robarts," *Globe and Mail*, Toronto, 16 November 1968.
25 *Toronto Daily Star*, 18 November 1968.
26 Ontario Committee on Taxation, *Report*, I, 269.
27 Ontario Department of Treasury and Economics, Taxation and Fiscal Policy Branch, *1969 Ontario Budget*, presented by the Honourable Charles MacNaughton, Treasurer of Ontario and Minister of Economics (Toronto, 4 March 1969), p. 7.
28 *Ibid.*
29 *Ibid.*, pp. 8–9.
30 *Ibid.*, p. 23.
31 *Ibid.*, p. 24.
32 *Ibid.*, pp. 28–9.
33 *Ibid.*, p. 56.
34 *Ibid.*, p. 57.
35 *Ibid.*, p. 59.
36 *Ibid.*, p. 58.
37 *Ontario Budget, 1970*, pp. 14–15.
38 *Ibid.*, pp. 6–7.
39 David M. Cameron, "The Politics of Education in Ontario, with Special Reference to the Financial Structure," (PH D thesis, University of Toronto, 1969), p. 69. (General acknowledgment, rather than for a specific item only.)
40 E.B. Rideout, "Memorandum on the County as an Intermediate Unit for School Finance," Department of Educational Research, Ontario College of Education, University of Toronto, July 1962. Mimeographed.
41 *Report of the Royal Commission on Education in Ontario, 1950*, J.A. Hope, chairman (Toronto: King's Printer, 1950), p. 303.
42 Ontario Committee on Taxation, *Report*, II, 33.
43 *Ibid.*, III, 35.
44 Cameron, "Politics of Education in Ontario," pp. 77–8.
45 Ontario Committee on Taxation, *Report*, III, 33–4.
46 Cameron, "Politics of Education in Ontario," p. 78.
47 Ontario Committee on Taxation, *Report*, II, 47.
48 Cameron, "Politics of Education in Ontario," p. 118.
49 Ontario Committee on Taxation, *Report*, II, 5.

50 E.B. Rideout, "The Financial Support of Education," *Canadian Education and Research Digest*, VIII, 2, June 1968, p. 95.
51 Ontario Committee on Taxation, *Report*, I, 46–7.
52 *Ibid.*, II, 90.
53 *Ibid.*, pp. 15–16.
54 *Ibid.*, p. 407.
55 *Ibid.*, p. 404.
56 Ontario Committee on Taxation, *Report*. A general acknowledgment is offered herewith as a substitute for numerous specific acknowledgments. Only direct quotations are subsequently footnoted in this section.
57 Ontario Committee on Taxation, *Report*, II, 53.
58 *Ibid.*, pp. 206–7.
59 J. Bascom St John, "The World of Learning," *Globe and Mail*, Toronto, 9 December 1963.
60 Cameron, "Politics of Education in Ontario," p. 111.
61 Ontario Committee on Taxation, *Report*, II, 119.
62 *Taxation in Ontario: A Program for Reform*, pp. 47–8.
63 *Ibid.*, p. 48.
64 *Ibid.*, p. 51.
65 *Ibid.*, pp. 40–2.
66 Ontario Department of Education, "Memorandum to W.M. McIntyre re brief from Ontario Farmers' Union (and meeting February 12, 11:00 a.m.)," W.G. Davis, 9 February 1968.
67 *Taxation in Ontario: A Program for Reform*, p. 40.
68 *Ibid.*, pp. 52–3.
69 *1969 Ontario Budget*, p. 61.
70 Ontario Committee on Taxation, *Report*, II, 124.
71 Ontario, Legislative Assembly, *Debates*, 28th leg., 2nd sess., 6 February 1969, p. 1074.
72 Ontario Committee on Taxation, *Report*, II, 125.
73 *Ibid.*, p. 141.
74 *Taxation in Ontario: A Program for Reform*, p. 55.
75 Ontario Committee on Taxation, *Report*, II, 146.
76 *Taxation in Ontario: A Program for Reform*, p. 56.
77 Ontario, Legislative Assembly, *Debates*, 28th leg., 1st sess., 7 March 1968, p. 556.
78 *Ontario Budget 1970*, pp. 15–16.
79 *Taxation in Ontario: A Program for Reform*, p. 72.
80 *Ibid.*, p. 62.
81 Ontario, Legislative Assembly, *Debates*, 27th leg., 5th sess., 8 May 1967, p. 3127.
82 *Ibid.*, p. 3118.
83 Cameron, "Politics of Education in Ontario," pp. 104–7.
84 Ontario, Legislative Assembly, *Debates*, 25th leg., 3rd sess., 5 February 1957, p. 144.
85 *Ibid.*, 26th leg., 1st sess., 2 February 1960, p. 115.
86 *Ibid.*, p. 116.
87 Ontario, Legislative Assembly, *Debates*, 27th leg., 2nd sess., 28 April 1964, p. 2549.
88 T.J. McKibbin, Clerk-Comptroller, Corporation of the City of Kingston, to the Honourable Wiliam E. [sic] Davis, Minister of Education, 11 November 1968.
89 Ontario Committee on Taxation, *Report*, I, 112.
90 J. Bascom St John, "The World of Learning," *Globe and Mail*, Toronto, 4 February 1963.
91 Ontario, *Revised Statutes of*

Ontario, 1960 (Toronto: Queen's Printer, n.d.), IV, 704.

92 Ontario Committee on Taxation, *Report*, II, 65–66.

93 *1969 Ontario Budget*, p. 63.

94 *Ibid.*

95 *Ibid.*, pp. 63–4.

96 *Ibid.*, p. 64.

97 *Ibid.*, pp. 64–5.

98 *Ibid.*, pp. 65–6.

99 *Ibid.*, p. 66.

100 *Ibid.*, pp. 66–7.

CHAPTER 10

1 Ontario, Treasury Board of Ontario, *Effective Management Through P.P.B.S.*, Honourable C.S. MacNaughton, chairman (Toronto, October 1969), p. 1.

2 *Ibid.*, p. 3.

3 Ontario Department of Education, Memorandum to the Inspectors Who Are Employed by the Department re the Financial Situation of Certain School Boards, 14 October 1960, G.A. Pearson, Superintendent of Elementary Education.

4 R.G. Ferguson, "School Administration's Guide to Budgeting," *School Administration*, IV, 11, November 1967, 32–5.

5 Robert Webb, "Ontario Faces Tough Task in Budgeting for 1969 Following Consolidation of School Boards," *School Administration*, November 1968, p. 23.

6 Frank MacKinnon, *Relevance and Responsibility in Education*, lectures delivered under the Quance Lectures in Canadian Education (Toronto: W.J. Gage, 1968), p. 78.

CHAPTER 11

1 Charles E. Phillips, *The Development of Education in Canada* (Toronto: W.J. Gage, 1957), p. 344.

2 Canada, *Statutes*, 6 Geo. 6, 1942–3, chap. 34.

3 D.E.M. Glendenning, "Impact of Federal Financial Support on Vocational Education in Canada" (PH D thesis, School of Education, Indiana University, September 1964), p. 61.

4 Privy Council 3165, Minute of a meeting of the Committee of the Privy Council, approved by his Excellency the Governor General on 1 May 1945.

5 Vocational Schools' Assistance Agreement, 27 February 1946.

6 Privy Council 8993, 21 January 1944.

7 Canada, *Statutes*, 9 Eliz. 2, 1960–1, chap. 6.

8 Technical and Vocational Training Agreement, 26 June 1961, between the Government of Canada and the Government of the Province of Ontario.

9 Ontario, Provincial Committee on Aims and Objectives of Education in the Schools of Ontario, *Living and Learning* (Toronto: Newton Publishing Company, 1968), p. 167.

10 Economic Council of Canada, Third Annual Review, *Prices, Productivity and Employment* (Ottawa: Queen's Printer, 1966), p. 197.

11 Canada, *Statutes*, 14–15–16 Eliz. 2, 1966–7, chap. 94.

CHAPTER 12

1 Robin S. Harris, *Quiet Evolu-*

tion: A Study of the Educational System of Ontario (Toronto: University of Toronto Press, 1967), p. 59.

2 C.B. Sissons, *Church & State in Canadian Education: An Historical Study* (Toronto: Ryerson Press, 1959), p. 118.

3 Harris, *Quiet Evolution*, p. 60.

4 Ontario, *Report of Royal Commission on University Finances*, I (Toronto: King's Printer, 1921), p. 29.

5 The Industrial Foundation on Education, *The Case for Corporate Giving to Higher Education*, Part I, Report no. 1 (Toronto, 15 December 1957), p. 23.

6 Carleton University, *The President's Report, 1956–57* (Ottawa), p. 6.

7 Ontario, Legislative Assembly, *Debates*, 25th leg., 3rd sess., 21 February 1957, p. 527.

8 *The Case for Corporate Giving to Higher Education*, Part II, Report no. 1, pp. 2–3.

9 *Carleton University President's Report, 1966–67*, p. 9.

10 University of Toronto, *President's Report for the Year Ended June, 1960*, pp. 9–10.

11 "University Education in Ontario," brief prepared for presentation to the Prime Minister of Ontario by the Ontario Council of University Faculty Associations, 19 December 1963, pp. 38–44. Mimeographed.

12 *Post-Secondary Education in Ontario, 1962–1970*, Report of the Presidents of the Universities of Ontario to the Advisory Committee on University Affairs, May 1962, revised January 1963 (Toronto: University of Toronto Press, 1963), p. 28.

13 J. Bascom St John, "Why the Secrecy on University Aid?" *Globe and Mail*, Toronto, 10 February 1964.

14 *Report of the Committee on Higher Education*, Lord Robbins, chairman, 1961–3 (London: Her Majesty's Stationery Office, 1963) [The Robbins Report], cited by J. Stuart Maclure, ed., *Educational Documents*, England and Wales, 1816–1963 (London: Chapman & Hall, 1965), p. 296.

15 J. Bascom St John, "University Cost Study," *Globe and Mail*, Toronto, 20 March 1964.

16 Ontario, Legislative Assembly, *Debates*, 27th leg., 3rd sess., 18 February 1965, pp. 574–5.

17 *Ibid.*, 22 February 1965, p. 660.

18 *Ibid.*, 28th leg., 1st sess., 10 June 1968, p. 4203.

19 *Ibid.*, 27th leg., 3rd sess., 19 February 1965, pp. 635–6.

20 Sir James Duff and Robert O. Berdahl, sponsored by the Canadian Association of University Teachers and the Association of Universities and Colleges of Canada, *University Government in Canada*, report of the commission (Toronto: University of Toronto Press, 1966), p. 82.

21 Presidents' Research Committee for the Committee of Presidents of Universities of Ontario, *From the Sixties to the Seventies: An Appraisal of Higher Education in Ontario* (Toronto, 1966), pp. 51–2.

22 *Report of the Committee on University Affairs, 1967*, Douglas T. Wright, chairman, p. 12.
23 *Ibid.*, p. 11.
24 Committee of Presidents of Universities of Ontario, *Collective Autonomy: Second Annual Review 1967/68* (Toronto, 1968), pp. 30–1.
25 Ontario, Legislative Assembly, *Debates*, 27th leg., 5th sess., 5 June 1967, p. 4327.
26 *Report of the Committee on University Affairs, 1967*, p. 15.
27 *Carleton University President's Report, 1966–67*, p. 9.
28 *Collective Autonomy*, pp. 28–9.
29 *Report of the Committee on University Affairs, 1967*, pp. 13–15.
30 *Collective Autonomy*, p. 32.
31 Ontario, Committee on University Affairs, "Extra-Formula Costs for 'Emerging' Universities," 10 January 1968.
32 *Report of the Committee on University Affairs, 1968–69*, p. 18.
33 Ontario, Committee on Taxation, *Report of the Ontario Committee on Taxation*, I: *Approach, Background and Conclusions* (Toronto: Queen's Printer, 1967), pp. 191–2.
34 *Post-Secondary Education in Ontario, 1962–1970*, pp. 28–9.
35 Ontario, Legislative Assembly, *Debates*, 27th leg., 2nd sess., 5 May 1964, p. 2817.
36 *Ibid.*, 22 April 1964, pp. 2334–5.
37 J. Bascom St John, "A Breach in University Autonomy," *Globe and Mail*, Toronto, 28 April 1964.
38 Ontario, Legislative Assembly, *Debates*, 27th leg., 3rd sess., 22 February 1965, p. 661.
39 *From the Sixties to the Seventies*, pp. 93–4.
40 *Ibid.*, p. 94.
41 Committee of Presidents of Universities of Ontario, *System Emerging: First Annual Review 1966–67* (Toronto, 1967), p. 28.
42 *Carleton University President's Report, 1966–67*, pp. 9–10.
43 Ontario, Legislative Assembly, *Debates*, 27th leg., 5th sess., 5 June 1967, p. 4299.
44 *System Emerging*, pp. 28–9.
45 *Ibid.*, p. 29.
46 *Report of the Committee on University Affairs, 1967*, pp. 32–4.
47 *Collective Autonomy*, pp. 35–6.
48 *Kitchener-Waterloo Record*, 10 May 1968.
49 Ontario, Department of University Affairs, "An Interim Formula for Providing Capital Funds for University Building and Expansion, Appendix B," 4 March 1969.
50 *Report of the Committee on University Affairs, 1967*, pp. 34–5.
51 V.W. Bladen, *Financing Higher Education in Canada*, Report of the Commission on the Financing of Higher Education in Canada to the Association of Universities and Colleges of Canada (Toronto: University of Toronto Press, 1965), p. 7.
52 *Ibid.*, pp. 7–8.
53 Claude T. Bissell, ed., *Canada's Crisis in Higher Education: Proceedings of a Conference*

held by the National Conference of Canadian Universities (Ottawa, 12-14 November 1956), p. 251. My translation of a section of an address by the Prime Minister of Canada, The Right Honourable Louis St Laurent. "Par contre, le gouvernement fédéral a le droit absolu de prélever des impôts indirects pour toutes fins et le pouvoir d'imposer des taxes directes pourvu qu'elles soient destinées à alimenter le Fonds du revenu consolidé du Canada. Il peut alors se servir de cet argent, avec l'approbation du Parlement, pour offrir des dons ou des octrois à des individus, à des institutions, à des gouvernements provinciaux et même à des gouvernements étrangers. Il s'agit là d'une prérogative royale que notre constitution ne restreint en aucune façon."

54 Ontario Council of University Faculty Associations, Submission to the Commission on the Financing of Higher Education, 8 January 1965, pp. 5–8. Mimeographed.

55 Ontario, Legislative Assembly, *Debates*, 27th leg., 5th sess., 5 June 1967, p. 4316.

56 *The Case for Corporate Giving to Higher Education*, Summary, Report no. 1, p. 2.

57 *Ibid.*, Part II, p. 22.

58 *The Case for Corporate Giving to Higher Education*, 1962 Supplement, Report no. 14, p. 9.

59 J. Bascom St John, "Colleges and Government," *Globe and Mail*, Toronto, 4 February 1964.

60 University of Toronto, *President's Report for the Year Ended June, 1960* (Toronto, 1960), p. 1.

61 *Financing Higher Education in Canada*, p. 45.

62 Ontario, Legislative Assembly, *Debates*, 27th leg., 3rd sess., 19 February 1965, p. 641.

63 Ontario Council of University Faculty Associations, Submission to the Commission on the Financing of Higher Education, p. 1.

CHAPTER 13

1 Ontario, *Statutes*, 18 Geo. 5, 1928, chap. 25, "An Act Respecting the Training of Apprentices."

2 Ontario, Legislative Assembly, *Debates*, 27th leg., 4th sess., 22 March 1966, p. 1768.

3 *Ibid.*, pp. 1768–9.

4 Department of Correctional Services, *Report of the Minister for the Year Ending 31st March, 1968*, Printed by Order of the Legislative Assembly of Ontario, Sessional Paper no. 37, 1969, p. 4.

5 *Annual Report of the Department of Reform Institutions, Province of Ontario for the Year Ending 31st March, 1948.* Part 1: Reformatories, Industrial Farms, Common Gaols. Printed by Order of the Legislative Assembly of Ontario, Sessional Paper no. 18, 1949, p. 5.

6 *Annual Report of the Department of Reform Institutions, Province of Ontario, for the*

Year Ending 31st March, 1955. Part 2: Training Schools. Printed by Order of the Legislative Assembly of Ontario, 1956, p. 7.

7 *Annual Report of the Department of Reform Institutions, Province of Ontario, for the Year Ending 31st March, 1959* (Toronto: Queen's Printer, 1960), pp. 7–11.

8 *Annual Report of the Department of Reform Institutions, Province of Ontario, for the Year Ending 31st March, 1960.* Part 1: Reformatories, Industrial Farms, Common Gaols. Printed by Order of the Legislative Assembly of Ontario, Sessional Paper no. 37, 1961.

9 Ontario, Department of Justice, *Ontario Fire College Calendar, 1969*, p. 4.

10 Ontario Economic Council, Tourist Industry Committee, *Ontario's Tourist Industry: Its Potentialities and Its Problems* (Toronto, December 1965), p. 4.

11 These publications do not include standard bibliographical information, but are obtainable from the Ontario Department of Tourism and Information, Parliament Buildings, Toronto.

12 Ontario, Department of Travel and Publicity, *Report for the Year 1960* (Queen's Printer, 1961), p. 30.

13 D.F. McOuat, "Our Provincial Archives," *Ontario History*, XLV, 1, Winter 1953, 31.

14 Ontario, Department of Travel and Publicity, *Annual Report for 1959.*

15 Barbara Froom, *Ontario Snakes* (Ontario Department of Lands and Forests, Conservation Information Section, Operations Branch, 1967).

16 D.H. Pimlott, J.A. Shannon, and G.B. Kolenosky, *The Ecology of the Timber Wolf in Algonquin Park* (Ontario Department of Lands and Forests, 1969).

17 Ontario, Department of Lands and Forests, Fish and Wildlife Branch and Research, *Wolves and Coyotes in Ontario.*

18 E.J. Zabitz, *Fifty Years of Reforestation in Ontario* (Ontario Department of Lands and Forests).

19 Ontario, Department of Lands and Forests, Reforestation Section, Timber Branch, *The Farm Woodlot*, Bulletin no. C14, revised 1969.

20 H.J. Gibbard, *Fur in Ontario* (Ontario Department of Lands and Forests, Fish and Wildlife Branch, Miscellaneous Publications no. 1, May 1964).

21 Department of Education, "Memorandum to Directors and Superintendents, 1962–63: 39," 25 February 1963.

22 Virginia Thorne, "OCLG – An Antidote for Apathy," *Municipal World*, LXXVIII, 5, May 1968, 133.

23 Canada, Parliament, House of Commons, Debates, 24th parliament, 4th sess., 30 May 1961, p. 5635.

24 Order-in-Council, 600/61.

25 Ontario, Department of Social and Family Services, *Report of the Minister, 1968–69* (Toron-

to: Queen's Printer), p. 112.

26 Ontario, Department of Civil Service, Staff Development and Research Branch, "The Senior Officers' Conference and Seminar" (Toronto).

27 *Report of the Royal Commission on Education, 1950,* J.A. Hope, chairman (Toronto: King's Printer, 1950), pp. 360–1.

28 Ontario, Legislative Assembly, *Debates,* 26th leg., 3rd sess., 10 April 1962, p. 2136.

29 *Ibid.,* 27th leg., 3rd sess., 27 January 1965, pp. 72–3.

30 R.S. Harris, *Quiet Evolution: A Study of the Educational System of Ontario* (Toronto: University of Toronto Press, 1967), p. 121.

31 *Ibid.,* p. 134.

32 *Ibid.,* pp. 123–4.

33 *Ibid.,* p. 134.

34 Ontario, Legislative Assembly, *Debates,* 27th leg., 5th sess., 17 May 1967, p. 3541.

35 *Ibid.,* 5 June 1967, p. 4265.

CHAPTER 14

1 Ontario, Legislative Assembly, *Debates,* 27th leg., 5th sess., 25 May 1967, p. 3815.

2 Canada, Council of Ministers of Education, "Operational Procedures. Agreed Memorandum on a Council of Ministers of Education," 1 May 1969. Draft copy.

3 Ralph Mitchener, "Education," *Canadian Annual Review for 1967* (Toronto: University of Toronto Press, 1967), p. 369.

4 *Ibid.*

CHAPTER 15

1 Ontario, Provincial Committee on Aims and Objectives of Education in the Schools of Ontario, *Living and Learning* (Toronto: Newton Publishing Company, 1968), p. 11.

2 "The Constitutional Limit on Educational Growth," *Globe and Mail,* Toronto, 19 August 1968.

3 The information about the Air Services Training School presented here is found in a brochure entitled *Airport Campus: The Department of Transport's School for Aviation Specialists,* produced by the Information Services Division, Department of Transport, in 1967.

4 Canadian Government Travel Bureau, *Summer Courses in Canada, 1969.*

5 Association of Universities and Colleges of Canada, *Universities and Colleges of Canada, 1969,* p. 353.

6 John J. Carson, "Executive Development: A Necessity, Not a Luxury," *Canadian Personnel and Industrial Relations Journal,* xv, 3, May 1968, 13–14.

7 *Ibid.,* p. 14.

8 *Ibid.,* pp. 15–16.

9 Canadian International Development Agency, *Annual Report 1967–68,* p. 34.

10 Marci McDonald, "A Life-or-Death Drama at the National Film Board," *Toronto Daily Star,* 4 October 1969.

11 A.S.R. Tweedie, "CEA/NFB Advisory Committee," paper presented at the Annual Conven-

tion of the Canadian Education Association, Toronto, September 1960. (Extract from *Canadian Film Institute Bulletin*, October 1960).

12 Hans Möller, "Audio-Visual Media in Canadian Schools," *Visual Education*, January 1969, pp. 16–17.

13 *The Canada Council, 1968–69, 12th Annual Report*, J.G. Prentice, chairman, 30 June 1969, p. 7.

14 For this and subsequent information, the writer acknowledges general indebtedness to *Universities and Colleges of Canada, 1969*, Association of Universities and Colleges of Canada.

15 *Ibid.*

16 Canadian National Commission for UNESCO, *Report of the Secretary-General to the Annual Meeting*, March 1969.

17 *Ibid.*

Contents of volumes in
ONTARIO'S EDUCATIVE SOCIETY

General index

Index of persons

www.ingramcontent.com/pod-product-compliance
Lightning Source LLC
LaVergne TN
LVHW090756070826
844660LV00022B/1003

* 9 7 8 1 4 8 7 5 9 8 6 1 7 *